DECISIONS
IN CRISIS

INTERNATIONAL CRISIS BEHAVIOR PROJECT

DECISIONS IN CRISIS

Israel, 1967 and 1973

MICHAEL BRECHER

With Benjamin Geist

UNIVERSITY OF CALIFORNIA PRESS

Berkeley · Los Angeles · London

University of California Press
Berkeley and Los Angeles, California

University of California Press, Ltd.
London, England

ISBN 0-520-03766-9
Library of Congress Catalog Card Number: 78-62850
Printed in the United States of America

1 2 3 4 5 6 7 8 9

In memory of my parents
Nathan and Gisela Brecher

CONTENTS

FIGURES AND TABLES

PREFACE

SOME OBSTACLES to a theory of international crisis behavior have been laid bare by a pioneer in this field:

So many studies of crisis have been published in the last fifteen years from so many different angles of inquiry that it is more difficult than it once was to be sure about the denotations and connotations of the term. Not only is there a heavy popular usage of the word in ordinary discourse but also there are indications that historical change has brought about an expansion of the variety of situations that are called readily by the crisis name.[1]

Accordingly, "the problem of simply providing satisfactory definitions" occupies an important place in the introductory chapter to this volume.

International crisis, as part of the study of foreign policy, has long been one of my major intellectual and practical concerns. This quest for knowledge about crisis has been stimulated by the earliest and one of the most innovative research projects at the state level of analysis, the Stanford Studies in Conflict and Integration, led by Robert North. Their contribution was seminal both in the application of a mediated stimulus-response model to interstate relations and in the effective use of quantitative methods to decipher decision-makers' perceptions. Yet the scope of that project

---

1. C. A. McClelland, "Crisis and Threat in the International Setting: Some Relational Concepts," Threat Recognition and Analysis Project (1975), pp. 1–2.

was limited largely to the crisis leading to the First World War, with peripheral excursions to Cuba 1962.[2] So too with the decision-making approach of Snyder, Bruck, and Sapin and its sole application, Glenn Paige's study of the U.S. Korean War decisions in 1950.[3] The bureaucratic politics paradigm, too, generated a major case study, Graham Allison's work on the Cuban Missile Crisis.[4] A wider canvas has been the exploration by Alexander George and several colleagues of eleven post–World War II cases of coercive

2. The Stanford studies generated important hypotheses on the impact of crisis-induced stress (many of which will be tested in this volume); evaluated components of crisis, with an emphasis on threat and time; explored the link between expression of hostility by one actor and perception of threat by another; and illuminated unintended consequences (escalation) of deterrence and defense policies. In the largest sense, "the Stanford scholarship makes a great contribution to theory building about crisis decision-making" (R. Tanter, "International Crisis Behavior: An Appraisal of the Literature," *The Jerusalem Journal of International Relations*, 3 (Winter–Spring 1978), 340–374. Publications of the Stanford group on crisis decision-making include: O. R. Holsti, *Crisis, Escalation, War* (Montreal, 1972); "Time, Alternatives, and Communications: The 1914 and Cuban Missile Crises," in C. F. Hermann, ed., *International Crises: Insights from Behavioral Research* (New York, 1972); "Cognitive Dynamics and Images of the Enemy: Dulles and Russia," in D. J. Finlay, O. R. Holsti, and R. Fagen, eds., *Enemies in Politics* (Chicago, 1967), chap. 2; "The 1914 Case," *The American Political Science Review*, 59 (June 1965), 365–378; O. R. Holsti, R. A. Brody, and R. C. North, "Measuring Affect and Action in International Reaction Models: Empirical Materials from the 1962 Cuban Crisis," *Journal of Peace Research*, 3–4 (1964), 170–190; O. R. Holsti, R. C. North, and R. A. Brody, "Perception and Action in the 1914 Crisis," in J. D. Singer, ed., *Quantitative International Politics* (New York, 1968), pp. 123–158; R. C. North, R. A. Brody, and O. R. Holsti, "Some Empirical Data on the Conflict Spiral," *Peace Research Society (International) Papers*, 1 (1964), 1–14; E. V. Nomikos and R. C. North, *International Crisis: The Outbreak of World War I* (Montreal, 1976); and D. A. Zinnes, "A Comparison of Hostile Behavior of Decision-Makers in Simulated and Historical Data," *World Politics*, 18 (April 1966), 474–502. For challenging critiques of the Stanford studies, see G. Hilton, "The 1914 Studies: A Re-assessment of the Evidence and Some Further Thoughts," *Peace Research Society (International) Papers*, 13 (1970), 117–141, and R. Jervis, "The Costs of the Quantitative Study of International Relations," in K. Knorr and J. N. Rosenau, eds., *Contending Approaches to International Politics* (Princeton, N.J., 1969), chap. 10. For a persuasive reply to the latter, see R. C. North, "Research Pluralism and the International Elephant," in Knorr and Rosenau, eds. (1969), pp. 218–242.

3. R. C. Snyder, H. W. Bruck, and B. Sapin, eds., *Foreign Policy Decision-Making* (New York, 1962); and G. D. Paige, *The Korean Decision* (New York, 1968), and "On Values and Science: The Korean Decision Reconsidered," *The American Political Science Review*, 71 (December 1977), 1603–1609.

4. See his *The Essence of Decision: Explaining the Cuban Missile Crisis* (Boston, 1971), and "Conceptual Models and the Cuban Missile Crisis," *The American Political Science Review*, 63 (September 1969), 689–718.

diplomacy and deterrence confronting the United States.[5] The most comprehensive work thus far, by Glenn Snyder and Paul Diesing, examined bargaining, decision-making, and system structure in sixteen international crises from 1898 to 1973.[6]

Several earlier studies attempted to apply a dynamic research framework to three crises of a small state in the Middle East, namely, Israel.[7] These crises were also used to generate hypotheses about state behavior in crisis conditions.[8] And in the conviction that knowledge about international crisis, as in other fields, must be cumulative, these findings were applied to thirty hypotheses about crisis behavior drawn mainly from the Hermann group effort.[9]

Viewed in the perspective of a long road to theory,[10] that stage of research resulted in:

1. The refinement of a framework for the analysis of state behavior, aspiring to be universal in time and space—given the availability of data.

2. The construction of an embryonic model of behavior with explicit parameters and linkages between independent and dependent variables.

3. The exploration of many decisions taken by two international actors, Israel and India, during their first three decades as independent states.

5. A. L. George, D. K. Hall, and S. A. Simons, *The Limits of Coercive Diplomacy: Laos, Cuba, Vietnam* (Boston, 1971), and A. L. George and R. Smoke, *Deterrence and Defense in American Foreign Policy: Theory and Practice* (New York, 1974).

6. G. H. Snyder and P. Diesing, *Conflict Among Nations: Bargaining, Decision Making, and System Structure in International Crises* (Princeton, N.J., 1977).

7. M. Brecher, *Decisions in Israel's Foreign Policy* (London, 1974, and New Haven, 1975), chaps. 6, 7, and 8.

8. M. Brecher, "Inputs and Decisions for War and Peace: The Israel Experience," *International Studies Quarterly*, 18 (June 1974), 131–177.

9. M. Brecher, "Research Findings and Theory-Building in Foreign Policy Behavior," in P. J. McGowan, ed., *Sage International Yearbook of Foreign Policy Studies*, 2 (Beverly Hills, 1974), pp. 49–122. The reservoir of 311 hypotheses was assembled by Hermann and Brady and published in Hermann's *International Crises: Insights from Behavioral Research* (1972). The publication of that volume was a milestone along the slow path to theory.

10. Stanley Hoffmann's still-haunting challenge to would-be theorists of international relations is contained in his "International Relations: The Long Road to Theory," *World Politics*, 11 (April 1959), 346–377.

4. The testing of many propositions about foreign policy behavior suggested by other scholars.

5. The generation of new hypotheses about war and peace decisions.

The results of these studies have been reported in two volumes and several papers[11] and in a doctoral dissertation on the 1967 Middle East Crisis.[12]

One of the major constraints has been the paucity of reliable data about the range, volume, and content of crises in any historical era or geographic region.[13] To help overcome this deficiency, the International Crisis Behavior Project (ICB) is engaged in "horizontal" research, a mapping of crises during the past half century. Preliminary investigation has uncovered 390 prewar and postwar crises and 79 intra-war crises.[14] By horizontal research is meant a comparison across crisis dimensions, actor attributes, and decisional unit characteristics in order to discover the frequency of different trigger mechanisms and also the distribution of crises by gravity, complexity, intensity, and duration, as well as by international

11. M. Brecher, *The Foreign Policy System of Israel* (London and New Haven, 1972); *Decisions in Israel's Foreign Policy* (1974); "Toward a Theory of International Crisis Behavior," *International Studies Quarterly*, 21 (March 1977), 39–74; "India's Devaluation of 1966: Linkage Politics and Crisis Decision-Making," *British Journal of International Studies*, 3 (April 1977), 1–25; *Israel, The Korean War and China* (Jerusalem, 1974, and New Brunswick, N.J., 1977); "Inputs and Decisions for War and Peace: The Israel Experience" (June 1974); "Research Findings and Theory-Building in Foreign Policy Behavior" (1974); "India's Decision to Remain in the Commonwealth," *The Journal of Commonwealth and Comparative Politics*, 13 (March and July 1974), 69–90, 228–230; "India's Decision on the Voice of America: A Study in Irresolution," *Asian Survey*, 14 (July 1974), 637–650; "Israel and the Rogers Peace Initiatives: Decisions and Consequences," *Orbis*, 18 (Summer 1974), 402–426; and "Images, Process and Feedback in Foreign Policy: Israel's Decisions on German Reparations," *The American Political Science Review*, 67 (March 1973), 73–102; J. G. Stein and M. Brecher, "Image, Advocacy and the Analysis of Conflict: An Israeli Case Study," *The Jerusalem Journal of International Relations*, 1 (Spring 1976), 33–58; and M. Brecher, B. Steinberg, and J. G. Stein, "A Framework for Research on Foreign Policy Behavior," *The Journal of Conflict Resolution*, 13 (March 1969), 75–101.

12. B. Geist, "The Six Day War: A Study in the Setting and the Process of Foreign Policy Decision-Making Under Crisis Conditions," Unpublished Ph.D. dissertation, The Hebrew University of Jerusalem (Jerusalem, 1974).

13. This has been partly overcome by some recently published inventories of international crises: R. L. Butterworth, *Managing Interstate Conflict, 1945–1974: Data with Synopsis* (Pittsburgh, 1976); L. Hazelwood and J. J. Hays, *Planning for Problems in Crisis Management* (Washington, D.C., 1976); and J. A. Moore et al., *Crisis Inventory* (Washington, D.C., 1975).

14. A tabular presentation is in Brecher, "Toward a Theory of International Crisis Behavior," *International Studies Quarterly*, 21 (March 1977), 46, Table 1.

system, time, size, and age of states, belief system, régime type, and levels of economic development and military capability. For example, the several hundred crises will be compared by outcome —those that lead to war, those that are resolved by peaceful means, those that end in stalemate, etc.[15] This part of the Project will facilitate the construction and testing of propositions about state behavior in crisis.

The ICB Project is currently engaged in "vertical" research— that is, studies in depth of a sample of twenty-five actor-cases.[16] They range from French and British decision-making in the 1938 Munich crisis to Syria's behavior in the Lebanese civil war of 1975–76. They encompass different types of international systems —tight bipolar, loose bipolar, and multipolar. All regional sub-systems are represented. So too are "old" states (pre–Second World War) and "new" states (created since 1945). The cases encompass large, medium, and small states; a diversity of cultures, religions, and ideologies; various types of political system; several levels of economic development and military capability; crisis decisional units of different structure and size; and crises of varied intensity and complexity. Some monographs will compare the behavior of two or more states, for example, India and Pakistan in the 1971 struggle over Bangladesh. Others will compare the behavior of one state in two or more crises, as with this first volume, the behavior of Israel in the 1967 and 1973 Crises.

These ICB studies are analyzing international crisis from the perspective of a single state, not of an international system or of all participants in the crisis, as with the Stanford studies of the 1914 Crisis. This volume, for example, focuses on the psychological setting for Israel's choices in the 1967 and 1973 Crises and the behavior of her decision-makers—but not on the perceptions and behavior of Egypt, Syria, Jordan, the U.S., or the USSR. To exam-ine any of these in depth would constitute a separate micro study of crisis. Nor do the ICB vertical studies purport to explain fully the reciprocal "conflict spiral" or *interaction* process. Rather, it is the behavior of one crisis actor, an *action* process, which is the

15. Preliminary findings in one region's crises are reported in H. Naveh and M. Brecher, "Patterns of International Crises in the Middle East, 1938–1975," *The Jerusalem Journal of International Relations*, 2–3 (Winter–Spring 1978), 277–315.

16. The procedures used in selecting the cases are set out in Brecher, "Toward a Theory of International Crisis Behavior" (March 1977), 47.

object of inquiry. This is evident in the Model of Crisis Behavior specified in Chapter 1 below. Such a focus, it should be emphasized, does not mean the exclusion of other participants in the crisis viewed systemically. Their actions or nonactions comprise stimuli, or inputs, to the behavior of the crisis actor under investigation, to the extent that they are perceived by its decision-makers. The international system and/or subsystem(s), too, are within the ambit of a micro study because they may impose constraints or make demands upon the crisis actor which affect its behavior.

The ICB design calls for each case study to apply the Model of Crisis Behavior and to use a multimethod of analysis, qualitative as well as quantitative. The goal is to accumulate a comparable body of findings about state behavior under crisis.

In essence, the Project has four objectives:

1. The discovery and dissemination of knowledge about international crises between 1938 and 1975.

2. The search for crisis patterns.

3. The testing and generation of hypotheses about the effects of crisis-induced stress on coping and choice.

4. The creation of a general theory of state behavior in international crises.

It is only through the imagination of the Canada Council and its Killam Program that this ambitious undertaking was initiated. The entire Project is being made possible by a generous Izaak Walton Killam Award. McGill University, as so often in the past, has continued to demonstrate unusual flexibility and understanding in granting me lengthy periods of leave for research.

The idea of a comparative study of Israel's behavior in the 1967 and 1973 Crises was conceived by Benjamin Geist and myself during the Yom Kippur War. I designed and directed the study and wrote the following segments: the introductory chapter on definitions, typologies, and model; the psychological environment for choice in 1967 and 1973 (Section B of Chapters 2, 3, 5, 6, 8, 9); the findings on crisis components and coping processes and mechanisms, derived from a comparative analysis of Israel's behavior in the two crises (Chapters 4, 7, 10, 11); and the concluding chapter on stress and choice. Geist, who had written a superior thesis on an Israeli crisis, assumed primary responsibility for the examination of the 1967 and 1973 decision flows (Section C of Chapters 2, 3, 5,

6, 8, 9) and of the military balance on the eve of the two wars (Appendix B). I prepared the final draft of the two decision flows.

Sheila Moser was involved in the work on this volume from the beginning and made invaluable contributions to its organization and contents.

I wish to express my appreciation to several scholars who read and made insightful comments on all or parts of earlier drafts of the book: Ernst Haas, Robert North, Janice Gross Stein, and Jonathan Wilkenfeld.

A number of graduate students rendered helpful research assistance, notably Mordekhai Raz, Mark Resnick, Judy Shribman Ron, and David Yoffe. Jacqueline Lieberthal and Nomy Margalit in Jerusalem, and Cathy Duggan and Ann Jackson in Montreal, transformed indecipherable manuscripts into impeccable typescripts.

During the past twenty-five years, my wife Eva has graciously tolerated a search for perfection and self-imposed deadlines. She encouraged—and has managed to survive in good spirits—another scholarly venture. Benjamin Geist wishes to thank his wife Aliza and also Michael, Daniel, and Abigail for their kindness and understanding about the pursuit of his academic interests.

MICHAEL BRECHER

Jerusalem, November 1978

CHAPTER ONE

DEFINITIONS, TYPOLOGIES, MODEL

DEFINITIONS

WHAT DISTINGUISHES a crisis from a noncrisis in international politics? Viewed from the perspective of a state,

> a crisis is a situation with three necessary and sufficient conditions, deriving from a change in its external or internal environment. All three conditions are perceptions held by the highest level decision-makers:

1. *threat to basic values*, with a simultaneous or subsequent

2. *high probability of involvement in military hostilities*, and the awareness of

3. *finite time for response to the external value threat.*[1]

This definition of crisis, which guides the case studies of the International Crisis Behavior Project (ICB), concentrates on the perceptions and behavior of a single state. Interaction among states

---

1. A *self-initiated* crisis is excluded; but a crisis may arise for actor A at time t_2 as a result of acts by other states (B, C, D, etc.) in response to acts initiated by A at time t_1. A crisis as defined here refers to the military-security (M-S) issue-area. However, breakpoints may occur in any foreign policy problem, and the study of international political, economic, and status crises might yield no less valuable findings. For these issues an appropriate change is necessary in the second condition specified above—namely, a perceived high probability of involvement in military hostilities. Thus an *economic* crisis requires "an expectation of adverse material consequences unless the response were drastic—and effective" (M. Brecher, "India's Devaluation of 1966: Linkage Politics and Crisis Decision-Making," *British Journal of International Studies*, 3 [April 1977], 1).

is explored in the form of reactions by the crisis actor to threatening physical and/or verbal acts by other states; that is, inputs from other states and the international system as a whole influence the behavior of the crisis actor by shaping its definition of the situation and its response. In other words, crisis decisions are made in the light of expectations about the behavior of other international actors. Moreover, a situational change, the precondition of crisis, may also be a destabilizing event in the international system. As such, a micro analysis of crisis incorporates some of the dimensions which are considered in a system-level analysis of international crisis.[2] Nevertheless, the state actor remains the central object of investigation— how its decision-makers perceive environmental change and how they choose, in the context of escalating or de-escalating perceptions of threat, time pressure, and probability of war.

The ICB definition builds upon, but differs significantly from, the widely accepted view of international crisis for a state enunciated by Charles Hermann:

A crisis is a situation that (1) threatens high-priority goals of the decision-making unit, (2) restricts the amount of time available for response before the decision is transformed, and (3) surprises the members of the decision-making unit by its occurrence. . . . Underlying the proposed definition is the hypothesis that if all three traits are present then the decision process will be substantially different than if only one or two of the characteristics appear.[3]

2. The most creative work on international crisis from the system perspective is that of Charles A. McClelland. See his articles: "The Acute International Crisis," *World Politics,* 14 (October 1961), 182–204; "Decisional Opportunity and Political Controversy, the Quemoy Case," *The Journal of Conflict Resolution,* 6 (September 1962), 201–213; "Action Structures and Communication in Two International Crises: Quemoy and Berlin," *Background,* 7 (1964), 201–215; "Access to Berlin: The Quantity and Variety of Events, 1948–1963," in J. D. Singer, ed., *Quantitative International Politics: Insights and Evidence* (New York, 1968), pp. 159–186; "The Beginning, Duration, and Abatement of International Crises: Comparisons in Two Conflict Arenas," in C. F. Hermann, ed., *International Crises: Insights from Behavioral Research* (New York, 1972), pp. 83–108; "Crisis and Threat in the International Setting: Some Relational Concepts," *Threat Recognition and Analysis Project Technical Report* (Los Angeles, June 1975); "Warning in the International Event Flow: EFI and ROZ as Threat Indicators," *Threat Recognition and Analysis Project Technical Report* (Los Angeles, July 1976); "The Anticipation of International Crises: Prospects for Theory and Research," *International Studies Quarterly,* 21 (March 1977), 15–38. Also noteworthy is O. R. Young, *The Intermediaries: Third Parties in International Crises* (Princeton, N.J., 1967), pp. 9–25, and *The Politics of Force: Bargaining During International Crises* (Princeton, N.J., 1968), chap. 1.

3. C. F. Hermann, *Crises in Foreign Policy: A Simulation Analysis* (Indianapolis, 1969), p. 414. Hermann's definition was derived from James A. Robinson's

The definition of crisis offered here differs on five essential points: (a) the omission of "surprise" as a necessary condition; (b) the replacement of "short" time by "finite" time for response; (c) the recognition that the situational change which induces a crisis may originate in the internal, as well as the external, environment of the crisis actor; (d) the concept of "basic values," rather than "high-priority goals," as the object of perceived threat; and (e) the addition of perceived "high probability of involvement in military hostilities." These definitional changes will now be elaborated.

a. There are high-threat, probability-of-war and finite-time situations in the perceptions of decision-makers that do not occasion surprise; that is, they are not unanticipated. Two illustrations will suffice. The situational change created by the Soviet Union in Berlin in 1961 and that brought on by Nasser's closing of the Straits of Tiran in May 1967 did not come as a surprise to American and Israeli decision-makers, respectively. But the perceived threat catalyzed a crisis atmosphere and stress in both cases, leading to changes in the American and Israeli behavioral response and decision-making processes.

(*The Concept of Crisis in Decision-Making* [Washington, D.C., 1962]) initial conception of international crisis as a decisional situation with three traits or components: "(1) identification of the origin of the event—whether external or internal for the decision-makers; (2) the decision time available for response—whether short, intermediate, or long; and (3) the relative importance of the values at stake to the participants—whether high or low." The quotation is from J. A. Robinson, "Crisis," in D. L. Sills, ed., *International Encyclopedia of the Social Sciences* (New York and London, 1968), vol. 3, p. 511, and is also in his "Crisis: An Appraisal of Concepts and Theories," in C. F. Hermann, ed., *International Crises*, 1972, p. 23. Hermann retained two of Robinson's traits, time and threat, but with significant changes: "restricted" or short time only; and threat to "high-priority goals," not values. And he replaced "origin of the event" with surprise. The first Hermann formulation is in his "Some Consequences of Crisis Which Limit the Viability of Organizations," *Administrative Science Quarterly*, 8 (1963), 61–82. See also his "International Crisis as a Situational Variable," in J. N. Rosenau, ed., *International Politics and Foreign Policy* (New York, 1969), pp. 409–421. The Hermann version has been adopted by many scholars. O. R. Holsti, for example, in his major work on the subject, wrote: "crisis—defined here as *a situation of unanticipated threat to important values and restricted decision time.*" He did not question its validity or utility, though he noted: "There are many usages of the term 'crisis'" (*Crisis, Escalation, War* [Montreal, 1972], p. 9 and p. 263, n. 13). Milburn, too, adopted that view of crisis. ("The Management of Crisis," in C. F. Hermann, ed., *International Crises*, 1972, p. 262). E. V. Nomikos and R. C. North, in their fascinating detailed narrative of the processes of conflict escalation in 1914, also accept Hermann's definition (*International Crisis: The Outbreak of World War I* [Montreal, 1976], p. 1).

Hermann and others were to become skeptical about the surprise component. His early simulation analysis led to a finding of "no significant relationship between either the time and awareness [surprise] dimensions or the threat and awareness dimensions; however, a significant correlation did occur between decision time and threat."[4] This was reaffirmed by Hermann in a later paper: "Consistent with this . . . is a review of the crisis literature that found the property of surprise mentioned less frequently than the other two traits."[5] The lower frequency of "surprise" and doubt about the adequacy of the overall Hermann definition of crisis are also evident in the findings of L. P. Brady: "In sum, . . . the absence of second-order interaction effects leads us to qualify our judgment concerning the typology's utility. . . . The eight-fold situational typology [of Hermann] is not as successful as we would have predicted."[6] McCormick went much further, questioning whether "surprise" could be operationalized at all: "Surprise . . . normally occurs only once when there is an unexpected outbreak of violence. . . . [W]e concluded that surprise is not measurable from content analysis."[7] And Hermann acknowledged, during a panel discussion on international crisis behavior (International Studies Association meetings, 1977), that, after extensive research, he concurred with the view that "surprise" was not a necessary—or universally present—condition of crisis. However, when it occurs it may increase the impact of time pressure.

b. The lack of universality of the short time condition, too, is demonstrated by the 1961 Berlin and the 1967 Middle East cases. The former lasted months, the latter three weeks, with Israel's decision-makers willing to delay a military response for another week or two. It was not the perceived brevity of time that influenced decision-making behavior, but rather the awareness of the finiteness of time for choice. A response could not be delayed indefinitely; that is, whether there was a week, a month, or many months, there was a realization that decisions for or against war had to be made within some time frame.

4. *Crises in Foreign Policy,* 1969, p. 69.
5. "Threat, Time, and Surprise: A Simulation of International Crisis," in C. F. Hermann, ed., *International Crises,* 1972, p. 208.
6. *Threat, Decision Time and Awareness: The Impact of Situational Variables on Foreign Policy Behavior,* Creon Publication 31 (Columbus, 1974), p. 58.
7. D. M. McCormick, *Decisions, Events and Perceptions in International Crises* (Ann Arbor, Michigan, 1975), vol. 1, p. 16.

c. For many Third World states, the situational change which triggers an international crisis has often occurred within the domestic environment, usually through physical challenges to the régime by strikes, demonstrations, riots, assassination, sabotage, and/or attempted coups d'état. Most new states are deeply penetrated political systems; and domestic situational changes, some of which derive from foreign sources, may give rise to an image of external threat. The assault on Chile's Allende régime in 1973 is a dramatic illustration of a widespread phenomenon in Africa and Latin America.

d. "High-priority goals" as the focus of threat, in Hermann's definition of crisis, has been broadened to "basic values." These include "core" values, which are near-constant and few in number, such as survival of the society and its population, political sovereignty, and territorial independence—though even the last two are not universal in time and space. A second value dimension is context-specific "high-priority" values: these derive from ideological and/or material interests as defined by decision-makers at the time of a specific crisis. "Core" values, by contrast, are shared by changing régimes and decision-making groups as well as by the attentive and mass publics of the state under inquiry. A crisis may be said to exist when the threatened values are not only "high-priority" for the incumbent elite but also include one or more "core" values. In short, this view differs from Hermann's in two respects: first, it is values, not goals, that are under threat in a crisis situation; and second, a crisis implies the involvement of a "basic value."

e. The most important change is the addition of "perceived high probability of war" as a necessary condition of crisis. In both cases cited above, decision-makers of the United States (1961) and Israel (1967) thought it very likely that they would be involved in military hostilities before the threat to values was resolved. Theoretically, the perceived probability of war can range from .001 to .999. Operationally, "high probability" may be designated as .50 to .99— that is, at least a 50/50 possibility. However, a marked change in the probability of war (e.g., from .1 to .3) may be just as salient to decision-makers as a move into the high-probability range—especially in cases where protracted conflict predisposes them to expect crisis. What is crucial to the existence of an international crisis is a high—or substantial rise in—perceived war likelihood. Threat and time pressure may coexist without a situational change being defined, or responded to, as an external crisis. Moreover, the

probability of war necessarily implies a perceived threat to values
—but the reverse does not obtain. Thus, probability of war is the
pivotal condition of crisis, with threat and time closely related, as
will be specified below in the model of behavior in international
crisis.[8]

The centrality of perceived high probability of war is also contained in the Snyder-Diesing definition of crisis:

An international crisis is a sequence of interactions between the governments of two or more sovereign states in severe conflict, short of actual
war, but involving the perception of a dangerously high probability of war.

In elaboration,

The centerpiece of [the] definition is "the perception of a dangerously
high probability of war" by the governments involved. Just how high the
perceived probability must be to qualify as a crisis is impossible to specify.
But ordinary usage of the term *crisis* implies that whatever is occurring
might result in the outbreak of war. The perceived probability must at
least be high enough to evoke feelings of fear and tension to an uncom-
fortable degree.[9]

While a *perceived high probability of war* is common to the
Snyder-Diesing and ICB definitions of crisis, there are important
differences. For Snyder-Diesing, crisis is an *interaction* process;
we focus on the perceptions and behavior of one state, an *action*
process. Secondly, they ignore the time component, both its duration and intensity, though we share the view that crises need not
be short—some last many months, even a year or more. And
thirdly, "the term *probability of war* excludes war itself from the

8. All five departures from the Hermann definition of crisis—omission of surprise, finite rather than short time, internal as well as external trigger mechanisms,
basic values instead of high-priority goals, and the high probability of war—seem
to be supported by empirical evidence. Their validity will be tested in this and
other case studies of the ICB Project. It will be evident that, with the first four
changes, the ICB definition of crisis is very similar to the original Robinson view
of crisis. One crucial difference remains—our emphasis on the perceived high
probability of war.

9. G. H. Snyder and P. Diesing, *Conflict Among Nations: Bargaining, Decision Making, and System Structure in International Crises* (Princeton, N.J.,
1977), pp. 6–7. This component was emphasized by Snyder in an earlier, less
crystalized definition of crisis: "International politics is pervasively conditioned
by the 'expectation of potential war'. . . . But in a crisis the element of potential
war is elevated from an underlying to a central and imminent position, and its
behavioral consequences tend to be starkly revealed" ("Crisis Bargaining," in
C. F. Hermann, ed., *International Crises*, 1972, p. 217).

concept 'crisis' . . . ," whereas the ICB Project develops the concept of intra-war crisis.

Others, too, define international crises as situations that *might* lead to war. McClelland, for example, views crisis as a "transition from peace to war. . . . A crisis refers to both a real prelude to war and an averted approach toward war. Crises are most commonly thought of as interpositions between the prolongation of peace and the outbreak of war."[10] But McClelland, as noted earlier, along with Schelling and Young, focuses on crisis at the systemic (macro) or interaction levels of analysis, not on the decision process within one crisis actor. Moreover, all three identify the *possibility*, not *probability*, of war.[11]

Crises are generally identified with situational changes which occur prior to the outbreak of large-scale hostilities. Preliminary research, however, has shown that there are developments during a war which logically fall into the category of triggers to an international crisis for a warring state. An intra-war crisis (IWC) manifests conditions 1 and 3 of the definition specified earlier—a threat to basic values and an awareness of finite time for response, generated by an environmental change. By its very nature, an IWC excludes the condition, perceived high probability of war. The replacement indicator is a perceived deterioration in a state's and/or an ally's military capability vis-à-vis the enemy—that is, an adverse change in the military balance. This replacement indicator may also be appropriate in a post-crisis period if the beginning of that period is synonymous with the outbreak of war—as

10. C. A. McClelland, "The Beginning, Duration, and Abatement of International Crises," in C. F. Hermann, ed., *International Crises,* 1972, p. 83. See also T. C. Schelling, *Arms and Influence* (New Haven, 1966), pp. 96–97, and O. R. Young, *The Intermediaries,* 1967, p. 10.

11. One more definition of crisis which may be noted is that of Edward L. Morse: "the sudden emergence (whether or not anticipated) of a situation requiring a policy choice by one or more states within a relatively short period of time, a situation requiring a choice between mutually incompatible but highly valued objectives" ("Crisis Diplomacy, Interdependence, and the Politics of International Economic Relations," in R. Tanter and R. H. Ullman, eds., *Theory and Policy in International Relations* [Princeton, N.J., 1972], p. 127). As Snyder and Diesing correctly comment: "We exclude the notions of suddenness and short time for decision from our own definition because they are not logically necessary and some empirical crises do not have these qualities" (G. H. Snyder and P. Diesing, *Conflict Among Nations,* 1977, p. 9, n. 7). Other substantive and procedural definitions of crisis are discussed in Robinson, "Crisis," 1968, pp. 510–511, and in G. W. Hopple and P. J. Rossa, "International Crisis Analysis: An Assessment of Theory and Research," 1978, unpublished paper, pp. 6–25.

in Israel's 1967 Crisis, when a favorable change in the military balance was responsible for the decline of stress. Six kinds of situational change have thus far been uncovered as triggers to actor-crises during a war:

1. *The entry of a new major actor into an ongoing war.* For example, the USSR into the Pacific War in August 1945, as a crisis for Japan, or the People's Republic of China into the Korean War in October 1950, as a crisis for the United States and South Korea.

2. *The exit of a major actor.* For example, France in June 1940, as a crisis for Great Britain and other allies in the war against Germany.

3. *Technological escalation during a war.* For example, the introduction of nuclear weapons with the Hiroshima A-bomb in August 1945, as a crisis for Japan, and the appearance of mobile, infantry-manipulated antitank and antiaircraft missiles by Egypt in October 1973, as a crisis for Israel.

4. *A major escalation, other than the introduction of a qualitatively advanced technology.* For example, the allies' invasion of Europe in June 1944, as a crisis for Germany.

5. *Defeat in battle which decision-makers perceive as significant.* For example, Stalingrad and El Alamein as crises for Germany during World War II, or Dien Bien Phu in May 1954 as a crisis for France during the first Vietnam War.

6. *A perceived high probability that a major actor will enter a war.* For example, Israel's crisis in 1956 arising from the Soviet threat to intervene in the Suez-Sinai War.

TYPOLOGIES

ICB research on crisis—this volume and others to follow—will focus on three comprehensive typologies: Dimensions of Crisis, Attributes of a Crisis Actor, and Characteristics of the Crisis Decisional Unit. Their essential contents will now be summarized.

The first crisis dimension is *source* or trigger mechanism(s). These fall into three broad categories:

1. Directed external hostile acts, whether verbal—such as threat of attack, retaliation, isolation, or sanctions—or physical. The latter include political acts, like subversion, alliance formation by adversaries, or severance of diplomatic relations; economic acts, such as embargo or blockade; nonviolent military acts—for example, mobilization of reserves, larger-than-normal war games, or the movement of forces closer to one's frontiers; and violent military acts, ranging from a limited force border crossing to a large-scale military attack.

2. Nondirected external changes, which may take the form of: (a) non-
    violent military acts, such as a change in specific weapons, weapon
    systems, or defensive capability; or (b) political acts, such as a chal-
    lenge to one's legitimacy emanating from another actor or an inter-
    national organization.

3. Hostile internal acts, whether verbal or physical. The former com-
    prise challenges to the régime or the specific incumbent élite by
    incitement to disobedience or the use of mass media to undermine
    legitimacy. The latter may take the form of sabotage, terrorism, riots,
    assassination, or an attempted coup d'état.

A second dimension of crisis is its *gravity*, measured by the
basic values which are perceived to be under attack. One is the
survival of a state's population—from genocide to deportation,
servitude, or forced assimilation. Another is political independence, which may be threatened by annexation or by one of several forms of external control—occupation, colonial or protector-
ate status, and the establishment of foreign bases. Other values
are territorial integrity, the autonomy of a political system, economic interest, influence in the international and regional sub-
systems, and societal stability. All of these may be threatened by
various acts. For example, the last, a high-priority value, may be
undermined by an enforced change in the ethnic balance, mass
emigration, the challenge to the legitimacy of a prevailing belief
system, and so on. Similarly, an actor's economic interests may
be impaired by enforced integration into another state's economy, the requisition of natural resources, or the loss of foreign
markets.[12]

The *complexity* of a crisis, a third dimension, may be defined
in terms of quantity and uncertainty. The former relates to the
scope of the decisional task posed by the crisis, ranging from one
to four issue areas; the perceived number of adversaries and allies,
from one to many states and international organizations; the number of input components; and the number of specific inputs oc-
casioned by the crisis. Uncertainty refers to adversaries, self, and

12. The hierarchy of values will vary among cultures, régimes, even historical
eras. For an instructive analysis of China's value hierarchy as it relates to crisis
behavior, revealing how different it is from western states in the period 1950s–
1970s, see D. B. Bobrow, S. Chan, and J. A. Kringen, "Understanding How
Others Treat Crisis: A Multimethod Approach,"*International Studies Quarterly,*
21 (March 1977), 199–224. See also J. A. Kringen and S. Chan, "Chinese Crisis
Perception and Behavior: A Summary of Findings," (unpublished paper, 1976).

others (notably allies), with respect to status, capability, intentions, reliability, scope of values threatened, range of alternatives for choice, and the constraints imposed by distance, time, and technology.

A fourth dimension of crisis is *intensity*, measured by the volume of acts during different periods and stress phases, and their quality, extending from grave to mild.

The *duration* of a crisis may be brief, from one to six days; medium, from one week to three months; or long, extending to more than six months.

Communication patterns constitute a sixth dimension of crisis. They encompass type of communication acts, whether verbal or physical, or both; type of contact, whether formal, third party, mass media, or face-to-face; the level of communication, from head of government to bureaucrats; the extent of formality; the extent of secrecy; and the role of the communication flow over time.

The *outcome* of a crisis is a seventh dimension for analysis. This focuses on the extent of conclusiveness, ranging from conclusive (that is, the termination of hostile acts and resolution of the value threat) to unterminated, an outcome in which hostilities end but the value threat remains. Outcome relates, too, to techniques, such as forcing surrender or submission by means of war, threats, or pressure, and pacific resolution via negotiations, mediation, adjudication, and the like. It also deals with substance—that is, a new equilibrium of power or partial loss of sovereignty or an imposed solution by outside actors. Outcomes are evaluated at that point in time when the three indicators—threat perception, awareness of time pressure, and expectation of military hostilities —decline in intensity to pre-crisis levels.

The dimensions of crisis are presented schematically in Table 1.

There are at least nine attributes of the crisis actor relevant to ICB research. One is *systemic context*—that is, the global and subsystem configuration in which the crisis occurs. This may be hegemonial, loose or tight bipolar, tripolar, polycentric; or theoretically, unipolar, unit veto, universal.[13] Another is *geographic context*,

---

13. These system categories were first delineated by M. Kaplan in his *System and Process in International Politics* (New York, 1957), chap. 2, and his "Some Problems of International Systems Research," in *International Political Communities, An Anthology* (New York, 1966), pp. 469–501.

TABLE 1
DIMENSIONS OF CRISIS

I Source (Trigger)	II Gravity	III Complexity
A. *Directed external hostile acts* Verbal Physical-political Physical-economic Physical-nonviolent military Physical-violent military B. *Nondirected external changes* Nonviolent military acts Political acts C. *Hostile acts: internal* Verbal challenges Physical challenges	A. *Values Threatened* Survival of population Independence as international actor Territorial integrity Autonomy of political system Economic interest Influence in international system(s) Societal stability	A. *Quantity* Range of adversary(ies) Range of ally(ies) Scope of input components Number of inputs B. *Uncertainty* Concerning adversary(ies) Concerning self Concerning ally(ies)

IV Intensity	V Duration	VI Communication Patterns	VII Outcome
A. *Volume* of acts B. *Quality* of acts	Brief Medium Long	A. *Type* of acts of contact B. *Level* C. *Extent* of formality of secrecy	A. *Conclusiveness* B. *Techniques* C. *Substance*

referring to both the location of the crisis actor—by continent and subregion—and to the regional combination of that state and its adversary(ies): for example, East Asia–North America (Japan–United States, 1941) or North Africa–North Africa (Algeria–Morocco, 1975). The *territorial size* of the crisis actor is a third attribute, ranging from large to mini states. So too with *population size,* which ranges from more than 50 million people (large) to less than one million (small). For the post-medieval era, the *age* or independent statehood of the actor may be classified as pre-1648; as modern, from Westphalia to the onset of World War I; as recent,

TABLE 2
ATTRIBUTES OF A CRISIS ACTOR

I Systemic Context	II Geographic Context	III Territorial Size
Global configuration Subsystem configuration	Continent, sub-continent location of crisis actor Regional combination of crisis actor and adversary(ies)	Large Medium Small Mini

IV Population Size	V Age—Independent Statehood	VI Belief System
Large Medium Small Mini	Pre-Western state system (pre-1648) Modern (1648–1914) Recent (1914–1945) Contemporary (1945–1975)	Christian Communist Hindu Jewish Muslim Shinto

VII Régime Type	VIII Economic Development	IX Military Capability
Competitive parties Dominant party— non-Communist Dominant party— Communist Military régime Traditional-monarchical	Post-industrial Modern Developing Undeveloped	Super power Great power Middle power Small power Mini power

from 1914 to 1945; and as contemporary, since the end of World War II.

The crisis actor's *belief system* is a sixth attribute which may be associated with different patterns of crisis behavior; it includes Christianity, Communism, Hinduism, Judaism, Islam, Shintoism, and others. Linkages will also be uncovered between régime type and crisis behavior; both the decisional process and choice among alternatives will be affected by whether the régime is a competitive or single-party system, Communist or non-Communist, whether it is controlled by a military junta, a traditional monarchy, etc. An eighth attribute is the level of *economic development*, ranging from post-industrial to undeveloped. Finally, there is the level of *military capability*, from superpower to minipower. The last two attributes will shape an actor's material capacity to respond to a crisis.

The actor attributes are presented schematically in Table 2.

The first of at least seven characteristics of the crisis decisional unit which impinge upon crisis behavior is its *structure*, whether institutional or ad hoc, or a combination of both. Another is its size, which may range from one to n persons. Relevant to behavior, too, is the *duration of prior decisional authority* by persons confronted with a crisis: Those with long experience may be better able to cope than those new to governmental responsibility. Another characteristic is *experience in dealing with crisis*, including the number of crises dealt with, from none to many; the cumulative time spent under crisis-induced stress, from less than one week to more than a year; the role played in previous crises, from nil to primacy in decision-making; and the relative failure or success in coping with past crises. All this will influence a decision-maker's tendency to conceptual rigidity—that is, to draw from past experience (analogize) or "the lessons of history."

The attitudinal prism and specific images of members of the decisional unit, that is, their *psychological environment*, will establish their predispositional response pattern to a crisis. Coping will depend on several aspects of information processing: the probe for information; its sources, both number and type; the number of organizations collecting and interpreting information; the receptivity to information by decision-makers, from open to biased; and the structure of the processing complex—that is, the hierarchical pattern and the size of the information-absorbing group. Finally, there is the *realm of options*, as perceived by the decisional unit. There are three theoretical possibilities. The decisional unit can act—by means of diplomatic, military, economic, and/or legal actions which escalate or de-escalate the crisis. It can delay a decision—from one day to the time the adversary acts. Or it can do nothing—that is, ignore the environmental change. In its behavior the decisional unit will perceive constraints on the exercise of options. They may flow from: the structure,

TABLE 3
CHARACTERISTICS OF THE CRISIS DECISIONAL UNIT

I Structure	II Size	III Previous Decisional Authority
Institutional	Large	Brief
Ad hoc	Medium	Medium
Combined	Small	Long

IV Crisis Experience	V Psychological Environment
Number of crises dealt with	A. *External*
Time under crisis-induced stress	Global system
Role in previous foreign policy crises	Subordinate system
Performance in past crises	Subordinate system (other)
	Dominant-bilateral relations
	Bilateral relations
	B. *Internal*
	Military capability
	Economic capability
	Political structure
	Interest groups
	Competing elites

VI Information Processing	VII Real and Perceived Options
Number of sources	A. *Real Alternatives*
Type of sources	Escalating or de-escalating acts
Number of collecting organizations	To delay decision
	To do nothing
Number of interpreting organizations	B. *Perceived constraints re options*
Time span	Decisional units
Size of processing group	Available resources
	Third-party pressures
	Type of political régime
	Ideological incompatibilities
	Domestic interest groups
	Information gaps
	Communication failures

size, and/or composition of the unit itself; limited resources; pressures from ally(ies), adversary(ies), or a superpower; the type of political régime; domestic pressure groups; information gaps; and communication failures. Any or all of these perceived constraints will affect behavior in a crisis.

The characteristics of the decisional unit are presented schematically in Table 3.

MODEL

The principal concepts of the analytic framework of research—foreign policy system, input, process, output, operational environment, communication network, psychological environment, attitudinal prism, image, issue areas, formulation, implementation, and feedback—have been elaborated elsewhere.[14] The approach, designated as "structured empiricism," is based upon three assumptions: (1) every international crisis can be dissected systematically through time in terms of a foreign policy system; (2) there are universal categories to classify relevant data; and (3) comparable findings can be used to test the utility of a model, as well as to generate and assess hypotheses about the crisis behavior of different types of states.

In essence, according to the framework, events within the operational environment or actions by international, transnational, or subnational actors come to the attention of a state's decision-makers via a communication network. In this way, they become inputs into a foreign policy system—that is, stimuli that are filtered through their attitudinal prisms and are specified as decision-makers' images. That psychological environment predisposes them to choose among perceived options. The formulation and implementation of decisions involve the working of bureaucratic and organizational processes. And from the implementation of choices, or decisions, consequences will ensue in the form of feedback to one or more of the environmental components, to the decision-makers, and/or to their psychological environment. Thus a foreign policy system is characterized by a ceaseless flow, from the opera-

14. M. Brecher, B. Steinberg, and J. G. Stein, "A Framework for Research on Foreign Policy Behavior," *The Journal of Conflict Resolution*, 13 (March 1969), 75–101, and M. Brecher, *The Foreign Policy System of Israel* (London and New Haven, 1972), chap. 1.

tional environment to implementing acts which create new, ongoing stimuli to various segments of the system.

A model of state behavior in international crisis has been constructed within this framework:[15]

1. The *independent* variable is *perception of crisis* as derived from decision-makers' images of stimuli from the environment. In operational terms, there are three independent —but closely related—perceptual variables: threat; time pressure; and high probability of involvement in military hostilities, or high probability of war.[16]

2. The *intervening* variable is *coping,* as manifested in four processes and mechanisms: information search and absorption; consultation; decisional forums; and the consideration of alternatives.

3. The *dependent* variable is *choice*—that is, decision.

The model (Figure 1) postulates a time sequence and causal links among its variables. The trigger events, acts, or environmental changes occur at time t_1. These are the *sine qua non* for an

15. As distinct from a taxonomy or framework, the most demanding construct, a model, requires a clear specification of variables and the hypothetical relations among them; that is, a rigorous attribution of cause-effect linkages. These need not be—but often are—quantitative in form. The purist kind of model would also specify the threshold level for each stress phase in quantitative terms. I restrict myself here to indicating the attributes of the choice patterns identified with different intensities of crisis-induced stress. Statements about relationships are phrased in terms of probability, namely, if variable a, b, . . . then effects x, y, . . .

This model is concerned with *crisis behavior*, especially *decision-making* under crisis, not with crisis warning and forecasting or with crisis management. Those are explored in a special issue. See R. A. Young, ed., "International Crisis: Progress and Prospects for Applied Forecasting and Management," *International Studies Quarterly,* 21 (March 1977), 5–248. Academic research on all three aspects is assessed in R. Tanter, "International Crisis Behavior: An Appraisal of the Literature," *The Jerusalem Journal of International Relations,* 3 (Winter–Spring 1978), 340–374.

16. These are not synonymous. Military hostilities may be brief, marginal in resource allocation, and peripheral in terms of the state's total responsive behavior during a crisis. War is of a qualitatively different order of significance in a state's reaction to a crisis. Yet in the perceptions of decision-makers, military hostilities invariably contain the seed of war, through noncontrollable escalation. Hence, "probability of war" or "war likelihood" are used interchangeably in the model with "probability of involvement in military hostilities."

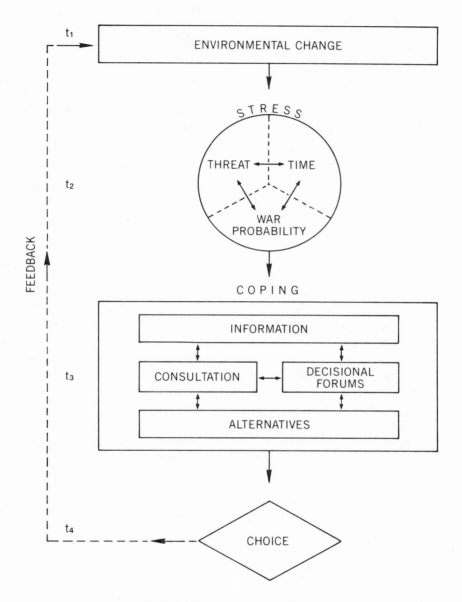

Figure 1. Model of International Crisis Behavior

international crisis viewed from the perspective of a single state actor; that is, they necessarily precede and stimulate changes in decision-makers' perceptions of threat (and later of time pressure and high probability of war as well). Perceptions of crisis, the composite independent variable, are generated and often expressed at time t_2. They are the cognitive reaction to the environmental stimulus, and they induce a feeling of stress. Decision-makers respond to threatening developments by adopting one or more coping strategies.[17] Whichever is selected, coping occurs within the broad time frame, t_3. Changes in perceptions of crisis affect not only coping mechanisms and processes, they also influence the content of decisions. In terms of the model, crisis-induced stress (the independent variable) at t_2 is mediated through coping (the intervening variable) at t_3 and shapes decisions (the dependent variable) at t_4. The direct link to choice is from the decisional forum, which selects one option after evaluation of alternatives in accordance with a set of decision rules.

The variables of the crisis behavior model and their interrelations may now be elaborated. According to Lazarus, "*Threat* refers to the anticipation of harm of some kind, an anticipation that is created by the presence of certain stimulus cues signifying to the individual [or group] that there is to be an experience of harm."[18] Threat perception incorporates the dimensions of activity (active–passive); potency (strong–weak); and affect (central–peripheral).

The notion of time pressure is closely related to uncertainty. Decision-makers may be uncertain, for example, about their adversary(ies) or the scope of information to be absorbed. Time pressure refers to the gap between available time and the deadline for choice. "Crisis time" cannot be equated with "clock time"; it depends on available time in relation to time pressure for decision. Thus, if a

17. Among these the most likely are:
1. A "satisficing" rather than "optimizing" decision strategy.
2. The strategy of "incrementalism."
3. Deciding what to do on the basis of "consensus politics."
4. Avoidance of value trade-offs.
5. Use of historical models to diagnose and prescribe for present situations.
6. Reliance on ideology and general principles as a guide to action.
7. Reliance on "operational code" beliefs.

From O. R. Holsti and A. L. George, "The Effects of Stress on the Performance of Foreign Policy-Makers," *Political Science Annual*, 6 (1975), 264.

18. *International Encyclopedia of the Social Sciences*, David L. Sills, ed., vol. 15 (London, 1968), p. 340.

problem can be resolved in twenty-four hours, and forty-eight hours are available, time will be less salient for behavior. Conversely, time will be more salient if, in a 48-hour clock time situation, a decision cannot be reached for ninety-six hours.[19] When decision-makers are uncertain, the pressure of time is likely to be greater.

The probability of war (or military hostilities), too, is related to uncertainty. If war is perceived to be certain, or as certain *not* to occur, the situational change which generates that image is the source of something other than a crisis: there must be some uncertainty about war involvement.[20] A sharp change in perceived probability of war may, as noted, be just as salient as high probability. Moreover, the saliency of changes in probability may also be a function of whether decision-makers are confronted with nuclear as opposed to conventional war. It is uncertainty about war, along with value threat and time pressure, that makes a situation a crisis and leads to "crisis-type" decision-making.

The three independent variables are logically separate: threat refers to value, time to temporal constraint, and war to means of goal attainment. One would expect, however, to find interrelations among the three components of crisis. It may be argued that the more active and stronger the threat and the more central the value(s) threatened, the higher will be the perceived probability that military hostilities will ensue. That, in turn, would lead to a more intense perception of crisis. Similarly, the more active, the stronger, and the more central (basic) the threatened value(s), the more limited will be the perceived time for response. Moreover, the greater the time pressure, the higher will be the perceived probability of war and the more intense the perception of threat. The reverse relationship also obtains: the higher the perceived probability of war, the more central, active, and strong will be the perceived value threat, and the more limited will be the time perceived to be available for response to that threat. In short, it is postulated that the three crisis components operate in mutually interacting relationships.

19. J. A. Robinson, "Crisis," in C. F. Hermann, ed., *International Crises,* 1972, pp. 24–25.
20. In the situations of May–June 1967 and September–October 1973, the major foci of this inquiry, there were feasible options from which to choose: to mobilize or not, to delay or fight, to pre-empt or await a first Arab strike, etc. And in both cases, war was not perceived by Israel's decision-makers as certain.

Two of these linkages, between threat and environmental stimulus and between threat and time, have been lucidly summarized as follows:

The immediate stimulus configuration resulting in threat merely heralds the coming of harm. Threat is thus a purely psychological concept, an interpretation of the situation by the individual. . . .

Another, less emphasized factor in the stimulus configuration is the imminence of the confrontation with harm. Threat is more intense when harm is more imminent.[21]

The composite independent variable, as noted, creates stress among decision-makers. The breadth of that concept is indicated by Lazarus, in the same excerpt:

As in the use of the term in engineering, where it is applied to forces exerted on inorganic objects, "stress" suggests excessive demands made on men and animals, demands that produce disturbances of physiological, social, and psychological systems. . . . "Stress," as the term is used in the social sciences, has been applied to phenomena as diverse as metabolic imbalance following surgery . . . [and] the societal disruptions produced by naturally occurring disasters. The term "stress" is thus loose, in that it is applied to a host of phenomena related only by their common analogy with the engineering concept, and, at the same time, exceedingly broad, in that it covers phenomena at the physiological, social, and psychological levels of analysis that may be described in a common theoretical language of causes, intervening processes, and effects.[22]

According to Janis and Mann,

Psychological stress is used as a generic term to designate unpleasant emotional states evoked by threatening environmental events or stimuli. A "stressful" event is any change in the environment that typically induces a high degree of unpleasant emotion (such as anxiety, guilt, or shame) and affects normal patterns of information processing.[23]

Holsti and George, who have contributed much insight into the psychological aspects of foreign policy decision-making, have remarked:

21. R. S. Lazarus, *International Encyclopedia of the Social Sciences,* 1968, pp. 340, 343.

22. Ibid., pp. 337–338. For a comprehensive analysis of psychological stress, see R. S. Lazarus, *Psychological Stress and the Coping Process* (New York, 1966).

23. I. L. Janis and L. Mann, *Decision Making* (New York, 1977), p. 50. The indicators of stress are the perceptual changes that also mark period-to-period transitions within a crisis, to be specified below. Thus, for example, higher threat and the onset of time pressure and perceived probability of war mean higher stress. And a decline in intensity of these perceptions is equated with less stress.

It is customary to regard "stress" as the anxiety or fear an individual experiences in a situation which he perceives as posing a severe threat to one or more values. . . . Psychological stress requires an interpretation by the subject of the significance of the stimulus situation. Psychological stress occurs either when the subject experiences damage to his values or anticipates that the stimulus situation may lead to it. "Threat," therefore, is not simply an attribute of the stimulus; it depends on the subject's appraisal of the implications of the situation. Thus, the perception of threat is regarded as the central intervening variable in psychological stress.[24]

Throughout this volume, *stress* and the term *crisis-induced stress* are used as code words for the perception of threat and/or time pressure and/or probability of war. It is those perceptions that set in motion the multiple coping processes and mechanisms leading to choice.

The first reactive (coping) step by decision-makers is to seek information about the threatening event(s) or act(s): Threat-induced stress may generate a greater than normal felt need for information and a consequent quest. The probe may be through ordinary or special channels; marginal, modest, or thorough; and may be related to the level of stress. The information may be received with an open mind or through a lens biased by ideology, memories of past experience, etc.; and it will be processed by n persons, in small, medium, or large groups. The kind of receptivity and size of the absorbing group, too, will vary with the level of stress. As indicated in Figure 1, changes in crisis-induced stress at t_2 cause changes in information processing at t_3; but the *precise effects* on the extent of the probe, the type of receptivity, and the size of the absorbing group will vary among

24. O. R. Holsti and A. L. George, "The Effects of Stress," p. 257. They thereby give "stress" an autonomy and significance greater than that specified in our model. For them, threat creates stress, the dependent variable. For us, threat, time, and war likelihood perceptions, as manifested in stress, serve as the independent variable in a two-step, or dual-linkage, model of crisis behavior, a point to be elaborated upon below. Earlier, in an extensive discussion of "Crisis, Stress, and Decision-Making," Holsti defined stress as *"the result of a situation that threatens important goals or values."* And he quoted, approvingly, "the most widely used definition of a stressful situation—one that 'seems to be threatening to most people.'" He also noted the lack of consensus on operational measures of stress: "Some define it as the stimulus (e.g., a severe threat), whereas others view it as the perceptual and behavioural response to threat." He adopted the latter; we identify stress with the perceptual reaction only; the behavioral response to the stimulus encompasses coping. See O. R. Holsti, *Crisis, Escalation, War,* 1972, pp. 11 and 37, respectively.

states, depending upon their diverse attributes, as noted in Table 2 above.

The initial acquisition of information leads to a process of consultation. This involves peer members of the high-policy elite, bureaucratic and military subordinates, and possibly others, such as persons from competing elites and interest groups. Consultation may be frequent or infrequent, ad hoc or institutional in form, within a large or small circle, comprising one or more groups and n persons. Coping involves, too, the activation of a decisional forum, which varies in size and structure. As with the several aspects of information processing, changes in the intensity of crisis-induced stress will have effects on the pattern of consultation and the size, type, and authority pattern of the decisional unit. Case studies will illuminate the variation by international crisis actor. Moreover, as specified in the model, consultation will occur before and/or simultaneously with the creation of the decisional unit to consider alternatives and make a choice.

Search and evaluation were defined by Holsti and George as follows:

Search refers to the processes of obtaining and sharing relevant information, and of identifying and inventing alternative options; [and] *analysis* (or evaluation) refers to the processes of examining relationships among the available information and evaluating the relative appropriateness of alternative options with reference to stated or alternative objectives and values.[25]

The search for and evaluation of options will depend upon the intensity of crisis-induced stress, especially the amount of time perceived by decision-makers as available before a decisional response must be made. Once again, the model specifies a causal link between perceptions of crisis at t_2 and the processing of alternatives at t_3. Just as changes in crisis-induced stress will affect one

25. O. R. Holsti and A. L. George, "The Effects of Stress," p. 271, n. 10. This follows the work of leading organizational theorists, Simon, March, and Cyert. It will be evident that the several processes identified by Holsti and George with the search stage of decision-making have been separated in the model: "obtaining" information is in our "information processing"; "sharing" information is in all our four coping mechanisms; and "identifying and inventing alternative options" is in our "search for alternatives." Information sought about the threatening event, act, and/or change at the outset is made available to the consultative circle and decisional forum and is revised during the consideration of alternatives.

or all aspects of coping in various ways, so too, the model posits, different patterns of choice will be associated with different levels of stress and will vary among states. The content of these choice patterns will emerge from case studies.

Figure 1 specifies a model of state behavior in the crisis as a whole. However, several choices will be made during a crisis. Moreover, stress changes, beginning with a more intense than normal perception of threat on the part of decision-makers and ending with de-escalation toward "normal" perceptions of threat, time pressure, and war likelihood. Thus a three-period model of crisis behavior was designed in order to specify the changes that take place within a crisis: from its inception, with low stress (pre-crisis period), through rising, higher, and peak phases of stress (crisis period), to a moderating, declining phase (post-crisis period).

In this volume, the word *crisis* used alone or with a date (for example, the 1967 Crisis or the 1973 Crisis), refers to the total phenomenon under inquiry, from the first trigger event, act, or situational change until the return of the perceptual indicators of threat, time pressure, and probability of war to noncrisis levels.

The *pre-crisis period* is marked off from a preceding noncrisis period by a conspicuous increase in perceived threat on the part of decision-makers of the state under inquiry. It begins with the event (or cluster of events) that triggers a rise in threat perception.

The *crisis period* is characterized by the presence of all three necessary conditions of crisis—a sharp rise in perceived threat to basic values, an awareness of time constraints on decisions, and an image of the probability of involvement in military hostilities (war likelihood) at some point before the issue is resolved. It, too, begins with a trigger event (or cluster of events). If war occurs at the outset of the crisis period or within its time frame, the third condition takes the form of a perceived decline in military capability vis-à-vis the enemy (or an adverse change in the military balance), i.e., increasing threat.

The *post-crisis period* begins with an observable decline in intensity of one or more of the three perceptual conditions—threat, time pressure, and war probability. If the onset of this

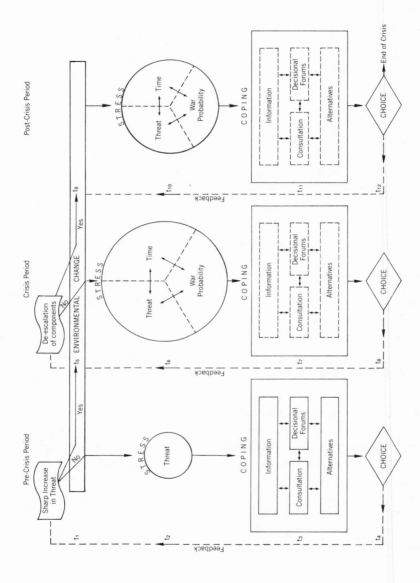

Figure 2. A Three-Stage Model of International Crisis Behavior

period is synonymous with the outbreak of war, the third condition is replaced by an image of greater military capability vis-à-vis the enemy (or favorable changes in the military balance), i.e., declining threat.

The post-crisis period (and the entire crisis) may be said to terminate when the intensity of relevant perceptions has returned to noncrisis norms. If, during the post-crisis period of Crisis A, threat perception re-escalates but with a different focus, this indicates an emerging pre-crisis period of a new crisis. If all three perceptual components rise simultaneously, this signifies that the post-crisis period of Crisis A is merging into the crisis period of Crisis B.

The three-stage model (Figure 2) follows the unified model in its central postulates: first, a time sequence from the trigger event or act (t_1), to perceived threat (t_2) (and, later, time pressure and probability of war), to coping (t_3), to choice (t_4), with feedback to the environment; and, second, a causal link from crisis-induced stress, mediated through coping, to choice, or decision. The three-stage model, however, goes further in trying to incorporate the pivotal concept of periods within a crisis, each with explicit indicators as noted above. Thus, whereas Figure 1 presents crisis as a total, integral phenomenon, Figure 2 monitors change from the beginning to the end of a crisis, through each period.

Viewed in this more elaborate frame, the sequence from trigger to choice is replicated three times: t_1-t_4 in the pre-crisis period; t_5-t_8 in the crisis period; and t_9-t_{12} in the post-crisis period. Among the independent variables, perceived threat alone is present in the pre-crisis period, as indicated. Stress will therefore be at its lowest and will have x effects on coping processes and mechanisms, and on decisions. The implementation of these decisions will generate feedback to the environment. As long as this does not induce a sharp increase in threat, the flow from trigger to choice will be repeated. The essentially unchanged—and low—level of crisis-induced stress may lead to n decisions by a state within the pre-crisis period. It is only when the feedback from decisions to the environment, or some other situational change—or both—trigger a sharp rise in threat and, with it, an awareness of time pressure and the likelihood of war that the onset of the crisis period can be identified.

As is evident in Figure 2, threat perception in the crisis period is conspicuously larger than in the pre-crisis period. Moreover, time and the probability of war become salient. Therefore, crisis-induced stress escalates, with consequences for both coping and choice. Their actual content will become known only as a result of empirical inquiry and will vary; thus the boundaries of coping processes and mechanisms, and of choice, are represented by broken lines. As long as the perceived crisis components do not reveal declining intensity, the flow from t_5 to t_8 will be replicated, within a crisis period encompassing rising, higher, and peak crisis phases. Just as the model predicts a distinctive pattern of choice in the low-stress pre-crisis period, so too it posits different choice patterns in the stress phases of the crisis period.

When feedback from one or more choices, or a situational change, triggers a decline in intensity among the perceptual components of crisis, another breakpoint has occurred—namely, the transition from crisis period to post-crisis period. As indicated, stress will lessen, and that in turn will affect coping and choice in forms and extent likely to be different from those in both the crisis and pre-crisis periods. In short, the model predicts at least three, and possibly more, patterns of choice. The broken lines there, too, indicate lack of *a priori* knowledge about the content of effects. Ultimately, a decision or cluster of choices in the post-crisis period will lead to a situational change that is perceived as no more threatening, time-constraining, or likely to confront the particular state with war than events or acts in noncrisis periods. At that point, the crisis ends.

The ICB model of crisis behavior includes two linkages: first, between different levels of crisis-induced stress and coping processes and mechanisms; and second, between stress levels and choice patterns.[26] One of the tasks of this volume, and of the ICB Project as a whole, will be to test the validity of the model as a guide to understanding the crisis behavior of states.

In the quest for knowledge and theory, one seeks to discover or confirm relationships which obtain for a number of nonidentical

---

26. As such, this model attempts to fill a major *lacuna* noted by two scholars on the borderland of international crisis behavior and psychology: "In evaluating the consequences of stress it is necessary to consider not merely the effect on formal process variables but also the ultimate effect on the substance of the resulting decisions. We advocate, that is, a *two-step* model for evaluating the impact of stress on the process and substance of policy-making" (O. R. Holsti and A. L. George, "The Effects of Stress," p. 269).

occurrences, phenomena, processes, etc. Thus, in the analysis of crisis behavior, one attempts to predict the probable outcome of decision processes which have been investigated and of those not yet analyzed which clearly fall within the scope of definition of the given universe of data—that is, crisis decisions. The ICB inquiry into international crisis behavior and the individual case studies are guided by an overarching research question and several that derive therefrom. All focus on the model and its core variables.

The central question addressed by this book may be stated thus: What is the impact of changing stress, derived from changes in perceptions of threat, time pressure, and the probability of war, on (a) the processes and mechanisms through which decision-makers cope with crisis; and (b) their choices? Following the model, the case studies of state behavior in crisis address nine specific questions. What are the effects of escalating and de-escalating crisis-induced stress:

on information: 1.   cognitive performance.

2.   the perceived need and consequent quest for information.

3.   the receptivity and size of the information-processing group.

on consultation: 4.   the type and size of consultative units.

5.   group participation in the consultative process.

on decisional   6.   the size and structure of decisional forums.
forums:
7.   authority patterns within decisional units.

on alternatives: 8.   the search for and evaluation of alternatives.

9.   the perceived range of available alternatives.[27]

27. An earlier formulation of twenty-two ICB research questions is to be found in M. Brecher, "Toward a Theory of International Crisis Behavior," *International Studies Quarterly*, 21 (March 1977), 59–60. Each question referred to a link between one of the three perceptual variables—threat, time pressure, probability of war—and one aspect of crisis behavior. The nine questions above encompass almost all of the original twenty-two questions but in a form which facilitates an analysis of the causal links between crisis components and coping specified in the model. The original set of questions served as the unifying thread for preliminary reports on nine cases, ranging in time from Holland in 1939–40 to Syria's behavior in the Lebanon civil war, 1975–76, in M. Brecher, ed., *Studies in Crisis Behavior* (New Brunswick, N.J., 1979). Some of the full-length ICB studies may not be able to address all of the research questions noted here because of data availability problems. They may focus on only one major aspect of coping, such as information processing.

These questions provide the focus for comparative inquiry. Findings will be used to generate new hypotheses on crisis behavior
and to assess others drawn from the literature.[28]

The independent variable, perception of crisis—or more precisely, perceptions of threat, time pressure, and probability of war
—is analyzed by quantitative and qualitative techniques. The
former combines several types of content analysis—for example,
of secretly communicated and recorded images prior to crisis decisions when they are available (as with Japan's decisions for war and
peace in 1941 and 1945), or of a sample of publicly articulated
statements by decision-makers before making their choices among
options. More specifically, content analysis will take one or all of
three forms, depending upon data availability:

1. *Intensity of crisis perceptions,* derived from all statements expressing
    an awareness of threat, time constraint, and probability of war.

2. *Analysis of attitudes,* based upon statements of friendship and
    hostility, satisfaction with the status quo, and demand for change in
    the status quo, the intensity of which is measured by the "pair com-
    parison" scaling method.[29]

28. The comparative thrust of the ICB Project and its Typologies for Research
on Crisis Behavior are similar in approach and design to the method of "focused
comparison" and the "typology of deterrence situations" in A. L. George and R.
Smoke, *Deterrence and Defense in American Foreign Policy: Theory and Practice*
(New York, 1974), pp. 95–97: "The method of 'focused comparison'. . . resembles
the statistical-correlational approach. . . . it proceeds by asking a limited number
of questions or testing a limited number of hypotheses. . . . But the focused comparison method also resembles the intensive case study approach . . . in that it ex-
amines each case in some depth. . . . All cases are approached by asking identical
questions. This standardized set of questions or hypotheses insures the compara-
bility of results. . . . With this method the investigator is able . . . to uncover similarities among cases that suggest possible generalizations; but he is also able to
investigate the differences among cases in a systematic manner. Analysis of differences can be just as useful as analysis of similarities for the development of theory.
. . . Comparison of cases can thus lead to what might be termed 'contingent generalizations'—'if circumstances A than outcome O'—which can be an important
part of theory and have important implications for practice. . . . What the focused
comparison method can offer in place of a high degree of formal verification may
be something more valuable—potentially a significantly greater degree of relevance to real policy problems. . . . Finally and most importantly, the capacity of
the focused comparison method to differentiate among cases offers a greater *diag-
nostic* potential. . . ." See also A. L. George, "Case Studies and Theory Development," in P. G. Lauren, ed., *Diplomacy: New Approaches in History, Theory and
Policy* (New York, 1979).
29. For examples in international relations research, see D. A. Zinnes, "'Pair
Comparison' Scaling in International Relations," in R. C. North, O. R. Holsti,
D. Zaninovitch, and D. A. Zinnes, *Content Analysis* (Evanston, Ill., 1963), chap.

3. *Advocacy analysis,* the coding of all goals enunciated by decision-
    makers in the dissected messages or statements and their measure-
    ment along a 9-point advocacy statement scale constructed by the
    analyst from expert knowledge of the specific crisis, through the use
    of prototype sentences.[30]

The quantitative (and qualitative) content analysis of statements,
speeches, messages, etc., is supplemented by interview data
where feasible, and by post facto sources of perceptions such as
memoirs and historical accounts of the crisis under investigation.

A reconstruction of the decision flow is another essential part of
the methodology of ICB case studies—because of the dynamic
character of the model. The link between perception of crisis,
coping or decision-making, and choice is not static. Nor is it one-
directional. Rather, as indicated by the feedback arrows in Figures
1 and 2, a continuous interaction is posited. The initial set of
decision-makers' images or their definition of the situation on the
eve of a crisis predisposes them to choice. These perceptions are
mediated through coping mechanisms in a decision-making process which begins with a quest for information and ends with an
evaluation of options. Once a decision is taken, its implementation
affects and may substantially change perceptions of the altered
environment. That, in turn, leads to new choices in response to
new stimuli which are filtered through changed coping mechanisms, in a ceaseless flow of perception, coping, and choice until
the crisis is resolved. Thus a detailed narrative of the decision flow
performs two important functions. First, it illuminates the responsive behavior of the crisis actor as decisions and actions
through time. Second, it provides the indispensable data for an
analysis of coping, or the decision-making process, throughout the
crisis and of the dimensions and patterns of choice by one international crisis actor.

Coping is explored through qualitative and quantitative methods. So too with choice. Each choice pattern is composed of several
different dimensions or traits of the option selected. They are not
additive. Most are perceptual—how the decision-makers view the
choice they made, after the evaluation of alternatives has narrowed
the options to the one which is transformed into a decision. First

5; and J. G. Stein, "Krishna Menon's View of the World—A Content Analysis," in
M. Brecher, *India and World Politics* (London, 1968), pp. 351–362.

30. For an illustration, see M. Brecher, *Decisions in Israel's Foreign Policy*
(London, 1974, and New Haven, 1975), chaps. 6–8.

among these dimensions is the *core input(s):* what is perceived as
the crucial stimulus(i) to each decision? A second is *cost,* the perceived magnitude of the loss anticipated from the choice—human,
material, political, and/or intangible losses. A third is the gravity or
importance of the choice, measured along a five-point scale, from
"decisive" to "marginal." A fourth is *complexity,* the breadth of the
decision's content: does it involve only military or political or other
issue-areas, one or more? The fifth dimension is *systemic domain,*
the perceived scope of reverberations of the decision, from domestic through regional to global. A sixth is the *process* associated with
choosing the selected option, designated as rational, affective, or
routine. *Activity* is another trait of choice—whether verbal or
physical, to act or to delay. And finally, is the choice *novel* or is it
based upon precedent in the crisis behavior of the state under
inquiry? Empirical data on coping and choice are coded. The findings facilitate the search for patterns, the generation and assessment of propositions, and the testing of the validity of a model of
crisis behavior.

   This volume will compare the behavior of a state in two international crises. In the pages that follow, we shall analyze Israel's
behavior during May–June 1967, culminating in the Six Day War,
and during the autumn of 1973, beginning with the eve of the Yom
Kippur War. The inquiry begins with the psychological environment of the principal decision-makers during the pre-crisis period
of each crisis. This is accompanied by a reconstruction of the decision flow for that period. It is followed by a comparative analysis of
the findings on crisis components and coping processes and mechanisms in both the 1967 and 1973 Crises (Part I). This is replicated
for the crisis and post-crisis periods (Parts II and III). The overall
findings on crisis and coping will be presented in Chapter 11,
along with an assessment of hypotheses derived from other cases
and the literature. In the concluding chapter, the links between
stress and choice will be examined, new hypotheses will be generated from our findings, and an application of the general model to
Israel's two cases will be offered (Part IV). Throughout, the inquiry
will be guided by the research questions indicated earlier.
   Israel, a relatively new state whose location and ideology placed
her in an environment of protracted conflict, is ideally suited to
crisis research in depth. A small state with a Western Democratic
political system and a high level of military capability, Israel has a
well-defined set of values which are shared by her predominantly

Jewish population. Perceptions of threat to basic values, notably to her survival as a sovereign state, have been ubiquitous since 1948. The studies of the 1967 and 1973 Crises will explore, inter alia, how her decision-makers behaved when the escalation of threat changed their perceived probability of war, in one case, and led to misperceptions of war likelihood, in the other. In both cases, however, all the necessary conditions of crisis were present, with different consequences for the patterns of choice.

The author is not unaware that confusion may arise from the interruptions of a "normal" chronological flow of events. But his decision to divide each crisis into three periods has a social scientific rationale. As noted earlier, the pre-crisis period is demarcated by the presence of a qualitative change in one perceptual condition —namely, threat. Such was the case between 7 April and 16 May 1967, and from 13 September to 4 October 1973. The crisis period, by contrast, manifests a qualitative change in all three perceptions, with threat sharply increased. This was evident from 17 May to 4 June 1967 and from 5 to 26 October 1973. Finally, in the post-crisis period, the three conditions experience a decline in intensity, and this obtained from 5 to 10 June 1967 and from 27 October 1973 to 31 May 1974. In the former crisis, although war was raging, the overwhelming Israeli military triumph in the early hours of the first day drastically reduced the intensity of threat perception: threat-induced stress was replaced by the stress of historic opportunities.

It is the ICB view that the demarcation of a total crisis—in these two cases, 7 April to 10 June 1967 and 13 September 1973 to 31 May 1974—into three periods can be established for any crisis in time and space by operationalizing the criteria specified in the definition of these three periods. This facilitates the attainment of several goals in the analysis of crisis behavior. First, it may clarify the causal link between decision-makers' images and their choices within each period. Second, it can illuminate differences in behavioral response across crises—for example, the decisions to mobilize and, later, to pre-empt in 1967, and the decisions *not* to mobilize until the eleventh hour and *not* to pre-empt in 1973. And third, comparative analysis will uncover findings which can generate new hypotheses about how different states behave in each of the three periods of diverse international crises. A rigorous comparison is facilitated by the brief time span—six years—between the two cases for the same state, and the cardinal fact that three of the four principal decision-makers in the 1967 and 1973 Crises were the same—namely, Moshe Dayan, Abba Eban, and Yigal Allon, with Levi Eshkol as Prime Minister in 1967 and Golda Meir in 1973.

Research for both cases was based upon a large number of primary and secondary source materials: reliable accounts of secret Israeli deliberations; extensive interviews with members of the decisional units and their consultative circles; private papers, memoirs, and diaries; and a content analysis of publicly articulated statements. The emphasis throughout is on the impact of changing perceptions of threat, time pressure, and the probability of war on coping and on choice.

PART ONE

PRE-CRISIS PERIOD

CHAPTER TWO

1967: 7 APRIL TO 16 MAY

ISRAEL'S most important foreign policy crisis prior to 1967 culminated in the Sinai Campaign of 1956.[1] In the 1967 Crisis, decisions were much more concentrated in time—barely a month, compared to six months. The level of intensity was much higher, and there were many more decisions, more closely integrated: All were focused on what decision-makers perceived to be the greatest threat since 1948.[2] A decade of "normalcy" in the protracted Arab-Israeli conflict was disturbed by a sudden sharp escalation of violence on 7 April 1967, when six Syrian MiG fighters were shot down over the Golan Heights. During the next three weeks, tension was sustained by a series of terror and sabotage incidents which, together, induced a higher level of perceived threat from Syria.

1. For a comprehensive analysis of Israel's behavior in that crisis, see M. Brecher, *Decisions in Israel's Foreign Policy* (London, 1974, and New Haven, 1975), chap. 6.
2. The War of Independence was the first direct Arab-Israeli military confrontation, but it is not comparable to the Sinai Campaign, the Six Day War, or the Yom Kippur War as a military-security crisis.

DECISIONS AND DECISION-MAKERS

There were three decisions in the 1967 pre-crisis period:

Decision Number	Date	Content
1.	7 May	Israel's Cabinet decided that if Syria did not heed her public warnings and if all other noncoercive methods of persuasion failed, Israel would launch a limited retaliation raid.
2.	15 May	Levi Eshkol, Prime Minister and Defense Minister, and Lieutenant-General Yitzhak Rabin, the Chief of Staff (COS) of the Israel Defense Forces (IDF), decided to alert regular army units and to move some to the Egyptian frontier.
3.	16 May	In the evening, Eshkol and Rabin decided on immediate limited mobilization of reserves.

Israel's decision-makers in the 1967 Crisis can be grouped into four categories: Cabinet ministers; other political leaders; the bureaucratic elite; and the military elite. The Cabinet was the core decisional unit.

Israel's first decision during the pre-crisis period—7 April to 16 May 1967—(and many decisions in the crisis period) was taken by a five-party coalition Government of eighteen ministers which had assumed office on 12 January 1966. The Labor Alignment of *Mapai* (the social-democratic Israel Workers' Party) and *Ahdut Ha'avoda* (the socialist-Zionist Unity of Labor Party) held a decisive majority (12). The other participants were the National Religious Party (*Mafdal* or NRP) (3); *Mapam* (the Left-socialist United Workers Party) (2); and the Independent Liberals (1). The pre-eminent Cabinet ministers were: Levi Eshkol, Prime Minister and, until 1 June 1967, Defense Minister; and Abba Eban, Foreign Minister. Other party leaders did not participate in the deliberations leading to the pre-crisis decisions. The most influential among Israel's civil servants and diplomats throughout the 1967 Crisis was Ya'acov Herzog. As Director-General of the Prime Minister's Office and trusted adviser, he provided Eshkol with ideas, drafted his cables and speeches, and often crystalized thinking at the Cabinet table. From the IDF the assessment and advice of Rabin and Director of Military Intelligence Major-General Aharon Yariv were influential with Eshkol and others. So too was the advice of Major-General

Meir Amit, Head of *Ha-Mosad,* Israel's Counter-Intelligence Service, and the advice of the Chief of Operations, Major-General Ezer Weizman.[3]

PSYCHOLOGICAL ENVIRONMENT

Attitudinal Prism[4]

There was a shared psychological setting among Israel's decision-makers and the consultative circle during the 1967 Crisis as a whole. It is relevant, therefore, to explore that attitudinal prism before analyzing the images of the principal decision-makers in each of the crisis periods.[5]

A major element of that prism was the *historical legacy of 1956–57,* when the United States compelled Israel to withdraw from Sinai, Sharm-e-Sheikh, and the Gaza Strip. A decade later this perceptual link was manifested—during the crisis period—in Israel's efforts to clarify the U.S. Administration's stand, notably by Eban on 26 May and Amit on 31 May–2 June, and in her yielding to Washington's "advice" on two occasions to delay action, on 23 and 28 May.

A second dimension of that prism was the *Ben-Gurion complex,* which warned that military action by Israel without great power

---

3. Appendix A contains biographical data on all persons who were involved in the deliberations and/or decisions taken in each of the three periods of the Crises of 1967 and 1973.

4. The "attitudinal prism" has been defined by M. Brecher (*The Foreign Policy System of Israel: Setting, Images, Process* [London and New Haven, 1972], p. 11) as follows: "Every decision-maker in foreign policy operates within a context of psychological predispositions. These comprise: (a) societal factors, such as ideology and tradition, which derive from the cumulative historical legacy; and (b) personality factors—the idiosyncratic qualities of decision-makers—that is, those aspects of elite attitudes which are not generated by their role occupancy. Together, these influences constitute the screen or prism through which elite perceptions of the operational environment are filtered."

5. There are two types of data which form the basis for the analysis of the psychological environment: (a) public articulated-perceptions, shortly before and during the crisis; and (b) indications of images during secret deliberations of the Cabinet and other forums engaged in the consultation process. The first source is the basis for describing the psychological setting in each period of the two crises under investigation—except for the post-crisis period of 1967. (The reason was that this lasted only six days and was synonymous with the War itself.) The analysis of public documents is supplemented by the less systematic indications of perceptions which are noted, wherever relevant, in the narrative of a decision flow.

support was fraught with danger. Ben-Gurion's own hesitations during the 1967 Crisis were shaped by this conviction. However, its importance went far beyond his individual view: this was the first Israeli security crisis in which Ben-Gurion was not the dominant decision-maker; since he, in 1956, would not act alone, the 1967 view was, "How can we act without great power backing?" Such was the gnawing fear which deterred some Cabinet ministers from an early response to Nasser's actions. As Moshe Carmel, Minister of Transport, recalled:

It was known that BG opposed taking military action, and that he had expressed the opinion that the general mobilization [19 May] had been a mistake, and that Israel had simply to dig in and await developments. I also think that Ben-Gurion did not believe that we were capable of waging this war alone. . . . He influenced quite a few ministers; for them he was after all still an authority on military matters. This was particularly so with the *Mafdal* and its leader, the late Haim Moshe Shapira, who was among the most adamant against taking independent action.[6]

Shapira himself vividly recalled the Ben-Gurion complex as a prominent part of the May–June psychological environment among Israel's decision-makers.[7]

Another component of the shared attitudinal prism was the *Holocaust syndrome*, the fear that Israel's survival was threatened. This was expressed on the eve of the Six Day War (henceforth also SDW) and in its midst by two high-policy decision-makers:

Only 25 years ago, a third of the Jewish people was cruelly annihilated by the murderous forces of the . . . Nazi enemy. . . . Only 19 years have passed since these survivors won their independence and began reconstructing the ruins of their national existence. . . .[8]

The State thus threatened with collective assassination was itself the last sanctuary of a people which had seen six million of its sons exterminated by a more powerful dictator two decades before.[9]

Rabin was no less blunt in asserting the psychological reality of the

    6. Interview, *Jerusalem Post*, 2 June 1972.
    7. Interview with Michael Brecher, 16 July 1968.
    8. Eshkol's letter to USSR Premier Kosygin on 1 June 1967, in reply to the Soviet Note of 26 May 1967. (English version in *Jerusalem Post*, 4 June 1967.)
    9. Eban Address to the UN Security Council, 6 June 1967, *Israel Information Services* (New York, 1967); and in A. Eban, *Voice of Israel* (New York, 1969), p. 301.

Holocaust syndrome: "I said at the time: 'We have no alternative but to answer the challenge forced upon us, because the problem is not freedom of navigation, the challenge is the existence of the State of Israel, and this is a war for that very existence.'"[10] Allon and Golda Meir added their support to the view that Israel's choice in May–June 1967 was "to live or perish." The former declared that, had the Arabs won, "they would have committed genocide."[11] And Meir remarked that, despite "the nonsense uttered by some of our generals," Israel was in danger of annihilation in June 1967.[12]

A fourth shared aspect was a sense of *surprise:* Israel's decision-makers were psychologically unprepared for an imminent full-scale war. According to Eban, "It seemed unthinkable, in the early days of May 1967, that war would descend upon Israel within a month; the crisis escalated suddenly, swiftly, without warning or foreknowledge."[13] Dayan's biographer wrote in a similar vein (emphasis added): "It is worth noting the starting point, and that is that, *like everybody else,* he was surprised by the events which began on May 14th. He thought, as did Chief of Staff Rabin, that war with Egypt is far away."[14] Rabin, too, vividly recalled the element of surprise: "In May 1967 there was no atmosphere of cooperation in the Arab world and it was *impossible to suppose* that in this setting the Arabs would strike against us."[15] Other ministers, including Allon and NRP leader Shapira, emphasized that imminent crisis and war were totally unanticipated.[16] Thus Israel's response to Egypt's first act—despatching troops to Sinai on 14–15 May—was to play down its significance. Only later was a grave threat perceived.

10. Y. Rabin, "Six Days and Five More Years," *Ma'ariv,* 2 June 1972.

11. *Jerusalem Post,* 15 June 1972.

12. Five years after the SDW, several IDF generals denigrated the Holocaust syndrome and denied that Israel had been in jeopardy in May–June 1967. They included the then Deputy Chief of Staff, Haim Bar-Lev (Interview, *Ma'ariv,* 18 April 1972 and 16 May 1973); Ezer Weizman; and the Quarter-Master General, Matityahu Peled, "The Character of Danger," *Ma'ariv,* 24 March 1972. Mrs. Meir was referring to this in the interview with the *Jerusalem Post,* 16 June 1972.

13. Interview with Michael Brecher, 8 August 1968.

14. S. Teveth, *Moshe Dayan* (Jerusalem and Tel Aviv, 1971), p. 560 (in Hebrew).

15. Y. Rabin, *Ma'ariv,* 2 June 1972.

16. Y. Allon, "Active Defense—A Guarantee for our Existence," *Molad,* 1 (July–August, 1967), 137–143 (in Hebrew), and H. M. Shapira, Interview with Michael Brecher, 16 July 1968.

Images

Of the eighteen formally equal Cabinet decision-makers, the most influential in the pre-crisis period, as noted, were Prime Minister Eshkol and Foreign Minister Eban. There is little evidence of their specific images at that time: these were to receive more frequent and cogent expression as the crisis escalated. Superimposed upon the four shared themes in the psychological setting, their salient perceptions during the pre-crisis period may be summarized.

ESHKOL

Eshkol's view of the external environment was marked by realism: he emphasized the primacy of Israel's self-reliant military capability, with international commitments being of supportive value only. Thus on 17 April, soon after a dramatic air battle over Syria, he stated in the Knesset: "When we ask the United States for arms we are told: 'Don't spend your money. We are here. The Sixth Fleet is here!' My reply to this advice is that the Sixth Fleet might not be available fast enough for one reason or another, so Israel must be strong on its own. . . ."[17] This image was to be reaffirmed frequently during the crisis period.

Eshkol perceived the Soviet Union in increasingly negative terms. By contrast, the United States was viewed by him as a patron and ally from the very outset. The Prime Minister's image of the cause of regional tension focused on Syria in the pre-crisis period: later it was to shift to Egypt and Nasser—and the related withdrawal of the UN Emergency Force. His perception of the Arabs was marked by extreme hostility and was saturated with the Second *Aliya* emphasis on force and retaliation: "The firm and persistent stand we have taken on behalf of our rights has strengthened the awareness among our neighbors that they will not be able to prevail against us in open combat. . . ."[18]

EBAN

The Eban image of the United States was no less positive, resting as it did on two pillars: his ambassadorial experience in Washington for almost a decade, which included securing the 1957 U.S.

17. *Divrei Haknesset*, 49 (22 May 1967), 2225–2227. English version in H. M. Christman, ed., *The State Papers of Levi Eshkol* (New York, 1969), pp. 77–89.

18. "Broadcast on Remembrance Day for Those Who Fell in Defense of Israel," State of Israel, *Government Press Office*, mimeo, 13 May 1967. English version in Christman, ed., *The State Papers of Levi Eshkol*, p. 70.

commitment to free passage through the Straits; and his perception of a continuous American commitment to the balance of
power and the territorial status quo in the Middle East. As early as
February 1967, he told a press conference: "I became impressed
by the conviction with which President Johnson, Secretary [of
State] Rusk and Secretary [of Defense] McNamara upheld the
status quo and the arms balance in our region. . . ."[19] The U.S.
role through the crisis was seen by him as falling into three stages:
(1) until 22 May, when Washington did not act fully in terms of
declared policy; (2) 22 May–5 June, a period of U.S. perplexity,
when she did not find a way to carry out her self-recognized obligations; and (3) after 5 June, when firm U.S. support for Israel was
perceived.[20]

The Foreign Minister's image of the Soviets, on the other hand,
began from a cold analytic posture and became increasingly hostile. In fact, his perceptions of the superpowers during the pre-
crisis period, as later, were essentially the same as Eshkol's—
namely, sharply negative towards the USSR and warmly positive
toward the U.S. The relationship between Israel and the UN had
deteriorated steadily during the decade that followed the Sinai
Campaign. Eban was aware of the inability—or unwillingness—of
the universal body to comprehend Israel's security complex, and
he became increasingly disappointed with its role throughout the
1967 Crisis. By contrast, he saw Israel's Sinai Campaign experience as cementing her tacit alliance with France: The Treaty of
Sèvres, a formal document signed by Britain, France, and Israel on
24 October 1956 to launch the Campaign, was, in his eyes, quasi-
legal; and he was to seek, in vain, French support in the 1967
Crisis.

On the tenth anniversary of that Campaign, Eban noted that
among other benefits were Israel's intensified relations with Africa
and Asia, and the fact that the Gaza border had become tranquil.[21]
His pre-crisis image, in short, encompassed a secure Israel, actively supported by one of the superpowers and bound by a network of
good relations with the overwhelming majority of members of the
international community.

19. Interview, *Jewish Observer and Middle East Review*, 17 February 1967.

20. Interview, *Ma'ariv*, 1 December 1967, and Israel, Ministry for Foreign
Affairs, Cables and Communications, Jerusalem, 1967.

21. "Abba Eban Reviews Diplomatic Results," *Jerusalem Post*, 28 October
1966.

DECISION FLOW

The fragile stability which had been achieved by the Sinai Campaign of 1956 still held a decade later, with no evidence of impending deterioration. From 1961 to 1964, Israel's main external concern was the dispute over the Jordan Waters:[22] The Carrier was completed in 1964, with Israel drawing her share; and the Arab states, realizing that they were too weak and divided to react with force, now turned to "summitry" at Nasser's initiative. During 1964–65 they tried, at three meetings of Heads of State, to coordinate their policies vis-à-vis Israel, setting up several inter-Arab organizations to channel, develop, and utilize their resources until the time was judged ripe for a "final" showdown with Israel: the Unified Arab Command, for military coordination; the Jordan Diversion Authority, to divert the headwaters of the Jordan River to Arab territory; and the Palestine Liberation Organization (PLO) and its military arm, the Palestine Liberation Army (PLA), for the organization, coordination, and control of the Palestinian movement. These efforts petered out. And with distrust growing between the "traditional" and "progressive" Arab camps, and among individual Arab states, 1966 was marked by the polarization and fragmentation of Israel's enemies: Syria was isolated; and Nasser's prestige was on the wane, with his Arab rivals led by King Faisal of Saudi Arabia trying to organize an anti-Nasser front under the aegis of the "Islamic Pact."[23]

The situation changed with the coming to power of a Left-wing *Ba'th* régime in Syria in February 1966. Beset by internal opposition and external isolation, the new rulers of Damascus decided to seek legitimacy in the radicalization of the Arab-Israeli conflict. This they did by proclaiming that the way to restore the rights of the Palestinians was by a guerilla-type War of Liberation, by giving active support to *fida'iyyun* incursions into Israel and by heating up the friction over the cultivation of the demilitarized zones on the Syria-Israel Armistice lines of 1949. At the same time, they sought and received Soviet support for their régime, thus breaking their extraregional isolation.

22. For an analysis of the Jordan water controversy see M. Brecher, *Decisions in Israel's Foreign Policy* (London, 1974), chap. 5.

23. See B. Geist, "The Six Day War: A Study" (unpublished Ph.D. dissertation, The Hebrew University of Jerusalem, 1974), chap. 13, for a more detailed analysis of inter-Arab rivalry in 1964–66.

In 1966, there were several Arab-Israeli flare-ups. Tension on the Syrian border led to the familiar pattern of artillery duels. Israeli retaliatory raids caused the Soviet Union to give full—and public—diplomatic support to the Syrian Government's claims. Israel was thereby deterred from mounting a major retaliatory raid against *fida'iyyun* bases in Syria. The largest across-the-border Israeli raid in 1966 was against the Jordanian village of El-Samu on 12 November, its justification being that most of the *fida'iyyun* activities originated from Jordan's territory. The condemnation of Syria in the UN was prevented by the use of the Soviet veto, while Israel was condemned for retaliatory acts. And Egypt's inter-Arab isolation was broken when, in November 1966, she signed a Defense Pact with Syria.

During January and February 1967, UN-initiated efforts were made to de-escalate the tension between Syria and Israel. For the first time since 1954, the Israel-Syria Mixed Armistice Commission (ISMAC) met, presided over by General Odd Bull, Chief of the United Nations Truce Supervisory Organization (UNTSO). But the three sessions that took place were taken up with wrangles over procedure and turned into platforms for inflammatory statements. As May 1967 approached, Odd Bull was still trying to arrange a fourth session, while on the borders the familiar conflict pattern was re-established. The Soviet Union again issued warnings about Israeli troop concentrations and aggressive designs against Syria. In Israel, internal pressures were mounting to "teach Syria a lesson" and bring some relief to the settlements near the Syrian frontier, which were exposed to periodic shelling from Syrian artillery on the Golan Heights. The somewhat higher friction in 1966 gave way to a few relatively low-level incidents—after the January 1967 UN call for a relaxation of tension and the reactivation of ISMAC.[24]

This stage of controlled tension was marred by a major outbreak of violence on 7 April. It started in the usual way. Israeli tractors working fields in the demilitarized zone were fired upon from Syria.

24. Figures for 1955–56 casualties are found in B. M. Blechman, "The Impact of Israel's Reprisals on Behavior of the Bordering Arab Nations Directed at Israel," *Journal of Conflict Resolution,* 16 (June 1972), 155–181. For a detailed description of incidents in 1965–66 and from January 1967 to prior to the SDW, see the *Middle East Record 1967*, 3 (henceforth, *MER*), D. Dishon, ed. (Jerusalem, 1971), pp. 166–178.

As the shelling spread to Israeli settlements, the Israeli and Syrian Air Forces went into action: six Syrian MiGs were shot down over the Golan Heights and Jordanian territory, and Israeli planes reached as far as Damascus.[25] At the end of April and beginning of May, tension escalated with the mining of roads well inside Israel and the use of mortars, for the first time, to shell an Israeli border settlement from Lebanon. Since these attacks occurred on the eve of Independence Day, they led to several public warnings by Israeli leaders about their possible effects. These warnings, especially those voiced on several occasions by Eshkol (Decision 1), and on 12 May by an IDF spokesman, incorrectly attributed to Rabin, were considered by the Israeli and world press to be the prelude to retaliatory action against Syria.[26] The Soviet Union contributed to this belief by "informing" Egypt, directly and indirectly, between 8 and 13 May, that Israel was concentrating large forces near the Syrian border—according to some sources, eleven or thirteen brigades—in order to mount a massive attack. To counteract this, the Soviets encouraged Nasser to make a show of force on the southern border of Israel.[27]

Three themes about the early May moves have been debated in the SDW literature: (1) Was Israel concentrating troops, with the intent of launching an attack on Syria? (2) Were the Soviet warnings part of a plan to involve the U.S. in a serious conflict in the

25. *MER*, pp. 176–177.

26. Ibid., pp. 179–180, 186–192. The *MER* is valuable for the empirical data on these warnings as well as for the evaluation of the context in which they were made in Israel and their effects on the international actors concerned. See also C. W. Yost, "The Arab-Israeli War: How It Began," *Foreign Affairs*, 46 (January 1968), 304–320. Briefly recapitulated, the Arab (and Soviet) version was that Israel had announced publicly that she would attack Syria with the avowed intent of toppling the Syrian régime. See *International Documents on Palestine 1967*, F. A. Jabber, ed. (Beirut, 1970), pp. 529–531, 538–541.

27. The most important warnings were direct, on 12–13 May. According to M. Heikal ("The 1967 Arab-Israeli War," *Sunday Telegraph* [London], 21 October 1973, excerpts in *Ma'ariv*, 9 November 1973), on the 13th, Sadat, then leading a parliamentary delegation in Moscow as President of Egypt's National Assembly, was told by no less a person than President Podgorny that "we have actual information that there are military concentrations directed against Syria"; he wired the news home the same day. Confirmation of these warnings was given by Premier Kosygin in his speech at the UN General Assembly on 19 June 1967 (*New York Times*, 20 June 1967) and by Nasser in his speeches of 22 May, 9 June, and 23 July 1967 (*International Documents on Palestine*, Docs. 318, 372, and 393; pp. 538, 596, and 620).

Middle East, thereby weakening her position in Vietnam? Or (3) Were they part of a carefully thought-out series of moves by Nasser (encouraged by the Soviets) that would regain for him some of his lost stature in the Arab world, without endangering Egypt too much?[28]

In fact, Israel did not concentrate large forces on the Syrian frontier, though some tank units were sent there as reinforcements after the 7 April flare-up. However, the intention to "teach Syria a lesson"—unless she desisted from supporting the campaign of terror—is evident in the 12 May briefing and other pronouncements, and in the contingent Cabinet decision of 7 May. As Eban later recalled:

Israel would reinforce defensive remedies on its own soil by minefields and barbed wire, and it would interpose a stage of verbal warnings to Syria before any military action was approved. Only if all this failed and violence had to be met by force would its response come into effect. Even then, it would be swift and of local scope falling short of a general confrontation and leaving the existing borders intact.[29]

There is no evidence of a well-planned Soviet exercise in brinkmanship. However, Moscow may have been interested in a limited, controlled increase in tension.[30] As for a carefully planned Egyptian scenario, almost all analysts agree that Nasser did not preplan the crisis, but rather utilized opportunities and raised the stakes from phase to phase, on the basis of ad hoc evaluations of

28. Theoretically, two other possibilities have also been suggested: J. Laffin (*Fedayeen: The Arab-Israeli Dilemma* [London, 1973], p. 23) states that the *Fatah* leadership assumed credit for the outbreak of the war. The Israeli "hard-liner" version of Ben-Gurion, Dayan, and Peres—doing their utmost to push Eshkol into a militant policy—was suggested by M. Rodinson, *Israel and the Arabs* (London, 1968), p. 188.

29. A. Eban, *My Country: The Story of Modern Israel* (London and Jerusalem, 1973), p. 164.

30. Eban stated in an interview with Michael Brecher in August 1968 that, in his opinion, the Soviet role was decisive in the crisis—that they caused the 1967 War. Eban's opinion is confirmed in his *An Autobiography* (Jerusalem and Tel Aviv, 1977), p. 320. This opinion is shared by many Israelis, including decision-makers and commentators. At the same time, there is great doubt whether it was their *intention* to cause a war. They intended to achieve a level of controlled tension, which then got out of hand. For a fuller treatment, see B. Geist, "The Six Day War," chap. 11. See also A. Ulam, *Expansion and Coexistence: The History of Soviet Foreign Policy, 1917–1967* (London, 1968), pp. 741–747.

the situation.[31] He may have been aware that there were no Israeli troop concentrations on the Syrian border. This was immaterial, for Israel, he believed, was preparing to mount a retaliatory action, and it was in his interest to forestall such an act: he had to do something to improve his tarnished image in the Arab world.[32]

The mounting tension led to a flurry of diplomatic activity. Israel's embassies in the states then represented in the Security Council were instructed on 9 May to draw to the attention of these governments the gravity of the situation. At the UN, on the 11th, Israel's Representative, G. Rafael, submitted a note to the President of the Security Council. In Washington, the next day, Ambassador Harman and Minister Evron held consultations with Lucius Battle, Assistant Secretary of State. The same day, the Director-General of the Foreign Ministry, A. Levavi, called the Soviet Ambassador's attention to the tense situation on the Syrian border, expressing Israel's deep concern about the increasing number of terrorist attacks. When Chuvakhin protested about Israeli troop

31. Possibly the clearest statement of this was given by Rabin in a speech three months after the War in an address at the Tel Aviv Mann Auditorium, 21 September 1967. Stenographic transcript in Hebrew in National Library of Israel; excerpts in *Jerusalem Post Weekly*, 9 October 1967. On the first half of the crisis period—16–26 May—he said: "In this phase, the Egyptians wanted to deter Israel, to demonstrate the deterrence of Israel before Syria and not to initiate or create conditions that would lead to war. . . ." Rabin contended that Nasser passed from phase one to two because of U Thant's challenge, "a step that could certainly not be accepted by Nasser, with all that it entailed." Y. Allon ("The Last Stage of the War of Independence," *OT* [November 1967], p. 7) shared Rabin's view: "The crisis that led right to the edge of war and then to war itself was the result of deterioration and not the result of cold and careful planning on Egypt's part."

32. One of the psychological problems facing Nasser was to show that this time he meant what he said and was prepared to back up words with deeds. In particular, there was the memory of the February 1960 incident when, in the wake of an Israeli retaliation at Tawfik on the Syrian border (Syria was at that time part of the United Arab Republic), Nasser moved his troops into Sinai, only to move them out again after a month. The memory of this incident played a significant role in the evaluations of the decision-makers, on both sides of the border, during the first days of the crisis. Thus, in Israel it was frequently used to support the "Nasser is bluffing" evaluation; while Nasser himself relied upon it, in his evaluation of how the Israelis would react to his—deterrent—move. Rabin stated in his address on 21 September 1967 (excerpts in *Jerusalem Post Weekly*, 9 October 1967): "It is possible that Egyptian perceptions at this stage included the experience of 1960, Israel's success, and that they believed Israel could be prevented from attacking, without a war." For Nasser's evaluation that this incident would be remembered as an indication of his intentions, see M. Heikal, "The 1967 Arab-Israeli War."

concentrations on the Syrian border, he was invited, as on previous
occasions, to see for himself. Again he declined.

In Egypt, a decision was taken to move troops into Sinai, in
order to divert Israel's attention from Syria. The Egyptian Army
was put on a state of full alert at 14:30 Cairo time on 14 May. By
that night, some units stationed along the Canal had crossed and
begun to move into the desert. In the afternoon, the parliamentary
delegation to Moscow, headed by Sadat, brought a Soviet warning
of Israeli troop concentrations on the Syrian border. Israel's Military Intelligence—and Chief of Staff (COS) Rabin—became aware
of Egypt's moves the same day. No reactive steps were taken. Prime
Minister Eshkol was informed on Monday, 15 May, at 09:30, one
hour before the Independence Day military parade was to begin.
Although the first Israeli assessment was that Nasser was putting
on a show, the situational change was considered serious enough
by Eshkol to forego a special reception and to call Eban and Ya'acov
Herzog to his home for consultations. Rabin had by now alerted
General Gavish, Officer in Command (OC) of the Southern Front,
and General Tal, Commander of a Division in the South, to stand
by for a possible reinforcement of the Sinai border.

The upshot of the initial consultations was the second Israeli
decision in the SDW pre-crisis period: Eshkol authorized a move
initiated by Rabin (in a telephone conversation with Gavish during
the afternoon) to reinforce the southern border with armored
units. The border until then was sparsely defended: There was
only one battalion on duty there at the time and "several dozen
tanks."[33] On the same day, Eban informed Egypt, through UN
Under Secretary-General Bunche, that Israel had no aggressive
intentions towards Syria.

There were further consultations in the evening among Eshkol,
Rabin, Weizman, and other high-ranking IDF officers. There was
no change in the early evaluation. Yet, to be on the safe side, Eshkol, Rabin, and Weizman agreed on the need to put regular army
units on the alert and on moving some of them to the South
(Decision 2).[34]

A disquieting change in the balance of military power on Israel's
southern front was becoming evident by the afternoon of the 16th:
According to IDF Intelligence reports, Egypt had poured 30,000

33. Gavish, Interview with D. Goldstein, *Yediot Aharonot*, 3 April 1970.
34. Weizman, Interview with D. Goldstein, *Ma'ariv*, 5 June 1973.

fresh troops, 200 tanks, and a large number of planes into Sinai—to strengthen the 30,000–35,000 troops already there. The General Staff was beginning to revise its estimates about Nasser's intentions; and Rabin reported these "cautiously revised estimates" to Eshkol.[35]

On Tuesday, 16 May, the Israeli perception changed. By the end of the day, the appreciation was one of "surprise," for some even "consternation," over the developments.[36] That morning, Eshkol, at a meeting with senior officials of the Defense Ministry, decided to send emissaries abroad to speed up arms deliveries.[37] During the day, he also held meetings to set in motion the mobilization of financial resources from world Jewry. Rabin presided over a meeting of staff and field commanders at General Staff Headquarters at 08:00. The mobilization of reserves was discussed but not yet decided on. General Tal was authorized to put regular units on alert.[38]

At the afternoon Cabinet session, which began at 16:00, the Prime Minister informed his colleagues that "the arraignment of the Egyptian forces in the Sinai and the general military activity testify to the establishment of an Egyptian *defensive* order there." The Foreign Minister reported on discussions with the Soviet Ambassador, as well as the optimistic evaluations of London and Washington—namely, that Nasser was acting demonstratively and that there was no cause for special concern. The consensus was that "Nasser did not have the capacity of starting a war," with the war in Yemen still going on; but it was also noted that "there was always the danger of an unexpected deterioration of the situation"; therefore, Israel should prepare for the worst contingency. The Cabinet approved, in principle, precautionary measures taken by the PM and the COS (Decision 2).[39]

35. W. Burdett, *Encounter with the Middle East: An Intimate Report of What Lies Behind the Arab-Israeli Conflict* (London, 1970), pp. 234–235.

36. Bitan, Interview with Michael Brecher, 8 August 1968.

37. The entries in Eshkol's *Appointment Book* (hereafter, *AB*) were first made in pencil, then erased and rewritten with pen, if the meeting actually took place. Thus it is a most accurate documentary source for his meetings throughout the SDW crisis. The *AB* carries the date, the hour, and the participants.

38. Israel, Ministry of Defense, *The War of Four Days, the Southern Command, 5 June–9 June 1967* (Jerusalem, 1969).

39. The quotations are, respectively, from Eshkol interview, *Yediot Aharonot*, 18 October 1967; Foreign Ministry sources; and *MER*, p. 194. See also S. Nakdimon, *Toward the Zero Hour: The Drama that Preceded the Six Day War* (Tel Aviv, 1968), p. 20 (Hebrew), and *Yediot Aharonot*, 16 June 1967. Eshkol was among the first to realize the seriousness of the situation. As he recalled in an interview in *Yediot Aharonot*, 18 October 1967: "When I was told that, according

Eshkol and Rabin then reported on Egypt's moves to the Knesset Foreign Affairs and Security Committee. The debate in the Committee developed around the appropriate limits of Israel's response, with the opposition, mainly *Gahal,* demanding strong deterrent measures. In the evening, after further information had been received about Egyptian troop movements, Eshkol and Rabin decided on the immediate mobilization of a reserve regiment of armor, as well as of some artillery (Decision 3).[40]

That same evening, the Egyptian Government took a decisive step—which proved to be the critical input into Israel's next decision and a trigger to her 1967 crisis period. At 22:00 hours Israeli (and Gaza) time, Brigadier Mukhtar handed over to General Rikhye, the Commander of UNEF, a written request from the Egyptian Commander-in-Chief, Mahmud Fawzi, that "for the sake of complete security of all UN troops which install observation posts along our borders, I request that you issue your orders to withdraw all these troops immediately." Orally, Mukhtar added that Rikhye "must order the immediate withdrawal of United Nations troops from El-Sabha and Sharm-e-Sheikh on the night of 16 May since United Arab Republic armed forces must gain control of these two places that very night." Noncompliance with that request might lead to immediate conflict between United Arab Republic and UNEF troops.[41] Rikhye refused, cabled the request

---

to every sign, war will not break out within a year, or within two years, I used to say: 'Wherefrom this certainty?' I used to say that this depends to a considerable extent on one man—a dictator, who can decide this matter."

40. All sources—see, for example, W. Burdett, *Encounter with the Middle East,* p. 235; T. Draper, *Israel and World Politics: Roots of the Third Arab-Israeli War* (New York, 1968), p. 75; D. Kimche and D. Bawly, *The Sandstorm, the Arab-Israeli War of June 1967: Prelude and Aftermath* (London, 1968), pp. 135–136; *MER,* p. 194; Nakdimon, *Toward the Zero Hour,* p. 20; and A. Tzimouki, "The Longest Month," *Yediot Aharonot,* 16 June 1967—agree that this decision was taken on 16 May. This was confirmed by Eshkol. The mobilization of the first reserves, as distinct from the alert and movement of regular units, was decided upon at the evening meeting, after having been approved, in principle, by the Cabinet.

41. Report on the Withdrawal of the United Nations Emergency Force, by U Thant, Secretary-General of the United Nations, 26 June 1967, *UN Monthly Chronicle,* 4:7 (July 1967), 135–161. It should be noted that U Thant's report of 18 May to the Security Council, which included an hour-by-hour description of the significant events, did not mention the key oral message; this was included later, in his 26 June report. Thus it is possible that the full extent of Egypt's demands was not known to Israel at the time.

to UN Headquarters, and asked for instructions from the Secretary-General.[42]

U Thant, after a short consultation with Ralph Bunche, made his crucial all-or-nothing decision within one hour of receiving the message. He called in Egypt's UN Representative, Ambassador El-Kony, and advised him that:

(ii)   The exact intent of General Fawzy's letter needed clarification. If it meant the temporary withdrawal of UNEF troops from the line or from parts of it, it would be unacceptable. . . .

(iii)   If it was the intention of the Government of the United Arab Republic to withdraw the consent which it gave in 1956 for stationing of UNEF on the territory of the United Arab Republic and in Gaza it was, of course, entitled to do so. . . . On receipt of such a request, the Secretary-General would order the withdrawal of all UNEF troops from Gaza and Sinai. . . .

(iv)   A request by the United Arab Republic authorities for a temporary withdrawal of UNEF from the Armistice Demarcation Line and the International Frontier, or from any parts of them, would be considered by the Secretary-General as tantamount to a request for the complete withdrawal of UNEF from Gaza and Sinai, since this would reduce UNEF to ineffectiveness.[43]

Analysis since the 1967 War has thrown considerable doubt on the formal-legal grounds on which U Thant later defended his widely criticized decision. Many commentators contend that it was U Thant's decision, rather than Egypt's move, that made the flow of events irreversible.[44] Certainly, it was another catalyst to perceptual change by Israel's decision-makers, increasing their image of threat, making them aware of a time dimension, and, for some, inducing concern about the possibility of war. Thus ended the 1967 pre-crisis period.

42. W. Burdett, *Encounter with the Middle East*, p. 216, has stated (he obviously interviewed Rikhye): "There was no doubt in Rikhye's mind that Mukhtar was talking about the evacuation of the entire Emergency Force from the entire Sinai Peninsula." According to R. Benkler ("General Rikhye's Truth," *Al Hamishmar*, 13 August 1971), Rikhye stated, four years later, that Nasser would not have attacked and that there was a chance to find a peaceful solution.

43. Report on the Withdrawal of the United Nations Emergency Force, by U Thant, 26 June 1967, *UN Monthly Chronicle*, 4:7 (July 1967), 135–161.

44. For a review of some of the literature on the U Thant controversy, see B. Geist, "The Six Day War," chap. 16. Typical of Israel's reaction was Interior Minister H. M. Shapira's remark in an interview with Michael Brecher in 1968: "We expected U Thant would resist Egyptian pressure to expel the UN, and were surprised at the UN response."

CHAPTER THREE

1973: 13 SEPTEMBER TO 4 OCTOBER

THE SIX DAY WAR was followed by a period of tranquility in the Arab-Israeli conflict. Then, in March 1969, Egypt launched a War of Attrition to compel Israel's withdrawal from Sinai. It was the fourth round of sustained violence—after the War of Independence (1948), the Sinai Campaign (1956), and the 1967 War. In the midst of the War of Attrition, Israel was confronted with another major foreign policy crisis which was induced by the U.S.-sponsored Rogers' Proposals. They called for a cease-fire and for negotiations under the auspices of UN Representative Jarring to carry out all the provisions of Security Council Resolution 242. Their (reluctant) acceptance by Israel in August 1970 led to a dissolution of her National Unity Government, established in June 1967, and another period of relative quiet on Israel's borders.[1] It was to last three years, when the Yom Kippur Crisis of 1973 descended upon the Jewish State.

The pre-crisis period began with an aerial battle on 13 September 1973, during which thirteen Syrian MiGs and one Israeli Mirage were shot down. This triggered an increase in perceived threat, notably by the IDF's OC Northern Command, Major-General Yitzhak Hofi, and Defense Minister Dayan. That period was to last until late in the night of 4 October, when information

---

1. The only component of the Rogers Proposals to be implemented was the cease-fire. For an analysis of Israel's crisis behavior in 1970, see M. Brecher, *Decisions in Israel's Foreign Policy* (London, 1974, and New Haven, 1975), chap. 8.

reached Israel that the remaining Soviet advisers and their families in Syria and Egypt were being withdrawn by a special airlift and that Egypt's offensive deployment along the Canal was now unprecedented in size and scope.

DECISIONS AND DECISION-MAKERS

There were two decisions during the 1973 pre-crisis period, along with several incremental reinforcement actions at the military-bureaucratic level.

Decision Number	Date	Content
1.	26 September	Defense Minister Dayan, in consultation with the Chief of Staff and the OC Northern Command, decided to signal Damascus that Israel would react vigorously against any Syrian military action—by issuing a public warning through the press and by despatching the Seventh Armored Brigade and some heavy artillery from the Negev to the Golan.
2.	3 October	The "Kitchen Cabinet" decided to delay consideration of the situation until the next regular Cabinet meeting, scheduled for Sunday, 7 October.

Israel's decision-makers in the 1973 pre-crisis period were few in number: Prime Minister Meir, Defense Minister Dayan, Deputy Prime Minister and Minister of Education Yigal Allon, and Minister Without Portfolio Yisrael Galili, the core members of the Kitchen Cabinet. Almost all key advisers were from the IDF: Chief of Staff David Elazar; Director of Military Intelligence Major-General Eliahu Zeira, or, in his absence, Director of Research within Military Intelligence, Brigadier-General Arye Shalev; the OC Air Force, Major-General Binyamin Peled; the Deputy Chief of Staff, Major-General Yisrael Tal; and Hofi from the Northern Command. From the bureaucratic elite the only active participant was Mordekhai Gazit, Director-General of the Prime Minister's Office.

PSYCHOLOGICAL ENVIRONMENT

Attitudinal Prism

As in 1967, there was a shared psychological setting among Israel's decision-makers and advisers during the 1973 pre-crisis period. Its content, however, was profoundly different. If the Arab attack on 6 October came as a surprise—to all but a few—the explanation is to be found at two levels of analysis: a pervasive "Conception" or general definition of the situation, and the specific images held by Israel's decision-makers in 1972 and the first nine months of 1973.

The Conception was crystalized with the passing of Sadat's "Year of Decision" (1971) without overt evidence of Egypt's capability or intent to launch an attack. The Conception's two pillars were astonishingly simple: (1) Egypt would not launch a war against Israel without superior air power, that is, sufficient to attack Israel in depth and to dislocate Israel's Air Force and its principal air fields; (2) Syria would not initiate a war against Israel without the active participation of Egypt. . . ."[2] Ergo, the Arabs would not launch a war. Underlying these premises was a set of (mis)perceptions— about the Arabs' capability and short-run goals, the balance of power, and the security provided Israel by the post-1967 borders.

The knowledge that Egypt's strategic doctrine emphasized the need for long-range bombers and missiles, able to threaten Israel's population centers and military airfields, as a precondition to a full-scale attack, was transformed into an immovable Israeli dogma that Egypt would not launch a war in the foreseeable future. Israel's intelligence community seemed unable to distinguish all-out war from limited war for limited political objectives. Moreover, Sadat's failure to act by the end of 1971 convinced Israel's military and political elites from January 1972 onwards that verbal threats by Egypt's President need not be taken seriously.[3] The expulsion of

2. Agranat Commission, Partial Report issued by the Committee of Inquiry— Yom Kippur War (Agranat Commission), Jerusalem, as published in the Hebrew press, 3 April 1974.

3. Bar-Lev interview with Michael Brecher, 29 July 1974. In reality, Sadat acknowledged that his decision for war had been made long before—though, in his memoirs, he gave several dates: July 1972; January, August 28–29, June 5, February, 1973 (In Search of Identity: An Autobiography [New York, 1978], pp. 232, 237, 242, 242, and 244, respectively). Parenthetically, he was explicit on his motives (p. 244): "I used to tell Nasser that if we could recapture even 4 inches of Sinai territory (by which I meant a foothold pure and simple) . . . [it would remove] the humiliation we had endured since the 1967 defeat. . . . [It] would restore our self-confidence."

almost 20,000 Soviet "advisers" from Egypt in July 1972 was read as a crucial indicator of Egypt's military weakness and as a signal of Sadat's determination not to become involved in a war with Israel, at least for several years. And when, in May 1973, the mobilization of Israel's reserves seemed to deter an imminent Egyptian attack, the invulnerability of Israel became an article of faith.[4] There was, too, an unshakable self-confidence that, even if by some remote contingency the Arabs attempted to attack, Israel's second-strike capability and her post-1967 hinterland would ensure a quick and overwhelming military victory.

The self-image of invulnerability was closely linked to the notion of secure borders, which most Israelis, including the attentive and mass publics, believed had been attained by the Six Day War. A lucid expression of this image of "secure borders" was contained in a postmortem by the then-Chief of Staff and later Prime Minister, Lieutenant-General Yitzhak Rabin:

> The present borders run along natural barriers: Egypt—the Canal; Jordan —the Jordan River, a less impressive barrier than the Suez Canal but nevertheless a barrier; and with Syria, there will no longer be a need to climb up mountains. The distance from the Egyptian border to Tel Aviv was once 130 kilometres and only 80 kilometres from the Gaza Strip. But the distance from our border on the Canal today to Cairo is only 130 kilometres. The distance from our border to Cairo was once something over 400 kilometres. Today the distance from the Egyptian border on the Canal to Tel Aviv is 400 kilometres.[5]

Chief of Staff Elazar conveyed the essence of the Conception in this way: "The central part of our conception was that Syria would not go to war alone. The most she would do is to retaliate for the loss of the thirteen planes [in an air battle on 13 September]. . . ."[6] Supplementing the political-strategic bases of the Conception was a set of military assumptions. In the words of Air Force Commander Peled: "Pre-war opinions were deep-rooted. . . . Some of these were: (a) no meaningful loss of ground will occur that will not quickly be regained," and (b) that after the enemy was blocked, Israel's offensive moves would be immediately decisive.[7] Sharing

4. According to Sadat, "I had no intention of starting a war in May, but my strategic deception plan . . . led the Israelis to believe that war was imminent" (*In Search of Identity,* p. 241).

5. "How We Won the War," *Jerusalem Post Weekly,* 4 October 1967.

6. Elazar, Interview with J. Stein, 20 April 1974.

7. B. Peled, "The Air Force in the War," *Military Aspects of the Israeli-Arab Conflict,* Proceedings of an International Symposium (Tel Aviv, October 1975).

this opinion was Deputy Prime Minister Allon, who declared publicly in June 1973, "They [the Arabs] have no military option at all."[8]

The official Commission of Inquiry into the early IDF setbacks during the Yom Kippur War summarized the role of the Conception thus:

We learned that the first and decisive part of this conception, which may well have been correct at one time, was not adequately reconsidered in view of the pressure of the changing political circumstances, and, in particular, on the basis of further information that reached the Director of Military Intelligence concerning the build-up of enemy strength with additional armaments systems. This "conception" had, therefore, in practice become obsolete. . . .[9]

The major effect of the Conception was to impair the ability of Israel's decision-makers and intelligence community to distinguish between "signals" and "noise," always a difficult task.[10] Secondarily, it led to misperception of the abundant signals between 26 September and 4 October indicating the concerted Arab intent and growing capability to launch an attack against Israel.[11]

---

8. Address at the Van Leer Jerusalem Foundation, 3 June 1973.

9. Agranat Commission, Partial Report, 3 April 1974.

10. A "signal" was defined by Roberta Wohlstetter as "a sign, a clue, a piece of evidence that points to the action or to an adversary's intention to undertake it, and by 'noise' is meant the background of irrelevant or inconsistent signals, signs, pointing in the wrong directions, that end always to obscure the signs pointing the right way." And she added with relevance to Israel's Yom Kippur Crisis: "Pearl Harbor . . . shows how hard it is to hear a signal against the prevailing noise, in particular when you are listening for the wrong signal, and even when you have a wealth of information" ("Cuba and Pearl Harbor: Hindsight and Foresight," *Foreign Affairs*, 43 (July 1965), p. 691). For studies of comparable erroneous evaluation of intelligence data, see J. J. Holst, "Surprise Signals and Reaction," *Cooperation and Conflict*, 1 (1966), 31–45; K. Knorr, "Failures in National Intelligence Estimates: The Case of the Cuban Missiles," *World Politics*, 16 (April 1964), 455–467; A. Shlaim, "Failures in National Intelligence Estimates: The Case of the Yom Kippur War," *World Politics*, 28 (April 1976), 348–380; B. Wasserman, "The Failure of Intelligence Prediction," *Political Studies*, 8 (June 1960), 156–169; B. Whaley, *Codeword Barbarossa* (Cambridge, Mass., 1973); and R. Wohlstetter, *Pearl Harbor: Warning and Decision* (Stanford, Calif., 1962).

11. According to Elazar's Memorandum to the Cabinet, May 1975, the IDF Intelligence Branch received, during that period, at least 400 significant items of information pointing to the possibility of war. Most, he added, were not brought to his attention until after the outbreak of war. Some of these signals will be noted in the discussion of the Decision Process during the pre-crisis period, to follow. There were also several notable indications of "noise":

1. On 25 September 1973, newly-appointed U.S. Secretary of State Kissinger hosted a lunch for Arab envoys to the UN; and, later that week, Israeli and Arab foreign

Images

The Conception provides a persuasive *general* explanation for
Israel's behavior in the 1973 pre-crisis period—and on the first day
of the crisis period. A more precise predictor of her decisions,
however, were the specific images of the setting held by Israel's
decision-makers. Not all were important—or even relevant—in
shaping their choices between 24 September and 4 October. Some
were articulated (secretly) during meetings of the Kitchen Cabinet
and between Dayan and IDF senior officers. Others were expressed in statements and speeches before diverse audiences
during the months preceding the 1973 Crisis. It is these composite
perceptions that will be examined, using both qualitative and
quantitative indicators, in order to discover the Israeli predispositions to choice.

Three persons were selected for image analysis relevant to the
pre-crisis period: Prime Minister Meir; Deputy Prime Minister
Allon; and Defense Minister Dayan.[12] During the pre-crisis period,
the primary objects of attention for all three lay at the regional
level—the "present situation," the possibility of war, and the Arabs
collectively, as well as the individual Arab states in the Near East
Core.[13]

---

ministers agreed—secretly—to meet under Kissinger's auspices sometime in November, after Israel's scheduled general elections, to seek agreeable procedures for
substantive negotiations. See B. Kalb and M. Kalb, *Kissinger* (Boston and Toronto,
1974), p. 512.

2.   Large-scale Egyptian army maneuvers, as in the preceding two years, were held at the
      beginning of October. And, as part of the Arab deception plan, they were "announced"
      as being due to end on 7 October. See M. Heikal, *The Road to Ramadan* (London,
      1975), p. 16.

3.   On 3 October, the military correspondent of *Al Ahram* wrote that Egypt's Commander-
      in-Chief had prepared a list of officers who wished to go on the "small pilgrimage" to
      Mecca. See M. Heikal, *The Road to Ramadan*, p. 32.

4.   The same newspaper reported that Rumania's Defense Minister would meet with his
      Egyptian counterpart in Cairo on 8 October. See M. Heikal, *The Road to Ramadan*,
      p. 32.

5.   On the 3rd, too, General Ismail ordered the immediate release of some reservists who
      had been called up in September for autumn "maneuvers." For a detailed narrative of
      the Arab deception plan, see M. Heikal, *The Road to Ramadan*, pp. 11–45.

12.   Foreign Minister Abba Eban was to play an important role in the decisional process of the 1973 post-crisis period and during the last few days of the crisis
period. He was not included at this stage of the analysis of the psychological environment because he was in the United States attending the UN General Assembly throughout the pre-crisis period—in fact, until 20 October.

13.   The selection of speeches and statements to be analyzed was affected by
data availability. Within that constraint, efforts were made to achieve represen-

MEIR

Prime Minister Meir perceived Israel's military situation several months before the Yom Kippur War as excellent; and she attributed this largely to the policy of her government during the preceding three years, since the cease-fire of August 1970: "Our policy was one of the factors that reinforced such welcome developments as the collapse of the [Arab] Eastern Command and the weakening of the power and activities of the terrorist organizations in Jordan."[14] Israel's main objective was defined by her as peace with security, to be achieved by direct negotiations. An essential component was secure borders, which "by their very location . . . deters a would-be aggressor . . . [and] can be defended by fewer casualties" (1 October).

The Arabs were perceived as solely responsible for the continuation of the conflict and were accused of adhering to the constant aim, the destruction of Israel, either by military pressure or by great power intervention. The Prime Minister's image of the adversary was concentrated on Egypt and the Palestinians. Less than a week before the Arab assault, on 1 October, she referred to President Sadat as a responsible leader of a great people. At the same time, she differentiated "the Palestinian people" from "the Arabs of the [occupied territories]," and "the terrorists." Those

---

tativeness—in audience, medium, type of presentation, and approximate equality of word volume for all the decision-makers. The dissected public documents with a word count were as follows:

				No. of Words
Meir	29 January	1972	Interview on *Galei Tzahal* (IDF Radio)	3,200+
	25 July	1973	Statement to the Knesset	4,000
	1 October	1973	Speech to the Council of Europe at Strassbourg	3,000
			Total	10,200
Allon	29 January	1972	Interview on *Galei Tzahal*	1,500
	November	1972	Speech to Labor Party Central Committee	4,300
	3 June	1973	Address at the Van Leer Jerusalem Foundation	6,000
			Total	11,800
Dayan	13 February	1972	Interview on U.S. TV, "Face the Nation"	2,500
	27 June	1973	Address to the Haifa Technion	2,000
	9 August	1973	Lecture to the IDF Command and Staff School	6,000
			Total	10,500

14. G. Meir, Statement to the Knesset, 25 July 1973, *Divrei Haknesset,* 68, 4274–4284. Unless otherwise indicated, all dates of speeches cited in this chapter are from 1973. The dates indicated in brackets in this section are from the speeches listed in note 13.

who raised "The Palestine Question" were viewed as seeking
Israel's destruction. The solution to the Palestinian problem was
defined by her, time and time again, as inexorably linked to Jordan:
"The Palestinian Arabs are entirely capable of attaining national
expression in Jordan. They need Jordan just as Jordan cannot exist
without them" (25 July). The refugee problem was dismissed as
the direct result of policies pursued by the Arab states since 1948.
And the crimes committed by the Palestinian terrorists were
viewed as endangering the entire world. Referring to the Schönau
incident, when Soviet Jewish refugees were taken hostage on a
train from Moscow to Vienna, she exclaimed: "The problem is
created by those who want to destroy the Jews and kill them" (1
October). By contrast, Israel's behavior in the West Bank and the
policy of "open bridges" were, for the Prime Minister, absolute
proof that Jews and Arabs could live together in peace in the
Middle East.[15]

Quantitative data on her public statements illuminate several
dimensions of the Meir attitude prior to the outbreak of the Yom
Kippur War. No less than sixteen topics were addressed. She
favored the open bridges policy, continued Jewish settlement in
the occupied territories, and the 1970 Cease-Fire Agreement. She
lauded the capability of the Israel Defense Forces, the pressure of
Jews and non-Jews alike in support of the right of Soviet Jewry to
emigrate, and United States' support of Israel. Soviet support for
the Arabs was decried. The Arabs were criticized for exploiting the
Palestinians, for engaging in terror, and for lacking the courage to
make peace. She also asserted that armaments were vital to Israel
and decried the fact that Israel had been denied even a single year
of genuine peace. Of her eighty-two attitude statements during
the pre-crisis period, more than one-third focused on three themes:
virulent hostility to terrorism, accompanied by advocacy of the
idea that it can be eliminated; hostility to the Arabs for exploiting
the situation of the Palestinians; and undisguised friendship for
the United States.

Of her twenty advocacy statements with Israel as the subject of
behavior, the largest group called for a dialogue with the Arabs in
the form of direct negotiations for peace. Second in frequency was

15. Introduced by Defense Minister Dayan soon after the Six Day War, the
policy was to permit free movement of persons and trade between the newly
occupied West Bank and the Kingdom of Jordan. The two points of crossing were
the Allenby and Damiya bridges across the Jordan River.

her stern admonition—"no accomodation with the terrorists under any circumstances." And the third most frequent theme was her categorical rejection of any proposal for an independent Palestinian state between Jordan and Israel. Closely related was her insistence that the Palestinians seek their national identity within an enlarged Jordan.

In her memoirs, Prime Minister Meir offered further (*ex post facto*) evidence that, until virtually the very last hours, she was skeptical about a high probability of war; that is, she misperceived the intent of Egypt and Syria, basing her image upon the advice of Israel's military and intelligence experts. Thus, in recalling the air battle of 13 September and reports of a Syrian build-up on the Golan Heights, she wrote: "Despite this, our intelligence people were very reassuring: it was *most unlikely*, they said, that there would be any *major* Syrian reaction." Similarly, the transfer of Syrian army units from the Jordanian border to the Israeli border on 26 September was interpreted as part of a recent détente between the two countries and as a Syrian gesture of goodwill towards Jordan.[16] At the Kitchen Cabinet meeting on 3 October, Mrs. Meir expressed disquiet: She repeatedly asked the Director of Research in the IDF Intelligence Branch about Arab military capability, regardless of intent—and about the possibility of a unilateral Syrian attack, with a view to dragging Egypt into war. On both points, Shalev persisted in estimating a "very low" probability of war.[17]

ALLON

The Deputy Prime Minister, by contrast, expressed dissatisfaction with the immobilism of Israel's policy and the complacency about Israel's ability to maintain indefinitely a posture of "no war, no peace." Less than a year before the Yom Kippur War, he warned: "Let us not put our hopes and trust in the illusion of all-powerful time. . . . The moment Israel adopts the policy that identifies the temporary with the permanent . . . there will be a sharp upheaval in a whole series of spheres and basic ideas. . . . On the external front the blame for the absence of peace in the area will be laid on our shoulders. . . . The Arab states will not

16. G. Meir, *My Life* (Jerusalem and Tel Aviv, 1975), p. 354; emphasis added.
17. S. Nakdimon, "The Days Before and After the War: New Revelations," (hereafter called "New Revelations"), *Yediot Aharonot,* 12 July 1974; Z. Schiff, *October Earthquake, Yom Kippur 1973* (Tel Aviv, 1974), p. 36.

only be quick to take advantage of the deterioration in our international standing, but they will also in all probability be more inclined to seek military solutions" (November 1972).

Allon correctly perceived Arab goals, but his evaluation of their options proved to be fundamentally wrong. "We cannot ignore the burdens of hostility in the hearts of the Arabs, from the abyss of frustration to the aspirations for revenge," he declared on 3 June 1973. As for the Egyptians in particular: "They fear that in the framework of a partial settlement . . . [involving] a partial Israeli withdrawal . . . they will lose their bargaining position with respect to the great powers, their vulnerability will grow, and they will lose their military option. They are mistaken, of course, because they have no military option at all." Like Meir's definition of the situation, Allon's profound error about the Arabs' military option was rooted in the pervasive Conception.

Most of his public attention in the pre-crisis period was focused on three issues: peace, the territories, and the Palestinians. These were inextricably linked: "Without a solution to the Palestinian problem," he declared four months before the October War, "peace is not imaginable."[18] Unlike Meir, he acknowledged the reality of a Palestinian community. "What is beyond argument," he asserted in November 1972, "is that a Palestinan population exists, whether or not we define it as a nation, recognized or not, that a Palestine problem painfully and distressingly exists." Like the Prime Minister, Allon differentiated among "Palestinians," "Palestinians of the territories," "local [Israeli] Arabs," and "terrorists." And he proposed different means to deal with each.

The Deputy Prime Minister stood apart in showing concern about normative and practical implications of Israel's continued occupation of the West Bank and Gaza. He warned against creeping annexation, especially its potential for corrupting Israel's society, the danger of a "Rhodesian process," as he candidly remarked. He envisaged a solution to the Palestine problem through an arrangement with Jordan—his preference lay with King Hussein's proposal for a Jordanian-Palestinian Federation. Yet he did not reject outright the idea of talks with the Palestinians of the territories. Towards the terrorists, however, his attitude was firm and uncompromising. He also called for "settlement [by Israelis] in

18. Address at the Van Leer Jerusalem Foundation, 3 June 1973.

certain sectors determined by strategic needs," and he opposed "settlement in areas in which we are prepared to compromise." Regarding Jerusalem and its surrounding areas he showed no compromise. The Golan Heights were perceived as strategically vital to Israel. The Gaza Strip he favored transferring to Jordan as an outlet to the sea. And in the Sinai Desert, which "must be demilitarized and jointly patrolled," Allon proposed that the border run from Sharm-e-Sheikh to "somewhere between El-Arish and Rafiah" (3 June).

The range of Allon's attitude statements was much narrower than Meir's—eight compared with sixteen topics. Three accounted for almost half of his sixty-one statements, and all of those expressed a desire for change in the status quo: for negotiations and a compromise peace settlement; for a solution to the problem of the Palestinians; and for improvement of conditions in the West Bank. There were expressions of friendship for the U.S.; of hostility to the USSR—for upsetting the regional balance of power; of criticism of the 1949–67 armistice lines; and of a willingness to meet King Hussein. He also indicated a perception of threat to Israel's existence. Conspicuously absent in the pre-crisis period, however, were images of time pressure for decisions and the probability of war.

Nevertheless, Allon, a distinguished commander in the 1948 War, was skeptical of the IDF Intelligence Branch estimate on 3 October that the likelihood of war was "lower than low." At the Kitchen Cabinet meeting that day, he pressed Shalev for evidence in support of this estimate. When informed, in reply to his query, that military life in Egypt was not routine, he asked for further data on Egyptian troop movements in the Canal Zone. And he sought an explanation for the evidence which contradicted the intelligence assessment of "routine maneuvers." Moreover, he sensed one of the major Egyptian tactical goals in launching an attack three days later: "The Egyptians might try to cross the Canal in order to occupy our forces and ease the pressure on the Syrians in the North."[19]

Allon's advocacy statements reveal his concentration on a few themes during the pre-crisis period. Israel, which was the subject in 90 of 104 statements, was urged to act in four spheres: (a) to

19. Nakdimon, "New Revelations," *Yediot Aharonot*, 12 July 1974.

change, that is, to make more positive, her behavior in the occupied territories, with a view to facilitating peace in the not-
too-distant future; (b) to take peace initiatives; parenthetically,
the Arabs, too, were urged to act in favor of peace; (c) to offer
far-reaching territorial concessions, within the framework of his
own plan; and (d) to accept the idea that no peace settlement
would be possible without a solution to the Palestine problem,
preferably within a federated Jordan. Allon's preoccupation with
the Palestinians is also evident in the frequency with which they
appeared as the target of his advocacy—twenty-two times, compared with nineteen for all other targets combined; and seventeen of those had as their target an Arab state, the West Bank, or
"the Arabs."

DAYAN

The Defense Minister's speeches and statements during the
1973 pre-crisis period were devoted overwhelmingly to the Arab-
Israeli conflict. Like almost all his colleagues in the high policy
elite, he seemed mesmerized by the appearance of security: "This
is the quietest autumn Israel has had for a long time," he declared
on 17 August 1972. "Tranquillity prevails on the various fronts, and
the departure of the Soviet military advisers and experts from
Egypt embodies great amelioration in our security status." Unlike
Allon, Dayan viewed that status quo as favorable to Israel—and
tenable for a long time. Moreover, the "no war, no peace" situation
could not be changed by Israel; and his advice was simply to
strengthen the existing military balance. He favored a peace settlement, but he argued that Israel had done everything possible in
the way of peace initiatives. And "we are also ready for interim
settlements, for peace in stages as well."

During the spring and summer of 1973, there was a striking
change in Dayan's evaluation—from a perception of high threat
and high probability of war to an image that war would not occur in
the near future, certainly not that year. His (then-secret) instructions to the General Staff on 21 May, soon after the war scare and
Israel's partial mobilization, read in part: "I speak now as a representative of the Government and also on the basis of information.
. . . Gentlemen, please prepare for war, Egypt and Syria are
threatening to launch a war." He prefaced this instruction by stating that "a renewal of war should be taken into account in the

second half of this summer."[20] On 1 June, he reportedly declared: "Sadat's war threats must be taken seriously."[21] By late July, however, the Conception had taken hold once more: "The next ten years will see Israel's borders frozen along their present lines, but there will be no major war."[22] And to the graduating class of the IDF Command and Staff School he was most reassuring on 9 August: "The total balance of forces is in our favor and outweighs all other Arab considerations and motives—and puts a break on the immediate renewal of hostilities. . . . Our military superiority is the double result of Arab weakness and our own strength. Their weakness derives from factors which, I believe, will not quickly change."[23]

As for the contents of an overall settlement, Dayan manifested more rigidity than any other Israeli decision-maker, an attitude of unqualified support for the status quo. Just a few months before the Yom Kippur War, he declared: "I would rather keep some of the territories even at the price of having no peace" (14 May). "On the Egyptian border . . . the key to security is the desert— the Sinai Desert" (17 August 1972). "As far as Syria is concerned we should not return most of the land." And with regard to Jordan, "I just cannot imagine how we could say, with our own decision, that Jews will not have the right to settle down near Hebron. I do think that Israel should stay forever, ever, ever and ever, on the West Bank, because this is Judea and Samaria; this is our homeland" (14 May). Within the conflict zone, Egypt was perceived as the crucial adversary. He expressed empathy for the Palestinians: "Had I thought that I [as a Palestinian] stand the chance to have a Palestinian state here, and beat the Israelis, I would do it. . . ." But toward the terrorists he was ruthless: "They should be crushed" (14 May). Like Meir and Allon, he rejected the idea of a third (Palestinian) state between the sea and the desert. And he warned the Arabs and the terrorists that the Palestinians would have to be resettled entirely within the Arab world: "Israel will not take them back, either willingly or under constraint" (27 June).

20. Agranat Commission, Partial Report, 3 April 1974; see also Hanoch Bar-Tov, *Dado—48 Years and Another 20 Days* (Tel Aviv, 1978), Vol. 1, pp. 269–270.
21. *Jerusalem Post*, 2 June 1973.
22. Interview, *Time*, 30 July 1973.
23. *Jerusalem Post*, 11 August 1973.

Dayan's scope of attitude articulation in the 1973 pre-crisis period included eleven topics, of which nine focused on the Arabs and the conflict. Approximately one-fourth of his attitude statements (fourteen of fifty-five) expressed hostility to and mistrust of the Arabs, who were accused of strangling all efforts at a compromise settlement. Moreover, he charged the Arabs with perpetuating the Palestinian problem—which, he added, long preceded the Six Day War. Third in frequency were his statements favoring negotiations and Israeli concessions for peace—namely, change in the status quo. He also indicated: a rejection of total Israeli withdrawal from the post-1967 territories for peace—that is, satisfaction with the territorial status quo; criticism of the UN's supervisory role along the borders; hostility to Lebanon's behavior, as well as to the USSR; a willingness to explore an understanding with King Hussein; and satisfaction with the existing balance of power in the region. He differentiated the West Bank Palestinians from the 1948 refugees; and he charged that the PLO wanted to eradicate the State of Israel.[24]

The most frequent advocacy statements by Dayan in the pre-crisis period, eleven of forty, related to Israel's future policy toward the occupied territories. The central themes were: to retain the West Bank; not to withdraw from anywhere prior to a peace settlement; to maintain control of Sharm-e-Sheikh; and to link territorial withdrawals in Sinai to a peace agreement with Egypt. There were statements urging Israel to attempt to achieve an overall peace settlement. Five were devoted to the necessity of absorbing all Arab refugees—from both the 1948 and 1967 wars—within the

24. A comparison of the quantitative data on the publicly articulated attitudes of the three decision-makers during the 1973 pre-crisis period reveals the following about the scope of their perceived interest and concern.

1. *Number of Topics:* Meir ranked first with 16, followed by Dayan (11) and Allon (8).

2. *Regional-Global Distribution:* Approximately 75 percent of all their attitude statements prior to 6 October 1973 were focused on the Middle East, especially on Israel's enemies, the Arabs or individual Arab states. Only 12 of Meir's 82 attitude statements were directed to the global level; they are sharply divided between expressions of friendship for the United States and hostility-threat perception toward the Soviet Union. So too with Dayan—4 of 55 attitude statements. Only 7 of Allon's 61 statements were focused at the global level—the UN, U.S., and USSR.

3. *Extent of Theme Concentration:* Dayan ranked first, with three themes: hostility to and mistrust of the Arabs; harsh criticism of the Arab states for perpetuating the Palestinian problem; and a positive attitude toward negotiations for

Arab world. Dayan advocated a peace agreement with Jordan on four occasions, with the remainder dispersed among the goal of an interim agreement, the emphasis on security and the status quo, caution about superpower intervention, and the need for realism. The targets of his advocacy statements were widely dispersed among the superpowers, the Arab states, and the Palestinians.

Among all Israeli decision-makers during the Yom Kippur Crisis, Dayan revealed (in then-secret deliberations) the most sustained perceptions of escalating threat—mainly from Syria—and, to a much lesser extent, of the possibility of war. During the pre-crisis period, these perceptions were first expressed at a General Staff meeting on 24 September, when Hofi, OC Northern Command, challenged the Intelligence Branch assurance of adequate warning of a possible Syrian attack: Dayan was reportedly concerned "in view of the threat to the Golan Heights settlements posed by the Syrian deployment."[25] He also called for the construction of an antitank barrier in the North.[26] In his memoirs, Dayan recalled his initial image in this way: "I was gnawed by the mounting suspicion that they [the Syrians] *could* be planning a more basic action." When "days passed [after the 13 September aerial battle] . . . and they did nothing . . . I expressed these anxieties to the officers of the General Staff at this September 24 meeting. . . . For if the Syrians were to succeed in overrunning our farm settlements in the Golan, it would be an unprecedented disaster."[27] Two days later, at the end of another meeting with Elazar, Hofi, and members of the General Staff, "I was still uneasy, and I decided to go up

---

peace—accounting for almost 60 percent of his attitude statements (31 of 55). Three themes accounted for 50 percent of Allon's statements (30 of 61): a positive view toward negotiations and a compromise peace settlement; the need to solve the Palestinian problem; and criticism of Israel's policy in the West Bank. Meir showed the widest dispersion. Three themes accounted for only 29 of 82 statements (35 percent): harshness toward terrorism; hostility to and mistrust of the Arabs; and friendship for the United States.

4. *Target:* The Arabs and specific Arab states were the most frequent target in the attitude statements of all three decision-makers. For Meir: Arab terrorist organizations (12), Egypt and the U.S. (8 each), of 66 statements with explicit targets. For Allon: the Arabs (13), the Palestinians (8), and the West Bank (8), comprised 29 of 45 statements. And for Dayan: all but 4 were targeted to the Arabs, Egypt, and other Arab states.

25. Agranat Commission, Partial Report, 3 April 1974.

26. C. Herzog, *The War of Atonement* (Jerusalem and Tel Aviv, 1975), pp. 60–61.

27. M. Dayan, *Story of My Life* (Jerusalem and Tel Aviv, 1976), pp. 382–383.

immediately to Northern Command," both to acquire firsthand
information and to strengthen Israel's deterrence credibility by
issuing a public warning to Syria (Decision 1). This he did at a
meeting with representatives of seventeen Golan settlements, at
Ein-Zivan.[28] The link between images and behavior was illuminated by Dayan's decision on the 26th, implemented the next day,
to despatch the Seventh Armored Brigade, stationed in the Negev,
along with some heavy artillery, to the Golan front.

At a regular meeting of the General Staff on the morning of 1
October, Dayan again conveyed his perception of growing threat:
"I said that of the various problems on our three fronts, my chief
anxiety was the possibility of a Syrian armored breakthrough to the
Golan. I expressed the situation in extreme terms: 'On the Jordanian border we have civilian settlements but no enemy. On the
Egyptian border we have an enemy but no settlements. On the
Syrian border we have both. If the Syrians get to our settlements,
it will be calamitous.'"[29] The next day, during a meeting with
Elazar, Dayan expressed his continuing perception of the Syrian
threat—in response to the intelligence estimate of no likelihood of
war; and he revealed its impact on his behavior: "As for the Syrians,
there were no signs of their intention to launch an attack, but
information had been received of further preparations. This increased my apprehensions, and I asked the chief of staff to let me
have a paper with details of the changes in the deployment of
Syria's forces and the information we had on them."[30]

During the Kitchen Cabinet meeting on 3 October, Dayan spoke
at length about the intentions and capabilities of Egypt and Syria.
The consequences of an attack in the South were dismissed as
minor—for the Egyptians, at worst, would be stopped in the
desert, far from Israel's civilian centers, and the IDF's second-
strike capability against Egypt was ample. Moreover, the probability of an Egyptian attack was very low. As paraphrased by Israel's
leading military correspondent, Dayan's perception was as follows:

28. Ibid., p. 383; Y. Ben-Porath et al., *Hamechdal [The Fiasco]* (Tel Aviv,
1973), p. 24.
29. *Story of My Life*, p. 384. A very similar version of Dayan's perception of
threat that day was reported by S. Nakdimon, "New Revelations," *Yediot
Aharonot*, 12 July 1974. Moreover, Meir recalled in *My Life*, p. 354, that Galili
phoned her in Strassbourg that day to convey Dayan's (and his) feelings that "as
soon as I got back we should have a serious discussion about the situation in the
Golan Heights."
30. *Story of My Life*, p. 384.

"If they cross the Suez Canal, they will sustain heavy losses and, in the second stage, the IDF will hit from all sides. They won't solve anything, and will be in a more difficult situation after the crossing, while at present—the Suez Canal protects them."[31] In the North, however, there was great danger to the Golan settlements. Dayan also seemed to perceive a higher probability of war, by remarking that the disposition and concentration of Syrian forces "is not normal defensive deployment"; further, that Syria had the military capability and intention—and temptation—to strike.

Despite these images of a growing Syrian threat and a higher probability of a Syrian attack, the Defense Minister made no recommendations. Nor did he object to the Kitchen Cabinet's decision not to consider the matter further until the regular Cabinet meeting set for the 7th. The reason lay in two other (competing) Dayan perceptions: (a) of the IDF's second-strike capability—to penetrate deep into Syria if she tried to seize the Golan; and (b) of Syria's proneness to miscalculation—namely, Dayan felt that any dramatic response by Israel to the Syrian build-up "would mobilize all Syria for war."[32] The lack of any sense of urgency—that is, of time pressure for decision—is evident in Dayan's stated rationale for requesting the 3 October meeting: "I had . . . thought it proper to bring this matter before the prime minister and any other ministers she wished to invite (two were present at that meeting) for a comprehensive review of the situation and of the steps we were taking to meet it."[33] Such were the perceptions of Israel's principal decision-makers on the eve of the 1973 crisis period.

The decision-makers' images in the 1973 pre-crisis period may now be summarized in terms of the most salient topics which emerged from the qualitative and quantitative analysis of their statements and speeches.[34]

1. *Definition of the Present Situation.* There was a striking difference here between Allon and Dayan. The Deputy Prime Minister criticized the immobilism of Israel's policy and expressed concern over its potential political and military repercussions. The

31. Z. Schiff, *October Earthquake*, p. 19.
32. S. Nakdimon, "New Revelations," *Yediot Aharonot*, 12 July 1974.
33. *Story of My Life*, p. 385.
34. For details of the quantitative analysis of the data, see note 24 above.

Defense Minister, by contrast, believed that the status quo could
—and should—continue for many years. Prime Minister Meir perceived the status quo as an achievement and shared Dayan's view
of its tenability.

2. *Possibility of War*. None of the three decision-makers envisaged the possibility of war in the autumn of 1973. Allon recognized
that mounting Arab frustration might induce an attack on Israel,
but he did not believe that an Arab military option was viable.
Dayan shared this view, with the self-assurance that the Arab
states understood that they could not defeat Israel on the battlefield. There were no references in the Meir statements to the possible outbreak of war.

3. *The Arabs*. Allon provided a detailed analysis of Arab attitudes and goals, in which he recognized their aspiration for revenge. Dayan perceived Arab objectives in stark terms—the
destruction of Israel. Meir shared Dayan's view.

4. *Egypt*. Allon revealed a profound understanding of Egyptian
fears, attitudes, and objectives. Meir criticized Sadat personally for
his ties with Moscow, his neglect of internal development, and his
callous attitude toward the lives of his own people. Dayan perceived Egypt as holding the key to war and peace.

5. *Superpowers*. Allon emphasized the need to limit superpower penetration of the Near East Core and perceived the
danger of an attempt to impose a solution of the Arab-Israeli conflict. Dayan's image was to the contrary: he viewed the superpowers and détente as a factor favorable to the preservation of the
status quo. Meir made no reference to the issue.

6. *The United States*. Before the Yom Kippur War, Dayan and
Meir perceived a consensus between U.S. and Israeli views and
their respective national interests.

7. *The Soviet Union*. Dayan argued that the Soviets had the
capability to encourage Arab belligerency, in contrast to the United States, which could play a positive role for peace. Meir frequently referred to the Soviets, in the context of Egyptian goals,
Soviet Jewry, and her own experience as a diplomat in Moscow.

8. *The Palestinians*. Allon's analysis of the Palestinian problem
was complex and profound. He warned that the Palestinians must
be treated as a potentially dynamic element in the Middle East,
and he cautioned against perpetuating their status as second-class
citizens. He was convinced that the Palestinians of the occupied

territories must be gradually encouraged to assume more responsibility for their own affairs. He did not accept the idea of an independent Palestinian state; rather, he favored the self-determination of Palestinians within Jordan. Dayan, too, differentiated among the Palestinians. While manifesting an empathy with the motivation of the terrorists, he advocated outright war against them. He also opposed repatriating any Arab refugees. And he was unwilling to withdraw from the West Bank. Meir, too, rejected an independent Palestine and, in general, perceived this issue in terms almost identical to Dayan's.

9. *Territories and Secure Boundaries.* Allon urged that Israel's territorial concessions be determined by strategic needs. He recognized that a peace settlement was impossible without far-reaching withdrawal by Israel. In this respect, he was far more generous than his colleagues. All three decision-makers expressed confidence in the deterrent power of "secure borders." Dayan argued that, with regard to Syria and Egypt, military security considerations should be the determinants of the extent of Israel's withdrawal. The Jordan border, however, was not, for Dayan, negotiable: the West Bank was perceived as part of the historic Jewish homeland—to the extent that he would have retained some of the territories, even at the cost of war. Meir shared Dayan's images.

DECISION FLOW

In September 1973, Israel was in the midst of a campaign for Knesset elections, scheduled for 31 October. Confidence had been restored after the war scare of May 1973.[35] Moreover, the Defense Minister had indicated a possible reduction in the three-year term

35. For a detailed description of the deliberations in the defense establishment on the April-June 1973 war scare, see H. Bar-Tov, *Dado,* Vol. 1, pp. 238–270. Dayan, Elazar, Zamir (Head of the *Mossad,* Israel's Intelligence Services abroad), and several other members of the General Staff decided that war was a distinct possibility: "The probability of war is higher than at any time since 1967" (Elazar). They therefore acted accordingly—in spite of AMAN's continued insistence on "very low probability" of war. The preparations for an Egyptian-Syrian attack were code-named "Operation Blue-White" and canceled only in early August 1973.

Meir and Dayan, retrospectively, designated the massing of Egyptian military power in May 1973 as the starting point of the pre-crisis period (Meir, *My Life,*

of military service.[36] The foreign policy platform of the ruling Labor-Mapam Alignment was based upon the "Galili Document," which adhered to the middle-of-the-road 1969 Alignment platform on the occupied territories.[37] The main opposition groups had formed the *Likud,* a Right-wing coalition led by Begin, Sharon, and Weizman, whose foreign policy platform called for the retention of the West Bank and most of the occupied territories in Sinai, as well as the Golan Heights.[38]

The trigger to the 1973 Crisis was an air battle arising from an Israeli photoreconnaissance mission along the Syrian frontier on 13 September, when thirteen Syrian MiGs were shot down against the loss of one Israeli Mirage. When Syria did not react immediately to this dramatic defeat, Israel's defence leadership became suspicious that Damascus "could be planning a more basic action."[39] This set in motion a series of incremental actions to strengthen IDF defenses in the North. Between 26 September and the outbreak of war on 6 October, the number of tanks in the

---

p. 353, and Dayan, *Story of My Life,* p. 381). The AMAN evaluation at that time had proved to be correct: War did not break out. And the Chief of Staff was accused of being overcautious and of wasting Israel's resources, to the amount of IL 61 million, the cost of a deterrent partial mobilization. See memorandum of Elazar to the Cabinet in May 1975, in response to the Agranat Commission's findings, *Ma'ariv,* 20 April 1976; and Nakdimon, "New Revelations," *Yediot Aharonot,* 19 July 1974. (Several decision-makers and advisers—Eban, Gazit, and Yariv—termed the Nakdimon series on Israel's 1973 decision process as entirely accurate.) See also "The October War As Seen Through the Eyes of Anwar Sadat," interviews with Sadat by Mussa Sabri in *Akhbar el Yom,* 10 September 1974; excerpts and the May war plan of Sadat were published in *Ma'ariv,* 13 September 1974. Israeli military intelligence evaluations in the summer of 1972 had predicted that, by May 1973, Egypt would be *ready* to go to war (A. Yariv, "Israeli Intelligence Believed Already in the Summer of 1972 that Egypt Would Be Ready for War in May 1973," *Ma'ariv,* 18 July 1975).

36. *Ha'aretz,* 21 July 1973.

37. The "Galili Document," which set forth a specific operational plan for 1973 to 1977, was a compromise between Dayan's demand for an activist policy in the territories and the dovish views of his opponents in the Alignment, mainly Allon, Bar-Lev, Eban, and Sapir. After the 1973 War, Heikal claimed that one of the reasons for Sadat's decision to go to war was the publication of the "Galili Document"; see Z. Schiff and E. Haber, eds., *Israel, Army and Defence, A Dictionary* (Tel Aviv, 1976), pp. 328–329. For an analysis of the Israeli policy spectrum on conditions for peace from 1967 to 1973, see M. Brecher, *Decisions in Israel's Foreign Policy,* pp. 460–462 and 515–517.

38. That remained the core of the *Likud* plank when it came to power after the ninth Knesset elections in May 1977.

39. Dayan, *Story of My Life,* p. 382.

Golan Heights front line was gradually increased from 70 to 177. Precautionary measures were also taken in the South, within the framework of a contingency plan called "Operation Dovecote." The number of tanks on the Bar-Lev line was increased to 276. And between 1 and 5 October, the regular army was gradually put on the highest state of alert.[40] No special defensive measures were taken along Israel's longest frontier, that with Jordan. As in 1956 and 1967, because of inter-Arab rivalries, Jordan's isolation within the Arab world, and the lessons of previous Arab-Israeli wars, the expectation was that even if war broke out with Syria and/or Egypt, Jordan would not join in the fighting.[41] Secondly, because of Israel's improved security position since the Six Day War, her military leaders believed that the Jordan front could be contained with the relatively small forces stationed on the West Bank.[42]

Foreign Minister Eban left for New York on 26 September to attend the UN General Assembly. His presence there, despite an intense election campaign at home, was important for another reason. Henry Kissinger, the newly appointed U.S. Secretary of State, had indicated the possibility of "corridor conversations" in New York between Egypt and Israel, with Kissinger or Under-Secretary of State Sisco acting as middleman. Eban later described the background of these diplomatic overtures in this way:

40. H. Bar-Tov, *Dado*, Vol. 1, pp. 289–324. Bar-Lev, the IDF Chief of Staff from 1968 until the end of 1971, vehemently defended the assumptions of "Operation Dovecote." In his view, the early disasters of the 1973 War could have been avoided if Israel's forces had been deployed according to plan, "with their fingers on the trigger." See Bar-Lev interview, *Ma'ariv*, 9 November 1973; interviews with freelance journalist Uri Millstein, 24 and 31 January, 26 June 1974; interview with M. Brecher, 29 July 1974; and "We Knew Where the Egyptians Would Attack and How—But We Made a Mistake About the Timing," *Ma'ariv*, 1 August 1975. Others, among them Allon, challenged these assumptions, stating that the massive Arab forces and their vast amount of sophisticated military equipment could not have been stopped during the first hours, even if everything had been prepared according to plan. See Allon interview with U. Millstein, 23 January 1974. See also A. Haselkorn, "Israeli Intelligence Performance in the Yom Kippur War," Discussion Paper, Hudson Institute, 17 July 1974; and interview with Major-General S. Gonen, who was OC Southern Command at the beginning of the 1973 War, in *Yediot Aharonot*, 21 September 1977.

41. This view was held despite the fact that, on 12 September, Sadat, Hussein, and Assad met in Cairo, and Syria and Jordan agreed to restore diplomatic relations.

42. These evaluations proved to be basically correct. Jordan was not informed of Egyptian and Syrian plans and stayed out of the War until 13 October, "to protect Syria's southern flank." On that day, Jordan sent her 40th Armored Brigade to Syria's aid.

The diplomatic sequence was as follows: the General Assembly, then talks with the Foreign Ministers. I had met him [Kissinger] privately for breakfast at the [Israeli] Embassy residence [in Washington], when he told me that, within two weeks [by mid-October] he expected to see [King] Hussein. The problem was that of acquiescence, what he called the attritional process. . . . He hoped this would bring Egypt to the nego- tiating table and then the other Arabs. The State Department had been pushing for an initiative in April [1973]. Sisco had made a speech in April. Kissinger said to me in August: "This can't go on, let's talk in October." He began with the Arabs in two rounds; one, a collective dinner party, for all of them who were willing to come (not all of them were willing to come). The Foreign Ministers who had diplomatic relations with America were there, and the Secretary-General of the Arab League was there, and they were anxious that he, Kissinger, the Wizard of Vietnam, should try to do something about the Middle East. More substantively, there was an individual talk with Zayyad [Egypt's Foreign Minister at the time]. Zayyad said there is not going to be a war. Kissinger told him that, after the Israeli elections, Eban could come back for talks, and the Egyptians agreed. And at our October 4th meeting Kissinger said: "You come back in November, let's hope Zayyad will come back, and then we shall see how we can get the negotiations going."[43]

On 4 October, Eban addressed the General Assembly about the UN role in the international system: He did not convey the slight- est expectation of war between Israel and her neighbors in the near future.

Prime Minister Meir left for Strassbourg on 30 September to address the Consultative Assembly of the Council of Europe. Two days earlier, Arab terrorists had taken hostage seven Soviet Jews who had just crossed into Austria. They threatened to kill them unless Austria immediately terminated her assistance to Soviet Jewish immigrants and closed down the Schönau transit camp. Chancellor Kreisky yielded the same day. The Israeli Cabinet, at a special session on 29 September, approved Prime Minister Meir's suggestion that she try to persuade Kreisky, at a personal meeting, to reverse his stand. It proved to be unsuccessful. Upon her return to Israel on Wednesday, 3 October, Meir reported to a special Cabinet meeting on her talks with Kreisky. There was also a discussion of steps to deal with the problem of Soviet Jewish

43. Interview with M. Brecher, 15 July 1974. This account was reaffirmed in Eban's *An Autobiography*, p. 498. According to William B. Quandt, the U.S. intelligence community, too, held the view that "the option of a political alter- native made an Arab-initiated war implausible" (*Decade of Decisions* [Berkeley, Los Angeles, and London, 1977], p. 168). See also B. Kalb and M. Kalb, *Kissinger*, pp. 455–457; and E. R. F. Sheehan, "Step by Step in the Middle East," *Foreign Policy*, 22 (Spring 1976), 3–70.

immigrants in the new situation. The security danger was not raised.[44]

It was, however, discussed by the Kitchen Cabinet just before the Cabinet session on the 3rd. That inner circle had been convened at Dayan's request in order to "share the responsibility" for decisions to be taken in response to Syrian and Egyptian military moves. Present were: the core group of political decision-makers —Meir, Allon, Dayan, and Galili; three IDF officers—Elazar, Peled, and Shalev, the last representing Zeira, who was ill at home; and six civil servants, notably Gazit.

Defense Minister Dayan, who opened the meeting, wrote later of his motivation: "We had received intelligence of weapons reinforcements on the Syrian and perhaps also on the Egyptian front and of the Syrian-Egyptian intention, or state of readiness to renew the war."[45] Shalev then presented the AMAN (Israeli Military Intelligence) assessment: events on the two fronts were unrelated; the Egyptian military activity was an exercise, while the Syrian dispositions were defensive. He acknowledged some behavior that did not fit this evaluation, notably the forward positioning of artillery and antiaircraft missiles; but on the Syrian front such activities had been observed before. Syria, he asserted, would not attack without Egypt, and there was no evidence to change the basic evaluation that Egypt was not ready to go to war. On the contrary, there was certain information that the Egyptian moves were annual maneuvers.[46] Allon questioned the basic AMAN assumption: "Is the routine [on the Egyptian side] really routine? I was told—yes. But they also told me two other important things; that a full alert had been declared in the IDF and that the entire Air Force was on alert. . . . And that we would know 48 hours in advance if war was to break out. . . ."[47]

Elazar supported the AMAN evaluation. Although he considered a joint Egypt-Syria attack possible, he believed it was im-

44. See Finance Minister Sapir interview with M. Brecher, 25 June 1974; Gazit interview with M. Brecher, 27 July 1974; Bar-Lev interview with U. Millstein, 26 June 1974; and S. Nakdimon, "New Revelations," *Yediot Aharonot,* 12 July 1974. The Agranat Commission later criticized the Prime Minister for not informing the Cabinet of the military situation at the 3 October meeting, but it absolved her in general: "The activities of the Prime Minister during the decisive days before the war bear witness to behavior fitting the responsibility placed upon her" (Agranat Commission, Partial Report, 3 April 1974).

45. *Story of My Life,* p. 385.

46. Agranat Commission, Partial Report, 3 April 1974; Dayan, *Story of My Life,* p. 385; S. Nakdimon, "New Revelations," *Yediot Aharonot,* 12 July 1974.

47. Allon, Interview with U. Millstein, 23 January 1974.

probable in the immediate future. He concluded by stating that the IDF's defensive deployment at that stage was sufficient, with some further reinforcement in the North. He hoped that, in the worst case, the IDF would be given sufficient early warning of an impending attack.[48] The Prime Minister also accepted the AMAN evaluation, after persistent questioning of the implications of the data put before her. She recalled the mood on 3 October and the decision of Israel's high policy elite in this way: "Nobody at the meeting thought that it was necessary to call up the reserves, and nobody thought that war was imminent. But it was decided to put a further discussion of the situation on the agenda for Sunday's [7 October] cabinet meeting" (Decision 2).[49]

48. H. Bar-Tov, *Dado*, Vol. 1, pp. 305–306.

49. *My Life*, pp. 354–355. As noted, Israel's Military Intelligence was well aware of Arab political and military activities throughout 1973. It was the mis-interpretation of the many signals of Arab preparation for war and the incorrect evaluation of Arab behavior that caused Israel's surprise. Briefly summarized, the main signals emanating from the Arab camp were:

1. Egypt and Syria decided, in April 1973, to go to war the following month. Operational plans were approved at a meeting of their Chiefs of Staff in Cairo on 21–22 April, and preparatory steps were set in motion. Israel responded by mo-bilizing IDF reserves. The Arab states did not go to war in May because Syria notified Egypt she was not yet ready.

2. During the summer of 1973, there were intensive Arab meetings at the highest political and military levels, among them: (1) the visit of a Syrian military delegation, led by Defense Minister Tlas, to Cairo, 6–8 June; (2) a nine-hour visit of Sadat to Damascus on 12 June, followed three days later by (3) a visit of Egyp-tian Defense Minister Ismail; (4) an Egyptian military delegation, led by Chief of Staff Shazli, was in Damascus from 6 to 9 August, to be followed (5) by a two-day consultation of the Heads of State in Damascus on 25–26 August; (6) two days later, on the 28th, Sadat went to Saudi Arabia for a seven-hour visit.

3. In September, after several exchanges of visits among senior military and political officials of the three countries, a meeting of Assad, Hussein, and Sadat took place in Cairo, from 10 to 12 September. This led to a formal resumption by Egypt and Syria of diplomatic relations with Jordan, which had been severed after the September 1970 civil war in Jordan. The frequency of consultations at the levels of Head of State, Defense Minister, and Chief of Staff, and the reconciliation with Jordan comprised an unusual pattern of behavior; but they were interpreted by AMAN as one of many intra-Arab reconciliations and as part of psychological warfare against Israel.

4. There were also military signals on the eve of the 1973 War. On 14 Septem-ber, the Lebanese press reported the transfer of Syrian army units from the Jor-danian to the Israeli front. A week later, the Beirut daily *Al Nahar* stated: "Cairo has informed a Palestinian personality [Arafat, at a meeting a few weeks earlier] that Egypt will shortly embark on an extensive military operation, with the pur-pose of generating American pressure on Israel." On the 24th, it was known by Israeli Intelligence that Syria had massed three infantry divisions, 670 tanks, and 100 artillery batteries on the Golan front—still in a defensive posture; this was

The next day, on 4 October, AMAN received information of a rapid build-up of Egyptian and Syrian forces and changes in their deployment from a defensive to an offensive posture. This was not, however, considered sufficiently serious to revise the previous day's appreciation. At General Staff Headquarters, defensive preparations for the coming winter were discussed, and a long meeting was devoted entirely to problems of discipline.[50]

On the 4th, too, Kissinger and Eban exchanged information on the military situation. The U.S. assessment, prepared by the CIA, reinforced the IDF evaluation: in spite of the signs, "an outbreak of major Arab-Israeli hostilities remains unlikely for the immediate future. . . ."[51] The meeting of the Foreign Ministers was devoted

---

interpreted as merely a response to the 13 September aerial battle in which thirteen Syrian MiGs had been shot down. Also on the 24th, a combined United States intelligence estimate (by the Central Intelligence Agency, the Defense Intelligence Agency, and the National Security Agency) of a possible Egyptian-Syrian attack was communicated to Israel: It was based on evidence of rare Egyptian maneuvers at the division level and indicated a much more complicated Egyptian field communications network than mere maneuvers. AMAN differed with the U.S. estimates. The following day, Syrian tanks began to move out of their usual defensive pattern, and United States Intelligence noted, for the second time in two days, that there was "something seriously suspicious about the nature of the Syrian redeployment" (B. Kalb and M. Kalb, *Kissinger*, p. 513).

On 1 October, Syrian tanks and artillery began to move from their bases around Damascus to forward positions on the Golan opposite Israel's defense line. The same day, a convoy of Egyptian missile trucks was seen entering the Canal Zone town of Ismailia. IDF soldiers stationed on the Bar-Lev line reported heavy Egyptian army traffic, including bridging equipment. The next day, Syria began to mobilize her reserves. Israel's aerial surveillance revealed that Syria's forces on the Golan had grown to 800 tanks and 108 artillery batteries; moreover, Syrian infantry were stationed on the forward front line. A revealing item from the Middle East News Agency reported that Egypt's Second and Third Armies had been placed on alert. The news was officially denied within minutes.

For analyses of Arab deliberations and actions on the eve of the 1973 War, see M. Heikal, *The Road to Ramadan* (London, 1975), passim; C. Herzog, *The War of Atonement* (Jerusalem and Tel Aviv, 1975), chaps. 2, 3, and 5; Michael I. Handel, "Perception, Deception and Surprise: The Case of the Yom Kippur War," *Jerusalem Papers on Peace Problems*, 19 (1976); Al-Haytham al-Ayoubi, "The Strategies of the Fourth Campaign," in N. H. Aruri, ed., *Middle East Crucible: Studies on the Arab-Israeli War of October 1973* (Wilmette, Ill., 1975), pp. 65–96; and Lt. Colonel Avi Shay, "Egypt Before the Yom Kippur War: War Aims and Plans of Attack," *Ma'arakhot*, 250 (July 1976), 15–38.

50. H. Bar-Tov, *Dado*, Vol. 1, pp. 311–313; C. Herzog, *The War of Atonement*, p. 283.

51. United States Government, House of Representatives, Report of Select Committee on Intelligence, September 1975, published in *Village Voice* (New York, 17 February 1976). The former U.S. President later recalled: "As recently

to preparations for the "corridor conversations," scheduled to begin in New York at the beginning of November. Eban recalled the content of his conversation with Kissinger, along with the prevailing intelligence estimates, as follows:

There were no American warnings [of an Arab military attack] specifically. There was a general knowledge that we shared with the U.S. Probably we told the U.S. about it rather than the other way around. There were joint discussions between the two governments of what they [the indicators] meant. There was absolutely no failure on the military, factual side of information. But there was, on both sides, a leniency about the interpretation of the facts. There were emphatic explanations in favor of contingencies other than war. And this was going on at the end of September, right up to October 5th. In my talks with Kissinger on October 4, five minutes were spent on the situation on the borders. Kissinger stated that there were heavy military concentrations, but according to U.S. military sources this did not mean intent, and he asked what was our appraisal. I had received for the purposes of our talk, from our intelligence people, a cable saying that it is true the concentrations are heavy but not uniquely so— there had been such concentrations before. The explanation was that there were maneuvers on the Egyptian front, and on the Syrian front they were hypochondriacally afraid of a strike from us. Then he [Kissinger] said, "since nothing dramatic is going to happen in all likelihood, let's get on to the negotiations."[52]

Late at night on 4 October, this evaluation began to change under the impact of accumulating information: first, news of a sudden and rapid exit of Soviet advisers and their families from Egypt and Syria; and secondly, the report of a special IDF aerial reconnaissance mission along the Canal, ordered that morning, which showed a considerable offensive Egyptian deployment, including the movement of bridging equipment toward three sectors of the Canal.[53] Bar-Tov noted in his biography of Chief of Staff Elazar: "Towards midnight of Thursday, October 4, the red lights lit up one after the other and the existing evaluations became insufficient to answer the questions raised."[54]

---

as the day before [the Egyptian-Syrian attack], the CIA had reported that war in the Middle East was unlikely, dismissing as annual maneuvers the massive and unusual troop movement that had recently been taking place in Egypt. They had similarly interpreted the dramatic step-up in Syrian military activity as a precautionary move because the Israelis had recently shot down three [actually thirteen] Syrian jets" (RN: The Memoirs of Richard Nixon [New York, 1978], p. 920).

52. Interview with M. Brecher, 15 July 1974.
53. Agranat Commission, Partial Report, 3 April 1974, and S. Nakdimon, "New Revelations," Yediot Aharonot, 12 July 1974.
54. H. Bar-Tov, Dado, Vol. 1, p. 313.

CHAPTER FOUR

COMPARISON AND FINDINGS[1]

AN INTERNATIONAL CRISIS has been defined as a "breakpoint" or basic shift along a continuum of relations between a state and other global actors. It is triggered by an event or events in the external or internal environment which generates three perceptual changes among a state's decision-makers—namely, images of a higher threat to basic values, of the probability of war, and of finite time for decisional response. These changes in perception, as noted in the model set forth in Chapter 1, lead to stress which, in turn, affects a state's coping mechanisms: information processing; the pattern of consultation; the type and structure of decisional forums; and the search for and evaluation of alternatives.

To what extent do the 1967 and 1973 Israeli cases fit this concept of crisis? How reliable is the operational definition of crisis as an organizing device to marshal the empirical data? And how valid is the model in illuminating the reality of a state's behavior under the stress induced by perceived threat, time pressure, and war likelihood?

1. The findings presented in Chapters 4, 7, and 10 are horizontal; that is, comparisons are made across crises—namely, between identical periods in the two Israeli Crises under inquiry: pre-crisis 1967–pre-crisis 1973, crisis 1967–crisis 1973, and post-crisis 1967–post-crisis 1973. The focus is static—namely, the comparison is *within-period*. By contrast, the findings to be presented in the concluding chapter about the impact of crisis-induced stress on coping mechanisms may be designated vertical. That is to say, they will, inter alia, focus on change from period to period *within a single crisis* and will be dynamic in character.

77

The conflict between Israel and her Arab neighbors has been protracted—three decades; but not every day, month, or even year has witnessed a crisis. Threat perception has been endemic. An image of the possibility of war has been constant. The pressure of time has been felt not infrequently. But, it is argued, only when the threat level is higher than normal, when war is perceived as probable, and the time for decision(s) is viewed as finite, all consequences of environmental change, can a crisis, within the conflict, be said to exist.

The reader will recall that the pre-crisis period is marked off from a preceding noncrisis situation by one indicator only—a conspicuous increase in perceived threat.

CRISIS COMPONENTS

Environmental Change

The trigger mechanism (or *source*) for the onset of the pre-crisis period was identical in both cases, a "directed external hostile act" of the "violent military" type. More specifically, it was an aerial battle, one on 7 April 1967, in which six Syrian MiGs were shot down, and another on 13 September 1973, when twelve Syrian MiGs and one Israeli Mirage were downed. For Israel's decision-makers each was the first link in a chain of events which, together, created a situational change triggering an increase in the perception of threat from Syria. But there was no awareness, as yet, of time constraints on decisions nor an expectation of war. And, in behavioral terms, there was no extraordinary activity, such as large-scale mobilization of reserves. The apex of the crisis lay in the future.

Threat to Values

During the decade from March 1957 (the end of the Sinai Campaign Crisis) to March 1967, there were few perceived specific threats to Israel's basic values. Notable were: the massing of three Egyptian divisions in Sinai and Gaza in February 1960, ostensibly, as in May 1967, to deter Israel from attacking Syria; and the reported use by Egypt of German scientists, especially in 1963–65, to produce surface-to-surface missiles, which posed a danger of high casualties and heavy destruction in Israel's heartland and in her major urban centers. The first was countered by Israeli signals of the IDF determination to respond—an effective demonstration of deterrence. The second was overcome by Bonn's diplomatic intervention, under Israel's pressure, to terminate the active involvement of German scientists in Egypt's military research.

The 7 April 1967 air battle was not unique. But the severe humiliation to Syria led to a sharp escalation of verbal hostility, including a renewed call by Syria's President on the 17th for "a popular war of liberation," Soviet warnings of Israeli troop concentrations on the northern border, and high-level Egypt-Syria consultations. The result was a sharp rise in Israel's threat perception, as evident in unmistakable public warnings—and private diplomatic activity—by Foreign Minister Eban (9 May), the Foreign Ministry to UNTSO Commander Odd Bull (10 May), UN Representative Rafael to UN Under-Secretary Bunche (10 May), Prime Minister Eshkol (11 May), Ambassador Harman to the State Department (11 May), Director-General of the Foreign Office Levavi to the Soviet Ambassador (12 May), an IDF spokesman's counterthreat of a major military operation against Syria (12 May), and warnings by Eshkol, Deputy Defense Minister Dinstein, and Minister Without Portfolio Galili (13 May).

The air battle on 13 September 1973, too, led to severe humiliation for Syria—but not to an escalation of verbal attacks from Damascus. Moreover, there was only one Israeli public warning indicating the presence of threat perception, made by Defense Minister Dayan on 26 September. In both cases, the value threatened was, at the outset, the security of border settlements from retaliatory action by Syria. By the close of the 1967 pre-crisis period, it had become Israel's deterrence credibility. In 1973, the threat changed to a probable joint Egypt-Syria attack to regain the Golan and Sinai territories which had been acquired by Israel in the Six Day War of 1967. In short, the values threatened in the two pre-crisis periods were not *grave* or basic. That is, they did not—yet—involve survival, political independence, territorial integrity, or societal stability.

Probability of War

The definition of crisis underlying this inquiry postulates that a perception of probability of war is *not* present during the pre-crisis period: that image-change occurs later. What does the evidence of

1967 indicate? Not until the last week of the pre-crisis period—
from 9 to 16 May—did the statements of Israeli decision-makers,
Eshkol, Eban, Rabin, and others, refer to the possibility of military
action, in the form of retaliation for Syrian border raids. In none
does one discern a perceived probability of war; rather, in all—
Eban (9 May), Eshkol (11, 13 May), Rabin (14 May)—there was a
threat of limited retaliation to counter terrorism.

    In 1973, apart from Dayan's public warning to Syria, none of the
public statements by Israel's decision-makers (as examined in
Chapter 3) made any reference to the possibility, let alone probability, of military action in any form. More pointedly, the persistent
evaluation by the Director of Military Intelligence and his Deputy
was of a "lower than low" probability of war. The question of border tension was not even discussed until three days before the
outbreak of war, and even then further consideration was set for a
regular Cabinet meeting due to take place on 7 October—the day
after the Syrian-Egyptian attack. While war and, certainly, limited
military action are always viewed as possible in a protracted conflict, the findings suggest the absence of a perceived probability of
war in the early period of both the 1967 and 1973 Crises.

                            Time Pressure

According to our definition, decision-makers do not perceive time
pressure—or even the salience of time—in their deliberative
process during the pre-crisis period. The findings for Israel's 1967
and 1973 Crises are in consonance with this postulate. Although
the trigger mechanisms were events on 7 April and 13 September,
respectively, there is no evidence of an awareness that time constrained—or in any way was relevant to—Israel's response. The
first Cabinet meeting to consider the escalating border violence in
1967 was the regularly scheduled session on 7 May. The decision
taken, in the form of a conditional threat of retaliation against Syria,
made no reference to time limit. The next meeting, set for the
14th, was delayed two days because, that year, Independence Day
fell on 15 May. Despite the news of Egyptian troop movements into Sinai, on 14/15 May, the Cabinet did not respond immediately
or concretely. Eshkol and Rabin decided on small-scale mobilization; but the perception of all was an Egyptian "show of force."
Threat had increased but was still moderate; war was, as always,

possible but of very low probability; and therefore time salience was not recognized in the making of any responsive decisions.

In the 1973 Crisis, the first Kitchen Cabinet meeting to consider the escalating threat occurred on 3 October. The decision, as noted, was to delay further deliberation. The next meeting of the Cabinet was an extraordinary session summoned by the Prime Minister on the 5th. By then, the crisis period had begun. In both cases, time salience was to become operative only in conjunction with a change in the other indicators—and that, in turn, required an environmental stimulus.

In the light of these findings, the concept of "pre-crisis period" (7 April–16 May 1967 and 13 September–4 October 1973) has been shown to be operationally viable. Both periods were characterized by an increase in threat perception, but no other crisis condition was present. One may postulate, therefore, that in any time frame in which high-policy decision-makers manifest a conspicuous increase in threat perception, unaccompanied by a high expectation of war and a higher salience of time, one has encountered a potential pre-crisis period of an international crisis.

What other similarities and differences may be discerned for the pre-crisis period? One is *duration:* in 1967 it was forty days; in 1973 it lasted twenty-two days. Another is *outcome:* the 1967 pre-crisis period led to the most intense perception of threat by Israel's decision-makers in the history of the state, and ultimately to war; in 1973 it led directly to war, the Egypt-Syria attack on 6 October. It is noteworthy that, although the direct outcome of the 1973 pre-crisis period was graver than its 1967 counterpart, threat perception in 1967 was much more intense. A third difference is the number of decisions: there were three in the 1967 pre-crisis period, and two in 1973. The time span of decisions was of almost equal duration, 7–16 May and 26 September–4 October, respectively. Of the two decisions taken in the 1973 pre-crisis period, one was to postpone deliberations. The number and content of decisions is another indicator of the greater intensity of threat perception in 1967.

COPING MECHANISMS

The model of crisis behavior (Figure 1) specifies that stress affects, inter alia, the ways in which decision-makers cope with crisis. The

coping mechanisms incorporated in the model comprise information processing, pattern of consultation, structure of decisional
forum, and consideration of alternatives. How did the threat-
induced rise in stress affect those mechanisms during the 1967 and
1973 pre-crisis periods?

Information Processing

As in noncrisis situations, the flow of information about Arab military activity in the 1967 pre-crisis period was channeled to a few
ministers—principally Eshkol and Eban. Similarly, the IDF Intelligence Branch was the sole source of information and appreciation
reports. The Cabinet Defense Committee was not yet a consumer
of information. In short, the increase in threat, especially on 15–16
May, did not raise the stress level sufficiently above the norm to
catalyze changes in information sources or processing. During the
1973 pre-crisis period, the early news of an Arab military build-up
was kept within the confines of the military elite—the Chief of
Staff, General Staff, senior officers of the Northern and Southern
Commands, and the Defense Minister. Under the impact of growing threat, the cumulating information was brought to the attention of the Kitchen Cabinet—but not the Cabinet proper—a few
days before the outbreak of war. The stress level, as in 1967, was
moderate until the end of the pre-crisis period, and therefore
changes in information processing were limited in scope.

TABLE 4

CONSULTATIVE MEETINGS BY TYPE AND SIZE:
PRE-CRISIS PERIODS

Number of Participants	1967			1973		
	Ad Hoc	Institutional	Total	Ad Hoc	Institutional	Total
small 2	–	5	5	2	1	3
3–4	2	–	2	–	2	2
medium 5–10	3	–	3	1	1	2
11–14	–	–	–	1	–	1
large 15–20	–	2	2	–	2	2
21+	–	–	–	–	–	–
Total	5	7	12	4	6	10

Consultation: Persons and Groups

Persons consulted in the pre-crisis period of 1967, apart from Cabinet members, were Y. Herzog from the bureaucratic elite, and four generals, Rabin, Yariv, Weizman, and Amit. In the 1973 pre-crisis period, consultation centered on the Kitchen Cabinet of Meir, Dayan, Allon, and Galili. The counterpart of Herzog— namely, M. Gazit—was the only participating civil servant, though others attended meetings. IDF advisers were Elazar, Zeira, or his deputy, Shalev, Tal, and two persons without a 1967 equivalent, the OC Air Force, Peled, and the OC Northern Command, Hofi. Thus, the political elite within the consultative circle was narrower in 1973, the Kitchen Cabinet versus the full Cabinet. The military elite was slightly larger, five compared to four. In both pre-crisis periods, however, the number of persons consulted was small.

Table 4 presents the data on consultative meetings in the pre-crisis periods by type and size.[2] The type of meeting has been designated as institutional or ad hoc. The former has the following attributes: permanence in organizational form; legal authorization to make decisions; and relative stability in composition.[3] All other group meetings are ad hoc. Both types of meetings are classified as large, medium, and small. The delineation of boundaries has been, of necessity, somewhat arbitrary, for the theoretical literature has not yet established precise boundaries. Therefore, we have used as a criterion the capacity for informal interaction. With up to four members, a group generally uses informal procedures for discussion. As a group expands, however, a formal or informal chairman is required to organize the discussion. The small-group literature suggests that when a group grows beyond ten, institutional procedures of discussion and decision are used.

The ratio of ad hoc to institutional meetings for the 1967 pre-crisis period is .7:1; and for 1973 it is virtually the same: .66:1. In 1967, the distribution by size of meetings for the pre-crisis period

2. Tables 4, 5, 7, 8, 10, and 11 are derived from the graphic representation of the 1967 and 1973 consultative and decision processes (Appendix C).

3. In Israel's foreign policy system there are several institutional groups: the Government or Cabinet; the Ministerial (Cabinet) Committee on Defense; the Prime Minister and Defense Minister together; the Defense Minister and Chief of Staff; the PM-DM and COS; and the General Staff. (Meetings between the PM and/or DM with any IDF officer(s) other than the COS are ad hoc, for they do not have any formal status. The Knesset Committee on Foreign Affairs and Security is an institutional consultative body which rarely makes decisions.)

TABLE 5
GROUP PARTICIPATION IN THE CONSULTATIVE PROCESS: PRE-CRISIS PERIODS

	1967			1973		
	Meetings with PM/DM alone	Meetings with PM/DM attended by two or more groups	Total	Meetings with PM and/or DM alone	Meetings with PM and/or DM attended by two or more groups	Total
ME	6	–	6	4	1	5
BE	2	1	3	2	1	3
M	–	2	2	1	–	1
PE	–	–	–	–	–	–
KC				–	1	1
U.S.				–	–	–
UN				–	–	–

BE = Bureaucratic Elite
DM = Defense Minister
KC = Kitchen Cabinet

M = Ministers
ME = Military Elite
PE = Political Elite

PM = Prime Minister
UN = United Nations
U.S. = United States

is 58% small, 25% medium, and 17% large. The comparable—and strikingly similar—pattern for 1973 is 50% small, 20% medium, and 30% large. The prominence of small meetings in both pre-crisis periods indicates that a moderate increase in stress, induced by the higher threat, was not intense enough to create a felt need by decision-makers for more authoritative consultation. This is also evident in the paucity of consultative meetings held during those periods—twelve in 1967 and ten in 1973. (Many more were held later, after all three crisis indicators had escalated.) In the largest sense, the data reveal surprise; that is to say, decision-makers did not anticipate the emerging security crises.

Table 5 presents the data on group consultation in institutional meetings. The number of participants noted is larger than the number of people active in the discussion at any specific meeting, for many were present in a technical or advisory capacity. The military elite predominated in the 1967 pre-crisis consultations: They participated in six out of a total of eleven meetings with the Prime Minister, and in all six no other group was present. The situation was similar in the pre-crisis period of 1973: There were ten meetings held by Meir and Dayan, of which five were with the military elite, with no other group present at four of them. Moreover, in 1967 they met with Eshkol alone three times as often as the bureaucrats; and in 1973 they met with the Prime Minister and/or the Minister of Defense more often than all other groups combined. All this suggests that an initial effect of increasing threat perception and of a moderate rise in stress for Prime Ministers and Defense Ministers in 1967 and 1973 was to seek more advice from, that is, consult more with, the IDF officers, the specialists on violence and on the routine procedures for response to a militarily threatening change in the environment.

Decisional Forums

Table 6 presents the substance of Israel's decisions during the pre-crisis periods of 1967 and 1973, the setting and size of the decisional meetings, and the specific decision-makers. The second and third decisions in 1967 were made by a small institutional group, the Defense Minister and the COS. The first decision, Israel's threat to launch a retaliation raid if Syria did not heed her public warnings, was taken in a large institutional forum—namely, the Cabinet. The size of the decisional unit thus ranged from two to eighteen. There were no decisions by ad hoc groups.

TABLE 6
DECISIONAL FORUMS:
PRE-CRISIS PERIODS

1967

Decision Number	Decision	Setting Institutional Small	Setting Institutional Large
1	Threat to Syria		C
2	IDF Alert	DM+COS	
3	Limited Mobilization	DM+COS	

1973

Decision Number	Decision	Setting Institutional Small	Setting Ad Hoc Small	Setting Ad Hoc Large
1	Warning to Syria, Brigade to Golan	DM+COS+ME		
2	Delay Further Discussion About Arab Military Build-up			KC+ME+BE

BE = Bureaucratic Elite   C = Cabinet   COS = Chief of Staff
DM = Defense Minister   KC = Kitchen Cabinet   ME = Military Elite

In the pre-crisis period of 1973, by contrast, the key decision on 3 October to delay further consideration of the altered security situation until the scheduled Cabinet meeting on the 7th was made by a large ad hoc group—namely, the Kitchen Cabinet together with members of the military and bureaucratic elites. The first decision, involving military movements, was made by the Defense Minister, in consultation with the Chief of Staff and other IDF officers. The decisional unit, then, ranged from one to eighteen persons. Four of the five pre-crisis decisions in both Crises were taken in institutional settings. Further, the Military was represented in all five decisions. This, too, indicates that a relatively low level of stress, the consequence of an initial increase in threat perception, led to a heavy reliance on institutional decisional forums dominated by the IDF, the guardians of standard operating procedures in the security field.

Alternatives: Search and Evaluation

In the 1967 pre-crisis period, a combination of (rising but still) low threat and low expectation of war, as well as available previously designed procedures, made unnecessary a search for or comprehensive evaluation of alternatives. This is particularly true for the last two decisions. Prior to the first decision, there was a modest Cabinet consideration of alternatives aimed at bringing about a de-escalation of tension.

The two pre-crisis decisions of 1973 were arrived at after limited discussion, less for the first than for the second. There was no search for new options. As in 1967 and on many other occasions, Syria was cautioned against any military action directed against Israel, and IDF defenses were strengthened; both were routine procedures. The decision to delay until 7 October a full Cabinet debate on Dayan's evaluation of the changing military situation was taken after some discussion, primarily because of a consensus perception in the Kitchen Cabinet and IDF Intelligence that the probability of war was very low. In summary, a moderate increase in stress, deriving from low levels of threat and war likelihood images, did not provide a stimulus, or create a recognized need, for careful evaluation of alternatives, let alone a search for new options.

PART TWO

CRISIS PERIOD

CHAPTER FIVE

1967: 17 MAY TO 4 JUNE

DECISIONS AND DECISION-MAKERS

FOR ISRAEL the 1967 crisis period began on 17 May and lasted until the Cabinet decision on 4 June to go to war. Following the three decisions of the pre-crisis period, there were fourteen others during the next nineteen days. They can be divided into three phases:

I
APPREHENSION AND MOBILIZATION:
17–22 MAY

Decision Number	Date	Content
4.	17 May	Eshkol and Rabin decided on further mobilization.
5.	19 May	Eshkol, as Defense Minister, and the General Staff decided on large-scale mobilization.
6.	19 May	The General Staff decided to change the disposition of the IDF forces from a defensive posture to a build-up toward offensive capability.
7.	21 May	The Cabinet approved the large-scale mobilization decision of 19 May.

II
DELAY AND DIPLOMACY:
23–28 May

Decision Number	Date	Content
8.	23 May	The Cabinet, acting as the Ministerial Committee on Defense, decided to postpone a decision on whether or not to go to war.
9.	23 May	The Cabinet, acting as the Ministerial Committee on Defense, approved Eban's journey to Washington to explore U.S. intentions.
10.	25 May	Eshkol approved a move to warn the U.S. Administration, through Eban, that there was a danger of an imminent Egyptian attack.
11.	26 May	The Cabinet, acting as the Ministerial Committee on Defense, decided to await Eban's return before taking a decision on the opening of the Straits.
12.	28 May	The Cabinet decided to opt for further waiting, to leave time for action by the maritime states.
13.	28 May	The Cabinet decided to keep the army on full alert.

III
RESOLUTION:
29 MAY–4 JUNE

Decision Number	Date	Content
14.	30 May	Eshkol, in consultation with other ministers and bureaucrats, decided to send Intelligence Head, Major-General Amit, to the U.S. to ascertain American intentions.
15.	1 June	Eshkol accepted the formation of a National Unity Government with Dayan as Defense Minister.
16.	2 June	Dayan approved military plans to strike along three lines of advance into Sinai, instead of one.
17.	4 June	The Cabinet decided to go to war.

Almost all decisions of the crisis period were taken by the eighteen-member, five-party coalition Cabinet and their advisers. The decisions on war were made by the National Unity Government, enlarged to twenty-one with the addition of two ministers from *Gahal* and one from *Rafi*. The Cabinet met almost daily throughout the 1967 Crisis, sometimes around the clock, and was engaged in what one civil servant termed "an exercise in collective cable reading."[1] Its composition was as follows:

ALIGNMENT

Mapai

L. Eshkol	Prime Minister (and Defense Minister to 1 June)
Z. Aranne*	Education and Culture
A. Eban*	Foreign Affairs
H. Gvati	Agriculture
P. Sapir*	Finance
E. Sasson*	Police
Y. S. Shapiro*	Justice
Z. Sharef	Industry and Commerce
Y. Yeshayahu	Posts

Ahdut Ha'avoda

Y. Allon*	Labor
M. Carmel	Transport
Y. Galili*	Without Portfolio (in charge of information)

Mapam

Y. Barzilai*	Health
M. Bentov	Housing

National Religious Party

Y. Burg	Welfare
H. M. Shapira*	Interior
Z. Warhaftig*	Religious Affairs

Independent Liberals

M. Kol*	Tourism and Development

As of 1 June:

Gahal

M. Begin*	Without Portfolio
Y. Saphir*	Without Portfolio

Rafi

M. Dayan*	Defense

1. Ya'acov Herzog, Interview with M. Brecher, 10 August 1968.
*Members of the Ministerial (Cabinet) Committee on Defense, as of 1 June 1967.

Other party leaders and persons who participated in the deliberations of the crisis period were:

S. Avigur	the "éminence grise" of Israel's military-security establishment.
D. Ben-Gurion	"Father of the Nation" and Prime Minister–Defense Minister for most of the period, 1948–63.
Z. Dinstein	Deputy Minister of Defense.
G. Meir	Secretary-General of *Mapai* during the 1967 Crisis.
S. Peres	Secretary-General of *Rafi* and a central figure in the 1967 domestic political crisis.
Y. Yadin	former Chief of Staff, archaeologist, and an Eshkol confidant.

Civil servants and diplomats of consequence during the crisis period, apart from Ya'acov Herzog, included: Aviad Yaffe, Eshkol's Head of Bureau; Harman and Evron at the Washington Embassy, who helped to decipher the attitudes and policy of the U.S. Administration; Levavi, who, in Eban's absence, often represented the Foreign Ministry in Cabinet discussions; Rafael, who implemented Israel's policy at the UN; and Moshe Bitan, Assistant Director-General of the Foreign Ministry in charge of U.S. affairs. From the IDF, Generals Rabin, Yariv, and Weizman continued to be actively involved in the consultation process. They were joined from 1 June by the newly appointed Deputy Chief of Staff, Major-General Haim Bar-Lev.

PSYCHOLOGICAL ENVIRONMENT

Attitudinal Prism

At the beginning of the crisis period, Israel recognized the gravity of the situational change—namely, the withdrawal of UNEF (17–18 May). Yet it required Egypt's closure of the Straits of Tiran (22–23 May) to restore the link between image and reality and to add the dimensions of time constraint and war likelihood to increased threat perception. And when that act was accompanied by a massive build-up of Egyptian military power in Sinai, Israel's decision-makers reacted with seeming suddenness: the unexpected Egyptian action had reawakened the Holocaust syndrome. That, together with the other two common elements of the psychological setting in the pre-crisis period—the historical legacy of 1956–57 and surprise—were now shared by the decision-making group as a whole. Day by day, the *Hamtana* (waiting period) accentuated their saliency.

The pervasive view of Israel's high-policy elite at the height of the crisis is evident from the prologue to the Cabinet decision of 4 June 1967: "After hearing a report on the military and political situation from the Prime Minister, the Foreign Minister, the Defense Minister, the Chief of Staff and the head of military intelligence, the Government ascertained that the armies of Egypt, Syria and Jordan are deployed for immediate multi-front aggression, *threatening the very existence of the state.*"[2] This was not mere rhetoric or form. The Holocaust psychology was deeply rooted in Israel's national consciousness, especially among non-sabras of European descent; and that included sixteen of the twenty-one Cabinet members.

Images

ESHKOL

Prime Minister Eshkol and Foreign Minister Eban played pivotal decision-making roles throughout the 1967 Crisis. Dayan joined the decisional unit on 1 June. But throughout the week before he entered the Government, he was the focus of personal-political attention; his images are therefore relevant from about 23 May.[3] Allon returned from the Soviet Union on 24 May, and from that day he was one of Eshkol's principal advisers on military issues. Thus the specific images of these four ministers during the crisis period will be explored in order to delineate the Cabinet's predispositions to choice.

Eshkol recognized the complex linkages affecting Middle Eastern international politics: "The state of inter-Arab relations and the relationship between the powers against the background of their

2. From the official text, as published in the *Jerusalem Post,* 5 June 1972 (emphasis added).
3. He requested—and received—permission from Eshkol as early as 20 May to visit army units in the South. On the 23rd, he attended the enlarged meeting of the Ministerial Committee on Defense—as a leader of the opposition *Rafi* party. Of his motivation and mood at the time, he later wrote in *Story of My Life* (Jerusalem and Tel Aviv, 1976), p. 252: "Rather than hang around the parliamentary or other cafes in Jerusalem, I preferred, as long as I was physically able, to take part in the fighting, even if only as a private."

global and regional policies . . . are inextricably linked with each other." By the beginning of the crisis period, his regional concern focused on Egypt. On 22 May, he declared: "The concentrations of Egyptian forces in Sinai have reached proportions which increase the tension in our region and arouse world concern. . . ." [4] And the following day, on 23 May: "Any interference with freedom of passage in the Gulf and the Straits constitutes . . . an act of aggression against Israel." As for Nasser's aim, it was "to attack Israel for the purpose of destroying her. . . ." [5] Jordan's place in Eshkol's image, by contrast, was secondary: she acted under pressure from Cairo.

Like his colleagues, the Prime Minister was optimistic about the outcome of a war. On 29 May, he told the Knesset: "Today our army is at the zenith of its strength in manpower, skill, fighting spirit, and military equipment. . . . if the necessity arises, they have the strength to defeat the aggressors. . . ." Further, "there is no doubt that the mobilization of the Israel Defense Forces and their readiness for any test constituted and continue to constitute a decisive factor in the stimulation of world political activity." [6] Eshkol's perception of the UN and its Secretary-General was candid and even bitter, especially after the withdrawal of UNEF. In his address to the Knesset on 22 May, he declared: "I must point out that Israel was a party to this international arrangement, reached in 1957, but the Secretary-General did not see fit to consult Israel before he adopted his hasty decision."

As for Moscow, Eshkol told Parliament on 22 May: "Particular responsibility rests with the Soviet Union, which has friendly relations in Damascus and in Cairo. . . ." [7] And in his letter to Premier Kosygin on 1 June, he stated bluntly: "The USSR has adopted the false claim and accusations of Israel's enemies." [8] By contrast, the Prime Minister's perception of the United States' role was positive, even warm: "The Government," he told the Knesset on 29 May, "was deeply impressed by the unambiguous stand of the United States in favor of the safeguarding of freedom of passage. . . ." [9]

    4. Statement in the Knesset, 22 May 1967, *Divrei Haknesset*, 49, 2225–2227. English version in H. M. Christman, ed., *The State Papers of Levi Eshkol* (New York, 1969), p. 85.
    5. Ibid., p. 86, and *Divrei Haknesset*, 49, 2267.
    6. *Divrei Haknesset*, 49, 2283–2285.
    7. The quotations are from *Divrei Haknesset*, 49, 2225–2227.
    8. Letter to USSR Premier Kosygin on 1 June 1967, in reply to the Soviet Note of 26 May 1967. English version in *Jerusalem Post*, 4 June 1967.
    9. *Divrei Haknesset*, 49, 2283–2285, and in Christman, ed., *The State Papers of Levi Eshkol*, pp. 95–104.

The next day he wrote to President Johnson "to welcome the assurance that the United States would take any and all measures to open the Straits of Tiran to international shipping. . . ." The patron image persisted: "One of the difficulties that I face is that I must call on my people to meet sacrifices and dangers without being able fully to reveal certain compensating factors such as the United States commitment and the full scope of your determination on the matter of the Straits of Tiran." [10]

Notwithstanding the widespread belief in Eshkol's hesitancy during the 1967 Crisis, his advocacy of Israel's objectives was the model of clarity:

22 May	"The status quo must be restored on both sides of the border."
29 May	"The Israel Government's statement at the United Nations Assembly on March 1, 1957 still expresses our policy with complete accuracy."
1 June	"This situation cannot be tolerated." [11]

EBAN

At the onset of the crisis, Eban expressed the Ben-Gurionist view about bargaining from strength: "With Israel weak," he cautioned on 17 May, "the Arabs will not make peace. With a strong Israel they will be compelled to make peace." [12] Moreover, his Weizmannist perception of mutual distortions of reality—by Israel and her neighbors—was replaced by an unequivocal perception of the cause of the 1967 Crisis. [13] Nor is there any doubt as to the prime mover of the threat. Referring to Nasser's 28 May speech, Eban declared: "Here, then, was a systematic, overt, proclaimed design at politicide, the murder of a State." [14] Among Egypt's provocative acts, the concentration of troops in Sinai heightened tension, but the blockade of the Straits was "the most electric shock of all." Indeed, on 30 May he warned Nasser that this was

10. Israel, Ministry for Foreign Affairs, Cables and Communications, 1967.

11. Statements in the Knesset, 22 and 29 May 1967, *Divrei Haknesset*, 49, 2225–2227 and 2283–2285, and letter to Kosygin on 1 June 1967.

12. Speech in Rehovot, 17 May 1967, reported in *Ma'ariv*, 18 May 1967.

13. For a discussion of that mirror image, see M. Brecher, *The Foreign Policy System of Israel: Setting, Images, Process* (London and New Haven, 1972), pp. 349–353.

14. Address to the UN Security Council, 6 June 1967, *Israel Information Services* (New York, 1967); also in A. Eban, *Voice of Israel* (New York, 1969), p. 301.

casus belli, terming free passage "a central and vital national interest . . . the kind of national interest for which a nation stakes all that it has, all its interests, and for which it is ready . . . to undertake every sacrifice."[15] Despite this emphasis on Egypt, Eban perceived Syria's primary role—in time. As for Jordan, her adherence to the Egypt-Syria alliance was a source of dissatisfaction, creating almost a sense of betrayal. But he perceived Israel's military capability in positive terms, though he devoted little public attention to it.

The Foreign Minister's image of the global and superpowers' context, during the crisis period, was very similar to that of Eshkol: "There is no doubt," he declared, "that the readiness shown by the big powers to protect the freedom of passage has been influenced . . . by their knowledge that . . . Israel will protect its rights."[16] The universal actor, however, was perceived with sarcasm and anger. On 30 May he declared: "The United Nations did not emerge from the events of the last two weeks with brilliance and credit. In fact, . . . the situation . . . in large measure arises from errors of UN judgement."[17]

On 30 May, too, he rebuked the Soviet Union: "It is not necessary for anyone to urge restraint on Israel. . . . The Soviet influence should in our view be applied in Cairo and Damascus." And on 19 June he delivered, retrospectively, a scathing attack at the General Assembly: "Its role in recent Middle Eastern history . . . is a sad and shocking story. . . . A Great Power which professes its devotion to peaceful settlement . . . has for fourteen years afflicted the Middle East with a headlong armaments race. . . ."[18] As for Britain and France, he perceived a strong undercurrent of unembarrassed sympathy from Prime Minister Harold Wilson, which was totally absent from his talks with President de Gaulle.

ALLON

Allon's views in May–June 1967 were consistent with his image of the Arabs and their pre-eminent leader of almost a decade earlier: "The blindness of the war situation," he remarked at the beginning of the crisis period, "prevents the Arab States from

15. Press Conference in Jerusalem, 30 May 1967, State of Israel, *Government Press Office* (mimeo).
16. Speech in Rehovot, 17 May 1967.
17. Press Conference in Jerusalem, 30 May 1967.
18. Ibid., and in A. Eban, *Voice of Israel,* pp. 329–330.

understanding how they have fallen victim to aggressive policy, which is not expressed on the battlefield but . . . in limitless arms, which are expensive to acquire and to maintain."[19] His respect for Nasser was undiminished, however: "I am not certain that Nasser, with his standing and prestige, could not permit himself an interim settlement. . . . Had he given a signal, I do not think a danger of patriotic competition would have arisen. . . ."[20] However, a leader with the prestige capable of making peace also has very strong aspirations: "The surging ambitions in Nasser overcame the clever statesman. . . ."[21]

In an article published soon after the Six Day War but written earlier in the spring, Allon gave trenchant expression to his perceptions and advocacy regarding pre-emptive war, the crucial issue of the crisis period:

I oppose a pre-emptive war morally and politically; morally, because as long as we can postpone the war without endangering Israel, there is no need to pre-empt, and by acting thus there is a possibility that the war will be postponed for many years. . . . Politically it would be an historic mistake to become involved in an aggressive war. In that case we would lose friends in the world and there is a possibility that we might face an embargo.

Yet he argued that Israel must retain the option to strike first:

Israel has the right—and even the obligation—to go to war in six possible situations:
1. The concentration of offensive [Arab] forces which constitute a threat to Israel;
2. when it seems that the enemy is preparing a surprise attack on Israel's air bases;
3. in case of an aerial attack on nuclear reactors and scientific institutions;
4. when terror and shelling are of such a magnitude that passive defense and retaliatory acts could not overcome them;
5. if Jordan joins a military alliance with any other Arab state and permits foreign troops to be stationed on her territory; [and] especially west of the Jordan River;
6. if Egypt blockades the Straits of Tiran.

19. See Y. Allon, *Masakh Shel Hol [Curtain of Sand]* (Tel Aviv, 1959), pp. 338–364, and M. Brecher, *The Foreign Policy System of Israel* (London and New Haven, 1972), pp. 361–366.
20. Interview, *Lamerhav*, 14 May 1967.
21. Y. Allon, "The Last Stage of the War of Independence," *OT* (November 1967), 5–13.

Allon also displayed prescience about the operational aspect of a pre-emptive strike in June 1967:

In a pre-emptive attack we must try, first of all, to attain air supremacy by destroying the airforce of the enemy on the ground, breaking his land forces, and reaching such an advantageous position on his territory that will serve against a renewal of aggression and as a bargaining counter in any future negotiations.

Moreover:

In case of a new war, we must avoid the historic mistake of the War of Independence and, later, the Sinai Campaign. We must not cease fighting until we achieve total victory, the territorial fulfilment of the Land of Israel, and a peace agreement which will bring about normal relations between Israel and her neighbors.[22]

The causes of the crisis were perceived by Allon thus on 2 June 1967: "As long as the Arab concentrations of forces do not draw back from their attack positions, as long as the border is not secure against a resumption of terror, and as long as the Eilat Straits are blockaded—the war is inevitable."[23] The order in which these causes was stated is not by chance, for, unlike Eban, he did not perceive the Straits as pivotal in the crisis: "The offensive concentrations in Sinai and, at a later stage, Jordan's joining the military pact—these became the central problem."[24]

Allon, as always, was very optimistic about a military victory: "I have no shadow of a doubt as to the final outcome, nor the outcome at each stage. . . . It is in our power," he concluded on 2 June, "not only to check the enemy, but to obliterate him." His advocacy was consistent with his militant image generally: "There are no preconditions for the opening of the Straits. . . . They must be opened to every ship, without any difference of flag or cargo. The aggressive forces must be moved away . . . [and] the terror activities . . . stopped. If all this is not granted, war will be forced upon us. . . ."[25]

22. Y. Allon, "'Active Defence': A Guarantee for Our Existence," *Molad*, 1 (July–August 1967), 137–143.

23. Interview with M. Brecher, 26 July 1968; and Y. Allon, *The Making of Israel's Army* (London, 1970), p. 91.

24. Y. Allon, "The Last Stage of the War of Independence," *OT* (November 1967), p. 7.

25. Speech in Tel Aviv, English summary, State of Israel, *Government Press Office*, Press Bulletin (mimeo.).

It is noteworthy that, in a speech during the height of the Crisis, Allon did not even mention the conflict-resolving efforts of the international community. The only indirect reference to the powers was the analogy drawn between the blockade of Eilat and a blockade of Marseilles, New York, or London, which Allon perceived as identical in provocation.

His perception of the Soviet role was even more harshly expressed (after the crisis) than that of Eshkol and Eban: "The Soviet Union went on perniciously with her anti-Israel argument, through a malicious neglect of the facts. . . ."[26] At the same time, he was certain that Moscow would not intervene in an Arab-Israeli war:

First, it was too risky—it could have meant confrontation with the United States; secondly, they were too weak in the Middle East militarily to risk war with Israel; it would have meant a military build-up equal to the size of the American build-up in Vietnam; thirdly, based on history I concluded they are not inclined to intervene; and finally, I counted on a short war, one not long enough to give the Russians time to intervene.[27]

Allon was also persuaded that the U.S. would not intervene, "provided we acted quickly." Moreover, "I profoundly believed there was no alternative to war and was prepared to risk American embarrassment." And "I knew that it was a U.S. objective interest for us to win; but they might be compelled to act if the war dragged on." He was not oblivious of France and Britain, but they were "secondary": "Even if Eban had reported that France would break diplomatic relations we would have gone to war."[28] In summary, for Allon the Soviets were hostile but would not intervene; neither would the basically friendly United States; and France, Britain, and the UN were of little consequence.

DAYAN

Dayan, like his colleagues, was profoundly influenced by the Sinai Campaign and its aftermath. The continuing role of historical legacy is evident in his image fifteen years after the Campaign:

We must learn some lessons from the Sinai Campaign . . . both from what we shouldn't have done and what we should do. One of the negative

26. Y. Allon, "The Last Stage of the War of Independence," *OT* (November 1967), p. 7.
27. Participants in Cabinet discussions during the crisis period confirmed to Michael Brecher that these views were also expressed by Allon in the secrecy of government meetings in May–June 1967.
28. Interview with M. Brecher, 26 July 1968.

lessons is that we should not retreat under pressure and we should not agree to a settlement that is temporary and, in our view, without substance. And we should not stop in the middle of our struggle before the true test that awaits us.[29]

In his memoirs, when reflecting on the eve of the SDW, Dayan also gave expression to his sense of identity with the long and painful history of Jewry:

I was completely absorbed by the problems with which we were suddenly faced. On the surface, these seemed to be political-military problems. But I knew in my bones that they were basically historical Jewish problems which were rooted in our past.[30]

Dayan, too, was skeptical of the global system's value in the 1967 Crisis. As early as 23 May, he objected to consultations with external actors, fearing pressure which would limit Israel's freedom of action.[31] On the role of diplomacy and the UN in resolving the conflict, he remarked on 3 June: "I will be happy and surprised if they do it."[32] As for the U.S. role, he recalled: "I will not detail the attempts—pathetic sometimes—which the United States made for free navigation, without any concrete result." The other superpower, however, was perceived by Dayan as the principal culprit, abetted by other anti-Israel forces: "The Russians incited, the Yugoslavs and Indians cooperated in, the French approved of, the closing of the Straits. . . ."[33]

The Sinai troop concentration was viewed as catalytic in the escalation of the 1967 Crisis. According to one of his biographers, Dayan predicted the major steps toward war as early as 16 May at a gathering of former IDF Chiefs of Staff.[34] Nasser's role was decisive, in his view: "The Six Day War broke out because the leadership of Abd-el-Nasser was put to the test. . . . Nasser became more and more infatuated with his own words and those of heads and representatives of other Arab states." And after the SDW he remarked: "The leaders of Egypt and the commanders of her army

29. *Ha'aretz*, 5 November 1971.
30. *Story of My Life*, pp. 251–252.
31. S. Nakdimon, *Toward the Zero Hour: The Drama that Preceded the Six Day War* (Tel Aviv, 1968), p. 51.
32. Press Conference, 13 June 1967, State of Israel, *Government Press Office* (mimeo).
33. *New Map—Other Relations* (Tel Aviv and Haifa, 1969), p. 11.
34. N. Lau-Lavie, *Moshe Dayan, A Biography* (London, 1968), p. 20.

were drunk with power, from the quantities of MiG aircraft and tanks. . . . They intoxicated themselves and were swept away by their enthusiasm."[35]

Other evidence as well points to his shared image of inevitable war: "I also knew war was inevitable. Diplomatic efforts within the international community would come to naught. And when war broke out, I had to be personally involved—even if only as a private soldier, though hopefully in a command function."[36]

Most revealing about Dayan's perceptions in the crisis period was his *tour d'horizon* before the Ministerial Committee on Defense on 13 June—the 1967 Crisis viewed on the morrow of its successful resolution:

I said that in the period preceding the war, the army and the government had made incorrect assessments in three basic areas. The first concerned the possible reaction to our military reprisals against Syria. We did not properly judge how far Egypt would consider herself bound to go to Syria's aid. . . .
The second . . . was to regard the entry of Egyptian forces into Sinai as window dressing. . . . The third . . . was the facility with which Nasser was able to order, and secure, the removal of UN forces from Sharm-el-Sheikh. . . .
The principal mistake in the crisis period had been Israel's failure to react at once to Egypt's blockade of the Straits . . . but to my mind . . . that was the opening shot. . . . We waited, and this plunged us into a complex situation. The government had maneuvered itself into a position whereby we had to be the first to open fire. . . .
Nor was the assumption correct that the United States was capable of lifting the blockade for us. . . . But even if America had managed to achieve some remedy in this field, this would in no way have corrected the disturbed balance of forces.[37]

There was therefore a broad consensus in the images held by the four Israeli decision-makers during the 1967 crisis period: the unreliability of global system action in the Crisis; UN powerlessness; USSR perfidy; and U.S. friendliness but ineffectiveness. There were, of course, shades of emphasis, notably Dayan's concern about Soviet behavior and Eban's greater attention to the UN and diplomacy. But a relatively homogeneous group image is apparent.

35. *New Map—Other Relations*, pp. 7, 11.
36. *Story of My Life*, p. 252.
37. Ibid., pp. 304–306.

DECISION FLOW

The 1967 crisis period was triggered by three dramatic events on 16 and 17 May: Egypt's request to withdraw UNEF, and U Thant's immediate response, which conceded Cairo's right to unilateral termination of the UNEF presence on her territory; the crossing of two additional Egyptian divisions into Sinai; and the overflight of Israel's nuclear research center at Dimona for a minute.[38] The crisis period may be divided into three distinct phases: (I) Apprehension and Mobilization, 17–22 May; (II) Delay and Diplomacy, 23–28 May; and (III) Resolution, 29 May–4 June.

I. Apprehension and Mobilization, 17–22 May

The events preceding 17 May were links in a chain of controlled tension that was part of a protracted conflict. Even the movement of Egyptian troops into Sinai on 14 and 15 May—and their reinforcement on the 16th—belong to the pre-crisis period: they were perceived by Israeli decision-makers as a repetition of February 1960, a show of force within the inter-Arab domain and not a threat to Israel's security.

The events of 17–22 May surprised Israel's political and military elites and induced precautionary acts that became part of the escalatory process of stimulus-response for both actors. And yet, until Nasser's closure of the Straits on 22/23 May, war was still not perceived as certain. That act was, for Israel, the watershed of the 1967 Crisis. In the words of Amit: "The basic evaluation was correct—Egypt was not ready for a war; and Nasser did not want a war. Until 23 May, I thought that there is a possibility for maneuvers, that there is leeway for alternatives. But when Nasser closed the Straits, I said: 'This is it, there is no way to avoid war.'"[39]

Wednesday, 17 May

Egypt's demand for the withdrawal of UNEF troops was broadcast by Radio Cairo at 06:00 hours, Israel time. By 11:00, the Ministerial Committee on Defense was in urgent session. The rest

38. The first two of these events occurred on the 16th, but they were unknown to Israel's decision-makers until the morning of the 17th. The significance of the second and third events was affirmed by Yariv in a conversation with Michael Brecher on 27 July 1977. Thus the beginning of the 1967 Crisis period is designated as 17 May.

39. Interview with B. Geist, 13 July 1973.

of the day was devoted to intense formal and informal consultations within the fairly large circle of participants in the deliberative
processes of the 1967 Crisis: the Cabinet—either in full or its
Defense Committee (comprising more than half its members); the
Knesset Foreign Affairs and Security Committee, broadening the
consultative circle to include the main Opposition parties; and the
military and foreign affairs elites. After the meetings of the Cabinet
Defense Committee and the Knesset Foreign Affairs Committee,
there were seven hours of small group consultations, involving
Eshkol, Eban, and Galili of the Cabinet; Rabin, Weizman, and
Yariv from the IDF General Staff; Herzog and Yaffe from the
Prime Minister's Office; and Levavi, Bitan, Tekoah, and Lourie
from the Foreign Office.

The upshot of these consultations was several reactive decisions
and moves in the military and diplomatic issue-areas. The Prime
Minister and the Chief of Staff decided to call up further military
reserves at a late evening meeting (Decision 4).[40] The Foreign
Minister instructed Rafael to bring to the attention of the Secretary-General the commitments given by his predecessor—Dag
Hammarskjöld—in February 1957, to prevent belligerency in the
Straits of Tiran and to undertake consultations in the UN if the
question of the removal of the UN Emergency Force was raised.[41]

40. Eshkol's *AB*, and M. Bar-Zohar, *Embassies in Crisis: Diplomats and Demagogues Behind the Six Day War* (Englewood Cliffs, N.J., 1970), p. 39.

41. U Thant noted in his 26 June 1967 report that Hammarskjöld took the
following position, in reply to a question on 26 February 1957 on the withdrawal
of the Force: "An indicated procedure would be for the Secretary-General to inform the Advisory Committee on the United Nations Emergency Force, which
would determine whether the matter should be brought to the attention of the
Assembly" (T. Draper, *Israel and World Politics: Roots of the Third Arab-Israeli
War* [New York, 1968], p. 190). The Israeli Cabinet was also informed of a relevant passage in Hammarskjöld's 5 August 1957 private memorandum: "Egypt
would declare to the United Nations that it would exert all its sovereign rights
with regard to the troops on the basis of a good faith interpretation of the tasks of
the Force. The United Nations should make a reciprocal commitment to maintain
the Force as long as the task was not completed. If such a dual statement was
introduced in an agreement between the parties, it would be obvious that the
procedure in case of a request from Egypt for the withdrawal of UNEF would be
as follows: The matter would at once be brought before the General Assembly. If
the General Assembly found that the task was completed, everything would be all
right. If they found that the task was not completed and Egypt, all the same,
maintained its stand and enforced the withdrawal, Egypt would break the agreement with the United Nations" (in R. Higgins, *United Nations Peace Keeping
1946–1967: Documents and Commentary, vol. I—The Middle East* [London,
1969], pp. 363–366).

Eban was told by Rabin that the IDF needed time to complete its defenses in the South. In fact, during the Cabinet session Rabin even suggested that Israel initiate a meeting of the Security Council, to gain time. Eban, after consultation with members of Israel's UN delegation, who were against it, rejected the idea.[42] His reasons were the possibility of an adverse decision and an expected Soviet veto, which might have encouraged Nasser even further. And "I knew from long experience that it was easier to turn on the tap of United Nations debate than to turn it off."[43] Instead, he tried, through Rafael and leading members of the Security Council, to induce U Thant to visit Cairo and Jerusalem.[44]

Events were overtaking decisions. The process imposed massive pressures on Israel's decision-makers, as they were to do during the next twenty days, as well as sharply limiting the practical possibility of keeping everybody concerned informed. By the time Rafael saw U Thant and Bunche the next day, the Egyptians had decided to demand total, immediate withdrawal of UNEF.[45]

In other capitals, as in Jerusalem, the mood was still tranquil. Eugene Rostow again advised Harman that Israel should not act. In Paris, Eytan was told by Herve Alphand, then Director-General

42. Foreign Ministry sources.

43. *An Autobiography* (Jerusalem and Tel Aviv, 1977), p. 324. Also cited in R. St. John, *Eban* (Garden City, N.Y., 1972), p. 413.

44. U.S. Ambassador Goldberg suggested it to U Thant the next day. The forthcoming visit—to Cairo only—was announced on Saturday, 20 May.

45. In a message in U Thant's Report on the Withdrawal of the United Nations Emergency Force, 26 June 1967, in *UN Monthly Chronicle,* 4:7 (July 1967), 140, addressed to the UN Secretary-General, the Foreign Minister of Egypt stated: "The Government of the United Arab Republic has the honor to inform Your Excellency that it has decided to terminate the presence of the United Nations Emergency Force from the territory of the United Arab Republic and Gaza Strip. Therefore I request that the necessary steps be taken for the withdrawal of the Force as soon as possible." Rafael's description of this meeting throws considerable light on Bunche's and U Thant's perceptions, on which they had based their fateful decision the day before. As he recalled in an interview in *Yediot Aharonot,* 4 June 1971: "I asked Ralph Bunche, what happened to the deceased Hammarskjöld's commitment of 1957 that no change will be made in the deployment of UNEF without a previous agreement of the General Assembly. Bunche answered that the Secretary-General had recently received an explanation from his legal adviser that the presence of UNEF is dependent only on the agreement of the host government. Bunche did not share our evaluations. He explained that through this announcement U Thant intends to bare the fact that Nasser's message is a bluff. He is convinced that faced with the situation that would be created by the departure of the Force Nasser will reconsider and back down." For another version see R. Bunche, Letter to the Editor, *New York Times,* 11 June 1967.

of the Foreign Ministry, who had just returned from Cairo, that Nasser was still interested in the presence of UNEF, as protection against Israel. In London the general appreciation was that, though the situation was dangerous, it would not reach a critical stage. Yet, by the end of the day the decisions regarding UNEF were taken and the facts already established.

Thursday, 18 May

The day began—and ended—in Israel with security consultations between Eshkol and Rabin. They were joined in the morning by Eban, Amit, Yariv, and other IDF officers. The daily intelligence estimate was that war was a remote possibility. While in consultation, around 09:00, President Johnson's first communication of the 1967 Crisis to Eshkol arrived. It was, in effect, outdated by this time, for it dealt with the Syrian situation; Johnson also warned Israel against retaliatory action:[46]

I want to emphasize strongly that you have to abstain from every step that would increase the tension and violence in the area. You will probably understand that the United States cannot accept any responsibility for situations that are liable to occur as a result of actions in which we were not consulted.[47]

That warning was to be repeated again and again in the coming days. The other item of discussion was Egypt's request for the *total* withdrawal of UNEF. This unexpected reaction of Nasser to U Thant's challenge turned apprehension into consternation. Eshkol and Rabin, later in the day, reportedly expressed their belief that there might be war.[48]

Eban called in the ambassadors of the U.S., U.K., and France to express Israel's objections to the removal of UNEF. He reminded them again of Western commitments made in 1957 and warned about the serious consequences of the upsetting of the status quo. In the afternoon he drafted a reply for Eshkol to Johnson's letter. The substance of the letter stated:

1.   The serious crisis presently threatening the Middle East originated in the attitude of Syria.

46. L. B. Johnson, *The Vantage Point: Perspectives of the Presidency 1963–1969* (New York, 1971), p. 290.
47. M. Gilboa, *Six Years–Six Days: Origins and History of the Six Day War* (Tel Aviv, 1969), p. 115 (in Hebrew).
48. Bar-Zohar, *Embassies in Crisis*, p. 46.

2. Egypt has spread out over the Sinai Peninsula an offensive force of at least 500 tanks. It is advisable to insist that that country return its forces immediately to the other side of the Canal.

3. The UN Force should not abandon its positions. The Secretary-General of the United Nations ought to inform Egypt that only the General Assembly can order the evacuation of the UNEF.

4. The United States should publicly reaffirm the guarantees it has given Israel in the past, notably from Johnson to Eshkol in 1964.[49]

Eshkol approved the calling up of further reserves and the speeding up of deliveries of war material that might be necessary —a constant source of concern to Israel's decision-makers. Eshkol and Rabin were "especially alarmed" by the report that U Thant was about to order UNEF's withdrawal, which raised the possibility of the closure of the Straits. Eshkol also held consultations on civil defense preparations; and he decided to acquire, at all costs, gas masks in sufficient quantities. (These were to be located and supplied at the height of the crisis, somewhat reluctantly, by the Federal Republic of Germany.)

The focus of the crisis on 18 May remained for the last time, until the outbreak of war, at UN Headquarters. In the forenoon, Rafael called upon U Thant and Bunche to warn against the removal of UNEF and the situation on the Israel-Syrian border. U Thant stated that he had seen no legal grounds for refusal and countered with the suggestion that UNEF be transferred onto the Israeli side of the border. Rafael refused on the spot.[50] The same suggestion was raised that day, and in the days to come, by the U.S., U.K., and—very strongly—by Canada.[51]

49. Ibid., pp. 44–45 and, in part, Gilboa, *Six Years–Six Days*, p. 145.

50. Rafael Interview, *Yediot Aharonot*, 4 June 1971; G. Rafael, "May 1967–A Personal Report," *Ma'ariv*, 18 and 21 April 1972; and C. W. Yost, "The Arab-Israeli War: How It Began," *Foreign Affairs*, 46: 2 (January 1968), 313.

51. "The first time I heard about the demand for the withdrawal of UNEF," recalled Israel's Ambassador to Canada during the 1967 Crisis, "was when Paul Martin [Canada's External Affairs Secretary] called me and told me that the Force was in danger, that its withdrawal would mean war, and that events are developing so fast that if something is to be done, it has to be done within hours. 'I propose, therefore,' said Martin, 'that you accept UNEF on your side of the border, as we originally proposed. I know that Israel is against it, and all the reasons for it, but this is no time for diplomatic niceties. You can call it a temporary step, or anything you wish, but the main thing is to save the Force.' I cabled this home and asked for instructions; I never received any" (Avner interview with B. Geist, 25 February 1973).

Rafael was immediately followed by El-Kony, with Foreign Minister Riad's note, calling for the termination of the UNEF presence. U Thant, after some hasty consultations with leading members of the Security Council, called, *for the first time,* a meeting of the UN Advisory Committee on UNEF for 17:00 New York time: he told them of his decision to evacuate UNEF. Serious misgivings were expressed, particularly by the representative of Canada, but no one challenged his decision, a fact that U Thant and his defenders later recalled to justify his action.[52]

Within the Arab world, 18 May marked the beginning of intra-Arab coordination. Noteworthy was Syria's announcement that the mobilization of her reserves was now completed. And Egypt let it be known that her secret missile bases were in a state of alert. That day also marked the first significant break in the intense hostility between the "progressive" and "traditional" régimes in the Arab world, with Saudi Arabia's Crown Prince openly supporting Syria on grounds of "our religion, Arabism, and brotherly bonds."

Friday, 19 May

On Friday, 19 May, "alarm bells rang at one and the same time in several chancelleries of the world."[53] In Israel, the adjustment to the unexpected gravity of the situation was rapid, although it was decided to continue, officially, the evaluation of "demonstrative moves" and to belittle the danger. The closure of the Straits was now considered a distinct possibility.

At eight o'clock in the morning, President Shazar left for an official visit to Canada; it had been decided upon the night before as part of the drive to underline the "business-as-usual" atmosphere. By 09:30, Eshkol and Rabin had returned to the Ministry of Defense, first for a consultation with the Chief Scientist of the Army and then for a meeting with the General Staff, where the daily intelligence report was evaluated. Gone was the appreciation that Nasser would not be ready for war until 1970. Gone, too, was the view that he would not risk war while he was tied down in Yemen. Instead, the report contained the new realities: the presence of

52. Canada's position was clearly stated in Parliament that day and a few days later: "It is now the prerogative of the UN rather than of the UAR Government to determine when the UN Force has completed its task of restoring peace and when it should be withdrawn" (House of Commons, *Debates, House of Commons, 2nd Session, 27th Parliament, vol. I, 8 May–5 June 1967*, pp. 342, 416).

53. M. Bar-Zohar, *The Longest Month* (Tel Aviv, 1968), p. 59 (in Hebrew).

70,000 Egyptian soldiers and 600 tanks in Sinai; an Egyptian infantry and two tank battalions recalled in secrecy from Yemen and sent straight into Sinai; Sharm-e-Sheikh occupied by Egyptian units; and the Gaza border manned by units of the Palestinian Liberation Army. The outcome of this meeting was the decision to order large-scale mobilization of reserves, effective immediately (Decision 5). Another decision was to replace the previous tactical plans for the build-up and disposition of Israeli troops along the border, with plans for a build-up to enable a pre-emptive strike into Sinai (Decision 6).[54]

The Foreign Minister decided on a last attempt to enlist Soviet support for a policy of restraint. He summoned Soviet Ambassador Chuvakhin and proposed "a reciprocal de-escalation of troops in the South." He asked "the Soviet Government to cooperate to this end," as well as in the prevention of sabotage from across the Syrian border; and he suggested international consultation on the consequences of the removal of UNEF. He added that everything now depended upon Egypt: "There will be no war unless the Egyptians attack our territory or violate our rights of free navigation." Chuvakhin replied that the present situation was created by Israel's aggressive propaganda against Arab states, especially Syria, and her attacks on Syria. "History will pass judgment on Israel for having played with fire." He was not prepared to discuss troop concentrations and acts of sabotage, because they were not within his competence. "As for UNEF, its presence on the territory of any state depended on the free consent of that state, which had full power to demand its removal." Eban came away from the meeting

54. Eshkol's *AB;* Eshkol's Broadcast to the Nation, 28 May 1967 (English version in *BBC,* 30 May 1967); Foreign Ministry sources; T. Draper, *Israel and World Politics,* p. 75; M. Bar-Zohar, *Embassies in Crisis,* p. 47. The transfer of Egyptian troops from Yemen to Sinai was, for Israel's decision-makers, a very significant indicator of Nasser's intentions: One of the pillars of the forecast that Nasser would not be ready to wage war against Israel for years to come was that a large part of his army—60,000 to 70,000 troops—was bogged down in Yemen. But there is some doubt whether in this field of military intelligence Israel's leaders had wholly accurate information. Nasser stated, in an interview in *Newsweek,* 10 February 1969: "In fact, three of our best divisions were in Yemen at the time, and had we been preparing for an attack, it would have been logical to bring them home first." Mohamed Heikal, in part of a series on the Six Day War, published in *Ma'ariv,* 9 November 1973, stated that sizable units, with armor, were returned from Yemen only toward the end of the crisis period; and it seems to be the correct version. In *The Third Arab-Israeli War* (London, 1972), p. 96, E. O'Ballance wrote that "on June 4 two infantry brigades and some logistic units, and about 10,000 soldiers, were in transit back to Egypt. . . ."

with the impression that "it was indecently clear that what the Soviet Union had in mind was not how to reduce tension, but how to bring it swiftly to the boil," and that Chuvakhin's demeanor "expressed an almost sadistic delight in Israel's predicament."[55]

Eban and Eshkol now proceeded, on a broad diplomatic front, to try to preserve Israel's freedom of navigation in the Straits. The Prime Minister wrote to de Gaulle: "Israel on her part will not initiate hostile acts but she is firmly resolved to defend her territory and her international rights. Our decision is that if Egypt will not attack us, we will not take action against Egyptian forces at Sharm-e-Sheikh—until or unless they close the Straits of Tiran to free navigation by Israel." This assurance was repeated the same day in a personal note by Eban to French Foreign Minister Couve de Murville. Eban reminded him that France had in the past confirmed, and identified herself with, former Foreign Minister Meir's statement of March 1957, in which Israel stated that: "Interference with free passage will be regarded by Israel as an attack entitling it to exercise the inherent right of self-defense under Article 51 of the United Nations Charter."[56] Israel's policy, he added, remained unchanged. A similar message was sent to Britain's Foreign Secretary, George Brown.[57]

Eshkol and Eban also acted to restrain all official Israeli public pronouncements so as not to aggravate the pressures now piling up on Nasser. And with the exception of *Ha'aretz* ("Tension Grows in the South"), the Israeli press still expressed the relatively tranquil mood of the preceding days.

U Thant decided to fly to Cairo. In Washington, the Administration was being urged to extend public support for the integrity and independence of Israel. Instead, President Johnson opted for "semi-quiet" diplomacy. George Brown announced the postponement of his visit to Moscow. And Moscow stated that she would not stand idly by if Israel attacked Syria.

55. Foreign Ministry sources. Also discussed in Eban, *An Autobiography*, p. 325.
56. Ibid., p. 327. Israel, Ministry for Foreign Affairs, Cables and Communications, Jerusalem, 1967.
57. The vigorous language of these Eban communiqués explains the virtual panic caused in Washington, London, Paris, and other capitals on 23 May by Nasser's announcement of the closure of the Straits. The Western powers expected Israel to go to war within hours. When she did not, and Eban's trip was announced, these powers could only conclude that Israel was hesitant; her credibility suffered as a consequence.

Saturday, 20 May

During the day, Eshkol and Rabin toured the southern front. The previous day's mobilization order was to be completed by nightfall. In the evening, Dayan received Eshkol's permission to tour IDF forces in the Negev. The first answer to Eshkol and Eban's communications came from Wilson. Although sympathetic in tone, it foreshadowed the line to be taken in Washington and Paris as well: support for the freedom of navigation, but international action only through the United Nations and only if the Egyptians in fact imposed an embargo:

I am on public record as saying that the Straits of Tiran constitute an international waterway which should remain open to the ships of all nations. If it appeared that any attempt to interfere with the passage of ships through the waterway was likely to be made, we should promote and support international action through the United Nations to secure free passage.[58]

Other communications from London stressed that Israel should not act prematurely.

In Paris, Israel's Ambassador suggested that de Gaulle add his prestige and influence to that of Johnson and put pressure on Kosygin to restrain the Egyptians. The French Government was reminded of its repeated commitments (in 1950, 1957, 1960, and 1964) to Israel's security and to the free passage of Israeli shipping in the Straits.[59]

In Washington, Harman and Evron had another meeting with Eugene Rostow and continued to press for a public statement of American support. But the reaction was cautious and hesitant. Rostow raised the suggestion that UNEF be placed on the Israeli side of the border; again the idea was rejected. All through the conversation, Rostow stressed that, at that stage, the crisis should be handled through the UN and that Israel should abstain from unilateral actions.

By the end of the day, the Israeli Government was biding its time, still slightly hopeful about possible developments, in spite of

58. Eban, *An Autobiography,* p. 327.
59. 1950: Tripartite Declaration; 1957: declarations in March at the UN; 1960: at de Gaulle's meeting with Ben-Gurion, where he stated that "if Israel is threatened, we shall not let you be destroyed." In 1964, de Gaulle repeated the same assurances to Eshkol, during the latter's visit to Paris.

the bad news beginning to arrive from Western capitals. Late in the evening, Eshkol was somewhat encouraged by the news of U Thant's forthcoming visit. Another encouraging sign was the passage of a cargo ship bound for Eilat through the Straits, unmolested.

Sunday, 21 May

Before the regular Sunday morning meeting of the Cabinet, Eshkol and Rabin met briefly to review the situation. The Cabinet session was, according to several accounts, acrimonious.[60] Much had happened since the last meeting of the Cabinet five days earlier, most of it unexpected, and all of it unpleasant.

The subjects discussed included: the concentration of Egyptian troops on the southern border—reported by Rabin to be by this time up to 70,000 men; the state of inter-Arab coordination; diplomatic efforts made by Eshkol and Eban; intelligence evaluation of possible developments, including an Egyptian surprise attack; Soviet intentions; and U Thant's forthcoming visit to Cairo. The predominant mood was that of emerging anxiety; and several Cabinet ministers strongly demanded that everything be done to avoid war. In Rabin's opinion there was no need for further mobilization: the Egyptian build-up was still defensive. The Cabinet approved the large-scale mobilization of 19 May (Decision 7). The Cabinet also approved Eshkol's intention to make a statement on the situation at the opening session of the Knesset the next day; but anxiety was such that several ministers, particularly H. M. Shapira, asked to be shown the draft of the Prime Minister's speech.[61]

Incoming cables at the Foreign Office showed a similar pattern: the advice of the Western powers was to lay the burden on the United Nations; and official France was covered in "thunderous silence."[62] One of the most important inputs to Israel's decisions on the 21st was a letter of caution from the State Department:

60. The following account is based upon: Foreign Ministry sources; S. Nakdimon, *Toward the Zero Hour,* p. 28; Z. Schiff, "The Three Weeks that Preceded the War," *Ha'aretz,* 4 October 1967; and M. Gilboa, *Six Years—Six Days,* p. 124.

61. W. Burdett noted in *Encounter with the Middle East: An Intimate Report of What Lies Behind the Arab-Israeli Conflict* (London, 1970), p. 237, that Herzog was instrumental in drafting a mild speech, so "that nothing should be said that might be seen as inflaming Nasser, lest in the future the world hold Israel responsible for overacting. . . ."

62. Eban Interview, *Ma'ariv,* 2 June 1972; and R. St. John, *Eban,* pp. 413–415.

"The United States' position is that the present grave problem should be handled, in a peaceful manner, preferably through the United Nations. . . ."[63]

In Washington, the answer to the first overtures of the U.S. to the Soviet Union arrived. Although recent developments were blamed on Israel for her aggressive intents, it did state that the Soviet Union was interested in the preservation of peace in the area. In Canada, Prime Minister Pearson used the occasion of Shazar's visit to sound out the Israelis on ways to save the UNEF presence, either through transferring to the Israeli side or through a considerable increase of the United Nations Truce Supervision Organization (UNTSO). Again, though informally, the first suggestion was turned down. The second—to which Israel was not totally averse—was soon to be overtaken by events.

The Arab world on 21 May was mainly concerned with the question: Will Nasser decide to close the Straits to Israeli ships? The Syrians and the Lebanese openly demanded it; so did the Jordanians and the Executive Committee of the Arab Socialist Union. The political consolidation of the Arab world continued; so did military preparations. Egypt now proclaimed total mobilization of reserves, and Nasser announced that he had accepted the President of Iraq's offer to send units of the Iraqi army, armor, and air force.

One other important event on the 21st, within Israel, was a meeting of *Rafi* leaders and sympathizers, convened by Shimon Peres. The meeting was attended by a galaxy of public figures, among them: Ben-Gurion and three former Chiefs of Staff—Dori, Zur, and Dayan. There seems little doubt that the meeting was called to lay the groundwork for an attempt to topple Eshkol and reinstate Ben-Gurion as Prime Minister and Minister of Defense. In any case, it marked the beginning of an internal crisis, a crisis of confidence in Eshkol's government and leadership that culminated in the formation of a National Unity Government and Dayan's appointment as Minister of Defense ten days later. A meeting between Ben-Gurion and Rabin later in the evening did not dispel the former's doubts about Israel's military prospects: He accused the Chief of Staff of escalating the crisis through wide-scale mobilization, at a time when the IDF was not adequately prepared and

63. R. St. John, *Eban*, p. 414.

Israel was without an ally. In Israel and the U.S., official optimism was still prevalent.

Monday, 22 May

On Monday, 22 May, Nasser decided to close the Straits. But during the day, until his decision became known, world attention was focused on Israel, specifically on Eshkol's anticipated statement. The major external input into his final draft was another Johnson letter, in answer to Eshkol's of 19 May, containing clarifications of the U.S. position. The President wrote that the United States would support "suitable measures in and outside the United Nations."[64] He referred to his contacts with Soviet leaders:

The Soviet leaders have no illusions about the pledge of the United States to prevent, either through the United Nations, or independently of that international organization, all aggression in the Middle East. This policy has been defined and confirmed by four American presidents: Truman, Eisenhower, Kennedy and myself. It is also contained in the three-power agreement of 1950.[65]

Johnson also suggested that Israel work toward renewal of the 1950 Tripartite Declaration, support for which was officially announced by the State Department.

In the afternoon, after appearing before the Knesset Foreign Affairs and Security Committee at 15:00, Eshkol read his prepared statement before the Knesset. It was a very cautious, moderate reaction to a dangerous situation; the possibility of the closure of the Straits was not mentioned once. He called upon the powers "to exercise their full influence," in order to remove the danger of conflagration in the Middle East, laying "particular responsibility" on the Soviet Union. He demanded a return to the status quo on both sides of the border and called for a complete cessation of acts of sabotage.[66] During the subsequent debate, many parliamen-

64. Eban interpreted Johnson's phrase as a retreat from previous statements: In 1963, President Kennedy's declaration spoke of *"adopting* other courses of action of our own," while Johnson wrote of *supporting* measures, presumably initiated by someone else. Eban elaborates on this in *An Autobiography,* p. 329. Harman's further clarification had elicited the response that the United States preferred to await the result of U Thant's visit to Cairo, before putting any pressure on Egypt.

65. Bar-Zohar, *Embassies in Crisis,* p. 68; and Foreign Ministry sources.

66. *Divrei Haknesset,* 49 (1968), 2225–2227; and Draper, *Israel and World Politics,* pp. 248–254.

tarians called for stronger measures to counteract Egyptian moves
—and for a clarification of the Government's position that it was
ready to go to war to defend Israel's rights.

In Washington, Harman warned Assistant Secretary of State
Battle that if Nasser were for a single moment to believe that the
United States' attitude were as indicated in the 21 May letter, he
would regard this as an invitation to interfere with shipping in the
Straits. In New York, Rafael handed U Thant an Eban letter which
emphasized Israel's determination to defend freedom of navigation. He also asked the Secretary-General not to commit himself in
matters which needed Israel's agreement.

During the day, there were other contacts between Evron and
Harman, and Evron and the Rostows. The Rostows reinforced the
tenor of Johnson's letter, making a public announcement conditional upon U Thant's trip, as well as on a Security Council debate.
Ways of defusing the crisis through some UN machinery were also
discussed, with the Americans suggesting a revitalization of the
Egypt-Israel Armistice Agreement and the Israelis giving an indication of a willingness to consider this.

Toward evening came news of further setbacks for Israel—the
French and British statements disavowing the 1950 Tripartite
Declaration. The French position was that the guarantees were
now outdated, while the British stated that they were only restat-
ing a policy announced by MacMillan in 1963 and reaffirmed by
Wilson in 1965. Their timing indicated the reluctance of two of the
signatory states to get involved in Israel's confrontation with the
Arabs.[67]

In Sinai, at the Bir Gafgafa airbase, Nasser made his fateful
announcement about the Tiran Straits:

Under no circumstances can we permit the Israeli flag to pass through the
Gulf of Aqaba. The Jews threaten war. We say they are welcome to war,
we are ready for war, our armed forces, our people, all of us are ready for
war, but under no circumstances shall we abandon any of our rights.
These are our waters.[68]

67. *New York Times, Davar,* and *Jerusalem Post,* 23–24 May 1967. It was also
reported over Radio Cairo on 22 May. The Tripartite Declaration had been dead
ever since the Sinai Campaign; its resurrection at this stage was a U.S. idea.
68. *International Documents on Palestine 1967,* F. A. Jabber, ed. (Beirut,
1970), p. 538.

Upon his return to Cairo, Egypt's President told the Soviet Ambassador that the Soviets were responsible for what had happened.[69]

The crucial role of the decision to close the Straits as a trigger mechanism for Israel's subsequent behavior in the 1967 Crisis was noted by President Johnson in his 19 June 1967 address: "If a single act of folly was more responsible for this explosion than any other, I think it was the arbitrary and dangerous announced decision that the Straits of Tiran would be closed."[70]

II. Delay and Diplomacy, 23–28 May

The second phase of the crisis period began and ended with Cabinet decisions to opt for diplomatic rather than military means to resolve the 1967 Crisis. Nasser had challenged the basis of Israel's security policy, the concept of deterrence—that is, the capability of the IDF to prevent encroachments upon Israel's vital interests. The announcement of the decision to close the Straits was, for Israel, a major escalation; in fact, it was a point of no return on the path to war.

Tuesday, 23 May

The news reached IDF Headquarters between 02:00 and 04:00. At 04:30, Rabin phoned Eshkol; Eban was informed by Army Headquarters at 05:00. Eshkol's first reaction was: "This cannot continue. We shall have to call upon the whole people and the whole Opposition."[71] Consultations with Herzog and Yaffe began at 06:10. At 06:40, they left together for a meeting at General Staff Headquarters in Tel Aviv, which began at 08:30. En route Herzog

69. M. Heikal (*Sunday Telegraph*, 21 October 1973, translated in *Ma'ariv*, 9 November 1973), purports to give a verbatim report of the discussion between Nasser and Soviet Ambassador Pozhidaev. Nasser is supposed to have said: "I want you to understand that you are the reason for everything that has happened today—the closure of the Straits—you are the reason. The confirmation by Moscow of the movements of the Israeli Army was the deciding factor that set everything into motion. When you told us that there are 11 Israeli regiments ready to attack Syria and occupy Syrian territory, we decided that matters cannot be left to fate. But now I realize that the Israeli concentrations in the North are thinned out and they are moving toward us. We have become the front."

70. *New York Times*, 20 June 1967.

71. Reported to B. Geist in confidential interviews, 1973.

suggested that Opposition leaders be brought into the consultations, and Eshkol readily agreed.[72] Some military leaders were of
the opinion that Israel's deterrent credibility was at stake. Others
expressed concern over large-scale war and destruction, along with
the view that war would be a matter of life and death for Israel.
This discussion was followed by a meeting of the Ministerial Committee on Defense, at 09:30, attended also by Eban's advisers,
along with Rabin, Weizman, Yariv, and Meir. After the departure
of three ministers, Aranne, Sapir, and Carmel, the meeting was
enlarged to include Coalition and Opposition leaders, who had
arrived in the interval: David Hacohen of the Labor Alignment,
then Chairman of the Knesset Foreign Affairs and Security Committee; Almogi, Peres, and Dayan from *Rafi;* and Begin, Ben-
Eliezer, Landau, Rimalt, and Serlin from *Gahal.* The ministers
who remained were Warhaftig and Galili. It was in that large forum
that most of the alternatives open to Israel for action were considered. However, the basic decision to wait and opt for diplomacy,
including the possibility of the Foreign Minister's journey to
Washington, was taken at the Ministerial meeting at 09:30. The
larger group was *not* informed of the decision authorizing a possible journey by Eban to the U.S.; and Eban's decision to see de
Gaulle en route was arrived at by neither forum, but rather in
the evening.

The Defense Committee meeting had begun with a review of
the military situation by Rabin. The Egyptian build-up was not yet
offensive, he observed; the pivotal 4th Armored Division was still
on the western side of the Canal, and nothing had yet moved on
the Jordanian front. He did not make a proposal for immediate
action but indicated that the sooner Israel acted the better. He

72. Herzog interview with M. Brecher, 10 August 1968, and Begin's Eulogy to
Herzog, March 1972. See also W. Burdett, *Encounter with the Middle East,*
p. 244; *MER,* p. 196; and S. Nakdimon, *Toward the Zero Hour,* pp. 43–46. The
following reconstruction of the 23 May decision process is based upon: Foreign
Ministry sources; Eshkol's *AB;* A. Eban, *An Autobiography,* pp. 332–338, and
his "Revelations from the Waiting Period," *Ma'ariv,* 6 May 1973; M. Begin,
"A Chapter from a Book to be Written," *Ma'ariv,* 18 June and 2 July 1971; J.
Serlin, Interviews, *Yediot Aharonot,* 26 May 1972 and 5 June 1972; A. Yaffe,
"The War of Twenty-Seven Days," *Nitzoz,* September 1967; R. St. John, *Eban,*
pp. 417–420; M. Gilboa, "The Crisis that Reached the Top," *OT,* 31 May 1973;
Nakdimon, *Toward the Zero Hour,* pp. 43–60; and Z. Schiff, "The Three Weeks
that Preceded the War."

also pointed out that if Israel were to take military action, it would not be feasible to strike at Sharm-e-Sheikh alone: "That would be to start the war at the worst and most difficult place."[73] The only viable alternative to an all-out assault would be to hit the Egyptian Air Force, then to occupy the Gaza Strip and hold. Although the IDF Command was certain of victory, "I cannot promise a walk-over," said Rabin. "This will not be similar to Sinai [1956]; it will not be easy. There will be sacrifices."[74] In reply to a question from Eban, whether anything would be lost by a few days' delay for intensive diplomatic activity, the military commanders present concurred that all nonmilitary possibilities should be exhausted first. They affirmed their agreement to a postponement of military action—for forty-eight hours—at the Ministerial Committee meeting and during the consultation with the larger group of the political elite.[75]

Eshkol expressed the view that Egypt's challenge could not remain unanswered. Already en route to Tel Aviv he had remarked to Yaffe that "it seems there is no way out."[76] Eban dominated the rest of the substantive discussion, by virtue of his mastery of the details of the commitments (as he saw them) made by the Western powers and other maritime states to Israel in 1957. And his views and proposals carried the day.

73. See A. Eban, "Revelations from the Waiting Period," *Ma'ariv*, 6 May 1973; and Nakdimon, *Toward the Zero Hour*, p. 48. Although Rabin later stated in an interview in *Ma'ariv*, 4 October 1967, and in "Six Days and Five More Years," *Ma'ariv*, 2 June 1972, that he perceived the closure of the Straits as a declaration of war, participants and observers at the 23 May meeting have stated that he did not propose war at that or at a later stage. There was *no* pressure on the 23rd from the military for "immediate action," as claimed by: W. Laqueur, *The Road to War, 1967: The Origins of the Arab-Israel Conflict* (London, 1968), p. 124; Draper, *Israel and World Politics*, p. 88; Nakdimon, *Toward the Zero Hour*, p. 49; Gilboa, *Six Years—Six Days*, p. 127; and D. Kimche and D. Bawly, *The Sandstorm, the Arab-Israeli War of June 1967: Prelude and Aftermath* (London, 1968), pp. 138–139. All noted that the military leaders agreed to further waiting, to explore political opportunities, as well as to give the IDF a little more time for preparations. Major-General E. Weizman (Interview, *Ma'ariv*, 5 June 1973) confirmed this as well, as did M. Bitan, in an interview with M. Brecher, 8 August 1968.

74. R. St. John, *Eban*, p. 418, and Eban, "Revelations from the Waiting Period."

75. It was, according to the very reliable Nakdimon (*Toward the Zero Hour*, p. 51), the main factor which persuaded *Rafi* and *Gahal* leaders to acquiesce in the Government's proposal of 23 May to opt for diplomatic action. See also Weizman, Interview, *Ma'ariv*, 5 June 1973.

76. Schiff, "The Three Weeks that Preceded the War," *Ha'aretz*, 4 October 1967.

"The question," Eban began, "is not whether we must resist, but whether we must resist alone or with the support and understanding of others." However, before Israel responded militarily, there were several powerful reasons for diplomatic activity: to explore Soviet intentions; to test the willingness of the Western powers to fulfil their 1957 commitments to break Israel's isolation; and to consult with friendly states, first and foremost with the United States, in order to assure their diplomatic support if victory were achieved on the battlefield. "Otherwise we may win a war and lose a victory."[77] And finally, diplomacy was designed to ensure U.S. support, especially the delivery of arms, in case of war. Eban analyzed the reactions of the Western powers to recent diplomatic moves. Then he read out a cable from Evron, which contained a formal request by Under-Secretary of State Rostow, on President Johnson's behalf, that Israel take no decision for the next forty-eight hours and that she consult with the United States. Again the President warned that he would not take any responsibility for actions on which he was not consulted. Eban suggested that Israel agree to this: the time could be put to good use to test the 1957 commitments; and "if we didn't do it, . . . they would say afterward that we missed an opportunity to solve our problem in cooperation with them."[78]

Eban's presentation contained elements that would satisfy everyone—the hawks and doves, even Ben-Gurion's followers. No one opposed the basic concept, though Dayan and Peres expressed

77. Eban, *An Autobiography*, p. 334. Not all have cast the "waiting period" in such a positive light. Teddy Kollek, in his memoirs a decade after the events, poured scorn on Eban's interpretation: "It seemed to us that Eshkol's hesitation about attacking derived from weakness, not wisdom. Later, his supporters gave statesmanlike reasons for the endless delay. . . . Much of this was nonsense (even after the American or British ships would have gone through, the Straits could have been closed again). It was good for some favorable editorials in newspapers and a few kind words on American television, yet it made no more difference in the United Nations than if we had attacked on May 15. . . . The fact that all turned out well was his [Eshkol's and, by clear implication, Eban's] good fortune and a result of Moshe Dayan's leadership and the army's state of preparedness" (T. Kollek, *For Jerusalem* [Jerusalem and Tel Aviv, 1978], p. 190).

78. Eban, *An Autobiography*, p. 335. For further details on Eban's views, see A. Eban, Interview, *Ma'ariv*, 2 June 1972. In a July 1968 interview with Michael Brecher, the then Foreign Minister stated that there was unanimity in the Cabinet on 23 May that war lay ahead; but nobody advocated going to war immediately. This is confirmed by other sources, including expressed opinions of those present at these meetings.

their belief that nothing would come of diplomatic maneuvers. Dayan stated that only Israel would open the Straits—though he was willing to let others have the honor (he was to express himself in a similar vein at his 3 June press conference). What he emphasized was that, in diplomatic contacts, no official Israeli commitments should be given to the principle of prior consultations. Further, "at the end of forty-eight hours, we should launch military action against Egypt. . . ."[79] It was clear to many, as Eshkol, Sapir, and others observed during the discussion, that forty-eight hours would turn into seventy-two or more.

Eshkol summed up the debate in the Ministerial Defense Committee by stating that the closure of the Straits was a warlike act and that every hour that passed was fraught with danger. He proposed cautioning Washington that a longer period of waiting might turn into a victory for Nasser. Thus the crucial ministerial session of 23 May ended with Israel's leaders opting for diplomatic action.

The most acrimonious discussion—in the Ministerial Committee only—revolved around implementation. H. M. Shapira suggested that Eban get in touch with those states which had committed themselves to freedom of navigation and possibly even visit them. Aranne opposed this, declaring that it would invite pressures on Israel for concessions; while Carmel opposed the whole idea, for it might tie Israel's hands. Eban countered that pressures could be applied just as well through ambassadors and that it was important that Israel's position be explained at the highest level abroad, directly by a high-ranking member of the Government. He emphasized that the most important place to visit was Washington, while Meir still believed that clarifications of de Gaulle's intentions had priority. A consensus was reached that U.S. intentions ought to be clarified. Then the question of the emissary was raised. Again the mistrust of Eban surfaced. Eshkol proposed that Meir be sent, but Eban vigorously opposed this and other suggestions, including the despatch of Amit. In the end, Eban's view triumphed.

The Ministerial Committee finally took the following formal decisions:

1.   The blockade is an act of aggression against Israel.

79. Dayan, *Story of My Life*, p. 254.

2. Any decision or action is postponed for forty-eight hours, during
    which time the Foreign Minister will explore the position of the
    United States [Decision 8].

3. The Prime Minister and Foreign Minister are empowered to decide,
    should they see fit, on a journey by the Foreign Minister to Washing-
    ton to meet President Johnson [Decision 9].[80]

Most of the participants now left for Jerusalem. Eshkol proceeded to work on his reply to the Knesset debate over his statement of
the previous day, but much had changed since then. His statement, delivered at eight o'clock in the evening, was short and
restrained and was devoted exclusively to the "announced" closure
of the Straits: "Any interference with the freedom of navigation in
the Gulf and the Straits . . . is an act of aggression against Israel."
The upshot of the past few days' consultations with other states
who supported the freedom of navigation was "that I can state that
the international support for these rights is serious and widespread. . . . I call upon the powers once again to act without delay
for the maintenance of the right of free passage to our southern-
most port. . . ."[81]

Eshkol proposed that the debate be continued, in secret, in the
Knesset Foreign Affairs and Security Committee. The vote expressed the growing national (as distinct from political) cohesion:
All parties except the Communists voted in favor, 89 to 4. Even the
minority resolutions submitted by the two Communist parties
affirmed Israel's right to freedom of passage.[82] Nasser had succeed-

---

80. Eban, "Revelations from the Waiting Period," *Ma'ariv*, 6 May 1973. The
English translation is quoted from his *An Autobiography*, p. 337; it also appears
in R. St. John, *Eban*, p. 420. St. John points out, correctly, that Eban's journey
was authorized (by delegation) by the Cabinet. What he fails to note is that: (a) the
decision was taken at the fairly brief Ministerial Committee meeting, and that
during the wider consultation forums with party leaders this was *not* mentioned;
and (b) the Ministerial Committee did not authorize his meetings with de Gaulle
and Wilson. Begin Interview, *Yediot Aharonot*, 2 June 1967, and M. Carmel, Interview, *Jerusalem Post*, 2 June 1972, carefully point out these distinctions.

81. H. M. Christman, ed., *The State Papers of Levi Eshkol* (New York, 1969),
pp. 89–94.

82. Moshe Sneh, the leader of *Maki*, the Israel Communist Party, explained
after the war in an interview in *Yediot Aharonot*, 16 June 1967: "On one side we
saw a pan-Arabic front, almost total, whose aim was to destroy Israel; on the other,
we saw a lone Israel, fighting for its very survival. There couldn't be and there
weren't any differences of opinion among us as to the fact that the Israel Communist Party would join the ranks with the whole nation in this campaign of
resistance."

ed in uniting Israeli society, an element that he always underesti-
mated in his calculations.

Earlier, at 18:00, there was a second informal meeting of seven
Cabinet members. Eban's proposed trip abroad was not discussed.
Throughout the afternoon and evening, the Foreign Office tried to
arrange a meeting between Eban and de Gaulle for the following
day. The cable also notified Paris of Eban's arrival in the morning.
When the Foreign Minister left Israel, however, he did not know
whether or not he would be able to see the French President.

When the news of Eban's journey to Washington became known
in the Knesset, there was great dissatisfaction in Opposition circles;
they had not been told during the consultations in Tel Aviv.[83] It
strengthened their resolve to take part in the decision-making
process in a formal capacity only: If they were to become an integral part of the process and share responsibility for decisions, they
would insist on proper authority.

At IDF Headquarters there was another meeting in the afternoon presided over by Rabin. The Chief of Staff felt faint, was
taken home, and was ordered complete rest for the next thirty
hours. His place was taken temporarily by Weizman.[84] On that
day, too, almost unnoticed at the time, Nasser raised the stakes
further: The first Egyptian statements were published denying

83. There was dissatisfaction among Coalition partners as well; see Carmel,
Interview, *Jerusalem Post*, 2 June 1972. The most extreme criticism of Eban's
meeting with de Gaulle came from Ben-Gurion, who later termed the mission "a
silly mistake" and claimed that "it could be that this meeting caused substantially,
maybe even decisively, de Gaulle's change of relationship and the imposition of
the embargo" (Interview in *Ma'ariv*, 13 November 1970). Just as Ben-Gurion earlier accused Eshkol of being the cause of the deterioration of relations between
France and Israel (see Gilboa, "The Crisis that Reached the Top," *OT*, 31 May
1973), so too, later, he blamed the Israeli side—Eban—for the failure. That he
was wrong is perhaps best shown by de Gaulle's views, expressed in remarks to
Wilson in Paris soon after the Six Day War—on 19 June 1967.

84. On the occasion of Rabin becoming a candidate for the Premiership, reports
about a document were published in *Ha'aretz* and *Ma'ariv* on 22 April, and in the
Jerusalem Post on 23 April 1974. The document, an *aide-memoire* prepared by
Weizman on 6 November 1967, stated, according to *Ha'aretz*, that "from the beginning Mr. Weizman felt that the COS's steadfastness is crumbling. Rabin got in
touch with Weizman at 8 in the morning [on the 23rd] and asked him to come to
his home immediately. . . . When he arrived . . . the COS told him in a weak
voice: 'I have involved the nation in the biggest and most difficult war because of
mistakes I have made.' He asked whether Weizman was willing to take over the
job, but Weizman refused and encouraged him. . . . [A]n army doctor told him
that the COS suffers from acute anxiety. It was decided to inform the Prime Minister and to let it be known that Rabin was suffering from nicotine poisoning."

Israel's right to a presence on the shores of the Gulf, that is, to Eilat.[85]

The procession of Arab leaders to Cairo reached a high point. By this time some members of the Security Council had lost their patience: Canada and Denmark insisted upon convening the Council, and it met the next day, 24 May. The U.S. Administration was galvanized into action on a broad diplomatic front by Nasser's announcement. Strong warnings were sent immediately to Syria and Egypt—through U Thant as well—that the United States Government supported Israel's right of navigation in the Gulf of Aqaba. The USSR was similarly informed. There were also immediate consultations with Britain.

The strongest pressure was put on Egypt. A message from Johnson to Nasser stressed in general terms the need to avoid fighting. He promised to send Vice-President Hubert Humphrey for talks with Egyptian, other Arab, and Israeli leaders "if we come through these days without hostilities."[86]

The U.S. Government note was stronger and more explicit. It warned against "misadventure or a miscalculation. Those in power in the area are likely to misunderstand or misinterpret the intentions and actions of others." Then it emphasized three aspects of the situation that "cause us special concern: the continual terrorist acts carried out against Israel with Syria's agreement, some of which at least are carried out from Syrian territory"; the removal of the UNEF; and the mobilization of forces on both sides. It continued: "We take this opportunity to reaffirm our continuous commitment to the freedom of passage in the Gulf of Aqaba for all ships. . . ." The verbal message was blunt and menacing:

The U.S.A. feels that: (1) the UNEF should remain in Gaza and Sharm-e-Sheikh until a decision is issued by the UN General Assembly. (2) No armed forces should proceed to Sharm-e-Sheikh until the UAR Government issues an official statement confirming the freedom of navigation in the Straits of Tiran, the entry to the Gulf of Aqaba, without any conditions. . . . (3) No Egyptian armed forces should enter the Gaza Strip. (4) The UN and its agencies should remain responsible for the administration of the Gaza Strip until the issue is settled. (5) The Egyptian military concentration which is now taking place in Sinai is a serious matter. The Egyptian forces in Sinai and the Israeli forces massed opposite them in the Negev should return to their previous positions.[87]

---

85. Radio Cairo, 11:30 GMT, 23 May 1967.
86. *The Vantage Point*, p. 291.
87. BBC, 26 June 1967.

In Washington, Johnson decided to publish a statement—after the release of the expected Soviet announcement. An early draft was read over the phone to Evron by Roche. It was a noncommittal text, mainly calling on both sides to abstain from aggravating the issue. Evron "lost his temper" and told his White House contact that if that is the best the President could do, he better not make any statements at all. Johnson was angry at first but later decided to make the statement stronger. The main part of the President's statement read:

The purported closing of the Gulf of Aqaba to Israeli shipping has brought a new and grave dimension to the crisis. The United States considers the Gulf an international waterway and feels that a blockade of Israeli shipping is illegal and potentially disastrous to the cause of peace.[88]

Moreover, units of the Sixth Fleet were ordered toward the Eastern Mediterranean.

Evron cabled home that the U.S. had decided to approach the Security Council because it was essential to use the UN platform before a unilateral position was adopted. He added the reassurances of a senior official that "we could rely on the President," and that the senior official confirmed that the President has told Premier Kosygin of United States commitments.[89]

In Moscow, after a meeting of the Soviet Government, *Tass* released its Statement on the Situation in the Near East. It stressed Israel's aggressive intentions toward Syria and praised the action of Arab states and the UAR "honoring its allied commitments for joint defense with Syria." The closure of the Straits was not even mentioned. The final passage stated:

But let no one have any doubt about the fact that should anyone try to unleash aggression in the Near East he would be met not only with the united strength of Arab countries, but also with strong opposition from the Soviet Union and all peace-loving states.[90]

In London, the British Government went into special, urgent session, under the impression that "at any moment it seemed that war might break out, with either side seeking to gain the advantage to be derived from a pre-emptive strike."[91] The British Cabinet

88. Evron, Interview with Michael Brecher, 3 March 1972, and *New York Times*, 24 May 1967.

89. Israel, Ministry for Foreign Affairs, Cables and Communications, Jerusalem, 1967, and Eshkol, Interview, *Ma'ariv*, 4 October 1967.

90. *New York Times*, 24 May 1967.

91. H. Wilson, *The Labour Government: A Personal Record 1964–1970* (London, 1971), p. 395.

decided to work, with other maritime nations, toward the assertion that the Gulf of Aqaba and the Straits were international waterways.

There was no official reaction from the French Government. As the tense day came to an end, world attention began to focus on Eban's forthcoming visit to Western capitals.

Wednesday, 24 May

On this day, discussions were held at the highest level in several capitals: their purpose was to try to gain time, for different reasons. U Thant finally met Nasser and continued his meetings with Egyptian Foreign Minister Riad. George Brown met with Kosygin and Gromyko in Moscow. British Minister of State Thomson began his talks with the American Administration in Washington. At the center of attention were Eban's meetings with de Gaulle and Wilson, in Paris and London. In New York, the Security Council met for the *first time* to deal with the crisis.

Eshkol spent the morning dealing with matters affecting the crisis tangentially—finance and internal security. He had lunch with Weizman, de facto COS during Rabin's illness, and he met with the General Staff for three hours in the afternoon. Mobilization was about to be completed; and Weizman used this opportunity to discuss military plans with the Prime Minister–Defense Minister. Three alternative possibilities were reportedly discussed: the occupation of the entire Sinai peninsula; part of Sinai, up to El Arish; or only the Gaza Strip. Bar-Lev, present at the meeting, claimed that the first alternative emerged as the dominant view; but his version is contradicted by two authoritative sources.

Weizman stated at the end of the meeting: "Mr. Minister of Defense, *Tzahal* is prepared and ready for war, as of tomorrow, that is, as of May 25."[92]

That afternoon, Allon returned from the first special visit by an Israeli Cabinet minister to the Soviet Union.[93] He immediately held a two-hour conference with Galili and, at General Staff Headquarters, with Bar-Lev. Eban left Israel at 03:30 in an empty El Al

92. See the article on the SDW in the *Encyclopaedia Hebraica*, vol. 23, pp. 725–726, and E. Weizman, Interview, *Ma'ariv*, 5 June 1973.

93. In an interview on 26 July 1968, Allon told Michael Brecher his reasons for not returning earlier: (1) In the USSR, it was very difficult to make correct judgments on what was happening in the Middle East. (2) He felt that unless his colleagues in the Cabinet called him back, he should not return. (3) He did not want to give the impression of panic.

plane, flying to France to load military equipment. During the forenoon, Eytan succeeded in arranging the meeting with de Gaulle. Eban knew that during the past few days the French had raised the question in official talks whether the economic value of trade through Eilat was sufficient to justify war. The time had come to put these doubts to the test.

The meeting with the French President began at noon, with Foreign Minister Couve de Murville also present.[94] De Gaulle asked Eban to present his case but first stated the basic French position:

Israel must not make war unless she is attacked by others. It would be catastrophic if Israel were to shoot first. The Four Powers must be left to resolve the dispute. France will influence the Soviet Union toward an attitude favorable to peace.[95]

Eban then spoke for twelve minutes. He had come to consult with Israel's great friend. "Israel was faced with Syrian terrorism, Egyptian troop concentrations and the blockade of the Straits; the last was an act which must be rescinded." He reminded de Gaulle of the strong French declarations of 1957 in favor of Israel's rights

94. The following version of Eban's meetings with de Gaulle and Wilson is based mainly on the recollections and reports of the participants: first and foremost, Eban himself in a series of books, articles, and interviews. See especially A. Eban, *An Autobiography*, pp. 341–344; R. St. John, *Eban*, pp. 420–426, which is based upon Eban's unpublished manuscript on the SDW; A. Eban, *My Country: The Story of Modern Israel* (London, 1973), p. 175; Interview, *Ma'ariv*, 1 December 1967, where he quotes verbatim passages from the discussion; Interview, *Ma'ariv*, 2 June 1972; and Interview, *Yediot Aharonot*, 22 April 1973. See also Israel, Ministry for Foreign Affairs, Cables and Communications, Jerusalem, 1967, quoted in M. Brecher, *Decisions in Israel's Foreign Policy* (London, 1974), pp. 381–382. Additional material comes from de Gaulle and de Murville. See de Gaulle's press conference of 27 November 1967, excerpts in the *New York Times*, 28 November 1967; *International Documents on Palestine 1967*, F. A. Jabber, ed., (Beirut, 1970), pp. 194, 212; M. C. de Murville, *Une Politique Étrangere 1958–1969* (Paris, 1971), pp. 469–471. Thirdly, see H. Wilson, *The Labour Government: A Personal Record 1964–1970*, pp. 396–397, and Geist's interview with Wilson in Jerusalem on 22 December 1972, during which Wilson confirmed the details of his discussion with Eban, as far as he remembered. There are also valuable secondary sources. M. Gilboa, *Six Years—Six Days*, pp. 136–140, gives a verbatim record of what was said during the meeting. M. Bar-Zohar, *Embassies in Crisis*, pp. 92–96; W. Burdett, *Encounter with the Middle East*, pp. 248–249; and S. Nakdimon, *Toward the Zero Hour*, pp. 65–68, all include verbatim accounts of the contents of these meetings.

95. R. St. John, *Eban*, p. 421. All quotations concerning the Eban–de Gaulle meeting, unless otherwise indicated, are from the above. This has been elaborated upon in Eban, *An Autobiography*, pp. 341–344.

in the Straits. In reply to de Gaulle's interposed question, "What are you going to do?", he stated: "Si la choix se pose entre l'abandon et la resistance, Israel va resister. La decision est prise" ["If the choice lies between surrender and resistance, Israel will resist. Our decision has been taken"]. But Israel would not act immediately. She wished to explore the attitude of the powers to their previous commitments. "If there is concerted international action . . . Nasser will yield. . . ."

De Gaulle emphasized again that Israel should not declare war —at least, she should not fire the first shot. He did not accept Eban's interposed remark that Nasser's acts had already opened hostilities: opening hostilities meant firing the first shot. He disengaged France from her 1957 position: 1967 was not 1957. He emphasized the importance of the role of the Soviet Union: "In our days there are no more Western solutions, and therefore coordination between the four powers has to be achieved, the Straits opened, and war is to be avoided." Specifically, he was skeptical about any Western naval action. The Soviet Union had to be part of any peaceful solution, to be achieved by a concerted action of the Big Four. "The more Israel looks to the West, the less will be the readiness of the Soviet Union to cooperate." He greatly minimized the closure of the Straits, placing it at the level of another "incident" in a long series of incidents since 1957. He upheld the freedom of the seas and suggested that an agreement could be sought "as in the Dardanelles."

Finally, Eban—in an obvious reference to arms supplies— thanked France for her "reinforcement of Israel's strength and spirit." De Gaulle's reply contained the first hint of the reversal of France's position in this matter as well: "Israel was not sufficiently established to solve all her problems herself."[96] He concluded by once again repeating his warning: Israel should not open hostilities; she should leave time for international consultation.

As he later recalled, Eban's immediate summary of the meeting was that "I had been an eye-witness to the death of solemn commitments." Expressions of support were vague, advice to abstain from "resistance" direct and specific. De Gaulle's solution was a four-power consensus with all that it entailed.

Eban then proceeded to London for an exchange of views with the British Prime Minister. Wilson was skeptical about four-power

96. Eban, Interview, Ma'ariv, 2 June 1972.

consultations; but, he added, he had declared the British Government's willingness to put the idea to the test. Eban stated that "Israel would not live without access to Eilat or under the threat of Egyptian encirclement. Israel's choice was either to fight alone or to join with others in an international effort to force Nasser's withdrawal." He had come to test the purpose of the maritime powers.

Wilson told him that the Cabinet's decision was that the blockade ought not to succeed. "Britain would join with others in an effort to open the Straits." He handed Eban a copy of a speech he had made that morning, at Margate, which included the following passage:

It is the view of Her Majesty's Government in the United Kingdom that the Straits of Tiran must be regarded as an international waterway through which the vessels of all nations have a right of passage. Her Majesty's Government will assert this right on behalf of all British shipping and is prepared to join with others to secure general recognition of this right.[97]

Wilson had already sent Thomson to Washington to discuss plans for common action—"nuts and bolts" talks. In reply to Eban's question, he stated that Britain would act within the UN, if possible, but could "take measures of her own outside the UN," if necessary.[98] When the talk ended, Eban noticed that Wilson had confined himself to an analysis of Britain's position: "He had not given me any counsel on the advisability or timing of Israel's resistance."

In Washington, the White House and the State Department kept officially silent. But unofficially a mood of caution and reserve was communicated. Publicly, members of the House of Representatives signed a statement calling on the President to do everything possible to defend Israel. On the other hand, the powerful Senate leaders, Mansfield and Dirksen, added their weight against any unilateral American action outside the UN. Ambassador Harman flew to Gettysburg to clarify with Eisenhower the commitments given by him in 1957 and to urge him to support Johnson. Eisenhower declared that, if he were asked by journalists, he would state that the Straits were an international waterway, as he and

97. Wilson, *The Labour Government*, p. 397. His speech was a verbatim passage from Great Britain's statement at the UN General Assembly, on 4 March 1957.
98. Eban, Interview, *Ma'ariv*, 2 June 1972.

Dulles stated in 1957, and that the denial of rights of free passage would be illegal.[99]

In New York, the Security Council convened at the request of Denmark and Canada. Two meetings were held during the day; but there was no vote taken, nor was a date fixed for the next meeting. In Moscow, George Brown met with Gromyko and Kosygin. It soon became clear that, while the Soviets were not interested in an outbreak of war, they were in no mood to cooperate with the Western powers in restraining Nasser, either within the United Nations, or through four-power consultation, or through pressure upon the Arab states.

Thursday, 25 May

From this day onward there was increasing pressure on Eshkol by Israel's military leaders—with the exception of Bar-Lev—to go to war; the time limit given to the political decision-makers on the 23rd was running out. The trigger seems to have been the news that the Egyptian 4th Armored Division had crossed into Sinai that morning. The first manifestation of IDF pressure occurred in a meeting at the armored division headquarters of Major-General Tal, at 11:15. The assembled officers presented to Eshkol the war plans of the Southern Command, which had been told that D-Day had been set for the morning of the 25th and then postponed twenty-four hours.[100] Then General Ariel Sharon expressed his dissatisfaction with the hesitations of the Government in the face of the increasing strengthening of the Arab forces. War could not be avoided any more; and the earlier the power of the Egyptian Army was broken, the more easily Israel's goals concerning the Straits would be achieved.[101] There was no doubt that Sharon was expressing the views of the field commanders.

During that morning's consultations, Yariv presented the daily intelligence appreciation, which showed the building up of a serious Arab military threat. As a result, Eshkol approved the sending of a cable to Eban informing him of the sudden escalation

99. At a press conference that Eisenhower held the next day, he added that "I can't recall that Egypt ever agreed to this." He urged caution: "None of us should be too hurried about getting into this thing. Any unilateral action by anyone would be a serious mistake" (*New York Times*, 26 May 1967).

100. Dayan, *Story of My Life*, p. 259.

101. A. Sharon, Interview, *Yediot Aharonot*, 20 July 1973.

and asking him to explain to President Johnson that the danger no longer lay simply in the closing of the Straits but also in the concentration of troops and in the prospect of an Arab attack on Israel.

In the evening, Eshkol approved a rather controversial and uncharacteristic venture in Machiavellian statesmanship, about which Dayan expressed disquiet (Decision 10).[102] The process was best described by Rabin:

After the closing of the Straits, in order to test where Israel stood and to what extent she was not to depend completely on herself, the Director-General of the Prime Minister's Office, the late Ya'acov Herzog, in a conversation with me, suggested that we send a telegram to the Foreign Minister, Abba Eban, who was then in Washington, and in it we would say that according to the information in our hands, there may occur the development of an Egyptian offensive initiated against Israel as the events evolve. And Mr. Herzog further suggested to me that we ask Mr. Eban to clarify to what extent the United States is prepared to make good on obligations, given in the past to Israeli leaders, for real help in such an event.[103]

It was typical of the hectic pace of consultations by that time that Eshkol accepted the idea and approved the second telegram to Eban as well, without thinking too much about its consequences. While the first telegram was merely informative, the second warned about an immediate attack. It stated:

As a result of events during the last twenty-four hours, be advised that *we expect a surprise attack from the Egyptians and the Syrians at any moment.* The United States Government should declare at once that any attack on Israel would be regarded as an attack on the United States. It should also issue instructions in that spirit to its forces in the area. It is recommended that you show this cable to the highest officials, the President himself or the Secretary of State.[104]

Immediately upon his arrival in Washington, Eban received the *second* telegram, signed by Eshkol: he was asked to convey the Israeli evaluations to the American leadership "in the most drastic and urgent terms." While deliberating whether to ask for further details, the *first* telegram was delivered to him, seemingly underscoring the contents of the one previously received. In spite of

102. *Story of My Life,* p. 263.
103. Y. Rabin, "Six Days and Five More Years," *Ma'ariv,* 2 June 1972.
104. Bar-Zohar, *Embassies in Crisis,* p. 109 (emphasis added).

his misgivings, as he later noted, he decided that he could not hesitate any longer and asked for his scheduled meeting with Dean Rusk to be advanced from 18:00 to 17:00.

The meeting, also attended by Eugene Rostow and Lucius Battle, was brief. Eban read the telegram to the Americans. Rusk, surprised, asked for an immediate adjournment in order to enable him to inform the President and the Secretary of Defense of this development. He remarked that there was support for Israel's cause but only if the U.S. did not have to act unilaterally; Israel's demand raised constitutional problems.[105]

Eban returned to the State Department for a working dinner, accompanied by Harman and Evron. The discussion was devoted almost exclusively to ways of opening the Straits. The Americans were rather optimistic about the planned maritime action. It provided for: (a) a declaration by maritime powers on the right of free passage, open to adherence by all, including Israel; (b) the enforcement of this declaration through a naval patrol by a group of maritime states; and (c) the two steps to be connected by a recourse to the Security Council. Eban was alarmed by an undertone of some possible limitations on Israel's rights in the Straits. At midnight, he sent Harman back to the State Department to make it clear, through E. Rostow, that the Israeli Government expected "absolute precision about where you stand in the matter." He was told: "On the determination of the United States to ensure that the Straits would be open Eban would have to hear from the President himself."[106]

After the dinner, Eban and Harman had a second meeting with Rusk. By that time the Secretary of State had seen the President, who had just returned from Canada, and had consulted General Earl Wheeler, Chairman of the Joint Chiefs of Staff. He told Eban that "the United States did not share the appraisal that any Arab state was planning an immediate attack on Israel."[107] The President had also told him that he did not have the authority to act

105. Eban interview with Michael Brecher, 22 July 1968. This is discussed in Eban's *An Autobiography,* pp. 349–350.

106. Israel, Ministry for Foreign Affairs, Cables and Communications, Jerusalem, 1967; Eban, Interview, *Ma'ariv,* 2 June 1972; and R. St. John, *Eban,* p. 428.

107. Israel, Ministry for Foreign Affairs, Cables and Communications, Jerusalem, 1967. The Americans did take the Israeli warning seriously, to the extent that the White House directed the State Department to summon the Egyptian Ambassador immediately and hand him a message from the President, which

without full coordination with Congress. What Israel was requesting (". . . any attack on Israel would be regarded as an attack on
the United States. . . .") had been stated only in the NATO treaty,
and even there only after a long and heated debate. Then he gave
the President's views on the crisis—views that were to be repeated,
sometimes in identical terms, twice the next day, in Johnson's
conversations with Evron and Eban. The President would act
to live up to American commitments, and he was taking a strong
political and diplomatic stand in Cairo, as well as in other capitals.
But it was absolutely essential for him to act with the approval of
Congress and public opinion; and in the meantime, Israel should
not take pre-emptive action. Thus the Israeli Government was
aware of the broad outlines of the American position the next
morning, Friday, 26 May.

Harman cabled to Jerusalem the results of the discussions
during the working dinner, while Eban sent Eshkol a short cable,
at 01:30 Friday, New York time, summarizing the results of the
three meetings. The latter cable emphasized the seemingly positive aspects of the talks:

It appears that the President is likely to discuss a program for opening the
Straits by the maritime powers, led by the United States, Britain and
perhaps others. . . . The second stage . . . would be the despatch of a
naval task force which will appear in the Straits. Some officials here
predict that the President will make a pledge that the Straits will be
opened, even if there is resistance.[108]

The growing clamor in Egypt and the Arab world to "wipe Israel
off the face of the earth" became an important input into the Israeli
decision process. It could no longer be ignored or discounted. The
air was full of martial songs, bloodcurdling threats, cries of exulta-
tion, and calls for total extermination of the Jews. Two illustrations
will suffice. Radio Cairo announced: "The Arab nation is determined to wipe Israel off the face of the earth and restore to Falastin

---

repeated the Israeli warning on Radio Cairo on 28 May 1967, and added: "We
have affirmed to them that our information does not confirm theirs in this respect,
but we do not want to leave anything to chance. I ask you, on behalf of President
Johnson, to inform Cairo immediately that the situation requires self-restraint
and abstention from carrying out any offensive military operation that may lead to
a large-scale explosion." The Americans also requested the Soviet Union to pass
along the warning, informing them of the Israeli message.

108. Israel, Ministry for Foreign Affairs, Cables and Communications, Jerusalem, 1967. Also partially quoted in Eban, *An Autobiography,* p. 350.

the Arab honor." Ahmad Shukeiry's answer to an interviewer's question as to what would happen to Israelis born in Israel: "Those who survive will remain in Palestine. I estimate that none of them will survive."[109]

Another significant event on the 25th was the announcement by Sixth Fleet Headquarters in Naples that six U.S. ships, with 2,000 marines on board, had sailed toward the eastern Mediterranean: the movements of the Sixth Fleet were carefully watched by Nasser and the Soviets as tangible evidence of American intentions.

Friday, 26 May

Eshkol presided over a six-hour meeting of the Ministerial Committee on Defense, in which Director of Military Intelligence Yariv gave the latest intelligence report, and Rabin evaluated the developments of the past ten days. The atmosphere was tense. The "doves," headed by Warhaftig, expressed doubts and fears about the feasibility of armed resistance. Further, it was necessary that all sectors of the nation be represented in the Government: Even to decide to postpone action required courage and daring—and the sanction of a National Unity Government. Ben-Gurion's views —partly included in Warhaftig's remarks—were discussed at length, sowing further doubt. The "hawk" view was expressed by the *Ahdut Ha'avoda* ministers. To Allon a delay in decision could be disastrous, while Carmel and Galili suggested that the Prime Minister be empowered to take appropriate action in case of necessity. Eshkol, in his summary of this security debate, stressed the change of Israel's primary focus from the Straits to the concentration of Egyptian forces along the border. If it were only the problem of the Straits, Israel could be satisfied with promised American assistance, he said; but there was now a greater danger.

On Sharef's suggestion, the Committee decided to wait for Eban's return from Washington with clarifications and to postpone discussions until then (Decision 11). Sapir then laid before the Committee plans for mobilizing resources—inside and outside Israel—to enable Israel to hold out, even during a prolonged siege.

After the session of the Ministerial Defense Committee, Allon met with Eshkol to persuade him of the necessity of an early Israeli

109. The first illustration is from BBC, 26–27 May 1967; the second, *New York Times*, 2 June 1967.

military initiative. He reportedly told him: "This is one of the great issues in Jewish history. I believe you can go down in Jewish history as another King David—if you decide to act now." He persuaded Eshkol to cable Eban instructions to emphasize, in his meeting with the U.S. President, not the closure of the Straits and its possible reopening, but the threat posed by the Egyptian army massed on Israel's border. According to Allon, this meeting was decisive in making up Eshkol's mind to go to war.[110]

At 16:00, the Knesset Committee on Foreign Affairs and Security convened to discuss the security situation. Again, Eshkol emphasized the change of focus from the Straits to the Sinai troop concentrations. Israel was still determined to exhaust all diplomatic possibilities, even though the results of Eban's contacts were not satisfactory. The prevalent atmosphere of hesitancy and doubt penetrated the Knesset Committee as well. At 19:00, *Mapam* leaders Ya'ari and Hazan met with Eshkol: The discussion centered around the warnings about the IDF's preparedness, which they had heard about from *Rafi* leader Shimon Peres the previous day and from Ben-Gurion that day. Eshkol finally retired after a meeting with Dayan, further consultations with leaders of world Jewry, and an evaluation of the military situation by Allon, Rabin, and others.

Friday, 26 May, was no less hectic and tense in Washington. Rusk phoned Harman, in an attempt to gain some time, and asked whether Eban would be staying until Saturday, for by that time the results of U Thant's visit to Cairo would be known. Eban phoned back immediately and told Rusk that he had to be back in Israel the next day. A Cabinet meeting was planned for Sunday, possibly the most crucial in the history of the state, and the Cabinet's decision would be heavily influenced by what President Johnson told him. The results of U Thant's mission were not decisive for Israel: Israel, in Eban's view, might have to face hostilities the next week. There was an act of blockade which had to be resisted.

Then, as planned, he went to the Defense Department for a meeting with McNamara, General Wheeler, and other Pentagon officials. While this meeting was in session, the cable containing Allon's suggestions arrived; Eban now emphasized the concentration of Egyptian armed forces in Sinai. But Wheeler again stated

110. See Allon, *Curtain of Sand,* pp. 368–372; Gilboa, *Six Years—Six Days,* p. 180; and Nakdimon, *Toward the Zero Hour,* p. 98.

that Israel would succeed, whoever took the initiative. To him the idea that Israel might have to act in desperation, in a mood of "now or never," was inconceivable, in view of the facts of the situation, especially Israel's air superiority. McNamara bluntly opposed the idea of a naval task force. For Israel, this was not a tactical question of using foreign ships to ply the Straits, but a *casus belli;* and the problem was first of all an Israeli one. General Wheeler expressed himself in similar terms: The breaking of the blockade by an international flotilla would not solve the problem. Because of fear of the charge of collusion, the Israelis were never told they should go to war; but neither did the Pentagon representatives say they should not.

Eban was informed of a further delay in the meeting with Johnson by W. Rostow. In the meantime, Eshkol cabled that he must return the following night: There were growing demands for a decision from political as well as military circles. Rostow called the President and informed him that Evron had given assurances that there would be no publicity given to his conversation with Eban. Johnson instructed him to fix the meeting for 19:00, and asked him to send Evron to see him. Late in the evening, Evron cabled the following report about his conversation with the President:

When I entered his room, the President told me that he fully understood the gravity of Israel's position. His reaction to the Foreign Minister would be in accordance with what Mr. Eban had heard from Rusk and others that morning, namely, that any American involvement would require Congressional support of the intentions and decisions of the President. The first step would have to be the laying of a Congressional basis for any support of Israel's position. The President emphasized that he was working energetically in that direction. The United States had pledged itself to preserve freedom of passage in the Straits of Tiran: and the United States would carry out that obligation. But anything involving even a possibility of force would be impractical and would boomerang unless the proper Congressional basis were laid in advance. The President agreed that the United Nations in its present composition would not be able to do anything; no result would come from its discussions. Yet those discussions were vital in order to give proper support to the President, in the Congress and the public, as well as in the international domain. The President spoke without confidence about the result of the Secretary-General's mission to Cairo, but said that it would be foolish to ignore the effect of his report. Any action by any member state before the report were published would be received badly in many places. The President spoke optimistically about the possibility of setting up a structure with the active support of Britain and other maritime powers after the conclusion of a quick debate at the United Nations. Here he mentioned several countries who might be willing to cooperate. He had taken counsel with some of his leading advisers. All of them could be described as friends of Israel. They had expressed their support in the following formulation: The objective is to open the Straits for navigation by all states including Israel and this objective shall be carried out. Mr. Johnson made it clear that the appraisal in Jerusalem about an imminent Egyptian surprise attack was not shared by the United States. Israel was a sovereign Government, and if it decided to act alone, it could of course do so; but in that case everything that happened before and afterwards would be upon its responsibility and the United States would have no obligation for any consequences that might ensue. He refused to believe that Israel would carry out unilateral action which was bound to bring her great damage. But, he added, this was Israel's affair. As President of the United States he must carry out American commitments to Israel in a way which seemed to him best, within the framework of American interests. He emphasized several times, that Israel could depend on him. He said that he was not a coward and did not renege on his promises, but he was not prepared to act in a manner which seemed to him to endanger the security of the United States, or to bring about the intervention of the Soviet Union, in the event, simply because Israel has decided that Sunday is an ultimate date.[111]

The formal meeting with Eban started a little late, around 19:15. Eban began by giving the President the essence of information which had reached him the previous day about the possibility of an Egyptian attack and a summary of Israel's concern.

Johnson reiterated that he had said publicly an illegal action had occurred and that the Gulf was an international waterway. The question was when and how to act. Only if the Congress and the American people felt that Israel had justice on her side could he respond firmly. Moreover, the UN channel must first be exhausted. He needed a very short time and British help to develop an effective solution. He suggested that "it would not be wise at this stage to call Nasser's hand. If your Cabinet decides to do anything immediately and to do it on their own, that is for them. We are not going to do any retreating. We are not back-tracking. I am not forgetting anything I have ever said." But there were constitutional constraints, and a statement to the effect that an attack on Israel is an attack on the United States was beyond his prerogatives. "What you can tell your Cabinet is that the President, the Congress and the country will support a plan to use any or all measures

111. Israel, Ministry for Foreign Affairs, Cables and Communications, Jerusalem, 1967.

to open the Straits. But we have to go through the Secretary-General and the Security Council and build up support among the nations. . . . Israel will not be alone unless it decided to go alone. . . . If you want our help in whatever ensues, it is absolutely necessary for Israel not to make itself responsible for the institution of hostilities."[112]

At the end of the meeting, the President handed Eban the following *aide-memoire:*

The United States has its own constitutional processes, which are basic to its actions on matters involving war and peace. The Secretary-General has not yet reported to the Security Council and the Council has not yet demonstrated what it may or may not be able or willing to do, although the United States will press for prompt action in the United Nations. I have already publicly stated this week our view on the safety of navigation and on the Straits of Tiran. Regarding the Straits we plan to pursue vigorously the measures which can be taken by maritime nations to assure that the Straits and the Gulf remain open to free and innocent passage of all nations. I must emphasize the necessity for Israel not to make itself responsible for the initiation of hostilities. Israel will not be alone unless it decides to do it alone. We cannot imagine that Israel will make this decision.[113]

Harman notified the Israeli Government:

The Foreign Minister left without being able to report on his talk with the President. Brings with him full protocol.[114]

112. Ibid., based upon Harman's record of the minutes with the President, and Evron's interview with Michael Brecher, 3 March 1972. President Johnson *(The Vantage Point,* pp. 293–294) corroborated in general the above account. He stressed his following remark to Eban: "The central point, Mr. Minister, is that your nation not be the one to bear the responsibility of any outbreak of war. Then I said very slowly and positively: Israel will not be alone unless it decides to go alone." Other sources on the Eban-Johnson and Evron-Johnson conversations are: Eban, *An Autobiography,* pp. 353–359, and his Interview, *Ma'ariv,* 2 June 1972; W. Burdett, *Encounter with the Middle East,* pp. 254–256; T. Draper, *Israel and World Politics,* pp. 90–91; S. Nakdimon, *Toward the Zero Hour,* pp. 106–108; and R. St. John, *Eban,* pp. 430–434.

113. Israel, Ministry for Foreign Affairs, Cables and Communications, Jerusalem, 1967.

114. Text of the cable, quoted in Eshkol's answer to a parliamentary question: *Divrei Haknesset,* 53, 9 December 1968, pp. 602–603. The Government had in the meantime received Evron's report of his talk with the President. But it was faced with a momentous decision: Every word of what the U.S. President had said counted, and it could only rely on a report of a meeting at the level of diplomats. Neither could it know that—substantially—Johnson repeated to Eban what he had said to Evron.

En route, Eban went to see Arthur Goldberg in New York. Security Council proceedings were coming to nought, he was told. And U Thant had been totally unsuccessful in Cairo, except for Nasser's promise not to start an armed assault. Goldberg stressed that Eban should pay particular attention to what the President himself had said: The alternatives open to America were now so fateful that the President's own words were decisive. At midnight, Eban began his journey back to Israel.

The 26th marked another escalation of the crisis by Egypt. Heikal wrote in his weekly column that morning that war was inevitable because Israel had no choice but to go to war; and hostilities could break out any moment. A more important input to Israel's decision process was Nasser's speech to a delegation of the Damascus-based Arab Workers Conference, which had come to Cairo to inform him of the Conference's resolution. The three significant elements of the speech were: his declaration that the closure of the Straits meant total war with Israel; his emphasis on the readiness of Egyptian and other Arab armed forces to win such a war; and his statement that the aim of the war would be the destruction of Israel—as compared with the aims of restoring the pre-1956 situation and supporting the rights of the Palestinians, stated in his Bir-Gafgafa speech four days earlier.

At UN Headquarters, U Thant submitted a report to the Security Council on the results of his mission to Cairo; his main recommendation was to gain time, a "breathing spell," in order "to allow the Council to deal with the underlying causes of the present crisis and to seek solutions."[115] In spite of the urgency, the Security Council was not convened until 29 May, three days later.

Another noteworthy event on the 26th was an announcement by Cairo Radio, quoting London sources, that a British ship arrived at Jordan's port of Aqaba without having been stopped and searched. Cairo Radio announced a compromise explanation (clearly in line with U Thant's suggestion to Nasser): Ships which pass through the Suez Canal would be allowed to pass through the Straits without inspection.[116]

115. Report of the Secretary-General of the United Nations, U Thant, to the Security Council, S/7906, 26 May 1967, *U.S. Senate Documents*, Doc. 33, p. 213.
116. All those concerned were playing a very careful game in the Straits. Israel had intended to sail a test ship through the Straits, and for this purpose an Israeli crew was flown to Massawa on 25 May. But the action was canceled on the Cabinet's orders: There was American pressure to cancel it, but the main reason was military—the action would have announced to Nasser the beginning of hostilities.

Saturday, 27 May

This day's events began with a concerted, deliberately dramatic move by the Soviet Union in both Israel and Egypt to prevent the outbreak of war. In Israel, the Government sat until after 4 o'clock the next morning (the 28th) to try to decide whether or not to go to war.

At 02:00 on 27 May, Bykov, First Secretary of the Soviet Embassy, phoned Yaffe at the Dan Hotel in Tel Aviv and insisted upon an *immediate* meeting between Eshkol and Ambassador Chuvakhin. The meeting began at 02:35 and lasted until about 4 o'clock in the morning. Levavi, Yaffe, and Bykov were also present.[117] The Ambassador gave Eshkol a Note from Prime Minister Kosygin, whose main passages were:

According to the latest information reaching the Government of the USSR, the tension on the borders of Israel, the UAR and Syria is mounting more and more. . . . It would be a tremendous error if circles eager for battle, unrestrained by serious political thought, gained the upper hand in such a situation, and arms were to begin to talk. We would like to appeal to you to resort to all measures to prevent a military conflict. . . . We are convinced that, however complicated the situation in the area of the borders of Israel, Syria and the UAR may be, it is necessary to find means to resolve the conflicts by non-military means, as it is easy to ignite a fire but putting out its flames may not be nearly as simple as those pushing Israel to the brink of war imagine.[118]

It was the most restrained Soviet official communiqué of the Six Day War Crisis until that date: it did not even mention the standard Soviet accusation that Israel was to blame for the tense situation.[119]

Eshkol replied that Israel had mobilized only in direct response to Egyptian and Syrian threats, and therefore the Soviet Government should direct her pressure toward these governments. But Chuvakhin was rudely insistent: His concern was Israel, and he

117. For details of the meeting, sometimes called the "pajama conference," because Eshkol and Yaffe decided to receive their callers dressed in pajamas, see A. Yaffe, "The War of Twenty-Seven Days," *Nitzoz*, September 1967, and W. Burdett, *Encounter with the Middle East*, pp. 262–264. The conversation took place in Russian.

118. *Jerusalem Post*, 4 June 1967.

119. The tone of Kosygin's letters to Eshkol during the 1967 Crisis was qualitatively more moderate than the harsh threats of destruction, put in the form of an ultimatum, in Bulganin's letter to Ben-Gurion on 5 November 1956. See M. Brecher, *Decisions in Israel's Foreign Policy*, p. 284.

demanded, four times, to know whether Israel would undertake not to fire the first shot. Eshkol would not commit himself. Finally, Israel's Prime Minister totally lost his temper and answered: Egypt had blocked the Straits, and her planes had penetrated over Israel—weren't these "first shots"? If Israel shot down such a plane, would that be the "first shot"? In great anger he told Chuvakhin:

The function of an Ambassador . . . was to promote friendly relations to the best of his ability, with the country to which he was accredited. It did not seem to him that Chuvakhin had cared or tried to do this. Since this was the case, he would be pleased to welcome a Soviet Ambassador who held this conception of his role.[120]

He questioned, sarcastically, the Soviet motives in their support for Syria: "Who are we to be compared with Syria, with its six million socialists?" He offered to travel to Russia, any time, to speak with Soviet leaders, in order to promote Soviet-Israeli friendship.[121]

At 09:30, Eshkol met a group of his colleagues including Meir, Galili, Allon, Sasson, Rabin, Yariv, Herzog, and Levavi to tell them about the "pajama conference."[122] Some interpreted Kosygin's message as an attempt to gain time while closely coordinating Soviet actions with the Egyptians, as proved by Egyptian War Minister Badran's visit to Moscow. Most thought Israel had no choice but to act. Rabin came away from the morning consultations

---

120. W. Burdett, *Encounter with the Middle East,* p. 263.

121. Interview in *Yediot Aharonot,* 7 July 1967. The offer to go to Russia, made —as far as can be established—on the spur of the moment, was taken quite seriously in Moscow. Kosygin notified Nasser, indicating that he would be willing to meet Eshkol, but only if "our Arab friends agree." Nasser, after a meeting with his advisers, in which opinions were divided on the possible effect of such a visit on Egypt's interests, chose a neutral attitude and answered that this concerned the USSR only and depended on her. The Russians finally decided to refuse the offer because it might harm the Soviet Union's position in the Arab world. An early report on these contacts was included in Heikal's weekly article in *Al-Ahram,* 20 October 1967, broadcast over Radio Cairo; BBC, 23 October 1967. A full description is in M. Heikal, "The 1967 Arab-Israeli War," *Sunday Telegraph* (London), 21 October 1973, excerpts in *Ma'ariv,* 9 November 1973.

122. Eshkol's *AB.* The meeting was considered one of the Alignment Political Committee. Part of the Eshkol method of consultations was to invite military leaders to meetings of this party forum. His predecessor, Ben-Gurion, had always insisted on a clear line of demarcation; his Director of Military Intelligence had never been allowed to appear even before the Foreign Affairs and Security Committee of the Knesset.

convinced that Eshkol had made up his mind to go to war; and he hinted at this when he returned to IDF Headquarters.[123] At a meeting of the Knesset Foreign Affairs and Security Committee, called for 11:45, Eshkol reported on his early morning conference with the Soviet Ambassador, thereby informing the Opposition as well.

The Cabinet session of 27 May, in which Israel's decision-makers came close to deciding to go to war, began late in the evening, around 22:30, and lasted for more than six hours. It was attended as well by Dinstein, Rabin, Weizman, Yariv, and Bar-Lev. The very fact of the Cabinet meeting was secret at the time. Parallel to it and in close vicinity, a session of the Knesset Foreign Affairs and Security Committee took place. It lasted until 3:30 the next morning. Eban, who went straight to the Cabinet session on arrival from abroad, around 22:00, attended both meetings and reported to both of them.

The Cabinet first heard reports by Yariv on the military situation and Levavi on international contacts. Eshkol reported on his talk with Chuvakhin. When Eban arrived, he gave a brief review of his talks in Paris and London and a long survey of his discussions in Washington. However, the accumulated information was unable to produce a consensus: The Cabinet divided evenly, 9–9, between those who advocated going to war immediately and those who opted for a further waiting period.

In order to reconstruct the essence—and the atmosphere—of the deliberative process on 27 May, it is well to note the reported views of the principal participants and groups at that meeting.[124] We may begin with Eban, whose report focused and shaped the discussion.

Eban acknowledged his failure to convince de Gaulle of Israel's view of the situation. The United States perceived her interest as vital that Egypt should not achieve a diplomatic victory. At the

123. Bar-Zohar, *Embassies in Crisis*, p. 132.

124. Sources for that Cabinet meeting are: Michael Brecher's interviews with three Cabinet ministers in July–August 1968: Allon, Eban, and Peres; Brecher's interview with H. M. Shapira in July 1968; Eban, *An Autobiography*, pp. 367–368; H. Bar-Lev, Interview, *Yediot Aharonot*, 5 June 1973; M. Begin, "A Chapter from a Book to be Written," *Ma'ariv*, 18 June and 2 July 1971; Eshkol, Interview with the editors of *Ma'ariv*, 4 October 1967; and S. Nakdimon, *Toward the Zero Hour*, pp. 117–123.

same time, there were some suspicions that Israel was trying to involve her in a military confrontation she did not want. American leaders did not promise anything concrete, but they were acting on the matter of the Straits. Wilson would cooperate, outside the UN as well, but only in concert with the U.S. Eban suggested that the Cabinet decide to wait another forty-eight hours. A further round of consultations with the U.S. was necessary because of steps undertaken by the U.S. in the wake of Israel's warning about an impending Egyptian attack. If Israel wanted to pre-empt on the 28th, said Eban, she should not have asked the Americans on the 25th to restrain Egypt.[125]

Eshkol stated that he was against the intervention of a third party; he did not see what another forty-eight hours would give Israel; the powers would continue to advise Israel to wait. Israel's deterrent power was being undermined; if she did not act, it would be considered a sign of weakness. But, as usual, he was willing to listen to what his colleagues had to say. After the war, he declared:

I know that if I would have pressed them I would have received the support of the majority. . . . Had I banged the table and insisted, no one would have resigned from the Government. I did not do that. . . . I do not regret it.[126]

Allon believed that Eban's journey was a mistake; its outcome had limited Israel's freedom of action. Time was working against Israel; and waiting for the international flotilla would lessen considerably Israel's chances for victory; moreover, it would be better if Israel acted alone, as it would have been better in 1956. Again he advocated a pre-emptive strike, and he expressed his certainty that Israel could win, even if she had to fight on three fronts, which he saw as a distinct possibility.[127]

Carmel agreed that a decision not to act would have very dangerous connotations. He felt that there was no prospect whatsoever that the Straits would be reopened. And even if, by some miracle, they were, that would not solve the main problem—the threat of the massed Egyptian troops poised along Israel's southern border.

125. S. Nakdimon, *Toward the Zero Hour*, pp. 119–121; Eban, Interview with M. Brecher, 8 August 1968.

126. Interview with the editors of *Ma'ariv*, 4 October 1967.

127. Y. Allon, "The Last Stage of the War of Independence"; *Curtain of Sand*, pp. 373–377; Interview with M. Brecher, 26 July 1968; Schiff, "The Three Weeks that Preceded the War"; Burdett, *Encounter with the Middle East*, pp. 264–266.

I feared their military initiative. . . . There was the overall military-political view of the necessity for us to take our fate in our own hands and to smash the aggressive Egyptian build-up.[128]

The Allon-Carmel views were opposed by the *Mafdal* and *Mapam* ministers. The former termed the Eban report encouraging; and in any case it would never be too late to fight. The latter agreed that Egypt, not the Straits, was the central problem but argued that Nasser would not attack; there was still time to exhaust diplomatic opportunities.[129]

For immediate action were: Eshkol, Allon, Carmel, Galili, Gvati, Sasson, Y. S. Shapira, Sharef, and Yeshayahu.

For a period of further waiting: Aranne, Barzilai, Bentov, Burg, Eban, Kol, Sapir, H. M. Shapira, and Warhaftig.

Eshkol suggested to his colleagues that they adjourn the deliberations, "sleep it over," and reconvene the next afternoon. This was accepted; though some, along with other political leaders and advisers, continued the discussion with Eshkol for another hour. Several of his colleagues later stated that Eshkol's 27 May behavior —not to press for a decision by a tired group of men—was typical of his essential humanity. His method, what some have termed "open deliberation," was to achieve a broad consensus, particularly on momentous decisions.

The meeting of the Knesset Foreign Affairs and Security Commitee was no less tense. There, too, opinions were sharply divided. Some members from *Mapai, Mafdal,* and *Mapam* supported Eban's suggestion for a further period of waiting. Others did not, arguing that the U.S. would not be able to assure free navigation permanently and that time was running out; they also rejected the American view that the Egyptian build-up was defensive. Deliberations ended as inconclusively as in the Cabinet.

Israel's frontiers were now "coming alive." An IDF border patrol vehicle hit a mine near the Gaza border, and seven soldiers were wounded. From that day on, there were to be almost daily incidents, increasingly violent, in which shots were fired and people were wounded or died.

128. "And Yet: We Were Faced with the Danger of Destruction," *Ma'ariv,* 21 April 1972; "Fighting for Survival—Struggling for Peace," *Davar,* 2 June 1972; and Interview, *Jerusalem Post,* 2 June 1972.
129. M. Bentov, "The Truth and Not 'Nightmares' Are of Educational Value," *Al Hamishmar,* 18 May 1972.

In Washington, there was relative calm after the previous day's feverish activities. Reports which reached Israel that day regarding the maritime action were still optimistic: E. Rostow told Harman that Britain and Holland had joined, and that Canada had promised a ship for the naval patrol; further, that the U.S. would act alone, if necessary. Reports from other capitals showed that Belgium and Norway, too, would sign the statement.

In London, the press was informed that the Cabinet had decided "to go to the UN," without any real hope that anything would come from that step. The British Government was still willing to act outside the UN, together with the U.S., but the latter was not prepared to do so. In Moscow, Kosygin met Badran, the Egyptian War Minister, for the second time. The world was tensely awaiting news from Israel.

Sunday, 28 May

The Israeli Cabinet reconvened at 3 o'clock in the afternoon of the 28th. In the interim, a spate of notes and other inputs to Israel's decision process arrived from abroad: All influenced Eshkol and, later, the Cabinet to opt for a further waiting period of two or three weeks (Decision 12). Of these, the most important were from the United States: a note from Johnson; a despatch from Rusk about Eban's discussions with Johnson and his advisers; and an addendum to this despatch, which was probably the most decisive in influencing Israel's leadership to leave more time for international action in the Straits to materialize. Additional information was contained in cables from Harman on his meeting with E. Rostow and other contacts. Other inputs were a message from Wilson and reports from Israeli Ambassadors Eytan in Paris and Remez in London on their contacts and discussions there.[130]

President Johnson's note was received at 11:00, Israeli time. He wrote that Moscow claimed to have information about Israel's preparations for military action, to provoke a conflict. "The Soviets state that if Israel starts military action, the Soviet Union will extend help to the attacked states." The President repeated his concern about the safety and vital interests of Israel and continued: "As your friend, I repeat even more strongly what I said yesterday to Mr. Eban: Israel just must not take pre-emptive military action

---

130. Eshkol's *AB;* M. Brecher, *Decisions in Israel's Foreign Policy,* pp. 398–400.

and thereby make itself responsible for the initiation of hostilities."[131] The British Prime Minister was more sympathetic. He said, inter alia: "We understand that you have reached the moment of decision. We urgently request you to maintain your attitude of restraint, as long as efforts are being made to solve the problem through diplomatic channels."[132]

The U.S. Secretary of State first despatched to Ambassador Barbour a résumé of Eban's talks in Washington, officially confirming their substance from an American source. Secretary Rusk's report to Ambassador Barbour ended: "During the course of the conversation Eban said: 'Can I take it that I can convey to my Prime Minister that you have decided to make every possible effort to assure that the Straits and the Gulf would be open to free and innocent passage?' The President responded 'yes.'" Only the words *every possible effort* might be construed as differing from Eban's report to the Cabinet: They were less firm than *decided to assure that the Straits would be open.* . . . To Johnson's letter, Rusk instructed Barbour to add the following explanation for Eshkol and Eban:

The British and we are proceeding urgently to prepare the military aspects of the international naval escort plan and other nations are responding vigorously to the idea. The Dutch and Canadians have already joined even before a text was presented to them. With the assurance of international determination to make every effort to keep the Straits open to the flags of all nations, unilateral action on the part of Israel would be irresponsible and catastrophic.[133]

The Israeli Cabinet session on 28 May was relatively short: It began at 15:00 and lasted for two to three hours. Eban reviewed the diplomatic contacts of the preceding hours and stated that Johnson was willing to reopen the Straits, even to do it alone. Several states—the U.K., Canada, and Holland—had already agreed to cooperate. It would take about two to three weeks. Eshkol was not as sanguine, but he agreed that Johnson's message had to be taken into consideration—and that a further waiting period of two to three weeks ought to be accepted in principle, though the

131. Israel, Ministry for Foreign Affairs, 1967, and Eban, *An Autobiography,* p. 370.
132. Bar-Zohar, *Embassies in Crisis,* p. 140.
133. Israel, Ministry for Foreign Affairs, 1967.

IDF would remain mobilized.[134] And there would be a continuous follow-up of Nasser's moves. Should the situation worsen, the Cabinet would be called into session immediately. That suggestion was supported by the *Mafdal* and *Mapam* ministers, while Allon and Carmel expressed doubts about the advantages of further waiting. They were also concerned about the military situation two to three weeks later. In this they were supported by Rabin.[135]

The Cabinet decided to delay military action, taking note of the promise of the President of the United States to undertake efforts to assure freedom of navigation in the Straits. At the same time, it decided to leave in force the mobilization of the reserves and the state of alert in the IDF (Decision 13). Although not formally inscribed as such in the Cabinet's final decision, the decision was to wait at least another two weeks. This is evident from Eshkol's cable to Johnson of 30 May: ". . . The international naval escort should move through the Straits within a week or two." It is also apparent from remarks to E. Rostow and Rusk by Israeli diplomats a few days later.[136]

The decisive role of U.S. pressure on that decision was confirmed by the Prime Minister some months after the Six Day War:

Had we not received Johnson's letter and Rusk's message, I would have urged the Government to make the decision to fight; but their communications pointed out not only that unilateral Israel action would be catastrophic but also that the United States was continuing with its preparations for multilateral action to open the Gulf to shipping of all nations. I could not forget that the latter was signed by the President who had once promised me face-to-face: "We will carry out whatever I ever promise you." I did not want him to come afterwards and say, "I warned you in advance and now you cannot make any claims whatever on the United States and its allies."[137]

The Cabinet also decided to reject the several suggestions voiced by Western states regarding the reactivation of UN machinery; and it empowered the Foreign Minister to attend the meetings of the Security Council, if he deemed it necessary. It also

134. During the day a small number of key personnel, needed on the economic front, were released.

135. Allon, Interview with M. Brecher, 26 July 1968; Carmel, "The Danger of Destruction," *Ma'ariv*, 21 April 1972; "Fighting for Survival," *Davar*, 2 June 1972; Interview, *Jerusalem Post*, 2 June 1972.

136. L. B. Johnson, *The Vantage Point*, p. 294.

137. Interview with the editors of *Ma'ariv*, 4 October 1967.

approved Sapir's journey abroad to organize an emergency financial appeal among world Jewry, to be directed personally by him.[138]
The Opposition was informed of the Cabinet's decisions by Eshkol
and Eban at a meeting of the Knesset Foreign Affairs and Security
Committee which began at 17:30. Begin went on record that the
Opposition was not informed in advance and that the decision to
delay was that of the Government alone.[139]

De Gaulle's answer to Eshkol's letter of 19 May was also delivered on the 28th; but its contents became known *after* the Cabinet
session and thus cannot be considered an input into the Cabinet
decisions of 28 May. President de Gaulle wrote:

> . . . For you the matter at issue is the threat which weighs upon your
> frontiers and the freedom of navigation in the Gulf of Aqaba. Indeed, it
> is legitimate to fear that the situation, suddenly tense and disturbing, in
> the region of which Israel is the geographical center, may deteriorate into
> an armed conflict. However, there is nothing to indicate that either of the
> parties at issue has any interest in such a development. It is not necessary
> for me to say that this is the case with Israel. Your message testifies to
> this fact in the most authorized fashion. It seems to me that this is also
> true for Syria and for Egypt. That is why it is essential in present circum-
> stances that no party should give a pretext for dangerous reactions. . . .
> As for the question of free navigation in the Gulf of Aqaba, I know the
> importance which this has for Israel. In this connection, you know how
> deeply France is attached to the maintenance of the status quo which
> ultimately seems to us to be essential in the Middle East both for Israel
> and for the other states in the region.
>
> My Government has moreover proposed that the four Great Powers
> which are members of the Security Council, should coordinate their
> action on the situation in the Middle East. The need is above all to insure
> that these Powers abstain from intervening in order to impose their own
> solutions; and that none of them undertakes any action or gesture which
> could be interpreted as taking sides. We hope that this initiative will first
> of all support a reduction of tension. Thereafter cooperation between
> these four states should take place for the establishment of peace and the
> settlement of the more burning questions which arise in the Middle
> East.[140]

138. For other sources on the 28 May Cabinet meeting, see L. Eshkol, statement in the Knesset, 29 May 1967; Burdett, *Encounter with the Middle East,*
pp. 266–267; Draper, *Israel and World Politics,* pp. 93–94; Gilboa, *Six Years
—Six Days,* pp. 155–157; and Nakdimon, *Toward the Zero Hour,* pp. 128–
129.
139. Interview, *Yediot Aharonot,* 2 June 1967.
140. Israel, Ministry for Foreign Affairs, 1967.

This letter finally convinced Israel's decision-makers in the Six Day War Crisis that France was advising Israel to acquiesce in Nasser's *fait accompli*. Indeed, the last sentence implied even further pressure, for, according to the Arabs, the "most burning question" in the Middle East was the very existence of the State of Israel, termed by Nasser a nineteen-year-old aggression.

The Cabinet also decided to inform the nation and the world of its delay decision and entrusted Eshkol, Eban, and Galili to draft the announcement. Eshkol broadcast the announcement live over *Kol Yisrael* at 20:30. The substantive contents were almost forgotten in Israel's history. What remained etched in everyone's memory was its mode of delivery and the disastrous effect it had on the nation's morale. The worst incident of the delivery was described thus:

"Furthermore," continues Eshkol, "lines of action were decided for the removal . . ." Eshkol suddenly stops. His breathing can be heard, picked up well by the sensitive mike, as well as his whisper: "What's this?" The word "removal" does not please him. And thus he includes in his deliberations his listeners who are in a state of high tension. He changes the word to "movement" (of military concentrations on the southern border of Israel).[141]

Eshkol's trials were not yet over. The Prime Minister knew that since the morning of 27 May, the General Staff had been expecting the decision to go to war: In contacts during the last two days, they had been led to understand that such a decision was imminent. Eshkol now had to tell them that the Cabinet had opted for further delay. Rabin told him that, as Defense Minister, it was his duty to inform them of the Government's decision. Eshkol proceeded to General Staff Headquarters, where most of Israel's military leaders

141. Nakdimon, *Toward the Zero Hour*, p. 130. The "stammering" incident came after days of mounting tension, with all of Israel—and the world—listening for the authoritative statement of what the Government of Israel intended to do. The mood of Israel's public, under the pressure of virulent assaults by Arab media of communication, was that Israel was faced with the question of survival. The announcement—the first one by Eshkol to the nation—came after days of attacks on him for his "hesitancy" and "indecisiveness" in the nation's hour of crisis. The mode of delivery seemed to underline this and strengthened the hands of the Opposition in their claim that Eshkol was not the right man to lead a nation fighting for its very existence. Many participants in the 1967 decision process testified after the War to the "disastrous" effect of this incident on public morale and as a contributory factor to the ouster of Eshkol from the Ministry of Defense.

were assembled, waiting for him. He was, as yet, completely unaware of the effect of his radio broadcast. He explained the reasons
for the Cabinet decision; again he emphasized the importance of
not isolating Israel, of securing the cooperation of the Western
powers. He also told them of his confrontation with the Soviet Ambassador. Then he asked for their opinions freely: "You can and
should say anything you like to me. Talk as if you were out of
uniform."[142]

Despite the previous indicators of dissatisfaction with the Government's hesitation, particularly among field commanders—the
25 May confrontation and Rabin's obvious reluctance to inform his
colleagues—Eshkol was totally unprepared for the storm that
broke. He was told by Sharon, M. Peled, and Avraham Yaffe—
with Allon, Rabin, and Bar-Lev standing aside silently—that there
was no way to avoid war any more and that every day that passed
might increase the losses. The generals expressed their concern
with the effect of further waiting on the IDF's and the public's
morale, and the possible effect on the enemy; and Yariv particularly stressed the dangers of a first Egyptian strike. Eshkol, clearly
shaken, tried to reassure the generals. According to Bar-Lev, he
answered substantially thus: "We have to have patience. I am sorry
that you feel the way you do. It is necessary to continue negotiations, in order to exhaust all other possibilities, before going to
war. This was also necessary in order to avoid a repetition of the
post-Suez [1956] Crisis, when Israel was forced to withdraw."[143]
After he left, he held another meeting with his Alignment colleagues (at 22:30), where again the Cabinet's decision was discussed.

In Egypt, the central event of 28 May was Nasser's press conference, broadcast live over Cairo Radio. It was one of his most brilliant performances. Incisive, biting and sarcastic, moving at times,
baring his teeth at the Western powers, particularly the United

---

142. Practically everybody who took part in that meeting has since published
—mostly in interview form—his version of what happened. While early descrip-
tions of this meeting as the "Revolt of the Generals" are nonsense, it was traumatic for all concerned, as attested to by most of the accounts. See Eshkol interview
with the editors of Ma'ariv, 4 October 1967; Yaffe, "The War of Twenty-Seven
Days"; Bar-Lev, Interview, Ma'ariv, 6 May 1973, and Yediot Aharonot, 5 June
1973; and A. Sharon, Interview, Ma'ariv, 20 July 1973, and Yediot Aharonot,
20 July 1973. Bar-Lev stated in his Ma'ariv interview that most of the generals
did not listen to Eshkol's radio statement before the meeting but they had heard
the reactions to it.
143. Interview, Yediot Aharonot, 5 June 1973.

States, he projected total confidence in the will and capacity of Egypt and the Arab world, and in the righteousness of their cause. While restating, in substance, the extreme Egyptian position—the threat to the very existence of Israel—he managed to avoid giving it an extreme formulation and even succeeded in putting the onus for a probable outbreak of war on Israel, leaving some doors open for possible ad hoc accommodation.[144]

Washington, on the surface, was relatively quiet on Sunday, 28 May. The Israeli Embassy was swamped with queries: "When will you react?"

NATO Headquarters in Paris and Brussels were put on a state of alert.

III. Resolution: 29 May–4 June

The deliberations of the week before the outbreak of war were dominated by Israel's domestic political crisis: This left very little time and energy for the critical foreign policy issues. The rest of the world seemed ready to accept the altered balance of power in the Middle East, with jubilation in one camp, resignation in the other. The momentum for action by the maritime states clearly had petered out by the end of that week, and all alternatives involved some compromise solution at the expense of Israel's vital interests in the Gulf of Aqaba. This final phase of the crisis period was divided in two: 29 May–1 June, characterized by growing pressure to form a National Unity Government, with Dayan as Minister of Defense; and 2–4 June, during which the decision process to go to war was consummated.

Monday, 29 May

The Israeli press reported Eshkol's stuttering radio broadcast, emphasizing its negative effect on morale. Even the pro-government daily *Davar* carried calls for a widening of the Government and for the co-option of Ben-Gurion or Dayan into the Government. In the late afternoon, Eshkol informed the Knesset that Israel had opted for a further waiting period and was continuing her diplomatic efforts. After describing the events of the previous week, he stated:

144. *Documents on Palestine*, pp. 328, 549.

The Government of Israel has repeatedly stated its determination to exercise its freedom of passage in the Straits of Tiran and the Gulf of Aqaba, and to defend it in case of need. This is a supreme national interest on which no concession is possible and no compromise is admissible.[145]

In Cairo, Nasser reaffirmed his ultimate aims in his last major policy statement before the Six Day War: "Just as we have been able to restore the pre-1956 situation, we shall certainly, with God's help, be able to restore the pre-1948 situation. . . . We want the full and undiminished rights of the people of Palestine."[146] In Syria, President Attasi, accompanied by Foreign Minister Makhus and Information Minister Muhammad Zubi, left for what even Radio Damascus termed a "hasty" visit to Moscow.

Conflicting signals reached Israel from the United States on the 29th. Rusk was continuing his efforts to mobilize wide support for the maritime declaration. Walt Rostow assured Harman that the maritime action plan was serious and that it would be transmitted the same day for President Johnson's approval, after which it would take ten to fourteen days to finalize detailed plans. On the other hand, Eugene Rostow, in his contacts with Harman and Evron, kept on emphasizing the Straits issue, thus minimizing what Israel now perceived to be her dominant problem—a direct military threat.

In New York, the Security Council convened for another inconclusive meeting. Elsewhere, West Germany finally informed Israel that the gas masks she sought would be delivered. And the French notified Israel that the USSR had turned down the four-power consultation formula because of disinterest on the part of the Arabs and U.S. involvement in Vietnam. That day, too, a Liberian tanker under an American captain tried to force the blockade. He disregarded Egyptian warnings and changed course only after an Egyptian torpedo boat fired a warning shot.

Tuesday, 30 May

The major event on the 30th was King Hussein's dramatic journey to Cairo and the signing of the UAR-Jordan Defense Agreement. In Israel, the internal crisis was reaching its climax; by then it dominated Eshkol's activities.[147]

145. *Divrei Haknesset*, 49, 2283–2285. The quotation is from Christman, ed., *The State Papers of Levi Eshkol*, pp. 95–104.

146. *Documents on Palestine*, p. 564.

147. Eshkol's *AB* shows that of his nineteen meetings on that day, twelve were with party leaders and personalities involved in the internal political crisis.

Early in the morning, Eshkol asked Eban to hold a press conference in order to clarify Israel's determination not to wait too long
for U.S. and/or Western action in reopening the Straits. He also
entrusted Eban with drafting a reply to President Johnson's letter
of 28 May. There were by now clear signs that U.S. "action," in the
sense of the use of force, was becoming more and more illusory.
Moreover, Harman cabled that contacts with several other maritime states—Canada, Denmark, and Norway—had shown that
support for the use of force had quickly evaporated—and that
Israel would be offered economic aid to compensate for the strain
of mobilization and waiting.

Uncertainty about U.S. intentions led Eshkol to decide to send
Meir Amit, the head of Israel's Intelligence Service, to Washington
(Decision 14). As Amit later recalled:

The American intentions were not clear; better stated, there was not
sufficient light. I believed that I could fathom their real intentions, and I
succeeded in this. A second aim of my mission was to make the Americans
realize, in direct contact, the seriousness of the situation, to make them
see that Israel had been forced into a situation where there was no way
out, and hear their reactions. Both aims were fully achieved: it became
clear that here, in Israel, there existed certain misperceptions. It became
totally clear that they [the U.S.] were not planning to do a thing.[148]

Eban's press conference was held around noon. He emphasized
the problems of the Straits and the "build-up of Egyptian troops on
the Israel frontier" and, repeatedly, the importance for Israel that
"these changes be rescinded . . . within the shortest possible
time." If international action would not materialize, Israel reserved
for herself the right of self-defense: "Normal rationality suggests a
policy: alone if we must, with others if we can." The press conference was also an occasion for an unparalleled attack by Eban on the
United Nations, and specifically on U Thant's decisions.[149]

In the afternoon, Eban formulated Eshkol's reply to Johnson,
which was sent the same day. The Prime Minister stated:

148. Interview with B. Geist, 13 July 1973. Amit was one of Eshkol's closest
advisers at the time and one of his main sources of information. Eshkol saw him
that day (the 30th) three times. Bitan, in an interview with M. Brecher on 8
August 1968, added a somewhat different reason for the Amit mission: "There
was a search for insight into Johnson's mind. We could not ask Johnson directly;
he would have had to say no. But we had to know. The U.S. and the USSR were
in communication, but we were not sure of what they said to each other." Amit's
contacts were with Pentagon and CIA circles, whose views were different from
White House policy.
149. Israel Government Press Office, 30 May 1967.

A point is being approached at which counsels to Israel will lack any moral or logical basis. I feel that I must make it clear in all candour that the continuation of this position for any considerable time is out of the question. . . . It is crucial that the international naval escort should move through the Straits within a week or two.

Eshkol reminded the President of commitments made a few days earlier and in 1957. He also stressed that history showed the futility of trying to appease an "aggressive dictator."[150]

The signing of the UAR-Jordan Defense Agreement—which placed Jordan's armed forces under Egyptian command—came as another surprise and shock to Israel's decision-makers. It caused a flurry of military consultations in the afternoon and gave added urgency to Amit's mission. Five years after the SDW, Rabin stated that "in my opinion Israel should have fought on the 30th of May."[151] And Eban recalled: "By his journey to Cairo on May 30 Hussein had made it certain that war would break out."[152] The Opposition was informed, as usual, at a meeting of the Knesset Foreign Affairs and Security Committee.

By the night of the 30th, Coalition and Opposition parties had practically united on the need for a National Unity Government. Only Eshkol himself and *Mapam* still held out. Nerves were strained to the breaking point. The following incident was symbolic of the atmosphere existing at the time: Michael Hazani, Member of the Knesset (MK) for the *Mafdal* (and later, Minister for Social Welfare), returned to the Knesset from a day-long tour of southern border settlements and started shouting in the corridors: "This cannot go on any longer. . . . The army is breaking up. . . . What are you doing? . . . Take a decision, and quickly. . . ." And Carmel told a group of Alignment Ministers and MK's standing in the corridors: "Everything is on fire. What are you discussing? What is it you are holding on to? There is no solution without the enlargement of the Government!"[153]

Messages of congratulation poured into Egypt from Arab governments, with the notable exceptions of Syria and Saudi Arabia. Hussein publicly invited Iraqi troops into Jordan, and President Aref agreed. Morocco promised to send troops. Rashid Karame,

150. Israel, Ministry for Foreign Affairs, 1967.
151. "Six Days and Five More Years," *Ma'ariv*, 2 June 1972.
152. Eban, *An Autobiography*, p. 380, and Interview with M. Brecher, 8 August 1968.
153. Nakdimon, *Toward the Zero Hour*, pp. 169, 170.

the Premier of Lebanon, came out with a strong statement of support. In Washington, the Israeli Embassy was informed by the
State Department that preparations for the formation of a multi-
national naval force, as well as the declaration in support of free
passage, were in an advanced state. Letters had been sent to
twenty-five states, and the Administration was now awaiting their
reactions. The significance of the sharp drop from the U.S. plan to
approach ninety states on 26 May could not have been lost. In New
York, the Security Council continued its futile debate. In Paris, official circles remained silent. In London, the British Cabinet, at its
weekly meeting, decided to soften its determined stand on action
to open the Straits, in the face of American hesitancy. Another significant development was the growing, shadowy confrontation between the naval forces of the two superpowers in the eastern
Mediterranean. Publicity was given to the fact that the main force
of the Sixth Fleet was concentrated in the Sea of Crete. The Fleet
was now within easy striking distance of the center of the conflict:
370 miles from Egypt, much less from Syria—one day's steaming
distance for warships, twenty minutes' flight time for many of the
planes on board the carriers. The Turkish authorities announced
that, in the first week of June, ten Soviet warships would pass
through the Dardanelles, on their way to the Mediterranean.

Wednesday, 31 May

This was a day of quiet, intense diplomacy in the capitals of the
world. In Israel, the domestic political crisis dominated. The main
inputs into her foreign-policy process were the news, evaluations,
and aftereffects of the Egypt-Jordan Defense Pact, and the weakening of the resolve on the reopening of the Straits. Israeli press
editorials that day and the next all dealt with the Pact, underlining
its serious implications.[154]

At 11:00, there began a long session of the Alignment's Political
Committee, which included members of the Cabinet and other

154. *The Jerusalem Post's* editorial of 1 June was entitled "Hussein Admits the
Wolf"; *Davar's* editorial of 31 May, entitled "Hussein with Nasser," stated that
"there is no doubt that Israel has to consider this development as a strengthening
of the threat to its well-being and to take it into account in all its political and
military activities. . . ." *Ha'aretz* echoed the same theme on 31 May: "Egyptian
Jordanian Defense Pact—A Sign of the Times." And the next day, Z. Schiff,
Ha'aretz's military correspondent, wrote about the "Danger from the East": "Our
deterrent power has been undermined not only in the eyes of the Arabs and ourselves, but in the eyes of friends as well, those near and far away."

party leaders. By now, it was clear to all but Eshkol himself that a new Minister of Defense had to be appointed. Eshkol met Dayan at 16:30 and offered to appoint him as Deputy Prime Minister, but Dayan refused: He was not interested in an advisory position; if he could not be responsible for defense matters, he preferred to serve in the IDF, for example, as Commander of the Southern Front. Eshkol accepted the suggestion, and by evening he received Rabin's reluctant agreement to replace Gavish with Dayan. For a few hours, Eshkol believed that his troubles were over.[155]

In Washington, disagreement was evident when W. Rostow called Evron to the White House to discuss a passage in Eshkol's letter of the previous day: It referred to "the assurances that the United States would take any and all measures to open the Straits of Tiran to international shipping." The President was disturbed by this formulation, which did not reflect accurately what he had said to Eban, since such a commitment went beyond presidential pre-rogative. Evron asserted that the statement was based upon a verba-tim report of the Johnson-Eban conversation prepared by Harman immediately after the meeting on 26 May. He added that these statements, reinforced by the letter from Rusk, particularly his addendum to the President's letter, which all reflected the same policy, had been decisive in Israel opting for a further waiting period on 28 May. The matter was not pursued any further, but the nature of the query itself, and its source, again cast doubts on the strength of the U.S. commitment.[156]

There were other disquieting indicators of the U.S. position. Rusk reportedly told the House of Representatives Foreign Affairs Committee that Washington was not planning any unilateral move, but only within the framework of the UN. And Goldberg stated in the Security Council that the purpose of a fresh U.S. resolution

155. Gavish stated in an interview in *Yediot Aharonot*, 3 April 1970, that Rabin informed him only at 6 o'clock the next morning, even then most reluctantly, that he would be replaced by Dayan; and Gavish refused point-blank to serve as Dayan's second-in-command, even when ordered to do so by Rabin. "I told him that under no circumstances would I do so. I got up, saluted and left." This was confirmed by Bar-Lev. Rabin's reluctance to accept the suggestion was also men-tioned by M. Peled in "The Beauty Is Untouched," *Ma'ariv*, 15 June 1973.

156. Dayan's version is in his *Story of My Life*, p. 268; and in Israel, Ministry for Foreign Affairs, 1967. There was, in fact, a substantial difference in the exact phrase used. The American version, as transmitted by Rusk on 28 May, referred to "every possible effort," while the Eshkol letter, as noted, referred to "any and all measures."

was "to insure a cooling-off period . . . without prejudice to the ultimate rights or claims of any party."[157] In London, Wilson and Brown made extensive statements in the House of Commons on the crisis, revealing a cautious retreat from the Prime Minister's Margate speech on 24 May. The Soviets continued to give all-out public verbal support to the Arab cause. However, in private contacts with Israeli and American diplomats they stressed their desire for a diplomatic solution of the crisis.

Thursday, 1 June

This was the day when Israel's internal agony ended: Everybody —including Eshkol—gave a sigh of relief and settled down to deal with a threat that most decision-makers and the public perceived as an issue of Israel's survival. It was well characterized thus:

Thursday, 1 June 1967, will be recorded as the longest day of Israel's first twenty years of existence. Every second was like 24 hours. The citizens of Israel wherever they were—the citizens of the home front, the regular and reserve soldiers on the front—are like a spring coiled to its utmost point of resistance. Nasser continues in his mad rush toward the borders of Israel and the news arriving from Washington underlines the weakening of hopes for the creation of an international naval force, supposed to break through the Straits.[158]

It was also the day that Eban withdrew his opposition to military action. There were several reasons. First, since 28 May there had been no U.S. pressure on Israel to wait for any length of time. Secondly, there was the Egypt-Jordan agreement and the encirclement of Israel, which "had shortened all previous ideas of the time available for an impending storm." Thirdly, the days of waiting had achieved their desired results—military action now by Israel would be greeted with relief, not condemnation, in most Western capitals. And finally, Amit's first report arrived on 1 June, stating: "From hints and scattered facts that I have heard, I get the impression that the maritime force project is running into heavier water every hour."[159]

By the time the *Mapai* Secretariat convened, at 10:00 on 1 June, several of its members had been informed by Peres that Dayan

157. *New York Times,* 1 June 1967.
158. Nakdimon, *Toward the Zero Hour,* p. 202.
159. Israel, Ministry for Foreign Affairs, 1967. Eban stated in an interview in *Ma'ariv,* 2 June 1972, that Amit, in his preliminary report, also wrote: "There is a growing chance for American political backing if we act on our own."

would accept the Ministry of Defense. Finally, in the afternoon, after further meetings with Coalition colleagues and Opposition leaders, and continuous reports about the debate in the Secretariat —all indicating the wish for the appointment of Dayan—Eshkol yielded. In a meeting at 16:15 hours, he offered the Defense Ministry to Dayan, either as a representative of *Rafi* or in his personal capacity, and Dayan accepted—on both counts. At 17:15, at a meeting of the Alignment ministers, Allon announced that, for the sake of national unity, he withdrew his candidacy for the Defense portfolio. Then Eshkol announced his decision to transfer it to Dayan. The decision was submitted to, and approved by, the *Mapai* Secretariat, which reassembled at 20:00 hours to hear Eshkol's further report. It was also approved in the *Rafi* caucus, which met about the same time in Ben-Gurion's home.[160]

The Cabinet met at 21:30 to formally approve the creation of the National Unity Government (Decision 15). And at 22:00, Dayan and Begin, the latter as Minister-designate Without Portfolio, joined the meeting. (The second representative of *Gahal*, Y. Saphir of the Liberal faction, joined the Cabinet deliberations the next day.) Eshkol and Eban reviewed the political situation, and Rabin gave a military account. After a brief exchange of views, the Cabinet decided to postpone the discussion of military matters to a meeting of the Ministerial Defense Committee, set for the morning of 2 June. Dayan, however, stated that if it would be decided not to attack, then 50 percent of the reserves ought to be released and the rest should dig in. This would also mean acceptance of the fact of the closure of the Straits.

In Cairo, Nasser met with Robert Anderson, President Johnson's personal emissary. Anderson left the same day for Lisbon and reported from there to Johnson that there was little chance to persuade Nasser to accept any compromise on the Straits. The concrete outcome of the meeting was that the U.S. and the UAR agreed to an exchange of vice-presidential visits, suggested by Johnson in his letter to Nasser of 22 May: Zahariyah Muhi-a-Din of Egypt would visit Washington on 7 June, with Humphrey's return visit

160. The events of those days made Eshkol bitter toward his colleagues. He felt betrayed by them, that they did not appreciate his role as Defense Minister during the four years he held the post, and that they lost their nerve under pressure. Always a skeptical man, he now trusted no one. For a good summary—pro-Eshkol—see A. Tzimouki, "Eshkol As I Knew Him," *Yediot Aharonot*, 25 February 1972.

thereafter to follow soon. Although the meeting was arranged secretly, it soon leaked to the press and became known to the Israeli Embassy in Washington the same day.

It was becoming clearer that the maritime force was breaking up before it ever assembled. Wilson arrived in Ottawa to try to persuade Canada to join the international maritime force with two destroyers. Pearson, under the pressure of sharp Egyptian protests, had by now retreated from his previous position of strong support for the freedom of navigation. In Washington, Rusk, leaving a meeting of the Senate Foreign Relations Committee, stated that the U.S. had no immediate plans to test the blockade or to act unilaterally. Both Rusk and Humphrey emphasized on that occasion the importance of action through the UN. E. Rostow again anxiously asked Harman about any Israeli intentions to send a ship through the Straits, stressing once more that the President had not yet decided what to do next. He also re-emphasized that it was a vital U.S. interest not only to prevent an Arab-Israeli war but also to prevent a diplomatic victory for Nasser, for that would endanger all the pro-Western Arab régimes, particularly Saudi Arabia.

At UN Headquarters there was intensive activity behind the scenes. Rafael met with Hans Tabor, President of the Security Council, and tried to persuade him to terminate the debate the next day; but Denmark's representative stated that it could not do so without a resolution, and there was no hope of arriving at one so soon. Rafael also tried (unsuccessfully) to persuade Lord Caradon not to submit a draft resolution which would touch upon the basic problems of the Arab-Israeli dispute. It was stopped only on Wilson's direct orders, after an Israeli intervention in London.

Friday, 2 June

The Ministerial Committee on Defense met from 09:15 until noon, with Eshkol, Allon, Dayan, Eban, Rabin, and their advisers continuing discussions for another hour. Present, too, were most of the IDF commanders. Yariv began with a report on the military situation. Then Rabin gave an overall view of Israel's military plans; the emphasis was on a decisive blow to the Egyptian army, with Sharm-e-Sheikh incidental to the strategic plan. Jordan's entry into a war was also considered a possibility. But in all these presentations, the focus was not on what the military aims were, but on how to achieve them. The implications of the plans were a deep thrust into Sinai and then action according to developments;

but no one spoke of how far the IDF should advance or where it should stop. Begin described the atmosphere at the meeting thus:

The commanders . . . revealed their basic concern that every additional day without a decision would increase our losses when the hour of implementation arrived. They had no doubts of victory. They expressed their belief not only in the strength of the army but also in its ability to rout the enemy.[161]

Again there was no decision. Begin asserted later that, after leaving the meeting, he and Dayan agreed they would leave the Cabinet if a decision were not taken.

Dayan devoted the rest of 2 June to briefings at Army Headquarters. There is consensus that his appointment gave a tremendous boost to the country's morale, including the High Command and the army: It was interpreted as a sign of Israel's determination to resist encroachment upon her vital interests. What is also certain is that the decision to break the Egyptain army with an all-out attack and then to occupy Sharm-e-Sheikh was finalized on the 2nd and subsequent days.[162]

The military plans of Israel and the changes effected during the crisis were summarized by the IDF historian as follows:

Two plans for counter-attacks were prepared in the period between the evacuation of UNEF and the closure of the Straits: a limited and a broad one. The starting point of both was the destruction of the Egyptian air force by surprise, and the difference lay in the deployment of ground forces. The broad plan envisaged the occupation of the forward area of Sinai, while avoiding a frontal attack on the Um Katef–Abu Ageila strongholds; while the limited one was directed toward the occupation of the Gaza Strip alone. After the blockade of the Straits by Abd el-Nasser, Prime Minister and Minister of Defense Levi Eshkol was presented with a plan to advance along the Northern axis, until the Suez Canal. . . . With this, the limited plan was put aside. . . . The final plan, which was approved by Defense Minister Moshe Dayan on June 2, 1967, stipulated— because of calculations connected with the "political clock" ticking away— a minimal span of time between the air force's first strike and the first breach of the ground forces in the Egyptian arena. The phase after the first breach was not planned in detail. In a plan of operations, prepared by Yitzhak Hofi, the Chief of the Operations Department, all that was

---

161. "The Meeting of 2 June 1967," *Ma'ariv,* 2 June 1972.

162. The role that Dayan played in influencing the outcome of the war was hotly debated in Israel. There is no question that he had a great influence in crystalizing military plans, but what remains controversial is whether or not the same decisions would have been taken anyway.

stated was that in the breaching phase, the forces are to establish a line—
not east of the line of El Arish–G'ebel Livni, i.e., short of the Canal and to
be in a stage of preparedness for moving toward the Suez Canal and
Sharm-e-Sheikh.[163]

To this should be added that, according to Ezer Weizman, Chief of
Operations, the broad plan was presented to Eshkol, there was a
consensus, but nothing was formally decided. Further, Gavish,
OC Southern Command, has stated that the limited plan was actually put aside on 2 June, under the impact of Dayan's appointment. And Sharon, OC of one of the three corps on the southern
front, stated that Dayan also decided, on assuming office, to order a
simultaneous advance by all three corps, along three axes, instead
of the existing plan of advancing along the northern axis (Decision
16).[164] Dayan was to write later about his dissatisfaction with existing IDF plans as early as 23 May, especially the concentration on
capturing the Gaza Strip, which "was not an outright military target" and would not attain the key goal—the destruction of much of
Egyptian military strength. He repeated these objections to Major-
General Amit, Head of *Ha-Mossad,* on the evening of the 26th.
And on 2 June, at a meeting of the inner circle—Eshkol, Eban,
Allon, and Rabin—he urged a full-scale attack on the 5th, "to destroy the Egyptian forces concentrated in central Sinai. We should
have no geographical aim whatsoever and we should not include
the Gaza Strip in our fighting plans. . . ." Just before that, he told
the General Staff that he envisaged a two-stage campaign—"first,
capture of northern Sinai; second, capture of the Straits and
Sharm-e-Sheikh."[165]

Another element of the public argument about Dayan's role revolved around the decision to go to war, with Dayan and Begin
and, more vociferously, their supporters claiming that the Cabinet's hesitancy came to an end with their entry.[166] Dayan's appointment made such a decision inevitable and possibly accelerated the
decision process.

On the evening of the 2nd, members of the Government fanned
out all over the country to inform and calm the public: The people

163. *Encyclopedia Hebraica,* vol. 23, p. 726.
164. See Weizman, Interview, *Ma'ariv,* 5 June 1973; Gavish, Interview, *Yediot
Aharonot,* 3 April 1970; and Sharon, Interview, *Yediot Aharonot,* 20 July 1973.
165. *Story of My Life,* pp. 256–258, 264, 271.
166. Dayan, Interview, *Yediot Aharonot,* 16 June 1967, and M. Begin, "A
Chapter from a Book to be Written," *Ma'ariv,* 18 June and 2 July 1971.

needed reassurances, and the proven valor of Dayan satisfied this yearning. Reports from all parts of the world served to reinforce the belief that the time for diplomatic efforts was over. A Note from the Soviet Government was more menacing than Kosygin's letter of 26 May. Although repeating Kosygin's statement that "the Soviet Government desires once again to state that it will do everything possible to prevent an armed clash," it continued with a threat: ". . . but if the Government of Israel should decide to take upon itself the responsibility for the outbreak of war, it will have to pay the price in full."[167] No less worrying was an official statement issued at noon in Paris, after a meeting of the French Cabinet. Bearing the unmistakable imprint of de Gaulle, it read:

La France n'est engagée à aucun titre ni sur aucun suject avec aucun des Etats en cause. De son propre chef, elle considéré que chacun de ces états a la droit de vivre. Mais, elle estime que le pire serait l'overture des hostilités. En conséquence l'Etat qui le premier et où que ce soit, emplorait les armes n'aurait ni son approbation ni, a plus forte raison, son appui.

[France is not involved in any form nor in any way with any of the States concerned. On her part, she considers that each of these States has a right to live. But, in her opinion the touchstone will be the opening of hostilities. As a result, the state which will be the first to open hostilities will have neither her approval nor her acclaim.][168]

The French Cabinet also decided to declare an embargo on arms deliveries to the Middle East, officially effective as of 5 June, but in fact, in some cases of equipment, effective immediately. The delivery of planes to Israel was stopped; that of spare parts and other vital equipment would now depend on the individual goodwill of French officials and the interests of the French High Command. It was yet another event that limited the perceived time available for action by Israel and thus achieved exactly the opposite effect of what de Gaulle intended. In Washington, the major event of that day was Wilson's talk with Johnson, with no joint communiqué being issued.

It was decided to bring Ambassador Harman back to Israel the same day to report the results of his discussions with U.S. officials. Harman asked that any decision be held up until his arrival, al-

167. A. Dagan, *Moscow and Jerusalem: Twenty Years of Relations Between Israel and the Soviet Union* (London, 1970), pp. 223–224.
168. *Documents on Palestine*, pp. 49–50.

though he already hinted guardedly that his report would not include new, positive developments. At the Israeli Embassy in Washington, Harman, Amit, and Evron had a final consultation about the Harman-Amit report to the Cabinet. All three agreed that their advice had to be that there was no alternative to war.[169] Just before he left for Israel, Harman had a final meeting with Rusk and E. Rostow. Although the Americans continued to assure him that the maritime plan was going well, that within seven to nine days plans would be completed, and that the Australians had promised ships for the naval patrol, there were also disquieting equivocations in their views on Soviet intentions and the probable U.S. response, and the interpretation of the 1957 American "commitments," regarding the Straits.

In Moscow, Gromyko again warned Israel, through Ambassador Katz, not to start a war and that Israel was endangering her future with her aggressive policy. In Paris, the French continued to insist that Nasser would not escalate further, that a compromise on the Straits could be achieved, and that the Soviet Union would have to play a decisive role in negotiations and ought to be persuaded to work together with the U.S. toward a reduction of tension.

Saturday, 3 June

Several crucial inputs—from the Near East core, the U.S., and France—crystalized the resolve taken at an ad hoc meeting of Israel's political and bureaucratic elites to propose military action at the Cabinet meeting, scheduled for the next day. At the same time, Dayan and his associates made an effort to create the impression that Israel would wait a little longer, a week or two, in order to regain the basis for tactical surprise. These efforts succeeded brilliantly.

Of all the rumors, statements, and declarations emanating from Arab sources about the flow of reinforcements to the fronts, one solid fact emerged that day: an Iraqi armored division had entered Jordan on its way to the Israeli border. This was perceived as a clear and present danger.

Another letter arrived on the 3rd from Johnson, in answer to Eshkol's letter of 30 May. The President again emphasized as "vital national interests of the United States" the right of free and innocent passage through international waterways, of which the Gulf of

169. Evron, Interview with M. Brecher, 3 March 1972.

Aqaba was one, and the territorial integrity and political independence of all countries in the Middle East. But there was no specific commitment for immediate U.S. action. On the contrary, Johnson repeated his warning: "I must emphasize the necessity for Israel not to make itself responsible for the initiation of hostilities; Israel will not be alone, unless it decides to go alone."[170] On the possibility of naval action the President was vague.

Harman and Amit arrived from Washington in the afternoon. Harman's full report about his contacts with the American Administration again showed that measures to be taken by the maritime powers were still under consideration but that nothing had been firmly decided. The evening meeting was held at Eshkol's Jerusalem home, beginning at 23:00. Present were: Allon, Dayan, Eban, Dinstein, Rabin, Yadin, Amit, Yariv, Herzog, Levavi, and Harman. The central issue was whether or not the United States and the Soviet Union would be aligned on the same side, against Israel, if hostilities began. Although Harman expressed the view that Israel ought to wait another week, because of the U.S. belief that they had been given that much time to complete their plans, there was a broad consensus that nothing further could be gained from additional waiting. Amit concurred and the day's events tended to support this assessment. Further, Amit's judgment was that if Israel decided to act alone, the U.S. would not resist. Those present agreed with Eshkol's and Eban's view that the U.S. would extend diplomatic support in the aftermath. There was also agreement that the Soviet Union would not intervene militarily.[171]

Military plans, too, were discussed at the meeting, especially those approved the previous day by Dayan. "It was decided to stage for the time being a holding operation against the Syrians in the North, and not to attack Jordan unless Jordan attacked first. . . . The main blow was to be directed against the Egyptians."[172] The meeting ended with unanimous agreement to recommend to the Cabinet the next day the decision to go to war.

170. Israel, Ministry for Foreign Affairs, 1967.

171. Israel, Ministry for Foreign Affairs, 1967, confirmed that Israel's decision-makers were by now convinced that the Soviet Union would not intervene directly; this was also confirmed in Herzog's interview with M. Brecher, 10 August 1968; Allon's interview with Brecher, 26 July 1968; and Amit's interview with B. Geist, 13 July 1973.

172. Laqueur, *The Road to War*, p. 158.

During that day (3 June), thousands of soldiers, released for the weekend, joined the crowds at the beaches, thus becoming a visible sign of relaxation of tension. Dayan, in personal meetings with correspondents, as well as in his two press conferences—one public, at 16:00, immediately followed by one for military correspondents—succeeded in convincing a hardened audience that war was not imminent; many of them so reported and left Israel the next day. Dayan's press conference was attended by hundreds of reporters and was immediately broadcast all over the world. Two of his statements made a particular impact on his audience. Asked about the loss of time because of the "long drawn out diplomatic action," he answered:

I accept the situation as it is. I know it is always easy to say last week we were in a better position. This is not the point. The point, I should think just now, is that it is more or less a situation of being too late or too early— too late to react regarding our chances in the military field—on the blockading of the Straits of Tiran—and too early to draw conclusions as to the diplomatic way of handling the matter.

On promises given by other governments, he stated:

I do not know whether we got such promises or not, but let me say that I, personally, do not expect and do not want anyone else to fight for us. Whatever can be done in the diplomatic way I would welcome and encourage, but if somehow it comes to real fighting I would not like American or British boys to get killed here, and I do not think we need them.[173]

At his meeting with military correspondents, he again emphasized the element of further waiting: "The Government of Israel had decided upon diplomatic steps and you have to give this a chance. Until when? Until the Government decides."[174]

In Washington, General Wheeler had told the President the previous day that war was now inevitable and that Israel would be victorious within two weeks, but the toll of destruction might be quite heavy. In New York, Wilson met with U Thant for two hours. Again, during a press conference, his statements were noncommittal. The problem was that of averting disaster; the matter was urgent, but he had no timetable for the issuing of the maritime declaration. In Paris, Eytan had a meeting with de Gaulle, who

173. *Jerusalem Post*, 4 June 1967.
174. Schiff, "The Three Weeks that Preceded the War."

tried to frighten Israel into following France's advice ("A war would be disastrous for Israel even if she won. There would be enormous losses . . ."). But by this time it had no effect on Israel's decision-makers.

Sunday, 4 June

On Sunday, 4 June, Iraq acceded to the Egypt-Syria-Jordan Pacts. An Iraqi division was advancing into Jordan, and two battalions of Egyptian commandos were flown there—clear indications to Israel's military leadership of an intent to attack at an opportune moment. By that time, however, no further stimuli were necessary to strengthen Israel's resolve. At a seven-hour meeting, broken up from time to time for group consultations, the Cabinet reviewed the situation once more and then decided to go to war.[175]

There were, in fact, three meetings, each flowing into the other: It all started at 8:30 as a meeting of the Ministerial Committee on Defense; this continued, at 11:00, as a full Cabinet meeting; and this then went on once more, after a pause, as a meeting of the Ministerial Committee on Defense. The deliberations were opened by Dayan, who reviewed the strength of the Arab armies confronting Israel. There were 100,000 Egyptian troops in Sinai, 60,000 in reserve; 1,000 tanks, mainly of the Soviet T-54 and T-55 types; and 400 interceptors and fighter-bombers. The Syrians had 50,000 men lined up on the border; 200 tanks; and 100 aircraft, 32 of which were MiG-21s. Jordan had 50,000–60,000 men, 250 Patton and Centurion tanks, and 24 British Hawker-Hunter fighters. They were reinforced by the Iraqi division, moving to take up positions on the Israeli border.[176]

The Cabinet then heard Eban's final evaluation of the international situation, including Johnson's message. The Foreign Minister emphasized that he believed the Americans were now committed,

175. Eshkol's *AB*. For details on the 4 June meeting, see Eban, *An Autobiography*, pp. 395–400; Nakdimon, *Toward the Zero Hour*, pp. 276–278; Kimche and Bawly, *The Sandstorm*, pp. 155–156; and Burdett, *Encounter with the Middle East*, pp. 309–316.

176. Carmel stated in an interview in the *Jerusalem Post*, 2 June 1972, that the review of the military situation was the crucial input into the Cabinet's decision: "When on June 4 practically all the ministers, excepting the two from *Mapam*, voted for immediate action . . . it was because of the information in our possession of a further build-up on the Egyptian and Syrian fronts and that Iraqi troops were advancing through Jordan to our lines. We felt that the noose was tightening around our necks."

at least to the extent that the 1956 situation would not be repeated: Israel would not be isolated after an armed clash. As for the Soviet Union, Israel could expect her to remain hostile politically, but there was no indication of armed intervention. Eban also told the Cabinet about de Gaulle's warning to Eytan the previous day, at which Israel had been notified of the arms embargo. He concluded by advocating military action, for Egypt had started the war by all known rules of international law.

Eshkol stated that Israel had to act soon and at her own initiative. He believed that Johnson had softened his stand and would give Israel political support. De Gaulle's actions worried and puzzled him. There was a movement toward a search for compromise, at Israel's expense. Interior Minister Shapira declared that he felt it necessary to recapitulate the views of Israel's elder statesman, Ben-Gurion, whom he had seen on Friday. Ben-Gurion said that it was very dangerous to initiate a war where Israel would have to fight alone, and mobilization had been a grievous mistake. Israel should hold out, even for several months, until she could find an ally who would stand by her side and enable her to take up arms against the enemy, as in the Sinai Campaign. Dayan rejected the implications of Shapira's statement—and Ben-Gurion's advice —by replying that, until somebody found Israel an ally, it was doubtful whether the country would still exist. He also rejected the idea of a test ship, for the same reason as that given by Rabin— it would be a clear signal to Nasser that Israel was about to attack. The time to act was now: There was increased danger on the Jordanian border, coupled with the possibility of a pre-emptive attack by Nasser, which could cause serious damage to Israel's hinterland. "Put bluntly, I [Dayan] said, our best chance of victory was to strike the first blow. The course of the campaign would then follow our dictates. . . . Considering the situation in which we found ourselves . . . it would be fatal for us to allow them to launch their attack."[177]

The *Mapam* ministers, Barzilai and Bentov, were taken aback by the change in attitude of colleagues who, until then, had advocated further diplomatic efforts (Eban and Shapira, among others). Yet they did not dissociate themselves from the general trend—after their proposed resolution for further delay and diplomacy received only two votes. Rather, they reserved the right to consult senior

177. Dayan, *Story of My Life*, pp. 275–276.

party colleagues, notably Ya'ari and Hazan. Begin supported the Prime Minister's proposal and suggested sending emissaries abroad, particularly to the U.S., to explain the real situation as presented to the Cabinet that day.

Eshkol called for a *formal* vote at the end of the meeting. Eighteen members of the Cabinet voted for the Dayan-initiated resolution. (Finance Minister Sapir was abroad.) The two *Mapam* ministers added their assent after consultation, thus making it unanimous. The resolution, the text of which was published five years later, stated:

After hearing a report on the military and political situation from the Prime Minister, the Foreign Minister, the Defense Minister, the Chief of Staff and the head of military intelligence, the Government ascertained that the armies of Egypt, Syria and Jordan are deployed for immediate multi-front aggression, threatening the very existence of the State.

The Government resolves to take military action in order to liberate Israel from the stranglehold of aggression which is progressively being tightened around Israel.

The Government authorizes the Prime Minister and the Defense Minister to confirm to the General Staff of the IDF the time of action.

Members of the Cabinet will receive as soon as possible the information concerning the military operation to be carried out.

The Government charges the Foreign Minister with the task of exhausting all possibilities of political action in order to explain Israel's stand to obtain the support of the powers.[178]

The Cabinet session ended at 15:00. The official communiqué was as innocuous as it could be under the circumstances:

The Cabinet at its weekly session . . . heard reports on the security situation by the Prime Minister and the Defense Minister-designate, and a survey of political developments by the Foreign Minister. . . .

The rest dealt with routine matters—approval of draft laws and ratification of treaties.

Dayan returned immediately to IDF Headquarters to supervise the final preparations. The forces on the borders of Syria and Jordan received strict instructions to stay in defensive position and to advance to limited strategic strongholds inside the enemy territory only if attacked. After a tour of the northern command,

178. Published by the Government of Israel on the 5th Anniversary of the SDW. See *Jerusalem Post*, 5 June 1972.

during which he told its commander, David Elazar, that because the campaign against Egypt would be difficult, he would have to do with the forces he had, Dayan returned to Army Headquarters and informed Ben-Gurion late at night of the Cabinet's decision. Ben-Gurion gave him his blessings.

Eshkol returned to his home and had a final consultation with Allon, Eban, Galili, and advisers. At 20:00 in Tel Aviv, he received the report of the Navy Commander about the first action of the War, the despatch of frogmen to the port of Alexandria, making 4 June the chronological first day of the 1967 War.

The pace of diplomacy was slowing down: Israeli diplomats and their counterparts abroad—Evron with W. Rostow in Washington, Rafael with Goldberg in New York—went over familiar ground.[179] A meeting between Tekoah and Chuvakhin can be characterized as one between two deaf men.

In the Arab states, as in the rest of the world and—seemingly— in Israel, it was a day of relative relaxation. The streets of Cairo filled again, diplomats and soldiers took off for a day of long-delayed relaxation, and journalists were leaving the scene in droves. In a speech at the ceremony of Iraq's accession to the Joint Defense Pact, Nasser declared that Egypt would regard a maritime declaration as an act of aggression and a prelude to hostilities. In an interview with Anthony Nutting, published in the *Sunday Times*, he declared that he planned no further escalation. King Hussein held a press conference to explain his decision to sign the Defense Pact. In Baghdad, President Aref opened a conference of the "Arab Oil Producing States." He threatened the oil companies that their property would be "seized, placed under tutelage, liquidated," if they supplied oil to Israel.

In Washington, Senator Mansfield released a report on the Senate Foreign Relations Committee's discussions with Humphrey, Rusk, and McNamara. There was a sharp distinction between the passage of American ships and the passage of Israeli ships through the Tiran Straits, in terms of a declaration and the use of force.[180] Italian and Japanese officials announced that their states would not sign the declaration for the time being. A French Government spokesman once more made it clear that France would not sign.

179. G. Rafael, "May 1967—A Personal Report," *Ma'ariv*, 18 and 21 April 1972.
180. *New York Times*, 5 June 1967.

British newspapers speculated that, after Wilson's return from the U.S., the British Cabinet would change its policy, since Wilson had not found energetic support for his initiative in Washington.

Intermittent firing broke out in Jerusalem early in the afternoon, in the vicinity of the Mandelbaum Gate. An additional Soviet destroyer passed through the Dardanelles, on its way to the Mediterranean. By now, a sizable British force had assembled off Aden: the aircraft carrier Hermes, four frigates, four minesweepers, and three other vessels. The bulk of the U.S. Sixth Fleet was still stationed off Crete. Full-scale war was hours away.

CHAPTER SIX

1973: 5 TO 26 OCTOBER

THE CRISIS PERIOD of 1973 was dominated by the Yom Kippur War, which was aptly termed the "October Earthquake."[1] Signals of its impending outbreak escalated on the morning of 5 October and culminated in information which reached IDF Intelligence at 03:40 on the 6th. These triggered all three necessary conditions of crisis: a sharp rise in threat perception, an awareness of time constraints on decisions, and an image of the higher probability of war, which became a near certainty on the morning of the 6th. War broke out at 14:00 that day. The crisis period—and the war—continued until 26 October, when the second UN-sponsored cease-fire took effect. At that point, all three crisis conditions declined in intensity, marking the beginning of a much longer post-crisis period.

DECISIONS AND DECISION-MAKERS

The 1973 crisis period encompassed the phase of perceived high threat, finite—and very short—time, and high probability of war, from 5 October until the outbreak of war, and the entire Yom Kippur War. There were eighteen discernible decisions (in addition to the two decisions taken in the pre-crisis period): six

1. The title of one of the earliest—and best—accounts of the Yom Kippur War, by Z. Schiff, Tel Aviv, 1974.

171

taken by the Cabinet, seven by the Prime Minister in consultation
with other ministers or the COS, three by her Kitchen Cabinet,
and two by the General Staff with the Defense Minister. Not all
were equally important. Some were of a formal, authorization
nature. The consultative process varied, as did the size of the
decisional unit.

Decision Number	Date	Content
3.	5 October, 09:00–10:00	The Chief of Staff and the Defense Minister, with members of the General Staff present, decided to place regular IDF forces on (the highest) alert "C" and the Air Force on full alert.
4.	5 October, noon	An extraordinary Cabinet meeting, with seven ministers present, approved all IDF measures taken thus far and empowered the Prime Minister and Defense Minister to mobilize all reserves, if necessary.
5.	6 October, 08:00–09:45	At a meeting of the Kitchen Cabinet, the Prime Minister decided against a pre-emptive strike.
6.	6 October, 08:00–09:45	The Prime Minister, with the Kitchen Cabinet, decided in favor of large-scale mobilization.
7.	7 October, 17:00–18:00	The Kitchen Cabinet empowered the Chief of Staff to decide about a counter-attack after he studied the situation on the southern front.
8.	8 October	The Defense Minister, in consultation with the Chief of Staff and the General Staff, decided to concentrate IDF action on the northern front, including the bombing of military targets deep inside Syria (Damascus, Homs, Latakia). This was subsequently approved by the Cabinet.
9.	9 October, morning	The Prime Minister, after consulting Dayan, Allon, and Elazar, decided to place Bar-Lev in charge of the Southern Command; that is, he was made de facto OC.
10.	9 October	The Prime Minister, after consulting Dayan, decided to fly to Washington on a secret mission (abortive decision).

Decision Number	Date	Content
11.	10 October, evening	The Kitchen Cabinet, in consultation with the General Staff, approved a plan to launch a general attack on Syria, in the direction of Damascus, but not to attempt to occupy Syria's capital.
12.	12 October, morning	The Kitchen Cabinet, in consultation with the Chief of Staff and several other generals, decided to postpone a decision on an attempted crossing of the Canal until Egyptian armor on the east bank had been defeated in battle.
13.	12 October, afternoon	The Prime Minister decided to accept a U.S. suggestion for a cease-fire in place.
14.	14 October, evening	The Cabinet approved a proposal to cross the Canal.
15.	19 October, morning	The Prime Minister approved Dayan's suggestion to press forward on the west bank of the Canal but not to advance on Cairo.
16.	21/22 October, midnight	The Cabinet decided to accept the U.S.-Soviet call for a cease-fire.
17.	22 October, evening	The Cabinet decided to continue IDF operations if Egypt did not obey the cease-fire.
18.	23 October, dawn	The Prime Minister approved continued IDF advances on the west bank of the Canal because of continuing Egyptian attacks.
19.	26 October, 04:00	The Cabinet, after a six-hour debate, decided to accept a second and third call for a cease-fire.
20.	26 October, evening	The Cabinet yielded to U.S. pressure on the issue of supplies to Egypt's encircled Third Army.

PSYCHOLOGICAL ENVIRONMENT

The analysis of Israel's psychological setting for decision during the 1973 crisis period is based upon two sets of data. One is twelve public documents—speeches, statements, press conferences, interviews—of Meir, Dayan, and Foreign Minister Eban, between 6 and 24 October, totaling 41,000 words. The other is the perceptions of key decision points during that period as recalled in the memoirs of Meir and Dayan.[2]

Attitudinal Prism

The pervasive prism among Israel's high policy decision-makers at the beginning of the crisis period—in fact, until the Egyptian-Syrian attack at 14:00 on 6 October—remained the "Conception." This, along with an image of a perfidious enemy, is evident in Prime Minister Meir's memoir on her perception of the day the war started:

Not only had we not been warned in time, we were fighting on two fronts simultaneously and fighting *enemies who had been preparing themselves for years to attack us.* We were overwhelmingly outnumbered—in guns, tanks, planes and men—and were at a *severe psychological disadvantage.* The shock wasn't only over the way in which the war had started, but

2. They are as follows:

			No. of words
Meir	6 October 1973	Address to the Nation on TV	700
	10 October 1973	Address to the Nation on TV	1,400
	13 October 1973	Press Conference in Israel	5,700
	16 October 1973	Speech to the Knesset	3,300
	23 October 1973	Speech to the Knesset	2,700
		Total	13,800
Dayan	6 October 1973	Address to the Nation on TV	800
	9 October 1973	Confidential briefing to Israeli editors	9,000
	20 October 1973	Interview on Israeli TV	400
	24 October 1973	Interview on Israeli TV	2,250
		Total	12,450
Eban	7 October 1973	Interview on U.S. TV, "Issues and Answers"	2,500
	17 October 1973	Press Conference with UN Correspondents Association	6,000
	24 October 1973	Press Conference in Israel	6,250
		Total	14,750

There were no statements or speeches by Allon during the crisis period, only one TV interview. In addition, several extracts from other speeches by the decision-makers during that period, which illuminate their images, are scattered through the qualitative analysis. All dates appearing in parentheses are from the above speeches. The Meir and Dayan memoirs are taken from Meir's *My Life* (Jerusalem and Tel Aviv, 1975), chap. 14, and Dayan's *Story of My Life* (Jerusalem and Tel Aviv, 1976), part VII.

also the *fact that a number of our basic assumptions were proven wrong;* the low probability of an attack in October, the certainty that we would get sufficient warning before any attack took place and the belief that we would be able to prevent the Egyptians from crossing the Suez Canal. The circumstances could not possibly have been worse.[3]

Images

MEIR

The Prime Minister touched upon half a dozen issues in her public statements of the crisis period: the outbreak of war; the Arab states involved in the fighting; Israel's aims; the cease-fire; Soviet culpability; United States aid; and the decision not to pre-empt. Her perceptions of some of these were recalled and elaborated in her memoirs, notably the last two. There were others: the nonmobilization of reserves on 5 October; her mood during the early days of the war; her confidence in victory; Arab aims; Jordan's role; UN Resolution 338; the U.S. President; and the Secretary of State.

Mrs. Meir termed the Yom Kippur War an unprovoked attack by the Arab world against Israel. The day selected by "the enemy" was regarded as especially evil: "It revealed both his ignorance and his malice" (16 October). In contrast to the pre-crisis period, when she had defined Israel's situation as favorable and had dismissed the idea of an Arab military option, she now argued that the October War was inevitable. This was so, not because of Israel's occupation of Arab territories, but because of the persistent Arab refusal to accept Israel's legitimate existence. The Egypt-Syria assault on 6 October was also used as the justification for not having returned the territories: "You can imagine," she told a press conference on the 13th, "what would have happened to us had we moved back to the June 4, 1967 lines, when this attack on us took place."

The Arab states participating in the war were an object of attention—but the Palestinians were not mentioned even once. She again accused Sadat of being ready to sacrifice a million lives to bring about the destruction of Israel, while Syria was described as inhuman, especially in the treatment of Israeli prisoners (13 October). She showed some understanding for the despatch of Jordanian troops to Syria; but she warned against further escalation.

3. *My Life*, pp. 359–360 (emphasis added).

As the war continued and Israel's military situation improved, there was a hardening in Meir's attitude: "In this war," she declared on the 16th, "our aim is clear and simple—to repel and break the enemy's power on both fronts." A similar development can be discerned in her attitude toward a cease-fire. On the 13th, she said: "When we come to a proposal of a cease-fire, we will consider it very seriously and decide, because our desire is to stop the war as quickly as possible." Three days later, by which time the IDF had established a beachhead west of the Canal, she set down a specific condition: "We shall not accept any cease-fire that does not include an exchange of prisoners."

The Soviet Union was accused of major responsibility for the outbreak of war and, in particular, was blamed for the large quantities of arms supplied to the Arabs: "It is a policy of irresponsibility not towards Israel alone but towards the Middle East and the whole world." For the United States there was praise, not only as an indispensable source of arms for Israel but also as an effective deterrent against active Soviet hostility. President Nixon was singled out for acting "in the finest tradition of his country, [in] succoring a nation that is locked in combat with aggressors" (16 October). According to Meir, a solution to the conflict could come only from Israel's neighbors: Israel was ready to compromise, but only after secure borders were assured. Last, but not least important, were her references to Jewry as the most reliable ally of Israel.

More illuminating, about both Meir's image of the politico-military situation a day before the surprise attack and the effect of history (experience) on her perceptions, is her recollection of an event and of a discussion with Dayan, Elazar, and Zeira at 10:00 on 5 October: "On Friday, 5 October, we received a report that worried me. The families of the Russian advisers in Syria were packing up and leaving in a hurry. *It reminded me of what had happened prior to the Six Day War,* and I didn't like it at all. Why the haste? . . . Was it possible that they were being evacuated? . . ." Meir's feeling of disquiet remained, despite the fact that "I was assured that we would get *adequate warning* of any real trouble, and anyway, *sufficient reinforcements were being sent to the fronts to carry out any holding operation* that might be required. Everything that was necessary had been done." Moreover, according to her (postwar) account, she conveyed a perception of escalating threat, time constraints, and the probability of war to an informal

Cabinet meeting at noon the same day: "No one seemed very alarmed [by the report of the evacuation of Soviet families from Syria]. Nevertheless, I decided to speak my mind. 'Look,' I said, 'I have a terrible feeling that this has all happened before. *It reminds me of 1967,* when we were accused of massing troops against Syria, which is exactly what the Arab press is saying now. And I think that it all means something.'"[4]

Notwithstanding that threatening information, Meir remained uncertain about the probability of war as late as Friday evening, the 5th. This belief was based partly upon the reassurances of her military advisers and partly upon the cumulative experience of apparent Arab intent and behavior in 1973. As she recalled during the Yom Kippur War: "No one in this country realizes how many times during the past year we received information from the same source that war would break out on this or that day, without war breaking out" (16 October).

The decision not to pre-empt was defined by the Prime Minister as a political decision, influenced mainly by prior experience, especially 1967, when Israel was accused of starting the Six Day War. "I regret not launching it [an interceptive strike] because there is no doubt that the [military] position would have been much better. I do not regret [the decision] . . . because at least we do not have that argument with the world" (13 October). "Will anyone dare, this time . . . to say the truth," she challenged the world three days later, "that responsibility for this awful war rests with them [the Arabs]?"

On that crucial decisional problem—to pre-empt or to take the first blow—Meir was typically candid about the perceptual inputs to choice.[5] One was world public opinion and prior experience, as noted. The other, more important, was the compelling need not to alienate the United States; or, stated more positively, the necessity to assure a flow of arms support.

The "U.S. factor" was clearly articulated on 16 November: "Had the situation as to who began hostilities not been clear beyond the

4. *My Life,* pp. 355–357 (emphasis added).
5. That a choice was available, at least on the Syrian front, is beyond doubt. Soon after learning, at 04:00 on the 6th, of the certainty of an Arab attack—at 18:00 that day, it was believed—Elazar asked the OC Air Force, Peled, to prepare an operational plan for an interceptive air strike against Syria. He was assured that this could be launched at 13:00 on the 6th, and he so informed the Prime Minister at the 08:00 Cabinet meeting.

shadow of a doubt, I question whether the vital equipment we received in the course of time would have flowed as it did, as it still continues to flow."

In her memoirs, she emphasized how vital was her image of the U.S. connection at the 08:00–09:45 meeting on 6 October: "*I had already made up my mind.* 'Dado' [Elazar], I said, 'I know all the arguments in favor of a pre-emptive strike, but I am against it. We don't know now, any of us, what the future will hold, but there is always the possibility that we will need help, and if we strike first, we will get nothing from anyone. I would like to say yes because I know what it would mean, but with a heavy heart I am going to say no.'"[6] When recalling the fateful decision, she reaffirmed that perceptual strand:

I remember going out to Lydda once to watch the Galaxies come in. They looked like some kind of immense prehistoric flying monsters and I thought to myself: "Thank God I was right to reject the idea of a pre-emptive strike! It might have saved lives in the beginning, but I am sure that we would not have had that airlift, which is now saving so many lives."[7]

Parenthetically, she did not reveal an awareness of time pressure in choosing not to pre-empt: She "had already made up [her] mind" before the deliberations on 6 October began.

There appears to have been a third perceptual component in the Prime Minister's approach to the decisional problem of pre-emption. Three times during the 6 October morning meeting she asked Elazar and Peled whether Israel's survival would be placed in jeopardy—and whether there would be long-run military disadvantages—if the decision were not to pre-empt. When they answered in the negative, her primary concern was set at rest, and the two external inputs—U.S. reaction and world opinion—held sway.[8] The costs of an interceptive air strike were evaluated by her as greater than any short-term military benefits.

The perception which shaped her choice, on the morning of 6 October, in favor of general mobilization (Elazar's advice) as against the option of partial mobilization (Dayan's recommendation) was clearly specified in her memoirs: "I had said [to the Kitchen Cabinet] . . . that I had only one criterion: if there really

6. *My Life*, p. 359 (emphasis added).
7. Ibid., p. 363.
8. Communicated to M. Brecher by a participant.

was a war [some doubt about its certainty remained], then we had to be in the very best position possible."[9] However, that was on Saturday, after the arrival of information about an imminent Arab attack. The much graver negative choice on Friday, the 5th, not to mobilize any reserves, and the competing images which conditioned that decision were illuminated in Meir's *mea culpa:*

Today I know what I should have done. I should have overcome my hesitations. I knew as well as anyone else what full-scale mobilization meant and how much money it would cost, and I also knew that only a few months before, in May, we had had an alert and the reserves had been called up, but nothing had happened. But I also understood that perhaps there had been no war in May exactly because the reserves had been called up. That Friday morning I should have listened to the warnings of my own heart and ordered a call-up. . . .

It doesn't matter what logic dictated. It matters only that I, who was so accustomed to making decisions . . . failed to make that one decision.[10]

From the very outset, despite the initial setbacks on both fronts, Meir remained confident of victory: "But even on the worst of those early days, when we already knew what losses we were sustaining, I had complete faith in our soldiers and officers, in the spirit of the Israel Defense Forces and their ability to face any challenge, and I never lost faith in our ultimate victory." And yet, "On the afternoon of 7 October, [when] Dayan told me that in his opinion the situation in the south was so bad that we should pull back substantially and establish a new defensive line, I listened to him in horror."[11]

Meir remained consistent about one of Israel's aims during the 1973 War. She perceived it thus: "Although we had neither wanted nor started the Yom Kippur War, we had fought and won it, and we had a war aim of our own—peace. . . ." And she recalled vividly her perception and goal on 20 October: "I remember driving back from the office through Tel Aviv's blacked-out streets on one of those nights when the Brezhnev-Kissinger talks about a cease-fire were going on in Moscow and taking a silent oath that, to the extent that it depended in any way at all on me, this war would end in a peace treaty obliterating, for all time, the famous three 'noes' of the Arabs ["No recognition; No negotiation; No peace"], declared in Khartoum after the Six Day War. . . ." She perceived Arab goals

9. *My Life,* pp. 358–359.
10. Ibid., p. 357.
11. Ibid., p. 360.

with no less consistency. To the Knesset she declared on 16 October: "Syria's aspirations are not limited to a piece of land but to deploying their artillery batteries once again on the Golan Heights against the Galilee settlements, to setting up missile batteries against our aircraft, so as to provide cover for the breakthrough of their armies into the heart of Israel. . . . The Arab rulers pretend that their objective is limited to reaching the lines of 4 June 1967, but we know their true objective: the total subjugation of the State of Israel." Her image of Jordan's role in the early days was indicated as follows: "For days I was tormented by the fear that a third front would be opened and that Jordan would join in the attack upon us."[12]

The Prime Minister's image of a hostile—and dangerous—Soviet Union was expressed frequently. Typical was her remark to the Knesset on 16 October:

The hand of the Soviet Union is obvious in the equipment, the tactics and the military doctrines that the Arab armies are trying to imitate and adopt. Above everything else, the Soviet Union's all-out support for Israel's enemies in the course of the war has been manifested in the airlift reaching our enemies' airfields and the ships calling at their ports. . . . Such conduct on the part of the USSR goes beyond the limits of unfriendly policy. It is a policy of irresponsibility not only towards Israel, but towards the Middle East and towards the world.[13]

As for the UN: "There was no question but that Resolution 338, passed with such indecent speed, was intended to avert the total destruction of the Egyptian and Syrian forces by us. . . ."[14]

There were several revealing perceptions of the United States in Meir's memoirs. One was the very high value she placed on American aid, then and later: "The airlift was invaluable. It not only lifted our spirits, it also served to make the American position clear to the Soviet Union and it undoubtedly served to make our victory possible." On Nixon she wrote: "I know that in the United States at that time many people assumed that the alert [on 24 October] was 'invented' by President Nixon in order to divert attention from the Watergate problem, but I didn't believe that then and I do not believe it now. . . . And I am still sure that President Nixon ordered

12. *My Life*, pp. 365, 363.
13. *Divrei Haknesset*, 68, 4474.
14. *My Life*, p. 369.

the U.S. alert on 24 October 1973 because, détente or no détente, he was not about to give in to Soviet blackmail. It was, I think, a dangerous decision, a courageous decision and a correct decision."[15]

Meir's perception of the importance of direct negotiations and, in that context, dependence upon the superpowers is revealing:

> Now that we were about to be placed under extreme pressure regarding a cease-fire, I felt more strongly than ever that we must make no substantive concession of any sort that did not include direct negotiations. . . .
> In the final analysis, to put it bluntly, the fate of small countries always rests with the super powers, and they always have their own interests to guard. . . . On 21 October there was every reason to believe that, given just a little more time, this would have happened [an "even more conclusive defeat of the Egyptian and Syrian armies"].[16]

As for the second cease-fire, Meir gave the most vivid expression of her image of dependence upon, and admiration for, the United States:

> "At least," I told the Cabinet that week, "let's call things by their right name. Black is black and white is white. There is only one country to which we can turn and sometimes we have to give in to it—even when we know we shouldn't. But it is the only real friend we have, and a very powerful one. We don't have to say yes to everything, but let's call things by their proper name. There is nothing to be ashamed of when a small country like Israel, in this situation, has to give in sometimes to the United States. And when we do say yes, let's for God's sake, not pretend that it is otherwise and that black is white." But we didn't agree to everything.[17]

Of Meir's fifty-five advocacy statements during the 1973 crisis period, Israel was the subject of action in fifty-one. The largest number concerned the cease-fire: She moved from opposition to any cease-fire to acceptance of a conditional cease-fire, from the 6th to the 25th of October. The idea of direct negotiations after the war was mentioned by her ten times, a striking preoccupation with the modalities of peace in the midst of a titanic struggle on the Sinai and Golan battlefields. She cautioned her people against panic. And she called for "defensible borders," manifesting a further concern with postwar negotiations.

15. Ibid., pp. 362, 370, 371.
16. Ibid., p. 369.
17. Ibid., pp. 371–372.

ALLON

During the 1973 crisis period, the Deputy Prime Minister, surprisingly, did not deliver any speeches. Only one interview was recorded, on 9 October, for the BBC's "Panorama" program. Two of Israel's war aims were mentioned. "The Israel Defense Forces will not stop at the cease-fire lines, if crossing them becomes necessary to destroy the Syrian and Egyptian enemy." Further, "Israel has no territorial ambitions in this war but will be more determined than ever before to insist on secure borders in any future settlement." And he shared with Meir and Dayan the image of the prohibitive costs of a pre-emptive strike on the 6th. Three days later, he declared: "It will soon become clear to all that the political advantage Israel gained thereby outweighs any military advantage the Arabs might have hoped to gain" from a surprise attack.[18] In fact, he was illuminating the causal link between image (in this case, of political advantage amply compensating for military costs) and behavior (the decision not to initiate the war).

EBAN

The Foreign Minister, like Meir, described the Yom Kippur War as a "brutal and unprovoked attack" directed against the very existence of Israel. "It is not a war about any specific territory, it is about Israel, its security, its sovereignty, its statehood, its existence, its life" (17 and 18 October). The assault was perceived as treacherous for two reasons: first, because it took place on the Day of Atonement; and second, because there was a negotiating possibility on the eve of the war, initiated by Secretary of State Kissinger in UN discussions at the beginning of October. Eban also shared the Prime Minister's self-satisfied image of Israel's policy since 1967 as being absolutely correct: "Imagine," he declared two days after the outbreak of war, "that in a moment of suicidal stupidity we had gone back to the previous armistice lines instead of negotiating boundaries in the framework of peace; then the attack of October 6 would have done such destruction to our vital security that perhaps Israel and all its people, and all its memories, hopes and visions which have enriched our history might now all be lost —swept away in a fearful massacre."

During the 1973 crisis period, one discerns changes in Eban's definition of Israel's war aims. At the beginning, he emphasized

18. *Jerusalem Post,* 12 October 1973.

simply the restoration of the 1970 cease-fire lines. This remained his goal on the 11th. A week later, however, he asserted the need "to create by the cease-fire . . . the minimal atmosphere in which a dialogue [toward an overall peace settlement] can go forward in an atmosphere of civility." He frequently spoke of Egypt's leader with hostility; for example: "When President Sadat said in an Egyptian newspaper that he admired Hitler, all the world smiled indulgently" (8 October). In that context, he held Egypt's President personally responsible for the Yom Kippur War and for its consequences—by drawing an analogy with the World War II experience: "In terms of Europe's history he suggests 1938 in order that 1939 should come at a later stage" (17 October).

Eban dismissed as most unlikely an imposed cease-fire, relying on the "fair play" of the United States toward Israel. Similarly, he opposed third-party mediation. Yet, in contrast to other Israeli decision-makers, the Foreign Minister did not describe the U.S. as the "friend of Israel." Rather, he explained her policy as designed to maintain a balance of power in the Near East Core. He condemned the Soviet Union and excluded the possibility of credible Soviet— or UN—guarantees. And the Western European powers were urged to support negotiations between the parties, but no more.

While Israel was the subject in the majority of Eban's advocacy statements during the crisis period, the proportion was the lowest among all four decision-makers, barely half. Other than Israel, the most frequent subject was "the parties." The central theme for both was—"negotiate a peace settlement." In this respect, Eban's advocacy in the crisis period was unique. There was also, however, an emphasis on the need to negotiate secure borders and a call to end the hostilities. In general, Eban's crisis period advocacies focused on peace and the path to a settlement. His was the largest variety of advocacy content, in part a function of his role as Foreign Minister.

DAYAN

Dayan's perception of the probability of war underwent a change during the night of 4–5 October. As he later recalled, news of the Soviet order to evacuate families of their advisers, and the arrival of passenger planes in Damascus and Cairo, "*strengthened* the probability that Egypt and Syria were about to launch a war."[19]

19. *Story of My Life*, pp. 385–386 (emphasis added).

The Agranat Commission, too, reported: "On that morning [5 October] the Defence Minister already *suspected* that the Egyptian exercise *might be* a camouflage for an attack."[20] The extent of upward revision in Dayan's estimate of the probability of attack is subject to controversy: One *ex post facto* report of his view indicated a 60–40 probability of attack; another suggested certainty of an Egyptian attempt to cross the Canal.[21] Dayan himself refers to a "strengthened" probability—but no more.

It was sufficient for him to approve, at the General Staff meeting on Friday the 5th at 09:00, Elazar's proposal of a "C" alert (the maximum) for the permanent army and the Air Force. But it was not enough for him to choose mobilization of reserves, even at an informal Cabinet meeting later that day. The reasons may be found in three other Dayan perceptions on 5 October: (a) that the defensive deployment of Arab forces could become offensive within hours and that Israel's mobilization could not prevent an attack by Egypt and Syria; (b) that Israel's mobilization would be misperceived by the Arabs—and the world—as an aggressive act; and (c) that Israel's "secure borders," especially in the South, and her second-strike capability would enable her to absorb an Arab attack without excessive cost, and with certain victory.

Unlike Meir and Elazar, Dayan was not persuaded of the certainty of war by the information input at 03:40 on the 6th: "The assumption that a war is actually going to break out was formulated on Saturday at 04:00. *Not* even then *with one hundred per cent certainty*. The assumption was that there was probably going to be a war. The information seemed accurate."[22] That perception, along with those noted in Chapter 3 regarding Arab miscalculation and world criticism of Israel, explains his strong objection to Elazar's two proposals throughout the morning of 6 October: general mobilization of the reserves and a pre-emptive air strike against Syrian airfields and missile emplacements. As is so often the case, images dictated choice and behavior. Even when presenting his case to the Prime Minister at the 08:00–09:45 meeting of the Kitchen

20. Agranat Commission, Partial Report, 3 April 1974 (emphasis added).
21. S. Nakdimon, "New Revelations," *Yediot Aharonot,* 19 July 1974. According to Bar-Tov, at 11 o'clock in the morning of 6 October, Dayan still asked Elazar what he would do with 100,000 mobilized reservists "wandering around"; he still was not certain that war was unavoidable (H. Bar-Tov, *Dado—48 Years and Another 20 Days* [Tel Aviv, 1978], Vol. 2, p. 30).
22. S. Nakdimon, "New Revelations," *Yediot Aharonot,* 26 July 1974.

Cabinet, Dayan clung to his image of what was necessary: "If you want to accept his [Elazar's] proposal I will not prostrate myself on the road and I will not resign; but you might as well know that it is superfluous."[23] How rooted was his perception that Israel's mobilization would be misread by the world and the Arabs as an aggressive act is evident in remarks attributed to him in private briefings during and after the Yom Kippur War: "If we knew *for sure* four days before the war, we would not have mobilized earlier. We would have hesitated to do so. If we had started to mobilize the reserves, the whole world would have charged—'the Arabs opened fire because they saw that Israel was going to attack.'"[24]

Furthermore, Dayan's rejection of a pre-emptive air strike flowed directly from his image of its (adverse) consequences and of the post–1967 "secure borders." At a press conference on the evening of 6 October, just hours after the outbreak of war, he declared:

We were faced with the dilemma of whether to open fire first and of course thereby to obtain a very important advantage, or not to do so and lose this military advantage, but make sure that the picture will be known, the true one, that the Egyptians and Syrians started the war. . . . It was a decision of the government not to strike first . . . in order to have the political . . . advantage at the expense of the military advantage. . . . I think it was the right decision . . . unlike six years ago [when] we couldn't have taken such risks; but after all Sinai is far away and we can allow ourselves such a tactic or strategy . . . and even if we shall have to evacuate or lose some positions it is far away . . .[25]

At a late stage in the war, on the 20th, the U.S. factor was cited by Dayan as a basic reason for the decision on the 6th not to intercept the Arab attack: "The Americans would not have helped us as they did." Once more, the link between images and decisions is evident. Another key to that crucial decision is found in Dayan's image of the world and Israel's place within it, as expressed a week after the outbreak of war: "We don't have that many friends and, if we had started the war, I doubt if we would have got applause, support and identification with our cause" (14 October). In the same speech, he gave other—domestic—reasons for that decision, one technical and one somewhat philosophical: "We would have

23. As cited in C. Herzog, *The War of Atonement* (Jerusalem and Tel Aviv, 1975), p. 53.

24. S. Nakdimon, "New Revelations," *Yediot Aharonot*, 26 July 1974.

25. Israel, Government Press Office, Press Bulletin.

had to keep the whole people [of Israel] under arms sitting on the line for years." Moreover, "this is a people that does not want war —that hopes for peace—that believes in peace. . . . And when it saw that we were managing to live with the Arabs of the Adminis-tered Territories, with open bridges . . . then this nation literally clung to this life of peace. . . ."

The Defense Minister's pre-crisis image of Israel's invincibility was undermined during the early days of the Yom Kippur War. "The halo of superiority," he told a group of Israeli editors in a then-confidential assessment on 9 October, "the political and military principle that, if they dared to start a war, they would be defeated, has not been proved." The enemy aim was defined in absolute terms: "The Arabs wish to annihilate us." And Israel was confronted by an enormous hostile bloc of Arab, Muslim, and Communist states. Self-reliance, which Dayan had perceived as a major asset during the pre-crisis period, now became the instinc-tive Israeli response to stress—a feeling of aloneness: "Israel can only rely on her own physical strength," he said sadly to the editors on the 9th, "no state would come to our aid should we ask them to." Nevertheless, he did not abandon his view that only the strength of the IDF could tip the scales: "The balance of forces and nothing else counts. . . ."

From the very beginning of the 1973 War, despite the initial setbacks on the battlefield, Dayan emphasized the necessity of ul-timate military victory. Yet he saw nothing wrong in withdrawing, temporarily, to new lines. Israel's war aim, he declared on the 14th, was "to smite the Arabs so hard that they would desire peace and not war." His reasoning was as follows: (1) "the Arabs want to de-stroy us"; (2) "if they cannot destroy us they would make peace"; and (3) "therefore, we have to show them very clearly that they cannot destroy us." At the same time, he remained skeptical about a genuine Arab interest in peace.

The link between the Middle East and the global system re-ceived considerable attention from Dayan during the 1973 crisis period. In that context, he emphasized, though sometimes reluc-tantly, the importance of American aid. This was perceived by him, in part, as restricting Israel's freedom of action—for example, with regard to the decision to bomb Syria beyond the front lines: "We took action against Damascus the first time, and I don't know what the American reaction will be like; and the reaction is very impor-tant to us at all times, especially in this situation." To the editors he

added: "Our purpose is to keep the Americans informed of everything, without covering up anything."

Dayan did not perceive a direct connection between Israel's dependence and Washington's dictation: "The United States won't
force Israel to seek a cease-fire," and "Israel's dependence on the
United States would not open the way to an imposed solution." On
the other hand, the Soviets were viewed as Israel's dangerous enemy, military and political: "If the Russians had not wanted the war
it would not have happened" (20 October).

Dayan told the newspaper editors, in confidence, on 9 October:
"At the moment it is not the time to consider political questions."
Unlike any of his colleagues, he displayed an awareness of the link
between Arab self-esteem, on the one hand, and, on the other, war
and peace in the Middle East: "Let them [the Arabs] keep their
honor and lose the war; and after salvaging their honor they should
be ready to make peace."

That preoccupation is overwhelmingly evident in the quantitative findings of our content analysis. No less than twenty-five of
ninety-four advocacy statements by Dayan during the crisis period
urged Israel to deny any territorial gain to the Arabs. In some instances there was a blunt admonition: "Throw the Egyptians across
the Canal." Moreover, he emphasized the need to remove Syria
from the war. And he advocated "reliance, the building of Israel's
military strength for a long mobilization." In short, a total of fifty-
one advocacy statements were directly related to the military
dimension of the Yom Kippur War—not unexpected, in view of
Dayan's role as Defense Minister. Unlike the Prime Minister, he
began to think aloud about a peace settlement only on the 20th;
within the next few days, he called upon Israel five times to negotiate, and upon "the parties" three times. Much earlier, however,
and often (ten times) he urged Israel not to refuse a cease-fire,
though not to take the initiative in bringing it about.

Dayan's perceptions during the 1973 crisis period are further illuminated by his memoirs. Seven themes, issues, and decisions
are clarified at specific points in time, from 6 to 22 October. The
dominance of the American factor in his image of mobilization and
pre-emption was acknowledged, first, on the deliberations of the
6th: "I feared that such moves would burden our prospects of securing the full support of the United States. . . . And if American
help was to be sought, then the United States had to be given full
proof that it was not we who desired war—even if this ruled out

pre-emptive action and handicapped us in the military campaign."
Then, in the context of a discussion with Kissinger on the 22nd, relating to the cease-fire: "It appeared that if we had started the war,
we would not have received a single, solitary nail from the United
States."[26]

During the early days of the War, Dayan's image focused overwhelmingly on *the War* itself—strategy, tactics, casualties, and
Arab fighting skills:

6 October   In my view we faced three difficult factors. The first,
                I said, was the very size of the enemy forces, lavishly
                equipped with weaponry accumulated during the pre-
                vious six years. The Egyptians and Syrians were not
                the Arab armies we had known in 1967. . . . Second was
                the enemy's anti-aircraft missile system, with the addi-
                tion of the SAM-6s. This weapons system presented a
                grave problem to our Air Force. . . . Third was our need
                to hold our frontier lines with small forces, since we
                neither wished nor were able to keep our population
                mobilized all the time. . . .
                   I concluded . . . that in Sinai we would ride out the
                immediate crisis, in the Golan we would face another
                two days of hardship, and then we would fight a war of
                armor against the Egyptians. . . . At the end of the
                meeting . . . I was tense and tired and could sense a
                gulf between me and my Cabinet colleagues. They had
                not liked what I had said about the Egyptian success,
                and certainly not my view about retiring to a second line.
                . . . They were seized by the optimism in the chief of
                staff's survey and above all by their own wishful
                thinking. . . . The battles were tough, heroic, and de-
                pressing. . . . Each one [stronghold] fought its individ-
                ual battle on its own. Each was a solitary, isolated isle,
                conducting a bitter and desperate struggle, a struggle of
                life or death, of surrender or breaking free. . . .

7 October   . . . As I flew back from Sinai to Tel Aviv, I could recall
                no moment in the past when I had felt such anxiety. If
                I had been in physical straits, involved in personal dan-
                ger, it would have been simpler. I knew this from ex-
                perience. But now I had quite a different feeling. Israel
                was in danger, and the results could be fatal if we did not
                recognize and understand the new situation in time, and
                if we failed to suit our warfare to the new needs. . . .
                The implication of this reality was that if we went on
                suffering heavy losses in incessant frontal attacks, we

26. *Story of My Life*, pp. 376–377, 444.

> might be left with an emaciated force in the midst of a
> campaign, while the Arabs, with their huge forces and
> arsenals, could hold on. . . . We had turned to America
> with urgent requests for planes and tanks, but who knew
> if and when we would receive them? And we, at all
> events, had to fight our own battles. No one would do
> the fighting for us. . . .

10 October   October 10th, the fifth day of the war, was the first day
> I stopped worrying whether somewhere along the fronts
> our forces might prove unable to stop the Arabs from
> breaking through into our territory. . . . We had
> reached a stage where we were able to initiate military
> moves with a choice of alternatives. . . . We now com-
> manded options. . . . As for the fighting standard of the
> Arab soldiers, I can sum it up in one sentence: they did
> not run away. . . .[27]

Dayan's perceptions of the Arab states involved in the fighting
also received attention. On the 10th, his definition of Israel's aim in
the North and his expectation of Syria's response was recalled thus:
"There was no intention of capturing Damascus or even of bombing it. It was our aim to hit the Syrians another hard blow, military
and political, so that they would lose forces as well as territory beyond the 1967 lines." As for his view of Jordan's likely behavior, "I
had repeatedly expressed the view that if we attacked in the direction of Damascus, Jordan would join in the war by employing her
forces on the Syrian front, rather than opening up a front of her
own."

Dayan's perception of the importance of Damascus in Israel's
political strategy, on 11–12 October, was stated clearly: "We had
no intention of capturing it, or bombing it—as long as the Syrians
refrained from bombing our cities. But it was most desirable that
Damascus should be within our artillery range. . . . It would demonstrate the Syrians' defeat."[28]

From 1956 onward, Dayan perceived the Soviets as hostile,
threatening, and dangerous; and this shaped his cautious behavior,
especially with respect to Syria, in both the Sinai Campaign and
the Six Day War. This image reappeared on 11–12 October, in the
midst of Israel's general offensive in the North: "The Russians had
harshened their tone as the Syrians kept retreating, and we had to
be very careful to prevent the bear from getting out of the forest.

27. Ibid., pp. 390–391, 401–406, 420.
28. Ibid., p. 428.

We had received reliable information that the Soviet Union was mobilizing three airborne formations to fly to the aid of the Arabs." And in the contest of feverish activity for a cease-fire on the 20th, "Moscow was trying to secure for the Arabs by political means what the Arabs themselves had failed to achieve by war."[29]

By contrast, Dayan had an acute perception of U.S. aid and its importance: "I hate to think what our situation would have been if the United States had withheld its aid, or what we would do if Washington were to turn its back on Israel one of these days." In reflecting on the airlift from 14 October to 14 November, he wrote: "We did not even receive full replacement for our losses. But the greatest gap remained between our requests and the measure in which they were granted. . . . We were troubled by the shortage of weapons, but we were no less disturbed by our isolation." And on 22 October, during the negotiations for the first cease-fire, his image of U.S. reliability was negative: "America found herself in a difficult situation at the moment because of the oil embargo, and her leaders would not hesitate to dissociate themselves from us if forced to choose between aid to Israel, which involved grave suffering for America, and reaching agreement with the Arabs, even at our expense."[30]

There were several expressions of Dayan's image of a cease-fire during the Yom Kippur War. On the 10th, he told the Southern Command: "If we could not drive them out at once, we should try to seize part of their territory west of the Canal. We would then have something with which to bargain, or at least even up the score." On the 19th, he became acutely aware of time pressure: "Feverish negotiations [are going on] between the Americans and the Russians to sponsor an agreed cease-fire resolution by the Security Council. . . . I . . . decided that before the cease-fire we had to capture the Mount Hermon positions on the Syrian front and reach a favourable line on the Egyptian front. . . . I said we should concentrate our attacks on the west bank of the Canal, but not press too far inland toward Cairo." The next day, "I urged Arik [Sharon], Bren [Adan], and Kalman [Magen] to secure the essential objectives with the utmost speed as the cease-fire was likely to go into effect in two or three days."[31]

29. *Story of My Life*, pp. 428–429, 440.
30. Ibid., pp. 420, 421, 422, 444.
31. Ibid., pp. 425, 439, 440.

As in Chapter 3, the most salient topics in the decision-makers' images during the 1973 crisis period will now be summarized. (Allon made only one public statement.)

1. *Definition of the Present Situation.* Only Dayan discussed the gravity of Israel's position on the battlefield.

2. *The Arabs.* Dayan's image of Arab military capability was radically altered; but he maintained the conviction that the Arabs wished to annihilate Israel. As with decision-makers of other states under stress, he viewed the alternatives open to the Arabs as unlimited, whereas Israel's options were perceived to be extremely limited. Meir engaged in highly personalized criticism of the Arabs as "malicious" and "ignorant." Eban used softer language to convey the same theme.

3. *Egypt.* Dayan was skeptical of Egypt's inclination toward a political settlement. Meir repeated her criticism of Sadat's Moscow ties, his callousness, and his neglect of his country's internal development. So too did Eban, noting Sadat's admiration for Hitler.

4. *Syria.* Meir termed Syrian leaders inhuman. Dayan was not certain that Syria would agree to sign even a cease-fire agreement. Eban did not make any reference to Syria.

5. *The Superpowers.* Dayan perceived asymmetry in superpower involvement, to Israel's disadvantage. Eban was confident that a cease-fire would not be imposed by them.

6. *The United States.* Dayan emphasized the importance of American public opinion. Both he and Meir viewed the U.S. in the friendliest terms, as a deterrent to the Soviet Union during the war and, hopefully, after the war, and as an honest broker bringing the parties together for negotiations. Eban perceived Washington primarily as a balancer.

7. *The Soviet Union.* Dayan accused the Soviets of being responsible for the outbreak of war; and, like Allon, he expected them to veto any UN cease-fire resolution. Meir shared Dayan's view. Eban condemned the Soviets, rejecting as well the idea of Soviet guarantees of a peace settlement.

8. *Territories and Secure Boundaries.* Allon asserted that Israel would be more determined than ever to insist upon secure boundaries. Dayan, strangely, did not mention territories or secure boundaries during the War. Meir and Eban believed that the 1973 War had nothing to do with territories and that it proved how dangerous a unilateral Israeli withdrawal to the 1949 armistice lines would have been—and would be in the future.

DECISION FLOW

1. 5–6 October

Three events triggered the 1973 crisis period: the hasty evacuation of Soviet dependents; the findings of a crucial Israeli air reconnaissance mission over Egyptian lines; and an intelligence report from the IDF Southern Command. As noted, information on the Soviet airlift of advisory personnel from Egypt and Syria, which reached AMAN during the night of 4–5 October, did not fit the existing evaluation of Arab intent. Preliminary analysis suggested three interpretations: (1) that the Russians were aware of an Arab plan to attack Israel and were attempting, openly and drastically, to prevent it; (2) that Egypt and Syria had requested the Soviet Union to withdraw all her advisers because of a deterioration in their relations; and (3) that Moscow was dissatisfied with her clients' behavior and had decided to act. The last two interpretations were unconvincing to Zeira, who conveyed his disquiet to the IDF Chief of Staff.[32] The results of the aerial reconnaissance mission along the Canal reached GHQ at the same time and "attested to the reinforcement of the Egyptian deployment in a threatening and warning manner."[33] This was further supported, at dawn on 5 October, by an intelligence report from the South showing that "the Egyptian army along the Suez Canal had reached a degree of

---

32. Nixon discerned a Soviet role: "It was hard for me to believe that the Egyptians and Syrians would have moved without the knowledge of the Soviets, if not without their direct encouragement" (*RN: The Memoirs of Richard Nixon* [New York, 1978], p. 921). Sadat confirmed Soviet knowledge by recalling in his autobiography that he told the Soviet Ambassador on 3 October: "I'd like to inform you officially that I and Syria have decided to start military operations against Israel so as to break the present deadlock." Assad conveyed the decision to the Soviet envoy in Damascus the next day. Sadat clearly implied Soviet discouragement by noting that the sole reply to his query, "What will the Soviet attitude be?", was an urgent request on the 4th for permission to land Soviet aircraft to evacuate the families of Soviet civilian advisers in Egypt (*In Search of Identity: An Autobiography* [New York, 1978], pp. 246, 247, 252). Zeira, then Director of Military Intelligence, was quoted, four years after the events, as having said to Elazar on Friday morning, 5 October: "I think that Israel is not going to war. But the situation today is fraught with more question marks than yesterday" (in S. Nakdimon, "Protocols of Discussions Among the Political and Military Leaders on 5th and 6th October 1973," *Yediot Aharonot*, 21 September 1977). See also Agranat Commission, Partial Report, 3 April 1974; S. Nakdimon, "New Revelations," *Yediot Aharonot*, 19 July 1974; A. Golan, "Albert," excerpt in *Yediot Aharonot*, 7 January 1977; and H. Bar-Tov, *Dado*, Vol. 1, pp. 314–316.

33. Agranat Commission, Partial Report, 3 April 1974.

emergency deployment and dispositions such as had never been observed previously by the IDF."[34] These included the strengthening of front-line forces along the Canal with dozens of artillery units, hundreds of tanks, and advanced preparations for a crossing.[35]

The direct result of these inputs was evident at the General Staff's weekly meeting on Friday morning. In Dayan's presence, the Staff "again decided to order 'C' Alert, the highest alert, for the army and a full alert for the Air Force" (Decision 3).[36] The "C" alert, declared at the beginning of the week, had been relaxed for some units on the previous day, 4 October.[37] At 09:45 on 5 October, Dayan, Elazar, and Zeira met with Meir to inform her of developments and IDF actions. At both meetings, the estimates of the probability of war were revised slightly upward, but it was still considered "low."[38] The outcome was a decision to convene a Cabinet meeting with those ministers present in Tel Aviv—it was the day before Yom Kippur—and to inform the United States of the situation, along with a request that the U.S. attempt to restrain Egypt through the Soviet Union. Although the warnings were transmitted, they did not achieve any effect, because of the prevailing CIA estimate of war as "unlikely" and because of communication failures between Washington and New York.

The Cabinet meeting on 5 October was attended by the Prime Minister, the Defense Minister, and five other ministers—Bar-Lev, Galili, Hazani, Hillel, and Peres—and by Elazar, Zeira, and Gazit. The Director of Military Intelligence reportedly declared that an attack was not likely, that "it was most improbable that the

34. Herzog, *The War of Atonement*, p. 47.
35. A. Golan, "Albert."
36. Dayan, *Story of My Life*, p. 386.
37. S. Gonen, Interview, *Yediot Aharonot*, 21 September 1977. H. Bar-Tov (*Dado*, Vol. 1, p. 315) contends that this was the first time the "C" alert was called since 1967. In view of the many critical situations and repeated warnings of the possibility of attacks in the past—as noted by Meir, Dayan, Elazar, and others—this is unlikely.
38. The summary paragraph of the AMAN intelligence report released at 13:15 on 5 October read: "In spite of the fact that the . . . emergency deployment on the Canal front could, seemingly, be an indicator for offensive intent, nevertheless, in our best judgment, there has been no change in the Egyptian appreciation of the balance between their and Tzahal's forces. Therefore, the likelihood that Egypt intends to renew hostilities is low" (quoted in Agranat Commission, Partial Report, 3 April 1974; see also Meir, *My Life*, p. 356). Dayan reportedly suggested, at one point in the meeting with Meir, the high probability of an Egyptian crossing of the Canal; but that was not the main thrust of his evaluation. See Nakdimon, "New Revelations," *Yediot Aharonot*, 19 July 1974.

Egyptians would cross the Canal in large forces, though they might open fire and attempt raids."[39] Elazar supported the AMAN estimate but added that there was no evidence that the enemy was not going to attack. Again he noted that he had ordered the highest alert in the regular forces, including the cancellation of all leaves on both fronts and in the Air Force, and he had alerted the mobilization centers, "but the mobilization of reserves and other measures were delayed until [the receipt of] further indicators."[40] Meir recalled about that meeting: "Not one minister . . . said a word about the need for total mobilization. [The experts] . . . said on Wednesday and on Thursday, even on that last Friday before the war, that war is unlikely."[41]

To be on the safe side, after Galili had raised the question, the Cabinet decided to empower the Prime Minister and Defense Minister to call up all the reserves, if necessary (Decision 4).[42] It also approved the despatch of a message to Kissinger, via Israel's Embassy in Washington, requesting him to inform Egypt, Syria, and the Soviet Union that Israel had no aggressive intentions but to indicate that, if attacked, she would respond forcefully. The message also contained the prevailing Israeli intelligence evaluation: that Syria was reacting to a perceived possible Israeli move against her, and that Egypt was engaged in maneuvers, which were expected to end on Sunday, 7 October. Inexplicably, the message was not sent until the evening. Brigadier-General Scowcroft, the Deputy Director of the National Security Council, received it at 17:30, that is, 23:30 Israeli time. The message reached Kissinger at 20:00 New York time.[43]

39. Dayan, *Story of My Life,* p. 386; according to Bar-Tov (*Dado,* Vol. 1, p. 320), this appreciation was voiced at the meeting of the General Staff, immediately following the Cabinet meeting. Bar-Lev, a former Chief of Staff, revealed soon after the Yom Kippur War that he learned of the seriousness of the situation for the first time at the 5 October Cabinet meeting (Interview, *Ma'ariv,* 9 November 1973). The highest level of U.S. decision-makers, too, did not anticipate war. According to Nixon: "The news of the imminent attack on Israel took us completely by surprise." Moreover, "I was disappointed by our own intelligence shortcomings, and I was stunned by the failure of Israeli intelligence. They were among the best in the world, and they, too, had been caught off guard" (*Memoirs,* p. 920).

40. Agranat Commission, Partial Report, 3 April 1974; Bar-Tov, *Dado,* Vol. 1, p. 320. The Agranat Commission added that these "further indicators" were supposed to arrive within hours, but in fact arrived only the next morning.

41. Interview, *Ma'ariv,* 16 September 1974.

42. Y. Galili, Interview with Y. Ben-Porath, *Yediot Aharonot,* 27 October 1978.

43. Ray Cline's testimony before the U.S. House of Representatives, Subcommittee on Intelligence, September 1975; Eban, Interview with M. Brecher,

This delay in informing Washington underlines the fact that, until the end of 5 October, time salience for Israel's decision-makers did not extend to hours and minutes. Nevertheless, the pace of consultation and action quickened. The IDF's Northern Command decided to prepare for a limited Syrian assault. The Southern Command undertook some preparations called for by Alert "C," but it denied requests made by the OC Armored Corps, South, General Avraham (Albert) Mendler, for additional forces. More serious, Mendler was unable to undertake some of the redeployment called for by "Operation Dovecote." Even as late as the morning of the 6th, he received instructions from the OC Southern Command not to undertake any movements (i.e., of tanks) to forward positions in Sinai that could arouse Egyptian suspicions of a planned Israeli attack.[44]

Between 03:30 and 04:00 on 6 October, the Director of Military Intelligence was notified that Egypt and Syria would attack Israel before sundown; he immediately informed the Defense Minister and the Prime Minister's military ADC.[45] The timetable of events from the receipt of this message until the outbreak of war at 14:00 is as follows:

03:30–04:00	The message was received by the Director of Military Intelligence, who informed Meir, Dayan, and Elazar.
04:00	Meir instructed ADC Lior to ask Dayan, Allon, Galili, and Elazar to be in her Tel Aviv office before 07:00.
04:05	Meir phoned Dayan, who informed her that he would meet with the Chief of Staff to assess the situation; the meeting at the Prime Minister's office was postponed to 08:00.
04:40	The Chief of Staff phoned Air Force Commander Peled and asked him to specify the earliest feasible time for a pre-emptive aerial strike against Syria. Peled indicated between 12:00 and 13:00. Elazar issued an order to prepare for such a strike.[46]

15 July 1974; A. Eban, *An Autobiography* (Jerusalem and Tel Aviv, 1977), pp. 500, 501; B. Kalb and M. Kalb, *Kissinger* (Boston and Toronto, 1974), pp. 458–459; M. Golan, *The Secret Conversations of Henry Kissinger: Step-by-Step Diplomacy in the Middle East* (New York, 1976), pp. 37–39.

44. A. Golan, "Albert"; Herzog, *The War of Atonement*, p. 45.

45. Dayan recalls 04:00 (*Story of My Life*, p. 375); Meir mentions 03:30 (Interview, *Ma'ariv*, 16 September 1974).

46. H. Bar-Tov, *Dado*, Vol. 2, pp. 9–10; Nakdimon, "New Revelations," *Yediot Aharonot*, 26 July 1974.

05:15   A General Staff meeting was held with Elazar, Zeira, Peled, Tal, and other ranking officers, but without the regional commanders. Zeira still estimated the probability of an attack to be "low," but this was rejected by Elazar and others. The Chief of Staff informed the meeting that he intended to propose full mobilization of the reserves and had given the necessary preparatory orders, including the mobilization of Civil Defense.

05:45   Dayan met General Shlomo Gazit, in charge of the Administered Territories, and they decided on an increased alert in his Command.

05:50   Dayan held a meeting with Elazar, Tal, Zeira, and others from the General Staff, as well as Lior. Elazar advocated almost total mobilization—"about 200,000 men"—and a pre-emptive strike by the Air Force either against Egypt and Syria or against Syria alone. Dayan rejected both ideas and was willing to agree only to mobilization of forces needed for defense.[47]

07:15   The Chief of Staff met with the OCs of Northern and Southern Commands, Generals Hofi and Gonen, and other members of the General Staff. He issued "general instructions" for war, emphasizing that the first phase would be a holding operation and that all forces must be ready to move over to a counter-attack as early as possible.[48]

08:00   The (enlarged) Kitchen Cabinet met at the Prime Minister's office in Tel Aviv. Present were Dayan, Galili, Allon (who arrived late), Bar-Lev, Elazar, Zeira, M. Gazit, and Zvi Zur, Assistant to the Defense Minister. The Prime Minister decided in favor of large-scale mobilization of reserves, but against a pre-emptive airstrike (Decisions 5 and 6).

10:00   Meir met U.S. Ambassador Keating and his Counsellor, Veliotis. Also present were Allon, Zeira, Aharon Kidron, Director-General of the Foreign Ministry, and Simha Dinitz, Israel's Ambassador to the U.S. The Prime Minister informed Keating that Israel had reliable evidence that the "attacks would start late in the afternoon and that we would not strike first."[49]

47. Nakdimon, "New Revelations," *Yediot Aharonot*, 26 July 1974; Dayan, *Story of My Life*, p. 376; H. Bar-Tov, *Dado*, Vol. 2, pp. 12–13.
48. Herzog, *The War of Atonement*, p. 53; H. Bar-Tov, *Dado*, Vol. 2, pp. 15–16.
49. *My Life*, p. 359; Keating and U.S. Embassy officials, Interviews with M. Brecher, 30 July 1974.

| 11:00 | Dayan joined the "Kedem" Operational Consultative Group chaired by Elazar to discuss preparations to stop the Egypt-Syria assault. |
| 12:00 | The Cabinet convened in Tel Aviv, with all members present except two *Mafdal* ministers—Burg and Warhaftig—who were in Jerusalem; Eban, who was in New York; and Sharef and Gvati. War broke out at 14:00 while the Cabinet was still in session. |

The consultative process during those fateful hours revealed the effect of intense time pressure. A realization that war had become a near certainty[50] led to a purely internal Israeli decision process without external, primarily U.S., pressure—unlike 1967.[51] The two major decisions—to order large-scale mobilization and not to pre-empt—were taken at the same meeting by the Prime Minister, almost intuitively, though she was formally empowered to do so during the previous day's Cabinet session.

50. "Near certainty" because there were still some doubts. For example, the late Pinhas Sapir emphasized that Dayan was skeptical about the outbreak of war until the last minute. He left the Cabinet session at 13:00 "for lunch," signaling his reservations about the thrust of the discussion (Interview with M. Brecher 25 June 1974; see also note 21 above). Dayan's actions during the next few days, notably his offer to resign on the 7th and his morbid assessment to Israel's editors on the 9th, testify to the trauma he experienced with the outbreak of war and the IDF's initial setbacks—and his surprise that it occurred at all.

51. For U.S. pressure on Israel in 1967, see Chapter 5 above. There is still a crucial, unresolved controversy about U.S. pressure on Israel in 1973, with significant implications for Israel's autonomy of decision about pre-emption on the eve of the Yom Kippur War. According to the Kalbs, Kissinger had warned Israeli Ambassador Dinitz and Minister Shalev in previous months—repeatedly and in the strongest terms—not to pre-empt. "'Don't ever start the war,' Kissinger would admonish them. 'Don't ever pre-empt!' He would then forecast absolute disaster if Israel ignored his counsel. 'If you fire the first shot, you won't have a dogcatcher in this country supporting you. You won't have presidential support. You'll be alone, all alone.'" Moreover, according to the Kalbs, the Secretary of State, in a phone conversation with Eban shortly after 06:00 New York time, 6 October, that is, shortly after 12:00 noon, Israeli time, which means almost three hours after the decision was taken, and after Keating's report of the decision reached him, "[added] the extra warning: 'Don't pre-empt!'" (B. Kalb and M. Kalb, *Kissinger*, pp. 459, 460). Quandt went further: "In the less than two hours that remained before the war began, Kissinger took charge, calling the Israelis to warn against preemption . . ." (*Decade of Decisions* [Berkeley, Los Angeles, and London, 1977], p. 166; see also pp. 169–170). No corroborating evidence has yet appeared, except for Dayan's ambiguous remark in his memoirs that, on the morning of the 6th, "Americans warned us not to take any provocative action" (*Story of My Life*, p. 379). The Kalbs' contention is highly improbable because of the time sequence noted above; that is, the decision on pre-emption was taken by Israel's decision-makers without U.S. pressure. In that context, Eban (*An Autobiography*, p. 502) recalled that telephone conversation as follows:

Elazar opened the meeting, which began at 08:00 on 6 October, advocating the mobilization of several army divisions and of the entire Air Force.[52] To the Prime Minister he said, pointedly: "I want you to know that our air force can be ready to strike at noon, but you must give me the green light now."[53]

Dayan recalled the deliberations thus:

We were faced with four principal issues: mobilization of reserves and reinforcement of the fronts; a possible pre-emptive strike by our Air Force; evacuation of children and women from our frontier settlements in the Golan Heights; and delivery of a warning to Egypt and Syria.

In our preliminary consultation [at a meeting], I told the chief of staff that I agreed to his request for the immediate mobilization of the reserves required for the defense of the two fronts on as full a scale as he found necessary. But I decided to bring before the prime minister the questions of a pre-emptive strike and the immediate mobilization of all the reserves needed under the contingency plan to go over to counter-attack. . . .

"He had been studying a report of our Prime Minister's talk with Ambassador Keating. He noted the Israeli decision to abstain from pre-emptive action. He wanted to put on record with me that this was an Israeli decision conveyed to the United States after it had been taken. He personally believed it to be the right decision, but the United States had no need to give advice on an issue which Israel had already determined for herself." The then-Foreign Minister also recreated the hectic, tense flow of events in New York during the two hours before the war. He received a cable from Galili shortly before 06:00, New York time, about the anticipated Egypt-Syria attack later in the day and the Prime Minister's assurance to the U.S. Ambassador that Israel would not pre-empt. According to Gazit, "There were no hints of any kind that I am aware of, from any source in the U.S. to any source in Israel, not to pre-empt. The only exception was at the meeting with Ambassador Keating where, after Mrs. Meir told him so, he remarked that it was important that we were certain that, in fact, we would not pre-empt. But nobody put pressure or suggested to Israel that she should not pre-empt in this situation" (Interview with M. Brecher, 27 July 1974). Ten minutes later, Eban informed Kissinger (who in the meantime had received Keating's report on his talk with Meir). During the next two hours of frantic activity, the Secretary of State informed President Nixon, Soviet Ambassador Dobrynin, UN Secretary-General Waldheim, and the Ambassadors of Egypt and Saudi Arabia, urging restraint upon the latter. Eban was on the phone with the Prime Minister and with the Director-General of Israel's Foreign Ministry, inquiring about Egypt's charge that Israel's navy had initiated the attack when the latter notified him that war had just broken out. (Gazit, Interview with M. Brecher, 27 July 1974. See also Eban, *An Autobiography*, pp. 501–503; and Nakdimon, "New Revelations," *Yediot Aharonot*, 26 July 1974.)

52. The Chief of Staff did not call for *general* mobilization but for units totaling 100,000 to 120,000 men; this was far less than Israel's entire reserves; H. Bar-Tov, *Dado*, Vol. 2, pp. 20–23.

53. Meir, *My Life*, p. 359.

The pre-emptive strike which the chief of staff recommended, after consultation with the Air Force, was to be directed against Syria alone . . . only against air bases deep inside Syria—and even that not before twelve noon.

I rejected the idea of a pre-emptive strike by the Air Force as well as the mobilization of more reserves than were required for immediate defense. . . .

These points were thoroughly reviewed at our meeting with the prime minister and it was finally resolved, at her decision, to order the mobilization of . . . 100,000 to 120,000 men, in addition to the regular army; not to carry out a pre-emptive air strike; to evacuate children and women from the Golan settlements; and to send a warning to Egypt and Syria through the United States. . . .[54]

Elazar's account of what took place in the discussion with Dayan before the 08:00 o'clock Kitchen Cabinet was diametrically opposed to the latter's memoir:

During my meeting with the Minister of Defense on the morning of Yom Kippur, I demanded again and again a full mobilization of reserves, but the Minister of Defense argued that a small deployment of two divisions would be sufficient. During the investigation, I was asked by the [Agranat] Committee if there was an agreement between the Minister and me to mobilize two divisions. My repeated answers were that during the meeting on the morning of Yom Kippur, it was not agreed to mobilize two divisions. I testified that at a certain point during this discussion, the Minister ordered his Military Secretary to ask the Prime Minister for approval by telephone to mobilize two divisions. I clarified that that would not be enough. The Minister cancelled his order to his Secretary and agreed that both proposals would be brought to the Prime Minister for her decision. . . . As a result of the disagreement between the Minister of Defense and me, the Minister decided to bring both proposals to the Prime Minister, and until her decision was made, he did not give his approval to any mobilization. . . . It should be noted that a request to the Prime Minister for the mobilization of reserves is the privilege of the Minister of Defense only.[55]

The essential difference between the two advocacies was cogently summarized as follows:

Elazar deduced his policy recommendations from the assumption of the worst case—the Arab intent to attack—and the subsequent necessity to increase Israel's defensive capability. Dayan deduced his proposals for partial mobilization and no pre-emption from a lower estimate of the

54. *Story of My Life*, pp. 375–376.
55. Memorandum to the Cabinet in May 1975; published in *Ma'ariv*, 20 April 1976.

probability of attack, reinforced by assumptions of miscalculation and escalation.[56]

Both men insisted upon clearly defined, explicit terms in the decision, and when they could not agree, Dayan passed the burden —for a crucial military decision—on to the Prime Minister. She recalled her consternation: "My God, I have to decide which of them is right?"[57]

The Prime Minister's decision in favor of Elazar's suggestion for large-scale mobilization was due to a single calculus, as noted earlier: "If there really was a war, then we had to be in the very best position possible." Similarly, as noted, she decided against a pre-emptive strike because "there is always the possibility that we will need help, and if we strike first, we will get nothing from anyone."[58] That decision, she later revealed, was made almost instantly: She made her calculation by drawing upon Israel's experience in the 1967 crisis period, before the Six Day War, when, even with Nasser's provocative acts, "we witnessed the 'great support' given to us by the whole world."[59] Elazar replied that it was, of course, reckless not to pre-empt but that it would not make things too difficult for Israel.[60]

The acrimonious debate between Dayan and Elazar was thus resolved and the orders given to mobilize. The Agranat Commission blamed Elazar for the delay; and it was the main reason for

56. J. Stein and R. Tanter, *Rational Decision-Making: Israel's Security Choices, 1967* (forthcoming). Quoted from manuscript, p. 402.

57. *My Life,* p. 358. For Dayan, it was a typical move of "sharing responsibility"; he did so several times in similar circumstances.

58. Ibid., p. 359.

59. Interview, *Ma'ariv,* 16 September 1974. Much insight into Meir's calculus in choosing not to pre-empt was provided by Gazit, who worked closely with her for many years in both the Foreign Ministry and the Prime Minister's Office: "Golda would tell you that she was afraid that this time she could not count on U.S. support. That is to say, she was concerned with the image of the U.S. and the possible loss of U.S. diplomatic and military support. Secondly, Golda had great confidence in the IDF's ability to win. She felt that in 1967 we were so successful that now, years later, with the large strides made in armament and, particularly, in view of the fact that neither Dayan nor Dado [Elazar] showed any apprehension or made a recommendation for a pre-emptive strike as a necessity, why should she then order it. And in that context, Dado said that a preventive strike would make things easier but he never said it would be essential. If Dayan and/or Dado would have said that a strike was essential, there is not doubt in my mind that Golda would have decided in favor of such a step" (Interview with M. Brecher, 27 July 1974).

60. Meir, Interview, *Ma'ariv,* 16 September 1974.

his resignation after the Commission's first interim report was published on 3 April 1974.[61]

At the 10:00 meeting with Keating, the Prime Minister informed the U.S. Ambassador that, "according to our intelligence, the attacks would start late in the afternoon and that we would not strike first. . . . We would not make a pre-emptive strike."[62] Keating recalled the incident vividly. He had received a phone call at 08:30 from the Prime Minister, asking for a meeting at 10:00:

The Prime Minister said to me that she had unqualified and undeniable evidence that the Arabs intended to strike massively against Israel by sunset of that day. The Prime Minister urged me to communicate this information to the Secretary of State and, through him, to contact Soviet officials and those of Egypt and of Syria and to tell them that Israel knew of their plans, was ready, but did not want war. I asked the Prime Minister: "In the light of the information is it Israel's intent, and has Israel made a decision, not to pre-empt?" And the answer was firm and clear: "Mr. Ambassador, we have decided not to pre-empt." Thereafter, Keating left to communicate this significant information to Washington.[63]

At the same time, U.S. Embassy personnel informed Washington that they expected to be notified by the Israeli Government within a few hours that there were too many risks involved and that it had decided to pre-empt massively. Thus, for several hours after the outbreak of war, the U.S. was not certain who attacked whom.[64]

The noon Cabinet meeting, in Meir's terse summary, "heard a full description of the situation, including the decision to mobilize the reserves and also my decision regarding a pre-emptive strike. Nobody raised any objections whatsoever."[65] One of the reasons for unanimity, and a key to Israeli decision-making throughout the 1973 crisis period, was noted by a participant: "The issue was discussed at the noon Cabinet meeting, but you must remember that Golda had great authority. Once she decided and gave her reasons, the others would accept her decision."[66]

61. Elazar asserted in his 1975 Memorandum to the Cabinet (published in *Ma'ariv*, 20 April 1976) that the Prime Minister approved the limited call-up of reserves "within minutes" of the beginning of the discussion, and the large-scale call-up within twenty minutes. Moreover, the delay arose from the Dayan-Elazar disagreement before the 08:00 meeting.

62. *My Life*, p. 359.

63. Keating, Interview with M. Brecher, 30 July 1974.

64. B. Kalb and M. Kalb, *Kissinger*, pp. 456–460. Nixon, however, reveals no uncertainty on this point, with his reference to "the news of the imminent attack on Israel . . ." (*Memoirs*, p. 920).

65. *My Life*, p. 359.

66. Gazit, Interview with M. Brecher, 27 July 1974.

Dayan confirmed the essence of the meeting more precisely:

The government approved what had been decided upon at my earlier
meeting with the prime minister, including partial mobilization—of
120,000 reservists. There was a brief discussion of how we might act if
Egypt alone opened hostilities, namely, whether to wait until Syria joined
in or to make an advanced strike on Syria. The Cabinet was also informed
that the United States had been in touch with Egypt, directly, and with
Syria, through the Soviet Union, telling them of Israel's report that they
intended to attack and asking for clarification. The Egyptians had not yet
replied, but America warned us not to take any provocative action, adding
that news had reached them that we were proposing to attack within six
hours. Nor had the United States received any response from the
Russians.[67]

Bar-Lev challenged the assumption that the attack would begin
at 18:00, on the grounds that it did not make military sense, and
he wondered whether the intelligence information might be
incorrect. The same objection was raised by Allon. But Elazar was
categorical about the timing.[68] While the Cabinet was still in
session, at 14:00, news arrived that war had broken out.[69]

During the next few hours, there were intense consultations
centering around Meir in the Prime Minister's office and Dayan at
General Headquarters (GHQ). In the evening, there was a second
Cabinet meeting; and from then on until the end of the 1973 crisis
period, as in 1967, there was a continuous round of Cabinet meet-

67. *Story of My Life*, p. 379.

68. S. Nakdimon, "The Events that Preceded the War," a series of articles
(hereafter "Pre-war Events") *Yediot Aharonot*, 14 December 1973; Schiff, *October Earthquake*, pp. 68–69. Schiff noted, p. 101, that the IDF had held a war
game in 1969 which showed the advantages to Egypt of an attack between 14:00
and 15:00. That lesson was forgotten. The error was apparently due to the ambiguous phrase in the intelligence report, "before sunset." "One of the great
puzzles that no one could explain," remarked Meir a year later, "was that it was
stated that war would break out at 6 in the evening and nobody knows why, on
what basis. The supposition is that, in the information received, the time of sunset
was mentioned and somebody concluded that this meant six in the evening"
(Interview, *Ma'ariv*, 16 September 1974).

69. The Air Force Commander was notified by Elazar at 12:30 that his proposal for an aerial strike had been rejected by the Cabinet. However, Peled, who
shared the skepticism of experienced former military commanders about the expected hour of attack, 18:00, ordered partrols into the air at 13:30. Two planes on
patrol from Sharm-e-Sheikh were immediately attacked by twelve Egyptian
MiGs, and in the engagement seven MiGs were shot down. Thus, strictly speak-
ing, hostilities began at 13:30 (Herzog, *The War of Atonement*, pp. 255–256). For
details on the planned pre-emptive air strike, see Peled as quoted in A. Avnery,
Red Sky (Tel Aviv, 1975), pp. 106–107 (in Hebrew).

ings, averaging two per day, at the Prime Minister's Tel Aviv office.[70] There were also many informal consultations at political and bureaucratic levels, and daily meetings of the Knesset Foreign Affairs and Security Committee, the first at 14:00 on 6 October, at which time Opposition Leader Begin proposed a political truce until the end of the war. The Prime Minister readily agreed.[71]

The second Cabinet meeting that day started at 22:00 and lasted until midnight, with the first three-quarters of an hour devoted to a report on the military situation by the COS and the Defense Minister. Elazar did not conceal the heavy losses sustained during the first hours of the fighting; but "despite this, [he] was relatively optimistic. . . . Israeli army reserves would reach both fronts within 24 to 48 hours. Their arrival would tilt back the balance of forces and enable us to retrieve the initiative."[72] Dayan's own evaluation was much less sanguine:

I felt heavy of heart, and I did not share the optimism of the chief of staff and GOC Southern Command. The Egyptians had already achieved powerful gains, and we had suffered a heavy blow. They had crossed the Canal, established bridges, and moved armor, infantry, and anti-tank weapons across them. Not only had we failed to prevent this, but we had caused the Egyptians relatively little damage.

The critical battlefield was the Canal Zone. . . . We would need a good deal of luck to end the next day's battles in our favor. After that, on the third and fourth days of the war, Monday and Tuesday (October 8 and 9) we should have all the planned armored force in the south, and we would be able to carry out tank warfare. It would not be simple, but the prospects for success were good.

It seemed to me, therefore, that in the south we should retire to a second line, fight the Egyptians within a belt of twelve miles from the Canal, and build up our strength. In the north, I expected that we would succeed in stopping the Syrians at the frontier. . . .[73]

70. Meir, Interview, *Ma'ariv*, 16 September 1974, and interviews with Meir aides during the 1973 Crisis by M. Brecher and B. Geist, 16 and 18 August 1977.

71. The Knesset, which had been formally dissolved because of impending elections, met only in special plenary sessions during the crisis period, on 16 and 23–25 October. At the 16 October meeting, the Prime Minister reported on the situation and indicated that the IDF had crossed the Canal. The tenor of Opposition speeches was that, while many questions had to be answered by the Government, this was not the appropriate time to raise them (*Divrei Haknesset*, 68, 4474 –4495).

72. Dayan, *Story of My Life*, p. 388. Confirmed in Gazit interview with M. Brecher, 27 July 1974.

73. *Story of My Life*, pp. 390–391. For Sadat's vivid account of the first day's fighting, see *In Search of Identity*, pp. 248–252.

The Cabinet was also informed of steps taken to keep Jordan out of the war; as in 1967, a warning was sent together with assurances that Israel would not start a third front.[74]

The issue of a cease-fire arose at the outset of the war. As Gazit remarked: "We were in favor of a cease-fire right from the beginning. But the decision . . . was not made on the first day. Even later, the request to the U.S. to arrange a cease-fire was not to arrange it on the ground but rather to restore the *status-quo-ante*."[75] Eban concurred—and shed more light on this controversial matter:

> On the first day of the war there was some discussion of a cease-fire, in a talk I had with Kissinger about its timing. Kissinger said, "We are working toward a cease-fire, the sooner the better." In that sense there was talk about it. But the Arabs were taking their time; they wanted a demonstration [of support] in the General Assembly, on Monday. I think it became clear on Monday how serious the situation was. Then a cable arrived from Mrs. Meir stating that we should wait for a cease-fire until Wednesday [the 10th], because by that time the situation should have turned to our advantage.[76]

This accords with the mood of optimism about the outcome that prevailed among Israel's decision-makers on the evening of the 6th. Moreover, at the UN, Israel, like the Arab States, did not request an urgent meeting of the Security Council: She merely conveyed to the Council's President and the Secretary-General a charge of Egyptian and Syrian aggression. The first meeting of the

74. Interviews by M. Brecher with Gazit, Yariv, and Peres, 27 July, 7 August, and 11 August 1974, respectively, and with senior officials of the U.S. Embassy, Tel Aviv, 12 August 1974.

75. Interview with M. Brecher, 27 July 1974. See also Quandt, *Decade of Decisions*, pp. 171–172.

76. Interview with M. Brecher, 15 July 1974. The contention that Israel asked for a cease-fire in place on 6 October was categorically denied in Brecher interviews with Gazit and Eban, as noted, and with Yariv, Keating, and other U.S. Embassy officials. Nixon (*Memoirs*, p. 921) wrote that, on that day, neither side wanted a cease-fire and that he saw no point in trying to impose one: "It would be better to wait until the war had reached the point at which neither side had a decisive military advantage." On the Arab side, there appear to have been differences over a cease-fire at the outset. According to Sadat, the Soviet Ambassador informed him on 6 October that Assad asked Moscow on the 4th to work for a cease-fire no more than forty-eight hours from the planned attack on the 6th. Assad reportedly denied this to Sadat, on the 7th. Brezhnev, in pressing Sadat to accept a cease-fire in the early days, told Tito that Syria had submitted three requests for a cease-fire. Egypt's President, by contrast, recalled that he had categorically rejected pressure for a cease-fire: on the 6th, from the Soviets; on the 13th, from Kissinger, via British Prime Minister Heath and the British Ambassador in Cairo; and from 16 to 19 October, from Kosygin (Sadat, *In Search of Identity*, pp. 252–254, 256–258, and 258–259). See also Quandt, *Decade of Decisions*, pp. 171–172.

Council did not take place until Monday, 8 October, in the evening. On that same date, there was also an inconclusive debate in the General Assembly at the initiative of the Arab States.[77]

II. 7–14 October

Sunday, 7 October, was a day of desperate fighting on both fronts to stop the advance of Syrian and Egyptian armor and infantry. IDF reserve units were thrown into battle as they arrived, and losses in manpower and equipment were mounting sharply. By the end of the day, the Syrian advance had been temporarily contained. On the southern front, the Egyptians were still advancing methodically, the Second Army in the northern sector of the Suez Canal and the Third Army in the southern section.

Early in the morning, Elazar reported to the Cabinet the estimates of front commanders that the advances of the Arab armies had been contained. He also reaffirmed his evaluation that the Egyptians could be thrown back to the other side of the Canal within a short time. Dayan was absent, having left for a tour of the fronts. After the Cabinet meeting, Elazar left for a similar tour.

At 16:00 and 17:00, respectively, when Dayan and Elazar returned, they met with Meir, Allon, and Galili. There was a sharp divergence in their assessment of the situation. The Defense Minister advocated a substantial retreat—evacuation of the Canal strongholds and the establishment of a new line "some distance from the Canal," to be held at all costs. The Chief of Staff, on the other hand, suggested a counterattack to begin the next morning. The meetings ended with a decision to empower the Chief of Staff to fly south, study the situation, and "decide about a counterattack" (Decision 7). But Dayan's evaluation was so shocking to the Prime Minister that she called a Cabinet meeting at 20:00; it approved the decision taken. The Prime Minister also decided to relieve former COS Bar-Lev from his duties as Minister of Industry and Commerce, and to send him to the northern front to assess the situation.[78]

77. Reports of UNTSO observers, confirming the Egypt-Syria attack, are in UN document S/7930/ADD. 2142. Eban spoke at both the General Assembly and Security Council meetings.

78. Dayan, *Story of My Life*, pp. 406–407; Meir, *My Life*, pp. 360–361; Herzog, *The War of Atonement*, p. 183; H. Bar-Tov, *Dado*, Vol. 2, pp. 63–73. In several Brecher-Geist 1977 interviews with Meir's 1973 aides, the profound effect of Dayan's pessimistic evaluation on Meir during that 7 October meeting was vividly recalled and emphasized, as it also was by Yisrael Galili in an interview

The heavy IDF losses in equipment—40 planes downed by missiles during the first twenty-four hours and 200 tanks—led to urgent requests for planes and tanks from the United States. However, only on Tuesday, 9 October, did these needs seemingly become so imperative that Israel put immense pressure on U.S. leadership, through several channels, for an immediate airlift of vital supplies. In reality, except for 155mm artillery shells, Israel's pre–6 October resources were adequate for the conduct of the 1973 War.[79] Nevertheless, to continue the war with rapidly dwindling stockpiles would have placed an intolerable strain on the IDF and its leaders. Secondly, and no less important, the fact of the U.S. airlift, in the face of an all-out resupply of Arab armies by the Soviet Union, was instrumental in restoring the diplomatic balance and laid the groundwork for an end to the war. At the same time, the negotiation process exposed Israel's dependence upon American support in a protracted conflict.

On the morning of 8 October, the southern part of the Golan Heights front collapsed and there was a danger that Syrian armor would reach Israeli Jordan Valley settlements. Furthermore, in the early afternoon, Syrian armored units suddenly appeared next to a military camp in the center of the Golan Heights (Nafekh); again there was grave danger that these units might reach Israeli Huleh Valley settlements by crossing over the B'not Ya'akov bridge, only six miles away. These advances were contained (a) by intensified IDF air attacks on Syrian armor; and (b) by using newly arrived reserve units in desperate blocking operations. By the evening, Syrian attacks were checked and the danger of a breakthrough was averted, with heavy fighting still continuing.

---

with Y. Ben-Porath in *Yediot Aharonot,* 27 October 1978. Dayan's assessment was offset by Elazar and, later, by Bar-Lev, who stayed on the northern front for twenty-four hours. Bar-Lev's view was that there was no reason to make territorial concessions. He reported to the Prime Minister on the 8th that "the situation is difficult but not lost" (Bar-Lev, Interview with U. Millstein, 26 June 1974).

79. Israel's request for arms was transmitted through three parallel channels: the Defense Ministry to the U.S. Embassy in Tel Aviv; Dinitz to Kissinger; and the Israeli Military Attaché in Washington, General Mordekhai Gur, to the Pentagon. Requests started on the second day of the war. Dinitz, during his first meeting with Kissinger on Sunday, 7 October, submitted a "modest" list of needed supplies (B. Kalb and M. Kalb, *Kissinger,* p. 464). From that day onward, in the words of the U.S. Chief of Naval Operations in 1973, "almost every day during the war's first week the Israeli Ambassador handed a new and larger shopping list to Henry Kissinger . . ." (E. Zumwalt, *On Watch, A Memoir* [New York, 1976], p. 433).

IDF operations on the Egyptian front that day were a dismal failure. The counterattack ordered by Elazar on the morning of the 8th did not achieve its aim—namely, to throw the Egyptians back across the Canal; and Israel again suffered heavy losses. The Agranat Commission issued a harsh verdict on the battle of 8 October:

Although in the *execution* of the operations of that day some of the effects of the initial surprise are still discernible, the IDF were by then in a position to determine the timing and plan of attack. . . . What caused— *inter alia*—the offensive to go wrong was an erosive deviation from the objective of the battle, as defined by the Chief of Staff, as well as a lack of control on the part of the Command, and its inability to read correctly the course of the battle.[80]

An early result was the Prime Minister's decision the following day to replace Gonen as OC Southern Command by Bar-Lev, as the Chief of Staff's Personal Representative (Decision 9).

The Security Council met for the first time during the 1973 Crisis on the evening of 8 October (New York time). Although the U.S. initiative was based upon an agreement reached in an exchange of messages between Nixon and Brezhnev the previous day, it soon became apparent that the cease-fire proposed by Ambassador Scali would not be accepted. Eban's very short speech was noncommittal, its main purpose being to reserve Israel's right of further communication. The Council adjourned without deciding anything, even the time for its next meeting, after less than two hours of discussion.[81]

The 9th of October became a turning point in U.S. and Soviet attitudes to the 1973 War: "From the perspective of Washington," wrote William B. Quandt, "the war entered a new and acute phase on October 9." Until then, the CIA evaluation was that Israel would be victorious within a week—Kissinger had called the Arab attack military madness. At that day's two meetings of the U.S. National Security Council's Action Group, Kissinger reported Israel's urgent needs for military equipment, received through

80. Third and Final Report of the Agranat Commission, 30 January 1975. See also articles by Z. Schiff, "The 8th of October: The Most Important Day of the War," *Ha'aretz*, 25 and 30 September 1974.

81. For the deliberations in and around the Security Council, see T. Draper, "The Road to Geneva," *Commentary*, 57:2 (February 1974), 23–39. Eban (*An Autobiography*, pp. 510–511) recalled receiving a cable from Meir on the 8th in the evening, advising him that "we could not possibly conceive of carrying out a cease-fire resolution so long as the enemy forces had not been repelled." See also M. Golan, *The Secret Conversations of Henry Kissinger*, p. 63.

Dinitz that morning. The Israeli Ambassador had also reported the heavy IDF losses, especially of planes on the Syrian front. Quandt continues: "The two recommendations that emerged from these sessions were presented to Nixon by Kissinger at noon. First, some arms must begin to reach Israel quickly, without violating the principle of maintaining a low American profile in the conflict. Second, a new formula for a cease-fire should be explored."[82]

The Soviet attitude toward the 1973 War had been relatively reserved thus far. While providing political support to the Arab cause publicly and in the UN, the style was restrained and mild.[83] Moscow revealed a readiness to cooperate in a political solution, stressing, as Brezhnev did on 8 October, "guaranteed security for all countries and peoples of the area." But after the early successes of the Arab armies, the Soviets decided to take a more active role. On 9 October, they began a massive supply of military aid by air and sea to Egypt and Syria, designed, as Galia Golan put it, "to supply the wherewithal for a total Arab victory now that the Arabs had proved their worth in battle."[84]

Dayan returned from the South with Elazar in the early morning of the 9th. His gloomy assessment of the situation on that front— overly pessimistic as events would show—received full expression in an off-the-record briefing for Israeli editors that evening.[85] Stating over and over again that Israel did not have the strength to push the Egyptians back across the Canal, he strongly urged that the IDF establish new defense lines near the Canal, dig in, and conserve its forces. The worst was over on the northern front, he argued, but the war in Sinai could be a drawn-out affair: "I don't think that the affair will be over in ten days," for the Egyptians "have unlimited equipment . . . , it's fantastic, it is terrible to fight against such a thing." Although unlikely, he did not rule out Egyptian gains in southern Sinai, at the Abu Rodeis oilfields, or even the occupation of Sharm-e-Sheikh.

Dayan had presented this morbid evaluation at the morning Cabinet meeting. The Cabinet approved a decision, taken by the

82. Quandt, *Decade of Decisions*, pp. 176–177.

83. Quandt reports that on both 6th and 7th October, Moscow suggested to Sadat that he accept a simple cease-fire at an early date—and that Kissinger was aware of this (*Decade of Decisions*, p. 174, n. 19).

84. G. Golan, *Yom Kippur and After: The Soviet Union and the Middle East Crisis* (Cambridge, England, 1977), pp. 85–86.

85. The verbatim text was published in *Ha'aretz,* 15 February 1974.

Defense Minister the day before, to concentrate IDF efforts on defeating the Syrians while containing Egyptian advances in the South. It also approved the bombing of military targets in Damascus and elsewhere well inside Syria, partly in retaliation for the use of ground-to-ground intermediate-range Frog-type missiles against targets inside Israel, and partly to ease the pressure on the IDF frontline (Decision 8).[86] The Cabinet also approved a request for large-scale military supplies from the United States. The only good news of the day was that Jordan and Lebanon had not—as yet—entered the War. Dayan believed that, if Syria could be beaten quickly, they would not do so.[87]

The response to Israel's early requests for arms during the Yom Kippur War was discouraging. The U.S. agreed to supply only two Phantom planes and electronic equipment—no tanks, artillery, or other weapons. On the 9th, Meir asked Allon to meet the U.S. Ambassador to clarify Israel's position and needs. At the meeting with Keating and Veliotis, Allon indicated that Israel had succeeded in stopping the Syrians in the North and was about to turn her attention to the Egyptians. However, in order to be able to do this, Israel required very substantial, indeed massive, U.S. military support. The word *airlift* was not mentioned, but it was clear from the context that military support of that magnitude would have to be transported in American planes.[88] As noted, the same request was submitted, through Dinitz, to Kissinger, and had reached the Secretary of State by 08:00 (New York time).

86. Yariv, Interview with M. Brecher, 7 August 1974; and Schiff, *October Earthquake*, p. 112. Syria fired fourteen Frog missiles at an Israeli military airport during the first three days of the war. They caused little damage; but the qualitative escalation of weapons was perceived—by Allon and Dayan, among others—as necessitating a commensurate response. See also Dayan, Confidential Briefing to Israeli Newspaper Editors, *Ha'aretz*, 15 February 1974.

87. Lebanon had secretly notified Israel that she would stay strictly neutral in fact, if not in word (Dayan, Confidential Briefing, *Ha'aretz*, 15 February 1974). However, a Lebanese radar station at El-Barik, halfway between Damascus and Beirut, kept the Syrians continuously informed of the movement of Israeli aircraft, until it was bombed on 9 October. On the Jordan dimension, Quandt wrote: "As the Syrian front began to weaken, King Hussein of Jordan came under great pressure to enter the war, if not by opening a new front, then at least by sending some of his troops to Syria. Israel conveyed an extremely harsh message to Hussein on October 9, warning of the consequences of opening a front along the Jordan River. Kissinger also urged Hussein to stay out of the fighting, stressing that a diplomatic effort was under way that, it was hoped, would succeed in ending the war in a few days" (*Decade of Decisions*, p. 177).

88. Keating, Interview with M. Brecher, 30 July 1974.

The Prime Minister, in consultation with the Defense Minister, decided on an even more drastic step—to fly to the U.S. for a secret meeting with President Nixon, in order to explain, face to face, Israel's needs in view of the strength of the Arab forces (Decision 10). She was dissuaded only when the President sent her a message of assurance on his decision to resupply Israel. Meir's immense relief is evident in her letter to Nixon on 10 October: "Early this morning I was told of the decision you made to assure us of the immediate flow of U.S. materiel. . . . I knew that in this hour of dire need to Israel, I could turn to you and count on your deep sympathy and understanding. . . ."[89]

The structure and style of Israel's decision-making unit during the early days of the 1973 crisis period was accurately portrayed by Schiff:

Grandma Will Decide
    Golda Meir almost unwillingly becomes the generalissimo. It is strange to see a warrior of seven campaigns and brilliant past-Chief of Staff of the IDF [Dayan] bringing clearly operational subjects to a Jewish grandmother for decision. Golda doesn't shirk responsibility. Of itself, neither appointed nor elected, a "War Cabinet" arises alongside Golda; but not her famous "Kitchen," which disbanded at the outbreak of war. Abba Eban is in the United States. Finance Minister Pinchas Sapir is also abroad to collect money. Agriculture Minister Haim Gvati is ill, while Justice Minister Shapiro—Golda's friend and veteran adviser—is not at home in war consultations. Yigal Allon and Yisrael Galili remain by her side and, with Golda, form the regular War Cabinet.
    Moshe Dayan oscillates between the Supreme Command, the war fronts, and the Cabinet Room. He reports to meetings where vital points are resolved but doesn't spend much time with the decision-makers. Dayan noticeably prefers battlefield tours to conference rooms and command bunkers.[90]

Moreover, Bar-Lev was acting as Commander in Chief on the southern front. In short, Cabinet sessions were, in most cases, attended by ten ministers: Meir, Allon, Galili, Hillel, Ya'acobi, and Zadok from the Labor Party, and Burg, Hazani, and Warhaftig from

89. Nixon, *Memoirs*, p. 922. Later, during her visit to Washington at the beginning of November, Meir reportedly said to Nixon: "There were days and hours when we needed a friend, and you came right in. You don't know what your airlift means to us" (Nixon, *Memoirs*, pp. 942–943). See also Meir, *My Life*, p. 362; Dayan, *Story of My Life*, pp. 411–412; and Schiff, *October Earthquake*, p. 150. Nixon also recalled conveying his decision to Kissinger on the 9th (*Memoirs*, p. 922).
    90. Schiff, *October Earthquake*, p. 148.

the NRP, with Dayan attending occasionally. Among them was an inner circle of four—Meir, Dayan, Allon, and Galili—who took decisions between Cabinet sessions.

On Wednesday, 10 October, the mood in Israel's decision-making group improved somewhat. Not only were there U.S. assurances about the resupply of military equipment, but also the Syrians had been pushed back beyond the 5 October cease-fire lines, with most of the armored equipment of their assault divisions destroyed or damaged. There was also more confidence about the southern front, for an Egyptian brigade probing in the direction of Abu Rodeis had been decimated. As Herzog noted, after 9 October "the Egyptians did not advance one yard during the remainder of the war."[91]

It was time to determine the next moves—to stop in place, continue the advance on the northern front in the direction of Damascus, or regroup and make a renewed effort in the South to push the Egyptians back. These options were considered at a series of meetings, beginning on the afternoon of 10 October and lasting for six hours: two at GHQ, the first attended by Dayan, and a third, extending beyond midnight at the Prime Minister's Tel Aviv office, with Dayan, Allon, Galili, Elazar, Tal, Zeira, and Peled present. The last of these discussions was recalled by Dayan as follows:

> On the southern front, the Egyptians had captured a strip along the east bank of the Canal, and if we could not drive them out at once, we should try to seize part of their territory west of the Canal. We would then have something with which to bargain, or at least even up the score. Bar-Lev of Southern Command said he agreed with the political considerations which called for the conquest of territory west of the waterline, but at the moment Southern Command was unable to do this. I replied that I thought it would be possible to transfer units from Northern to Southern Command, and Bar-Lev agreed that we should plan an action which would give us a hold west of the 1967 lines.
>
> Various places were mentioned. . . . At all events, the guideline of our next step was clear to me. Either in the Golan Heights or in Sinai we had to go over to the attack. And indeed, after midnight, at a meeting with the Prime Minister, it was resolved that our forces would attack on the Syrian front with the objective of advancing as far as possible in the direction of Damascus. There was no intention of capturing Damascus or even of bombing it.[92]

91. *The War of Atonement,* p. 199, and, more generally, chap. 14. See also Dayan, *Story of My Life,* chaps. 31 and 32.

92. *Story of My Life,* pp. 425–426.

The upshot of the discussions was a decision to press the advance on the northern front (to begin at 11:00, the next day, 11 October), in order to put Damascus within IDF artillery range, though not to occupy it, and thus exert powerful pressure for a cease-fire with Syria (Decision 11). As for the southern front, it was decided to prepare forces for an attack across the Canal, to occupy territory, and thus balance Egyptian gains on the Sinai side of the Canal.

Israel's decision-makers were now beginning to be aware again —as they were in the 1967 War—of the ticking of the political clock. Dayan recalled: "There was now 'powerful pressure,' according to our representative in Washington, for an unconditional cease-fire. The Soviet Union had approached President Nixon with this suggestion, and the United States, in its anxiety to avoid deterioration in her relations with Russia, was likely to respond positively. This would mean victory for the Arabs. . . . I felt we should do whatever we could to prevent an immediate cease-fire decision."[93]

The attack on the northern front began, as planned, at 11:00 on 11 October, but it proved to be heavy going. The Syrian defenses were not broken. In fact, their forces in the prewar defense perimeter around Damascus, which had not participated in the initial attack on 6 October, were now strengthened by the remnant of their assault troops, together with a brigade of tanks from Jordan, an Iraqi division, and troops from other Arab states.[94] During the next three days, the IDF advanced ten kilometers beyond the line of 5 October, putting its long-range artillery within range (twenty-five miles) of the outskirts of Damascus. From 13 until 22 October, the day Syria accepted a cease-fire, heavy fighting continued, but the Syrian front line held. The IDF improved its position mainly on the southern part of the Golan Heights.[95] A stronghold on Mount Hermon was recaptured by Israeli forces during the last day of the War.

Israel's actions in the North were calculated mostly in terms of Soviet behavior. On 9 October, Moscow began a massive resupply

93. *Story of My Life*, pp. 426–427. See also Quandt, *Decade of Decisions*, pp. 177–178.
94. See Appendix B on the 1973 military line-up; Herzog, *The War of Atonement;* Schiff, *October Earthquake;* and Meir, Speech to the Knesset, 16 October 1973, *Divrei Haknesset*, 68, 4474.
95. Herzog, *The War of Atonement*, chap. 10.

of the Arab armies, first and foremost that of Syria. This was accompanied by increasingly threatening verbiage as Israeli troops advanced into Syria.[96] In the South, fighting continued, with limited Egyptian attacks repulsed by Israeli forces, causing heavy losses in men and equipment to the Egyptians.

The idea of an IDF counterattack across the Canal had been discussed, heatedly, from the beginning of the War. With the enemy contained, the commanders on the southern front, headed by Bar-Lev, considered the various alternatives on the evening of the 11th. Bar-Lev decided in favor of a crossing between the territories held by the Second and Third Egyptian Armies, at Deservoir—but only after Egypt had transferred a major part of her forces still on the west side, committed them to battle, and saw them defeated.

These recommendations were put the next day before GHQ, with Dayan, Elazar, and Bar-Lev present. Because of Dayan's indecision, the issue was brought before the Kitchen Cabinet. Present were Meir, Dayan, Allon, Galili, Elazar, Bar-Lev, and several other generals. While the discussion was going on, news arrived that Egyptian armored forces on the west bank had begun to cross the Canal. On Bar-Lev's suggestion, the Israeli decision on the IDF crossing was postponed until after the breaking of the expected Egyptian attack (Decision 12). The high level of stress among the decision-makers is evident in the accounts of these events.[97]

On the Prime Minister's instructions, Eban met with Kissinger in Washington on the evening of Friday, 12 October; also present were Dinitz and Shalev. Eban again demanded the speeding up of U.S. arms deliveries, with Kissinger replying that everything was

96. G. Golan, *Yom Kippur and After*, chap. 3.

97. H. Bar-Tov, *Dado*, Vol. 2, pp. 180–193; Herzog, *The War of Atonement*, p. 202. According to Schiff, *October Earthquake*, pp. 190–192, Dayan's outburst on military versus political decisions was directed at Bar-Lev, not Elazar. Bar-Lev stated that, at his request, the plan for a crossing was prepared on the 11th. He accepted it and submitted the plan to GHQ and then to the Prime Minister. During the meeting, news arrived that the Egyptians would attack on the 13th and 14th. He then suggested that the crossing be postponed until the IDF "had succeeded in breaking what could be broken. . . . There was no argument about this" (Interview with U. Millstein, 31 January 1974; confirmed in Bar-Lev, Interview with M. Brecher, 29 July 1974). Dayan, so explicit on so many other points, is silent on the decision process about the crossing, stating only: "After a thorough review, we decided on a Canal crossing . . ." (*Story of My Life*, p. 429).

being done to get the airlift into motion. When Eban's report of his meeting reached Meir, indicating further delay, she despatched a personal note to President Nixon, asking for the immediate, direct delivery of military supplies. Nixon summoned the National Security Council on the 13th and, after discussion, ordered the use of American military cargo planes immediately. The former President recalled the incident, so crucial for Israel, as follows:

> The way that we worked was that he [Kissinger] would come in with options; and the option that he presented was that the Defense Department thought we should send three of these big cargo planes; and then, of course, he gave his own opinions as to their reasons and reasons which he thought I ought to have before me; that politically it would be perhaps dangerous for us to sent a greater number and that it would destroy the chances for negotiation in the future if our profile was too high. . . . And I said: "Look, Henry, we're going to get just as much blame for sending three if we send thirty, or a hundred, or whatever we've got, so send everything that flies. The main thing is—make it work."[98]

It was the cumulative stress from two sources—delay of the U.S. airlift, while the Arab armies were being lavishly resupplied, and continued fighting on both fronts, with reinforcements pouring in from Saudi Arabia, Iraq, and Jordan—that led Meir to agree on 12 October to a renewed Soviet proposal for a cease-fire in place (Decision 13).[99] The cable was transmitted by Eban and Dinitz directly in Washington that day. Eban recalled the episode:

98. From the verbatim text of Nixon's television interview with David Frost, 12 May 1977. On the Kissinger-Schlesinger controversy over the delay of U.S. arms deliveries to Israel in 1973, see also E. Luttwak and W. Laqueur, "Kissinger and the Yom Kippur War," *Commentary*, 58:3 (September 1974), 33–40. Admiral Zumwalt, no friend of Kissinger, wrote: "It was Henry himself who stalled the airlift. I do not mean to imply that he wanted Israel to lose the national war. He simply did not want Israel to win decisively. . . ." The policy of the U.S., Secretary of Defense Schlesinger told Zumwalt, was to "maintain a low profile and avoid visible involvement . . ." (Zumwalt, *On Watch*, pp. 433–435). Nixon, in his *Memoirs* (p. 927), unreservedly supported Kissinger's version. He recalled his reaction, on 12 October, to the Pentagon's continued hesitation about which planes to use for the airlift: "I became totally exasperated. I said to Kissinger, 'Goddamn it, use every one we have. Tell them to send everything that can fly.'" Earlier that day he had told Schlesinger: "Whichever way we have to do it, get them in the air, *now*." For a detailed description of the U.S. decision process, as well as an assessment of American interests, see Quandt, *Decade of Decisions*, pp. 176–183.

99. According to M. Golan, *The Secret Conversations of Henry Kissinger*, pp. 65–83, Meir decided on acceptance in consultation with Dayan and Elazar. Israel's gains on the Syrian front were cited as the principal stimulus to Meir's decision. See Insight Team of *The Sunday Times* (London), *The Yom Kippur War* (London, 1975), p. 279. This was also noted by Quandt, *Decade of Decisions*, p. 180 and n. 35, referring to "a highly–placed Israeli source."

I went to Washington on the 12th to try to get a cease-fire in place,
immediately. Things were not going too well. We had had some successes
in the North, but in an exhausting way. In the South we were in the
mountains. . . . Then Kissinger worked out a scenario with the Soviets,
but they wanted an Israeli retreat to June 1967. The British were involved. But by October 14, and according to my instructions, I refused it
—to Kissinger's surprise.[100]

Quandt's account of this Israeli decision, as viewed from Washington, is revealing:

Prime Minister Meir, under pressure from the United States to accept a
cease-fire in place, apparently appalled by the mounting casualties, and
realizing that American arms might not be readily forthcoming if she
refused, finally agreed to accept a cease-fire in place. Her acceptance was
accompanied by an urgent personal appeal to President Nixon to order an
immediate resupply of arms to Israel. She went so far as to raise the
specter of an Israeli military defeat. On October 12, late in the evening,
Ambassador Dinitz met with Kissinger at the White House. He conveyed
Israel's acceptance of the principle of a cease-fire-in-place and Golda
Meir's urgent request for arms.[101]

According to I. Disentshik of *Ma'ariv*, the request for a cease-fire,
to be submitted by the British, came from Meir but on condition
that the British were not told the source of the request.[102]

Kissinger tried to arrange a cease-fire through the British UN
Delegation, but he couldn't get the necessary agreement. His
scenario called for a British proposal without prior consultation
with Sadat. But the British did consult with Sadat. Egypt's President told the British Ambassador at a dawn meeting on the 13th
that a cease-fire was unacceptable.[103] The issue never came before
Israel's Cabinet or even the Kitchen Cabinet. "In fact," noted Matti
Golan, "till this very day her [Meir's] desperate telegram has not
been entered into the official records of the government."[104]

    100. Eban, Interview with M. Brecher, 15 July 1974. See also Eban's *An Auto-
biography*, pp. 514–515, and his "Kissinger Told Me That He Went To Sleep
Quietly After He Received the Israeli Intelligence Appreciation on the Eve of
October 5," *Ma'ariv*, 21 September 1977.
    101. Quandt, *Decade of Decisions*, pp. 181–182.
    102. I. Disentshik, "You Don't Ask for a Cease-fire with Your Back to the
Wall." *Ma'ariv*, 21 September 1977.
    103. Sadat's account, with the clear message—"Please tell Kissinger . . . I
haven't agreed to a cease-fire proposed by the Soviet Union or any other party.
. . ."—is contained in his *In Search of Identity*, pp. 256–258.
    104. M. Golan, *The Secret Conversations of Henry Kissinger*, p. 96.

Superpower involvement had become more pronounced. And with the primary military danger contained, it played an increasing role in Israel's decision-making process. On the one hand, Israel was finally notified on Saturday, 13 October, that the U.S. would deliver military supplies, even refueling fighter planes—Phantoms and Skyhawks—in the air. The first huge transport planes, Galaxy C5s and C141s, landed at Lod the next day.[105] On the other hand, Soviet pressure became more intense. Israel's Government was notified that Ambassador Dobrynin had informed Kissinger of the alert of two Soviet airborne divisions—and of Kissinger's reply that the U.S. would not want the Soviet Union to do anything irresponsible.[106]

There were other noteworthy military movements. On the previous day, during an Israeli naval attack on the Syrian port of Latakia, a Russian freighter, the Ilya Michnikov, had been sunk. In its wake, the Soviet navy had concentrated missile boats to protect the port, and units of the U.S. Sixth Fleet were ordered close to Israel's coastline.[107] As in 1967, movements of the Sixth Fleet were used to signal U.S. political decisions. And as in 1970, Israel shied away from giving the Soviets grounds for direct intervention; the IDF ceased the attacks on Latakia.

Another recurrent legacy of the past became a focus of decision. Allon had, for years, been advocating that Israel encourage the creation of an independent Druze State in the southern region of Syria, including parts of the Golan Heights. After the Six Day War, he had stated publicly that Israel had erred in not reaching Mount Druze, the center of the Syrian Druze minority. At a Cabinet meeting of 13 October, he urged a push toward Mount Druze, but the idea was dropped because of Dayan's sharp opposition.[108]

105. Nixon recalled with pride that there were more than 550 American missions during the next few weeks, "an operation bigger than the Berlin airlift of 1948–49" (*Memoirs,* pp. 927–928). For an informative discussion of the details of the U.S. airlift, see Quandt, *Decade of Decisions,* pp. 183–185. He adds that its impact on Israel's military decisions during the Yom Kippur War was minimal.

106. Dayan, *Story of My Life,* pp. 428–429; G. Golan, *Yom Kippur and After,* pp. 90–95; Schiff, *October Earthquake,* p. 196.

107. Schiff, *October Earthquake,* pp. 196–199; Zumwalt, *On Watch,* pp. 436–437; G. Golan, *Yom Kippur and After,* pp. 108–109.

108. The Druzes are an Arabic-speaking ethnic and religious minority of several million who live in Syria, Lebanon, Jordan, and Israel. Israel's Druze minority is accepted as loyal, and Druzes serve in the IDF. Druzes living in Arab states serve in their armies, though in Syria there is some resentment toward them.

The expected Egyptian attack on the east bank of the Canal began at 06:00 on 14 October and lasted until 15:00, with close to one thousand tanks, hundreds of artillery pieces, and scores of planes taking part. It was a major IDF victory, with 260 Egyptian tanks destroyed or damaged, against the loss of only a few Israeli tanks. Bar-Lev phoned the news to Meir in the evening and strongly urged her to approve the crossing of the Canal, planned for the next day. The Prime Minister brought it before the Cabinet, then in session. Elazar explained the proposal, and it was passed unanimously (Decision 14).[109]

III. 15–23 October

The crossing of the Canal was to begin at 19:00 on the 15th. In fact, the first IDF units crossed by rubber boats and floats at 01:30 on the 16th; and it took another day-and-a-half of heavy fighting to enlarge the beachhead and complete a pontoon bridge. At one stage, when the fighting around the bridgehead became very heavy, Dayan suggested withdrawal; but he accepted Bar-Lev's decision to continue as planned, subject to a bridge being completed quickly.[110]

Meir had called a Cabinet meeting for 19:00 on the 15th. Because of the delays in crossing, ministers stayed all night, awaiting information from the front. News of the Canal crossing was announced by the Prime Minister during the first Knesset session since the outbreak of the Yom Kippur War, on the afternoon of 16 October. The main thrust of her speech was the justification of Israel's policy since 1967, the "evil role" of the Soviet Union, and Israel's war aims. On the subject of feelers for a cease-fire, she stated, disingenuously: "Until now there has not been offered to the Government of Israel any suggestion from any source for a cease-fire. This being the case, we do not have to discuss the subject."[111] By contrast, Sadat publicly stated for the first time on the

---

Schiff notes that Dayan opposed the idea of Druzes serving in the army "as an unnecessary burden on the IDF; anyway, he isn't at all certain that the Druzes are really interested" (*October Earthquake*, p. 200).

109. Schiff, *October Earthquake*, p. 215; Herzog, *The War of Atonement*, pp. 208–209; Bar-Lev, Interview with U. Millstein, 26 June 1974.

110. Schiff, *October Earthquake*, p. 238.

111. *Divrei Haknesset*, 68, 4474–4476.

16th that Egypt would agree to a cease-fire—if Israel would return to the 4 June 1967 borders. He also disclosed, ominously, that Egypt possessed surface-to-surface missiles "aimed at Israel's largest cities."

Premier Kosygin's unexpected and unannounced arrival in Cairo the same day heralded a sharp escalation in superpower involvement in the war. While both superpowers, mainly with the help of monitoring devices and satellites, were generally well-informed of what took place on the Arab-Israeli battlefield, there was no photographic coverage of battlefield events available on the 16th. Such photos reached Kosygin on the 18th, and he immediately showed them to Sadat. Egypt's President did not mention the IDF crossing to the Soviet Premier on the 16th, though he was aware of it; and on the 17th they did not meet.[112] Yet Kosygin's efforts to persuade Sadat to accept a cease-fire failed.

The Israeli Defense Minister remained in the South to observe IDF advance and blocking actions, while the Chief of Staff shuttled back and forth between the fronts, GHQ, and Cabinet meetings in Tel Aviv. Dayan phoned the Prime Minister every evening to report on the progress. On the evening of 17 October, after another day of heavy fighting, Israel's armored brigades crossed to the west side of the Canal on a pontoon bridge.

This change in the balance of military power was immediately reflected in diplomatic activity. Kosygin, using the photographic evidence of the seriousness of Israel's penetration, persuaded Sadat on the 18th to accept a cease-fire.[113] The same day, after a delegation of Arab Foreign Ministers from nonbelligerent states had met with Nixon and Kissinger to explore the U.S. position on a cease-fire, the Organization of Arab Petroleum Exporting Countries (OAPEC) declared an oil embargo.

Use of the oil weapon had no effect on the outcome of the war; this was decided on the battlefield and in Washington and Moscow. The main effect of the oil embargo was a sharp increase in the price of oil, causing economic hardship all over the world. However, the panic caused in Europe and Japan contributed substantively to growing pressure on Israel after the 1973 War, causing her isolation in many diplomatic forums, including the UN.

    112. See G. Golan, *Yom Kippur and After,* pp. 107–108; Schiff, *October Earthquake,* pp. 240, 250; Herzog, *The War of Atonement,* p. 232.
    113. M. Heikal, *The Road to Ramadan* (London, 1975), pp. 235–236.

Parallel to Kosygin's role in Cairo on the 18th, USSR Ambassador Dobrynin called upon Kissinger and demanded a cease-fire, linked to a gradual Israeli withdrawal from all occupied territories. Kissinger accepted the call for a cease-fire but not withdrawal.[114] These proposals were communicated by General Scowcroft to Dinitz, who immediately informed Meir in Tel Aviv and Eban in New York. Eban cabled Meir that Israel ought to accept the call for a cease-fire in principle, even a reference to Resolution 242, on condition of an exchange of prisoners. In any case, she should suggest to Kissinger that Israel needed to gain time to complete her military activities. Eban repeated these suggestions to Kissinger in a telephone conversation two hours prior to his (Eban's) departure for Israel on the 18th. He was not informed of Kissinger's intended trip to Moscow.[115]

These inputs reached Israel on the morning of 19 October. Dayan stated that Ambassador Dinitz "informed us of feverish negotiations between the Americans and the Russians to sponsor an agreed cease-fire resolution by the Security Council, and it was clear that only a few days remained before the end of the war."[116] This was reinforced later in the day by a message from Nixon to Meir, explaining that a cease-fire also served U.S. interests. He reminded her that the U.S. had supplied Israel's needs in aircraft and other vital equipment and would continue to do so; moreover, he was submitting to Congress a request for 2.2 billion dollars for emergency defense assistance to Israel.[117]

114. For Nixon's negative response to the Soviet proposal, see his *Memoirs*, pp. 930–931.

115. Interview with M. Brecher, 15 July 1974.

116. Dayan, *Story of My Life*, p. 439.

117. Nixon, Interview with David Frost, 12 May 1977, and his *Memoirs*, p. 931; Quandt, *Decade of Decisions*, p. 188. The way the amount of $2.2 billion of U.S. assistance was arrived at highlights the effect of time pressure on U.S. decision-making: "It was an interaction process. The Israelis made it clear from the outset that they really did not have the resources to pay for this. The U.S. Embassy [in Tel Aviv] made it clear to Washington that the cost would have a very adverse effect on the Israeli economy. They urged Washington very strongly to make the first billion dollars—which was the estimate of what was needed at first—a straight grant and worry about what was coming later. It was a fight for survival. As to how the sum was arrived at: It was clear to everybody that the minimal figure for the airlift was one billion. It was also clear that the airlift would go on and that they would need much more in the later stages of the war. Nobody knew what the figure was. The Israelis calculated at some stage 3.5 billion; some put it even higher. We knew that this was an exaggeration, but we did not know what was the correct figure. . . . It was probably a compromise

At a meeting between the Prime Minister and the Defense Minister, it was decided to press forward on the west bank of the Canal but not to press too far inland toward Cairo (Decision 15). On the northern front, an all-out effort would be made to recapture former IDF positions on Mount Hermon before a cease-fire came into effect.

The dramatic events of 19 October, involving the two superpowers, had no immediate effect on Israel's decision-makers; they were not aware of them. Summarized briefly, the "hot line" between Moscow and Washington was activated that morning. Brezhnev notified Nixon that the Soviet Government was about to take a decision from which there would be no retreat, and he urged that Kissinger come to Moscow immediately. The President agreed, perhaps in part because, by that time, the Americans knew of a considerable Soviet military build-up, including the introduction into Egypt of MiG-25 squadrons flown by Soviet pilots.[118]

Bernard and Marvin Kalb noted that, prior to his departure, Kissinger

> talked at length with Dinitz about a cease-fire scenario. In rough terms, Kissinger knew what the Russians were proposing, and what the Egyptians were willing to accept, however reluctantly: a cease-fire-in-place, linked to an Israeli withdrawal to the 1967 line. The Israeli Ambassador rejected this proposal as unrealistic. He recommended instead a cease-fire linked to direct negotiations between the two sides that could lead to withdrawal and peace. Kissinger set his sights on achieving a solution that accented direct negotiations. If Brezhnev really needed American cooperation to rescue his Arab clients and to preserve détente and its dividends, then the Russians might be made to pay a high price.[119]

Dinitz informed Jerusalem of his talk with Kissinger, adding that the Secretary of State intended to provide sufficient time for Israel to complete her military victory.[120]

---

between the figure the Israelis said they needed and what Washington calculated they needed" (U.S. Embassy officials, Interview with M. Brecher, 12 August 1974).

118. An American intelligence memorandum quoted in Zumwalt, *On Watch*, p. 439, noted that: "If the Soviets were going to introduce troops, they would want their own people doing reconnaisance in advance."

119. B. Kalb and M. Kalb, *Kissinger*, p. 483. This is also discussed in Eban, *An Autobiography*, pp. 524–525.

120. Kissinger repeated on several occasions that one of the reasons he agreed to go to Moscow was that it gave Israel another ninety-six hours to improve her military position; see, for example, his talk with American Jewish intellectuals, as reported in *Yediot Aharonot*, 15 February 1974. Quandt, by contrast, indicated as the primary goal, "to obtain Soviet and Arab agreement to a cease-fire resolu-

Kissinger arrived in Moscow on the evening of 20 October. The next day an agreement was hammered out, according to which U.S. and USSR representatives would submit a draft resolution to the Security Council calling for an immediate cease-fire in site, linked to Resolution 242. Most of the day's negotiations were taken up by the Soviet insistence on linking the cease-fire to a call for total Israeli withdrawal to the 4 June 1967 borders. However, because of the rapidly worsening plight of the Arab armies, the Russians suddenly dropped that demand and accepted Kissinger's proposals. The basic framework of a peace conference under joint superpower auspices was also agreed upon. And the Soviet Union promised to undertake efforts to expedite an exchange of prisoners of war.[121] As a result, the UN Security Council passed Resolution 338 on 22 October 1973:

The Security Council
1. Calls upon all parties to the present fighting to cease all firing and terminate all military activity immediately, no later than 12 hours after the moment of the adoption of this decision, in the positions they now occupy;
2. Calls upon the parties concerned to start immediately after the cease-fire the implementation of Security Council Resolution 242 (1967) in all of its parts;
3. Decides that, immediately and concurrently with the cease-fire, negotiations start between the parties concerned under appropriate auspices aimed at establishing a just and durable peace in the Middle East.

Israel was kept informed, from time to time, of the progress of the Moscow talks on the 20th; but then, because of a "technical hitch" in transferring news from Moscow, she received no further reports.[122] By that time, it had become sufficiently clear to the Israeli Government that they had only a day or two until a cease-fire agreement was imposed; Southern Command was so informed by Elazar.[123] Finally, Israel was notified of the U.S.-Soviet agreement on a cease-fire when General Haig, Kissinger's deputy, called on Dinitz on the 21st and presented him with the text. It

---

tion that could serve as the basis for a subsequent diplomatic effort" (*Decade of Decisions,* p. 191).

121. Nixon, *Memoirs,* p. 936; G. Golan, *Yom Kippur and After,* pp. 112–118; Meir's speech to the Knesset, 23 October 1973. *Divrei Haknesset,* 68, 4507–4510.

122. Nixon tried to assuage Meir's hurt feelings by sending her a letter, while Kissinger was en route to Israel, "expressing my regret that there had not been more time for consultation . . ." (*Memoirs,* p. 936).

123. Schiff, *October Earthquake,* pp. 267–270.

was not open to argument. Dinitz immediately cabled it to Tel Aviv, as well as phoning the Prime Minister to convey its content. The news reached Israel around 17:00.

Upon receipt of the messages, Meir called a Cabinet meeting, which began at 22:00. While the Cabinet was still in session, at 01:00 on 22 October, a message arrived from Nixon, in which he urged the Israeli Government to accept the text of the cease-fire agreement to be submitted the next day. The Cabinet decided unanimously to accept the cease-fire (Decision 16).[124] The next day, Meir described the reasons for its acceptance, in a speech to the Knesset:

In connection to paragraph 2 of the proposed decision [the reference in Resolution 338 to Resolution 242], the Government instructed its representative at the UN to include in his speech in the Security Council, a passage to clarify that our agreement to this paragraph is given subject to its meaning as specified by Israel when she decided, in August 1970, to respond to the U.S. initiative for a cease-fire. Israel's agreement to a cease-fire with Egypt is subject to Egypt's agreement and not subject to Syria's agreement to a cease-fire with her, and vice versa. We saw fit to respond to the U.S. initiative and that of U.S. President Nixon, because:
a. Israel, by her very nature, does not want war. . . .
b. The proposal for a cease-fire has come when our situation on both fronts is firm; when our achievements are of great value and justify an agreement to a cease-fire, despite the enemy's achievement on the east bank of the Canal.
c. We responded to the U.S. call and that of its President in appreciation and esteem of the positive policy of the U.S. in the Middle East at this time.[125]

Meir notified the U.S. Government of Israel's acceptance at 03:00 on 22 October and then informed the Knesset Foreign Affairs and

---

124. Dayan, *Story of My Life*, p. 411; Ben-Porath et al., *Hamechdal [The Fiasco]* (Tel Aviv, 1973), pp. 220–222 (in Hebrew). The message was transmitted, simultaneously, through Dinitz and Keating. It reached Israel while Eban was briefing the Knesset Foreign Affairs and Security Committee, which was suspended immediately. Yariv stated that the Cabinet erred in interpreting Nixon's message as straight pressure; it contained no appeal, but also no threats. Israel should have insisted on another twelve hours (Interview with M. Brecher, 7 August 1974). The scene was repeated in Cairo. At exactly the same time, Sadat received through Ambassador Vinogradov a message from Brezhnev, urging him to accept the agreed proposal for a cease-fire in place. But Brezhnev's message also contained assurances that the Soviet Union would enforce the cease-fire, if necessary, on her own. See Heikal, *The Road to Ramadan*, pp. 238–240; G. Golan, *Yom Kippur and After*, p. 115.

125. *Divrei Haknesset*, 68, 4507–4508.

Security Committee of the Cabinet's decision, in terms of a *fait accompli.*

At Israel's request, Kissinger paused in Tel Aviv, en route from Moscow to Washington, to clarify the agreement reached with the Soviet Union; Kosygin flew to Cairo for the same purpose. During his four-hour visit on 22 October, Kissinger met first with Meir alone and then with Meir, Eban, Dayan, Allon, and Galili and reported on his Moscow talks. Dayan's memoir version is as follows:

> As to a cease-fire agreement, we made the categorical demand that there be an exchange of prisoners. We considered this a prime condition: "No prisoner exchange, no cease-fire." Kissinger was unwilling to agree to such an extreme formula. He promised to act and to ask the Russians to help. He cited promises which he had received from Moscow but he avoided giving us an iron-clad undertaking that there would be a prisoner exchange. His reassurances were bound by such expressions as "We'll work for it." "We'll try." "We'll make a supreme effort." As for getting exit permits for the Jews of Syria, he was even less forthcoming.
>
> The impression created was that we were treading a tightrope which soared above a canyon of monstrous danger but which stretched toward a gleam of light in the distance. We would reach that light only if we learned to tread along the thin cord with wisdom. . . .
>
> Furthermore, the United States supported the cease-fire because a continuation of the war would lead to the radicalization of the Arab world, to the fall of moderate governments, and their replacement by extremist regimes.[126]

The results of the discussion with Kissinger were brought before a Cabinet meeting that evening. The Cabinet decided that "if the Egyptians failed to live up to the cease-fire, the Israel Defense Forces will 'repel the enemy at the gate'" (Decision 17).

Israel announced at 18:05 her acceptance of a cease-fire which was to go into effect on 22 October at 18:52. Radio Cairo had announced Egypt's acceptance at 14:30 the same day. Syria announced at 06:15 on 23 October her acceptance in principle and on condition that Israel withdraw to her pre–4 June 1967 borders.

Fighting continued on the Sinai front, however, with conflicting views on responsibility. IDF forces in the rear of the Third Army received orders and ceased fire at 19:00, while those on the outskirts of Ismailia continued for another four hours in order to extricate their dead and wounded. But when the Egyptians continued to send commando and infantry teams during the night to destroy

126. *Story of My Life,* pp. 443–444.

Israeli tank concentrations, in order to open an escape route for the Third Army, fighting was resumed at dawn with the Prime Minister's approval (Decision 18). There are strong indications that Israel's military leaders were hoping for such an eventuality in order to complete the encirclement of the Third Army.[127] This was attained by midnight 23 October. And the IDF gained control of part of the town of Suez, as well as the port of Adabiyah, thus sealing the Third Army off from all supplies.

IV. 23–26 October

Israel came under mounting U.S. pressure to stop the fighting, including a phone call from Kissinger to Meir on the evening of the 23rd; the Secretary of State emphasized his commitment toward the Soviet Union on a cease-fire.[128] At UN Headquarters, the Security Council passed another cease-fire resolution (339) on 23 October, this time calling for the immediate despatch of UN observers to supervise it:

The Security Council,
Referring to its Resolution 338 (1973) of 22 October 1973,
1. Confirms its decision of an immediate cessation of all kinds of firing and of all military action, and urges that the forces of two sides be returned to the positions they occupied at the moment the cease-fire became effective;
2. Requests the Secretary General to take measures for immediate despatch of United Nations observers to supervise the observance of the cease-fire between the forces of Israel and the Arab Republic of Egypt, using for this purpose the personnel of the United Nations now in the Middle East and first of all the personnel now in Cairo.[129]

Sadat, fearing that IDF advances since the first cease-fire call would erase all his gains in the field, now called upon the Soviet

127. Bar-Lev, Interview with M. Brecher, 29 July 1974, and Interview with U. Millstein, 31 January 1974. Bar-Lev indicated that Israel needed another day to place the IDF in a strong advantageous position. A message to Nixon from Brezhnev on the "hot line" at 11:00 A.M. (New York time), 23 October, charged the Israelis with rupturing the cease-fire: "I sent a reply that, according to our information, Egypt was the first party to violate the cease-fire" (Nixon, *Memoirs*, p. 936).
128. Ben-Porath et al., *Hamechdal [The Fiasco]*, p. 220; Quandt, *Decade of Decisions*, p. 194.
129. The Resolution was passed by 14 to 0; China did not participate in the vote. Within twelve hours, UN observers despatched from Cyprus, Cairo, and Jerusalem were on the scene.

and U.S. leaders to send troops to ensure the cease-fire.[130] His letter to Nixon reached Washington at 15:00, 24 October (21:00 Israeli time). Six hours later, a letter reached the President from Brezhnev; it warned that if Israel would not observe the cease-fire and the U.S. refused to cooperate in enforcing it, "we should be faced with the necessity urgently to consider the question of taking appropriate steps unilaterally. Israel cannot be allowed to get away with the violations."[131]

Nixon recalled this grave incident as follows:

The note had an ominous sound to it because he, in effect, said that the United States and the Soviet Union should move in as the Egyptians had requested. He knew we had rejected that and he said ". . . if you cannot restrain the Israelis. . . ." It's my recollection he said: "It will be necessary for us to move unilaterally . . . into the situation." Now that to me was a code word. For the Soviet Union to move any kind of forces into the Mid-East would, first, tip the balance so that Israel would have been down the tube. But even more important, it would have established the precedent where the Soviets had a presence in the Mid-East. . . . And so it ran the risk of a great power confrontation. . . . I just said, in my reply: "We would not agree to go in. Second, we would be glad, of course, to participate in a UN group with a number of advisers. And third, we took a very dim view—I used stronger words than that—a very dim view of any unilateral action on their part of moving in."[132]

The U.S. also signaled Moscow by placing most of her armed forces on "Defensive Condition 3," including the Strategic Air Command with its nuclear capability. This became known almost immediately. And CIA reports reached Washington that, in the early hours of 25 October, a Soviet ship suspected of carrying one or several nuclear warheads had docked in Alexandria.[133]

By the afternoon of the 25th, the crisis of superpower confrontation began to abate when it became known that the USSR had accepted the American formula (at 15:00) for the setting up of a UN

130. Sadat's version of the renewed fighting from 22 to 24 October, markedly at variance with all others, is in his *In Search of Identity*, pp. 265–267.

131. B. Kalb and M. Kalb, *Kissinger*, p. 490.

132. Interview with David Frost, 12 May 1977. Nixon's perception of the danger of a nuclear confrontation with Moscow and his decision to order a nuclear alert, including the text of his messages on the 24th to Brezhnev and to Sadat, explaining U.S. opposition to superpower forces in the Middle East, are recalled vividly in his *Memoirs*, pp. 937–941.

133. Zumwalt, *On Watch*, pp. 443–448; B. Kalb and M. Kalb, *Kissinger*, pp. 493–494; Nixon, Interview with David Frost, 12 May 1977; F. Kohler, L. Gouré, and M. Harvey, *The Soviet Union and the October 1973 Middle East War, The Implications for Detente* (Miami, 1974), p. 65.

Emergency Force "composed of personnel drawn from state members of the United Nations except permanent members of the Security Council."[134]

Parallel to these UN efforts, U.S. pressure was put on Israel to accept the second cease-fire call, without the surrender of Egypt's Third Army and, in fact, with a flow of supplies to the beleaguered force. In Israel, Keating and Veliotis went to see Meir and Allon to communicate the urgency of the situation. In Washington, Kissinger kept in constant touch with Dinitz and, by phone, with the Israeli Foreign and Defense Ministers. There was even, reportedly, a phone conversation between Nixon and Meir.[135] The Americans argued that it was in the highest U.S. and Israeli interests to accept the cease-fire. There were too many unknown factors: Soviet intervention, the effect on détente, and future peace talks. In terms of the future, it would be better to keep the Third Army alive. There was no talk of stopping the airlift.

The Israeli decision process (leading to Decisions 19 and 20) was recalled by Dayan as follows:

We were first told by the Americans that they had information that we were attacking the Third Army. This, they said, was a breach of the cease-fire agreement, and we had apparently failed to understand the grave

---

134. The full text of Resolution 340, passed on 25 October by a vote of 14 to 0 (with China not participating) is:

The Security Council,

Recalling its Resolutions 338 (1973) of 22 October and 339 (1973) of 23 October 1973,

Noting with regret the reported repeated violations of the cease-fire in non-compliance with Resolutions 338 (1973) and 339 (1973),

Noting with concern from the Secretary General's report that the United Nations military observers have not yet been enabled to place themselves on both sides of the cease-fire line,

1. Demands that immediate and complete cease-fire be observed and that the parties return to the positions occupied by them at 16:50 hours GMT on 22 October 1973;
2. Requests the Secretary General, as an immediate step, to increase the number of United Nations military observers on both sides;
3. Decides to set up immediately under its authority a United Nations Emergency Force to be composed of personnel drawn from State/Members of the United Nations except the permanent members of the Security Council and requests the Secretary General to report within 24 hours on the steps taken to this effect;
4. Requests the Secretary General to report to the Council on an urgent and continuing basis on the state of implementation of the present resolution, as well as Resolutions 338 (1973) and 339 (1973);
5. Requests all Member States to extend their full cooperation to the United Nations in the implementation of the present resolution, as well as Resolutions 338 (1973) and 339 (1973).

On the behind-the-scenes maneuvering at the UN, see T. Draper, "The Road to Geneva."

135. U.S. Embassy officials, Interview with M. Brecher, 12 August 1974.

steps the United States was likely to take against us. Half an hour later, following a strong denial from Jerusalem, our Washington embassy received a correction: The Americans had discovered in the meantime that indeed it was not we but the Egyptians who were continuing hostilities! However, they added, this information was not "relevant." The crux of the problem was the situation itself—the isolation of the Third Army, with all the complications that arose therefrom. The Americans could not allow this Egyptian army to be destroyed, or left hungry, or weakened by thirst, or taken prisoner. If the Third Army could not receive supplies in any other way, the Soviet Union would send them, and such a move, they said, would be tantamount to Soviet military intervention. It would be a blow to American prestige. No matter how, the Third Army had to be saved from its plight. . . . Finally, the Americans presented their demand more or less in the form of an ultimatum. It had crystallized into the requirement that we grant a one-time permit allowing an Egyptian supply convoy of non-military equipment, food, and water to pass through our lines to the Third Army. If we did not agree to this proposal, we would find ourselves in a crisis situation with the United States. Israel gave approval for one hundred supply trucks to be sent from Cairo.[136]

At the Cabinet meeting, which began late at night on 25 October and lasted until 04:00 on the 26th, Meir, as noted, gave U.S. pressure as the reason for Israel's acceptance of the cease-fire call. Eban's recollection of the deliberations and the reasons for acceptance was as follows:

Yes, consideration was given to the possibility that American supplies would be stopped, though this was not said in the [Nixon] letter. It was a matter of casualties if the war goes on, the Soviet threat, and a break with the U.S. The continuation of good relations with the U.S. was more important than a greater military victory. If we had two or three more weeks . . . but these were just not available. If it would have been a matter of two or three days, Nixon might have gone along with it, because he wanted an American success vs. a Soviet one.

The threat of Soviet intervention was real and visible. This time, unlike in 1967, there was a concentration of troops, and they were now operating in UN interests, come as it were, to carry out the world's will—there has to be an end to the war. The feeling was that there could very well be a Soviet military intervention in the Middle East, unless the U.S. put up a very strong show. All that night [the 25th] we sat up, until 04:00 o'clock, while the Security Council was waiting. In the Cabinet there was a consensus that the Soviets might intervene unless the Cabinet responded, it was that persuasive. There was physical evidence of Soviet strength.

The Cabinet meeting of the 25th lasted until 04:00 in the morning. The entire meeting was devoted to the question, do we accept the second

136. *Story of My Life*, pp. 447–448. See also Quandt, *Decade of Decisions*, p. 198 and n. 71, and H. Bar-Tov, *Dado*, Vol. 2, pp. 339–341.

cease-fire or do we not? The decision was unanimous. The decisive factor was the Soviet threat, and the preparedness of the U.S. for a confrontation. This was different from 1956 and 1967 because the evidence was there. The Soviets then solved it by retiring from the idea of Soviet intervention and accepting this rather innocuous form (Resolution 340).[137]

The Yom Kippur War ended on 26 October, and with it the 1973 crisis period. For Egypt it was a prestige victory, along with a major military defeat. As against the two Egyptian footholds on the eastern side of the Canal, Israel held a substantial enclave on the western side; and on the northern front, the IDF had not only expelled all enemy soldiers from positions gained during the first days of surprise, but it had also advanced to within artillery range of Syria's capital.

The cost to both sides, for a short war, was high. In absolute terms, the Arab armies lost several times more than Israel.[138] Material losses were made up so quickly by the superpowers that, within several weeks, Israel and Syria were better equipped than before the war. But in relative terms, Israel's losses in manpower, dead, and wounded were a heavy blow to a small nation.

The 1973 War followed the pattern of its predecessors. Israel's war aims were victory on the battlefield, destroying as much as

137. Interview with M. Brecher, 15 July 1974. Also noted in Eban, *An Autobiography*, pp. 528–530.

138. The armies of Egypt and Syria lost the following equipment during the war:

	Egypt	Syria
Planes		
Fighters	222	117
Bombers	1	0
Helicopters	42	13
Tanks	1,000	1,113*
Armored Personnel Carriers	450	400
Artillery units	300	250
SAM Batteries	44	3
Missile boats	6	3
Torpedo boats	4	1

*Includes Iraqi, Saudi Arabian, and Jordanian equipment.

See S. Gazit, "Arab Forces Two Years After the Yom Kippur War," in *Military Aspects of the Israeli-Arab Conflict* (Tel Aviv, 1975), pp. 189–195. Figures for Israel are not known precisely. COS David Elazar has stated that the ratio of losses in tanks was 4:1 in Israel's favor; that of aircraft, 5:1 (D. Elazar, "The Yom Kippur War: Military Lessons," in *Military Aspects of the Israeli-Arab Conflict*, pp. 245–250. This would mean approximately the loss of over 500 tanks and about 80 planes. Other sources put the number of Israeli aircraft lost at between 94 and 112; see Avnery, *Red Sky*, pp. 259–270.

possible of her opponents' military capability. The Arab war aims
were victory if possible, but, if not, to use the fighting as an extension of diplomacy to break a political stalemate. As long as the Arab
side had the upper hand, there was no pressure from the international system, specifically from the superpowers. But the moment Israel began to triumph on the battlefield, there was intense
pressure from the superpowers, directly and through the UN, for a
cease-fire, coupled with demands for Israel's retreat to prewar
positions. The Soviet Union used military threats to achieve her
aims; the U.S. used pressure. There were two differences in the
military domain between the Six Day War and the Yom Kippur
War: (a) because the latter lasted three weeks instead of six days,
both sides had to be resupplied by their superpower patron during
the war; and (b) the Soviet military threat was much more credible
in the Yom Kippur War, because of the build-up of an impressive
Soviet military presence at or near the scene of fighting: a vast
armada in the Mediterranean, including landing craft with tanks
and troops; squadrons of MiG 25s in Egypt, as well as brigades
armed with ground-to-ground missiles; alerted airborne divisions
near airfields around the Mediterranean; and—possibly—nuclear
warheads for missiles in Alexandria. As in the 1967 War, so in the
1973 War the military moves of both superpowers were carefully
calculated to signal political aims and interests to the other side.
And in both cases, at the height of the crisis, there was a direct
confrontation between them, including, in 1973, the resort to a
nuclear alert.

CHAPTER SEVEN

COMPARISON AND FINDINGS

THE 1967 AND 1973 crisis periods will be compared, as in Chapter 4, on two levels: first, in terms of the four crisis components and, in that context, as they relate to several variables of the Typologies for Crisis Research (Tables 1, 2, and 3 in Chapter 1); and second, with a focus on the effects of escalating stress on Israel's coping mechanisms.

CRISIS COMPONENTS

Environmental Change

A cluster of events on 16 and 17 May 1967 served as the *source* for the crisis period: Egypt's first step leading to the withdrawal of UNEF; U Thant's reply acknowledging her right to withdraw UNEF; and the Egyptian overflight of Israel's nuclear research center at Dimona. These catalyzed a sharp change in all three perceptual strands and in Israel's behavioral response. Evidence may be found in the large number and importance of decisions, which included all four basic decisions of the 1967 Crisis as a whole: large-scale mobilization (19 May); postponement of a decision on war (23 May); further delay (28 May); and a pre-emptive strike (4 June).

In 1973, the change from pre-crisis to crisis period was triggered by the arrival during the night of 4–5 October of news of two developments: the sudden and rapid Soviet airlift of advisers and their families from Egypt and Syria; and evidence of an offensive Egyptian deployment along the full length of the Canal. All three perceptual components of crisis—threat, time, and probability of war—escalated on the morning of the 5th; the last even more sharply at 04:00 on the 6th, with the information of an imminent Arab attack. As in 1967, the 1973 crisis period included all core decisions: (by implication) not to mobilize (5 October); not to pre-empt (6 October); to cross the Canal (14 October); and to accept the UN cease-fire resolutions (21 and 26 October).

Threat to Basic Values

The intensity of threat perception by Israel's decision-makers changed on 17 May 1967, in the light of the probable withdrawal of UNEF and the overflight of Dimona. The former was viewed as the removal of a barrier between adversary armies and as the un-freezing, or heating up, of a dormant frontier between two states in a protracted conflict; the path for an Egyptian attack was now open. The latter was seen as a grave threat to Israel's deterrent capability. Later in the crisis period, the decision-makers believed that Israel's very survival was at stake.

Evidence of a sharp increase in threat perception is pervasive at the verbal level. It was manifest in the tone and substance of Eshkol's speeches to the Knesset on 22, 23, and 29 May, his broadcast to the nation on the 28th, his letter to Kosygin on 1 June, and in several letters to Western leaders—Johnson (18 and 30 May and, via Eban, 25 May), de Gaulle and George Brown (19 May), along with a formal diplomatic note to the Powers (21 May). It may also be discerned in Eban's speech (17 May) and press conference (30 May), and in the reports of his face-to-face discussions with de Gaulle and Wilson (24 May), Rusk (25 May), McNamara, Wheeler, and Johnson (26 May); in Allon's interview (4 June); and in Dayan's press conference (3 June), as well as his memoirs (1976).

Events during the night of 4–5 October 1973 led to a sharp increase in threat perception among Israel's decision-makers. During the first thirty hours of the crisis period, the value threatened was peace. Then, for three days, several other values were seen as jeopardized, notably the lives of Israel's soldiers and the nation's reputation for military invincibility. As the war continued, the basic value threat took the form of a spiraling cost in human life.

Evidence of threat perception may be found in Meir's addresses to the nation (6 and 10 October), her press conference on the 13th, and two speeches to the Knesset on 16 and 23 October; and in Dayan's TV speeches (6, 20, and 24 October), and especially in his confidential briefing to Israeli editors on the 9th. The *gravity* of perceived threat at the height of the 1967 crisis period (27 May–4 June) was qualitatively higher than at the peak of the 1973 crisis period (6–9 October) because, heavy casualties notwithstanding, the issue of Israel's survival was not in question in 1973.

Probability of War (or Shift in Military Balance)

By 17 May 1967, and increasingly thereafter, the likelihood of war came to permeate the cognitive map of Israel's decision-makers. The findings at the action level are striking: decisions for partial and large-scale mobilization of IDF reserves (17, 19, 21 May); the formulation of a National Unity Government on 1 June and, particularly, the replacement of Eshkol by a charismatic military leader, Dayan, as Defense Minister; the despatch of special envoys abroad (Eban to Paris, London, and Washington, 24–26 May; and Amit to Washington, 30 May–2 June); and prolonged mobilization of reserves at grave economic cost (19 May–4 June). A high probability of war was perceived by most Israeli decision-makers—and many other persons—from Nasser's closing of the Straits (22–23 May), with a steadily rising likelihood during the next thirteen days. Eshkol, Eban, Allon, and Rabin testified to this in many statements, interviews, and writings during the decade following the 1967 Crisis. Some, like Dayan and Rabin, reportedly perceived a high probability of war as early as 16 and 17 May. Eshkol's statements to the Knesset and his letters to Heads of Government of the great powers reveal an escalating expectation of war. So too do Eban's speeches and press remarks during the crisis period, and the difference between Allon's interviews on 14 May and 4 June. The evidence is overwhelming.

In 1973, the perceived probability of war increased from the early hours of 5 October until 04:00 on the 6th and then rose traumatically until the Egyptian-Syrian attack. During the next three days, there was grave concern about an adverse change in the military balance, for the Egyptians had crossed the Canal and had destroyed the Bar-Lev line, and Syrian forces had come alarmingly close to Israeli settlements on the Golan Heights and to the B'not Ya'acov bridge leading to the population centers of the Huleh Valley.

Time Pressure

Another consequence of the three events that converged at the outset of the 1967 crisis period was an emerging awareness of the time dimension. A quick response was regarded by Israel's decision-makers as necessary to maintain her deterrent credibility. That led to the decision for further mobilization on 17 May and, in response to the actual withdrawal of UNEF on the 18th, to the large-scale mobilization decision on the 19th. While it is difficult to determine the relative importance of the three perceptual changes, there is no doubt that decision-makers began to perceive time as constraining, finite, and, at the beginning of the crisis period, short. Time salience was also apparent in the deliberations of 23 May and in the response to the closing of the Straits—the decision to delay by only forty-eight hours the basic choice of war or acquiescence. The Cabinet discussions and decision of 27–28 May again revealed a perception that time was limited—Israel could not wait indefinitely. On that occasion, however, the time for decision was finite but no longer short. No deadline was specified in the "further delay" decision. Eshkol wrote to Johnson on 30 May that "it is crucial that the international naval escort should move through the Straits within a week or two." Eban told a press conference the same day that the waiting period could be counted in days or weeks, not months or years. Thus, toward the end of the 1967 crisis period, time was perceived as finite but not brief. And in reality, Israel's decision-makers waited a week after the 28 May decision. They might well have waited longer but for other situational changes which made time more salient: the Jordan-Egypt alliance on 30 May and the movement of Iraqi troops into Jordan on 4 June. In addition, there was a growing awareness of the steadily increasing economic and morale cost of prolonged mobilization, along with vocal demands by the generals for a military riposte. In Eshkol's words to Johnson: "The time is ripe for confronting Nasser. . . ."

Far more than in 1967, time pressure was felt by Israel's decision-makers in the 1973 crisis period. The gap between the uncertainty about war and its actual outbreak could be measured in hours, thereby imposing a demand for immediate response regarding mobilization and pre-emption. Secondly, Egyptian and Syrian advances on 6 and 7 October created an acute sense of the need for a rapid military triumph, leading to the controversial decision on the 8th to counterattack in Sinai. The pressure of time was no more starkly evident than in the last days of the Yom Kippur War, which witnessed the (unsuccessful) pleas to Kissinger to delay the coming into effect of the first cease-fire (22 October) in order to provide time for a decisive IDF victory over Egypt. Time constraints also led to an Israeli decision to press forward vigorously on the west bank of the Canal and to attempt to recapture the positions on Mount Hermon in the Golan. And finally, a seemingly clear signal of intended direct Soviet military intervention, on the 24th, created an awareness of grave danger and total time constraint if Israel rejected the second cease-fire. In short, all of the seventeen Israeli decisions in the 1973 crisis period were made under a recognized time constraint.

Thus the crisis periods in 1967 and 1973 were characterized by the presence of the crisis components set out in our definition—a sharp increase in threat to basic values, a probability of war (or change in the military balance), and an awareness of time salience. This supports the general proposition that the convergence of these three perceived conditions, brought about by changes in the environment of a state actor, marks the beginning of the crisis period in an International Crisis.

Other similarities and differences in the crisis periods of the two cases may be noted. One similarity is *duration:* In 1967, the crisis period lasted nineteen days, from 17 May to the morning of 5 June; in 1973, it lasted close to twenty-two days, from the early hours of 5 October to the 26th. There was a difference in the *outcome:* The 1967 crisis period culminated in the decision to launch a pre-emptive strike, leading to the Six Day War and Israel's greatest military triumph since independence; in 1973, the crisis period, the Yom Kippur War itself, ended with a cease-fire and led to a protracted period of negotiations. The *number of decisions* was similar: fourteen during the crisis period of 1967 and seventeen in 1973. The *time span* of decision in both cases was coterminous with the entire crisis period: In 1967, it began with a partial mobilization decision on 17 May and ended with the pre-emption decision; in 1973, it began with the IDF alert decision on 5 October and concluded with the acceptance of the cease-fire on 26 October.

COPING MECHANISMS

Information Processing

As the 1967 Crisis became more intense, Israel's decision-makers felt a greater need for more information. Thus, from 17 May, Yariv, the Head of AMAN, reported directly to the Prime Minister. Moreover, senior IDF officers were invited to meetings of the Cabinet and its Committee on Defense from the 23rd onward. The closing of the Straits of Tiran on 22–23 May led to a further sharp increase in stress and a consequent perceived need for new, authoritative information, to be obtained by extraordinary methods. First, Eban was sent urgently to Paris, London, and Washington (24–26 May) to elicit information at the highest level about the Western Powers' intentions. Then, following the Jordan-Egypt Military Pact on 30 May, when the probability of war was seen as rising daily, the Cabinet despatched Amit to Washington, particularly to tap the attitudes and intentions of the Pentagon and the CIA. And finally, Harman was called to Jerusalem for the critical inner circle meeting on the evening of 3 June. The Evron and Eban reports were crucial for the 28 May decision to extend the "waiting period." Amit's and Harman's information weighed heavily in the decision to pre-empt. Among conventional sources, the telephone and cable media between Jerusalem and Israel's Washington Embassy were utilized to a much greater extent than in noncrisis situations, especially from 26 May onward.

In 1973, the felt need for information was narrower in scope but more intense: It focused on the battlefronts and Washington. Special measures were taken to ensure a flow of reliable information to the Prime Minister and the group around her as speedily as possible. Dinitz was immediately returned to Washington on 5 October, with Eban as a second source of information from the U.S. Galili and Gazit were put in charge of all contacts on the Israeli side. Dayan and Elazar shuttled back and forth between Cabinet and other meetings and the two fronts, in order to supply the Tel Aviv terminal with firsthand accounts of rapidly changing developments. Allon did so as well several times.

Information was channeled to the decision-makers as follows: Meir kept in constant touch by telephone with Eban and Dinitz in the United States, and with Dayan, Elazar, and Bar-Lev on the battlefronts. Cabinet members tended to stay around the Prime

Minister's office in Tel Aviv even between meetings, in order to get the latest information as soon as possible. There were three parallel channels of information: with the U.S. President (Meir-Dinitz)[1] or the State Department (Meir-Gazit-Dinitz-Kissinger, or Meir-Kissinger); through the U.S. Embassy in Tel Aviv (Allon or Gazit-Keating, Veliotis); or through the Defense establishment (Allon-Gur-Pentagon).

As the focus of decision shifted from the battlefield to the bargaining table, the lack of information led to increased stress. An especially dramatic illustration of this was Meir's unconcealed anger at Kissinger when no direct contact with Israel took place during his visit to Moscow on 20–21 October. However, unlike 1967, the Prime Minister did not despatch envoys to glean additional information: The Kissinger-Dinitz cooperation, along with Eban's presence in the U.S., were considered adequate to keep the decisional unit well-informed.

As the 1967 Crisis became more intense, the group which received secret information grew markedly in size—from a small restricted circle to the entire formal policy elite. The Cabinet Defense Committee was not a consumer of information until the enlarged Committee meeting on 23 May. However, during the last week of the crisis period, all information flowed to the Cabinet. It engaged, as Herzog remarked, in a "collective reading of cables" on the path to choice. In 1973, the Cabinet's role was even more important: It processed information daily throughout the crisis period, though on occasion the Cabinet, as an institution, may not have been informed of a major step until it was taken—for example, Meir's 12 October agreement in principle to a cease-fire in place. Moreover, Eban, on his return from the U.S., and on other occasions, reported to the Knesset Committee on Foreign Affairs and Security.

In noncrisis "normal" situations, correspondence between Israel's Prime Minister and other Heads of Government is infrequent, apart from ritual messages. During the 1967 crisis period, by contrast, communication with external actors was an important

1. It is unclear whether there were any direct phone conversations between Nixon and Meir during the War. President Nixon stated (in his 12 May 1977 television interview with David Frost) that "I had several conversations with her," but this was denied in interviews with members of the Prime Minister's entourage. A source close to Meir stated that there were phone conversations transmitted through Dinitz while he was at the White House.

aspect of Israel's pattern of behavior. Notable were Eshkol's several letters to and from Johnson (19, 25, 30 May, and 22, 28 May, 3 June, respectively), de Gaulle (19 May, and 28 May), Wilson (19 May, and 20 May), and Kosygin (1 June, and 4 June), and to the Four Powers (21 May). To these must be added Eban's face-to-face discussions with de Gaulle, Wilson, Johnson, and Rusk (24–26 May). Insight into the attitudes of the Powers was a basic objective of those high-level exchanges; and the information thus acquired was invariably processed by the Cabinet soon after, with spillover effects on the ensuing deliberations.

During the 1973 Crisis, the external actor whose attitudes and behavior were considered most important by Israel was the United States. The Prime Minister felt it imperative to speak directly with the U.S. President twice—on 9 October and immediately after the War. She was dissuaded the first time only after the receipt of a direct message from Nixon. And she hurried to Washington a few days after the cease-fire took effect. There was also an exchange of notes between Nixon and Meir on 9, 21, and 24 October, and there was almost daily communication between the Secretary of State and the Government of Israel. On Meir's insistence, Kissinger stopped on his way home from Moscow on 22 October, so that Israel's decision-makers could acquire information about the cease-fire and discuss U.S.-Israeli relations with him.

During the 1967 crisis period, especially from 23 May onward, the volume of incoming information increased markedly. Cables from Israel's diplomatic missions were much more frequent and longer than usual. Moreover, a few high policy decision-makers, notably Eshkol, Eban, and Galili, had to process an abnormally large number of messages from Heads of Government and Foreign Ministers. Thus, while the amount of information increased, effective processing became more difficult—especially since the time available for considered response decreased. Although quantitative data are not available, interviews with Foreign Office personnel revealed that the volume of incoming messages to the Foreign Ministry was more than double, and in wordage more than triple the amount in noncrisis periods.

Quantitative data are not available for 1973 either. On the basis of interviews, however, it can be stated that the U.S.-Israeli flow of information through the three channels mentioned above was of a very high volume. These were handled by Gazit, Allon, and Galili, while almost all other messages were shunted to the Foreign

CRISIS PERIOD

Office bureaucracy. There was virtually no counterpart to the frequent exchanges with Heads of Government and Foreign Ministers of other powers. Therefore, the processing of information was less complex than in the 1967 crisis period.

Consultation: Persons and Groups

With the escalation of stress, a larger number of persons was consulted during the 1967 crisis period. The Cabinet added three members on 1 June: Begin and Saphir from *Gahal* as Ministers Without Portfolio, and Dayan from *Rafi* as Defense Minister. Moreover, six other party leaders were consulted: Avigur, Ben-Gurion, Dinstein, Meir, Peres, and Yadin. Six more civil servants, too, were involved: Bitan, Evron, Harman, Levavi, Rafael, and Yaffe. Finally, Bar-Lev was added to the IDF generals, Rabin, Yariv, Weizman, and Amit. In short, Israel's consultative circle was enlarged from twenty-four in the 1967 pre-crisis period (Cabinet–18, bureaucrats–2, and military elite–4) to thirty-nine in the crisis period (Cabinet–21, bureaucrats–7, military elite–5, and other–6), an increase of 62 percent.

The increase in the consultative circle from the pre-crisis to the crisis period was much larger in 1973 than in 1967: from the Kitchen Cabinet of four to seven available Cabinet ministers on 5 October, to the full Cabinet of eighteen thereafter. Dinitz joined Gazit from the bureaucratic elite. There was a change in composition, though not in the number of persons, in the military elite, because of the exit of Zeira and Hofi and the addition of Yariv and Bar-Lev. In summary, the consultative group in 1973 grew from ten (Kitchen Cabinet–4, bureaucrat–1, and military elite–5) to twenty-five (Cabinet–18, bureaucrats–2, and military elite–5), an increase of 150 percent. The consultative circle during the two crisis periods as a whole, thirty-nine in 1967 and twenty-five in 1973, was somewhat larger on occasion because several other generals and sometimes the entire General Staff were consulted. Thus, in terms of coping with crisis, a noteworthy effect of escalating stress, in both cases, was a marked increase in the size of the consultative circle. In 1967, this was accompanied by a broadening of the group as well, to include other politicians and public figures. And in 1973, the ministerial segment of the consultative group grew rapidly, from four on 3 October to eighteen on the 6th.

TABLE 7
CONSULTATIVE MEETINGS BY TYPE AND SIZE: CRISIS PERIODS

Number of Participants	1967			1973		
	Ad Hoc	Institutional	Total	Ad Hoc	Institutional	Total
small 2	21	10	31	9	33	42
3–4	23	–	23	5	3	8
medium 5–10	21	3	24	11	14	25
large 11–14	1	3	4	1	5	6
15–20	1	5	6	–	13	13
21+	–	9	9	–	17	17
Total	67	30	97	26	85	111

Table 7 presents quantitative data on consultative meetings held by the Prime Minister and/or Defense Minister in the 1967 and 1973 crisis periods, by type and size. In both periods, the two principal institutional forums for consultation were the largest (the Cabinet) and the smallest (Defense Minister [DM] and Chief of Staff [COS]). In 1967, there were nine Cabinet meetings, in addition to five of the Ministerial Committee on Defense, and ten of the DM-COS. During the 1973 crisis period, the comparable figures were thirty (17 + 13) and thirty-three.

The ratio of ad hoc to institutional meetings in the 1967 crisis period was 2.2:1—and really higher, because ad hoc meetings on the domestic political crisis are not included. The ad hoc institutional ratio in 1973 was 0.3:1. That is, institutional settings for consultation were far more important during the 1973 crisis period than in 1967. And approximately 56% of the consultative meetings were small, 25% were medium-sized, and 19% were large in 1967. For the 1973 crisis period, the comparable figures are 44% small, 23.5% medium, and 32.5% large.

More than four-fifths (83%) of all small and medium-sized meetings in the 1967 crisis period were ad hoc, compared to a third in 1973. Two reasons may be adduced for this difference. One is the fact that, for most of the 1967 crisis period, Eshkol served as both Prime Minister and Defense Minister; all of his meetings with a single person, except the COS, were ad hoc. Meetings between

TABLE 8
GROUP PARTICIPATION IN THE CONSULTATIVE PROCESS: CRISIS PERIODS

	1967			1973		
	Meetings with PM alone	Meetings with PM attended by two or more groups	Total	Meetings with PM and/or DM alone	Meetings with PM and/or DM attended by two or more groups	Total
ME	19	31	50	40	28	68
BE	13	31	44	–	1	1
M	8	20	28	19	4	23
PE	4	6	10	3	–	3
KC				1	8	9
U.S.				2	2	4

BE = Bureaucratic Elite
DM = Defense Minister
KC = Kitchen Cabinet

M = Ministers
ME = Military Elite
PE = Political Elite

PM = Prime Minister
U.S. = United States

Prime Minister Meir and Defense Minister Dayan in 1973, however, were coded as institutional. The second, more substantive
reason relates to the different character of the two periods. In
1967, the crisis period was prewar, with many diplomatic and
political negotiations, requiring frequent informal consultation. By
contrast, hostilities broke out twenty-four hours after the onset of
the 1973 crisis period, and a greater need was felt for formal procedures—consultative as well as decisional—to cope with the
grave problems created by the Egypt-Syria attack.

Large institutional groups exceeded large ad hoc groups overwhelmingly in both crisis periods: seventeen of nineteen consultative meetings in 1967 and thirty-five of thirty-six meetings in 1973.
There were several reasons. One is structural: As indicated in
Chapter 4, when a group expands beyond ten members, informal
procedures are no longer adequate for discussion. Secondly, escalating stress requires a larger formal consensus to cope with the
multiple problems created by an international crisis, especially the
need to take fateful decisions under time constraints. And thirdly,
both Prime Ministers rarely saw the need to circumvent established consultative procedures, which are highly institutionalized
in Israel's political system. The effect of increasing stress on this
aspect of coping with crisis, then, was to reinforce the reliance on
established institutional frameworks for large and small consultation—namely, the Cabinet and the Ministerial Committee on
Defense.

Israel's military and bureaucratic elites were the most frequently consulted groups in the 1967 crisis period, as is evident in Table
8. The many meetings between Eshkol and other ministers on the
domestic struggle for control over the Defense Ministry are not
included. This explains, in part, the disparity between bureaucratic and military elite consultation, on the one hand, and ministerial consultation on the other. The Military met alone with the
Prime Minister almost as often (nineteen times) as did Bureaucrats
and Ministers (twenty-one times). And when civil servants were
consulted, military officers were usually present. During the 1973
crisis period, too, the Prime Minister and/or Defense Minister met
mainly with IDF officers: The Military Elite (ME) participated
altogether in sixty-eight meetings, while consultations with Ministers took place only twenty-three times. The Ministers met with
the PM and/or DM alone nineteen times, while the Military Elite
met them alone forty times. Thus, the ME met the PM and/or DM

twice as many times alone as did the Ministers and three times as much together with other groups as did the Ministers. Yet, Ministers played a much more active role than Bureaucrats, who never were consulted alone by the Prime Minister and/or Defense Minister. Other groups were marginal in the 1973 crisis period pattern of consultation, though two are not evident in 1967—namely, the Kitchen Cabinet and U.S. officials.

A striking aspect of the data in Table 8 compared across the two periods is the much higher proportion of consultations with the Military in 1973 (68 of 108, that is, 63%) than in 1967 (50 of 132, that is, 38%). This may be explained by the war–no war difference between the two crisis periods. For all but the first thirty hours, the 1973 crisis period was synonymous with the Yom Kippur War; in 1967, the political and diplomatic dimensions of the crisis required more attention from Eshkol than did military issues. That is, the Prime Minister turned more frequently for advice to the Military, absolutely and relatively, in 1973 than in 1967. This contrast also explains the conspicuous consultative role of Bureaucrats in 1967—forty-four meetings—and their virtual non-role in 1973. Members of the Political Elite (PE) were not often consulted in either crisis period, especially during the 1973 War. And Ministers were consulted with virtually the same frequency in the two periods, though much more so alone in 1973.

In terms of coping with crisis, these findings indicate that:
1. The escalation of stress in a prewar (nonviolent) phase of an international crisis led Israel's decision-makers to seek advice from both civil servants and military officers.
2. War-induced higher stress created an overwhelming reliance on the group skilled in violence.
3. Other politicians were increasingly ignored as stress continued during the war phase of a crisis.
4. War-induced escalation of stress strengthened the search for legitimation by the senior decision-maker(s) by consulting alone with ministers.

Decisional Forums

Israel's decisional unit in the 1967 crisis period ranged from one to the enlarged Cabinet of twenty-one. In reality it was nineteen, for two ministers were not present at Cabinet meetings in the last phase of the crisis period, 1–4 June. In 1973, the decisional unit showed great variation in size, ranging from one (the Prime Minister), through four (the Kitchen Cabinet), through seven (available ministers), to the full Cabinet of eighteen.

Table 9 specifies the decisions taken during the two crisis periods, the decision-makers, and the structural setting in which each decision was made. The principal forums for decision-making in the 1967 crisis period followed the same pattern as consultation. Eleven of the fourteen decisions were made in large, institutional settings: the Cabinet, its Defense Committee, or the General Staff with the Defense Minister present. One decision was taken in a small institutional setting and two in medium ad hoc forums.

In 1973, by contrast, the patterns of decisional forums and consultation were markedly different: There were more than three times as many institutional as ad hoc consultative meetings, compared to an equal distribution of ad hoc and institutional decisional forums (nine to nine). The Cabinet dominated institutional settings, making six of the nine decisions, while the Kitchen Cabinet was the key ad hoc forum, making seven of the nine decisions. The Prime Minister and the Defense Minister each participated in three of the small and medium-sized decisional forums, once together.

A noteworthy feature of the 1967 crisis period was that three large institutional groups each made two decisions at a single meeting: the General Staff (Decisions 5 and 6), the Ministerial Committee on Defense (8 and 9), and the Cabinet (12 and 13). In every case, the first decision was basic and the second was essentially an implementing provision. In the 1973 crisis period, there was one paired-decision case (5 and 6). However, in contrast to 1967, those decisions were both of core significance.

Decisions in the 1967 crisis period were made in a variety of forums: the Cabinet; the Cabinet acting as the Ministerial Committee on Defense; the Defense Minister; the Chief of Staff; the General Staff; the Military Elite; Bureaucrats; and Ministers. The Cabinet as such, or in its capacity as the Ministerial Committee on Defense, made eight of the fourteen decisions, including three of the four strategic ones (Decisions 8, 12, and 17). The fourth (Decision 5) was made by the Defense Minister and the General Staff. The Prime Minister participated in all but two decisions. In the 1973 crisis period, the decisional forums comprised: the Prime Minister; the Cabinet; the Defense Minister; the Chief of Staff; the General Staff; the Military Elite; Ministers; and the Kitchen

TABLE 9
DECISIONAL FORUMS: CRISIS PERIODS
1967

Decision Number	Decision	Setting Institutional Small	Setting Institutional Large	Ad Hoc Medium
4	Further Mobilization	DM+COS		
5	Large-scale Mobilization		DM+GS	
6	Defensive to Offensive IDF Posture		DM+GS	
7	Mobilization Decisions Authorized		C	
8	Decision on War Postponed		MCD+	
9	Eban to Washington		MCD+	
10	U.S. Is Warned Egyptian Attack Imminent			ME+BE
11	Await Eban Report		MCD+	
12	War Decision Again Delayed		C	
13	IDF Alert Renewed		C	
14	Amit to Washington			M+BE
15	National Unity Government		C	
16	Military Plans Crystalized		DM+GS	
17	Launch Pre-emptive Air Strike		C	
		1	11	2

BE = Bureaucratic Elite	DM = Defense Minister	MCD = Ministerial Committee on Defense	
C = Cabinet	GS = General Staff		
COS = Chief of Staff	KC = Kitchen Cabinet	ME = Military Elite	
	M = Ministers	PM = Prime Minister	

Cabinet. The Cabinet—or its informal inner circle, the Kitchen Cabinet—made thirteen of the eighteen decisions.

There were several major differences in decisional forums during the two crisis periods. One was the prominent role of the Kitchen Cabinet in 1973. It was, in effect, the successor to the Ministerial Committee on Defense, which had ceased to exist in the Meir régime. Another was the nonparticipation of Bureaucrats in any decisional forum of the 1973 crisis period. As noted, their role in consultations during that period was minimal. In 1967, by contrast, they played an active role in both the consultative and decisional processes. Thirdly, while the General Staff was frequently consulted in the 1973 crisis period, it was not a key decision-making organ and was much less important than in 1967, when it was the forum for three decisions (5, 6, and 16).

TABLE 9 (*Continued*)

DECISIONAL FORUMS: CRISIS PERIODS

1973

Decision Number	Decision	Institutional			Ad Hoc		
		Small	*Medium*	*Large*	*Small*	*Medium*	*Large*
3	Highest IDF Alert		DM+COS +ME				
4	Empowered Mobilization by PM and DM			C			
5	Not to Pre-empt					KC+ME +BE	
6	Large-scale Mobilization					KC+ME +BE	
7	COS Empowered to Counterattack					KC	
8	IDF Concentration on North		DM+GS				
9	Bar-Lev Appointed OC South					PM+DM+ COS+M	
10	Meir to Washington (abortive)	PM+DM					
11	General Attack on Syria					KC	
12	Canal Crossing Postponed					KC	
13	Accept Cease-fire in Place (abortive)	PM+M					
14	Crossing of Canal			C			
15	Advance West of Canal Short of Cairo					KC+ COS	
16	Accept First Cease-fire			C			
17	Continue IDF Operations			C			
18	Continue IDF Advance West of Canal					PM+DM +ME	
19	Accept Second Cease-fire			C			
20	Supply Third Army			C			
		1	2	6	1	7	1

Two other themes merit attention. An examination of the data in Table 9 reveals no correlation between decisional forums and kinds of issues about which they made choices. Thus, in 1967, the Cabinet made military decisions (13 and 17), a political decision relevant to the crisis (15), and a political-military decision (12). The Ministerial Committee on Defense made political decisions (9 and 11) and one with political-cum-military implications (8). This blurred multi-issue-area focus of decision was also evident in 1973. The Cabinet made narrow-gauge military decisions (4 and 17) and some with political-cum-military dimensions (13, 16, 19, and 20); so too with the Kitchen Cabinet. There was no clear association between decisional forum and issue. The second theme which emerges from the data is that, even in periods of high stress, whether war was anticipated or actually taking place, the Military did not dominate Israel's decisional forums. Rather, it was civilian structures, notably the Cabinet and its Defense Committee, which played the pivotal decision-making role in both the 1967 and 1973 crisis periods.

In terms of coping with crisis, larger rather than smaller decisional forums were preferred by Israel's decision-makers at high levels of stress. This was more conspicuous in 1967—for eleven of fourteen decisions. In 1973, only two of the eighteen forums for decision were small.

There is evidence, too, of an association between stress and intragroup tension and leadership: As stress increased in the 1967 Crisis, tension grew within the decision-making group. This began to emerge at the 21 May Cabinet meeting. Disagreement reached its peak with the 9–9 vote at the Cabinet session on the 27th. Harmony was gradually restored under the impact of a series of threatening acts by the Arabs and perceived American non-opposition to an Israeli pre-emptive strike. Harmony increased steadily during the last week of the crisis period, 27 May to 4 June. Because the 1973 crisis period coincided, almost entirely, with the Yom Kippur War, tension was high at all times. There was continuous stress among military commanders, caused by mutual recriminations and fundamental differences of opinion on tactics. At the highest political level, however, largely because of the difference in the personalities of Prime Ministers Eshkol and Meir, stress was lower in 1973 than in 1967.

Alternatives: Search and Evaluation*

The first decision of the 1967 crisis period, like those in the pre-crisis period, was made in accordance with routine procedures. Search for alternatives was initiated only when threat increased sharply and the routine procedures could no longer cope with the environmental changes. There was a careful evaluation of alternatives, in nonquantitative cost-benefit terms, leading to the four strategic decisions. The key alternatives considered for each were: Decision 5 on 19 May—no mobilization, an approach to the Powers, warning signals to the Arab states, especially Egypt, or some combination thereof; Decision 8 on 23 May—an immediate small or large-scale pre-emptive strike; Decision 12 on 27–28 May—the same alternatives; and Decision 17 on 3–4 June—a further delay to permit organized international naval action.

The 1967 decision to pre-empt (17) was made after careful evaluation of all known data. The close of the "waiting period" was signaled by the appearance of an end to U.S. restraint on military action by Israel. One IDF estimate of cost for further delay, on 28 May, was two hundred additional casualties per day. The benefit of delay was assessed as twofold: continued direct U.S. support for Israel's claims vis-à-vis the Straits, and a steady increase in support by world public opinion. By 4 June, the cost was estimated to be far greater than any benefit from continued delay.

The first two decisions of the 1973 crisis period were made after a modest cost-benefit evaluation. Increased preparedness and authority to mobilize were weighed in terms of the perception of the enemy's intent as against the economic burden for Israel; as noted, the cost of the May 1973 partial mobilization was estimated to be 61 million Israeli pounds. Moreover, Dayan argued on 5–6 October that premature action would benefit Israel's adversaries. Several wartime decisions, too, were arrived at after cost-benefit evaluations—notably Decision 8 to concentrate on repelling the Syrians, and Decisions 12 and 14 about crossing the Canal only after weakening the enemy's armored strength. In general, the decisions on military moves from 8 October onward were calculated to save lives and military equipment as much as possible, in view of the first two days' heavy losses: 1,000 dead and nearly 300 tanks and 50 planes lost. By contrast, the two strategic decisions of 6

*The substance of all decisions mentioned in this discussion is indicated in Table 9.

October 1973 (5 and 6) were taken mainly on the basis of historical legacy and intense time pressure.

Escalating stress during the 1967 crisis period led to increasing attention to options concerned with immediate rather than long-term objectives. After the initial despatch of Egyptian troops to Sinai, and after the withdrawal of UNEF, Israel's decision-makers weighed alternatives to meet the specific short-term challenges. After 22 May, they were preoccupied with the goal of lifting the blockade of the Straits. And from 28 May to 4 June, they focused on countering Egypt's massive concentration of forces on Israel's Sinai border. Among the leaders, only Eban emphasized the longer-range goal of American and world public opinion support for Israel in the political struggle which would follow a war. The consideration of long-term aims was more apparent in the 1973 crisis period deliberations. The decision not to pre-empt (5) was taken primarily in terms of long-range concerns, notably future U.S. military, economic, and political support in the Arab-Israeli conflict. These concerns were also in the forefront, though not as decisive, in the decisions to cross the Canal (14); not to advance to Cairo (18); and to accept the calls for a cease-fire (19).

As stress increased during the 1967 Crisis, Israel's decision-makers perceived the range of alternatives open to them to be steadily narrower. As noted above, several options were weighed in Phase I. These declined from 23 May onward. But only with the failure of the U.S.-U.K.-sponsored international flotilla project did the conviction become universal that Israel now had only one viable choice—namely, to respond to Arab threats with large-scale military action. The range of perceived alternatives in the 1973 crisis period was a product of the fortunes of war. During the first three days of fighting, all energies were devoted to containing the enemy's advance: There were no alternatives in that phase of very high stress. Once an equilibrium had been established on both fronts and the initiative for military moves passed into IDF hands (from 10 October on), the range of choices expanded and, as indicated, alternatives were evaluated.

Despite the increase in stress from 23 May 1967 onward, Israel's decision-makers did not make premature choices among alternatives during the 1967 crisis period. They deliberated on the 23rd and opted for diplomacy. They again opted for delay on the 28th— for another week before deciding to pre-empt. In 1973, there was one noteworthy premature choice—namely, Meir's agreement in principle to a cease-fire in place (Decision 13 on 12 October). Fortunately for Israel, neither Egypt nor Syria was prepared to accept. Another case of premature closure would seem to have been Decision 7 on 7 October to empower the Chief of Staff to decide upon a counterattack in the South on the 8th. Dayan had advocated retreat into Sinai, and Elazar had urged a counterattack. The attack proved to be a costly failure. However, the Agranat Commission concluded that it was a necessary move, "primarily by the fact that [it] contained and blocked the enemy's bridgeheads, preventing him from completely achieving the first stage of his plan."

During the 1967 crisis period, there was a steadily growing reliance on group decision-making processes. This was accompanied by a greater consideration of alternatives. The early Eshkol-Rabin decisions were either in accord with routine procedures or, primarily, were extensions of earlier decisions. However, as the decisional forum moved to a group, under the impact of higher stress, there emerged a wider search for alternatives in the near-daily discussions within the Cabinet or its Defense Committee from 23 May to 4 June. The 1973 evidence reveals a similar pattern. A large part of the 6 October noon Cabinet meeting was devoted to a debate on what would happen if Syria attacked and Egypt did not. Moreover, as the 1973 crisis period evolved, there was continuing reliance on a large group, the Cabinet, to evaluate alternatives and make choices.

The effects of stress on this aspect of coping were different in two important respects during the crisis periods: first, the somewhat greater attention to short-run goals in the high-stress *pre-war* crisis period of 1967 than in the high-stress *wartime* crisis period of 1973; and second, the evidence of premature closure in 1973, compared to patient consideration of alternatives throughout the 1967 crisis period. Each was associated with the absence (1967) or presence (1973) of war—or, more precisely, with the expectation or reality of military hostilities. This suggests that war-induced stress has distinct effects on Israel's coping with crisis.

PART THREE

POST-CRISIS PERIOD

CHAPTER EIGHT

1967: 5 TO 10 JUNE

DECISIONS AND DECISION-MAKERS

AT THE CONCLUSION of the Six Day War, Israel was the strongest and most secure state in the Near East Core. The post-crisis period of 1967 was synonymous with the War itself and generated nine further decisions. All but two were taken by the 21-member National Unity Government, which had been formed on 1 June. The decisions were as follows:

Decision Number	Date	Content
18.	5 June	The Cabinet decided to notify Jordan that Israel would not initiate military action against her.
19.	5 June	The Cabinet decided to delay a decision on an attack on the Old City of Jerusalem.
20.	6 June	The Cabinet, acting as the Ministerial Committee on Defense, approved encirclement of the Old City but delayed a decision on entry.
21.	7 June	Eshkol and Dayan, in consultation with other ministers, approved plans to attack the Old City.
22.	7 June	The Cabinet, acting as the MCD, approved Dayan's plan to stop the advance into Sinai short of the Suez Canal.
23.	7 June	The Cabinet, acting as the MCD, decided to advance on the Syrian front to the international border only, subject to developments in the international arena.

24.	8 June	The Cabinet, acting as the MCD, decided to delay a decision on the Syrian issue, in effect, not to attack Syria.
25.	9 June	The Cabinet aproved Dayan's orders to advance up to the escarpment of the Golan Heights.
26.	10 June	Eshkol, Dayan, and Eban decided to accept the Security Council call for a cease-fire on the Syrian front.

PSYCHOLOGICAL ENVIRONMENT

Attitudinal Prism

The gestation period for Israel's decision to go to war, especially the *Hamtana* (waiting) from 23 May to 4 June, was perceived by much of the politically conscious world as one of grave peril for Israel. Arab elites and attentive publics viewed that peril as a unique opportunity to destroy the Jewish state and reveled in that expectation. Soviet-bloc elites approved Nasser's deeds—short of war—and his policy goals—except for the destruction of the State of Israel. But most actors in the global system observed the escalating tension as a "time of troubles" for Israel—in fact, a real threat to her survival. The result was a wave of sympathy, among non-Jews as well as Jews, not confined to the Western world. It was the peak of pro-Israel sentiment in the history of the State, not excluding the days and weeks following the Declaration of Independence in May 1948. Fear gave way to a sense of relief when Israel's decision to pre-empt terminated the uncertainty and initiated a sweeping military triumph. For Jewry, the weeks of waiting and the outbreak of war had produced a trauma of collective identification with Israel under siege. As for the universal actor, U Thant's behavior placed in jeopardy the UN's *bona fides* as a third party in the Arab-Israeli conflict. In addition, the most important bilateral link of the preceding decade, with France, and the military, political, and economic components of the internal environment had been affected.

All of these changes were acutely perceived by Israel's decision-makers, as is amply revealed by the extracts from their speeches. Yet their image-attentiveness was not equally focused on (1) sympathetic world opinion, (2) the rallying of Jewry, and (3) the international organization. The first was welcomed as an additional but marginal support for Israel during and after the crisis. But the behavior of non-Jewish states or publics is always subconsciously suspect in a pre-eminent Israeli "we-they" view of the world. Thus the sympathetic attitude tended to be perceived as a deviation from the norm of antagonism or indifference to Israel. The demonstrable fact of UN weakness was viewed by Israeli decision-makers as further proof of the illusory quality of the world body's—or indeed any external—guarantees as a viable path to peace. The pledges and guarantees of 1957 had proved defective, and this created an unshakable belief that the fruits of victory must not be squandered, as they were after the Sinai Campaign.

Among all the territories acquired as a result of the Six Day War, Jerusalem stands apart in the psychological environment of Israel. From 1948 to 1967, Israelis identified with Jerusalem as the Jewish people had done for three thousand years: This was the cradle of their culture, religion, and nation. But the de facto compromise of partition between the New and Old City had gradually become accepted as the basis for coexistence. The Six Day War and its related decisions transformed the nature of the commitment, making a reunited Jerusalem the heart of Israel. The collective and individual outpouring of affection for the liberation of "The Western Wall" demonstrated the overwhelming power of this identification. Decision-makers perceived this national mood and shared it. And the worldwide support of Jewry exceeded the expectations of most Israeli leaders, even those accustomed to view the Jewish people as Israel's only reliable ally.

None of the decision-makers failed to perceive President Johnson's role during the "waiting period" and, after the War, his pro-Israeli sentiments for a just settlement. The view was that only the United States could counteract the menacing Soviet presence in Egypt and Syria. And the deep-rooted image of Soviet animus towards Zionism, Israel, and Jewry was strengthened by Russia's escalating flow of military assistance to Israel's adversaries.

Images

ESHKOL

During the post-crisis period—that is, the six days of the 1967 War—Eshkol's perceptual net spread over many issues, regional and global. Four of them, all deriving from developments on the battlefield, are evident in secret Cabinet and Defense Committee deliberations: (1) how to respond to Jordan's initiation of hostility on the morning of the 5th; (2) what to do about the Old City of

Jerusalem; (3) how far the IDF should advance on the Golan
Heights; and (4) whether or not to occupy the headwaters of the
Jordan River. The first two emerged within hours after the War
began and were the center of attention at a Cabinet meeting on the
evening of 5 June. Eshkol led off with the remark: "We shall have
to consult tonight on what to do about Jordan, if they keep on with
their attack. The Jordanians opened fire and we have warned them
two—three times, through the proper go-betweens. They did not
respond." Later, he mused aloud: "This may be an opportunity to
enter the Old City." And, at the end of the debate, in reply to
Aranne's question, "If the Old City is occupied—when and to
whom does one return it?" he declared, "Nonetheless, there has to
be a counter-attack, against the shelling from Jordan. Let's leave
the military aspect to the Army. We shall notify the COS and the
Defense Minister of the Government's will."

At a meeting of the Ministerial Committee on Defense, two days
later, Eshkol agreed with Dayan's proposal to limit the IDF advance on the northern front to the international border, because of
concern about possible Soviet intervention. At the same time, his
long-term involvement in agriculture, land reclamation, irrigation,
and security found expression: He demanded the occupation of the
headwaters of the Jordan River system, a source of Arab-Israeli
tension since 1948.

Much is revealed about Eshkol's perceptions in three public
statements during and immediately after the 1967 War. On the
5th, he railed against "the aggressive ruler of Egypt . . . [and] his
plan and his preparations to attack Israel in order to destroy her.
. . . Arrogantly and braggingly, Nasser has made a mockery of
international law. . . ." He exuded confidence in the IDF—
"mighty, resourceful and well-trained defense forces, equipped
with top-quality weapons. . . ." Uncertainty about the attitude of
other states to the War—and a challenge—are evident, too: "Today we shall know who will lend us his support. These days are a
testing time for the nations of the world—whether they will join in
the heavy campaign, lend a loyal hand to our defense, and help us
check the aggressor." And finally, the ever-reliable ally, world Jewry, was commended: "This solidarity of the Jewish people with the
State of Israel elates us and inspires us with confidence."[1] On the
7th, in an address to Israel's spiritual leaders, he made two other

---

1. Broadcast to the Nation, 5 June 1967. English version in H. M. Christman,
ed., *The State Papers of Levi Eshkol* (New York, 1969), p. 109.

perceptual points. One related to the Old City: "Out of consideration for the sanctity of the city, and in accordance with our policy of
avoiding casualties among the civilian population, we have ab-
stained from any answering action inside the city, despite the
casualties incurred by our soldiers and citizens." The other image
was of Jordan's costly aggression: "The criminal actions of Jordan's
Government shall stand before the court of international opinion
and before the judgment of history."[2]

Eshkol gave renewed expression to the Holocaust syndrome, at
the beginning of his statement to the Knesset on 12 June: "A week
ago . . . the existence of the State of Israel . . . hung in the balance." The image of security in the aftermath of war followed: "The
aggression of the enemy has been repulsed, the greater part of his
power has been broken, his military machine destroyed, the bases
for aggression cleared. The threat of war has been lifted from our
country."[3] The IDF was defined once more as a citizen's army,
with a sacred mission: "Our forces are a people's army: when they
fight, the entire nation fights; when they fight, the whole of Jewish
history watches them. When our army fights, it fights not only for
the life of the people, but for its redemption."

The UN was ridiculed ("the impotence of international organization") and was charged with facilitating Nasser's closure of the
Straits with the Security Council remaining silent even then. The
rallying to Israel's cause was commended: "In the days that preceded the battles, the world's anxiety for Israel's survival became a
mighty manifestation. . . ." Hostile Soviet behavior was treated
rhetorically: He asked "how her policy is compatible with open
support for the aggressor during the fighting." And the rejection of
the status quo ante was proclaimed: "To the nations of the world I
want to say: be under no illusion that the State of Israel is prepared
to return to the situation that reigned up to a week ago. . . . The
position that existed up till now shall never again return."

EBAN

Foreign Minister Eban's perceptions, as articulated in the secret
deliberations, ranged over half a dozen issues. On the morning of

2. Address to the Chief Rabbis and Spiritual Leaders of all of Israel's Communities, 7 June 1967. English version in Christman, ed., *The State Papers of
Levi Eshkol*, p. 114.
3. Statement in the Knesset, 12 June 1967. English version in Christman, ed.,
The State Papers of Levi Eshkol, p. 119. The following passages are from Christman, pp. 121, 129, 130, and 131.

the 5th, immediately after Israel's pre-emptive air strike, he perceived three external sources of danger:

1. The Soviet Union might intervene on Egypt's behalf if it felt that the United States was hostile to Israel's reaction.

2. A cease-fire resolution would be adopted, calling not only for an end of the shooting, but for a return to previous positions.

3. Foreign governments and world opinion would forget the background of developments from 22 May onward, and seize upon the scope and range of our reactions on 5 June, as excuse for laying a burden of culpability on Israel.[4]

At the Cabinet meeting that evening, Eban voiced concern about the international repercussions of occupying the Old City of Jerusalem: "Can the fighting cause damage to the Holy Places? If the military situation makes it mandatory to occupy the Old City," he continued, "it should be done without declaring what will happen afterwards. Her holiness has to be assured." As for the priorities: "Military discussion has to precede the political one."

On the same day, he told a press conference in Tel Aviv: "The pattern of aggression which is now unfolding, in a culminating stage, did not, of course, begin this morning. . . . In our view, the actual hostility began with the act of the blockade." On Israel's goals, he stated that "Government policy includes no aims of conquest." Further, "our single objective is to frustrate the attempts of the Arab armies to conquer our land and so to break this siege and ring around us."[5]

For the rest of the post-crisis period—and beyond—Eban was at the UN. There, on the 6th, he began one of the great speeches of his career by evoking the pervasive Israeli image: "I have just come from Jerusalem to tell the Security Council that Israel, by its independent effort and sacrifice, has passed from serious danger to successful resistance." Like Eshkol, he defined Nasser's aim and Israel's perception as destruction: "Here was a clear design to cut the southern Negev off from the main body of our State. For Egypt . . . predicted that Israel itself would soon expire." He referred to "the hostile threat," "an alarming plan of encirclement," and freedom of passage being "suddenly and arbitrarily choked. Israel was and is breathing with only a single lung." He spoke about "an

4. Israel, Ministry for Foreign Affairs, Cables and Communications, Jerusalem, 1967.
5. English text of A. Eban's Press Conference, Tel Aviv, 5 June 1967. Israel, Government Press Office (mimeo).

apocalyptic air of an approaching peril. And Israel faced this danger alone." And with that he invoked the Holocaust syndrome: "Here, then, was a systematic, overt, proclaimed design at politicide, the murder of a State. . . . And the State thus threatened with collective assassination was itself the last sanctuary of a people which had seen six million of its sons exterminated . . . two decades before."

Eban reaffirmed that "our margin of general security was becoming smaller and smaller." His image of the UN was rhetorically devastating: "People in our country and in many countries ask: What is the use of a United Nations presence if it is, in effect, an umbrella which is taken away as it begins to rain?" As for UNEF: "Nothing became it less than the manner of its departure." Sinai he perceived as "a natural geographic barrier" between Egypt and Israel. He conveyed Israel's puzzled concern at the "relative lack of preoccupation on the part of friendly Governments and international agencies with this intense concentration. . . ."

Eban reaffirmed his (and Israel's) perception of the three main courses of the 1967 Crisis: "the sabotage and terrorist movement, emanating mostly from Syria, and the heavy troop concentrations accompanied by dire, apocalyptic threats in Sinai," and "the most electric shock of all . . . , the closure of the international waterway. . . ." The vital interest in Elath was emphasized: "There will not be—there cannot be—an Israel without Elath. We cannot be expected to return to a dwarfed stature, with our face to the Mediterranean alone." He also noted the universally shared Israeli perception of "a relative stability on the Egyptian-Israeli frontier for ten years," and declared: "Suddenly this pattern of mutually accepted stability was smashed to smithereens." He echoed Eshkol's image of world support for Israel in distress: "When danger threatened we could hear a roar of indignation sweep across the world." He restated his oft-made "iron law": "There will never be a Middle East without an independent and sovereign State of Israel in its midst." And he concluded by chiding the Soviet Union: "I think we have an equal duty to bring substantive proof for any denunciation that we make, each of the other."[6]

ALLON

Labor Minister Allon was acutely conscious of three issues during the 1967 War: the Old City of Jerusalem; the extent of advance

6. Address to the UN Security Council, 6 June 1967. Reprinted in A. Eban, *Voice of Israel* (New York, 1969), pp. 299–312.

by the IDF toward the Canal; and the extent of advance by the IDF on the Golan Heights. Along with Begin, his was the most militant advocacy regarding the Old City. Thus, at the 5 June Cabinet meeting, he declared:

From the military point of view this [Jordan's shelling of Jerusalem] is cause enough to attack the Old City. [And further:] The argument falls into several parts. First, the liberation of the Holy Places. Second, the elimination of a military obstacle. Third, the fate of Mount Scopus. The liberation of the Holy Places will be achieved without damaging them. The elimination of the military obstacle of the Jordanian attack from the Old City solves the political problem. Regarding Mount Scopus, there is a real danger of its occupation. Therefore, positive decisions on these three points can be justified in political terms. The Holy Places are within the walls. To avoid damaging them the Old City has to be surrounded from the direction of Nebi Samuel, the French Hill and Mount Scopus. This will also take care of an Arab attack on the Mount.[7]

The next day, Allon (and Begin) pressed this view, in contrast to the more cautious encirclement advocacy by Dayan.

On the 7th, Allon revealed militancy once more, urging an IDF advance to the shore of the Suez Canal. Similarly, on the 8th and 9th, he perceived an historic opportunity to achieve a "natural frontier" in the North by opening a third front and advancing on to the Golan Heights.

DAYAN

From the outbreak of the Six Day War (the post-crisis period), Defense Minister Dayan perceived danger and advocated caution, whereas Allon saw opportunity and pressed for immediate action. This was evident in secret deliberations on the three crucial issues: the Old City, the IDF advance in Sinai, and the advance into Syria. Thus, at the Cabinet/Defense Committee meeting on 6 June, Dayan opposed a direct attack on the Old City, indicating a willingness to gamble that its inhabitants would surrender within hours or days; the City would fall by itself, thereby avoiding the risks, military and political, of street-to-street fighting. He also proposed that the IDF stop short of the Canal, on the grounds that the Egyptians would not stop fighting and the Soviets might intervene; and, on the West Bank, the IDF should advance no further than the line of hills dominating the descent toward the Jordan River.

7. U. Benziman, *Jerusalem, City Without Walls* (Jerusalem and Tel Aviv, 1973), p. 11 (in Hebrew).

The next day, Dayan revealed to his Cabinet colleagues his perception of danger arising from an advance all the way to the Canal:
"If *Tzahal* [IDF] will reach the Canal, the war will never finish.
The Egyptians will not be able to allow themselves the occupation
of the bank by *Tzahal,* neither will the Soviets acquiesce in this. It
is possible that they will intervene, maybe by indirect military
means. . . . If we reach the Canal, Nasser will refuse a cease-fire,
and the war will continue for years." And, after the 1967 War,
Dayan recalled: "I did not want to reach the Canal; I issued orders
to stop some distance from it. The army presented me with an accomplished fact."

As for the Syrian front, Dayan strongly insisted that the IDF
stop at the international border—i.e., advance a few hundred
meters only and capture the Syrian artillery positions that had
been sowing destruction on Israeli settlements for years, particularly the Tel-Azaziyat stronghold. On the 8th, he repeated his perceptions and advocacy to the Ministerial Committee on Defense:
The war might last for years; the Syrians would not stop fighting;
and the Soviet Union would not allow an attack on Syria and the
endangering of its régime. Thus an attack on the Golan Heights
would snap the line of political tolerance, drawn to the breaking
point, and the Soviets would intervene militarily. He added that
the Syrian fortifications were very strong and an attack would
cause grave losses; Israel's Air Force was too strained and worn
out, and should not be further burdened; and there were still insufficient IDF forces opposite the Syrians to assure a quick victory.

Dayan's general image of the War and his own role in it was
elucidated in an interview he gave soon after its conclusion:

My main contribution [was] to keep the finger on the military and operative pulse, to know what happens on our side, and on the enemy's side, to
know the political conditions, and to bring the Government from time to
time the military moves.[8]

In his memoirs, Dayan recalled his Six Day War images—and
behavior—on some of the key issues. Nine years after the War, he
remained consistent about the Canal. The challenge from Jordan
on 5 June remained, in his memory, an unwanted diversion from
the main tasks: "We now had no option but to engage in full-scale
action against Jordan, reluctant as we were to divert resources

8. Interview, *Ma'ariv* and *Yediot Aharonot,* 13 June 1967.

from the fighting in Sinai."[9] As for Syria, his 1967 caution was reaffirmed, and his change of perception and decision clarified:

The night before [8 June] . . . I opposed such action [against Syria] in the most extreme terms. But conditions changed. At midnight that night, after I had had my say . . . I learned that Nasser had agreed to a cease-fire. At three in the morning, Syria announced that she, too, accepted a cease-fire. There was also an intelligence report that Kuneitra was empty, and that the Syrian front was beginning to collapse. These announcements and reports prompted me to change my mind. At 7 A.M. I gave the order to go into action against Syria.[10]

The perceptions held in the 1967 post-crisis period by Israel's four principal decision-makers may be categorized thus: Allon saw an historic opportunity and urged his colleagues to decisive action. Eban viewed the patterns for decision in a global setting and expressed concern about world reactions toward Jerusalem. Dayan, as in 1956, was preoccupied with the Soviet danger and insisted on military self-restraint by the IDF, in the North and in the South—lest Moscow be provoked to intervention. And Eshkol supported the Defense Minister's estimates of the situation, except for a vocal determination to achieve control over the headwaters of the Jordan River in the Golan Heights.

DECISION FLOW

Introduction

The 1967 War lasted five and one-half days. There were three campaigns: against Egypt, against Jordan, and against Syria. The first two were fought simultaneously; that against Syria when the others were practically over. The campaign against Egypt, the largest and bloodiest, lasted four days and three hours; against Jordan, two days and eight hours; and against Syria, one day and nine hours. The War's outcome was decided within three hours of its beginning, with the Israeli Air Force's devastating strike (99 percent successful) against the Egyptian Air Force and the achievement of total air superiority over the main antagonist. It was a

9. *Story of My Life* (Jerusalem and Tel Aviv, 1976), pp. 293–294.
10. Ibid., p. 306.

modern war, where every second counted. Israel's military and political decision-makers raced the clock for three reasons: to establish facts before the Arab states and their powerful allies could prevent an Israeli military victory by imposing a cease-fire; to prevent the escape of enemy forces, particularly the withdrawal of equipment; and to forestall an infusion of weapons into the Arab armies, including direct intervention by external powers. The major aim was to break the might of the neighboring Arab states, so that the menace to Israel's security would be removed for many years. A second goal appears to have been the occupation of territory as a bargaining element in future peace negotiations.[11]

Monday, 5 June

The order to move was given by Major-General Hod at 07:10 from Air Force Headquarters, with Dayan and other military leaders (Rabin, Bar-Lev, and Yadin) in attendance. At 07:45, all Egyptian airfields in Sinai and some in northern Egypt, including Cairo, were hit simultaneously by a massive wave of Israeli planes; Israel's skies were left for the next two hours practically defenseless— twelve planes to defend all of Israel's airspace.[12] The attack order to the ground forces on the southern front was given by Gavish at 07:47.

During the next two hours, some members of the Government —Eshkol, Allon, and Eban among them—joined Dayan in the War Room at IDF Headquarters to await the outcome of the crucial air strike and first reports of the ground fighting. Thirty-five minutes before Dayan went on the air, at 10:30, to announce that Israel

11. A formal decision to return all of Sinai to Egypt—in exchange for a peace treaty and effective guarantees—was reportedly adopted unanimously at the 19 June 1967 session of the Cabinet. This was revealed by Weizman in a speech before the Herut Center on 14 January 1973, four years prior to that party's rise to power, at the time of his confrontation with Begin for party leadership: "The Government of Israel resolved, on 19 June 1967, that for peace with Egypt—the Sinai border is the international border. . . . I checked this morning: I am not mistaken" (text of speech in *Yediot Aharonot*, 19 January 1973). For the relevance of the Cabinet decision to the Golan Heights, see Y. Harif, "In the Argument Around the 'Separation of Forces' on the Syrian Frontier, Washington Bases Itself on an Israeli Document of 19 June 1967," *Ma'ariv*, 22 March 1974.

12. See Y. Ben-Porath and U. Dan, *Mirage Contre MiG* (Paris, 1967), p. 64; and R. S. Churchill and W. S. Churchill, *The Six Day War* (London, 1967), pp. 78–82.

was at war, Hod had informed him that "there is nothing more to worry about. We have achieved most of our aims."[13]

Trying to keep Jordan out of the War had immediate priority. Eshkol and Eban, acting on a Cabinet directive (Decision 18), prepared a message to King Hussein, which stated: "We shall not initiate any action whatsoever against Jordan. However, should Jordan open hostilities, we shall react with all our might, and the King will have to bear the full responsibility for all the consequences." The message was transmitted through General Odd Bull, Head of UNTSO, at 09:30, and reached Hussein within half an hour.[14] It was also sent through several other channels.[15] In fact, these attempts continued even after the Jordanians opened fire and occupied UN Headquarters in Jerusalem, as the first step of an all-out attack. Jordan was informed that, if she would cease firing and evacuate Government House, Israel would be prepared to guarantee the 1949 armistice borders with Jordan—through UN machinery and a certain friendly power.[16] Of the messages sent to Heads of Government, the one to President Johnson was the most important; in it Eshkol illuminates the expectations of Israel's decision-makers at the onset of the 1967 War and their dependence on Washington:

13. Quoted in M. Gilboa, *Six Years—Six Days: Origins and History of the Six Day War* (Tel Aviv, 1969), p. 206 (in Hebrew). For an Egyptian version of the air attack, see M. H. Heikal, "The 1967 Arab-Israeli War," *Sunday Telegraph* (London), 21 October 1973. Heikal notes: "The attacks ended at 11:45 (10:45 Israel time). By that time 85 per cent of the Egyptian Air Force had been destroyed and the battle lost."

14. See Gilboa, *Six Years—Six Days,* p. 233; and King Hussein, *My "War" with Israel* (New York, 1969), pp. 64–65. The text of the message is found in A. Eban, *An Autobiography* (Jerusalem and Tel Aviv, 1977), p. 406, and R. St. John, *Eban* (Garden City, N.Y., 1972), p. 452. The episode was also related in O. Bull, *War and Peace in the Middle East* (London, 1976), p. 113. Hussein, op. cit., p. 65, answered the UNTSO Commander: "They started the battle. Well, they are receiving our reply by air."

15. Arab broadcasts of *Kol Yisrael;* Eshkol's Broadcast to the Nation at 12:00 on 5 June and his statement to the Knesset that afternoon; Eban's verbal communication to the Ambassadors of the U.S., Great Britain, France, and the Soviet Union; and letters to the Heads of Government of the Four Powers. In the letter to Wilson (St. John, *Eban,* p. 452), Eshkol repeated Israel's desire "to avoid any engagement with Jordan, unless Jordan makes conflict irresistible."

16. Quoted from an article by Y. Rabin, "Analogies with the Present and the Future," *OT,* 3 June 1971; also confirmed in an interview with Major-General Narkiss, then Commander of the Central Front, including Jerusalem (*Ma'ariv,* 8 June 1972).

I am grateful . . . for your undertaking to provide effective American support to preserve the peace and freedom of Israel in the Middle East. . . . We rely on the courage and determination of our soldiers and citizens. But our trials are not over, and we are confident that our people can count on the fealty and resolution of its greatest friend. I hope everything will be done by the United States to prevent the Soviet Union from exploiting and enlarging the conflict.[17]

Israel also began to deal with the danger of a one-sided call for a cease-fire. Before nine o'clock in the morning, Rafael woke Tabor, then President of the Security Council (it was 03:00 in New York), and asked for an urgent meeting to notify the Council of Egypt's "aggressive design" and Israel's reaction; Rafael preceded El-Kony by twenty minutes with his announcement. Instructions were also sent to Israeli Ambassadors to explain her position to their host countries and to point out that "Israel's survival was at stake, and that when victory was won our objectives would be security and peace."[18] At 13:00, Eban told a press conference in Tel Aviv that Israel's moves were a reaction to Egyptian air movements and to the shelling of Israeli border settlements from the Gaza Strip.

As the fighting on the Jordanian front spread, Allon and Begin began to press Eshkol to use this historic opportunity to "free Jerusalem and to unite it." Eshkol agreed to Begin's demand to call an immediate Cabinet meeting.[19] It was to be discussed at three special sessions during the next forty hours. The Cabinet assembled in a shelter. Again it was divided between "activists" and "moderates," along the lines of the 27 May meeting; this time, however, Eshkol did not side with the "activists." Some advocated taking the Old City immediately (Allon and Begin), while others were concerned with the international implications of such a step (Aranne, Eban, and H. M. Shapira). The Cabinet deferred a decision until a meeting the next day at which Dayan would be present (Decision 19), in order to hear about the military aspects. The mood, especially the stress created by this historic opportunity to unite Jerusalem, was vividly recalled by Teddy Kollek in his memoirs:

17. Israel, Ministry for Foreign Affairs, Cables and Communications, Jerusalem, 1967.
18. St. John, *Eban*, p. 453.
19. See Gilboa, *Six Years—Six Days*, p. 225; and Benziman, *Jerusalem, City Without Walls*, p. 11.

I reached the Knesset building about five in the afternoon. The mood
was momentous and exciting. Cabinet ministers, Knesset members, party
leaders, and journalists were milling around the halls, and a Cabinet
meeting was expected to take place at any moment. The one question
discussed everywhere was whether our army should counter-attack and
take East Jerusalem. To advance on the Jordanian-held sector of Jerusalem was, of course, more of a political risk than a military one. Each of
us knew in his heart that once we took the Old City, we could never give
it up. Thus it was truly an historic decision that had to be taken that day.
People were standing in line in the Knesset lobby to ask Ben-Gurion his
opinion on the question. He was clearly in favor of taking the Old City.[20]

The attack on the Old City's surroundings was to begin several
hours later, at 02:00 on 6 June. The Cabinet also approved Eban's
journey to New York to head Israel's delegation to the Security
Council.[21] He left at midnight. After the Cabinet meeting, Eshkol
told the Knesset: "Since the morning our ground and air forces had
been forced to return battle. . . . The fighting is now taking place
beyond the borders of Israel in Sinai. I will not give details now, for
obvious reasons, neither numbers, nor places, nor names. But I
can say that our forces are pushing the enemy back."[22]

The full extent of the debacle during the first hours did not penetrate to the highest Egyptian level. To King Hussein, Nasser stated
that Egypt was bombing Israeli air bases and launching "a general
offensive in the Negev." He asked him to occupy as much land as he
could, "for I have been informed that the Security Council is intervening tonight to stop the war."[23] Finally, at 16:00, the Egyptian Air
Force Commanders informed Nasser of the disaster. At meetings
held until late at night, Nasser demanded an immediate strong
counterattack; but, in his phrase, the Supreme Command had developed a "thrombosis of the heart." Finally, he decided to publish a
charge that Israel was fighting in collusion with Anglo-American air
forces. In the afternoon, Radio Cairo announced that Israeli planes
had bombed and sunk several ships in the Suez Canal, including a
French oil tanker, thus blocking part of the waterway, and the
station put the blame for the stoppage of traffic on Israel.

Jordan joined the war in the morning, first by shelling West
Jerusalem, then by sending planes to bomb the coastal city of

20. T. Kollek, *For Jerusalem* (Jerusalem and Tel Aviv, 1978), p. 193.
21. Gilboa, *Six Years—Six Days*, pp. 226–227; and Israel, Ministry for Foreign
Affairs, Cables and Communications, Jerusalem, 1967.
22. *Divrei Haknesset*, 1967, 49, 2319.
23. King Hussein, *My "War" with Israel*, p. 71.

Netanya. During the day, shelling spread along the whole frontier extending to the outskirts of Tel Aviv. Israel's first response was an air strike, which destroyed the small Jordanian Air Force within three hours, most of it on the ground. A counterattack was initiated after the Jordanian occupation of UN Headquarters—which was retaken two hours later. At noon, Hussein summoned the U.S. and British Ambassadors and accused their countries of supporting Israel: His radar station had detected planes taking off from aircraft carriers and landing at an Israeli airfield near Megiddo. The Ambassador's denials did not convince him. The next morning, he accepted Nasser's proposal to publish a charge of Anglo-American collusion with Israel.

Syria's behavior was that of controlled delay. General Riad's calls for Syrian reinforcements to Jordan were either ignored or evaded. A similar call for a coordinated air strike on Israeli targets in the morning was answered by repeated evasions. The Syrians contented themselves with two air strikes of small strength and the shelling of Israeli border positions; actual warfare was left to the Syrian radio stations. Israel's response was limited to air strikes. By the end of the day, air superiority had been established on that front as well. The border with Lebanon was quiet, with the exception of an incursion by a single Lebanese plane, which was shot down. Of the reinforcements under way from Algeria, Iraq, Sudan, Morocco, Tunisia, and Saudi Arabia, only two squadrons of Algerian MiGs reached the front, to be destroyed. The Arab states now decided, at a conference in Baghdad, to implement the oil boycott. It was to last in fact for one week, de jure for three months, and was never complete: Algeria kept the oil flowing to France.

News of the outbreak of fighting reached Washington a few minutes before 03:00 New York time on 5 June. The first and foremost concern of the U.S. Government was to verify the Soviet position and to assure the nonintervention of the superpowers. In a telephone conversation with Rusk, at 05:09, President Johnson approved the despatch of a message to Gromyko, which stated: "We feel it is very important that the United Nations Security Council succeed in bringing this fighting to an end as quickly as possible and are ready to cooperate with all members of the Council to that end."[24] At 07:57, McNamara informed the President that the "hot

24. L. B. Johnson, *The Vantage Point: Perspectives of the Presidency 1963–1969* (New York, 1971), p. 297.

line" from Moscow was active—the first time since it had been in-
stalled in 1964. Kosygin's message "expressed Soviet concern over
the fighting. Kosygin said that the Russians intended to work for a
cease-fire and that they hoped we would exert influence on Israel.
I replied, in part, that we would use all our influence to bring hostilities to an end, and that we were pleased the Soviets planned to
do the same."[25]

At the United Nations, the Americans and Russians agreed to
support a call for an immediate cease-fire. Goldberg also agreed to
support a Soviet proposal to call for the withdrawal of troops to the
1956 armistice lines, provided "that such a withdrawal be accompanied by a commitment of all parties to refrain from 'acts of force
regardless of their nature.'" Goldberg made it clear to El-Kony
that this meant the lifting of the blockade and the withdrawal of
troops of both sides from Sinai. El-Kony, not aware of the actual
state of affairs, refused to accept this proposal; and Fedorenko did
not press him until the afternoon. Neither did the Americans put
any pressure on Israel or the Arab states to accept; and Rafael did
all he could to prevent a resolution. The Council session broke up,
after several hours of deliberation, without tabling a resolution.[26]

In London, the Cabinet decided to support a resolution for an
immediate cease-fire, and Lord Caradon acted accordingly. In the
afternoon, Wilson assured a delegation of Arab Ambassadors that
the British Government would stay neutral in the conflict. So did
Brown in a statement to the House of Commons: "The Government's attitude . . . is that the British concern is not to take sides,
but to ensure a peaceful solution to the problems of the area."[27] De
Gaulle reacted with chagrin: "They have not listened to France."[28]
And the French embargo was announced immediately. During the
afternoon, he expressed great concern to Moscow over the developments and again suggested Four-Power consultations to defuse
the crisis. In Moscow, after an all-day meeting of the Politburo, the

25. Johnson, *The Vantage Point*, p. 298; and Eban, Interview, *Ha'aretz*, 5 June
1970. For a detailed description of the exchanges on the hot line during the war,
see L. Velie, *Countdown in the Holy Land* (New York, 1969), chap. 1.

26. See A. Lall, *The United Nations and the Middle East Crisis, 1967*, 2nd ed.
(New York, 1970), pp. 46–51; Rafael, Interview, *Ma'ariv*, 4 August 1967, and
"May 1967—A Personal Report," *Ma'ariv*, 18 and 21 April 1972.

27. British Parliamentary Debates, Hansard, House of Commons, 2nd
Session, 27th Parliament, 5 June 1967, cols. 629–631.

28. M. Bar-Zohar, *Embassies in Crisis: Diplomats and Demagogues Behind the
Six Day War* (Englewood Cliffs, N.J., 1970), p. 210.

Soviet Government accused Israel of aggression, declared "resolute support" for the Arab states, and expressed confidence "in the success of their just struggle." It called upon the Israeli Government to "immediately and unconditionally cease hostilities . . . and withdraw its troops beyond the armistice line." The statement concluded: "The Soviet Government reserves the right to take all steps that may be necessitated by the situation."[29] In an exchange of notes between the Soviet and Israeli Governments, Eshkol explained Israel's action as a reaction to "wicked aggression which Nasser has been building up against us," and he called for Soviet understanding of Israel's "mortal struggle to defend our existence and forestall Egypt's avowed intention to repeat against the Jewish People in Israel the inhuman crimes committed by Hitler." Kosygin's note, handed over by Chuvakhin at the same time that he received Eshkol's letter to Kosygin, requested that "Israel stop the fighting and evacuate the territories it has conquered."[30] The Soviet Mediterranean flotilla remained north of Crete, shadowing the main force of the U.S. Sixth Fleet, which also did not move.

Tuesday, 6 June

The main Israeli counterattack in the Jerusalem area began at 02:00. By morning, units of armor and parachutists had encircled part of the Old City; by noon, they linked up with the isolated garrison on Mount Scopus. In the morning, too, Dayan gave orders to advance upon and occupy part of the West Bank, until the line of the hills dominating the descent to the Jordan Valley. But he kept to his original plans as regards the Old City: encircling it, so that it would fall without having to fight a house-to-house battle. In Sinai, the IDF was advancing rapidly; by the evening, it had broken through the second line of Egyptian defenses. The Gaza Strip, cut off from the rest of Egyptian forces the previous day, was occupied after a heavy day's fighting.

The Cabinet met as the Ministerial Committee on Defense at 16:00. There was a review of the diplomatic situation by Levavi, followed by a preliminary discussion of postwar policy, with the aim of permanent peace. The rest of the meeting was devoted to

29. *International Documents on Palestine 1967*, F. A. Jabber, ed. (Beirut, 1970), Doc. 57, p. 5607; *New York Times*, 6 June 1967.
30. *Jerusalem Post*, 7 June 1967.

the political considerations of the military advances, with Dayan demanding clear-cut decisions. Eshkol supported Dayan's caution, especially his insistence that the IDF stop short of the Canal and on the hills overlooking the Jordan River; these suggestions were adopted. As for the Old City, Dayan proposed to complete its encirclement but without entering it: In his opinion, the Arabs would begin to flee and the City would fall by itself, thus avoiding the dangers—military as well as political—of street-to-street fighting. This, too, was supported by Eshkol but was vigorously opposed by Begin and Allon, who demanded that the Old City be taken by nightfall. Finally, it was decided to surround the Old City but not to enter it that night (Decision 20). The Syrian front was barely mentioned.[31]

While Israel's decision-makers were preoccupied with the battles now raging on two fronts, her diplomats were being made aware of a possible political debacle. In Washington, Evron was told by Walt Rostow: "You ought to know that now the greatest danger for Israel could be the overweening pride in your victory. You ought to begin to give serious thought to the [Arab] refugee problem if you want peace in the Middle East."[32] And by the time Eban arrived in New York, at 18:00 New York time, there had been intensive efforts at UN Headquarters to achieve unanimous support for an unconditional cease-fire. Goldberg was adamant in his previous day's position; and Fedorenko tried hard, but in vain, to convince the Arab delegates to accept a cease-fire: They rejected anything that would imply Arab withdrawal or compromise on the Straits issue.[33] Nevertheless, the Soviet delegate accepted a resolution calling for an unconditional cease-fire. Voted on unanimously at 19:10 New York time, before Eban arrived at UN Headquarters, it stated:

31. See Gilboa, *Six Years—Six Days*, p. 227; Benziman, *Jerusalem, City Without Walls*, pp. 19–20; and S. Nakdimon, "The Moves that Preceded the Occupation of the Old City," *Yediot Aharonot*, 4 June 1971. U. Narkiss explained in an interview in *Ma'ariv*, 4 June 1971: "The Defense Minister's intention at the time was to surround the Old City and to wait until it surrenders. . . . We waited until early Wednesday morning. And then, when it became clear that the Arabs would not surrender of their own free will and there was the danger that a decision to stop fighting in Jerusalem would be passed, I got the order to take the city."

32. Bar-Zohar, *Embassies in Crisis*, pp. 233–234.

33. See Lall, *The United Nations and the Middle East Crisis, 1967*, pp. 51–56; St. John, *Eban*, p. 457; and *New York Times*, 7 June 1967.

The Security Council
1. Calls upon the Governments concerned as a first step to take forthwith all measures for an immediate cease-fire and for a cessation of all military activities in the area;
2. Requests the Secretary-General to keep the Council promptly and currently informed on the situation.[34]

The Security Council was at the center of world attention. Eban's concern was as much to assure a favorable public opinion for Israel as to place Israel's case before the UN—which he did brilliantly. He accepted a call for a cease-fire, on condition that the Arab states accepted it as well. As to the future: "The situation to be constructed after the cease-fire must depend upon certain principles. The first of these principles surely must be the acceptance of Israel's Statehood. . . . The second principle must be that of the peaceful settlement of disputes."[35]

In the early hours of the 6th, the charge of collusion was coordinated by Nasser with the Heads of other Arab states. The specific charges, broadcast by Arab radio stations, were that "U.S. and British aircraft carriers have been providing protective air-cover over Israeli territory. The Jordanian radar network has recorded that U.S. aircraft have actually taken part in operations against Jordanian forces." By the end of the day, six Arab states—the UAR, Syria, Algeria, Iraq, Yemen, and Sudan—broke off diplomatic relations with the United States and Great Britain (the UAR and Algeria had broken off relations with the U.K. in 1965, over the Rhodesia issue). Despite Arab pressure, through their envoys in Moscow, the charge was disbelieved in the USSR, as elsewhere.

For Jordan, the situation had quickly become desperate. As King Hussein later recalled: "At 2 P.M. on Tuesday, 6 June, the situation was perfectly clear. For me, this so-called war was lost."[36] At 12:30, Hussein sent a personal telegram to Nasser, describing in the starkest terms the destruction of Jordan's army. "This is happening because we have no air support. . . . I beg you to reply immediately." He also informed Nasser of the strong American denials of their participation in the fighting. Nasser finally answered at 23:15. Admitting for the first time the loss of his Air Force, he

34. Lall, *The United Nations and the Middle East Crisis, 1967*, p. 52.
35. Abba Eban's Speech before the UN Security Council, 6 June 1967. Text published by Israel Information Service, New York, 7 June 1967.
36. King Hussein, *My "War" with Israel*, p. 80.

agreed to a call for a cease-fire.[37] But Hussein vacillated, and this contributed to the confusion of his forces: Riad had ordered the withdrawal of Jordanian troops to the east bank of the Jordan River, but Hussein, after hearing about the cease-fire ordered by the Security Council, contermanded those orders and told his troops to hold out. This confusion spilled over into the political arena as well.

In Washington, the hot line came alive again at 06:40 New York time. President Johnson recalled simply: "The Soviets felt the Security Council should press for a cease-fire."[38] But according to Velie:

> The message was ominous. Kosygin had dropped the let's-both-keep-hands-off line of the previous message. Now, he wanted the U.S. to get into the act, to use its influence with the Israelis to halt their advance in the Sinai and to withdraw to their borders. With this demand came a thinly veiled threat—the suggestion that the Russians might have to intervene. In effect, Kosygin was saying: get them out of there, or *we* will![39]

Johnson replied, after deliberations for two hours, that "the United States would not act unilaterally. The place to seek an end to the Arab-Israeli war was at the United Nations. The method was a UN cease-fire resolution."[40] The President also denied the collusion charge to Kosygin—as did Goldberg to the Security Council in the afternoon. "I told him," recalled Johnson, "that since his intelligence knew where our carriers and planes were, I hoped he would emphasize the facts to Cairo."[41]

---

37. *International Documents on Palestine,* Doc. 352, p. 586; and Doc. 360, p. 519.
38. Johnson, *The Vantage Point,* p. 299.
39. Velie, *Countdown in the Holy Land,* p. 4. Velie also noted (p. 7): "At the outbreak of war on Monday, the Sixth Fleet's two aircraft attack carriers, the USS America and the USS Saratoga, had ostentatiously abandoned all jetfighter exercises to assure the watchful Russians that the U.S. was sitting out the Arab-Israeli War, in line with the Monday hot line agreement. Now, just as ostentatiously, the aircraft carrier America steamed east from Crete at twenty knots under a state of alert—known as readiness condition three—two steps away from the call to battle stations. On her flight decks were 100 aircraft, including F-4 Phantom jetfighter bombers and A-4 Skyhawk attack jets. A Soviet destroyer that had been shadowing the America for days would undoubtedly inform Moscow at once of the carrier's movements. The Russians would know the Americans meant business."
40. Ibid., p. 6.
41. Johnson, *The Vantage Point,* p. 299.

Israel's representatives in Washington and New York kept on emphasizing that an historic opportunity for a permanent settlement had been created. Israel needed time to finish the job. This argument was accepted by the U.S., though, for a while, Rusk supported the Soviet drive for a cease-fire, coupled with withdrawal.

In London, Wilson told the House of Commons that Great Britain would stop arms deliveries to the Middle East for a trial period of twenty-four hours, subject to the other powers following suit. The embargo was lifted the next day, since there was no response from other states. In Moscow, the Politburo accepted the call for an unconditional cease-fire, while dissociating itself from the Arab charges of collusion. Simultaneously, it decided to increase the pressure on Israel, to threaten her with a break of diplomatic relations. The Soviets also decided to call an urgent meeting in Moscow of the leaders of Communist states to coordinate their support for the Arab states.

Wednesday, 7 June

News of the cease-fire resolution reached Israel in the first hours of 7 June. Begin, who heard it over the radio at 04:00, phoned Dayan: "Though yesterday we agreed to continue with surrounding the Old City, the Security Council's decision changes everything. We cannot wait any longer. I suggest that a telephone poll of Cabinet members be taken to change yesterday's decision."[42] Dayan agreed and suggested that Begin contact the Prime Minister. Begin woke Eshkol at 06:30 and demanded immediate action to take the Old City, in fear that the cease-fire would come into force before the Old City was taken. Eshkol concurred.

Between 07:30 and 09:50, members of the Cabinet and advisers from the army and Foreign Office assembled in Eshkol's office, with Dayan, who was the first to arrive, coming and going between meetings. Dayan told his colleagues that orders had been issued to take the Old City. Nevertheless, the ministers decided to add their own weight: Instructions were issued again, through the lines of command, to take the Old City, "and the earlier the better for Israel" (Decision 21).[43]

42. Benziman, *Jerusalem, City Without Walls*, p. 20.
43. Ibid., pp. 20–21; U. Narkiss, Interview, *Davar Hashavua*, 1 June 1973; and Nakdimon, "The Moves that Preceded the Occupation of the Old City." Although

The liberation of the holiest places of Jewry and Israel released a traumatic wave of emotion, unparalleled in the history of the state. People whose affective attachment to religion and the past had been indifferent embraced each other with tears in their eyes; and the joy of the religious and traditional people knew no bounds. After 1,900 years, the Western (Wailing) Wall, the only solid link with the past still in existence, was in the hands of the Jews; and the freedom of worship denied for so many years (despite the 1949 Armistice Agreement with Jordan) was now theirs. The pilgrimage to the Wall began immediately: Cabinet ministers, the Chief Rabbis, Dayan, Rabin and other high-ranking officers, Ben-Gurion, the Prime Minister—all hurried to be among the first to touch the holy stones. Dayan expressed the emotions—and the future policy towards Jerusalem—simply:

We have returned to the holiest of our places; we have returned never to be parted from them again. To our Arab neighbors we extend at this hour . . . the hand of peace. And to the followers of other religions, the Christians and the Moslems, I solemnly promise that their freedom of worship and all their religious rights will be safeguarded. We have not come to Jerusalem to conquer the holy places of others or to constrict the freedom of other religions, but to assure its unity and to live here with others in understanding.[44]

By noon, the Old City had been taken; and by the evening, all of the West Bank was in Israel's hands. Jordan's army was shattered, with its Air Force and about 70 percent of its armor destroyed. The cease-fire on the eastern front went into force at night.

In Sinai, the first Israeli troops reached the vicinity of the Canal by evening. Sharm-e-Sheikh was occupied by a small naval unit in the morning, without a shot being fired: The Egyptian garrison had already withdrawn. Forty-five minutes later, a small force of parachutists, led by Weizman, arrived.[45] On the Syrian border, the artillery duel continued, as did the strafing of Syrian positions by

---

these consultations—and the decision—did not take place within the formal framework of a Cabinet meeting, it may, because of the participants, be considered the third Cabinet session on the Old City during the War.

44. *Ha'aretz* and *Jerusalem Post*, 8 June 1967.

45. The decision to take Sharm-e-Sheikh was made the night before, by Dayan, when he noted that in the hurry of war Sharm-e-Sheikh, the cause of it all, had been forgotten, with the possibility of a cease-fire resolution getting nearer every minute. See E. Weizman, "A Chapter from My Memoirs," *Ma'ariv*, 26 September 1973.

the Israeli Air Force. But there were no attacks. The Lebanese border was quiet.

The IDF advance in Sinai was also discussed during the morning meetings. Dayan told his colleagues that he had given orders to stop short of the Canal—and this was approved by the Cabinet (Decision 22). His fear of Soviet intervention was not entirely without foundation. In the morning, Chuvakhin had delivered another, more menacing note from the Soviet Government:

> The Government of the Soviet Union expresses its decisive condemnation of the traitorous attack by Israel upon a neighboring Arab state—the UAR. . . .
> This attack has conclusively proved the nature of the policies implemented by ruling circles in Israel, who for the sake of their own narrow interests are willing to gamble with their whole destiny. . . .
> If the Israeli government does not comply immediately with the general demands of the nations concerning the immediate cease-fire which was decided upon by the Security Council, the Soviet Union will re-examine her relations with Israel and will reach a decision regarding the continuation of diplomatic relations with Israel, who by her actions has placed herself in opposition to all the peace-loving nations. It is understood that the Soviet government will examine the position and take other necessary steps resulting from the aggressive policy of Israel.[46]

At noon, Eshkol and Dayan reported to the Knesset Foreign Affairs and Security Committee. At 21:30, the question of a cease-fire was discussed by the Ministerial Committee on Defense; by that time, U.S. Ambassador Barbour had transmitted his Government's concern about a possible further advance across the Jordan. The Committee decided to authorize an advance to the banks of the Jordan River, to accept the second call for a cease-fire issued by the Security Council, and to make advances in Sinai conditional on the acceptance of the cease-fire by the Egyptians (a condition considered not likely to materialize). The specter of Soviet intervention was again discussed, with Dayan sticking to his views and Allon pressing for an advance to the Canal, asserting that the Soviets would not intervene; he interpreted the threat of a break in diplomatic relations as a sign that they would not intervene directly. Although Allon advocated going up on the Golan Heights, the prevailing view, finally adopted, was that the IDF should advance to the international border. If, during the fighting, it would seem

---

46. A. Dagan, *Moscow and Jerusalem: Twenty Years of Relations Between Israel and the Soviet Union* (London, 1970), pp. 229–230.

necessary to get a foothold on the Syrian escarpment (an advance of 4–5 kms.), the matter would be submitted to the Prime Minister and Minister of Defense for their approval (Decision 23).[47]

The Security Council reassembled at 13:00 New York time on the 7th, at Fedorenko's urgent request. He submitted a draft resolution calling *only* for a cease-fire, as the previous resolution had, but this time adding a time limit—20:00 GMT, 7 June 1967—and he asked for an immediate vote. After a short debate, the Council voted unanimously to accept the resolution; before the vote, President Tabor informed the Council that Jordan had accepted the cease-fire. El-Kony, after the vote, stated that his delegation's understanding of the resolution was that Israel should not only cease fire but also withdraw to the armistice demarcation lines. This interpretation was not supported by the delegates of the Soviet Union and Bulgaria, both of whom spoke after him; and Eban denied it, while again accepting the cease-fire: "We welcome, we favor, we support, we accept the resolution calling for immediate measure to institute a cease-fire." But he pointed out that he had yet to hear a similar sentence from the other side, a single sentence stating that "We Syria, we Iraq, we UAR welcome and accept the cease-fire resolution." In fact, radio broadcasts and press reports from Cairo indicated that the UAR rejected the resolution. Eban welcomed the Jordanian acceptance of the cease-fire but pointed out that the Jordanian army was under Egyptian command; thus the acceptance by it alone could not be effective.[48]

In Washington, Johnson announced the formation of a special committee of the National Security Council, with Rusk as its chairman and McGeorge Bundy as its executive secretary, to coordinate the Administration's efforts "to help build a new peace."[49] Officially, the word went out to keep a low profile; Johnson said during a meeting of the National Security Council: "One thing we should do now is to develop as few heroes and as few heels as we can."[50] In London, Brown, in a statement to the House of Commons,

47. See Gilboa, *Six Years—Six Days*, p. 232; D. Kimche and D. Bawly, *The Sandstorm, The Arab-Israeli War of June 1967: Prelude and Aftermath* (London, 1968), pp. 203–204; and Z. Schiff, "The Three Days of the Campaigns," *Ha'aretz*, 9 June 1967.

48. United Nations, Report by U Thant to the Security Council, S/7896, 19 May 1967; *U.S. Senate Documents*, Doc. 30, pp. 213–214.

49. *New York Times*, 8 June 1967.

50. Johnson, *The Vantage Point*, p. 300.

called the charge of collusion "a downright lie."[51] De Gaulle kept
on pressing for an immediate cease-fire and insisting upon Four-
Power deliberations to defuse the conflict. During a long speech in
the National Assembly, Foreign Minister Couve de Murville suggested an international convention for the Straits of Tiran, similar
to that worked out for the Bosphorus and the Dardanelles.

Thursday, 8 June

After fierce fighting at the approaches to the Canal, Egypt accepted the unconditional cease-fire. Sporadic fighting continued
until noon the next day. The front with Jordan was quiet. The
Syrian front remained static; Syria accepted the cease-fire, in the
wake of Egypt. During the 8th, there occurred the "Liberty" incident: The Israeli Air Force and Navy mistakenly attacked and
heavily damaged an American intelligence ship, stationed off the
shore of Sinai, near El-Arish; thirty-four American sailors lost their
lives, seventy were wounded.[52]

The biggest problem facing the Government of Israel that day
was what to do about the Syrians. From their positions on the Golan
Heights, the Syrians had for years menaced the border settlements
and from time to time had sown death and destruction. Now they
had kept successfully out of the war, for all purposes. No decision
was taken that day: Dayan had until now resisted Allon's demand,
which was supported by the General Staff, to open a third front,
together with Eshkol's demand to occupy the sources of the Jordan
River, near Tel Dan; and he continued to do so on the 7th. As yet,
he was uncertain whether the Egyptians would accept the cease-
fire. He was also afraid of a drawn-out war, in which a large part of
the IDF would be immobilized along the Canal. Further, he was

51. British Parliamentary Debates, Hansard, 7 June 1967, Cols. 1065–1079.
52. Johnson later recalled his reaction thus: "For seventy tense minutes we
had no idea who was responsible, but at eleven o'clock we learned that the ship
had been attacked in error by Israeli gunboats and planes. . . . There was a possibility that the incident might lead to even greater misfortune, and it was precisely
to avoid further confusion and tragedy that I sent a message to Premier Kosygin
on the hot line. I told him exactly what had happened and advised him that the
carrier aircraft were on their way to the scene to investigate. I wanted him to
know, I said, that investigation was the sole purpose of these flights, and I hoped
he would inform the proper parties. Kosygin replied that our message had been
received and the information had been relayed immediately to the Egyptians"
(*The Vantage Point*, pp. 300–301).

concerned about the threat of direct Russian intervention; and he
believed that there was no certainty that the Americans would
prevent an intervention under these circumstances.

The discussions between Eshkol and the advocates of an attack
—Allon and Rabin—continued at a series of meetings. Eshkol and
Allon were contacted by telephone by representatives of the Huleh
Valley settlements, who demanded action against the Syrians. Eshkol summoned a meeting of the Ministerial Committee on Defense, which began at 19:00. A delegation from the settlements had
arrived in the meantime in Tel Aviv. Eshkol agreed to let them put
their case before the Committee. Deliberations continued till late
at night. Allon was for action; so were the *Mapam* ministers; and
there was a hesitant but growing consensus among others as well
to opt for action. But because of Dayan's continued stringent opposition, to which Eshkol reluctantly added his weight, the matter
was not put to a vote; and no formal decision was taken. In effect, it
was a decision to delay an attack on Syria (Decision 24).

Yet, the military plans for an attack were completed during the
day;[53] and *Kol Yisrael* began to broadcast calls in Arabic to the
people and soldiers of Syria to liberate themselves, to obey Israeli
army instructions, "and to keep out of the way of its advance."[54]

The Security Council reconvened at 14:50 New York time (20:50
Israeli time), at the insistence of the U.S. and the Soviet Union.
Tabor informed the Council that Kuwait had refused to abide by
the cease-fire; there was no reply from Iraq; and though the fighting had stopped along the Jordanian frontier, Jordan had reported
that Israel was bombing Mafraq, in Jordan. The Foreign Minister
of Israel had answered that Iraqi troops were in the area. After
Goldberg presented a U.S. draft resolution, the Secretary-General
interrupted the proceedings to announce that the UAR had accepted the cease-fire; and El-Kony read a statement informing the
Secretary-General that his Government had "decided to accept the
cease-fire call, as it has been prescribed by the resolutions of the
Council on 6 and 7 June 1967, on the condition that the other party
ceases fire."[55]

53. Elazar, Interview, *Yediot Aharonot*, 9 June 1972.
54. British Broadcasting Corporation (BBC), *Summary of World Broadcasts,
Part 4, The Middle East and Africa*, Reading, England, 9 June 1967.
55. Lall, *The United Nations and the Middle East Crisis, 1967*, p. 65; UN
Document 8/7953, 8 June 1967.

The operative paragraphs of the U.S. draft resolution read:

The Security Council
1. *Insists* on an immediate scrupulous implementation by all the parties
concerned of the Council's repeated demands for a cease-fire and cessation of all military activity as a first urgent step toward the establishment
of a stable peace in the Middle East;
2. *Calls* for discussions promptly thereafter among the parties concerned,
using such third party or United Nations assistance as they may wish,
looking toward the establishment of viable arrangements encompassing
the withdrawl and disengagement of armed personnel, the renunciation
of force regardless of its nature, the maintenance of vital international
rights and the establishment of a stable and durable peace in the Middle
East.

The Soviet draft resolution, by contrast, suggested that the
Security Council

1. *Vigorously condemns* Israel's aggressive activities and its violations of
the aforementioned Security Council resolutions, of the United Nations
Charter and of United Nations principles;
2. *Demands* that Israel should immediately halt its military activities
against neighboring Arab States and should remove all its troops from the
territory of those States and withdraw them beyond the armistice lines.[56]

More important, Eban informed his colleagues that U.S. officials
had hinted to him that an Israeli action against Syria would not be
opposed by Washington, though they warned against an advance
on Damascus.[57]

Friday, 9 June

Syria informed the President of the Security Council at 01:00 New
York time that she accepted the cease-fire. But the artillery duel
along the northern border continued; and at 09:40, Israel moved
against the formidable fortified positions on the Golan Heights,
first by concentrated air attacks, then—at 11:30—with infantry and

56. Texts in Lall, *The United Nations and the Middle East Crisis, 1967*,
pp. 63, 66.
57. Israel, Ministry for Foreign Affairs, Cables and Communications, Jerusalem, 1967; St. John, *Eban*, p. 461: "Eban . . . said he had been given the definite
impression in Washington that some action against Syria would not be received
'without sympathy provided it was limited in time.'" And President Johnson (*The
Vantage Point*, p. 301):"We did know Israel's military intentions towards Syria. . . ."

armor. By night, after an uphill frontal assault, the Syrian line was broken. The IDF held the heights bordering on Israel and stopped there. Dayan had given the order to attack directly to Major-General Elazar, OC Northern Command, at 07:00. His orders were to begin the attack at 11:30, at the latest, and to advance until the former Mandatory borders. Then Dayan asked that Eshkol be informed. Elazar asked Rabin for confirmation upon his arrival at Northern Command headquarters. Eshkol was furious and would not answer. After half an hour, Dayan again contacted Eshkol's office and insisted on an answer. This was reluctantly given by Eshkol's military aide-de-camp, Lior. ("What do you expect? After all, Eshkol's position on the matter itself is known to you.") Eshkol now decided to call for an urgent meeting of the Ministerial Committee on Defense.

The meeting started at 09:30. Dayan announced that he had given the order to assault the Golan Heights and that this was approved by the Prime Minister. Although the National Unity Government survived the shock and gave its approval (Decision 25), the debate was acrimonious: Nothing had changed since the previous night, when Dayan had still refused to move. The then-Minister of Justice, Y. S. Shapiro, summed it up after the War:

Possibly in time of peace and dealing with a different problem it would have been permissible to draw the inevitable conclusion from what had happened. But it was not possible to raise such suggestions [the dissolution of the Government] in times of war, and this was understood by all members of the Cabinet. If these matters would have become public knowledge during the fight in Golan, it would have constituted a public and national disaster in the country, as well as abroad. As opposed to the prestige of the individual, the prestige of the Government is sometimes a matter of security, and vital. Furthermore, regarding the matter at hand itself, the Minister of Defense knew that the majority supported it and that he was fulfilling the wish and demand of the majority.[58]

It is still unclear what made Dayan change his mind within several hours. However, in an interview immediately after the SDW, Dayan declared:

The war developed and spread to areas that were not pre-planned by anyone, not even by myself. But it was possible, in the circumstances created, to include these areas in accordance with developments.[59]

58. Gilboa, Six Years—Six Days, p. 238.
59. Interview, Ma'ariv and Yediot Aharonot, 13 June 1967.

Rafael informed the President of the Security Council at 05:30 New York time (11:30 Israeli time): "Although the Damascus Government had agreed to accept the Security Council's call for a cease-fire, the Syrian artillery continues to bombard sixteen Israeli border settlements, and Israeli forces have advanced to silence the Syrian guns."[60] This expressed the political aims and limits of the advance and correctly reflected Dayan's orders. The Council met at noon New York time and accepted—immediately and unanimously—a draft resolution introduced by Tabor. It noted the acceptance of the cease-fire by Israel and Syria, and "the statements made by the representatives of Syria and Israel about continued hostilities; demanded that hostilities cease forthwith, and called upon the Secretary-General to arrange 'immediate compliance' with previous calls for a cease-fire and to report to the Security Council not later than two hours from now."[61] The Council deliberated, broke up for brief pauses, and was recalled urgently several times; it stayed in session, with intervals lasting from two to four hours, for the next twenty-four hours. U Thant was able to inform the Council by 18:00 New York time that both Israel and Syria had agreed to stop fighting immediately; but messages arriving within an hour stated that fighting was still going on and spreading. At this stage, reports from UNTSO observers were still scarce; not until early next morning did U Thant receive any reliable information from Odd Bull and his staff.

The emergency meeting in Moscow was attended by the leaders of the Soviet bloc, as well as Yugoslavia. The communiqué, signed by all except Rumania, stated:

> The socialist countries declare that they are in complete and full solidarity with their [the Arab states'] just struggle and will render them assistance in repelling aggression and defending their national independence and territorial integrity.
>
> If the Government of Israel does not halt the aggression and withdraw its troops behind the armistice line, the socialist states that signed this statement will do everything necessary to help the peoples of the Arab countries deal a resolute rebuff to the aggressor, protect their legal rights, extinguish the hotbed of war in the Near East and restore the peace in the area.[62]

60. Lall, *The United Nations and the Middle East Crisis, 1967*, p. 72.
61. Ibid., Appendix 6.
62. *International Documents on Palestine*, Doc. 89, p. 98.

Given the circumstances, the statement was relatively devoid of threats, except for the use of the word *assistance*. What was also decided, and soon became clear, was that: (1) the Soviet bloc states would break off diplomatic relations with Israel; (2) the armies of Syria and Egypt would be replenished as soon as possible; (3) an all-out diplomatic effort would be made to compel Israel to withdraw; and (4) public opinion would be forcefully brought into line with official policy, even by drastic measures.[63]

Saturday, 10 June

During the day, Israeli forces advanced along several lines to occupy a large area of the Golan Plateau, including the town of Kuneitra, the Plateau's administrative and military center. The cease-fire became effective at 18:30, arranged by General Odd Bull; the war was over. Yet this was also the day when the two superpowers came closest to direct confrontation. In the political field, it was the tensest, most dramatic day of the 1967 War.

The extent of the advance on the Golan Heights was discussed by Israel's decision-makers during the whole night of 9–10 June, culminating in a meeting of the Ministerial Defense Committee, at 04:45, which lasted till about 07:00. Everybody was aware of the race against the clock. Consultations centered on Eshkol, Dayan, and their advisers. At 10:30, Eshkol and Dayan flew by helicopter to the scene of the battle and directed the political moves from there until the cease-fire came into effect. Dayan flew back to Tel Aviv for a meeting with Odd Bull. Discussions and decisions were shaped by advances on the front, on the one hand, and by cables from New York and Washington, on the other. Dayan still resisted, in the morning, going beyond the line of first fortifications along the Golan Heights. Eshkol demanded that the fighting continue until noon, in order to remove all danger from the Huleh valley settlements. But no decision was taken as to where the army should stop: The Cabinet did not decide to occupy the Golan Heights; this became a function of military advances.[64]

---

63. For Hungary, see the article cited by David Giladi, *Ma'ariv,* 5 June 1973; for Poland, *New York Times,* 16–21 June 1967; Gomulka had to initiate a sharp attack against "deviationists," including an accusation that the Jews in the party hierarchy were guilty of double loyalty. In Czechoslovakia, the events of June 1967 were instrumental in the downfall of the hard-line Novotny régime and the coming to power of Dubcek. See also U. Ra'anan, "Soviet Global Policy and the Middle East," *Midstream,* 15:5 (May 1969), 3–13.

64. D. Elazar (Interview, *Yediot Aharonot,* 9 June 1972) confirmed that he

At 08:26, the Syrians—in total reversal of their practice hitherto —announced that the town of Kuneitra had been captured. In effect, Israeli troops were not even near the town at that time; they captured it only at 14:30. The Syrian aim was obviously to force the hands of the Russians—for once Kuneitra fell, the road to Damascus was open. But Syrian troops also heard the broadcast, and, according to reconstructions made after the war by several observers, it had a disastrous effect on their morale. They broke and began to flee towards Damascus, with the population of the town fleeing as well. The broadcast also became a license for the IDF to advance and occupy the town; by that time, it was the goal of three Israeli columns advancing from different directions.[65] Revised Syrian announcements several hours later (11:05: "Our forces are still fighting inside Kuneitra") could not undo the damage. The Israeli High Command's final aim, with Eshkol's and Dayan's approval, became the occupation of Kuneitra and the establishment of a line which would include certain strategic crossroads and points. Parachutists were flown in by helicopter. The strategic crossroad of Butmiya was occupied at 17:30, one hour before the agreed-upon cease-fire was to come into effect.

With the rapid IDF advance on the Heights came increasingly heavy pressure to stop the fighting from three sources of the U.S. Administration: from Rusk and Eugene Rostow through Harman; from Walt Rostow through Evron; and from Goldberg through Rafael. In Washington, Israeli diplomats were informed of renewed Soviet threats through the hot line and were told that there was a real danger of direct Soviet intervention. In New York, Goldberg warned Rafael that Fedorenko was getting ready to announce that the Soviet Union intended to intervene, and this had to be prevented at all costs: Even if they would not carry out their threat, the fact that the fighting would stop after such an announcement would be used by the Soviets to claim that they had saved the Arab cause.[66]

---

received orders on 9 June to advance and hold only the Syrian escarpment, i.e., 4–5 kms. beyond the international border. He also confirmed that he received no orders to occupy Kuneitra and the territory around it; these were developments of the fighting.

65. *Middle East Record, 1967,* 3 (Jerusalem, 1967), p. 230; St. John, *Eban,* p. 462; and N. Safran, *From War to War: The Arab-Israeli Confrontation 1948– 1967* (New York, 1969), pp. 380–381.

66. Johnson (*The Vantage Point,* p. 301) wrote: "We used every diplomatic resource to convince Israel to work out an effective cease-fire with Syria."

Eshkol and Dayan decided to call Odd Bull to an urgent meeting with Dayan in Tel Aviv at 14:15, at which Dayan agreed to the UN Commander's proposed "cessation of all firing and troop movements at 16:30 GMT" (Decision 26). The Syrians also agreed. The agreement was immediately cabled by Israel to Washington and New York, and by Odd Bull to U Thant, thus defusing the potential Soviet threat. Rafael was able to give the information to U Thant, who read it immediately, minutes before Fedorenko was scheduled to speak. The cease-fire came into effect at 18:30, though sporadic firing continued for several hours. In the afternoon, Chuvakhin, accompanied by Bykov, "stormed" into Eban's office and read out the Soviet Note announcing the severance of diplomatic relations between the USSR and Israel:

The news had just been received that the Israel armies, ignoring the decision of the Security Council regarding military action, are occupying Syrian territory, and are moving towards Damascus. . . . The Soviet Union declares that in the light of the continued aggression by Israel towards the Arab states, and the grave violation of the decision of the Security Council the Soviet Union has decided to sever diplomatic relations with Israel.[67]

Eban assured Chuvakhin that Israel had no intention of moving towards Damascus, but he would not clarify Israel's intentions after the cease-fire.[68] At the same hour, Katriel Katz, the Israeli Ambassador in Moscow, was called to the Kremlin by Vasili Kuznetzov, First Deputy Foreign Minister, who handed him a copy of the Note and requested that the Israeli diplomatic staff leave as soon as possible. Within the next two days, the Soviet move was followed by Bulgaria, Czechoslovakia, Hungary, Poland, and Yugoslavia. Rumania did not follow suit; the German Democratic Republic had had no diplomatic relations with Israel.

As noted, the Israeli decision process on 9–10 June was, to a large extent, a sensitively conditioned response to what was happening in Washington and at UN Headquarters in New York. Especially important was the reactivation of the hot line from Moscow at 08:00. President Johnson recalled those fateful minutes:

On the morning of June 10 we thought we could see the end of the road. But new word from Moscow brought a sudden chill to the situation. I was told that the hot line was active again. . . .

67. Dagan, *Moscow and Jerusalem*, p. 236.
68. St. John, *Eban*, pp. 462–463; and Gilboa, *Six Years—Six Days*, p. 244.

. . . Kosygin said a "very crucial moment" had now arrived. He spoke of the possibility of "independent decision" by Moscow. He foresaw the risk of a "grave catastrophe" and stated that unless Israel unconditionally halted operations within the next few hours, the Soviet Union would take "necessary actions, including military." Thomson, at Rusk's request, read the original Russian text to make certain that the word "military" was indeed the correct translation. Thomson said it was. In an exchange between heads of government, these were serious words: "very crucial moment," "catastrophe," "independent decisions," "military actions."

The room was deathly still as we carefully studied this grave communication. I turned to McNamara. "Where is the Sixth Fleet now?" I asked him. "It is approximately three hundred miles west of the Syrian coast."

"How fast do these carriers normally travel?" I asked. "About twenty-five knots. Travelling normally, they are some ten to twelve hours away from the Syrian coast," McNamara said.

We knew that Soviet intelligence ships were electronically monitoring the Fleet's every movement. Any change in course or speed would be signaled instantly to Moscow. There are times when the wisdom and rightness of a President's judgement are critically important. We were at such a moment. The Soviets had made a decision. I had to respond.

The Fleet was under orders to stay at least one hundred miles from the Syrian coast in its cruising pattern. I told McNamara to issue orders at once to change the course and cut the restriction to fifty miles. The Secretary of Defense gave the orders over the phone.

We all knew the Russians would get the message as soon as their monitors observed the change in the Fleet's pattern. That message, which no translator would need to interpret to the Kremlin leadership, was that the United States was prepared to resist Soviet intrusion in the Middle East.[69]

Between 08:00 and 10:00, the situation in the other two centers of action—New York and Israel—also stabilized. The Security Council resumed its deliberations at 08:10. Within a short time, U Thant was able to report the news of the Dayan–Odd Bull meeting. A further report from Odd Bull followed closely, announcing the acceptance of the cease-fire by both sides for 16:30 GMT. The Council adjourned in the forenoon, to await a report from the Secretary-General on the implementation of the cease-fire. It reconvened at 21:00 at Soviet insistence and stayed in session until 02:39, 11 June, to deal with allegations of continued shooting and fighting. But it did not pass any resolution, since it was becoming clear that the fighting was dying down. Thus did the last period of the 1967 Crisis draw to a close.

69. Johnson, *The Vantage Point*, pp. 301–302.

CHAPTER NINE

1973-74: 27 OCTOBER TO 31 MAY

THE 1973 CRISIS PERIOD came to a dramatic end on 26 October. In the early morning that day, the second cease-fire took effect, after a nuclear confrontation between the superpowers had been averted. Those two events set in motion a decline in Israel's level of threat perception and in her decision-makers' image of time pressures on decisions. At the same time, with the IDF bridge-head on the west bank of the Canal secure and Egypt's Third Army encircled on the east bank, Israel's leaders perceived a marked improvement in the balance of military power on the day active hostilities ceased. Thus, all three conditions of crisis underwent a qualitative change, marking the end of the crisis period.

The post-crisis period of 1973 lasted over seven months. It continued until the signing of the first Disengagement of Forces (Interim) Agreement with Egypt on 18 January 1974 and then, after a re-escalation of violence, the signing of a similar agreement with Syria on 31 May 1974. As the psychological environment and the character of the decision process were similar during the negotiations for both agreements, it should be sufficient to analyze them in depth only until 18 January 1974. The negotiations with Syria will be summarized in an epilogue.

DECISIONS AND DECISION-MAKERS

Four substantive Israeli decisions were taken during the first phase, 27 October–11 November 1973; and eight decisions were taken between 12 November 1973 and 18 January 1974. The decisional unit for both phases was the Cabinet. During the second phase, however, some decisions were taken by a negotiating team composed of Meir, Allon, Dayan, and Eban. These decisions were authorized later by the Cabinet.

There were two changes in the decision-making group during the post-crisis period: Minister of Justice Y. S. Shapiro resigned on 30 October; and, within the military-bureaucratic elite, Yariv, who joined the Cabinet after the 31 December 1973 elections, played a central role in the negotiations.

Decision Number	Date	Content
21.	30 October	The Cabinet sanctioned Meir's resolve to visit the U.S. in order to enlist President Nixon's direct support for Israel's objectives.
22.	8 November	The Cabinet approved the amended version of the Six-Point Agreement, as formulated by Sisco and the Israeli negotiating team.
23.	20 November	The Cabinet decided, upon advice from Eban, to clarify U.S. intentions regarding the forthcoming Geneva Peace Conference and to instruct Yariv on the negotiations with Egypt at Kilometer 101.
24.	25 November	The Cabinet decided, in principle, to participate in the opening session of the Geneva Peace Conference, formally chaired by the UN.
25.	2 December	The Cabinet approved Meir's authorization to Dayan to put forward to the U.S. "personal" suggestions for a disengagement agreement: an Israeli withdrawal from both sides of the Canal, thinning out of forces, and a UN buffer zone, in return for Egypt's "assurances of no more war."
26.	14 December	The Cabinet decided to insist that the text of the U.S.-Soviet invitation to Geneva specify that any future invitation to the Geneva Conference require the approval of all original participants.
27.	17 December	The Cabinet approved participation in the Geneva Conference but decided not to sit in the same room with Syria's delegates unless the latter released the list of Israeli prisoners of war.

Decision Number	Date	Content
28.	21 December	The Cabinet decided to accept the U.S.-Soviet request to start the negotiations at Geneva on 26 December, before the Knesset elections.
29.	2 January 1974	The Cabinet authorized Dayan to place before Kissinger Israel's conditions for a disengagement agreement with Egypt.
30.	15 January	The Cabinet decided, on Meir's initiative, to abandon Israel's demand for a clear-cut Egyptian declaration of nonbelligerency as part of the Disengagement Agreement.
31.	17 January	The Cabinet decided to accept the Disengagement Agreement with Egypt.

PSYCHOLOGICAL ENVIRONMENT[1]

Attitudinal Prism

The attitudinal prism of Israel's decision-makers in the post-crisis period was essentially the same as that which obtained during the crisis period.

1. The data base for the content analysis of Israel's psychological environment during the 1973 post-crisis period was fourteen documents of approximately 40,000 words. These were as follows:

			No. of words
Meir	3 November 1973	Press Conference	4,000
	1 December 1973	Interview on Israeli Radio	5,200
	22 January 1974	Speech to the Knesset	2,500
		Total	11,700
Allon	11 November 1973	Interview on Israeli TV	1,500
	26 November 1973	Address at the Van Leer Jerusalem Foundation	6,500
	5 December 1973	Speech to Labor Party Central Committee	4,500
		Total	12,500
Dayan	30 October 1973	Speech to the Knesset	3,000
	10 November 1973	Lecture at Labor Party College, Beit Berl	700
	24 November 1973	Address to Israeli lawyers, Beit Hapraklit	3,700
	9 December 1973	Interview on U.S. TV, "Face the Nation"	2,000
		Total	9,400
Eban	30 October 1973	Interview on U.K. TV, "Panorama"	1,300
	9 November 1973	Reaction to Statement of EEC	800
	16 November 1973	Interview on U.S. TV, "Today Program"	1,800
	28 December 1973	Interview in Histadrut daily, Davar	3,000
		Total	6,900

Images

MEIR

No basic changes in the Prime Minister's image of the Arab-Israeli conflict are apparent during the post-crisis period. Indeed, she was consistent throughout the 1973 Crisis. She repeated her belief that Israel was reasonable and wanted peace. And she recalled, as so often, the tragic experience of the Jewish people over the generations. However, in contrast to her self-confidence in the pre-crisis period, Meir tended to emphasize the dangers of the existing situation for Israel. She was embittered by international pressure, the role of the Security Council, and, especially, Soviet threats, all of which denied to Israel the fruits of a complete military victory, which had been within her grasp. The Soviet Union was perceived as a destabilizing factor in the region and, generally, as the state which, by its policy, transformed local conflicts into global ones. The attempt to compel Israel to withdraw to the 22 October cease-fire lines which, she asserted, never existed in reality, symbolized for her the denial of a (costly) total triumph.

The Prime Minister's confidence in the United States is central to her oft-stated image: "I am not surprised that Americans think that other people also have a right to live" (3 November); though "I cannot say that the talks [which she held in Washington early in November after the second cease-fire took effect] have settled all our differences of opinion" (13 November).

Of all the Arab states involved in the conflict, Meir expected the most from Egypt. The Six-Point Agreement of 11 November was seen as the first positive step toward an overall settlement: "The ice has been broken," she declared on 16 November; "the freezing point has been passed." References to Syria were made only in the context of prisoners of war, then her—and Israel's—highest priority. As for the Palestinians, nothing had changed: "We will not agree to a Palestinian state on the West Bank" (3 November). Notable was the lack of attention to the new Arab weapon, oil. And there were no changes in her attitude toward negotiations. As always, since 1967, she believed that Israel must retain Jerusalem, the Golan Heights, and Sharm-e-Sheikh. Yet they were not beyond discussion: "Both sides are free to argue their points as they wish.

Quotations appearing in the analysis of the psychological environment are cited in the text by date. Moreover, some extracts from other speeches and statements are incorporated into the qualitative analysis of that period.

And in these arguments, with the exception of Jerusalem and maybe one or two other points, we hope that compromises can be made" (3 November). On the issue of a peace conference, there was a change over time. "As far as I am concerned it can be today," she said on 3 November. Yet, on the 16th, when there was a specific proposal about the date, she expressed reservations, on the grounds of Israel's impending general election.

Israel was the subject of action in the majority of Meir's advocacy statements, twenty-five of thirty-nine, just as in the earlier periods of the 1973 Crisis. The proportion directed toward "the parties" and others is much higher than in the case of Allon or Dayan, suggesting a higher level of demand that other international actors take steps to seek a solution for the Arab-Israeli conflict. In content, her most frequent advocacy dealt with the prisoner-of-war issue. The dominant theme directed to Israel was peace negotiations—which held the same primacy for her as it did during the pre-crisis period. In both periods, too, her insistence that there be no other state between Israel and Jordan ranked third in frequency. The principal targets of Meir's statements were Egypt and Israel, eight each of twenty-eight clearly-designated targets in the content analysis.

In contrast to the crisis period, the Meir memoirs contain few perceptual themes on the period after the Yom Kippur War. One was a sense of betrayal by social democrats in Israel's darkest hour:

I was still enraged over the refusal of my socialist comrades in Europe to let the Phantoms and Skyhawks land for refuelling as part of the airlift operation. . . . I phoned Willy Brandt [and said] . . . I need to know what possible meaning socialism can have when not a single socialist country in all of Europe was prepared to come to the aid of the only democratic nation in the Middle East. Is it possible that democracy and fraternity do not apply in our case?[2]

And, at a November meeting of the Socialist International, "I told my fellow-socialists, 'Not one inch of your territory was put at our disposal for refuelling the planes that saved us from destruction. . . .'"[3]

A second image was of Kilometer 101 talks and the Six-Point Agreement: "For the first time in a quarter of a century, there was direct, simple, personal contact between Israelis and Egyptians.

2. G. Meir, *My Life* (Jerusalem and Tel Aviv, 1975), p. 375.
3. Ibid., p. 376.

They sat in tents together, hammered out details of the disengagement and shook hands."[4] A third focus was the postwar protest movement in Israel:

Much of the outcry was genuine. Most of it, in fact, was a natural expression of outrage over the fatal series of mishaps that had taken place. . . . It was a call to eliminate from the scene everyone who could possibly be held responsible for what had happened and to start all over again with new people, younger people, people who were not tainted by the charge of having led the nation astray. . . . But part of the outburst was vicious, and some of it was demagoguery, pure and simple, and the making of political capital by the opposition over a national tragedy.[5]

The Prime Minister's image of Kissinger and his role was effusive:

I admired his intellectual gifts, his patience and his perseverance were always limitless, and in the end we became good friends. . . . One of the most impressive of Kissinger's many impressive qualities is his fantastic capacity for dealing with the minutest details of whatever problems he undertakes to solve. . . . Of course, even with that really brilliant mind and with that astounding capacity for hard work, if Kissinger had been the foreign minister of Gabon, he wouldn't have gotten far with the Syrians, but he had everything: intelligence, diligence, stamina *and* the fact that he represented the greatest power in the world, which made for a very effective combination indeed.[6]

ALLON

During the post-crisis period, the Deputy Prime Minister referred frequently to Israel's military achievements in the Yom Kippur War. At the same time, he was realistic about its political implications: "In my opinion, the Arabs rightly claim credit for having— through the deployment of forces—withdrawn the Arab-Israeli conflict from its deep freeze . . . and placing it at the head of the items on the international agenda" (26 November). As for the postwar political situation, he declared on 5 December: "This is the hour of truth. . . . We won the military battle but we find ourselves in a tense political situation, more complex . . . than ever." Israel's self-reliance had long been a source of pride and a primary value for Allon. His concern about the extent of dependence upon the United States during the 1973 War led him to a "dissonance-reducing" assessment of Israel's performance: "It has been clearly

4. Ibid., p. 377.
5. Ibid., p. 378.
6. Ibid., pp. 372, 373, 374.

proved that little Israel is capable of defending herself even when forced to fight on more than one front simultaneously. . . . We are, with all due respect, no less an independent state than many a European country, insofar as the concept 'independence' is defined in the 'seventies of this century" (26 November).

Allon's image of the roles of the superpowers was basically asymmetrical. He expressed Israel's gratitude for American aid, but he observed that the U.S. had gained much from the War while contributing only what was essential for Israel's survival. Despite his advocacy of the renewal of diplomatic relations with Moscow in a speech on 11 November, he severely criticized Soviet behavior. He was also acutely conscious of the salience of Soviet threats for Israel's foreign policy decisions. With an implied reference to the 1956 and 1967 Crises, he remarked: "Regardless of whether these threats are substantive or not, they cannot be ignored at certain moments which might be regarded as fateful" (26 November). His most scathing comments were directed at Europe: "All told, just like parasites, they, too, will benefit if big brother does the work for them. These are the European countries that quake in their boots when the Americans so much as think of withdrawing one brigade of the U.S. army stationed in Central Europe. Yet we never requested even a single American company" (26 November).

In the post-crisis period, too, Allon was acutely aware of the global salience of Middle East developments. "From now on, much more than ever . . . , every step we take must be weighed not only in the context of Arab-Israel relations, but also in the context of great power relations, and the entire world" (5 December). Earlier, he reiterated an oft-expressed aversion to external penetration of the region: "The time has come for the Middle East to enjoy genuine sovereignty instead of the present quasi-sovereignty of each nation, depending to so large a degree on the goodwill of the big powers" (11 November).

As in the pre-crisis period, Allon analyzed Arab frustration, leading to their decision to seek redress of grievances by force. And he (begrudgingly) recognized a basic improvement in their military performance during the 1973 War: "But even the new military standards of the Arab army cannot tip the scales against us" (26 November). Allon acknowledged that the Arab oil weapon had been used more effectively than he had believed possible. There was only one indirect reference to the Palestinians during that period. More attention was devoted to territory and security. His views were consistent: He favored compromise but rejected a return to the old (1949, that is, pre–4 June 1967) armistice lines. "We do not insist on geographic symmetry," he said on 26 November. "For obvious reasons, however, we do insist on strategic symmetry, since we view this . . . as a temporary military settlement." And he cautiously welcomed the opportunity to negotiate a peace settlement, although he anticipated a difficult diplomatic struggle.

In the vast majority of Allon's advocacy statements, sixty-one of sixty-seven, Israel was the subject. The most frequent theme was his admonition to do everything for peace. Second in order of frequency was the call to stabilize the cease-fire. He also urged Israel: (1) to learn from past experience; (2) to accept a territorial compromise, but with secure boundaries; (3) to be aware of U.S. interests and her behavior in the future; and (4) to prepare for the next war, since no political-military situation is permanent. The most frequent target for Allon's advocacy after the 1973 War was the Arabs in general, followed by the great powers.

EBAN

During the pre-crisis and crisis periods, the Foreign Minister had been the eloquent defender of Israel's policy toward the Middle Eastern conflict since 1967. Now, with no less eloquence, he gave expression to the trauma of the Yom Kippur War and the need for change in Israel's perceptions: "The war has shaken Israelis out of the images and ways of thought in which they had lived for over six years. . . . Since all these became suddenly obsolete in a single week, the intellectual and emotional shock is hard to sustain. We are summoned almost overnight to a far-reaching reconstruction of our conceptual world" (27 November). In the same speech, Eban attacked the assumptions underlying Israel's security doctrine since 1967:

[First,] that policy should be directed not only to making the enemy unable to fight us again but also to the hope of making him unwilling to fight us again.

[Second,] the illusion that the cease-fire could exist indefinitely, in a diplomatic vacuum. . . .

[Third,] the illusion that a million Arabs could be kept under Israeli control forever, provided that their economy and social welfare were sufficiently advanced.

[Fourth,] the illusion that Zionism forbade a sharing of national sovereignty between two nations in the former Palestine Mandate Area.
    [Fifth,] the illusion that Israel's historic legacy was exclusively a matter
of geography. . . .
    [Sixth,] the fallacy that a nation could not be strong unless it demon-
strated its toughness at any contingency.

While this was, for Eban, a period of review and reflection, he
noted the feeling of immense pride in Israel for the achievements
of the IDF. And, in his view, it was this achievement, not the Arab
willingness to negotiate, that led to a cease-fire. Further, the manner in which it was established indicated that the cease-fire was a
vital phase in a peace process. Eban reaffirmed his belief that a
return to the 4 June 1967 lines was out of the question. He explained the "Israeli security obsession" by reference to the Jewish
fate in history, the trauma of World War II, and the many lives lost
in the wars of 1948, 1956, 1967, and 1973. He favored secure
borders, but he also criticized some of the "excesses" of that concept. He rejected the idea of "historic" boundaries but refrained
from specifying any borders. Leaving all options open, he maintained that everything was negotiable and to be negotiated.
    The coming Peace Conference at Geneva he perceived with a
mixture of hope and realism. As to Palestinian participation, he
shared the view of his colleagues that, logically, the Palestinian
representatives should participate in the Jordanian delegation. He
was critical of Britain and France and rejected as unjustifiable the
claim for their participation at Geneva. Nor did he have any kind
words for the UN. In general, he rejected the idea of international
peace forces.
    Even more than in the crisis and pre-crisis periods, Eban de-
voted attention to the superpowers, especially the United States.
Once more, the link between image and choice received public
confirmation. On 24 October, recalling the decision not to pre-
empt, he emphasized that "our relations with the United States
would not have developed as affirmatively as they have if we had
struck first, and this would have had the very greatest significance
for the future prosecution of the war."
    Most of Eban's advocacy statements during the post-crisis
period, thirty of thirty-five, were directed to Israel. The most
frequent theme, as in the crisis period, was to negotiate secure
boundaries. The call to negotiate disengagement ranked second.
Eban also called on Egypt to initiate peace proposals. He was

unique in his criticism of the November 1973 pro-Arab declaration of the EEC; almost certainly, this was a function of his role as Foreign Minister. So too was the fact that his advocacy revealed once more the largest variety in both options and targets. The most frequent target was Europe, followed by the Arabs, the Palestinians, and Jordan.

DAYAN

During the post-crisis period, the Defense Minister continued to emphasize Israel's military strength—"the principal element in the cease-fire." However, he no longer argued that a military victory alone could compel the Arabs to negotiate; the superpowers had now become the dominant factor in the peace process. He anticipated that Moscow and Washington would attempt to use the cease-fire as a point of departure for talks leading to a settlement—and this expectation ran parallel to his own ideas about what should and would happen. Accordingly, Dayan adopted a moderate, though vague, posture on Israel's concessions: "We must be ready for this whole subject to be put to a test and by this I mean the problem of Jerusalem, Gaza, Syria, the territories, and other things. Everything is now on the table. . . . I am ready to make concessions" (10 November). As time passed, there was a hardening in Dayan's attitude. Two weeks later, he declared: "We do not have to come down from the Golan Heights nor to move from the Jordan [River], nor from the hills of Schem [Nablus]. . . . The [new] city of Yamit [south of Gaza on the Mediterranean] is one thousand times more important than it was before. And if our relations with the Arabs are based on a naval blockade, such as they imposed on Bab-el-Mandeb, then God forbid that we move from Sharm-e-Sheikh." Thus, a month after the 1973 War, Dayan reaffirmed the views expressed before the War.

Dayan's attitude toward the United States remained ambivalent. On 25 October, when the second cease-fire took effect, he expressed deep appreciation for American aid. Yet, "Israel did not give into every demand the U.S. made on it" (30 October). And later he acknowledged candidly: "We have differences of opinion with the Americans" (24 November). At the same time, he perceived America as a counterweight to Soviet pressure: "The U.S. alert [on 24 October] in the face of Soviet demands was no play-acting . . ." (10 November). His image of the United Nations remained hostile.

About Egypt's apparent willingness, now, to reach a settlement, he displayed optimism. He also devoted attention to the Palestinians, specifically those of the West Bank, as in the pre-crisis period: "It is certainly absurd that we should sit down to talk with the Egyptians, and even the Syrians, and not with the Palestinians; not for the establishment of a third state in the area, nor the return of territories or refugees, but on how we can live together" (30 November). Dayan also referred to other international actors. He treated the EEC with disdain: "The Nine of Europe made ponderous pro-Arab declarations in the hope of getting more oil" (30 November). He also referred to Japanese pressure on Washington because of Arab oil blackmail. And he was aware of the African abandonment of Israel. Yet, on the whole, Dayan's image of the external world was concentrated on superpower behavior toward the Arab-Israeli conflict. Finally, he warned the nation against undue optimism: "The worst thing that can happen is . . . to cling to the past world of 1967 and refuse to see the harsh reality of 1973" (10 November).

Israel was the subject in all but one of Dayan's thirty-five advocacy statements during the post-crisis period. The most frequent theme was his call for a readiness to engage in political struggle in the near future. Closely related was his urging Israel to be prepared "to fight" at the Geneva Peace Conference. The territorial issue, particularly opposition to withdrawal—from almost everywhere—was his second most frequent specific advocacy. More than his colleagues, Dayan seemed preoccupied with tasks of the near future.

The United States was the overwhelming focus of attention in Dayan's memoirs on the 1973 post-crisis period. There are also revealing images of Sadat and Egypt, the Kilometer 101 talks, the first Interim Agreement, Syria, the UN, peace prospects, and the danger of the resumption of war.

Dayan's recollection of U.S. behavior begins on 26 October with a perception of confrontation and ends on 5 January 1974 with one of many image statements on American aid. "An endless exchange of telephone calls . . . took place between Washington and Jerusalem—with the Americans occasionally resorting to a tone that could not be described as the acme of civility—while the Israeli Cabinet met for urgent consultation. Finally, the Americans presented their demand more or less in the form of an ultimatum [to permit continued Egyptian supplies to the Third Army]. . . . When Abba Eban was Israel's Ambassador in Washington, he used to describe Israeli-American relations as 'very special.' This they certainly were." Dayan's realistic perception of probable U.S. behavior emerged in the context of the blockade of Bab-el-Mandeb, on 7 December: "My reading of the position was that America would go to war over U.S. interests but not over an international principle such as freedom of navigation. There was clear evidence of this position in the explanation demanded by Congress after the presidential [order] placed U.S. forces on alert in October." Moreover, "I also knew that if we insisted on staying put for another year, Israel's position vis-à-vis the United States would be far from rosy."[7]

On the perennial issue of U.S. arms support, "I told him [Vice-President Ford] briefly . . . what would have happened if these arms had not been sent to us. We would have managed, I said. We would have held firm, but the war would have been tougher and our casualties heavier." "I told the Prime Minister [on 10 December] that we were likely to face considerable difficulty in securing all the weapons and equipment we needed."[8]

The potential for U.S. pressure was clearly perceived, as were disagreements: "There was no need to be hasty [about peace terms and withdrawal]," he told Meir on 10 December.

We should exercise patience, remain on the west bank of the Canal, and on no account evacuate the Canal Zone within the framework of a military agreement that lacked political elements. Moreover, it was essential that the United States be involved in the negotiations so that she would share responsibility for its implementation. We would have differences of opinion with the United States, since she wanted to hasten the disengagement of forces arrangement in the hope that this would help her get oil from Saudi Arabia. . . .

I had not felt any tendency in Washington to press us to concede on issues vital to us. It was explained to me, albeit indirectly, that the Americans did not demand that we surrender our basic interests, but they expected us to advance toward peace. The time might come when they would exercise real pressure, but for the moment I did not think they would try to force us to abandon our position by deliberately keeping us short of weapons. They were spurring us to compromise, but they were not going to sell us out.[9]

On the U.S. role in overseeing a settlement: "The disadvantage of this procedure [Egyptian pledges to the U.S. rather than to Israel] was, of course, the absence of direct contact between the

7. M. Dayan, *Story of My Life* (Jerusalem and Tel Aviv, 1976), pp. 448, 455.
8. Ibid., pp. 457, 458.
9. Ibid., p. 458.

Egyptians and us, but it had the advantage of securing the involvement of the United States, if not as actual guarantor at least as a partner to the arrangement." And finally: "It was difficult to avoid the impresson [after a meeting with Schlesinger on 5 January 1974] that the American arms policy toward Israel was to give us a little now as a hint that if we reached agreement with the Egyptians, we could expect a long-term agreement on arms deliveries. . . . Our problem was that America was our only friend—with the accent on 'only.' "[10]

Egypt's leader was perceived by Dayan in the post-crisis period as being in a weak bargaining position and dependent on a settlement: "President Sadat was in fact anxious to reach an arrangement with us. The main reason was his distressing military predicament. . . . The one thing of which Sadat was certain was that his armed forces were powerless to break the Israeli siege. . . . [And] Sadat understood that his achievements in this war were all behind him, and he had to end it, even at the cost of concession and compromise." Moreover, "Egypt was far more anxious for us to quit 'Africa' and remove ourselves from the Canal than we were to go, and this was therefore the time to reach a military-political arrangement with her." "However, I felt there was little chance that Egypt would accede to our demand that she undertake to end belligerency. The Egyptians were insisting that we evacuate most of Sinai even before the phase of peace, and they were unlikely to obligate themselves to non-belligerency at this stage. . . ." As for eastern Sinai, Dayan's image in mid-December 1973 reveals much about his subsequent behavior:

Our presence [there] was not too disturbing [to the Egyptians]; for they could continue, together with the other Arab States, to maintain a position at least of no peace. Sadat, like his predecessors, would echo the slogan from time to time that for him, too, the Palestinian problem was the heart of the matter and that Jerusalem took priority over Sinai. . . . [It] solved the practical side of the problem—securing for Egypt what was the most important part of Sinai for her—and paid the required lip service to the symbolic side.[11]

On the substance of an interim agreement, Dayan made his views known to Kissinger on 7 December: "Removing ourselves from the Canal would be the greatest concession on our part, and

10. *Story of My Life,* p. 465.
11. Ibid., pp. 450–451, 455. 462–463.

it was being demanded of us in the very opening phase of the negotiations. In return we were being offered a very poor exchange, a temporary cease-fire. . . . Therefore, I said, if we were to withdraw 6 to 10 miles east of the Canal, the move should be made within the framework of an agreement that would ensure the termination of hostilities. On this basic issue there should be formal undertakings as well as practical steps—the opening of the Canal cities." He reaffirmed this to Kissinger in Jerusalem ten days later, noting that, in his view, "these actions were of greater consequence than a formal guarantee to end the war, for they represented not simply a verbal obligation but the practical implementation of a peaceful pattern of life, a pattern which was incompatible with a continuation of hostilities." And early in January, as he told Kissinger, "my disengagement of forces proposal . . . was devised as a total concept and not as a patchwork quilt. It had a specific logic and would work properly and fulfill its purpose only if it were implemented in its entirety. . . . It was aimed at creating a new situation and opening a new page in the relations and realities between Israel and Egypt."[12]

About Syria, Dayan expressed the widespread Israeli image: "Assad was very stubborn, and his real aim, even if he did not say so explicitly, was to destroy Israel." On the prospects of peace, Dayan was not optimistic: "As for a peace arrangement with Egypt," he told Schlesinger on 9 December, "I feared that Egypt would make a final settlement between us conditional upon our reaching an arrangement with Syria and Jordan. . . . Sadat would insist on a prior solution to the problems of the Palestinian refugees and of Jerusalem." He repeated this to Kissinger, adding: "I believed that the key to an arrangement with every Arab state, and particularly Egypt, was the creation of conditions which reduced the Arab motivation for war and promoted the normalization of life. With Egypt, this applied to the Canal Zone."[13]

Throughout the post-crisis period Dayan perceived a danger that the war would be resumed: "The situation between October 24, 1973 and January 18, 1974 . . . also held the ever-present possibility of a renewal of full-scale war. There were three variations on how it might break out, two Egyptian and one Israeli. One Egyptian plan was to attack our units west of the Canal from the

12. Ibid., pp. 454, 462.
13. Ibid., pp. 460, 457, 462.

direction of Cairo. The other was to cut off our Canal bridgehead by a link-up of the Second and Third Armies on the east bank." On the Israeli side: "The only feasible possibility was the destruction of the Third Army. It was cut off, exposed to our Air Force, and we could assemble for this operation enough armor to give us superiority. The various possibilities could become realities if the Egyptians were to start a war of attrition against our forces west of the Canal. This condition did not present itself."[14]

Dayan's recorded image of Kissinger is instructive—and almost identical to Meir's: "I am very much impressed by his wisdom, his broad-ranging knowledge, his prodigious capacity for work, and his ability to set things in perspective. . . . But if he had been Secretary of State of a small country—Belgium or Holland, for example —without having at his disposal the power of the United States, he surely would not have accomplished such striking feats. His greatness stems primarily from his knowledge of how to use the powerful lever of the United States to exert pressure and to retaliate, to influence, and to promise guarantees."[15]

As in Chapters 3 and 5, we will now compare, by topic, the decision-makers' images during the 1973 post-crisis period.

1. *Definition of the Present Situation.* Allon and Meir perceived radical changes in Israel's political reality, following the Yom Kippur War. All four decision-makers emphasized Israel's military achievements. Eban's was the most profound analysis of the new political environment.

2. *The Arabs.* Allon dealt at length with Arab goals and achievements, admitting that they had succeeded in unfreezing the conflict by drawing world attention to its intensity. He also acknowledged the qualitative improvement in the Arab armies and the positive psychological effects of the war on their self-image. Dayan expressed cautious optimism that the Arabs would now be more willing to arrive at a political settlement. Eban and Meir both tended to direct their attention to specific Arab states.

3. *Egypt.* Dayan now believed that Cairo would be more amenable to a political settlement. So too did Meir. Allon barely mentioned Egypt.

14. *Story of My Life,* pp. 468, 469.
15. Ibid., pp. 443.

4. *Syria*. Allon noted a marked improvement in Syrian military deployment during the war. Dayan and Meir perceived a settlement with Syria as highly improbable. Eban discussed Syria only in the context of a prisoner-of-war exchange.

5. *The Superpowers*. Allon expressed resentment about the less-than-sovereign status of Middle East states. Yet he recognized the salience of superpower relations to the future of the Arab-Israeli conflict. Like Dayan in the pre-crisis period, he viewed their performance during the 1973 War as asymmetrical. Dayan, by contrast, now perceived the powers as a positive factor. So too did Eban. Meir made no reference to the superpowers during this period.

6. *The United States*. Allon qualified his appreciation of American aid during the war with remarks to the effect: (a) that Washington provided only what was essential for Israel's survival; (b) that it denied Israel a near-certain total military victory; and (c) that the Americans attained significant influence in the Arab world. Dayan perceived the U.S. as an important counterweight to Soviet threats. He and Meir noted continuing Israeli disagreements with Washington but emphasized that no pressure had been imposed. Eban's image of the U.S. was essentially the same.

7. *The Soviet Union*. Allon made an extensive and critical analysis of Soviet motivation and action. He also emphasized the impact of Soviet threats on the process of Israel's decision-making in the conflict. Dayan, too, was suspicious of Soviet motives, though he recognized the Russians' interest in playing a role in a Middle East settlement. Meir perceived the Soviets as a destabilizing factor in the region and as the crucial barrier to Israel's consummation of her military triumph.

8. *The Palestinians*. Dayan advocated negotiations with the Palestinians of the West Bank, but not for independence or the return of refugees. Meir was confident in her rejection of a third state between the sea and the desert, as was Dayan. Eban seemed to favor Palestinian participation in the Geneva Conference through the Jordanian delegation; and he criticized Israel's policy toward the Palestinians of the territories. Allon made no reference to the Palestinians.

9. *Territories and Secure Boundaries*. All four decision-makers expressed a willingness to make larger territorial concessions—if strategically located demilitarized zones were agreed upon. Allon

insisted on strategic—but not geographic—symmetry. Dayan noted only those territories on which he was *not* willing to compromise. Meir expressed a hope that a compromise could be reached, apart from Jerusalem. And Eban, while recognizing Israel's need for strategic depth, indicated that substantial border changes were possible in the context of negotiations.

DECISION FLOW

The cease-fire achieved on 26 October was very precarious. Egypt demanded the fulfilment of a Soviet promise to rescue the encircled Third Army.[16] Israel insisted upon an immediate exchange of prisoners. And the oil embargo led to growing fear in the industrialized states, notably in Western Europe and Japan. In military terms, the Arabs had been beaten but, unlike 1967, not shattered; in the North and South, two large armies were left facing each other fully armed and capable of causing considerable damage to each other. Indeed, shooting continued on both fronts until the day the disengagement agreements were signed.[17] Thus, the 1973 Crisis was not over; it now entered the post-crisis period. Israel's decision-makers perceived a lower order of threat once the guns were silenced, and time pressure in decision-making declined markedly. Yet the "unfinished business" of the Yom Kippur War remained.

Prime Minister Meir's visit to the U.S., from 31 October to 5 November 1973, was approved by the Cabinet on 30 October (Decision 21). The journey was mainly her own initiative. She had expressed the desire to go even during the war and now felt the urgent necessity to explain Israel's immediate needs—a continued supply of arms and the return of the prisoners of war. As Gazit

16. The Israeli Cabinet decision on 26 October to allow the passage of a one-time convoy of 100 trucks to the Third Army, together with the cease-fire, marked the end of the 1973 crisis period. However, the fate of the Third Army remained the focal point of U.S.-Israeli controversy during the first phase of the post-crisis period—that is, until the Six-Point Agreement of 11 November.

17. On the southern front, during the first two months after the cease-fire, there were 452 incidents initiated by the Egyptians, in which 15 Israeli soldiers died and 265 were wounded (Dayan, *Story of My Life*, p. 467). On the northern front, 54 Israeli soldiers fell in battle and 176 were wounded until the signature of the Interim Agreement with Syria on 31 May 1974 (Meir, Government Statement to the Knesset, 30 May 1974, *Divrei Haknesset*, 70, 1459–1462).

remarked: "It was natural for her to go, certainly after the cease-fire. Golda went to Washington to 'touch base,' to have discussions with American leaders, particularly in view of the U.S.-Soviet confrontation of 24 October. Of course, Golda was prepared to enter into negotiations with the Egyptians to achieve the release of the prisoners of war, based upon the fact of our strong position on the western bank of the Canal."[18]

Meir met Nixon on 1 November, and this was followed by several long bargaining sessions with Kissinger on the 1st and 3rd; the earlier meeting with the Secretary of State lasted all night. The President reaffirmed the United States' strong support for the existence of Israel but warned of the dangers of another nuclear confrontation.[19] He made it clear that the U.S. could not have allowed the destruction of the Third Army. At the same time, he indicated his belief that a new basis for peace talks had been created, which would involve Israel in territorial concessions, though the U.S. would work to assure her secure boundaries. Sadat, in Nixon's opinion, was peace-oriented, and it would be in the best interest of Israel as well if the U.S. would improve her relations with Egypt and Syria. Meir indicated that Israel would not return to the positions of 22 October.[20]

It was Kissinger who first raised the issue of IDF withdrawal to the 22 October lines. He, too, insisted that the U.S. would not permit the destruction of the Third Army, arguing that this would have put the clock back, since it would be a humiliation to the Egyptians, leading to their inability or unwillingness to begin meaningful negotiations. Playing on fear and uncertainty, he emphasized Israel's isolation, the grave effect of the oil embargo,

18. Interview with M. Brecher, 27 July 1974.
19. Nixon refers briefly to his meeting with Meir in *RN: The Memoirs of Richard Nixon* (New York, 1978), pp. 942–943. According to U.S. Embassy sources in Tel Aviv (Brecher interviews with Ambassador Keating and other officials, 12 August 1974), it was only during her stay in Washington that the Prime Minister became aware of the enormity of the issues involved for the U.S.: the alert; the confrontation with Moscow; the airlift; the traumatic effect of all these decisions on the Americans; and the limits of support Israel could expect. She was made to realize that, from the U.S. perspective, there was much more involved than the Arab-Israeli conflict and that Israel would have to make concessions in exchange for continued American support.
20. *My Life*, pp. 375–376. See also M. Golan, *The Secret Conversations of Henry Kissinger* (New York, 1976), pp. 105–106, and E. Sheehan, "Step by Step in the Middle East," *Foreign Policy*, 22 (Spring 1976), 3–70.

and the dangers of a Russian intervention. He demanded the opening of a "humanitarian" corridor to the Third Army, under Egyptian control. He also suggested a staged Israeli withdrawal from the west bank of the Canal into Sinai as a meaningful step toward peaceful negotiations.

Meir rejected out of hand the proposal to withdraw to the lines of 22 October; nobody, she asserted, including the UN Observers, knew where those lines were. As to IDF withdrawal from the west bank of the Canal, she suggested a mutual return to the lines of 5 October. Yet she made a substantial concession on the issue of the Third Army: Israel would allow a corridor, with a UN checkpost, but under IDF control. In return, she insisted upon an immediate exchange of prisoners of war.[21] According to William B. Quandt, the atmosphere in the Kissinger-Meir meetings was strained. Meir suspected that the fruits of victory were about to be snatched again from Israel by friends, while Kissinger insisted that U.S. policy would not be determined in Israel. On 2 November, after their all-night meeting, he summoned the "Washington Task Force" and declared that he would work for a moderate peace agreement and thereby limit Moscow's influence in the Middle East, as well as put an end to the oil embargo. "If, God forbid, that effort should fail, the oil crisis would get worse and international isolation would befall the U.S. and Israel. The Arabs had to be convinced that it is preferable to deal with Washington than with Moscow."[22]

It was during this tense series of meetings that the draft of a six-point agreement between Israel and Egypt was worked out. With slight modifications, this draft was signed by Israel and Egypt at Kilometer 101 on 11 November—after Kissinger had secured Sadat's acceptance during his visit to Cairo on 6–7 November. As Dayan recalled it, Sisco, who brought the draft from Cairo, "met with representatives of our government, and after a discussion of several hours and the introduction of certain changes, we agreed to

21. Gazit, Interview with M. Brecher, 27 July 1974; and Yariv, Interview with M. Brecher, 7 August 1974. Both accompanied Meir on that visit to Washington. Meir recalled: "They were not easy or pleasant talks, but then we were not discussing pleasant matters" (*My Life*, p. 376).

22. W. B. Quandt, *Decade of Decisions* (Berkeley, Los Angeles, and London, 1977), pp. 215–216. Excerpt published in *Yediot Aharonot*, 21 September 1977. See also B. Kalb and M. Kalb, *Kissinger* (Boston and Toronto, 1974), pp. 502–505.

accept it. The next day the amended draft agreement was brought before the Cabinet and approved" (Decision 22).[23]

There were other dramatic incidents before the signature. At the Cabinet meeting on the 7th, at a meeting of the Knesset Foreign Affairs and Security Committee immediately thereafter, and at a further Cabinet session on 10 November, objections were raised about the lack of clarity on certain points in the draft agreement. These concerned (1) the authority of UN personnel in the corridor with Egypt and the UN's seeking control of the axis where the UN checkpost was established, while Israel remained firm on the issue of complete control; and (2) the lifting of the blockade at Bab-el-Mandeb on vessels bound for Eilat. Kissinger, in China at the time, dealt with these problems on the basis of messages sent to him. He agreed that the corridor would remain under exclusive Israeli control. The lifting of the blockade could not be included in the agreement, but he assured Israel that Sadat had given his word that the blockade would be lifted de facto, and it was.[24]

The text of the Six-Point Agreement was as follows:

A. Egypt and Israel agree to observe scrupulously the cease-fire called for by the United Nations Security Council.

B. Both sides agree that discussions between them will begin immediately to settle the question of the return to the October 22 positions in the framework of agreement on the disengagement and separation of forces under the auspices of the United Nations.

C. The town of Suez will receive daily supplies of food, water and medicine. All wounded civilians in the town of Suez will be evacuated.

D. There shall be no impediment to the movement of nonmilitary supplies to the east bank.

E. The Israeli checkpoints on the Cairo-Suez road will be replaced by United Nations checkpoints. At the Suez end of the road, Israeli officers can participate with the United Nations to supervise the nonmilitary nature of the cargo at the bank of the Canal.

F. As soon as the United Nations checkpoints are established on the Cairo-Suez road, there will be an exchange of all prisoners of war, including wounded.[25]

23. *Story of My Life*, p. 451.

24. Yariv, Interview with M. Brecher, 7 August 1974; M. Golan, *The Secret Conversations of Henry Kissinger*, pp. 114–115; and Quandt, *Decade of Decisions*, p. 214.

25. The text was submitted by Ambassador Scali, in the form of a letter from the Secretary of State to Secretary-General Waldheim on 9 November 1973 and was published the next day. Bernard and Marvin Kalb (*Kissinger*, pp. 502–505)

There was little discussion of issues on the Syrian front; both sides sensed that progress would first have to be made in the Israel-Egypt negotiations. The one attempt at negotiation failed. Mohamed Ismail, Syria's Deputy Foreign Minister, had come to Washington from UN Headquarters on 2 November. During his talks with Kissinger, he offered "informally" to exchange Israel's prisoners of war for the strongholds which had been reoccupied by the IDF on Mount Hermon and the return of some 15,000 Syrian villagers to their homes in the territory held by Israel. But before the specifics could be explored, the offer was withdrawn.[26]

The talks at Kilometer 101 continued from 28 October to 29 November 1973, when they were broken off by Egypt because of alleged Israeli intransigence. Altogether, eighteen meetings were held between Israeli and Egyptian delegations, headed by Generals Yariv and Gamassi, with Tal filling in while Yariv was in Washington with Meir. At first, the discussions concentrated on the implementation of the Six-Point Agreement. During the second stage, after the prisoner-of-war exchange was carried out on 15 November, substantive negotiations began on a disengagement of forces. Israel offered a retreat to the east bank of the Canal in return for a thinning out of forces and reopening of the Canal, and Egypt insisted upon a much deeper IDF retreat and control of both banks. There were parallel political negotiations between Meir and Kissinger in Washington from 1 to 4 November and on 21 November between Eban and Kissinger in Washington. According to Yariv, there were two reasons for moving the talks to Geneva: (1) Israel was interested in putting a political stamp on what were talks between officers on a military agreement; and (2) Kissinger's interest in making the Kilometer 101 talks part of a process toward a disengagement agreement.[27] Dayan was less satisfied with this form of contact:

---

claim that the six-point draft was prepared by Kissinger. The Egyptian viewpoint was communicated in discussions held by Kissinger with the newly-appointed Egyptian Foreign Minister Ismail Fahmi, on 29–30 October. According to Quandt (*Decade of Decisions,* p. 214), Fahmi brought with him an 11-point proposal, outlining Egypt's agreement to the end of belligerency with Israel, in exchange for the return of all of Sinai before a peace conference.

26. Eban, Interview with M. Brecher, 15 July 1974; and Gazit, Interview with M. Brecher, 27 July 1974. See also Meir, Statement to the Knesset, 20 December 1973, *Divrei Haknesset,* 68, 4798 and 4829–4830.

27. Interview with M. Brecher, 7 August 1974.

The progress of the Yariv-Gamassi talks at Kilometer 101 had not been to my liking. It had seemed to me that we were about to make vital concessions without receiving anything appropriate in exchange and without a suitable settlement and that I was unable to prevent it. The head of our delegation at the time reported directly to the Prime Minister. The basic points were brought before the Cabinet for consideration and decision, but I had found little support there for my suggestions . . . [and] it was not possible to secure these objectives in the negotiations between Yariv and Gamassi and without United States mediation and acceptance of responsibility. With all my occasional reservations about Kissinger and his moves, I was not unmindful of his achievements.[28]

From that early post-crisis phase emerged the pattern of future Israeli-Arab-U.S. negotiations: Kissinger's shuttle diplomacy; the painstaking search for common ground, sometimes to an absurd, microscopic degree; Israel's insistence on a political *quid pro quo* for territorial concessions, "a piece of peace for a piece of territory"; and a progressively deeper U.S. involvement, in the form of assurances, as well as economic and military aid, to both sides.

Phase II: 12 November 1973–18 January 1974

In the second phase of the post-crisis period, diplomatic efforts concentrated on the preparations for a peace conference in Geneva, whose outlines had been agreed upon at the 21 October meeting between Kissinger and Brezhnev.[29] Although the idea of a disengagement of forces between Israel and Egypt was discussed in some detail during December, the speedy conclusion of the agreement in January 1974 came as a surprise to all concerned.

The principal events in the Israeli decision flow during that phase were:

1. Foreign Minister Eban's discussions in Washington on 21 November about the opening of the Geneva Conference, and the Conference's approval by the Cabinet on 25 November.

2. Defense Minister Dayan's discussions in Washington on 7–8 December about the disengagement of forces on the southern front.

28. *Story of My Life*, p. 451.
29. H. Kissinger, News Conference, 21 March 1974, as quoted in *Statements on the Middle East* (hereafter *Statements*), 29 November 1973–24 June 1974, U.S. Information Service, Tel Aviv, 1974, p. 95.

3. Secretary of State Kissinger's second visit to the Near East and his
    talks with Israeli and Arab leaders on Geneva and disengagement,
    from 12 to 19 December.
4. Dayan's second journey to Washington and further discussions on
    disengagement, on 4 January 1974.
5. Kissinger's third visit, from 11 to 18 January 1974, to meet with
    Israeli and Arab leaders, which ensured a disengagement agreement.

Kissinger had informed Israel's leaders, during his brief stopover
in Tel Aviv on 22 October, of his agreement with the Soviets on
the Geneva Peace Conference. At that time, he had made it clear
that the Conference would be chaired by the U.S. and the USSR.
As to matters of substance, these emerged at the Kilometer 101
talks between Yariv and Gamassi. After the Six-Point Agreement
had been concluded on 11 November, these talks became the first
stage on the road to a disengagement agreement. In Yariv's words,
"If all the pieces fell into place, they might lead to the beginning of
a long process of negotiation toward a peace settlement."[30] At a
meeting with Gamassi on 22 November, Yariv submitted, informally, Israel's most far-reaching proposal thus far, approved by a
Cabinet meeting on 20 November (Decision 23): an IDF withdrawal of 10 to 12 kilometers from the Canal; a thinning out of
troops on both sides of the Canal and the stationing of UN forces in
evacuated areas; the Canal's speedy reopening to Israeli shipping
as well; and the rehabilitation of Egypt's Canal cities. Egypt,
however, insisted on "an Israeli retreat from the west bank of the
Canal to a depth of 35 kilometers in the Sinai; a 15-kilometer UN
buffer zone between the forces; an area of thinned-out army forces
for 10 kilometers on each side of the buffer; a detailed timetable for
further Israeli retreat until the complete evacuation of the Sinai;
opening of the Canal and the rehabilitation of the cities when the
Israeli retreat reached a line 60 kilometers from the Canal."[31]

The talks were broken off on 29 November. In Yariv's view this
was because all concerned were more interested by then in moving
the talks to the political level.[32] According to Quandt, "Gamasay
discovered that Yariv had gone back to his original proposal that

30. Interview with M. Brecher, 7 August 1974.
31. M. Golan, *The Secret Conversations of Henry Kissinger*, pp. 119–120.
32. Yariv, Interview with M. Brecher, 7 August 1974. For Soviet interests, see
G. Golan, *Yom Kippur and After: The Soviet Union and the Middle East Crisis*
(Cambridge, England, 1977), pp. 153–154.

both sides should withdraw from territory gained in the war. This reversal of position angered the Egyptians and led to the breakdown of the talks."[33]

Parallel to the Kilometer 101 talks, Israel's Cabinet decided, on 20 November, to instruct Eban in Washington to negotiate the details of the Geneva Conference (Decision 23). His instructions were to make it clear that (a) Israel would not enter into substantive discussions at Geneva before the general elections, now rescheduled for 31 December 1973; and (b) that Israel would not accept a separate Palestinian delegation at the Peace Conference. Kissinger informed Eban that Egypt was now demanding that the Conference be held under UN auspices. When Eban resisted the idea, Kissinger proposed that Secretary-General Waldheim act as host at the opening session, with the U.S. and the Soviet Union as co-chairmen. The first session would determine the procedure for future meetings whose subject would be the disengagement of forces. Because of Kissinger's concern with "keeping up momentum," he proposed that the Conference convene on 11 December.

The Cabinet approved Kissinger's suggestions, conditionally, on 25 November, insisting upon the postponement of the opening session until 18 December, in order to lessen the anticipated pressure on Israel for substantive discussions before her general elections (Decision 24).[34] The Cabinet decision also noted that, upon receipt of the official invitation, further clarification would be necessary before final approval by Israel.

The main purpose of Dayan's visit to Washington on 7–8 December was to seek American agreement to long-term delivery of arms, in particular the tanks and planes which Israel needed to balance Soviet rearmament of Arab forces. The U.S. had, within two months of the beginning of the airlift, delivered or sold to

33. Quandt, *Decade of Decisions*, p. 219.
34. When the Conference was finally opened on 21 December, a Friday, and continued on the Sabbath, it caused an uproar in Israel's religious circles (Meir, Statement to the Knesset, 20 December 1973, and subsequent discussion, *Divrei Haknesset*, 68, 4796–4833, and *Ha'aretz*, 26 December 1973). The full text of the statements by the Secretary-General of the United Nations, Dr. Kurt Waldheim; the Foreign Minister of the USSR, Andre Gromyko; U.S. Secretary of State, Dr. Henry Kissinger; Egyptian Foreign Minister, Ismail Fahmi; the Prime Minister and Foreign Minister of Jordan, Zeid el-Rifai; and the Israeli Foreign Minister, Abba Eban, at the Opening Session, are in M. Medzini, ed., *Israel's Foreign Relations, Selected Documents, 1947–1974* [hereafter *Selected Documents*] (Jerusalem, 1976).

Israel military equipment worth about one billion dollars;[35] but Israel was not getting the type and number of tanks and planes and some other heavy equipment that she had requested. The second purpose was political discussions on the form of disengagement (Decision 25). Israel's official position until then had been to insist upon an exchange of territories, in effect a return to the 5 October lines. Dayan recalled that he now put before Kissinger his "personal view," for which he had the approval of the Prime Minister, as follows:

As to the topographical structure of the arrangement, I thought there should be a strip separating the two parties, a buffer zone put under the control of the UN forces. To my mind, the United States, too, had an active role to play in the agreement, particularly on the matter of Bab-el-Mandeb, which was an international waterway used also by our oil tankers. It was up to the U.S. to guarantee freedom of shipping through these straits, and she was not without the power to meet the possible objection of a couple of Egyptian frigates! I told Kissinger that if Egypt failed to accept our political terms, we would remain in our present military positions and Egypt would eventually accept the arrangement she now rejected. I said this even though I knew that it was not only Egypt that was interested in an immediate arrangement. America was too, in order to put an end to the hysteria in Europe over oil.[36]

Dayan reported to the Prime Minister, the Cabinet, and the Knesset Foreign Affairs and Security Committee upon his return to Israel, on 10 December. The Secretary of State now set out on another round of face-to-face negotiations in the Middle East.

Kissinger arrived in Israel on 16 December, after having talked with the leaders of Algeria, Egypt, Saudi Arabia, Syria, Lebanon, and Jordan within a period of three days. In Cairo, he obtained Sadat's agreement to attend the Peace Conference and his promise

35. Statement by Kenneth Rush, Counsellor to President Nixon for Economic Policy, before the Senate Committee on Foreign Relations, 13 December 1973, as quoted in U.S. Information Service, *Statements*, p. 15.

36. *Story of My Life*, pp. 454–456; present at the meeting were Dayan, Zvi Zur, Dinitz, Gur, Kissinger, and Sisco. Dayan had advocated these policies consistently since 1967. The main political concession he expected in return was "assurance of no more war," a price that Kissinger believed Israel would not get in that phase: "You are asking for the impossible" (as quoted in Sheehan, "Step by Step in the Middle East," p. 24). There is little doubt that Sheehan was correct in asserting that Dayan's ideas were instrumental in breaking the impasse in the disengagement negotiations. He also played a decisive role in the final stages of the negotiations in January 1974.

to help persuade the Syrians to do the same.[37] But Sadat insisted that the invitation to the Conference contain some reference to the rights of the Palestinians to attend at a future date.

The discussion turned upon some crucial sentences in the letter of invitation to the Conference, to be issued by the U.S. and the USSR. The first draft contained a reference to "the question of the Palestinians"; but this was dropped after Kissinger's talk with Dayan and Dinitz on 7 December, where both insisted, on Meir's instructions, that Israel would not go to Geneva "if there is any doubt on the Palestinians." Kissinger informed Sadat after the meeting that the U.S. did not favor Palestinian participation at the first session. The second draft, shown to Sadat on the 14th, included a reference to future participation in the Conference of "organizations and groups." This was dropped at Israel's insistence on the 16th. Thus the relevant sentence in the final draft read: "The parties have also agreed that the question of other participants from the Middle East area will be discussed during the first stage of the Conference."[38]

Kissinger was less successful in Damascus on the 15th. Assad insisted that "any disengagement must involve all of the Golan Heights"; that "there should be disengagement before the Conference convenes"; and that until then he would not release the list of Israeli prisoners of war—"Why should I give up this card? What am I getting for it? Brezhnev never mentioned that to me."[39]

There was still another source of apprehension on the Palestinian issue, before Kissinger arrived. On 13 December, Nixon sent a message to Meir in which he

indicated that he was disturbed by her attitude, and denied that the UN Secretary-General would have more than a symbolic role. Regarding the

37. For Sadat's version of his meeting with Kissinger on 11 December, with his assertion, "I am going to liquidate the Israeli Deversoir pocket" (on the West Bank of the Canal), and Kissinger's reported reply, "I know you're ready for it; I knew it before I came to see you. . . . You must know, however, that if you do this the Pentagon will strike at you . . . ," see *In Search of Identity: An Autobiography* (New York, 1978), p. 268.

38. See the debate in the Knesset on 20 December, in particular the Prime Minister's opening statement and her summary at the end of the debate, *Divrei Haknesset,* 68, 4796–4799 and 4829–4833. The quotations are taken from the verbatim texts in Sheehan, "Step by Step in the Middle East," pp. 24–30.

39. Sheehan, "Step by Step in the Middle East," pp. 26–28; the quotations are from the verbatim protocols cited there.

Palestinians, Nixon argued that the mention of Palestinian participation in the conference did not prejudice the outcome and that, in any case, the participation of additional members . . . would require agreement of all the initial participants. . . . Nixon concluded his letter by warning the prime minister that the United States would not understand Israel's refusal to attend the Geneva conference and that he would no longer be able to justify support for Israel if Israel did not send its representatives to Geneva.[40]

The pace of Kissinger's negotiations in Israel was hectic, then as later. He had a three-hour meeting with the Prime Minister, which began at 18:00. At 21:30, there was a working dinner with Meir, Eban, Sisco, and their aides. This was followed by a Cabinet meeting starting at 01:00 on 17 December and lasting for another three hours. There were further meetings in the morning with the "negotiating team"—Meir, Allon, Eban, and Dayan; also present were Elazar, Yariv, Gazit, Dinitz, Sisco, Keating, and their aides.[41]

On Israel's participation in the Geneva Peace Conference, the sometimes heated debates turned upon three issues:

1. *The reference to the Palestinians*, which was the most difficult to solve. Israel insisted that no reference, not even the phrase "organizations and groups," be included in the letters by the superpowers, and that invitations to future participants be issued only with the agreement of *all* participants at the opening session (Decision 26). As noted, the second condition was explicitly accepted in Nixon's message of 13 December.

2. *The role of the UN at Geneva*, particularly in view of the latest Security Council resolution (Resolution 343, of 15 December 1973). Meir's suspicions were quieted by Kissinger's repeated assurances and Nixon's message that the UN role would be only ceremonial. As she indicated to the Knesset on 20 December:

> In the written and oral contacts with the President of the United States . . . and Dr. Kissinger, the main conditions and political framework of the Conference were well clarified. During these contacts we agreed to the definition of the UN's role.
>
> UN auspices are limited to the assembling of the Conference. The Secretary-General of the UN, Dr. Waldheim, will call the Conference and preside at the opening ceremony. The Secretary-General of the UN sent

40. Quandt, *Decade of Decisions*, p. 222.
41. B. Kalb and M. Kalb, *Kissinger*, pp. 526–528; Dayan, *Story of My Life*, p. 459.

the invitations to the Conference at the request of the United States and the Soviet Union. . . .[42]

3. *Israel's insistence on receiving—in advance—the list of prisoners of war held by Syria and on visits by the Red Cross in Damascus.* Dayan urged that Israel not attend the Conference if this condition were not fulfilled. The Cabinet, however, decided in favor of Meir's proposal that Israel attend but refuse to sit with the Syrian delegation in the same room (Decision 27). The problem was solved when Damascus announced publicly, on 18 December, that it would not attend the Conference. Thus the Prime Minister's formula saved Israel from being accused of aborting the Peace Conference.[43]

After contacts with Gromyko in Moscow and Sadat in Cairo, Kissinger secured Egypt's agreement to delete the phrase "organizations and groups"; but Sadat refused to grant Israel a right to veto future PLO participation. This problem was solved only when the U.S. gave Israel a secret "Memorandum of Understanding," promising that no other parties would be invited to future meetings at Geneva "without the agreement of the initial participants," even to the extent of using a U.S. veto.[44]

These problems were the focus of discussion at the Kissinger meetings on 16 December and at the Cabinet meeting which authorized Israel's participation at the opening Geneva ceremony. The negotiations with Kissinger on the 17th were devoted mostly to clarifying the disengagement proposals. Here is Dayan's reconstruction:

• I felt that the only solution in keeping with Isaiah's "Fear not, O Jacob" was to return to my old proposal of an interim settlement, a plan which I had been advancing, without success, ever since the Six Day War. I now explained that while Golda was right in saying that what was called disengagement was in fact a unilateral withdrawal of our

42. *Divrei Haknesset,* 68, 4796–4799.

43. Dayan, *Story of My Life,* pp. 459–460; M. Golan, *The Secret Conversations of Henry Kissinger,* pp. 127–128; Sheehan, "Step by Step in the Middle East," p. 29. According to Quandt (*Decade of Decisions,* p. 223), Assad notified Kissinger on 10 December that he would not attend the first stage but might reconsider later.

44. Sheehan, "Step by Step in the Middle East," p. 31; M. Golan, *The Secret Conversations of Henry Kissinger,* p. 127; Meir, Statement to the Knesset (and the debate which followed), 20 December 1973, *Divrei Haknesset,* 68, 4796–4833.

forces, what we needed in exchange was not a parallel withdrawal by the Egyptians but an agreement. Such an agreement had to contain three essential provisions:

• Disengagement was to be effected within the framework of an Israeli-Egyptian non-belligerency pact.

• Our withdrawal was not to be exploited by the Egyptians to strengthen their front-line forces: their tanks should not be brought in as our tanks pulled out.

• The area was to be restored to normal. This important proviso meant the rebuilding of the Suez Canal cities; return of the civilian population to the Canal area; renewal of industrial activities, such as the refineries and the operations of the oil pipeline from the Gulf of Suez; and a significant reduction in the size of the Egyptian army.[45]

The next day, 18 December, Waldheim issued letters of invitation to the agreed-upon participants. The opening session on 21 December was attended by Secretary-General Waldheim; the co-chairmen, Kissinger and Gromyko; and the delegations of Egypt, Israel, and Jordan, headed respectively by Foreign Ministers Fahmi and Eban, and Prime Minister Zaid al-Rifai. Following the opening speeches by all participants, Egypt and Russia insisted that, at least formally, meetings should begin on disengagement talks in Geneva on 26 December and not on 7 January, as had been previously agreed upon. When Meir received this request, she summoned the Cabinet, which decided to accept (Decision 28). Thus, on 26 December, an Israeli military delegation, headed by General Gur, began totally procedural meetings in Geneva with an Egyptian delegation, headed by General Ismail.[46]

A side dividend at Geneva was a meeting between Gromyko and Eban, arranged by Kissinger at Eban's request. The substance of the discussion was reported by G. Golan as follows:

The Soviet Foreign Minister received Eban with smiles and fond reminiscences. He repeated his public remarks about Israel's right to security and territorial integrity, pointing out that the Soviet Union felt

45. *Story of My Life*, pp. 460–462.

46. *Ha'aretz*, 21–23 December 1973; M. Golan, *The Secret Conversations of Henry Kissinger*, chap. 4. Dayan stated in his memoirs that "our military delegation had to kill time until after the general elections." He gave strict instructions to the head of the delegation and his deputy, Colonel Sion (Dayan's son-in-law), to prevent any official proposals. Moreover, on the basis of the "bitter experience from the talks at Kilometer 101," they were answerable to him alone and were to receive instructions only from him (*Story of My Life*, p. 463).

that it even had a stake in this matter, given its support in 1948, adding that since 1948 the Soviets had never questioned Israel's right to sovereign existence and independence. Gromyko suggested that Israel recognize that its security was best protected not by territories acquired at the expense of other countries but by Soviet-American guarantees which both superpowers were willing to provide, now that the United States and the Soviet Union were cooperating.

In the private part of their talk, Gromyko reportedly suggested that Soviet-Israel contacts be continued, and he raised the issue of renewed diplomatic relations with Israel. Gromyko tied such a step to "significant progress" in Israel's contacts with the Arabs, stressing the word "significant." He amplified that such progress meant at Geneva, perhaps in the disengagement with Egypt, and that it was necessary so as to justify such a move to Soviet "public opinion." It is more likely that Gromyko meant justification to present to the Arabs and the Third World, although the renewal of Egyptian-American relations should have been sufficient "justification" for a similar Soviet move.[47]

The 31 December elections returned the ruling Labor-*Mapam* Alignment to power, though it declined from 58 to 51 seats in the 120-member Knesset. Nevertheless, the Government, reassured of legitimacy, could now return to the process of negotiation.

When Dayan met Kissinger again in Washington on 4 and 5 January 1974, he carried with him revised proposals for a disengagement agreement. These were worked out first in a meeting of the "negotiating team"—Meir, Allon, Eban, and Dayan—with Elazar on 1 January, and approved by the Cabinet the next day (Decision 29). As described by Dayan, the following demands and suggestions were contained in the proposals:

Four [provisions] were military and dealt with deployment of forces, limitation of forces, timetable for the implementation of the new deployment, and the budget required to fortify and provide the necessary services, such as access roads, for the new lines.

Other provisions related to three areas. First, the proposed apparatus for supervising the agreement—UN observers and other measures. Second, non-military matters which should be included in the agreement: cessation of hostilities, civilian rehabilitation of the Canal Zone, freedom of passage through the Bab-el-Mandeb Straits, reduction of Egyptian and Israeli troop strength, and renewal of passage through the Suez Canal, including Israeli cargoes. Third, an agreement between Israel and the United States which should contain items of bilateral concern, such as

47. G. Golan, *Yom Kippur and After,* pp. 165–166. See also, A. Eban, *An Autobiography* (Jerusalem and Tel Aviv, 1977), pp. 551–554; M. Golan, "The Revealing Meeting of Eban with Gromyko," *Ha'aretz,* 4 October 1974; and Nakdimon, "New Revelations," *Yediot Aharonot,* 16 August 1974.

arms supplies and economic aid, as well as matters directly affecting Israel and the Egyptians in which America was involved as a third party. The latter would include guarantees over Bab-el-Mandeb and other matters on which Egypt would agree to give undertakings to the United States but not to us. The disadvantage of this procedure was, of course, the absence of direct contact between the Egyptians and us, but it had the advantage of securing the involvement of the United States, if not as actual guarantor at least as a partner to the arrangement. . . .

. . . I told him [Kissinger] that the proposal I had brought with me, approved by my government, would no doubt be endorsed by the next government to be formed on the basis of the election results. . . . We . . . considered our suggestions as being the first step toward peace and not merely a disengagement of forces.

The map and proposals were presented by Dayan to Kissinger as a "total concept. . . . It could be accepted or rejected, but there was no point in arguing over each of its provisions."[48]

During their second meeting, on 5 January, Kissinger tried to persuade Dayan that Israel should withdraw to the Mitla and Gidi passes, as such a move would have military and psychological importance. Despite Dayan's refusal, Kissinger was sufficiently encouraged by the Israeli proposals to initiate another round of negotiations. Neither Kissinger nor Dayan—nor Sadat, for that matter—expected that the agreement would be signed within ten days.[49]

The sequence of meetings and decisions in the last phase of negotiations leading to an interim agreement with Egypt, the first "real" Kissinger shuttle, was as follows:[50]

11 January	19:30	Kissinger arrives in Aswan and holds his first meeting with Sadat.
12 January	11:00	Second meeting with Sadat.
	18:00	Kissinger arrives in Israel.
	19:00	Working dinner with Allon, Dayan, Eban, Dinitz, Gazit, and aides. (Meir was ill.)
	midnight	Israeli Cabinet meets and authorizes the presentation of a proposal to Kissinger for the disengagement of forces.

48. Dayan, *Story of My Life*, pp. 463–464.
49. B. Kalb and M. Kalb, *Kissinger*, p. 530.
50. *New York Times* and *Ha'aretz*, 11–19 January 1974; M. Golan, *The Secret Conversations of Henry Kissinger*, chap. 6; Dayan, *Story of My Life*, chap. 36.

13 January	morning until afternoon	A U.S.-Israeli team works out the details of the proposal to be submitted to Sadat: size and disposition maps, forces, and timetable.
	early evening	Kissinger, Dayan, Sisco, and Elazar finalize their agreement on the maps prepared by the IDF.
	late evening	Kissinger arrives in Aswan with maps and other Israeli proposals.
14 January	10:00	Third Kissinger-Sadat meeting—Israeli proposals are discussed.
	morning-afternoon	Egyptian officials—Gamassi, Fahmi, and aides—work out with Americans an Egyptian response, to be called an "American plan" because of Sadat's refusal to consider an "Israeli" proposal.
	evening	Fourth Kissinger-Sadat meeting, where this plan is approved.
	midnight	Kissinger arrives in Israel; he conveys an outline of the Egyptian counter-proposals to Eban, Dinitz, and Evron, en route to Jerusalem.
15 January	07:00	At a meeting of Meir, Allon, Dayan, Eban, Galili, Dinitz, and Gazit, a tendency to accept the Egyptian proposals emerges.
	09:00–13:00	Israeli and American officials review these proposals in detail.
	13:15	Kissinger meets with Meir, who, after emphasizing Israel's security needs, indicates acceptance of the proposals.
	17:30	Israel's Cabinet meets for five hours and approves the Prime Minister's suggestions to give up the demand for a clear-cut Egyptian statement on the end of a "state of belligerency" and to authorize the American Secretary of State to proceed with the negotiations. The Cabinet reserves final consent until Kissinger's return from Egypt (Decision 30).
	22:30–03:00	Further discussions by the Cabinet on details of the proposed disengagement agreement.

16 January	14:00	Kissinger arrives in Aswan for a fifth meeting with Sadat; the Egyptian President accepts Israel's demand for a reduction of Egyptian forces on the east bank of the Canal to ten battalions.
	20:00	Sixth Kissinger-Sadat meeting, where the proposals are finalized and approved.
	midnight	Kissinger arrives in Israel and holds discussions with Eban and Dinitz en route to and in Jerusalem.
17 January	10:30	Kissinger meets with Allon, Dayan, and Eban to discuss Egypt's proposals.
	13:00	Kissinger meets with Meir to finalize the agreement.
	15:00–18:00	Israel's Cabinet decides to approve the agreement (Decision 31).
	19:00	Kissinger is notified of the Cabinet's decision.
	21:00	(15:00 New York time): Presidents Nixon and Sadat and Prime Minister Meir, in a simultaneously timed statement, announce news of the disengagement.
18 January	12:30	At Kilometer 101, Elazar and Gamassi sign the agreement; General Siilasvuo witnesses it on behalf of the UN.

The first and basic issue—the extent of Israel's withdrawal—was settled within two days. At the outset, Sadat demanded an IDF withdrawal to the Mitla and Gidi Passes. But when Kissinger returned with an Israeli counterproposal to withdraw twenty kilometers from the Canal, Sadat agreed, except for the southern end, where the city of Suez would have remained within shelling distance of IDF artillery. Israel, on Dayan's initiative, accepted that reservation and redrew the line accordingly.

The next problem was the size of forces to remain in the areas of the thinned-out forward lines—the size of military units, the number of tanks and guns, and the distance of missile sites from the Canal. Bargaining lasted until the last moment, with Meir agreeing to ten battalions only on 17 January, just before the Cabinet meeting which approved the Disengagement Agreement as a whole.

The third problem was the presence, size, and composition of the UN Force in the proposed buffer zone. Israel demanded, on the basis of the May 1967 experience with UNEF, that Egypt should not be able, unilaterally, to remove such a Force; that any such proposal come before the Security Council—where the U.S. had a right of veto; that the UN Force be strong enough to prevent violations of the agreement; and that the Force not include soldiers from states which had no diplomatic relations with Israel. Of these bargaining demands only the third was accepted, and even that was not spelled out in the Disengagement Agreement; it was arranged on the basis of an agreement between Kissinger and Waldheim.

Israel's main political demand was that the agreement would end the "state of belligerency" between the two states; but finally, under U.S. pressure, she had to accept the innocuous phrase, "maintenance of the cease-fire." This was done at the Cabinet meeting of 15 January, probably the most significant Israeli concession in the negotiating process. Other political demands by Israel were: the reopening of the Canal and free passage of Israel-bound goods; and a U.S. guarantee against a renewed blockade of Israel-bound shipping through the Straits of Bab-el-Mandeb (this blockade had been imposed during the Yom Kippur War and was rescinded by Egypt during the first negotiating phase of the post-crisis period). Neither demand was incorporated into the official agreement, because of Egypt's domestic constraints and her sensitivity vis-à-vis other Arab states. Rather, they became the subject of another U.S.-Israeli "Memorandum of Understanding."

There were several such informal bilateral agreements—between the U.S. and Egypt as well as the U.S. and Israel. One dealt with the limitation of forces: On the basis of written Israeli and Egyptian commitments to the United States, Washington undertook "American commitments" to the other side. Another dealt with political issues: The U.S., in a separate "Memorandum of Understanding," assured Israel of the reopening of the Canal and the right of passage of Israel-bound goods.[51]

The text of the separation of forces (disengagement) agreement, which was signed on 18 January 1974, is as follows:

51. These were renegotiated in August 1974, for Sadat's agreement in January 1974 did not commit him to a specific timetable; the first Israel-bound vessel passed through the Suez Canal in October 1975.

A

Egypt and Israel will scrupulously observe the cease-fire on land, sea and air called for by the UN Security Council and will refrain from the time of the signing of this document from all military or para-military actions against each other.

B

The military forces of Egypt and Israel will be separated in accordance with the following principles:
1. All Egyptian forces on the east side of the canal will be deployed west of the line designated as line A on the attached map. All Israeli forces including those west of the Suez Canal on the Bitter Lakes will be deployed east of the line designated as line B on the attached map.
2. The area between the Egyptian and Israeli lines will be a zone of disengagement in which the United Nations Emergency Force will be stationed. The UNEF will continue to consist of units from countries that are not permanent members of the Security Council.
3. The area between the Egyptian line and the Suez Canal will be limited in armament and forces.
4. The area between the Israeli line, line B on the attached map, and the line designated as line C on the attached map, which runs along the western base of the mountains where the Gidi and Mitla Passes are located, will be limited in armament and forces.
5. The limitations referred to in paragraphs 3 and 4 will be inspected by the UNEF. Existing procedures of the UNEF, including the attaching of Egyptian and Israeli liaison officers to the UNEF, will be continued.

C

The detailed implementation of the disengagement of forces will be worked out by military representatives of Egypt and Israel, who will agree on the stages of this process. These representatives will meet no later than 48 hours after the signature of this agreement at Kilometer 101 under the aegis of the United Nations for this purpose. They will complete this task within five days. Disengagement will begin within 48 hours after the signature of the completion of the work of the military representatives, and in no event later than seven days after the signature of this agreement. The process of disengagement will be completed not later than 40 days after it begins.

D

This agreement is not regarded by Egypt and Israel as a final peace agreement. It constitutes a first step toward a final, just and durable peace according to the provisions of Security Council Resolution 338 and within the framework of the Geneva Conference.[52]

52. Medzini, ed., *Selected Documents,* pp. 1110–1111. For a detailed explanation of Israel's reasons for the signing of the Agreement, see Meir, Statement to the Knesset, 22 January 1974, *Divrei Haknesset,* 69, 10–12; English text in Medzini, ed., *Selected Documents,* pp. 1111–1116. See also Kissinger, News Conference, 22 January 1974; text in U.S. Information Service, *Statements,* pp. 43–48.

The Agreement was hailed by President Nixon as "the first significant step toward a permanent peace in the Mideast."[53] Israel's reaction was hopeful but reserved. Dayan summed it up thus:

On the whole I was satisfied with this agreement with the Egyptians. I did not expect us to attain more, under the circumstances, and I also felt that it had intrinsic merit. It put an end to the war—up to its signature there had been fighting at one point or another along the front—and the essential conditions were included in its articles. From the territorial point of view, the new line—the Mitla and Gidi Passes and the hills in front of them—was the best possible, once we had pulled back from the Canal beyond artillery range. And under the reduction of forces clause, the military strength which the Egyptians would be maintaining east of the Canal was indeed minimal.

The Disengagement Agreement also embodied political content of great importance. Certain undertakings were given, and if carried out— and I hoped they would be—they would contribute much toward the normalization of life in the area and serve to defuse war tensions. They would bring about the opening of the Suez Canal to navigation, including the passage of Israeli cargoes; removal of the blockade threat at Bab-el-Mandeb; rehabilitation of the Canal cities; demobilization of part of the Egyptian army and of our own reservists; and an improvement in the relations between the United States and Egypt, particularly over the oil problem.[54]

In short, with the signing of the Disengagement Agreement, all of the indicators of crisis—perception of threat, time pressure, and probability of (the renewal of) war—had de-escalated to the Israeli-Egyptian norm. Israel's 1973 Crisis, as it focused on Egypt, was over.

EPILOGUE[55]

The achievement of a disengagement agreement with Syria was both easier and more difficult than that with Egypt. It was easier because the military outcome of the Yom Kippur War for Syria was

---

53. Nixon, Statement on 17 January 1974, in U.S. Information Service, *Statements*, pp. 41–42. The positive role of Meir and Sadat, and especially the herculean efforts of Kissinger, were warmly praised, then and later. See Nixon, *Memoirs*, pp. 982, 1005.

54. *Story of My Life*, pp. 469–470.

55. As noted, it was found sufficient to summarize the decision flow of the Israel-Syria Disengagement Agreement. For details of the negotiations, see Meir, Government Statement to the Knesset, 30 May 1974 (and the following debate), *Divrei Haknesset*, 70, 1459–1509; Dayan, *Story of My Life*, chap. 37; M. Golan, *The Secret Conversations of Henry Kissinger*, chap. 6; and Quandt, *Decade of Decisions*, pp. 229–245.

unqualified defeat. She failed to regain an inch of territory on the Golan Heights. Moreover, she had retreated beyond the 6 October line, with the IDF now entrenched close to Damascus. But dis-engagement was more difficult because an Israeli withdrawal of even a few kilometers on the Golan Heights (altogether 65 kms. in length and 24 kms. at their widest point, a tiny area of 625 sq. kms. adjacent to and protecting the densely populated northern part of Israel) would have placed towns and villages in Israel within Syrian artillery range.[56] Moreover, several Arab states attempted to exert pressure, through the U.S., by linking an Israeli-Syrian agreement to a termination of the oil embargo.

The process of negotiations was complicated by a crisis of confi-dence in the Government of Israel caused by the war. Its leaders, especially Dayan, were under heavy pressure to resign. There were spontaneous demonstrations for change, some of them led by young war heroes. It took Meir two-and-a-half months to form a new coalition. Dayan, who had tendered his resignation in March 1974, withdrew it when Israel received news that Syria "had decided to resume the war immediately."[57] The new Meir Govern-ment lasted less than a month, from 13 March until 11 April 1974; but it remained in office as a caretaker government until the sign-ing of the Disengagement Agreement with Syria on 31 May. The Prime Minister resigned because of a continuous public atmos-phere of nonconfidence. Her successor was Yitzhak Rabin. Shimon Peres replaced Dayan as Defense Minister. Thus, the last phase of negotiations with Syria was conducted by members of the outgoing Meir Government, with Rabin and Peres joining Israel's negoti-ating team.

The first problem facing Kissinger, to whom all parties turned as a mediator, was to get the list of Israeli prisoners held in Syria. It was made absolutely clear that, for Israel, this was a *sine qua non* for negotiations. The second problem was to find a basis for accom-modating the sharply conflicting demands of Israel and Syria. These were solved during two visits to the Middle East. The first was in February, when Kissinger received the list of prisoners

56. Nixon noted another reason for greater difficulty in the negotiations with Syria: "The Egyptian-Israeli disengagement had been easier because Sadat had adopted the attitude that if major issues could be resolved, the minor ones could be settled at the ongoing Geneva Conference. But the hatred between the Syrians and the Israelis went too deep for them to be able to think this way" (*Memoirs*, p. 1005).
57. Dayan, *Story of My Life*, p. 500.

(which he handed over to Meir on 27 February). The second was in May, when, in a shuttle lasting thirty-three days, he achieved an overall disengagement agreement. It may have been the greatest achievement of Kissinger's career.

The Secretary of State arrived in Jerusalem on 2 May 1974, after preliminary negotiations in Washington during March with Dayan and Syrian representatives. It took another twenty-seven days of shuttling between Jerusalem and Damascus, with side trips to Riyadh, Amman, and Cairo, to attain the Disengagement Agreement. Negotiations on the Israeli side were conducted by Meir, Allon, Dayan, Eban, Rabin, and Peres, advised by Gur (the newly appointed Chief of Staff), Gazit, Dinitz, and Evron. Kissinger's entourage of forty included Under-Secretary of State Sisco, and Atherton, Bunker, and Saunders. Three times—on 13, 18, and 27 May—the talks were at the point of collapse. During the final phase, pressure was exerted on Israel's Cabinet through phone calls from Nixon to Meir.

The first significant Israeli concession was the return of part of Kuneitra, to divide the principal town on the Golan Heights into Israeli, UN, and Syrian zones. The bargaining over precise boundaries, even to the extent of control over a few hundred square meters, and the presence of soldiers in the vicinity of Kuneitra, continued for another two weeks. Israel's main concerns were: (a) to retain the strategic hills next to Kuneitra; and (b) to create a demilitarized buffer zone, in order to protect nearby Kibbutz Meron Hagolan. The final agreement gave Israel control over two of the three strategic hills. Assad accepted this on 18 May, on condition that heavy weapons would be forbidden there.

The second focus of bargaining was the size of a UN buffer zone and the thinning out of forces on both sides. Israel's main goal was to minimize the threat of Syrian artillery on her settlements. Agreement was reached on the number of troops and heavy weapons in the thinned-out zones, including a limitation on the quantity of artillery.

A third Israeli demand was a Syrian commitment to include a cessation of terrorist activities in the cease-fire. Damascus refused. The solution was another U.S. "Memorandum of Understanding," made known by Meir in the Knesset on 30 May 1974:

The Government of the United States has informed us of its position on the first paragraph of the agreement, and this is: "Raids by armed groups or individuals across the demarcation line are contrary to the cease-fire. Israel, in the exercise of its right of self-defense, may act to prevent such actions by all available means. The United States will not consider such actions by Israel as violations of the cease-fire and will support them politically."[58]

The Agreement was announced on 29 May and was signed in Geneva on the 31st by Israeli and Syrian military delegations.[59]

The guns on the Golan Heights ceased firing the same day.

58. *Divrei Haknesset*, 70, 1460; English Text in Medzini, ed., *Selected Documents*, pp. 1131–1136.

59. The text of the "Agreement on Disengagement between Israel and Syrian Forces" may be found in Medzini, ed., *Selected Documents*; Sheehan, "Step by Step in the Middle East," and *New York Times*, 30 May 1974.

CHAPTER TEN

COMPARISON AND FINDINGS

THE 1967 AND 1973 post-crisis periods will now be discussed, as in Chapters 4 and 7, in terms of the four crisis components and several variables of our typologies. Moreover, comparative findings will be presented on Israel's coping mechanisms during the two periods.

CRISIS COMPONENTS

Environmental Change

In 1967, the trigger mechanism (or *source*) was Israel's pre-emptive air strike against Egypt, launched at 07:45 on 5 June. Within less than three hours, Egypt's airfields were in rubble and most of her planes had been destroyed on the ground. The post-crisis period continued until the close of the Six Day War, with stress de-escalation interrupted only briefly by the appearance of possible Soviet military intervention, on 6 and 9 June; but that threat was quickly countered by a display of U.S. deterrent capability and intent. In 1973, two events combined to usher in the post-crisis period. One was the termination of the U.S. nuclear alert and, along with it, the danger of direct superpower military confrontation and/or intervention in the Arab-Israeli War. The other was the coming into effect of the second UN cease-fire on 26 October. In short, the basic difference in environmental change, setting in motion the post-crisis period, was a major IDF triumph at the outset of war

(1967), compared with the end of fighting after Israel's advances on both fronts (1973). The perceptual consequence for Israel was almost identical—namely, that of a positive shift in the Israeli-Arab military balance.

Threat to Values

The decline in perceived threat is one indicator of change from a crisis period to a post-crisis period. This became manifest, as noted, within three hours of Israel's 1967 pre-emptive strike: News that Egypt's Air Force had been decimated on the ground was immediately perceived by Israel's decision-makers as certain triumph in the 1967 War; and total air supremacy on both the Egyptian and the Jordanian fronts meant security for Israel's heartland and centers of population. Israel's survival was no longer in jeopardy. Evidence of this reduced threat perception is present at the *verbal* level: in Eshkol's broadcast to the nation (5 June) and his recollections (4 October); in Eban's press conference (5 June), his speech to the Security Council (6 June), and his unpublished and published accounts of the 1967 Crisis (1969, 1977); in Allon's study of the IDF (1970); and in Dayan's speech (6 June), as well as his memoirs (1976). Military leaders, too, notably Rabin, Weizman, Peled, and Yariv, acknowledged the sharp reduction in threat perception by 10:45 on 5 June.

This change and its consequences are also evident at the level of behavior. From that time onward, the issues upon which Israel's decision-makers focused were not value threats but opportunities for goal attainment: the liberation of Jerusalem, the maximal destruction of Arab military power, and the enhancement of Israel's security by the establishment of secure borders—ultimately, the Suez Canal in the South, the Golan Heights in the North, and the Jordan River in the East. The seven meetings of Israel's Cabinet or its Committee on Defense during the 1967 War, the post-crisis period, were devoted primarily to those goals, not to value threats which, apart from possible Soviet intervention, had receded from the decision-makers' perspective.

In the post-crisis period of 1973, Israel's decision-makers perceived less threat: (a) from the Arabs, with Egypt's Third Army encircled on the east bank of the Canal and Damascus within IDF artillery range; and (b) at the global level, because of the pulling back of Washington and Moscow from a near collision. With the decline in threats to basic Israeli values, other aims became more pertinent. One was a viable military-political agreement with Egypt which would ensure tranquility. Another was to make (minimal) territorial concessions from the post-1967 status quo. As for Syria, the initial Israeli objective was the return of IDF prisoners of war. After the signing of the Interim Agreement with Egypt in January 1974, the primary goal became the termination of Syria's war of attrition and, with it, Israel's mounting casualties. Israel has always placed a high value on the welfare of her soldiers, and there was evidence of ill-treatment of IDF prisoners in Syria. Their release remained a constant Israeli preoccupation in all negotiations with Egypt and Syria via Kissinger—for example, during Meir's meetings in Washington from 1 to 4 November and the Cabinet's refusal on 17 December 1973 to sit with the Syrians at the Geneva conference table. Negotiations over the POW issue ended with Kissinger handing over the list of IDF prisoners in Syria on 27 February 1974. The second goal was reached with the signing of the Israel-Syria Interim Agreement on 31 May 1974.

Israel perceived other threats to her security during the post-crisis period: first, in the territorial concessions she was being called upon to make; and, second, in her fears that the U.S. would curtail arms supplies. However, the termination of military hostilities led to a marked reduction in the scope and severity of those value threats. In sum, the difference between the two post-crisis periods concerning threat was that in 1973 Israel's military triumph was less dramatic, her casualties were much higher, including many more prisoners, and an uncertain political future was perceived.

Probability of War (or Change in the Military Balance)

The definition of crisis given in Chapter 1 specifies a decline in the perceived probability of war as another indicator of the onset of the post-crisis period. Or, as in 1967, when the post-crisis period was synonymous with war, the probability-of-war indicator is replaced by a perceived improvement in the balance of military power. As noted, this occurred within hours of Israel's air strike. Not only were Israel's decision-makers aware of less threat, because of the ensuing air supremacy, they also perceived a dramatic and overwhelming shift of the military balance in their favor. With each passing day, Israel's military position and security were enhanced. That, in turn, strengthened the image that the 1967 Crisis had been successfully resolved.

From the late morning of 5 June, the atmosphere of post-crisis was evident in personal and group behavior. The knowledge of military triumph reduced the stress level for all. Deliberations in the Cabinet and other forums were free from the obsessive Holocaust syndrome of the late crisis period. Eshkol's normal "chairman of the board" type of leadership reappeared. So too did Eban's natural role of supreme advocate for Israel at the UN and international forums generally. And political considerations replaced purely military-security criteria in evaluating alternative courses of action. The atmosphere of post-crisis was no less apparent in the tone of confidence and self-assurance displayed by Eshkol (5 and 7 June), Eban (5 and 6 June), and Dayan (7 June). Although the war continued, Israel's victories had already made her militarily secure, seemingly into the indefinite future.

By the end of the 1973 crisis period—that is, by the end of the Yom Kippur War—Israel's leaders perceived a positive shift in the military balance: The IDF was firmly entrenched on the west bank of the Canal; Egypt's Third Army was surrounded and in danger of being destroyed; and in the North, the outskirts of Damascus were within the range of IDF artillery. Israel had once again proved her military superiority. However, whereas in 1967 she had destroyed enemy armies, this was denied her in 1973 by massive external pressure, both Soviet and American. The perception of a positive shift in the power balance may be noted in Allon's speeches of 11 and 26 November and 5 December, and in Dayan's 10 November statement. At the same time, the probability of renewed war was perceived by Dayan. And a concern that Syria's war of attrition in the first half of 1974 might re-escalate to full-scale hostilities always lurked in the background. It vanished only with the signing of the Israel-Syria Interim Agreement on 31 May 1974, marking the formal—and de facto—end of the post-crisis period.

Time Pressure

Unlike threat perception, which declined sharply on 5 June, time remained salient throughout the decision-making process during the Six Day War. However, the pressure was perceived in a fundamentally different frame of reference than in the crisis period. From 17 May to 4 June, especially after 22 May, time constraints were related to the awesome issue "to live or perish." As such, time had the effect of intensifying crisis-induced stress. From 5 to 10 June, by contrast, time constraints were related to unique, unanticipated opportunities to attain the long-cherished high-value goals of a reunited Jerusalem under Israeli control and secure "natural" borders with the three major adversaries, Egypt, Jordan, and Syria. Thus, Cabinet deliberations over the Old City (5, 6, and 7 June) reveal an acute awareness of the time limit for decisive Israeli action; but it was not the gnawing fear of time pressure associated with high threat. So too with the discussions over the IDF advance to the Canal. Dayan perceived a danger of Soviet intervention, but that threat, unlike the Arab threat in the crisis period, was not linked to—and compounded by—the time dimension. The same was true of the decision process prior to the attack on the Golan Heights. There, however, time became highly salient during the last hours of the War—because of the danger of imminent Soviet intervention and because Eshkol, in particular, insisted on delaying Israel's acceptance of the cease-fire until the IDF had reached strategic goals, such as the Banias headwaters of the Jordan River. In brief, time during the 1967 post-crisis period was viewed as increasingly central to the attainment of basic value goals.

Israel's decision-makers in the 1973 post-crisis period, by contrast, did not feel time pressure as salient to military objectives. The cease-fire lines of 26 October left Israel in an advantageous position. They were more interested in using this situation to make political gains. Time salience was indeed felt in the efforts to secure prisoner exchanges and in response to U.S. pressure to yield immediately on the issue of continued supplies to Egypt's Third Army: That was done within twenty-four hours. The rapid negotiations conducted by Kissinger also placed pressure on Israel to reach decisions quickly. His presence in the area heightened the salience of time: An agreement was reached within ten days of his first shuttle—11 to 18 January 1974.

The post-crisis periods in 1967 and 1973 were marked off from the crisis periods by a decline in threat perception, a positive shift in the military balance, and the lessening of time pressure. This was induced, in both cases, by an environmental change—and a marked improvement—in Israel's military capability, more so in 1967 than in 1973.

The *outcome* in 1967 was, apart from a transformation of the balance of military power, Israel's acquisition of territory much larger than her 1949–67 base and the beginning of a six-year period of "secure borders." In fact, the 1967 post-crisis period—that is, the Six Day War—made Israel the most powerful international actor in the Near East Core. In 1973, the outcome was fundamentally different. The Disengagement Agreements led to tranquility on the borders with Egypt and Syria. There was also an improvement in Israel's relations with the U.S., badly strained between March and August 1975, following the impasse in Kissinger-mediated negotiations for a second Israel-Egypt Interim Agreement. And the pressure on Israel for further concessions eased during the last year of the Ford Administration in Washington—not to be revived until the spring of 1977, and to continue under Carter through 1978. There were also differences in the *number* and the *time span* of decisions: nine decisions in the post-crisis period of 1967, eleven in 1973; the latter were taken over a much longer period of time—seven months, compared to six days.

COPING MECHANISMS

Information Processing

During the 1967 post-crisis period, information was sought about American and Soviet intentions, especially about the danger of direct military intervention and the timing of a UN-sponsored cease-fire. However, with a reduction in perceived threat and an awareness of military triumph, the felt need for more information declined. Israel's decision-makers became less dependent on information about the attitudes of non–Middle East actors when making their choices concerning the Old City of Jerusalem on 5, 6, and 7 June and concerning the extent of IDF advance on all three fronts.

In terms of information flow to the decision-makers, however, there was no change from the crisis to the post-crisis period: A large daily volume of information relevant to the unique opportunities for goal-attainment was funneled directly to the Cabinet or its Committee on Defense—from the UN, from Israel's embassies in Washington, Paris, London, and Moscow, from Heads of Government, from the battlefronts, and from the world press. High values continued to be at stake, though in the perspective of positive potential, not negative threat; and time salience was perceived. Thus the pattern of "collective cable reading" continued unchanged, with radio-derived news about an impending cease-fire and Soviet pressure constituting an added information input, as in the deliberations leading to the IDF entry into the Old City of Jerusalem.

During the prolonged 1973 post-crisis period, there was persistent U.S. pressure on specific issues, beginning with the freeing of Egypt's Third Army from IDF encirclement, and continuous American intervention in the search for an interim agreement with Egypt. This led to an intensely felt need for information about U.S. intentions and likely behavior—and to more frequent visits of high policy Israeli decision-makers to Washington. Notable were Meir's discussions with Nixon and Kissinger soon after the cease-fire (1–4 November), followed by Eban (20–24 November) over the Geneva Conference, and Dayan (5–7 December and 4–5 January 1974) about the terms of an agreement.

Another major source of information, especially about Arab intentions, demands, and possible concessions on interim agreements, was Secretary of State Kissinger. As a deeply involved mediator, he alone had access to all the principal decision-makers and was able to transmit (his own version of) the parties' attitudes and bargaining positions—to Israel, as well as to Egypt and Syria. In 1973, the processing of information by Israel was fundamentally different than in the 1967 post-crisis period. The decline in threat-induced stress, combined with a marked lessening of time pressure, made it unnecessary for all members of the Cabinet to process all information hour by hour or even day by day. Rather, there was a two-stage process: All information went to the four-person Negotiating Committee, Meir, Dayan, Eban, and Allon, later enlarged to include Peres and Rabin; this group then reported—as fully as it deemed appropriate or necessary—to the Cabinet as a whole. The full Cabinet, then, received a selection of information in the 1973 post-crisis period; it was not the primary consumer, as in the 1967 post-crisis period and in both crisis periods.

Consultation: Persons and Groups

The number of persons consulted in the 1967 post-crisis period was much less than in the crisis period. The enlarged Cabinet of twenty-one was the principal consultative forum. Among the civil servants, only Y. Herzog and Yaffe remained within the circle; others, like Harman and Evron in Washington, Rafael in New York, and Levavi and Bitan in Jerusalem, became mere transmitters of information and decisions. The four IDF commanders consulted during the crisis period remained active throughout the Six Day War. In brief, the consultative group declined from thirty-nine to twenty-seven (Cabinet–21, bureaucrats–2, and military elite–4).

During the extended negotiations of the 1973 post-crisis period, the Cabinet remained the principal forum of consultation. Opposition leader Begin, too, was consulted. Among the civil servants, Gazit and Dinitz were joined by Evron. Three generals were actively involved: Elazar, Tal, and Yariv. Thus the consultative group contained twenty-four members (Cabinet–17, other party leaders–1, bureaucrats–3, and military elite–3). This was only one more than in the 1973 crisis period. The impact of declining stress on the size of the consultative circle was, then, mixed: It became smaller in 1967, marginally larger in 1973. Perhaps the duration of the post-crisis period or the nature of the issues to be considered can explain this. Changes in stress do not seem to account for changes in the size of the group.

Table 10 presents the number and size of all ad hoc and all institutional consultative meetings during the two post-crisis periods. The ratio between the two kinds of meetings in 1967 was 4.3:1; and in 1973, it was 2.2:1. The relatively high frequency of ad hoc meetings becomes more apparent when compared to the data on the crisis period: then there were only twice as many ad hoc as institutional meetings. (The gap is exaggerated, however, because records of small institutional group meetings—that is, those held by the Defense Minister—were not readily available for the 1967 post-crisis period.) In 1973, the contrast between periods is even sharper: Institutional consultations exceeded ad hoc meetings in the crisis period by 3 to 1—that is, eighty-five to twenty-six; in the post-crisis period, the figures were reversed—twenty-nine institutional and sixty-three ad hoc meetings. This clear preference for ad hoc consultation in both post-crisis periods seems to indicate that, with decreasing stress, brought about by a de-escalation of threat and/or time pressure and/or probability of war, Israel's decision-makers did not perceive the need for legitimation prior to formal decision-making. Further, the high frequency of ad hoc consultation correlates with declining stress, not with war: During the Six

TABLE 10
CONSULTATIVE MEETINGS BY TYPE AND SIZE:
POST-CRISIS PERIODS

Number of Participants	1967			1973		
	Ad Hoc	Institutional	Total	Ad Hoc	Institutional	Total
small 2	6	–	6	27	4	31
3–4	13	–	13	18	2	20
medium 5–10	6	–	6	17	–	17
large 11–14	4	4	8	1	–	1
15–20	–	1	1	–	–	–
21+	1	2	3	–	23	23
Total	30	7	37	63	29	92

Day War, the 1967 post-crisis period, there were more than four times as many ad hoc as institutional consultations; during the Yom Kippur War, the 1973 crisis period, institutional meetings far outnumbered ad hoc consultations. There is, in short, a high correlation between stress and the ad hoc-institutional ratio of consultation. A de-escalation of stress is also associated with a declining number of consultative meetings, in both the 1967 and 1973 cases, perhaps because less stress leads to less perceived need for support from peers and subordinates. Finally, the difference in the total number of post-crisis consultative meetings (thirty-seven in 1967, ninety-two in 1973–74) can be partly explained by the difference in duration of the two periods—six days in 1967, eighty-four in 1973; the former involved much more intense consultation.

As for the size of consultative meetings in the post-crisis periods, 51% were small, 16% medium, and 33% large in 1967. The distribution was similar in 1973—55.5% small, 18.5% medium, and 26% large. In 1967, there were almost as many large ad hoc as large institutional meetings. In 1973, the pattern was altogether different: All but one of the twenty-four large consultations were institutional; in fact, all but one were within the Cabinet. When declining stress was accompanied by the absence of war, the disposition was to consult the formal body, the Cabinet, rather than any large informal group.

The pattern of consultation in the 1967 post-crisis period was very different from the crisis period. The Military, as evident from the data in Table 11, never met alone with the Prime Minister,

TABLE 11
GROUP PARTICIPATION IN THE CONSULTATIVE PROCESS: POST-CRISIS PERIODS

	1967			1973		
	Meetings with PM alone	Meetings with PM attended by two or more groups	Total	Meetings with PM and/or DM alone	Meetings with PM and/or DM attended by two or more groups	Total
ME	–	8	8	4	16	20
BE	4	14	18	–	23	23
M	10	14	24	9	13	22
PE	–	4	4	1	–	1
KC				1	4	5
U.S.				19	25	44
UN				2	1	3

BE = Bureaucratic Elite   M = Ministers   PM = Prime Minister
DM = Defense Minister   ME = Military Elite   UN = United Nations
KC = Kitchen Cabinet   PE = Political Elite   U.S. = United States

undoubtedly because Eshkol had ceased to hold the Defense portfolio. Since the military elite, including Dayan, were busy with the
operational conduct of the war, the Prime Minister met mainly
with ministerial colleagues and bureaucratic advisers during that
post-crisis period: In fact, they accounted for all single-group
meetings with him and 70 percent of the meetings when two or
more groups were present. Like IDF officers, other politicians
played a minimal role in consultation with the PM because opposition leaders had been incorporated into the National Unity Government.

During the 1973 post-crisis period of protracted negotiations,
U.S. Secretary of State Kissinger was the person most frequently
consulted by Israel's Prime Minister and Defense Minister—alone
more often than all others combined, and more than any other
when two or more groups were present. Among Israeli groups,
Ministers reportedly met more often alone with the Prime Minister and/or Defense Minister than did all others combined, 9 to 6.
IDF officers and civil servants were usually present at meetings
with one or more group(s), especially with U.S. officials, providing
the specialized knowledge required for the extraordinarily minute
negotiations which characterized that period. Other political
leaders and the UN were virtually ignored. Many more consultations were recorded in 1973—one hundred and eighteen compared to fifty-four; but, as noted, the 1973 post-crisis period lasted
almost three months, the 1967 post-crisis period, six days.

Decisional Forums

In the post-crisis period of 1967, as is evident from Table 12, the
decisional forum ranged from one, the Defense Minister, to the
nineteen (of twenty-one) members of the National Unity Government present in Israel. In the 1973 post-crisis period, there was no
variation: The Cabinet as a whole made or approved all the decisions. The principal forum for the assessment of options in 1967
was large, formal, and institutional—that is, the Cabinet or its
Defense Committee. In 1973, by contrast, this function was per-
formed primarily by Israel's Negotiation Team—Meir, Dayan,
Allon, and Eban, later joined by Peres and Rabin—assisted by IDF
specialists and civil servants.

There were several decisional forums in the 1967 post-crisis
period: the Chief of Staff and the Ministerial Defense Committee,

TABLE 12
DECISIONAL FORUMS:
POST-CRISIS PERIODS
1967

Decision Number	Decision	Setting Institutional Large	Ad Hoc Small	Ad Hoc Large
18	Warning to Jordan	C		
19	Attack on Old City Delayed	C		
20	Encircle Old City	COS+MCD		
21	Enter Old City			M+BE
22	Cease Advance East of Canal	COS+MCD		
23	Not to Cross Syrian Border	COS+MCD		
24	Attack on Syria Delayed	COS+MCD		
25	To Scale Golan Heights		DM*	
26	Cease-fire Accepted		M	

1973

Decision Number	Decision	Setting Institutional Large
21	Meir to Washington	C
22	Sign Six-Point Agreement	C
23	Eban re Geneva Conference, Yariv re Km. 101	C
24	Postpone Geneva Conference to 18 December	C
25	Terms of Disengagement	C
26	Insist Veto Right Over New Geneva Parties	C
27	Won't Sit With Syria at Geneva	C
28	Start Negotiations 26 December	C
29	Disengagement Proposal to Kissinger	C
30	Yield on Egyptian Declaration of Non-belligerency	C
31	Accept Interim Agreement	C

*Cabinet Approved
BE = Bureaucratic Elite   DM   = Defense Minister
C   = Cabinet   M   = Ministers
COS = Chief of Staff   MCD = Ministerial Committee on Defense

the Cabinet, the Defense Minister, and Ministers along with Bureaucrats. The first of these made four of the nine decisions; the Cabinet, three others. In the 1973 post-crisis period, there was only one decisional forum: the Cabinet made or approved all eleven decisions. All decisions in both post-crisis periods, except for one in 1967, were made in large settings. This suggests the hypothesis that, as stress declines, routine procedures for choice are reintroduced by Israel's crisis decision-makers.

Alternatives: Search and Evaluation

All of Israel's decisions during the 1967 post-crisis period were influenced by the changing circumstances of war. In particular, the rapid IDF advance, the danger of Soviet intervention, and mounting pressure for a cease-fire made time highly salient. Three decisions, in fact, were dominated by perceived intense time constraints: Decision 18—to prevent Jordan's entry into the war; Decision 21 on Jerusalem; and Decision 25 on the Golan Heights —the last two in the face of an apparently imminent cease-fire. A careful search for alternative paths is not facilitated by a pervasive awareness of severely limited time. And the 1967 post-crisis decisions do not reveal the search dimension. Yet, within the time available, there was an evaluation of instantly understood alternatives. This was most striking regarding Jerusalem: The decision-makers considered with care the alternatives to direct attack on 5, 6, and 7 June and decided in favor of two options—delay and encirclement—before the perceived danger of an imposed cease-fire led to a frontal assault on the Old City. Similarly, they evaluated—and chose—alternatives to a direct attack on the Golan (Decisions 23 and 24) before time pressure led to the decision to scale the Heights. In both of these issues, political concerns were central to the process of evaluating alternatives. And the alternative to immediate acceptance of the call for a cease-fire was assessed (and chosen) in that case for economic reasons—namely, control over the headwaters of the Jordan river system.

During the 1973 post-crisis period, by contrast, time salience was very low, almost to the point of irrelevance, except for the issues of the encircled Egyptian Third Army and Israel's prisoners of war. Only Decision 21—to endorse Prime Minister Meir's visit to Washington—was greatly influenced by the time factor. And even there the alternative—not going—was carefully assessed. During the prolonged negotiations, leading first to the Six-Point Agreement and then to the Interim Agreement, there were no time constraints on the consideration of alternatives. And, as the narrative of the 1973 post-crisis decision process revealed (Chapter 9), Israel's decision-makers examined options very carefully at every decision point. The most striking example was the decision cluster relating to the Geneva Conference. Throughout, the alternatives of not attending at all, delay, and attending subject to conditions (such as not sitting with the Syrian delegation) were considered—and chosen—before making the final decision to participate. The same process of evaluating alternatives is evident in Cabinet discussions prior to the decision concerning the terms of an agreement with Egypt. Neither threat nor time—nor a probable resumption of war—constrained the consideration of alternatives. In 1973, it was a more leisurely process than in 1967, because of the difference in time salience. In both, stress had declined, though in 1967 the awareness of possible missed historic opportunities influenced the evaluation of alternatives, through "positive" stress. Search was much more in evidence in 1973 during the miniscule negotiations. The evidence from both post-crisis periods indicates that de-escalation of stress leads to a careful evaluation of alternatives, and more so when time salience is low.

PART FOUR

CONCLUSIONS

CHAPTER ELEVEN

CRISIS AND COPING: OVERALL FINDINGS

THE PERCEPTIONS and behavior of a single actor, Israel, in two international crises, 1967 and 1973, have been analyzed in terms of the model and related research questions set out in Chapter 1. Comparative findings for each of the three periods of the crises were indicated in Chapters 4, 7, and 10. Overall findings will now be presented, using the same format. The pertinent research questions will first be recalled, to be followed by: (1) relevant findings from other crises and from experimental psychology, small group research, and organizational behavior; (2) total findings from this study, qualitative comparisons for the two crises as a whole and period-by-period changes within a crisis under the impact of changing stress (dynamic intracrisis analysis to complement the static analysis in earlier chapters), and a quantitative analysis of coping mechanisms used in the decision-making process for each of the fifty-seven decisions; and (3) the testing of hypotheses from the crisis literature.

In the concluding chapter, some dimensions of choice in Israel's crisis experience will be explored. And in that light, a revised dynamic model of Israel's crisis perceptions and behavior in 1967 and 1973 will be specified.

PSYCHOLOGICAL ENVIRONMENT
FOR CRISIS BEHAVIOR

Mistrust of Arab intentions has been endemic in Israel since the earliest days of the *Yishuv* (the name of the Jewish community in Palestine before independence). Yet even a predisposition to "worst case" analysis did not induce a perceived probability of war in early May 1967 or at the beginning of October 1973. This sanguine outlook derived from two sources: a decade of tranquility, in the first case, and in the second, an incorrect assessment of Arab military capability. All the senior decision-makers viewed Israel's military situation in 1973 as secure, with the Arab confrontation states lacking a military option. Neither short-term intention nor Arab capability was viewed as constituting a danger of war against Israel. During the last few days in each pre-crisis period, all the decision-makers, especially Meir and Dayan in 1973, manifested disquiet and an emergent perception of threat. Nevertheless, Arab behavior at the outset was seen as a "show of force" (14–16 May 1967) and as "normal" maneuvers (3–4 October 1973).

One of the research questions posed at the beginning of this volume concerned the impact of changing crisis-induced stress on cognitive performance. Holsti and George provide an admirable summary of the consensus findings on the effects of stress on individual performance in foreign policy decision-making: "The overwhelming preponderance of historical and experimental evidence indicates that intense stress . . . impairs cognitive performance." Studies of U.S. foreign policy decision-making, they add, support the "inverted U" or curvilinear relationship between intensity of stress and quality of performance. More specifically, in the context of psychological environment, high stress leads to a reduced span of attention and greater cognitive rigidity. These, in turn, have adverse consequences. The first induces a lower cue awareness and a greater reliance upon past experience in the search stage. The second tends to a decline of general cognitive ability, including creativity and the capacity to cope with complexity. There is, too, a reduced tolerance for ambiguity and an increased emphasis on stereotyping. Moreover, the situation is defined in simplistic, zero-sum terms, and complex problems are viewed in terms of cognitive and emotional predispositions. Intense interaction also leads to fatigue, and that in turn impairs cognitive performance.[1]

Two hypotheses relating to these findings are:

1. "The greater the stress, the greater the conceptual rigidity of an individual, and the more closed to new information the individual becomes."[2]

2. "The greater the crisis, the greater the propensity for decision makers to supplement information about the objective state of affairs with information drawn from their own past experience."[3]

In the 1967 Crisis, stress increased sharply after Nasser's closing of the Straits on 22–23 May: That act was perceived as a grave threat to basic values—namely, Israel's deterrent capability and her access to Africa and Asia. Blockade and the ensuing massive Egyptian military build-up made Israel's decision-makers more acutely conscious of the Holocaust with each passing day, viewing Arab verbal threats and behavior as an intended re-enactment of the Nazi destruction of European Jewry. To the Holocaust syndrome were added two other attitudinal strands from past experience. One was the Ben-Gurion complex, the oft-stated view of the Father of the Nation that it was imperative for Israel to secure active great-power support before embarking on war; that is, it

1. O. R. Holsti and A. L. George, "The Effects of Stress on the Performance of Foreign Policy-Makers," *Political Science Annual*, 6 (1975), 277–281.

2. A combination of Propositions 1 and 2, in H. B. Shapiro and M. A. Gilbert, *Crisis Management: Psychological and Sociological Factors in Decision-Making* (Arlington, Va., 1975), pp. 19, 20. The first half of the hypothesis is derived from J. W. Moffitt and R. Stagner, "Perceptual Rigidity and Closure as a Function of Anxiety," *Journal of Abnormal and Social Psychology*, 52 (1956), 355. The second half is derived from O. R. Holsti, *Crisis, Escalation, War* (Montreal, 1972), pp. 15, 19: "Time pressure . . . impedes the use of available information"; "Unpleasant information and that which does not support preferences and expectations is most likely to fall by the wayside." Supported by psychological findings, as cited by Holsti and George, "The Effects of Stress," pp. 279–280; by evidence from the 1914 Crisis, in Holsti, *Crisis, Escalation, War*, pp. 15, 19; and in the Korean and Cuban Crises, in G. D. Paige, "Comparative Case Analysis of Crisis Decisions: Korea and Cuba," in C. F. Hermann, ed., *International Crises: Insights from Behavioral Research* (New York, 1972), p. 49.

3. G. D. Paige, *The Korean Decision* (New York, 1968), p. 295; T. W. Milburn, "The Management of Crisis," in C. F. Hermann, ed., *International Crises*, p. 274; and psychological findings cited in Holsti and George, "The Effects of Stress," p. 281.

would be folly to fight alone. The other lesson was derived from the Sinai Campaign—namely, the gap between pledges and practices by many international actors regarding freedom of passage through the Straits of Tiran. Together these perceptual elements created widespread gloom about the likely outcome of the 1967 Crisis, including increasing fear in late May and early June for the survival of Israel and her people. Israel's decision-makers were psychologically prone to reliance on past experience as a guide to coping with current threats to basic values.

That proneness first became manifest with the "show of force" interpretation of Egypt's initial despatch of troops to Sinai on 14–15 May, 1967. Rabin and the IDF General Staff perceived Nasser's action and intent as a replay of the February 1960 affair; that is, as a symbolic gesture of support for Syria in the face of Israel's threat of retaliation. Similarly, U Thant's immediate compliance, on the 16th, with Egypt's demand to withdraw UNEF was viewed as a continuation of the UN's pro-Arab stance from the Hammarskjöld era. Nasser's closing of the Straits and the steady growth of Egypt's military power in Sinai during the last week of May were viewed as indicators of the unchanging Arab goal—politicide. Moreover, the signing of a Jordan-Egypt Defense Pact on the 30th called forth the memory of an identical encirclement of Israel in October 1956, on the eve of the Sinai Campaign. And the rapid erosion of the Anglo-American-sponsored international naval flotilla was viewed as confirmation of the deeply rooted belief that Israel would have to ensure her own survival. In short, the psychological environment of Israel's decision-makers in 1967 was dominated by a reliance on past experience which created a greater conceptual rigidity. At the same time, they maintained an open mind to information inputs throughout the Crisis, as will be elaborated below.

The perception-stress link in Israel's Yom Kippur Crisis operated essentially the same way. The self-assured Conception, which was shared by Israel's decision-makers before and during the pre-crisis period, changed drastically with the evidence of growing threat to basic values, near-certain war, and very short time to respond—only ten hours before the joint Egypt-Syria attack on 6 October. Stress was made more intense by the severe setbacks and heavy casualties on both fronts during the first three days of the War. Yet at no time during the 1973 Crisis was there a reversion to the Holocaust syndrome. From the 11th onward, certainly with the crossing of the Canal on the 16th, optimism about the outcome began to be apparent.

There was also frequent reliance on the "lessons of history" during the 1973 Crisis. AMAN evaluations of Arab intent and likely behavior during the four days preceding the War were based partly on past experience—the abortive crisis of May 1973—and partly on the rigid outlook of the Conception. Meir's decision on 6 October against a pre-emptive strike was influenced partly by her memories of the Six Day War, especially the widespread view abroad in 1973 that Israel's pre-emption in 1967 was aggression. The emphasis by all decision-makers upon the American factor, too, was partly a result of consciousness of the crucial U.S. role in the 1956 and 1967 Crises and Wars. And the suspicion of Soviet-American collusion toward the end of the Yom Kippur War was reinforced by the experience of their joint pressure in 1956–57, which had denied Israel a greater sense of security derived from the territorial gains of the Sinai Campaign. That proneness to perceive events, options, and the behavior of other states in a "lessons of history" syndrome, during the 1973 Crisis, replicated the 1967 pattern of conceptual rigidity and reliance on information about past experiences.

Despite increasing stress in the 1967 Crisis from 17 May to 4 June, Israel's decision-makers seemed to be acutely aware of their complex environment. They did not exaggerate or minimize, nor did they have illusions about: U Thant's response to Cairo's demand to withdraw UNEF; Nasser's bravado; intra-Arab rivalries; Soviet mischief in misleading their (the Soviets') clients; the limited capability of the Western Powers in organizing a naval flotilla; de Gaulle's criticism of Israel's claims vis-à-vis the Straits; the deterioration in Israeli morale; and the economic cost of waiting. In 1973, too, the environment was complex. Israel's leaders were uncertain about, but aware of the significance of: Jordan's possible full-scale entry into the Yom Kippur War; the danger of direct Soviet intervention; multiple U.S. commitments and goals; and West European reaction. Increasing stress during both crises did not impair this dimension of cognitive performance.

Israel's decision-makers were subject to intense strain and fatigue, especially during the two crisis periods. These were the product of around-the-clock discussions, the need to process a large volume of information, and the growing sense of fatefulness in the deliberative processes in which they were engaged. In the 1967 Crisis, this was conspicuous at the 27/28 May Cabinet Meeting that resulted in a 9–9 deadlock over the issue of war or further delay. Fatigue and an awareness of escalating danger were even more in evidence during the early and closing days of the Yom Kippur War from 6 to 9 and 20 to 26 October. As will be noted later, extreme fatigue did not impair group cognitive performance, as measured by the care with which alternatives were evaluated. However, the high stress derived from fatigue did affect individual performance. This w̄as evident in Eshkol's stammering broadcast to the nation on 28 May 1967 and in his stubborn clinging to the Defense portfolio at the height of a national crisis. Similarly, Rabin's breakdown from 23 to 25 May revealed extreme fatigue and an inability to cope with the then sharply escalating stress. And in the early stressful days of the 1973 War, the crisis period, Dayan lost his customary self-assurance and became ridden by doubts. He advocated a substantial IDF retreat and exuded acute morbidity about the future in his report to the editors of Israeli newspapers on 9 October. Nevertheless, all three decision-makers overcame the temporary effects of extreme fatigue and were able to restore a high level of cognitive (and decision-making) performance.

In summary, evidence from Israel's 1967 and 1973 Crises about stress and cognitive performance is mixed. As stress increased, her decision-makers relied more heavily on past experience—that is, they manifested greater conceptual rigidity than in noncrisis situations. There were some notable examples of impaired performance, cognitive as well as behavioral, due to extreme fatigue and strain. Thus the second hypothesis noted from the literature is strongly supported, while the first is partly so: New information was not only not rejected; it was sought in both crises (to be noted below). As for the findings indicated by Holsti and George, many are not supported by Israel's crisis experience. High stress did not lead to a reduced span of attention and, with it, a lower cue awareness. Nor did it create a reduced time perspective, a reduced tolerance for ambiguity, or a tendency to premature closure. The situations confronting them were not defined by Israel's crisis decision-makers in simplistic, zero-sum terms. And while complex problems were viewed, in part, through predispositional lenses, these did not determine the decision-makers' approach. On balance,

then, intense and increasing stress impaired cognitive performance in Israel's two crises but not drastically or fundamentally.[4]

COPING: PROCESSES AND MECHANISMS

Information

The second and third research questions, relating to information,
were: What is the impact of changing crisis-induced stress on: (2)
the perceived need and consequent probe for information; and
(3) the receptivity and size of the information-processing group? A
major consequence of high or increasing stress, according to the
Holsti-George summary of findings from other crises and the
literature, is a restricted search for information.[5]

What does the evidence reveal about the stress-information
nexus in the 1967 and 1973 Crises? In 1967, the greater felt need
for information was expressed in several forms: first, in the direct
reporting from AMAN to the Prime Minister, when threat began
to escalate; second, in a growing exchange of letters between Eshkol and Eban, on the one hand, and Heads of Government and
Foreign Ministers of the Four Powers, on the other; third, in the
special missions of Eban and Amit, the former to Paris, London,
and Washington, the latter to Washington; and fourth, in the recall
of Harman, as well as Amit, to provide the latest reliable information before the strategic decision to pre-empt was taken on 4 June.
Thus a correspondence is evident between rising stress and a more
thorough probe for information, deriving from a greater felt need.
The reverse relationship also obtained: The felt need for information declined in the 1967 post-crisis period as threat-induced
stress de-escalated—in the very midst of war. Concern about
external actors' likely behavior was in evidence only with regard to
Soviet intentions and U.S. response, the sole dimension of possible
re-escalating crisis for Israel's decision-makers during the Six
Day War.

4. It should be noted, however, that Holsti and George acknowledge that parts
of their analysis and illustrations, which are drawn largely from U.S. experience,
may have more limited application for small states ("The Effects of Stress," p. 256,
n. 1).

5. O. R. Holsti and A. L. George, "The Effects of Stress," pp. 277–283, 288–
292.

In 1973, too, the link between changing stress and felt need for information can be discerned: in the search for reliable information from the battlefront, most thoroughly during the phases of high stress—6–9 and 20–26 October; in the increasingly agitated demand by Meir for information about the U.S. airlift, from 7 to 14 October; in the Israeli decision-makers' bitterness over the lack of information about the Kissinger-Brezhnev cease-fire arrangement on 19–21 October; in the gravely felt need for information about the likely U.S. response to Soviet threats of direct military intervention, on 23–24 October; and in the need to overcome uncertainty about U.S. intentions and probable action regarding Egypt's Third Army. After the 1973 cease-fire, apart from the Third Army issue, the marked decline of threat and time pressure provided a fillip for a thorough search for information.

Information during the 1967 pre-crisis period was processed by Eshkol and Rabin and, at their discretion, by the Cabinet when it met to approve the early decisions on partial mobilization. As stress increased, especially from 23 May onward, all information about the crisis was elevated to the Cabinet—the top of the decisional pyramid. And for the next thirteen days, it was engaged in daily, often hourly "collective cable reading." Nothing seems to have been withheld. So it remained until the end of the 1967 Crisis: The premier decisional forum received all the information necessary in order to make the required crucial choices during the Six Day War. As stress increased, the receptivity to information became more objective and open. In the post-crisis period of de-escalation of stress, there was a greater tendency for the processing group to revert to biased receptivity—that is, to filter information through a prism dominated by past experience, ideology, etc.

The same pattern of size is evident for 1973. During the low-stress pre-crisis period, information was restricted to a segment of the high-policy elite, the Kitchen Cabinet. With the outbreak of war, and the sharp escalation of stress, information from the battle-front and overseas moved upwards to the full Cabinet. It remained so for most of the Yom Kippur War, the crisis period. As stress declined, however, the information flow changed. Everything went to the four-, later six-person negotiating team, which informed the Cabinet on a selective basis whenever legitimacy and appraisal of its recommendations were required. The 1967 pattern of more open receptivity, however, was not repeated during the

1973 Crisis: most of the incoming information was processed by decision-makers through a biased lens.

As with the growing felt need for information and its elevation to the full Cabinet when stress escalated, Israel's reliance on extraordinary channels for information has been documented in the narrative of the decision flow in the two cases, in Chapters 2, 3, 5, 6, 8, and 9 above. It has also been noted in the period-by-period findings, in Chapters 4, 7, and 10. The greater felt need for information inexorably led the decision-makers to resort to special channels. Suffice it to recall the Eban and Amit missions to Washington during the very high stress crisis period in 1967, as well as the summoning of Harman to Jerusalem on the eve of the decision to pre-empt. In 1973, the counterpart was Meir's frequent and distressed telephonic communications during the high stress wartime crisis period with Ambassador Dinitz in Washington and Foreign Minister Eban in New York, as well as with U.S. officials. When threat-induced stress declined, during the 1967 post-crisis period, normal channels of information flow obtained, even with regard to the tense Johnson-Kosygin "hot line" exchanges over superpower intervention. This was also true in the 1973 post-crisis period, apart from Meir's visit to Washington just after the cease-fire, when threat-induced stress arising from the Third Army issue was high.

The search for more information, with rising stress, also took the form of increasing communication with other international actors. This was highlighted in the 1967 crisis period by the fourteen letters exchanged between Eshkol, on the one hand, and, on the other, Johnson, de Gaulle, Wilson, Kosygin, and the Four Powers. No such communication took place in the pre-crisis period of low stress. More generally, in-coming and out-going cable communications contained more than triple the volume of words in noncrisis situations. In the high stress wartime crisis period of 1973, Meir exchanged notes with Nixon three times and tried to speak with him by phone at least twice. Moreover, there was daily, sometimes more frequent, communication with Kissinger. And the cable traffic, as in 1967, rose markedly.

Consultation: Persons and Groups

Two more research questions were posed earlier about consultation by actors during international crises: What are the effects of

changing stress (4) on the type and size of consultative units, and
(5) on group participation in the consultative process? The only
relevant finding from experimental work on groups is that, "as
stress increases, both the frequency and intensity of interaction
tend to rise." This, in turn, leads to standardized patterns of
behavior.[6]

What does Israel's experience indicate about the stress-consulta-
tion nexus? The escalation of stress in 1967, as noted, was accompanied by a larger number of persons consulted. This was even
more pronounced in 1973. Declining stress led, in 1967, to a
contraction of the consultative circle. In 1973, it was virtually
unchanged.

The overall data on consultative meetings by type and size are
contained in Table 13.

TABLE 13
CONSULTATIVE MEETINGS BY TYPE AND SIZE:
OVERVIEW OF CRISES

Number of Participants	1967			1973		
	Ad Hoc	Institutional	Total	Ad Hoc	Institutional	Total
2	27	15	42	38	38	76
3–4	38	–	38	23	7	30
5–10	30	3	33	29	15	44
11–14	5	7	12	3	5	8
15–20	1	8	9	–	15	15
21+	1	11	12	–	40	40
Total	102	44	146	93	120	213

The ratio of ad hoc to institutional consultations for the 1967
Crisis as a whole was 2.3:1. In 1973, it was .78:1. The major difference in type of consultation is the very high frequency of institutional groups in 1973, at both ends of the size scale. There would
appear to be a twofold explanation, which also may shed light on
the ad hoc–institutional ratio in the two crises. One is Prime
Minister Meir's much greater dependence than Eshkol's upon

6. O. R. Holsti and A. L. George, "The Effects of Stress," p. 289.

military advice (Eshkol, it will be recalled, was also Defense Minister during most of the 1967 Crisis). Furthermore, while Meir's meetings with Dayan in 1973 were all coded as small institutional meetings, there was no Dayan counterpart as Defense Minister until 1 June 1967.

As noted earlier, there were fewer ad hoc than institutional meetings in the 1973 crisis period. The reverse obtained in the 1967 post-crisis period. Both were periods of war. And acute time pressure was perceived in both war periods. Thus the presence or absence of military hostilities and time pressure do not seem to influence the choice of ad hoc or institutional group(s) for consultation by the most senior Israeli decision-makers. Declining crisis-induced stress in the post-crisis periods, however, does indicate a preference for ad hoc group consultation.

In 1967, 55% of the consultative meetings were small, 23% were medium-sized, and 22% were large. For the pre-crisis period, when stress was low, the breakdown was 58%, 25%, and 17%, respectively. For the crisis period, when stress had increased sharply, the distribution was almost identical—56%, 25%, and 19%. And for the post-crisis period, when stress was declining in intensity, 51% of consultative meetings were small, 16% were medium-sized, and 33% were large. In short, the Prime Minister–Defense Minister spent more than half of his consultation time with small groups in all three periods.

The pattern of consultation was similar in the 1973 Crisis: Overall figures were 50% small, 21% medium, and 29% large; for the pre-crisis period—50% small, 20% medium-sized, and 30% large; for the crisis period—44% small, 23.5% medium-sized, and 32.5% large; and for the post-crisis period—55.5% small, 18.5% medium-sized, and 26% large. Thus the size of group consultation in the two Israeli crises shows little variance by period. Nor did it change with escalation or de-escalation of stress. (The figures are drawn from Tables 4, 7, and 10.)

It is also noteworthy that the finding from experimental research, which relates increasing stress to a rise in the frequency of interaction, is supported by Israel's experience in both crises. Moreover, declining stress was accompanied by a reduction in consultative meetings: in 1967, 12 consultations in the low stress pre-crisis period, 97 in the high stress crisis period, and 37 in the moderate declining stress post-crisis period; in 1973, the comparable figures were 10, 111, and 92.

TABLE 14
GROUP PARTICIPATION IN THE CONSULTATIVE PROCESS: OVERVIEW OF CRISES

	1967			1973		
	Meetings with PM alone	Meetings with PM attended by two or more groups	Total	Meetings with PM alone	Meetings with PM and/or DM attended by two or more groups	Total
ME	25	39	64	48	45	93
BE	19	46	65	2	25	27
M	18	36	54	29	17	46
PE	4	10	14	4	–	4
KC				2	13	15
U.S.				21	27	48
UN				2	1	3

BE = Bureaucratic Elite
DM = Defense Minister
KC = Kitchen Cabinet

M = Ministers
ME = Military Elite
PE = Political Elite

PM = Prime Minister
UN = United Nations
U.S. = United States

The ranking of groups in Israel's consultation process may be correlated with escalation and de-escalation of stress in the two crises. The military elite predominated in the 1967 pre-crisis period, the military and bureaucratic elites in the crisis period, and Ministers along with Bureaucrats during the post-crisis period. In 1973, the military elite had a slight edge at the outset and was pre-eminent during the crisis period, when its involvement was greater than all other groups combined. During the post-crisis period of negotiations, consultations with the U.S. (Kissinger) ranked first, with Bureaucrats, Ministers, and the Military closely bunched together (based upon the data in Tables 5, 8, and 11).

For the 1967 and 1973 Crises as a whole, as is evident in Table 14, members of the military elite met *alone* with the Prime Minister and/or Defense Minister more frequently than did any other group; in 1973, it was almost as often as all other Israeli groups combined. The Military met with the senior political leader(s) alone slightly more often than they did when others were present. Bureaucrats were rarely consulted alone in 1973. In terms of overall group consultation, the military elite stands apart in 1973, a further indicator of the character of that crisis compared to 1967.

In 1967, the outcome of the war was determined within hours. Thus the Prime Minister concentrated on its political dimension. In 1973, there were grave setbacks during the early days. The continuous need to make tactical military choices on both fronts necessitated frequent consultations with the Military until the end of the Yom Kippur War, the outcome of which remained blurred even after the tide of battle had turned.

Israel's Cabinet met frequently for consultation, as well as decision-making, during the three-week 1967 Crisis—much more than in noncrisis situations, when it normally convenes once a week. Moreover, as stress increased, especially from 23 May onward, the sessions became longer: for example, they went almost around the clock on 27–28 May. Apart from formal government meetings, there was a myriad of discussions among the inner circle. All this revealed a greater felt need for face-to-face consultation among the decision-makers under the impact of growing crisis-induced stress.

A correlation between the intensity of that need and changing stress is also evident in the 1973 Crisis. During the crisis period, the Yom Kippur War from 6 to 26 October, the Cabinet met daily on the average, sometimes twice a day, and the Knesset Security and Foreign Affairs Committee once a day. Moreover, Ministers felt the need to congregate around the Prime Minister's office in Tel Aviv, sometimes staying all night. And as in 1967, there were many informal small-group discussions. As stress declined, during the post-crisis period, the felt need for consultation declined. Cabinet meetings reverted to the norm, with occasional special sessions.

Decisional Forums

The analysis of settings for crisis decisions in 1967 and 1973 focuses on two other research questions: What are the effects of changing crisis-induced stress (6) on the size and structure of decisional forums, and (7) on authority patterns within decisional units? Consensual findings from the literature and other crises were summarized by Holsti and George as follows: "In high stress situations decision groups tend to become smaller." Moreover, high stress induces greater group cohesion, which often leads to more harmony and emotional support for its members. Face-to-face interaction may increase in frequency and intensity, and in "group think," a tendency to group concurrence and the subordination of dissent, as pressure for conformity grows under the impact of threat.[7]

The findings from our study of two Israeli crises are varied with regard to these themes. An overview of decisional forums in the two Israeli crises is presented in Table 15. Sixty-nine percent of the 1967 decisions, including the four crucial ones, were made in large institutional settings: either the Cabinet or its Defense Committee, or the General Staff. A similar pattern is also evident in the 1973 data: Fifty-five percent of the decisions were taken in large institutional settings.

Cabinet approval of de facto choices was provided in many decisions, but those approvals were decisions, not merely rubber-stamp authorizations. This post hoc support was given for one of two reasons: (1) to legitimate a previous action taken under time pressure; and (2) to share responsibility and/or credit.

During the Six Day War, most military decisions were taken by the Ministerial Defense Committee, an institutional group; for example, approval of Dayan's insistence on 7 June that the IDF advance stop short of the Canal. In the Yom Kippur War, the Kitchen

---

7. O. R. Holsti and A. L. George, "The Effects of Stress," pp. 286–290.

Cabinet (an ad hoc group led by Prime Minister Meir) made many military decisions. Two reasons can be adduced for this difference in decisional forum. First, the two Prime Ministers had a different conception of the Cabinet's role. Second, the psychological environment was totally different. Three hours after the Six Day War started, the decision-makers knew that the war had been won; the main question was how far to advance. Thus the Cabinet was able to delegate authority to the MCD and the Chief of Staff. In October 1973, by contrast, the decision-makers had to weigh defensive measures cautiously in the face of an enemy whose military capability was overestimated by the Defense Minister during the long, agonizing early days.

Although medium-sized groups met with the Prime Minister as often as did large groups during the entire 1967 Crisis, as is evident in Table 13, they rarely made a decision—only two at thirty-three medium-sized meetings, compared with nineteen decisions at thirty-three large meetings; that is, medium-sized groups were called by the Prime Minister almost entirely for consultation. Both decisions by medium-sized groups, as indicated in Table 15, were taken under severe time pressure: Decision 10—to warn the United States of the danger of an imminent Egyptian attack; and Decision 14—to send Amit to Washington. The deliberate task of making a decision in 1967 was always assigned to large institutional groups.

The same pattern obtained during the 1973 Crisis: nineteen of sixty-three large meetings served as decisional forums, compared with nine of forty-four medium-sized meetings. As in 1967, medium-sized groups, ad hoc or institutional, were called together primarily for consultation. On two occasions, decisions were taken by a medium-sized institutional group, both under extreme time pressure: Decision 3 on 5 October—to put the IDF on maximum alert; and Decision 8 on 8 October—to concentrate IDF forces in the North. All decisions by medium-sized ad hoc groups in 1973, too, were taken under time pressure. As in 1967, the explicit task of making a choice among options, when time was less salient, was given to large institutional groups, notably the Cabinet. This was especially true for the 1973 post-crisis period.

Almost all decisions by small institutional groups, in both crises, were made in the pre-crisis period and the early phase of the crisis period, when stress was relatively low. The highest frequency of decisions in 1967 was in the post-crisis period, the Six Day War: at least one, and sometimes two or three, per day. In 1973, this

TABLE 15
DECISIONAL FORUMS BY TYPE AND SIZE:
OVERVIEW OF CRISES
1967

Decision Number	Setting					
	Institutional			Ad Hoc		
	Small	Medium	Large	Small	Medium	Large
1			X			
2	X					
3	X					
4	X					
5			X			
6			X			
7			X			
8			X			
9			X			
10					X	
11			X			
12			X			
13			X			
14					X	
15			X			
16			X			
17			X			
18			X			
19			X			
20			X			
21						X
22			X			
23			X			
24			X			
25				X		
26				X		
Total	3	0	18	2	2	1

occurred in the crisis period, the Yom Kippur War. Thus the largest clusters of decisions correlated with the highest levels of war-induced tensions.

Viewed in terms of the first research question relating to this coping mechanism, the size of Israel's decisional unit increased, more so in 1967 than in 1973, as threat perception escalated and as time pressure became more intense. This finding is contrary to the evidence from other international crises and experimental research, as noted earlier.

TABLE 15 (*Continued*)
DECISIONAL FORUMS BY TYPE AND SIZE:
OVERVIEW OF CRISES

1973

Decision Number	Institutional			Ad Hoc		
	Small	Medium	Large	Small	Medium	Large
1	X					
2						X
3		X				
4			X			
5					X	
6					X	
7					X	
8		X				
9					X	
10	X					
11					X	
12					X	
13				X		
14			X			
15					X	
16			X			
17			X			
18						X
19			X			
20			X			
21			X			
22			X			
23			X			
24			X			
25			X			
26			X			
27			X			
28			X			
29			X			
30			X			
31			X			
Total	2	2	17	1	7	2

As crisis-induced stress escalated in 1967, there was an increasingly felt need for more effective decision-making authority and leadership. It began on 21 May and mounted as threat perception and the expectation of war grew. Dissatisfaction reached its peak after Eshkol's stammering fiasco on the 28th. The demand for his replacement as Defense Minister acquired a relentless pressure until it was satisfied on 1 June. In short, under the impact of rising stress, Israel felt the need for a trusted military leader (Dayan) in control of the Defense Ministry and the IDF.

In 1973, the felt need for authority was satisfied by Meir. The Prime Minister, who by her own admission hardly knew the difference between a division and a corps, was asked to decide upon military moves on 5, 6, 7, 10, 12, and 14 October. Some of these involved choosing the views of Elazar or those of Dayan. When she did so, such was the force of her personality and acknowledged authority that no one challenged her recommendations for decision. As far as is known, the Cabinet did not take a formal vote on decisions. Rather, after (sometimes) lengthy debates, Meir's summaries were accepted, usually unanimously. During the first few days, the Defense Minister's advocacy was sharply divergent from that of the Chief of Staff, as well as that of several ministers. However, Dayan accepted Meir's resolution of these differences at all times.

Alternatives: Search and Evaluation

This aspect of the inquiry into Israel's 1967 and 1973 Crises focused on two other research questions derived from the model: What are the effects of changing stress (8) on the search for, and evaluation of alternatives, and (9) on the perceived range of available alternatives? A major finding from other empirical studies is that high stress leads to a reduced time perspective which, combined with cognitive rigidity, leads to a higher value being placed upon immediate goals, with less attention to the distant future, along with a lower resistance to premature closure. Another finding is that there is a restricted search for alternatives. And the evaluation of alternatives and their consequences tends to be less constrictive, the assessment of costs and benefits less rigorous, and analysis is reduced under the pressure for rapid closure.[8]

8. O. R. Holsti and A. L. George, "The Effects of Stress," pp. 280, 291.

Our findings with regard to search and evaluation for each period of the two crises were presented in Chapters 4, 7, and 10. It is sufficient here to summarize the main themes.

In both pre-crisis periods, there was a resort to routine procedures for evaluating alternatives, because of perceived low threat and very low war likelihood, and because of the availability of standing operating procedures for response to similar challenges. The increase in threat at the outset of the 1967 crisis period led to a substantive initiation of search for options.

A very large part of decision-making time in the high stress crisis period of 1967 was devoted to search for and evaluation of alternatives. The time constraints of the post-crisis period virtually eliminated the search stage. Moreover, many of the 146 meetings between Eshkol and his ministers, as well as between Eshkol and members of the military and bureaucratic elites, were devoted to one or both of these tasks. The pattern of evaluation in 1973 was the same, except that decisions were the outcome of a continuous flow of 213 meetings and consultations.

The postulated inverse relationship between stress and the quality of evaluation of alternatives is not apparent for the 1967 decision-making group as a whole. When stress was relatively low, until 23 May, decision-makers evaluated alternatives with care and made sound decisions—mobilization in stages, diplomacy, and delay. The sharp rise in stress did not lead to a decline in the evaluation process or its outcome. There was a further delay decision on the 28th and, when all the information had been processed, the decision on 4 June to pre-empt. Similarly, the stress of war opportunities did not lead to hasty evaluation of options and premature decisions concerning the Old City, the extent of advance in Sinai, and whether or not to scale the Golan Heights. In all those decisional situations, costs and benefits were carefully weighed; there was no evidence of premature closure; and decisional performance was of uniformly high quality.

In 1973, too, increasing stress did not generally lead to deterioration in the consideration of alternatives. There was, however, variety in the extent of cost-benefit evaluation: *moderate* regarding the highest alert decision and the authorization to mobilize; *rushed,* because of intense time pressure prior to the core decisions in favor of large-scale mobilization and against pre-emption; and *careful* before the decisions to concentrate on the North, and to cross the Canal. A notable exception occurred during the peak stress phase of the crisis period, 6–9 October, particularly with respect to the decision to launch a counterattack in Sinai on the 8th: Options were not carefully weighed, nor were costs and benefits carefully assessed; stress took its toll.

The escalating stress of the (prewar) 1967 crisis period led to a perception of steadily narrowing options, until the *ein breira* (no alternative) situation leading to the 4 June decision to pre-empt. In 1973, too, rising stress, caused by setbacks during the first phase of the (wartime) crisis period, led to a perception of no alternative. Later, as the military situation improved, the range of alternatives for Israel widened. Despite the increasing stress, Israel's decision-makers did not make premature choices during the 1967 crisis period: Alternatives were evaluated, and in many instances with great care, from 19 May onward. In 1973, there were several examples of premature choice: Decisions 7, 10, and 13, respectively. In 1967, there was a growing reliance on group decision-making— with an overall effect of a greater consideration of alternatives, although there were some lapses in specific decisional situations. The same pattern is evident in 1973, with the full Cabinet replacing the Kitchen Cabinet as the principal deliberative and decision-making body.

The evidence reveals that more attention was given to immediate than to long-term objectives by most of the decision-makers in 1967. Foreign Minister Eban was the exception with his emphasis, during the crisis period, on U.S. and world public opinion and governmental support for Israel in the political struggle which would follow a war. An awareness of long-term aims was more apparent in the 1973 deliberations, notably in the decision of 6 October not to pre-empt and in such decisions as not to advance close to Cairo, and to accept the calls for a cease-fire. All post-crisis decisions were influenced by long-range goals of direct negotiations toward a permanent peace settlement.

In the 1967 post-crisis period, threat-induced stress de-escalated almost at once, but rare opportunities to attain long-cherished goals emerged and created high tension. Moreover, the rapid changes created by war made time highly salient. One result was to discourage a search for new options: Decisions 18, 21, and 25 illustrate the effect of perceived time constraints on the search for options. By contrast, the evaluation of known alternatives was careful prior to several key choices: Decisions 19, 20, and 21 on whether to enter the Old City of Jerusalem; and Decisions 23 and 24 concerning an attack on the Golan Heights. Thus, declining crisis-induced stress in 1967 led to little search but did not undermine the evaluation process.

The lengthy 1973 post-crisis period was characterized by moderate and declining stress in which time salience was at a minimum, except over IDF POWs and, at the outset, Egypt's Third Army. The result was a limited search for, and a careful evaluation of, alternatives. This was especially noticeable in the process of arriving at decisions concerning the terms of an interim agreement with Egypt (Decisions 25, 29, and 30). The careful consideration of, as well as limited search for, alternatives was facilitated by low stress, which was the result of absence of threat, time, or war likelihood pressures.

The increasing stress in the 1967 crisis period led to greater attention to immediate than to long-term objectives: how to counter the withdrawal of UNEF, the blockade of the Straits, and Egypt's Sinai military build-up. In the post-crisis period, the focus was much more on long-term political goals. In 1973, long-term goals were more apparent, especially in the evaluation prior to the decisions (1) not to pre-empt, (2) to cross the Canal, (3) to continue the IDF advance west of the Canal, and (4) to accept the second cease-fire.

EVIDENCE AND HYPOTHESES

The effects of changes in perceptions of threat, time, and war likelihood on Israel's coping mechanisms in the 1967 and 1973 Crises have been presented in qualitative terms. These will now be supplemented with quantitative findings. Each of the fifty-seven decisions (twenty-six in 1967, thirty-one in 1973) was coded,* in chronological sequence, for various dimensions of all the four coping mechanisms.[9]

*The coding was done, independently, by Brecher and two assistants. Overall inter-coder reliability was .81. Differences were resolved through the technique of direct discussion and persuasion.

9. These findings are presented with some diffidence, partly because of the novelty of the exercise and partly because of the following acknowledgment by an authority (Lazarus) on the subject: "In reality, we know too little about coping processes to offer any dependable recommendations or interventions to facilitate adaptation under stress for either individuals or groups. Most theoretical treatments, including mine, are descriptive and classificatory, not deterministic, and the

Information   Was the quest for information thorough, modest, or
Processing: marginal? Were the decision-makers receptive to
                     information made available to them; in other words,
                     was their evaluative disposition open or biased—that
                     is, filtered through a prism heavily influenced by past
                     experience, ideology, etc.?

Consultation   How broad was the consultative circle, ranging from
Pattern: one to n groups? What was the distribution of consul-
                     tative meetings held by Israel's Prime Minister and/or
                     Defense Minister, between ad hoc and institutional
                     consultations, for each decision? (Precise data are
                     drawn from Appendix C.)

Decisional   Was the choice-selecting group small (1–4 persons),
Forums: medium-sized (5–10), or large (more than 10)?
                     Was it an institutional or ad hoc forum?

Alternatives: What was the extent of the search for options before
                     reaching the decision—extensive, limited, or pro
                     forma? And was the evaluation of alternatives careful,
                     moderate, or little?

The data on the coping performance for each decision were then clustered into five stress phases corresponding to time periods within each of the two Israeli crises as follows:

1. Low stress—synonymous with the pre-crisis period of both crises.

2. Rising stress—17–22 May 1967 and 10–20 October 1973.

3. Higher stress—23–27 May 1967 and 5, 21–26 October 1973.

4. Peak stress—28 May–4 June 1967 and 6–9 October 1973.

5. Moderate, declining stress—synonymous with the post-crisis periods.

The demarcation of stress phases and the selection of break-points are based upon the findings of the analysis of the psychological environment for choice—that is, of the changing articulated perceptions of threat, time pressure, and probability of war by

---

latter is what is badly needed." During the same reflective address, in Israel, a year after the Yom Kippur War, Lazarus noted, inter alia: (a) Israel's "benign appraisal" of her situation vis-à-vis the Arabs between the 1967 and 1973 Crises— that is, the "Conception," resulting "in inadequate preparatory coping actions which, in turn, contributed to the difficulties in the conduct of that war"; and (b) the post-1973 reappraisal, in the form of blame cast on Israel's political and military leaders, and self-criticism, direct actions which "were largely reactive in their coping efforts" (R. S. Lazarus, "The Psychology of Stress and Coping: With Particular Reference to Israel" [Tel Aviv, 1975], pp. 26–27, 24, 25).

Israel's senior decision-makers—in section B of Chapters 2, 3, 5, 6, 8, and 9 above. It may be noted at the outset that the intensity of stress in 1967 follows a normal bell-shaped curve, in the sequence of the five phases, as specified. In 1973, by contrast, a bimodal distribution is discerned.

The underlying question of this segment of the analysis may be stated thus: Are there patterns of coping which correspond with different levels of stress, induced by differing intensities of perceived threat, time pressure, and war likelihood (or of change in the military balance)? The findings are presented in Tables 16–20.

The decisions in the lowest stress phase, the findings on which are reported in Table 16, were as follows:

1967	1. To issue a threat of retaliation against Syria	7 May
	2. To place the Israel Defense Forces (IDF) on alert	15 May
	3. Limited mobilization	16 May
1973	1. To warn Syria and to despatch the Seventh Brigade to the Golan Heights	26 September
	2. To delay further discussion of the military situation until the regular Cabinet meeting on the 7th	3 October

Findings:

In the low stress phase, there was a modest-to-thorough probe for information, largely involving the IDF's Intelligence Branch (AMAN), before reaching specific military-type decisions (alert, mobilization) or warnings to Syria. However, decision-makers' receptivity to new information was heavily biased, primarily due to the strong effect created by Arab, especially Syrian, military activity. The information was processed, for the most part, by a small group.

The consultative circle, too, was narrow, mostly institutional and small.

The decisional forum was predominantly institutional, but divided between small and large groups.

There was limited search for options; and the assessment of alternatives was little to moderate.

The rising stress phase, the lowest of three in the crisis period, is located, as noted, in different chronological time zones during the two crises: at the outset of the 1967 crisis period, 17–22 May; and

TABLE 16
COPING: LOWEST STRESS PHASE
7–16 May 1967
26 September–4 October 1973

Decision Number	Information			Consultation			Decisional Forums			Alternatives	
					Number of Meetings			Structure			
	Probe	Receptivity	Processing Group	Number of Groups	Ad Hoc	Institutional	Size	Ad Hoc	Institutional	Search	Evaluation
1967											
1	Thorough	Biased	Large	–	–	–	Large		X	Limited	Moderate
2	Thorough	Biased	Small	3	1	3	Small		X	Pro forma	Little
3	Modest	Biased	Small	3	2	3	Small		X	Pro forma	Little
1973											
1	Thorough	Open	Small	2		3	Small		X	Pro forma	Moderate
2	Modest	Biased	Small	4	2	2	Large	X		Limited	Moderate

after the initial sharp escalating phase accompanying the unanticipated Syria-Egypt attack in 1973, 10–20 October. In both of these
phases, however, the level of the three crisis indicators was higher
than in the pre-crisis periods of 1967 and 1973.

The decisions in the rising stress phase, the findings on which
are reported in Table 17, were as follows:

1967	4.	To order further mobilization of IDF reserves	17 May
	5.	To institute large-scale mobilization	19 May
	6.	To shift the IDF from a defensive to an offensive posture	19 May
	7.	To authorize the mobilization decisions	21 May
1973	11.	To launch a general attack on Syria	10 October
	12.	To postpone the IDF crossing of the Suez Canal	12 October
	13.	To accept a cease-fire in place (abortive)	12 October
	14.	To cross the Canal	14 October
	15.	To advance west of the Canal short of Cairo	15 October

Findings:

During the rising stress phase there was a slight decline in the
  search for information; receptivity was much greater, and there
  was a marked broadening of the processing community.

There was, too, a broadening of the consultative circle, along with a
  shift to ad hoc group consultation; however, this tendency differed in the two crises: There was more ad hoc consultation
  before every decision in the 1967 prewar rising stress phase;
  more institutional group consultation before every decision in
  the 1973 *wartime* rising stress phase.

This difference was also present with respect to decisional forums:
  mostly large and all institutional in 1967, mostly medium and all
  but one ad hoc in 1973. In terms of the stress levels, the forum
  continued to be entirely institutional in 1967, when both phases
  were prewar, and moved to ad hoc groups from a prewar to wartime 1973 situation.

There was an increase in the search for options, though it was still
  not thorough, and the evaluation of alternatives was more
  careful.

TABLE 17
COPING: RISING STRESS PHASE
17–22 May 1967
10–20 October 1973

Decision Number	Information			Consultation			Decisional Forums			Alternatives	
	Probe	Receptivity	Processing Group	Number of Groups	Number of Meetings		Size	Structure		Search	Evaluation
					Ad Hoc	Institutional		Ad Hoc	Institutional		
1967											
4	Modest	Biased	Small	5	5	4	Small		X	Pro forma	Careful
5	Thorough	Open	Large	4	8	25	Large		X	Limited	Moderate
6	Thorough	Open	Large	4	8	2	Large		X	Limited	Careful
7	Marginal	Biased	Large	5	5	3	Large		X	Pro forma	Moderate
1973											
11	Thorough	Open	Medium	5	1	5	Medium	X		Extensive	Careful
12	Thorough	Open	Medium	4	1	4	Medium	X		Limited	Careful
13	Modest	Biased	Small	5	2	6	Small	X		Limited	Moderate
14	Thorough	Open	Large	5	2	5	Large		X	Limited	Careful
15	Modest	Biased	Small	5	1	18	Medium	X		Limited	Careful

The second highest stress phase in 1967 followed directly from the rising but still relatively low level of stress at the outset of that crisis. It extended from 23 to 27 May. The counterpart in 1973 combines two time segments: the initial escalation of threat and the introduction of time pressure and awareness of war likelihood at the very beginning of the crisis period, on 5 October; and the re-escalation of threat and time indicators toward the end of the crisis period (which was also the end of the Yom Kippur War), from 21 to 26 October. Both in 1967 and 1973, crisis-induced stress was very high during those phases, though not at their peak.

The decisions in the higher (second highest) stress phase, the findings on which are reported in Table 18, were as follows:

1967	8.	To postpone a decision on military response to Egypt's massing of troops	23 May
	9.	To send Foreign Minister Eban to Washington	23 May
	10.	To warn the U.S. that an Egyptian attack was imminent	25 May
	11.	To await Eban's report on his discussions in Paris, London, and Washington	26 May
1973	3.	To place the IDF on highest alert	5 October
	4.	To empower the Prime Minister and Defense Minister to order up to full mobilization of IDF reserves	5 October
	16.	To accept the first cease-fire	21 October
	17.	To continue IDF operations	22 October
	18.	To continue the IDF advance west of the Canal	23 October
	19.	To accept the second cease-fire	26 October
	20.	To supply Egypt's encircled Third Army	26 October

Findings:

The second highest stress phase manifested a more thorough probe for information; there was a sharp decline in receptivity; and the processing group increased even more.

There was, too, a further broadening of the consultative circle; there were more institutional consultations overall, but a difference between the two crises: near-equality in 1967, more institutional than ad hoc meetings in 1973.

TABLE 18
COPING: HIGHER STRESS PHASE
23–27 May 1967
5, 21–26 October 1973

Decision Number	Information			Consultation			Decisional Forums			Alternatives	
				Number of Groups	Number of Meetings			Structure			
	Probe	Receptivity	Processing Group		Ad Hoc	Institutional	Size	Ad Hoc	Institutional	Search	Evaluation
1967											
8	Modest	Open	Large	5	3	3	Large		X	Extensive	Careful
9	Thorough	Biased	Large	6	3	3	Large		X	Extensive	Moderate
10	Marginal	Biased	Medium	5	6	4	Medium	X		Limited	Moderate
11	Thorough	Biased	Large	4	1	1	Large		X	Limited	Moderate
1973											
3	Modest	Biased	Small	2	2	2	Medium		X	Pro forma	Moderate
4	Thorough	Biased	Large	4	2	1	Large		X	Limited	Moderate
16	Thorough	Biased	Large	6	3	16	Large		X	Extensive	Careful
17	Thorough	Biased	Large	6	2	4	Large		X	Extensive	Careful
18	Modest	Biased	Large	3	2	1	Large	X		Limited	Moderate
19	Thorough	Biased	Large	6	2	5	Large		X	Limited	Careful
20	Thorough	Biased	Large	6	2	5	Large		X	Limited	Careful

The trend to large, institutional forums for decision was very
striking.

There was a more extensive search for options; but evaluation of
alternatives was slightly less careful.

The peak stress phase in 1967 was coterminous with the week
preceding the Six Day War, when the central problem of choice
was whether or not to launch a pre-emptive strike. In the 1973
Crisis, it was the early days of setback after the surprise attack by
Egypt and Syria. Thus, one was a prewar phase of peak stress, the
other, war-induced perceptions of maximum threat and time
pressure.

The decisions in the highest stress phase, the findings on which
are reported in Table 19, were as follows:

1967	12.	To delay a pre-emptive decision again	28 May
	13.	To renew the IDF alert	28 May
	14.	To send Director of Counter-Intelligence Amit to Washington	30 May
	15.	To form a National Unity Government	1 June
	16.	To crystalize military plans	2 June
	17.	To launch a pre-emptive air strike	4 June
1973	5.	Not to pre-empt	6 October
	6.	To order large-scale mobilization of IDF reserves	6 October
	7.	To empower the Chief of Staff to launch a counterattack in the South	7 October
	8.	To concentrate IDF firepower in the North	8 October
	9.	To appoint former Chief-of-Staff Bar-Lev OC South	9 October
	10.	To authorize Prime Minister Meir to visit Washington (abortive)	9 October

Findings:

The quest for information was the most thorough during the highest stress phase; receptivity increased as well, much more so in
the prewar peak phase of 1967 than in 1973, when threat was at
its highest; the processing group remained broad, only slightly
less so than in the second highest stress phase.

TABLE 19
COPING: HIGHEST STRESS PHASE
28 May–4 June 1967   6–9 October 1973

Decision Number	Information			Consultation				Decisional Forums		Alternatives	
	Probe	Receptivity	Processing Group	Number of Groups	Number of Meetings		Size	Structure		Search	Evaluation
					Ad Hoc	Institutional		Ad Hoc	Institutional		
1967											
12	Thorough	Open	Large	9	19	7	Large		X	Extensive	Careful
13	Thorough	Biased	Large	7	2	12	Large		X	Limited	Moderate
14	Thorough	Open	Medium	5	9	3	Medium	X		Limited	Little
15	Thorough	Biased	Large	4	2	2	Large		X	Extensive	Little
16	Thorough	Open	Large	6	4	2	Large		X	Limited	Careful
17	Thorough	Open	Large	8	16	5	Large		X	Extensive	Careful
1973											
5	Modest	Biased	Medium	6	7	4	Medium	X		Limited	Careful
6	Modest	Biased	Medium	6	7	4	Medium	X		Limited	Careful
7	Modest	Biased	Large	6	1	12	Medium	X		Limited	Moderate
8	Thorough	Open	Large	4	3	4	Medium		X	Extensive	Careful
9	Thorough	Biased	Large	4	2	3	Medium	X		Limited	Moderate
10	Thorough	Biased	Small	4	3	6	Small		X	Limited	Little

The consultative circle, too, became broader; but there is no clear
trend in the ad hoc–institional distribution of consultation.

Overall, the size of decisional forums during the peak phase of
stress reveals a split, but there was a marked difference by crisis:
in 1967, the trend to large decisional forums noted for the next
highest stress phase continued; moreover, the trend of very few
small decisional forums continued in both crises, almost all
institutional in 1967, and ad hoc in 1973.

The limited-to-extensive trend in the search for options continued;
and evaluation of alternatives was careful on the whole.

The fifth phase, which was synonymous with the post-crisis
periods, was characterized by moderate and declining stress; that
is, the perceptual indicators of threat, time, and war likelihood
show less intensity and move downward in the direction of the
pre-crisis levels, ultimately to those of noncrisis situations. In
1967, this phase was very short (six days) and was dominated by
war. In 1973, it was a very long (twelve week) postwar negotiation
phase. Yet the two may be taken together, as with the other four
stress phases of the 1967 and 1973 Crises, because of their shared
declining level of stress. The focus of inquiry is identical: What
were the effects of changing stress on Israel's coping mechanisms
in crisis?

The decisions in the moderate, declining stress phase, the findings on which are reported in Table 20, were as follows:

1967	18. To warn Jordan against military intervention	5 June
	19. To delay an attack on Jerusalem's Old City	5 June
	20. To encircle the Old City	6 June
	21. To enter the Old City	7 June
	22. To halt the IDF advance east of the Canal	7 June
	23. Not to cross the Syrian border	7 June
	24. To delay an attack on Syria	8 June
	25. To scale the Golan Heights	9 June
	26. To accept a cease-fire	10 June
1973	21. To authorize Prime Minister Meir to visit Washington	30 October
	22. To accept the Six-Point Agreement	8 November

TABLE 20
COPING: MODERATE, DECLINING STRESS PHASE
5–10 June 1967   26 October 1973–18 January 1974

Decision Number	Information			Consultation			Decisional Forums			Alternatives	
	Probe	Receptivity	Processing Group	Number of Groups	Number of Meetings Ad Hoc	Institutional	Size	Structure Ad Hoc	Institutional	Search	Evaluation
1967											
18	Modest	Open	Large	5	2	2	Large		X	Pro forma	Little
19	Thorough	Biased	Large	3	3	1	Large		X	Extensive	Careful
20	Thorough	Biased	Large	5	7	1	Large		X	Extensive	Careful
21	Modest	Biased	Large	6	18	2	Large	X		Pro forma	Careful
22	Thorough	Biased	Large	4	8	1	Large		X	Limited	Careful
23	Thorough	Biased	Large	4	8	2	Large		X	Limited	Careful
24	Thorough	Biased	Large	5	1	5	Large		X	Extensive	Careful
25	Modest	Biased	Small	5	6	2	Small	X		Pro forma	Careful
26	Modest	Open	Small	4	6	2	Small	X		Limited	Careful
1973											
21	Thorough	Biased	Large	4	0	2	Large		X	Pro forma	Careful
22	Thorough	Biased	Large	6	9	3	Large		X	Limited	Careful
23	Thorough	Open	Large	7	6	4	Large		X	Limited	Careful
24	Modest	Open	Small	4	1	2	Large		X	Limited	Moderate
25	Thorough	Biased	Small	6	3	3	Large		X	Limited	Careful
26	Modest	Biased	Small	6	8	5	Large		X	Limited	Careful
27	Thorough	Biased	Large	4	7	2	Large		X	Limited	Moderate
28	Marginal	Biased	Small	4	1	1	Large		X	Pro forma	Little
29	Thorough	Biased	Small	5	22	10	Large		X	Limited	Careful
30	Thorough	Open	Large	6	6	1	Large		X	Limited	Careful
31	Thorough	Open	Large	5	6	1	Large		X	Pro forma	Moderate

23.	To send Foreign Minister Eban to Washington; General Yariv to Kilometer 101	20 November
24.	To postpone the Geneva Peace Conference to 18 December	25 November
25.	To specify the terms of disengagement	2 December
26.	To insist upon Israel's right of veto over new participants in the Geneva Conference	14 December
27.	Not to sit with Syria at Geneva	17 December
28.	To start negotiations 26 December	21 December
29.	To submit a disengagement proposal to Kissinger	12 January
30.	To yield on Egyptian Declaration on Non-belligerency	15 January
31.	To accept the Interim Agreement	17 January

Findings:

The quest for information remained thorough, but it declined somewhat from the peak phase; receptivity, too, declined; and processing became narrower, though formally most of the situations indicated a large processing group. In reality, almost all of the 1973 decisions were preceded by small-group information processing—by the four-member Negotiating Team.

The consultative circle, too, became narrower; and there was a strong shift to ad hoc consultation.

The decisional forums were overwhelmingly large, mainly due to the decline in time pressure and threat from the peak stress phase.

There was a decline in the search for options; but with less time pressure and threat, the evaluation of alternatives was more careful.

Thus, five distinctive patterns of coping are evident in Israel's crisis experience in 1967 and 1973. The trends within each, from phase to phase, are presented schematically in Table 21.

In the light of these qualitative and quantitative findings, it remains for us to assess relevant hypotheses, derived from other crises and the literature, about the effects of changes in crisis-induced stress on coping.

TABLE 21
STRESS AND COPING
(in percentages)

Stress Phases	Information		Consultation			Decisional Forums		Alternatives	
	Thorough Probe	Open Receptivity	Average Number of groups*	Total Number of meetings*	Ad Hoc	Medium or Large	Institutional	Limited or Extensive Search	Careful Evaluation
Low	60	20	3.0	16	44	40	80	40	–
Rising	55	55	4.7	105	31	78	55	78	67
Higher	64	9	4.8	73	36	100	82	91	45
Highest	75	42	5.75	139	54	92	59	100	50
Moderate declining	65	30	4.9	180	71	90	85	70	75

*Refers to absolute numbers.

Information*

3. "The greater the crisis [that is, the higher the stress], the greater the felt need for information."[10]
4. "The greater the crisis, the more information about it tends to be elevated to the top of the organizational [decisional] pyramid."[11]
5. "The higher the stress in a crisis situation, the greater the tendency to rely upon extraordinary and improvised channels of communication [and information]."[12]
6. "In crises, the rate of communication by a nation's decision makers to international actors outside their country will increase."[13]
7. As crisis-induced stress increases, the search for information is likely to become more active, but it may also become more random and less productive.[14]

Our findings on Israel's crisis behavior in 1967 and 1973, as presented in Chapters 4, 7, and 10, and as summarized in this chapter, especially with regard to the data on information processing in Tables 16–21, support all of these hypotheses, except the last part of Hypothesis 7, which refers to the possibility of less efficiency.[15]

Consultation

8. "The longer the decision time [in a crisis], the greater the consultation with persons outside the core decisional unit."[16]
9. "The greater the crisis, the greater the felt need for face-to-face proximity among decision makers."[17]

*Hypotheses 1 and 2 relate to the psychological environment for choice and were noted and evaluated in that section of this chapter.

10. Paige, *The Korean Decision*, p. 292.
11. Ibid.
12. O. R. Holsti, "Time, Alternatives, and Communications: The 1914 and Cuban Missile Crises," in C. F. Hermann, ed., *International Crises*, p. 75.
13. C. F. Hermann, "Threat, Time, and Surprise: A Simulation of International Crisis," in C. F. Hermann, ed., *International Crises*, pp. 202–204.
14. J. C. March and H. Simon, *Organizations* (New York, 1958), p. 116.
15. O. R. Holsti, too, hypothesizes that as crisis-induced stress rises, information processing becomes less efficient ("Foreign Policy Formation Viewed Cognitively," in R. Axelrod, ed., *Structure of Decision* [Princeton, N.J., 1976], pp. 20–21).
16. Paige, "Comparative Case Analysis of Crisis Decisions," in C. F. Hermann, ed., *International Crises*, p. 52.
17. Paige, *The Korean Decision*, p. 288; and I. L. Janis, *Victims of Groupthink* (Boston, 1972), pp. 4–5.

These hypotheses, too, are supported by the evidence from Israel's 1967 and 1973 crisis behavior, except for an absence of change in the size of the consultative circle from the crisis period to the post-crisis period in the second case.

Decisional Forums

Several hypotheses focus on escalating stress, on the one hand, and, on the other, on intragroup personal contact, leadership, and conflict and consensus within the decision-making group. The first hypothesis has been noted above, in the context of consultation (Hypothesis 9).

10. The longer the crisis, the greater the felt need for effective leadership within decisional units.[18]
11. "The longer the decision time, the greater the conflict within decisional units."[19]
12. "The greater the group conflict aroused by a crisis, the greater the consensus once a decision is reached."[20]
13. "The longer the amount of time available in which to make a decision, the greater will be the consensus on the final choice."[21]

Israel's crisis behavior in 1967 and 1973 also supports these hypotheses, in which continuation of a crisis, decision time, and group conflict may be equated with our notion of crisis-induced stress. However, our findings do not support three important hypotheses on the structure of decisional forums and their authority pattern:

---

18. Paige, *The Korean Decision,* p. 289, and his "Comparative Case Analysis of Crisis Decisions," in C. F. Hermann, ed., *International Crises,* pp. 52, 305.

19. Paige, "Comparative Case Analysis of Crisis Decisions," p. 52. Also supported by U.S. Foreign Service officers' perceptions. See H. H. Lentner, "The Concept of Crisis as Viewed by the United States Department of State," in C. F. Hermann, ed., *International Crises,* p. 133. The Lentner proposition reads: "Crises raise tensions among the policy makers involved and heighten the stress and anxiety they experience."

20. Shapiro and Gilbert, *Crisis Management,* p. 55, derived from findings on business and government decision-making groups, reported in H. Guetzkow and J. Gyr, "An Analysis of Conflict in Decision-Making Groups," *Human Relations,* 7 (1954), 367–381.

21. Shapiro and Gilbert, *Crisis Management,* p. 56, derived from Paige, "Comparative Case Analysis of Crisis Decisions," in C. F. Hermann, ed., *International Crises,* p. 52, and R. L. Frye and T. M. Stritch, "Effects of Timed versus Non-Timed Discussion Upon Measures of Influence and Change in Small Groups," *Journal of Social Psychology,* 63 (1964), 141.

14.   "Crisis decisions tend to be reached by ad hoc decisional units."[22]
15.   "In high stress situations decision groups tend to become smaller."[23]
16.   In crises, decision-making becomes increasingly centralized.[24]

Alternatives

The literature on crisis contains many hypotheses about stress in relation to alternatives:

17.   As stress increases, decision-makers become more concerned with the immediate than the long-run future.[25]
18.   "The greater the reliance on group problem-solving processes, the greater the consideration of alternatives."[26]
19.   During a crisis the search for alternatives occupies a substantial part of decision-making time.[27]
20.   The relationship between stress and group performance in the consideration of alternatives is curvilinear (an inverted U)—more careful as stress rises to a moderate level, less careful as stress becomes intense.[28]

The findings from Israel's behavior in the 1967 and 1973 Crises indicate strong support for these four hypotheses. At the same time, the findings do not support other propositions dealing with stress and alternatives.

22. Paige, *The Korean Decision*, p. 281.
23. Holsti and George, "The Effects of Stress," p. 288, and Hermann, "Threat, Time, and Surprise," in C. F. Hermann, ed., *International Crises*, p. 197. Hypotheses 14 and 15 are so widely reported in the literature, and our findings from Israel's crisis behavior are in such direct conflict, that it was considered necessary, not only to note the lack of support, but also to generate a new hypothesis (No. 10 in the following chapter) from our very clear evidence.
24. Lentner, "The Concept of Crisis as Viewed by the United States Department of State," in C. F. Hermann, ed., *International Crises*, p. 130.
25. O. R. Holsti, "The 1914 Case," *The American Political Science Review*, 59 (June 1965), 365, and *Crisis, Escalation, War*, pp. 14–17, 200; and G. T. Allison and M. H. Halperin, "Bureaucratic Politics," in R. Tanter and R. H. Ullman, eds., *Theory and Policy in International Relations* (Princeton, N.J., 1973), p. 50.
26. Shapiro and Gilbert, *Crisis Management*, p. 83, derived from Paige, "Comparative Case Analysis of Crisis Decisions," in C. F. Hermann, ed., *International Crises*, p. 51.
27. J. A. Robinson, "Crisis: An Appraisal of Concepts and Theories," in C. F. Hermann, ed., *International Crises*, p. 26, based upon H. Simon, "Political Research," in D. Easton, ed., *Varieties of Political Theory* (Englewood Cliffs, N.J., 1966), p. 19. C. F. Hermann, "Threat, Time, and Surprise," in his edited *International Crises*, p. 210, and Holsti, *Crisis, Escalation, War*, p. 121, hypothesize that the search for options, under stress, is reduced.
28. Shapiro and Gilbert, *Crisis Management*, p. 36. Milburn, "The Management of Crisis," in C. F. Hermann, ed., *International Crises*, p. 264; and psychological findings cited in Holsti and George, "The Effects of Stress," p. 278.

21. Despite the rise in stress, choices among alternatives were not, for the most part, made in 1967 and 1973 before adequate information was processed; that is, there was not a tendency to premature closure.[29]

22. As time pressure increased, the choice among alternatives did not become less correct.[30]

23. Finally, decision-makers did not generally choose among alternatives with an inadequate assessment of their consequences.[31]

It has been suggested that Israel is unique. Under these crisis conditions, one would have expected to find little convergence between her crisis behavior and that of large and small states in 1914 or of a superpower later. Yet this exercise of relating our findings to those of the crisis literature in general produces a striking convergence. Israel's behavior in 1967 and 1973 supports seventeen of twenty-three propositions about the effects of crisis-induced stress—notably, through higher threat perception and time pressure, which also have supportive findings from other major international crises of this century involving great and small powers in a multi-state crisis (1914) and a superpower in two recent crises (the U.S. in 1950 in Korea, and in 1962 in the missile crisis in Cuba). Thus, these propositions appear to reflect trends in behavioral response to crisis affecting (1) information processing, (2) consultation, (3) the structure, size, and performance of decision-making groups, and (4) the search-evaluation-choice process.

29. Hermann, "Threat, Time, and Surprise," in Hermann, ed., *International Crises*, p. 210, and Holsti, *Crisis, Escalation, War*, p. 121.

30. Shapiro and Gilbert, *Crisis Management*, pp. 36–37.

31. D. G. Pruitt, "Definition of the Situation as a Determinant of International Action," in H. C. Kelman, ed., *International Behavior* (New York, 1966), p. 411; and psychological findings cited in Holsti and George, "The Effects of Stress," pp. 278–279.

CHAPTER TWELVE

STRESS AND CHOICE

THE ANALYSIS of stress and choice is generally confined to process —that is, to the procedures used by individuals and groups to select one among several perceived options directed to a specific goal. Janis and Mann, in a major work on decision-making, state:

If we have no dependable way of objectively assessing the success of a decision, how can we apply and test the implication of propositions specifying favorable and unfavorable conditions for decision-making activity? Our answer is that all such propositions . . . on the effects of low and high levels of psychological stress can be firmly anchored in observable measures by examining the *quality of the procedures* used by the decision maker in selecting a course of action.[1]

In the model of crisis behavior specified at the beginning of this volume, the procedures for choice comprise information processing, consultation, decisional forum, and the search for and evaluation of alternatives. The *overall* effects of changing stress, induced by changes in perceptions of threat, time, and probability of war, on each of these coping mechanisms have already been summarized for the 1967 and 1973 Israeli crises. *Period-by-period* effects within each crisis have been indicated.

We now confront the second half of the central research question posed earlier: What are the effects of changing crisis-induced stress, mediated through coping mechanisms, on dimensions of

1. I. L. Janis and L. Mann, *Decision Making* (New York, 1977), p. 11.

choice? In order to answer that question and thereby test the utility of the model, three analytic exercises are necessary with respect to each of the choices made by Israel during those two international crises. The first, an examination of the effects of changes in the perceptual indicators of stress on coping mechanisms, was attempted in the preceding chapter. The second is to discover whether distinctive patterns of choice are discernible at different levels of crisis-induced stress. Stated in terms of the model, are changes in stress associated with distinctive choice patterns; or do decision-makers tend to choose differently at various levels of stress? The third task is to present our findings on the impact of changing crisis-induced stress (the dependent variable), filtered through coping mechanisms (the intervening variable), on patterns of choice (the dependent variable).

DIMENSIONS OF CHOICE

Israel's decisions in two international crises have been dissected from that point in time at which options for each problem were narrowed to the most likely choice. Various dimensions of the selected option, the decision, will be explored:

Core inputs: the crucial stimuli to each decision as perceived by the decision-maker(s).

Costs: the perceived magnitude of the loss(es) anticipated from the choice which was made—human (casualties); material (equipment and economic); political (deterrence credibility, alliance potential); and intangibles, such as morale and unity; these were coded as a qualitative composite: low, medium, or high.

Importance: the perceived value of the decision at the time of choice, measured along a five-point ordinal scale: 5–decisive; 4–significant; 3–important; 2–consequential; 1–marginal.

Complexity: the number of issue-areas involved in the choice, ranging from one to four—namely, Military-Security (M-S), Political-Diplomatic (P-D), Economic-Developmental (E-D), Cultural-Status (C-S).

Systemic Domain: the perceived scope of reverberations of the decision, ranging from Domestic alone to Bilateral, Regional, Superpower, and Global—any one or all of which may constitute the Domain.

Process: the mental procedure associated with the selected
                          options, as distinct—but not necessarily different
                          —from the procedure attending the evaluation of
                          all other options considered *prior* to choice; this
                          was coded as Routine (following established
                          procedures for response to similar challenges);
                          Affective (an assessment dominated by reliance on
                          past experience, ideology, rooted beliefs, emotion-
                          al preference, etc.); and Rational (a calculus based
                          upon the measurement of costs and benefits,
                          qualitatively and/or quantitatively).

Activity: the thrust of the decision; coded as to act, to delay,
                          or to not act.

Novelty: the presence or absence of innovation, in terms of
                          reliance on precedent and past choices; coded as
                          yes or no.

Coding was done independently by the author and another specialist on Israel's crisis behavior, with an inter-coder agreement of .85.[2] The findings are specified in terms of the nine choice dimensions for each of the five stress phases, in Tables 22–27. The focus may be stated in the form of a question: Are patterns of choice to be discerned at different levels of perceived threat, time pressure, and probability of war?

The decisions in the lowest stress phase, the findings on which are reported in Table 22, were as follows:

1967   1. To issue a threat of retaliation against Syria   7 May

         2. To place the Israel Defense Forces
            (IDF) on alert   15 May

         3. Limited mobilization   16 May

1973   1. To warn Syria and to despatch the Seventh
            Brigade to the Golan Heights   26 September

         2. To delay further discussion of the military
            situation until the regular Cabinet
            meeting on the 7th   3 October

Findings:
There was only one input in four of the five decisions—namely, hostile Arab acts.

2. The coding is based upon the voluminous data on the psychological environment for choice throughout this volume (Section B of Chapters 2, 3, 5, 6, 8, and 9,
as well as the comparative findings on the psychological setting (Section A of
Chapters 4, 7, 10, and 11).

TABLE 22

DIMENSIONS OF CHOICE: LOWEST STRESS PHASE
7–16 May 1967   26 September–4 October 1973

Decision Number	Core Inputs	Costs	Importance	Complexity	Systemic Domain	Process	Activity	Activity	Novelty
1967									
1	Arab Hostility	Low	2	M-S	Bilateral	Routine	Act	Both	No
2	Arab Hostility	Low	1	M-S	Regional	Routine	Act	Physical	No
3	Arab Hostility	Low	3	M-S	Regional	Routine	Act	Physical	No
1973									
1	Arab Hostility	Low	1	M-S	Bilateral	Routine	Act	Both	No
2	Past Experience								
	Cost of Mobilization								
	Rooted Belief	Low	1	M-S	Regional	Affective	Delay	Verbal	No

M-S = Military-Security

Costs were perceived as low in all five decisions.

The perceived importance of decisions was in the bottom third of the five-point scale, an average value of 1.6; three decisions were at point 1, and none was viewed as crucial—that is, at points 4 or 5.

The scope of choice was narrow, all five decisions being confined to one issue-area.

There were no anticipated reverberations beyond the Middle East region, in any of the five decisions.

The process for arriving at choice was overwhelmingly routine.

There was a decisional disposition to act: All but one decision called for activity; the thrust of activity was physical (mobilization, alert, movement of forces) more often than verbal, with two decisions combining both forms of activity.

There was no novelty, no unprecedented decisions.

In short, the pattern of choice at minimal crisis-induced stress was characterized by physical activity decisions in the military sphere, assessed as of little importance, narrowly perceived as to scope of effects, with a low cost, no novelty, one core input, and a heavy reliance on routine procedures.

The decisions during the rising stress phase, the data for which are presented in Table 23, were as follows:

1967	4. To order further mobilization of IDF reserves	17 May
	5. To institute large-scale mobilization	19 May
	6. To shift the IDF from a defensive to an offensive posture	19 May
	7. To authorize the mobilization decisions	21 May
1973	11. To launch a general attack on Syria	10 October
	12. To postpone the IDF crossing of the Suez Canal	12 October
	13. To accept a cease-fire in place (abortive)	12 October
	14. To cross the canal	14 October
	15. To advance west of the Canal short of Cairo	15 October

Findings:

A marked change occurred in the core inputs to choice. There was much greater variety than in the lowest stress phase; Arab

TABLE 23

DIMENSIONS OF CHOICE: RISING STRESS PHASE
17–22 May 1967   10–20 October 1973

Decision Number	Core Inputs	Costs	Importance	Complexity	Systemic Domain	Process	Activity	Activity	Novelty
1967									
4	Hostile Arab Acts	Medium	3	M-S	Regional	Routine	Act	Physical	No
5	Hostile Arab Acts, Past Experience	High	5	M-S	Regional, S-P, G	Affective	Act	Physical	No
6	Hostile Arab Acts, Past Experience	High	3	M-S	Regional	Affective	Act	Physical	No
7	Hostile Arab Acts	High	1	M-S	Regional	Routine	Act	Verbal	No
1973									
11	Military Capability; Bargaining Potential	High	2	M-S, P-D	Regional	Rational	Act	Physical	No
12	Military Capability	Medium	2	M-S	Regional	Rational	Delay	Physical	Yes
13	Military Capability; Costs	Very High	3	M-S, P-D	Regional, G, S-P	Affective	Act	Both	Yes
14	Military Capability; Status	Very High	4	M-S	Regional	Rational	Act	Physical	Yes
15	Possible Soviet Intervention	Low	3	M-S, P-D	S-P	Rational	Not to Act	Physical	No

G   = Global   P-D = Political-Diplomatic
M-S = Military-Security   S-P = Superpower

hostility and relative military capability were present in each of four decisions; other inputs were past experience, bargaining potential, status, and superpower pressures. Moreover, in the (wartime) 1973 rising stress phase, the perceived balance of Arab-Israeli military capability replaced hostile Arab acts as the pervasive core input.

Perceived costs increased sharply, with only one of nine decisions viewed as low, two very high, and four high.

The gravity of decisions almost doubled in that phase, to midpoint on the scale, with an average of 2.95. Two of the nine choices were viewed by decision-makers as "crucial"—one as "decisive" (point 5), and another as "significant" (point 4).

The scope of choice (complexity) was much broader than in the lowest stress phase: Three of the nine decisions, compared to none, spilled over from the Military-Security to the Political-Diplomatic issue-area.

There was a broadening, too, of the systemic domain in which reverberations were viewed as likely, from the Middle East region to superpower and global spheres; that is, transregional implications were perceived in the choices of that phase.

There was also a striking change in the process to choice, from almost all to only two of nine decisions using routine procedures. In the (nonwar) higher stress phase of 1967, there was a shift to affective evaluation. And when that higher stress was accompanied by a change from nonwar to wartime conditions in 1973, the process to choice was overwhelmingly rational calculus.

While the disposition to act remained very high, two decisions called for delay or nonaction. The thrust of activity remained physical, with one decision solely verbal and another partly so.

There was some tendency to novel choice: Three of nine decisions lacked a precedent in Israel's experience, all in a wartime 1973 phase, compared to none in the (nonwar) lowest stress phase of both crises.

In short, the pattern of choice in the second lowest stress phase was distinctive: There was a perception of more important but not crucial decisions; a moderate awareness of their political implications; an embryonic extension to global and superpower segments of the systemic domain; a sharp increase in perceived costs; a tendency to unprecedented choice; the greatest variety of core inputs; and declining resort to routine procedures to choice.

TABLE 24
DIMENSIONS OF CHOICE: HIGHER STRESS PHASE
23–27 May 1967

Decision Number	Core Inputs	Costs	Importance	Complexity	Systemic Domain	Process	Activity		Novelty
1967									
8	U.S. Pressure	Very High	5	M-S, P-D	G, S-P, Regional	Affective	Delay	Physical	Yes
9	Need for Information re U.S., U.K., French Attitudes	Low	2	P-D	G, S-P, Regional	Rational	Act	Verbal	No
10	U.S. Attitudes	Very High	2	P-D	S-P, Regional	Rational	Act	Verbal	Yes
11	Need for Information about U.S. Attitudes	High	2	P-D	S-P, Regional	Rational	Delay	Verbal	No

G   = Global
M-S = Military-Security

P-D = Political-Diplomatic
S-P = Superpower

TABLE 24 (Continued)

DIMENSIONS OF CHOICE: HIGHER STRESS PHASE

21–26 October 1973

Decision Number	Core Inputs	Costs	Importance	Complexity	Systemic Domain	Process	Activity		Novelty
1973									
3	Hostile Arab Acts	Medium	3	M-S	Regional	Routine	Act	Physical	No
4	Hostile Arab Acts; Costs	High	1	M-S	Regional, G, S-P	Routine	Delay	Physical	No
16	Pressure from both Superpowers	High	4	M-S, P-D	Regional, G, S-P	Rational	Act	Both	No
17	Hostile Arab Acts; Opportunity	Medium	3	M-S	Regional, G, S-P	Rational	Act	Physical	No
18	Opportunity	Medium	3	M-S, P-D	Regional, G, S-P	Routine	Act	Physical	Yes
19	U.S. Pressure	High	5	M-S, P-D	Regional, G, S-P	Rational	Act	Both	No
20	U.S. Pressure	Low	4	M-S, P-D	Bilateral, S-P	Rational	Not to Act	Physical	Yes

G   = Global   P-D = Political-Diplomatic
M-S = Military-Security   S-P = Superpower

The data on choice dimensions during the second highest stress phase are reported in Table 24. The decisions were as follows:

1967	8.	To postpone a decision on military response to Egypt's massing of troops	23 May
	9.	To send Foreign Minister Eban to Washington	23 May
	10.	To warn the U.S. that an Egyptian attack was imminent	25 May
	11.	To await Eban's report on his discussions in Paris, London, and Washington	26 May
1973	3.	To place the IDF on highest alert	5 October
	4.	To empower the Prime Minister and Defense Minister to order up to full mobilization of IDF reserves	5 October
	16.	To accept the first cease-fire	21 October
	17.	To continue IDF operations	22 October
	18.	To continue the IDF advance west of the Canal	23 October
	19.	To accept the second cease-fire	26 October
	20.	To supply Egypt's encircled Third Army	26 October

Findings:

The dominant input in this phase was U.S. pressure or attitudes, present in seven of Israel's eleven choices. The pressure of other powers was perceived in two decisions, Arab hostility in three, opportunity to attain goals in two, and costs in one. More generally, the key stimulus to choice was the American factor, with a remnant of Arab hostility and an emerging perception of opportunity for gain.

The perceived costs remained considerable, with six of eleven choices estimated as high or very high; all high-cost decisions were in 1973.

The importance of decisions continued to rise, with an average of 3.1, just above midpoint on the scale. Moreover, the number of choices viewed as "crucial" by the decision-makers was double that of the rising stress phase: two at point 5 and two at point 4— that is, four of eleven decisions.

Complexity, too, increased markedly, with eight of eleven decisions involving political as well as military content.

The data also reveal a considerable broadening of the systemic domain: Perceptions of reverberations in the superpower arena were present in seven of eleven decisions, and at the global level in four.

There was a slight rise in reliance on routine procedures to choice —in three of eleven decisions. At the same time, an increasing resort to rational calculus is evident—in the making of six choices.

There was a greater disposition to delay or not to act as the crisis indicators rose—three decisions with passive activity and one with nonactivity. There was also a much stronger tendency to verbal activity—three decisions wholly so and two others with combined physical and verbal activity.

There was slightly more novelty—four of eleven decisions being without precedent in Israel's crisis behavior.

Another distinctive pattern of choice is apparent. With higher stress came: a further increase in the perceived importance of decisions; a greater tendency to delay or not to act; more verbal activity; more complexity, with a larger political-diplomatic presence; a much more acute perception of the external domain; an almost unchanged perception of high costs; a modest increase in novel choice; an awareness of U.S. pressure as pre-eminent; and a heavier reliance on rational calculus in proceeding to choice.

Decisions in the peak stress phase, the findings on which are presented in Table 25, were as follows:

1967	12. To delay a pre-emptive decision again	28 May
	13. To renew the IDF alert	28 May
	14. To send Director of Counter-Intelligence Amit to Washington	30 May
	15. To form a National Unity Government	1 June
	16. To crystalize military plans	2 June
	17. To launch a pre-emptive air strike	4 June
1973	5. Not to pre-empt	6 October
	6. To order large-scale mobilization of IDF reserves	6 October
	7. To empower the Chief of Staff to launch a counterattack in the South	7 October

TABLE 25

DIMENSIONS OF CHOICE: HIGHEST STRESS PHASE
28 May–4 June 1967

Decision Number	Core Inputs	Costs	Importance	Complexity	Systemic Domain	Process		Activity	Novelty
1967									
12	U.S., U.K., French Pressure; Economic Costs	Very High	5	M-S, P-D, E	G, S-P, Regional	Rational	Delay	Both	Yes
13	Hostile Arab Acts	High	2	M-S	Regional	Routine	Act	Physical	No
14	Need for Information about U.S. Attitude	High	3	M-S, P-D	S-P	Rational	Act	Verbal	Yes
15	Past Experience; Ideology	Low	4	M-S, P-D, C-S	Domestic, Reg., G, S-P	Affective	Act	Verbal	Yes
16	Past Experience	High	2	M-S	Regional	Rational	Act	Physical	No
17	Past Experience; Domestic Constraints; Deterrence Credibility	Very High	5	M-S, P-D, E	Regional, G, S-P	Rational	Act	Physical	No

C-S = Cultural Status
E = Economic
G = Global

M-S = Military-Security
P-D = Political-Diplomatic
S-P = Superpower

TABLE 25 (*Continued*)
DIMENSIONS OF CHOICE: HIGHEST STRESS PHASE
6–9 October 1973

Decision Number	Core Inputs	Costs	Importance	Complexity	Systemic Domain	Process	Activity		Novelty
1973									
5	U.S. Attitude; World Public Opinion; Past Experience; Military Capability	High	5	M-S, P-D	G, S-P, Regional	Rational	Not to Act	Physical	Yes
6	Hostile Arab Acts	High	4	M-S	Regional, G, S-P	Affective	Act	Physical	No
7	Ideology	Medium	4	M-S	Regional	Routine	Act	Physical	Yes
8	Cost in Equipment and Lives	High	3	M-S	Regional	Rational	Act	Physical	Yes
9	Past Experience; Need for Information	Low	2	M-S	Domestic	Affective	Act	Verbal	Yes
10	Need for Information about U.S. Attitude; Military Capability; Costs; Past Experience	Medium	4	M-S, P-D	S-P	Affective	Act	Verbal	Yes

E = Economic
G = Global
M-S = Military-Security
P-D = Political-Diplomatic
S-P = Superpower

8.   To concentrate IDF firepower in the North   8 October

9.   To appoint former Chief of Staff Bar-Lev as
     OC South   9 October

10. To authorize Prime Minister Meir to visit
     Washington (abortive)   9 October

Findings:

The most striking change occurred in the content, variety, and
   number of perceived key stimuli to choice: There was more than
   one input in eight of the twelve decisions; much greater variety,
   with emphasis on past experience, the need for information, and
   the awareness of cost; and, in substantive terms, an emphasis on
   the "lessons of history" (in six of twelve decisions), information,
   ideology or doctrine, and cost calculations (in three decisions
   each). External stimuli were less salient, with pressure from the
   Powers perceived in only two decisions; and Arab hostility re-
   emerged as highly salient—in four decisions.
Perceived costs increased, with eight of twelve decisions in the
   high or very high category.
The importance of decisions was the highest of any stress phase:
   The average decisional value was 3.6; and no less than seven of
   the twelve choices were viewed at the time to be "crucial"—
   three at the "decisive" point 5 on the scale, and four at the "significant" point 4.
The complexity of choice, too, increased: The Economic-Developmental (E-D) issue-area emerged in Israel's crisis decision-
   making in two of the twelve decisions; three issue-areas were
   present in two decisional situations; and two issue-areas in three
   others.
The focus of systemic domain changed somewhat: The awareness
   of superpower reverberations remained high—in seven of the
   twelve decisions; so too with the global system, in five; and the
   regional arena was present in no less than nine decisions.
There was change, too, in the process to choice—a decline in
   reliance on routine procedures, only two decisions, and a noticeable rise in the resort to affective calculus in four decisions.
More activity was displayed—in ten of twelve decisions. The
   thrust to verbal activity was very marked (in five decisions), a
   result of the perceived need for more information, when confronted with momentous, high-value problems of choice.
Unprecedented decisions continued to increase—eight of twelve
   in this stress phase.

In short, Israel's choices during the highest stress phase in 1967 and 1973 were characterized by: a sharp rise in the number of decisions perceived to be "crucial," along with the highest average decisional value; more active-oriented choices, with a verbal thrust; broader complexity; a narrowing of systemic domain; a further increase in perception of costs; a marked growth in novel decisions; greater variety and content of inputs to choice; and a greater disposition to affective-based decisions.

The data on choice in the post-crisis stress phase, the findings on which are presented in Table 26, were as follows:

1967	18.	To warn Jordan against military intervention	5 June
	19.	To delay an attack on Jerusalem's Old City	5 June
	20.	To encircle the Old City	6 June
	21.	To enter the Old City	7 June
	22.	To cease the IDF advance east of the Canal	7 June
	23.	Not to cross the Syrian border	7 June
	24.	To delay an attack on Syria	8 June
	25.	To scale the Golan Heights	9 June
	26.	To accept a cease-fire	10 June
1973–4	21.	To authorize Prime Minister Meir to visit Washington	30 October
	22.	To accept the Six-Point Agreement	8 November
	23.	To send Foreign Minister Eban to Washington, General Yariv to Km. 101	20 November
	24.	To postpone the Geneva Peace Conference to 18 December	25 November
	25.	To specify the terms of disengagement	2 December
	26.	To insist upon Israel's right of veto over new participants in the Geneva Conference	14 December
	27.	Not to sit with Syria at Geneva	17 December
	28.	To start negotiations 26 December	21 December
	29.	To submit a disengagement proposal to Kissinger	12 January
	30.	To yield on Egyptian Declaration of Non-belligerency	15 January
	31.	To accept the Interim Agreement	17 January

TABLE 26
DIMENSIONS OF CHOICE: MODERATE, DECLINING STRESS PHASE
5–10 June 1967

Decision Number	Core Inputs	Costs	Importance	Complexity	Systemic Domain	Process	Activity	Activity	Novelty
1967									
18	Past Experience; Military Capability	Low	3	M-S, P-D	Regional	Rational	Act	Verbal	Yes
19	Anticipated, G, S-P Pressure	Medium	2	M-S, P-D, C-S	Domestic, G, S-P	Rational	Delay	Physical	Yes
20	Anticipated, G, S-P Pressure	Medium	2	M-S, P-D, C-S	Regional, G, S-P	Rational	Delay	Physical	Yes
21	Ideology; Domestic Pressure; Opportunity	High	4	M-S, P-D, C-S	Domestic, Regional, G, S-P	Affective	Act	Physical	No
22	Soviet Pressure	Low	3	M-S, P-D	Regional, S-P	Affective	Not to Act	Physical	No
23	Soviet Pressure	Low	3	M-S	Regional, S-P	Affective	Not to Act	Physical	Yes
24	Soviet Pressure; Military Capability	Medium	1	M-S	Regional, S-P	Rational	Delay	Physical	No
25	Opportunity	Very High	3	M-S	Regional, G, S-P	Rational	Act	Physical	Yes
26	G, S-P Pressure	Low	3	M-S, P-D	Regional, G, S-P	Rational	Act	Both	No

C-S = Cultural Status
G = Global
M-S = Military-Security

P-D = Political-Diplomatic
S-P = Superpower

TABLE 26 (*Continued*)
DIMENSIONS OF CHOICE: MODERATE, DECLINING STRESS PHASE
26 October 1973–18 January 1974

Decision Number	Core Inputs	Costs	Importance	Complexity	Systemic Domain	Process	Activity	Activity	Novelty
1973									
21	U.S. Pressure; POWs	Low	3	P-D	Regional, S-P	Affective	Act	Verbal	No
22	U.S. Pressure	Low	4	P-D, M-S	Regional, S-P	Rational	Act	Verbal	Yes
23	Military Strategy; U.S. Pressure; Information Search	Low	3	P-D, M-S	Regional, S-P	Rational	Act	Verbal	Yes
24	Pending Elections	Low	1	P-D	Regional, G, S-P	Affective	Delay	Verbal	Yes
25	Arab Hostility; Military Strategy	Medium	3	P-D, M-S	Regional, G, S-P	Rational	Act	Verbal	No
26	Arab Hostility; Hostility to Palestinians	Medium	3	P-D	Regional, G, S-P	Affective	Delay	Verbal	Yes
27	POWs; Ideology	Low	1	P-D	Regional, G, S-P	Affective	Not to Act	Verbal	Yes
28	Pending Elections	Low	1	P-D	Regional, G, S-P	Affective	Delay	Verbal	No
29	Military Strategy	Medium	3	M-S, P-D	Regional	Rational	Act	Both	Yes
30	U.S. Pressure	High	3	M-S, P-D	Regional, G, S-P	Rational	Act	Verbal	Yes
31	Military Strategy	Medium	1	M-S, P-D	Regional	Rational	Act	Both	Yes

C-S = Cultural-Status   P-D = Political-Diplomatic
G   = Global   S-P = Superpower
M-S = Military-Security

Findings:

There was a decline from the peak stress phase in the number of core inputs to choice, with more than one input in eleven of twenty decisions (six of nine decisions in 1967, five of eleven in 1973). The variety was, however, as large, with anticipated U.S. pressure and Soviet pressure the most frequent, in seven and six decisions, respectively. Other stimuli were military capability or strategy (in six decisions), pending elections (three), prisoners of war (two), ideology (two), opportunity for gain (two), past experience (one), and information need (one).

Cost perception declined sharply to medium-low, in seventeen of twenty decisions.

There was also a marked decline in perceived importance of decisions: The average decisional value was 2.5, a sharp reduction from the peak phase (3.6) and lower than all three stress phases of the crisis period; but it remained higher than the average for the pre-crisis period; this decline is evident for both the short, wartime 1967 post-crisis period and the long, negotiation 1973 phase. Not a single decision in the post-crisis phase was perceived to be "decisive," point 5 on the scale, and only two were at point 4.

Complexity revealed an increase from the peak stress phase, with twelve of twenty decisions involving two or more issue-areas; and complexity was of the same order in the moderate phase of both crises, though 1967 witnessed the extension to the Cultural-Status (C-S) issue-area as well.

The domain of expected reverberations from decisions widened; in fact, it was the broadest of all stress phases in both crises. There was more than one domain in seventeen of twenty decisions; and pervasiveness of the superpower domain is also evident—in seventeen decisions (eight of nine in 1967, nine of eleven in 1973).

There was a slightly greater disposition to rational choice than at the highest level of stress—in twelve of twenty decisions (six of nine in 1967, six of eleven in 1973); so too with affective calculus —eight of twenty; and there was no resort to routine procedures.

The tendency to make action-type decisions dropped sharply in only half of the twenty decisions. The thrust to verbal activity rose sharply in the 1973 moderate phase: in all eleven decisions. The combined data for the two crises shows a slight increase in that phase as a whole: thirteen of twenty decisions.

Resort to unprecedented decisions remained high in thirteen instances.

In summary, the pattern of choice during the post-crisis moderate stress phase revealed: a decline in the perceived importance of decisions, with an average value lower than the lowest of the three stress phases of the crisis period; a similar decline in action choices; a sharp rise in verbal activity in the decisions; an increase in both their complexity and systemic domain; a sharp reduction in perceived costs; a continued high proportion of unprecedented choices; a decline in the number of inputs; and a higher disposition to rational and affective procedures to choice.

The composite findings on stress and choice are set out, in proportional terms, in Table 27.

NEW HYPOTHESES ON CRISIS BEHAVIOR

The impact of changes in crisis-induced stress, as mediated through coping, on Israel's choices will now be summarized through two time sequences: first, within each of the five stress phases, from changes in stress (time t_2),[3] through coping (t_3), to choice (t_4); and second, from one phase to another through both crises for each of the coping mechanisms and patterns of choice at different levels of stress. These findings are presented in a combined horizontal (short-time) and vertical (long-time) format in Table 28.

Coping Mechanisms

Information-Processing

As crisis-induced stress rises:

1. The quest for information about the threatening event(s) tends to become more thorough.[4]
2. Decision-makers' receptivity to new information tends to become more open.

3. Environmental change, the trigger to perceptions of threat, time pressure, and probability of war, is the first development; that is, it occurs at time t_1.
4. This is the operational counterpart of a well-known hypothesis which was tested earlier, concerning the link between rising stress and greater felt need for information.

TABLE 27
STRESS AND DIMENSIONS OF CHOICE
(in percentages)

Stress Phases	More than One Core Input	Very High or High Cost Estimation	Importance*	Complexity†	Systemic Domain‡	Rational Process	Activity		
							To Delay or Not to Act	Verbal	Novelty
Low	20	–	–	–	–	–	20	60	–
Rising	67	67	22	33	22	44	22	22	33
Higher	18	55	36	45	91	55	36	45	36
Highest	58	67	58	50	42	50	17	42	66
Moderate Declining	35	10	10	60	85	60	50	65	65

* The proportion of decisions perceived as point 5 ("decisive") or point 4 ("significant").
† More than one issue area.
‡ More than one level of expected reverberations.

As crisis-induced stress declines:[5]

3. The quest for information becomes more restricted.
4. Receptivity becomes permeated by more bias.

Consultation

As crisis-induced stress rises:

5. The scope of consultation by senior decision-makers broadens steadily.
6. Decision-makers increasingly use ad hoc forms of consultation.
7. The frequency of high-level consultation increases sharply.

As crisis-induced stress declines:

8. The consultative circle becomes narrower.
9. Consultation relies heavily on ad hoc settings as high-level consultation reaches its peak.

Decisional Forums

As crisis-induced stress rises:

10. There is a heavy reliance on medium-large and institutional forums for decisions.

As crisis-induced stress declines:

11. There is a maximum reliance on large, institutional forums for decision, regardless of whether it is a war or postwar phase.

Alternatives

As crisis-induced stress rises:

12. The search for options tends to increase.
13. The evaluation of alternatives becomes less careful.

5. Virtually the entire literature on crisis is concerned with the effects of *increasing* stress or more intense crisis on behavior. Only four of the 311 hypotheses on crisis in the Hermann inventory (C. F. Hermann, ed., *International Crises* [New York, 1972], pp. 304–320) refer explicitly to the consequences of *decreasing* stress or less intense crisis. Exceptions are found in the work of Charles McClelland and Edward Azar. See, for example, McClelland, "The Beginning, Duration, and Abatement of International Crises: Comparisons in Two Conflict Arenas," in C. F. Hermann, ed., *International Crises*, pp. 83–105, which generated the four hypotheses referred to; and Edward E. Azar, "Conflict Escalation and Conflict Reduction in an International Crisis: Suez, 1956," *The Journal of Conflict Resolution*, 16 (June 1972), 183–201. There is also a brief discussion of the declining phase of crisis in G. H. Snyder and P. Diesing, *Conflict Among Nations* (Princeton, N.J., 1977), pp. 14–21, 497–503.

TABLE 28
STRESS, COPING, AND CHOICE: OVERALL PATTERNS

STRESS PHASE	COPING: PROCESS AND MECHANISMS				CHOICE
	Information	Consultation	Decisional Forums	Alternatives	
Low	modest to thorough search; heavily biased receptivity; small processing group	narrow base; institutional type; few meetings	predominantly institutional	little search; moderate evaluation	Pattern I one core input—Arab hostility; low cost; low importance; Military-Security issue area only; regional effects; routine procedure to choice; physical activity; no novelty—reliance on precedent
Rising	slight decline in search; much greater receptivity; broader processing group	broader; ad hoc, 1967; institutional type, 1973; very sharp rise in frequency	large institutional, 1967; medium ad hoc, 1973	more search; much more careful evaluation	Pattern II most variety of core inputs; sharp increase in perceived costs; marked rise in importance; moderate awareness of political implications; global and superpower reverberations; less resort to routine procedures; continued physical activity; some tendency to novel choice
Higher	more thorough search; sharp decline in receptivity; further growth of processing group	same breadth; tendency to institutional type; decline in meetings	striking rise in large institutional forums	further increase in search; a little less careful evaluation	Pattern III pre-eminence of superpower (U.S.) input, with declining variety of stimuli; continued high costs perceived; higher importance; higher political content; much greater awareness of superpower and global implications; more reliance on rational procedures to choice; more nonaction verbal activity; slight rise in novelty

TABLE 28 (*Continued*)
STRESS, COPING, AND CHOICE: OVERALL PATTERNS

STRESS PHASE	COPING: PROCESS AND MECHANISMS				CHOICE
	Information	Consultation	Decisional Forums	Alternatives	
Highest	most thorough search; marked increase in receptivity; large processing group	broadest; more ad hoc; sharp rise in frequency	large institutional, 1967; medium ad hoc, 1973	most search; slightly more careful evaluation	*Pattern IV* increase in variety and number of inputs; increase in perceived costs; maximum importance; broader complexity, extending to economic sphere; more regional and domestic focus in systemic domain; increased reliance on affect in choice; more active; great increase of unprecedented decisions
Moderate Declining	slightly less thorough search; reduction in receptivity; unchanged processing group	narrowing of circle; increase in ad hoc meetings; most consultations	overwhelmingly large institutional	decline in search; most careful evaluation	*Pattern V* decline in number and variety of inputs; sharp decline in perceived costs; marked reduction in perceived importance; broadest complexity; wider systemic domain; more analytic and affective procedures to choice; sharp reduction in activity, with highest verbal-type action; continued resort to novel decisions.

As crisis-induced stress declines:

14. The search for options tends to become less extensive than in all
     three phases of the crisis period.
15. The evaluation of alternatives reaches its maximum care, more so
     when time salience is low.

Stress and Choice

Core Inputs
As crisis-induced stress begins to rise:

16. The number and variety of core inputs to decisions increases
     sharply.

As crisis-induced stress declines:

17. The number and variety of core inputs are reduced.

Costs

18. When decision-makers operate under stress, they assess their
     decision as costly.
19. When decision-makers operate under low or declining stress, they
     perceive their decisions as of small cost.

Importance
As crisis-induced stress rises:

20. Decision-makers tend to perceive their decisions as more and more
     important.

As crisis-induced stress declines:

21. The perceived importance of decisions declines from the levels in
     the three phases of the crisis period.

Complexity
As crisis-induced stress rises:

22. The complexity of issue-areas involved steadily rises.

As crisis-induced stress declines:

23. The number of issue-areas involved in decision-making reaches its
     maximum.

Systemic Domain
In situations of peak crisis-induced stress:

24.   The heretofore steadily-broadening systemic levels of anticipated reverberations from decisions become narrower.

As crisis-induced stress declines:

25.   Systemic domain rises from the peak crisis phase.

Process

As crisis-induced stress rises:

26.   The selected option tends to be chosen by rational calculus.

As crisis-induced stress declines:

27.   Decision-makers resort mainly to rational procedures to ultimate choice.

Activity

As crisis-induced stress rises:

28.   There is a tendency for decisions to be continuously active.
29.   The activity implied by the decisions moves from physical to verbal.

As crisis-induced stress declines:

30.   There is a sharp increase in decisions to delay or to not act.

Novelty

As crisis-induced stress rises:

31.   There is a steady increase in resort to choices without precedent.

As crisis-induced stress declines:

32.   Unprecedented choices remain at their peak.

From the findings uncovered in the preceding analysis of stress, coping, and choice, and from the summary in Table 28, one may also induce associational propositions between the dependent variable, choice, and the intervening variable, coping. Several illustrations follow.

Proposition 1

As the number and variety of core inputs to choice increases, up to the peak crisis phase, the search for information and its receptivity also increase, along with a broadening of the consultative circle, an enlargement of the decisional forums, and an increase in both the search for and evaluation of alternatives.

Proposition 2

As stress moves downward from the peak, an inverse relationship develops between the number and variety of core inputs, on the one hand, and information search and the consideration of alternatives, on the other.

Proposition 3

There is a direct relationship between the perceived importance of a decisional problem and the pattern of information—that is, between the thoroughness of the probe and the openness of processing.

Proposition 4

As decision-makers perceive their problem of choice to be more important, they engage in steadily increasing consultation, resort to large institutional forums for decision-making, search more extensively for options, and evaluate alternatives more carefully.

Proposition 5

The same direct association is evident between the perceived complexity of choice, on the one hand, and the patterns of consultation, decisional forum, search for options, and evaluation of alternatives, on the other.

Proposition 6

As stress rises, there is a direct relationship between changes in procedures for decision-making, from routine to affective to rational, on the one hand, and, on the other, an increasing probe for information to which decision-makers are receptive.[6]

On the basis of this analysis, it may be concluded that changes in crisis-induced stress, as mediated through changes in coping mechanisms, led to choice patterns with distinctive content traits

---

6. As with the dearth of hypotheses on declining crisis-induced stress and coping, there are none in the Hermann inventory or, to the best of our knowledge, elsewhere which relate crisis-induced stress, rising or declining, to substantive aspects of choice, the second part of the dual linkage or two-flow model.

or dimensions. Stated differently, the model has been tested with the evidence of Israel's behavior in the 1967 and 1973 Crises and has been found to be valid.

The three-stage model of crisis behavior specified in Chapter 1, as adapted to Israel's behavior in 1967 and 1973, may now be presented graphically (Figure 3).

A model of state behavior in international crisis has been specified and operationalized. Its utility has been demonstrated through hypothesis-generation. And its claim to validity is supported by the prediction of choice patterns with distinct content traits in different stress phases. It is highly probable that other international actors experience different effects of changing stress on their coping processes and choice patterns. However, it is reasonable to conclude that these are discoverable through a model-directed systematic empirical analysis of state behavior in crisis, with a potential for more effective crisis management in the future.

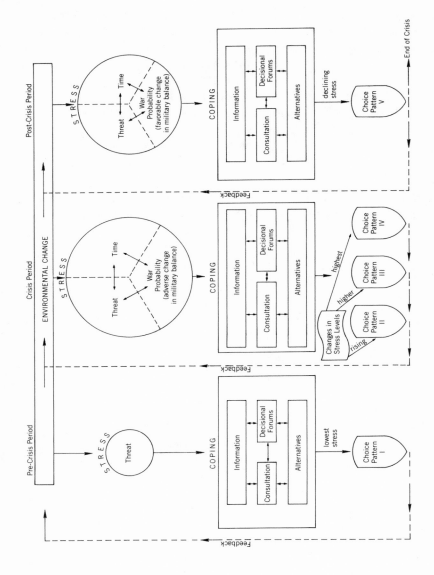

Figure 3. A Three-Stage Model of Israel's Crisis Behavior: 1967 and 1973

DECISION-MAKERS AND THE CONSULTATIVE CIRCLE

THE 1967 AND 1973 CRISES

Members of the Government

ALLON, YIGAL
Ahdut Ha'avoda
Alignment
Israel Labor Party
(ILP)

born 1918 in Palestine; in the 1948 War, commander of the *Palmah;* joined the Cabinet as Minister of Labor in November 1961; held that post in May–June 1967; Deputy Prime Minister and Minister of Education during the 1973 Crisis.

BURG, S. YOSEPH
National Religious
Party (NRP) or *Mafdal*

born 1909 in Germany; joined the Cabinet in October 1951 as Minister of Health; apart from June 1958–December 1959 and December 1976–May 1977, a member of every Israeli Government thereafter; in May–June 1967 he was Minister of Social Welfare, and in 1973 he was Minister of Interior.

DAYAN, MOSHE
Mapai
Rafi
Alignment
ILP

born 1915 in Palestine; IDF Chief of Staff, 1953–1958; joined the Cabinet in December 1959 as Minister of Agriculture; resigned in October 1964 and returned as Minister of Defense on 1 June 1967; held that position in 1973.

EBAN, ABBA
Mapai
Alignment
ILP

born 1915 in South Africa; Israel's Ambassador to the United States, 1949–1959; Ambassador to the United Nations, 1950–1959; joined the Cabinet as Minister Without Portfolio in 1959; Minister for

Foreign Affairs from January 1966 to
May 1974.

GALILI, YISRAEL
Ahdut Ha'avoda
Alignment
ILP

born 1911 in Poland; a commander of the
Hagana prior to 1948; joined the Cabinet
in January 1966 as Minister Without Portfolio and held that position until 1977.

GVATI, HAIM
Mapai
Alignment
ILP

born 1901 in Poland; Minister of Agriculture, 1964–1974.

KOL, MOSHE
Progressive
Independent Liberal

born 1911 in Poland; Minister of Development and Tourism, 1966–1977.

SAPIR, PINHAS
Mapai
Alignment
ILP

1909–1975. Born in Poland; joined the
Cabinet in November 1955 as Minister of
Commerce and Industry; Minister of
Finance, 1963–1968 and 1969–1974.

**SHAPIRO, YA'ACOV
SHIMSHON**
Mapai
Alignment
ILP

born 1902 in Russia; joined the Cabinet in
1966 as Minister of Justice; held that
position until his resignation immediately
after the cease-fire of 26 October 1973.

SHAREF, ZE'EV
Mapai

born 1906 in Rumania; Secretary to the
Government, 1948–1957; Minister of
Commerce and Industry, 1966–1969 (also
Minister of Finance 1968–1969); Minister
of Housing, 1969–1974.

WARHAFTIG, ZERAH
NRP

born 1906 in Poland; Minister for Religious Affairs, 1961–1974.

Bureaucratic Elite

EVRON, EPHRAIM

born 1921 in Palestine; in 1967 he was
Minister in the Washington Embassy;
in 1973 he was Deputy Director-General
of the Foreign Ministry.

Military Elite

BAR-LEV, HAIM

appointed IDF Deputy Chief of Staff on
1 June 1967; and as de facto OC Southern
Command on 9 October 1973. (See also
Members of the Government for the
1973 Crisis.)

YARIV, AHARON — born 1920 in Latvia; Director of Military Intelligence (AMAN), 1962–1971; special consultant to the Prime Minister, 1972–1975.

THE 1967 CRISIS

Members of the Government

ESHKOL, LEVI
Mapai
Alignment
ILP

1895–1969. Born in Russia; joined the Cabinet in October 1951 as Minister of Agriculture and Development; member of every Government from 1951 to 1969; June 1963–1 June 1967, Prime Minister and Defense Minister; from 1 June 1967 until his death in 1969, Prime Minister.

ARANNE, ZALMAN
Mapai
Alignment
ILP

1899–1970. Born in Russia; joined the Cabinet as Minister Without Portfolio in January 1954; Minister of Education and Culture, June 1963–December 1969.

BARZILAI, YISRAEL
Mapam
Alignment

1913–1970. Born in Poland; joined the Cabinet in November 1955 as Minister of Health and held that position in May–June 1967.

BEGIN, MENAHEM
Herut
Gahal
Likud

born 1913 in Poland; leader of the Right-wing underground resistance organization, IZL, before 1948; the leading Opposition figure until 1967; joined the Cabinet as Minister Without Portfolio on 1 June 1967. (See 1973 Crisis list.)

BENTOV, MORDEKHAI
Mapam
Alignment

born 1900 in Poland; a member of the Provisional Government in 1948–1949 as Minister of Labor and Construction; Minister of Housing, January 1966–December 1969.

CARMEL, MOSHE
Ahdut Ha'avoda
Alignment
ILP

born 1911 in Poland; Brigade Commander in the 1948 War of Independence; joined the Cabinet in November 1955 as Minister of Transport and held that portfolio in 1967.

SAPHIR, YOSEPH
Liberal
Gahal

1902–1971. Born in Palestine; Minister of Transport, December 1952–June 1955; on 2 June 1967 he became Minister Without Portfolio.

SASSON, ELIAHU
   Mapai
   Alignment

1902–1978. Born in Syria; joined the Cabinet as Minister of Posts in November 1961; in 1967 he was Minister of Police.

SHAPIRA, HAIM MOSHE
   NRP

1902–1970. Born in Poland; a member of every Government from 1948 to 1970, except from June 1958 to December 1959; in 1967 he was Minister of Interior.

YESHAYAHU, YISRAEL
   Mapai
   Alignment

1910–1979. Born in Yemen; in 1967 he was Minister of Posts.

Other Party Leaders and Persons Consulted

AVIGUR, SHAUL
   Mapai
   Alignment

1899–1978. Born in Latvia; involved in security matters since 1948; member of highest *Mapai* organs; in May 1967 he was an intermediary in the Eshkol-Dayan negotiations.

BEN-GURION, DAVID
   Mapai
   Rafi

1886–1973. Born in Poland; Prime Minister and Defense Minister, 1948–1963 (except for January 1954–February 1955; resumed PM post in November 1955); in May–June 1967 he was Israel's elder statesman and leader of *Rafi*.

DINSTEIN, ZVI
   Mapai
   Alignment
   ILP

born 1926 in Palestine; Deputy Minister of Defense in 1967.

MEIR, GOLDA
   Mapai
   Alignment
   ILP

See 1973 Cabinet list. In 1967 she was Secretary-General of the Israel Labor Party and a confidant of Eshkol.

PERES, SHIMON
   Mapai
   Rafi
   Alignment
   ILP

See 1973 Cabinet list. He was a central figure in the 1967 domestic political crisis.

YADIN, YIGAEL
   non-party

born 1917 in Palestine; Chief of Operations, IDF, in 1948 War of Independence; Chief of Staff, 1949–1952; a trusted military adviser of Eshkol; became Eshkol's link to Defense Minister and General Staff after 1 June 1967.

Bureaucratic Elite

BITAN, MOSHE
born 1918 in Czechoslovakia; in 1967 he was Assistant Director-General of the Foreign Ministry, in charge of the United States desk.

HARMAN, AVRAHAM
born 1914 in England; in 1967 he was Israeli Ambassador to the United States.

HERZOG, YA'ACOV
1921–1972. Born in Ireland; in 1967 he was Director-General of the Prime Minister's Office and Eshkol's closest bureaucratic adviser.

LEVAVI, ARYE
born 1912 in Russia; in 1967 he was Director-General of the Foreign Ministry.

RAFAEL, GIDEON
born 1913 in Germany; in 1967 he was Israel's Representative to the UN.

YAFFE, AVIAD
1923–1977. Born in Palestine; in 1967 he was Eshkol's Political Secretary and Head of the Prime Minister's Bureau.

Military Elite

AMIT, MEIR
born 1921 in Palestine; senior officer in IDF for many years; in 1967 he was Head of *Ha-Mossad* (Counter-Intelligence Service) and one of Eshkol's most important sources of information on military-security matters.

RABIN, YITZHAK
born 1922 in Palestine; in 1967 he was Chief of Staff and principal military adviser to Eshkol.

WEIZMAN, EZER
born 1924 in Palestine; Commander of the Israeli Air Force; in 1967 he was Chief of Operations of the IDF.

THE 1973 CRISIS

Members of the Government

MEIR, GOLDA
Mapai
Alignment
ILP
1898–1978. Born in Russia; Minister of Labor, 1949–1956; Foreign Minister, 1956–1966; Prime Minister, 1969–1974. (See Other Party Leaders, 1967.)

ALMOGI, YOSEPH
  Mapai
  Rafi
  Alignment
  ILP

born 1910 in Poland; joined the Cabinet as Minister Without Portfolio in November 1961; in 1973 he was Minister of Labor.

BAR-LEV, HAIM
  ILP

born 1924 in Austria; Chief of Staff, IDF, 1968–1971; Minister of Commerce and Industry, 1972–1977. (See also the Military Elite for the 1967 and 1973 Crises.)

HAZANI, MICHAEL
  NRP

1913–1975. Born in Poland; Minister of Welfare from September 1970 until his death in 1975.

HILLEL, SHLOMO
  Mapai
  Alignment
  ILP

born 1923 in Baghdad; joined the Cabinet as Minister of Police in 1969, and served in that position in 1973.

PELED, NATAN
  Mapam
  Alignment

born 1913 in Russia; joined the Cabinet as Minister of Immigration and Absorption in 1970 and served in that position in 1973.

PERES, SHIMON
  Mapai
  Rafi
  Alignment
  ILP

born 1923 in Poland; joined the Cabinet as Minister Without Portfolio in December 1969; in 1973 he was Minister of Transport and Communications; Minister of Defense, 1974–1977; Acting Prime Minister, March–May 1977. (See also Other Party Leaders and Persons Consulted in 1967.)

SHEMTOV, VICTOR
  Mapam
  Alignment

born 1915 in Bulgaria; joined the Cabinet as Minister Without Portfolio in December 1969; in 1973 he was Minister of Health.

Other Party Leader

BEGIN, MENAHEM
  Herut
  Gahal
  Likud

(See also the 1967 Members of the Government list.) In 1973 he was Leader of the Opposition, having resigned from the Cabinet in August 1970.

Bureaucratic Elite

DINITZ, SIMHA — born 1929 in Palestine; in 1973 he was Israeli Ambassador to the United States.

GAZIT, MORDEKHAI — born 1922 in Turkey; in 1973 he was Director-General of the Prime Minister's Office.

Military Elite

ELAZAR, DAVID — 1925–1976. Born in Yugoslavia; Chief of Staff, 1972–1974; resigned following the publication of First Agranat Report.

HOFI, YITZHAK — born 1927 in Palestine; in 1973 he was OC Northern Command.

PELED, BINYAMIN — born 1928 in Palestine; in 1973 he was Commander of the Israeli Air Force.

TAL, YISRAEL — born 1924 in Palestine; in 1973 he was Deputy Chief of Staff.

ZEIRA, ELIYAHU — born 1928 in Palestine; he was Director of Military Intelligence, 1972–1974, and was replaced after the publication of the First Agranat Report.

THE MILITARY LINE-UP: 1967 AND 1973

THE MILITARY LINE-UP IN 1967[1]

Arab Forces

On the eve of the 1967 War, political fragmentation within the Arab world gave way to unity—the goal being to crush Israel. During the crisis period, there were many pious declarations of military support for the front-line Arab states. In fact, they received very little—partly because of the gap between stated and real intentions[2] and partly because the war was over within six

---

1. The data are based on the following sources: Israel, IDF Information Office, *This Was Goliath* (Tel Aviv, October 1967); N. Safran, *From War to War: The Arab-Israeli Confrontation 1948–1967* (New York, 1969), chaps. 4, 5, and 7, and Appendices B and C; *Middle East Record 1967*, D. Dishon, ed. (Tel Aviv, 1971), pp. 205–207; International Institute for Strategic Studies, London, *The Military Balance 1966–67*, and *1967–68* (London, 1966 and 1967, respectively); A. Legler and W. Liebisch, "Militärische, Ereijuisse im Nahen Osten, Junie 1967, Eine Documentation," *Bibliothek für Zeitgeschichte Jahres-Bibliographie* (Stuttgart, 1967), pp. 321–395; Edgar O'Ballance, *The Third Arab-Israeli War* (London, 1972); and Major Yonah, "The Background of the Six Day War in the Eyes of the Arabs: Egypt and Her Entry Into the War," *Ma'arakhot*, 191–192 (June 1968), 37–40, 73–103. For an analysis of the military balance, 1967–1973, including the qualitative aspects, see Ahmed S. Khalidi, "The Military Balance 1967–73," in N. H. Aruri, ed., *Middle East Crucible: Studies on the Arab-Israeli War of October 1973* (Wilmette, Ill., 1975), pp. 21–63.

2. The story of the Kuwaiti regiment, as told by Mohamed Heikal, was typical of this gap: "One of the strangest incidents of the day centered around a battalion of the Kuwaiti Regiment which had been sent to Egypt as a propaganda move to demonstrate Arab solidarity. It had been despatched to El Arish on the understanding that it would not be involved in any trouble. . . . But the only welcome the Kuwaiti's got at El Arish came from Israeli planes strafing the station. The moment they got out of the train they were ordered to make their way back to Suez" ("The 1967 Arab-Israeli War," *Sunday Telegraph* [London], 28 October 1973).

days.[3] Thus, the data on Arab forces are limited to those of Egypt, Jordan, and Syria (Lebanon stayed out of the war), plus the Iraqi forces which had been despatched to Jordan prior to the outbreak of hostilities.

Land Forces

In early June 1967, Egypt's estimated regular armed forces were 180,000–200,000 men (not including the National Guard). Of these, about 30,000–35,000 were stationed in Sinai. An expeditionary force of approximately 30,000–40,000 was fighting in Yemen. Syria's armed forces comprised about 60,000–70,000 regulars and 40,000–45,000 reservists. Jordan's Arab Legion consisted of about 50,000–55,000 regulars, and its National Guard units consisted of 15,000–20,000 men.

	Egypt	*Jordan*	*Syria*	*Iraq*	*Total*
TROOPS					
Infantry Brigades	6	6	6	1	19
Mechanized Brigades	8	1	2	1	12
Armored Brigades	8	2	2	2	14
Special Troop Battalions	15		2	1	18
ARMOR					
Tanks and self-propelled guns	1,380	200	500–550		2,080–2,130
Armored Personnel Carriers	1,160	250	500	200	2,110
ARTILLERY	1,200	200	1,200		2,600
SA-2 BATTERIES	18		10		28

Air Forces

	Egypt	*Jordan*	*Syria*
Fighters	400	22	100
Bombers	70		6
Helicopters	60	3	10
Transport	90	6	5
Trainers	120		20–30

3. Of the Arab countries without a direct border with Israel, small units from Iraq already in positions in Sinai took part in the fighting. Of the reinforcements under way from Algeria, Iraq, Sudan, Morocco, Tunisia, and Saudi Arabia, only two squadrons of Algerian MiGs reached the front. There were some air strikes by Iraqi planes from an Iraqi airfield. An Iraqi division, reinforced by a battalion of Palestinian troops, which had entered Jordan on 4 June, reached the Jordan River on the day of the cease-fire with Jordan, having been slowed down and severely mauled on the way by Israeli air strikes.

Naval Forces

	Egypt	Syria
Destroyers	8	
Submarines	12	
Motor Torpedo Boats	32	12
Missile Boats	18	4

Israeli Forces

Published estimates of Israel's armed forces in May 1967, including those in the IISS *Military Balance,* erred on some important items, as noted by Yitzhak Rabin. The following data are taken from Safran's estimates (with some adjustments based on the judgments of M. Brecher and B. Geist) from other sources mentioned in Note 1 to this Appendix.

TROOPS		ARMOR	
Infantry Brigades*	23	Tanks and self-	
Armored Brigades*	8	propelled guns	1,050
Artillery Brigades	12	Armored Fighting	
*including mechanized units		Vehicles	1,000

The number of men in the IDF, on full mobilization, was estimated to be 270,000–300,000.

PLANES		NAVAL UNITS	
Fighter-Bombers	200–230	Destroyers and Frigates	4
Bombers	25	Submarines	2
Trainers/		Motor Torpedo Boats	12
Ground Attack Planes	60		
Transport	20		
Helicopters	25		

The Forces Committed on 5 June 1967

In the opening air strike, Israel committed her entire Air Force to the destruction of the main protagonist, the Egyptian Air Force; twelve planes were left to protect Israel's air space. After the destruction of the larger part of Egypt's Air Force and airports, all of Jordan's twenty-two Hawker Hunter fighters were destroyed, and half of Syria's Air Force. The principal task of Israel's Air Force from the second day was mainly ground support.

During the first four days of the war, Egypt, and then Jordan, joined the battle. Syria stayed out, her army contained by the reduced units of Israel's Northern Command, as well as by air strikes.

Israel's land assault on the Sinai front on 5 June involved the larger part of her mechanized infantry and armored strength. Organized in three IDF Corps, they advanced along three axes in the northern part of Sinai. On her eastern border, as Jordan began an artillery bombardment all along the line and an infantry attack in Jerusalem, Israel committed five infantry and three armored brigades; of these, two infantry and one armored brigade were assigned to the battle for Jerusalem.

By 5 June, Egypt had concentrated close to 100,000 combatants in Sinai, including some who were hastily recalled from Yemen. Two reinforced divisions were placed in the northern approaches to Sinai, including the Gaza Strip. Two divisions controlled key positions in the second line and around the strategic crossroads of Bir Hama and Bir Hassna, while the Fourth Armored Division held the mountain passes leading to the Suez Canal. Forces of more than one division strength controlled a third line, further south. In addition, the so-called "Shazli Task Force," composed of three brigades and two hundred tanks, was poised opposite the southern Negev, with orders to cut off the southern part of Israel, including Eilat.

Jordan committed almost all of her armed forces in the developing battle. Two of the armored brigades, kept in the Jordan river valley until 5 June, were seriously weakened by air strikes as they advanced. By the second day of fighting, King Hussein admitted that the war was lost and asked for a cease-fire.

The Qualitative Balance

It is always misleading to compare military data on a one-to-one basis. First, there are significant differences between plane and plane, tank and tank, missile and missile, their concentration or dispersal, their tactical use, etc. Secondly, leadership, training, technology, motivation, and organization cannot be quantified but are of crucial importance nonetheless.

In June 1967, Israel had two qualitative advantages over her adversaries: surprise and motivation. The devastating air strike on the 5th caught Arab leaders totally by surprise and ensured Israel's aerial supremacy for the rest of the war. In fact, Israel's victory was certain within the first three hours. As to motivation, the concentrated outpouring of hatred during the crisis period had convinced Israelis, from the Cabinet to the man in the street, that once again they were fighting for survival. The superior quality of IDF leadership and training, the quick exploitation of the tactical advantages gained on the first day—air supremacy and the breakthrough of the Arab front line—led to disarray and retreat among the Arab land forces.

The armies of Egypt and Syria had been equipped with sophisticated Soviet weapons in the years prior to the 1967 War, including MiG-21 fighters, SA-2 missiles, and the latest models (T-54 and T-55) of Russian tanks, at the time. Israel's military experts admitted after the Six Day War that Soviet armor was superior to Israel's. But these weapon systems were not yet fully integrated into the Arab armies and were used, if at all, less effectively in battle conditions. Moreover, in sharp contrast to 1973, the Egyptian army was badly led in 1967.

The combined Arab armed forces were superior to the IDF quantitatively and, regarding weapons, qualitatively as well. "Because of this, knowledgeable and qualified observers did not anticipate anything approaching the actual course of the war."[4] The combination of superior motivation, leadership, and training, and the tactical exploitation of surprise, speed, and air superiority more than made up for those advantages.

II. THE MILITARY LINE-UP IN 1973

Arab Forces

Two years after the Yom Kippur War, Major-General Shlomo Gazit, the IDF's Director of Military Intelligence, provided the following figures for the Arab armed forces facing Israel in the 1973 War. The figures were "based on what we knew before the war, and especially on whatever we found out after the war when a lot of documents and thousands of prisoners fell into our hands."[5]

Two Egyptian armies faced Israel across the Suez Canal: the Second Army in the north and the Third Army in the south. They

4. Safran, *From War to War*, p. 319.
5. S. Gazit, "Arab Forces Two Years After the Yom Kippur War," in *Military Aspects of the Israeli-Arab Conflict*, Proceedings of an International Symposium, October 12–17, 1975 (Tel Aviv, 1975), pp. 188–195.

included five infantry, three mechanized, and two armored divisions. In addition, several Arab states despatched expeditionary forces to the Suez front when war broke out; thus the IDF had to fight a formidable adversary. (See pp. 420–21.)

Overall, according to Dayan, the "Arabs have, on both fronts, 820,000 soldiers"; while Meir's estimate was 800,000.[6]

Arab Air Forces

	Egypt	Syria	Jordan
Fighters	653	388	55
Bombers	39		
Helicopters	160	58	6
Transport	61	6	11
SAM Batteries	146	34	

Arab Naval Forces

	Egypt	Syria
Destroyers	5	
Frigates	3	
Submarines	12	
Missile Boats	19	9
Torpedo Boats	34	13
Mine Sweepers	14	4

Israeli Forces

There are no official figures on the overall strength of Israel's armed forces and her equipment—planes, tanks, guns, and missiles. Most of the educated guesses on Israel's military strength in October 1973 are based on the figures for July 1973, published by the IISS. They are quoted here from the Institute's annual survey, *The Military Balance 1973–74.* The Egyptian military intelligence assessment of Israel's armed strength, as of 1 September 1973, tended to be higher; these figures will be quoted in parentheses; they are taken from documentary evidence cited in Lt. Colonel Shay's article in *Ma'arakhot*, 250 (July 1976).

6. Respectively: Dayan, Interview on Israeli Television, 14 October 1973, Hebrew text in *Ma'arakhot*, Special Edition, 232–233 (November 1973); and Meir, Speech to the Knesset, 16 October 1973, *Divrei Haknesset*, 68, 4474, English text in M. Medzini, ed., *Israel's Foreign Relations, Selected Documents 1947–1974*, pp. 1044–1051.

Arab Land Forces on the Egyptian Front

TROOPS*	Egyptian	Algerian	Kuwaiti	Lybian	Moroccan	Sudanese	Tunisian	Total
Infantry Brigades	15	1			1	1		18
Mechanized Brigades	15							15
Armored Brigades	10	1		1				12
Additional Infantry Battalions			1			1	1	3
Special Troop Battalions	24							24
S/S Rocket Brigades	2							2
ARMOR								
Tanks	2,200	130		100	12	30		2,472
Armored Personnel Carriers	2,985	30				30		3,045
ARTILLERY (units)	2,200	18		18		12–14		2,248–50
S/S SCUD LAUNCHERS	9							9
S/S LUNA LAUNCHERS	12							12

*The number of personnel in each Arab military unit is fluid: a division ranges from 11,000 to 17,000 soldiers; it usually includes three to four brigades and each brigade usually is composed of three to four battalions, as well as auxiliary units; a mechanized brigade in Egypt and Israel includes about 3,500 men (International Institute of Strategic Studies, *The Military Balance 1973–74*).

Arab Land Forces on the Syrian Front

TROOPS	Syrian	Iraqi	Jordanian	Kuwaiti	Moroccan	Saudi Arabian	Total
Infantry Brigades	9	2	6	1	1	2	21
Mechanized Brigades	5	2	3				10
Armored Brigades	10	4	6			1	21
Special Troop Battalions	7	2	3			1	13
Additional Armored Car Battalions						1	1
S/S Rocket Brigades	1–2						1–2
ARMOR							
Tanks	1,650	500	480	40	30	36	2,736
Armored Personnel Carriers	1,500	700	550	40–50	12		2,802–12
ARTILLERY (units)	1,200	180	320			54	1,754
S/S LUNA LAUNCHERS	36						36
AML 90						40	40

TROOPS

Infantry Brigades	14 (18)
Additional Infantry Battalions	(22)*
Mechanized Brigades	9 (6)
Armored Brigades	10 (10)
Additional Forces, Including Tank Battalions	(6)
Artillery Brigades	3 (37 artillery and 15 antiaircraft and missile battalions)

---

*Some of these are listed in *The Military Balance* as Para-Military Forces: 4,000 Border Guards and 5,000 *Nahal* soldiers.

ARMOR

Tanks	1,700
Armored Fighting Vehicles	3,000

The estimate for number of troops is 314,000 on full mobilization —that is, regulars, conscripts, and reserves—and about 125,000 without the reserves.

PLANES[7]		NAVAL UNITS	
Fighters (including fighter-interceptors, 2 fighter-bombers)	403 (395)	Submarines	3
		Destroyers	1
		Fast Patrol Boats	13
Trainers	85 (96)	Motor Torpedo Boats	9
Transport	30 (50)		
Helicopters	42 (80)		

COS Elazar stated that the ratio of the number of tanks was 2.5:1 in the enemy's favor; that of planes, 2:1.[8] This would imply about 2,000 Israeli tanks and 650 Israeli aircraft of all types, numbers larger than those enumerated by the Institute.

The Forces Committed on 6 October 1973

The Egyptian leadership decided during the planning stage "to strike the strongest possible blow [in the first assault] that we are capable of."[9]

7. For more detailed data, see *Flight* magazine figures, quoted in A. Avnery, *Red Sky* (Tel Aviv, 1975), pp. 79–80. These added up to 601 planes.

8. "The Yom Kippur War: Military Lessons," in *Military Aspects of the Israeli-Arab Conflict*, pp. 245–250.

9. Heikal, Interview with General Hafez Ismail, published in *Al Anwar* (Beirut), 18 November 1973; quoted in A. Shay, "Egypt Before the Yom Kippur War: War Aims and Plan of Attack," *Ma'arakhot*, 250 (July 1976), 18.

The Egyptian High Command allotted to the first assault wave, on the northern (Second Army) sector, three infantry divisions and three additional tank brigades; to the southern (Third Army) sector, two infantry divisions, two additional tank brigades, and one mechanized brigade. One mechanized and one infantry brigade, supported by several commando battalions, were allotted the task of conquering the Ras-Sudar-A-Tur section of the Sinai coast (south of the Third Army's section); and one infantry brigade, supported by several commando battalions, was ordered to conquer, in an independent effort, a triangle in the northernmost section of the Suez Canal front.[10]

Along the Canal were arrayed almost the total artillery force of Egypt, 2,000 units, which, at 14:00 on 6 October, opened a barrage along the entire front, firing 3,000 tons of shells at a rate of 175 shells per second, for 53 minutes. The first assault was also supported by a wave of 240 Egyptian planes, sent to bomb airfields and missile sites. In sharp contrast to the Syrians (see below), the Egyptians committed mostly infantry forces in the first assault, and only a small part of their armor by night; about 100,000 Egyptian soldiers and 400 tanks (of a total of 2,200) had crossed the Canal.

The IDF's defense, along the first line, comprised 436 soldiers in a series of fortifications, the Bar-Lev Line, "7–8 miles apart and three tanks actually on the water-front."[11] In the second line, there were 275 tanks, divided almost equally among three brigades. These tanks were not in position. Major-General Mendler, the Commanding Officer, had orders to move them into position, according to the guidelines of "Operation Dovecote," at 16:00 on the 6th, in order not to create unnecessary tension until the last moment before the attack, expected at 18:00. Israeli armor suffered heavy casualties while moving forward—from aerial bombardment as well as from Egyptian infantry units equipped with antitank missiles by then in large numbers on the east bank of the Canal. "On Sunday [7 October] at 5:00 in the morning, there were about 110 tanks and about 500–550 soldiers defending the state on the southern front."[12]

10. Shay (July 1976), and C. Herzog, *The War of Atonement* (Jerusalem and Tel Aviv, 1975), pp. 150–151.

11. Herzog, *The War of Atonement*, p. 151. Bar-Lev mentioned 352 soldiers in fourteen fortifications along the Canal, "and that included cooks, medics, radiomen, drivers and other service personnel," three tanks and five batteries of artillery, with several battalions of artillery in the second line ("We Knew Where the Egyptians Would Attack and How—But We Made a Mistake About the Timing," *Ma'ariv*, 1 August 1975).

12. Interview with Major-General Gonen on the fourth anniversary of the Yom Kippur War (Hebrew calendar), *Yediot Aharonot*, 21 September 1977.

The Syrian Front

On 6 October, Syria had concentrated along the front line of the Golan Heights three infantry divisions, which together included 540 tanks. The two supporting armored divisions had 460 tanks. All told, the Syrian Army on the Heights disposed of approximately 1,500 tanks. In addition, they had moved 140 batteries of artillery to the front line.[13]

These five divisions were opposed on 6 October by two IDF armored brigades: the Barak Brigade in the southern part of the Golan Heights and the 7th Armored Brigade in the northern part, together with 177 tanks; there were also eleven batteries of artillery and two battalions of infantry.[14]

The Qualitative Balance

In 1973, in contrast to 1967, the Arab armies were better trained and equipped, and they had higher motivation because they were fighting to regain occupied territories. Israel's army, because it was convinced it could not afford a single defeat, fought with the same commitment as in previous wars.

In the 1973 War, the Arab armies had the advantage of surprise, tactical as well as strategic. Egypt had meticulously planned the first assault across the Canal for four years—and carried it out well. But after 14 October, when the massive Egyptian armored attack in Sinai was stopped (250 tanks destroyed against marginal IDF losses of 5 tanks destroyed and 10 damaged), some of the organizational weaknesses of Egypt's army, and Israel's qualitative superiority, reasserted themselves. That prompted Bar-Lev to inform Meir: "Golda, it will be all right. We are back to being ourselves and they [the Egyptians] are back to being themselves."[15]

According to Egyptian sources, as well as military analysts, Egyptian field commanders reported to GHQ accurately as long as the battle went reasonably well. But as of 14 October, old habits of misreporting resurfaced. Thus the crossing of the Canal by Israeli forces was brought to the notice of Egypt's GHQ sixteen hours after it actually took place, though front-line observations had been reported at least six hours earlier.[16]

13. Herzog, *The War of Atonement*, pp. 61, 63–64.
14. *Ma'arakhot,* Special Edition (September 1974).
15. Bar-Lev, Interview, *Ma'ariv,* 21 September 1977.
16. See excerpts from the top-secret Third Army daily journal of messages, captured during the war and published in *Ma'ariv,* 14 September 1975.

There was a massive, concentrated use of antitank and anti-aircraft missiles by the Egyptians: Sagger missiles by Egyptian infantry who had crossed the Canal, and the Strella and SAM 2, 3, 6, and 7 missiles fired by infantry or from static or mobile batteries. The latter provided an effective umbrella against the known superiority of the Israeli Air Force during the first week of the war.

For Israel, perhaps the greatest qualitative difference in the 1973 War was surprise: It took a week until the IDF recovered; much of the confusion and many of the losses of that week were attributed to this factor.[17] However, by quickly adapting tactics—for example, making the destruction of SAM missile batteries by infantry and armor the first priority after crossing the Canal—the superior technical proficiency of Israeli armor and air power was reasserted.[18]

17. See Major-General Y. Tal, Deputy Chief of Staff in 1973, Interview, *Yediot Aharonot*, 21 September 1977.

18. For analyses of the military aspects of the 1973 War, see Herzog, *The War of Atonement;* Z. Schiff, *October Earthquake, Yom Kippur 1973* (Tel Aviv, 1974) and his articles on the battle of 8 October and on the encirclement of the Third Army, *Ha'aretz,* 25 and 30 September 1974, and 14 September 1975; Shay, "Egypt Before the Yom Kippur War"; *Ma'arakhot,* 232 and 233 (November 1973), and special issue on the first anniversary of the war, No. 240 (September 1974); M. Heikal, *The Road to Ramadan* (London, 1975); the series of interviews with Sadat by M. Sabri, ed., *Akhbar el-Yom,* 1974; Insight Team of *The Sunday Times* (London), *The Yom Kippur War* (London, 1974); E. Monroe and A. H. Hockley, *The Arab-Israel War, October 1973, Background and Events* (London, 1974), Adelphi Paper No. 111 (Winter 1974); and Martin Van Creveld, *Military Lessons of the Yom Kippur War: Historical Perspectives* (London and Beverly Hills, 1975).

DECISIONAL PROCESSES, 1967 AND 1973 CRISES

A Graphic Representation

APPENDIX C maps the day-by-day decisional processes of the 1967 and 1973 Crises. More precisely, it specifies: (1) the date of meetings; (2) which group(s) participated; (3) the type of meeting, whether institutional or ad hoc; (4) the number of participants; and (5) the structural setting for each decision. It also indicates, for 1973 only, whether the Prime Minister or Defense Minister, or both, were present at the meeting. In addition, the graphs are designed to portray the consultative and decisional process through time, with emphasis on the changing size, structure, and type of group deliberation and decision.

DECISIONAL PROCESS: 1967 CRISIS

PRE-CRISIS

Column headers for NUMBER OF PARTICIPANTS: 2, 3-4, 5-6, 7-8, 9-10, 11-12, 13-14, 15-16, 17-18, 19-20, 21+

DATE	Setting	Decision
7.5	C*	①
15.5	ME	
	ME	
	M.BE	
	ME	②
	ME	
16.5	BE	
	ME	
	C	
	ME	③
	WJ.M	
	BE	

CRISIS

DATE	Setting	Decision
17.5	MCD.ME	
	C.ME	
	ME	
	M	
	ME	
	BE	
	ME	④
18.5	ME	
	ME.M.BE	
	M.BE	
	ME.M.BE	
	M.BE	
	ME	
	ME	
	ME	
19.5	ME	
	GS	⑤⑥
	ME.BE	
	M.BE	
	M.BE	
20.5	ME	
	BE	
21.5	ME.BE	
	MCD.ME	
	C.ME	⑦
	MCD.ME	
22.5	BE,ME	
	M	

CRISIS (continued)

DATE	Setting	Decision
23.5	BE	
	GS.BE	
	MCD.ME.BE.PE	⑧⑨
	C.ME.BE.PE	
	PE	
	M.BE	
24.5	ME**	
	GS.BE	
25.5	M	
	ME	
	ME.BE	
	ME.BE.M	
	ME.BE	⑩
	M.ME.BE	
26.5	MCD.ME.BE	⑪
	M	
	PE	
	PE	
	WJ.M	
	M.ME,BE	
27.5	SOVIET AMBAS.	
	ME	
	ME	
	M.ME.BE.PE	
	M	
	PE	
	ME	
	C.ME.BE	
28.5	C.ME	⑫⑬
	ME	
	GS	
	M.PE	
29.5	M.BE	
	M	
	ME.BE	
	ME	
	M.BE	
30.5	M	
	BE,ME	
	BE,ME	
	BE,ME,M	⑭
	ME	

SOURCE: DAILY APPOINTMENT BOOK OF PRIME MINISTER ESHKOL

CRISIS

DATE	CRISIS	2	3-4	5-6	7-8	9-10	11-12	13-14	15-16	17-18	19-20	21+
31.5	BE	▫	▫									
1.6	M ***	▫										
	C.ME ⑮	▪	▪	▪	▪	▪	▪	▪	▪	▪	▪	▪
2.6	M.BE	▫	▫									
	BE.PE	▫	▫	▫								
	MCD.ME.BE	▫	▫	▫	▫	▫	▫	▫	▫	▫	▫	▫
	ME.M.BE	▫	▫	▫	▫							
	BE	▫	▫									
	M.GS ⑯	▪	▪	▪	▪	▪	▪	▪	▪	▪	▪	▪
	BE	▫	▫									
	BE	▫										
	WJ	▫										
	ME	▪										
	BE	▫										
	BE	▫										
	BE	▫										
3.6	BE	▫										
	M.BE	▫	▫	▫	▫	▫						
	M.BE	▫	▫	▫								
	PE.BE	▫	▫									
	PE.BE	▫	▫									
	M.ME.BE	▫	▫	▫	▫	▫	▫	▫				
4.6	MCD.ME	▫	▫	▫	▫	▫	▫	▫				
	C.ME ⑰	▪	▪	▪	▪	▪	▪	▪	▪	▪	▪	▪
	MCD.ME	▫	▫	▫	▫	▫	▫	▫				
	BE.PE	▫	▫	▫	▫	▫						
	ME	▫										

POST-CRISIS

DATE	POST-CRISIS	2	3-4	5-6	7-8	9-10	11-12	13-14	15-16	17-18	19-20	21+
5.6	C.BE.ME ⑱	▪	▪	▪	▪	▪	▪	▪	▪	▪	▪	▪
	M	▫										
	M.BE	▫	▫									
	M	▫	▫									

POST-CRISIS

DATE	POST-CRISIS	2	3-4	5-6	7-8	9-10	11-12	13-14	15-16	17-18	19-20	21+
5.6	C. ME ⑲	▫	▫	▫	▫	▫	▫	▫	▫	▫	▫	▫
	M.ME.PE.BE	▫	▫	▫	▫	▫	▫					
6.6	BE	▫	▫	▫								
	BE.M.PE	▫	▫	▫	▫	▫						
	BE.M	▫	▫	▫								
	BE.M.ME	▫	▫	▫	▫	⋄	⋄	⋄	⋄	⋄	⋄	⋄
	BE	▫	▫									
	BE	▫	▫									
	MCD. BE ⑳	▪	▪	▪	▪	▪	▪	▪	▪			
	M.BE	▫	▫									
	BE	▫	▫									
	M.BE	▫	▫									
	M	▫										
7.6	M	▫										
	M.BE	▫	▫									
	M.BE	▫	▫	▫	▫							
	M.BE ㉑	▫	▫	▫	▫	▫	▫					
	M.ME.BE	▫	▫	▫	▫	▫	▫					
	MCD ㉒㉓	▪	▪	▪	▪	▪	▪	▪				
8.6	M.PE	⋄	⋄	⋄	⋄	⋄	⋄	⋄				
	M.BE.ME	▫	▫	▫								
	ME.BE	▫	▫									
	PE.BE	▫	▫									
	M.ME	▫	▫									
	MCD.PE ㉔	▪	▪	▪	▪	▪	▪	▪				
9.6	M	▫										
	MCD ㉕	▪	▪	▪	▪	▪	▪	▪				
	M	▫										
	M	▫										
	M	▫										
	M	▫	▫	▫								
10.6	MCD.PE.BE	▪	▪	▪	▪	▪	▪	▪	▪			
	M ㉖	▫	▫									

* A regular Cabinet meeting was held on 7 May, when decision① was taken . The next Cabinet meeting was on the 16th. Whatever *ad hoc* meetings took place between 7 and 15 May were not relevant to Israel's 1967 crisis decision process.
   The number of participants for institutional meetings denotes the number invited. Not all invitees attended all meetings.

** From 24 May through 1 June there was a series of meetings which dealt exclusively with the domestic political struggle to replace Eshkol as Defense Minister. Unless the meeting also dealt with foreign policy issues it has been excluded from the graph.

*** As of this meeting the Cabinet was enlarged to include Dayan, Begin, and (as of 2 June) Y. Saphir.

DECISIONAL PROCESS:1973 CRISIS

KEY

C = CABINET	☐ Each box represents two persons except for the box indicating 21+
KC = KITCHEN CABINET	⊡ Meetings with Prime Minister
GS = GENERAL STAFF	⊠ Meetings with Defense Minister
M = MINISTER(S)	▨ Meetings with PM and DM
ME = MILITARY ELITE	☐☐ Institutional meeting
BE = BUREAUCRATIC ELITE	☐ ☐ *Ad Hoc* meeting
PE = OTHER POLITICAL ELITE	① FORMAL DECISIONAL SETTING and number of decision
US = KISSINGER AND SISCO	

PRE-CRISIS

DATE			NUMBER OF PARTICIPANTS
	PRE-CRISIS	TYPE	2 / 3-4 / 5-6 / 7-8 / 9-10 / 11-12 / 13-14 / 15-20 / 21+
24.9	GS		
26.9	ME		
	ME	①	
1.10	GS		
2.10	ME		
	M		
3.10	KC, ME, BE	②	
4.10	ME		
	BE		
	BE		

CRISIS

DATE			
5.10	ME.BE	③	
	M		
	ME		
	C.ME,BE	④	
	M		
	M		
6.10	M		
	GS		
	ME		
	ME.BE		
	M		
	KC,ME,BE	⑤⑥	
	GS		
	C.ME.BE		
	PE		
	PE		
	C.ME.BE		
	GS		
7.10	ME		
	ME		
	C.ME.BE		
	ME		
	ME		
	M		
	KC.ME	⑦	
	ME.M		
	M		
	C.ME.BE		
	ME		
8.10	M		
	C.ME.BE		
	ME	⑧	
	ME		
	C.ME.BE		
	ME		

CRISIS (continued)

DATE			
9.10	ME		
	M.ME	⑨	
	C.ME.BE		
	M		
	ME		
	M	⑩	
	C.ME.BE		
	ME		
10.10	ME		
	ME		
	GS		
	KC.ME	⑪	
	C.ME.BE		
11.10	C.ME.BE		
	ME		
12.10	ME		
	KC.ME	⑫	
	C.ME.BE		
	M		
	M	⑬	
13.10	C.ME.BE		
14.10	C.ME.BE	⑭	
15.10	C.ME.BE		
	M		
	GS		
	C.ME.BE		
16.10	M		
	M		
	ME		
	ME		
	C.ME.BE		
17.10	ME		
	ME		
	ME		
	C.ME.BE		
18.10	ME		
	ME		
	C.ME.BE		
19.10	ME		
	M		
	KC.ME	⑮	
	C.ME.BE		
	ME		

CRISIS

DATE	CRISIS	NUMBER OF PARTICIPANTS
		TYPE · 2 · 3-4 · 5-6 · 7-8 · 9-10 · 11-12 · 13-14 · 15-20 · 21+
20.10	ME	☒☐
	ME	☒☐
	ME	☒☐
	ME	☒☐
	KC.M	☒☐☐☐
	M	☒☐
	C.ME.BE	☒☐☐☐☐☐☐☐☐☐
21.10	ME	☒☐☐☐☐☐☐
	ME	☒☐
	ME	☒☐☐
	ME	☒☐☐
	M	☒☐
	M	☒☐
	ME	☒☐
	US	☐☐
	ME	☒☐☐☐
	C.ME.BE (16)	☒☐☐☐☐☐☐☐☐☐
22.10	ME	☒☐
	PE	☐☐☐☐☐☐☐☐☐
	ME	☒☐
	US	☐☐
	KC.US.ME	☒☐☐☐☐
	C.ME.BE (17)	☒☐☐☐☐☐☐☐☐☐
	KC.ME	☒☐☐
23.10	ME.BE	☒☐☐☐☐☐
	ME (18)	☒☐☐☐☐☐☐
	C.ME.BE	☒☐☐☐☐☐☐☐☐☐
24.10	KC	☒☐☐☐
	ME	☒☐
	C.ME.BE	☒☐☐☐☐☐☐☐☐☐
25.10	ME	☒☐☐
	M.US	☐☐☐
26.10	C.ME.BE (19)(20)	☒☐☐☐☐☐☐☐☐☐

POST-CRISIS

DATE	POST-CRISIS	NUMBER OF PARTICIPANTS
27.10	M.ME	☒☐☐
30.10	C.ME.BE (21)	☒☐☐☐☐☐☐☐☐☐
1.11	US	☐☐
	US	☐☐☐
	US	☐☐
2.11	US.ME.BE	☐☐☐☐
	ME.BE	☐☐☐☐
3.11	US.ME	☐☐☐
5.11	C.ME.BE	☒☐☐☐☐☐☐☐☐☐
7.11	US.M.ME.BE	☒☐☐☐☐☐
	C.ME.BE	☒☐☐☐☐☐☐☐☐☐
8.11	PE	☐☐
	US.M.ME. BE	☒☐☐☐☐☐
	C.ME.BE (22)	☒☐☐☐☐☐☐☐☐☐
9.11	PE.BE	☐☐☐☐☐☐☐☐☐
	US	☐☐
10.11	C.ME.BE	☒☐☐☐☐☐☐☐☐☐
12.11	ME	☐☐
13.11	ME.UN	☒☐☐
	UN	☒☐
14.11	US	☐☐
17.11	C.ME.BE	☒☐☐☐☐☐☐☐☐☐
19.11	KC.ME	☒☐☐☐
20.11	C.ME.BE (23)	☒☐☐☐☐☐☐☐☐☐
22.11	M.ME	☒☐☐
23.11	M	☐☐
25.11	C.ME.BE (24)	☒☐☐☐☐☐☐☐☐☐
27.11	KC	☒☐☐☐

POST-CRISIS

DATE	POST-CRISIS	NUMBER OF PARTICIPANTS
		TYPE · 2 · 3-4 · 5-6 · 7-8 · 9-10 · 11-12 · 13-14 · 15-20 · 21+
2.12	UN	☒☐
	C.ME.BE (25)	☒☐☐☐☐☐☐☐☐☐
3.12	US.BE	☒☐☐
7.12	US.BE	☒☐☐☐☐☐
	US.BE.ME	☒☐☐
	US.BE	☒☐☐
8.12	M	☒☐
9.12	US.BE.ME	☒☐☐
	US	☒☐
	M	☒☐
10.12	M	☒☐
	C.ME.BE	☒☐☐☐☐☐☐☐☐☐
	PE	☒☐☐☐☐☐☐☐☐☐
14.12	US	☒☐
	C.ME.BE (26)	☒☐☐☐☐☐☐☐☐☐
15.12	US	☒☐
16.12	US	☒☐
	US	☒☐
	US.BE	☒☐☐
	US.M.BE	☒☐☐☐☐
17.12	C.BE	☒☐☐☐☐☐☐☐☐☐
	US	☒☐
	US.M.ME.BE	☒☐☐☐☐☐
	C.BE (27)	☒☐☐☐☐☐☐☐☐☐
18.12	US	☒☐
21.12	C.ME.BE (28)	☒☐☐☐☐☐☐☐☐☐
23.12	C.ME.BE	☒☐☐☐☐☐☐☐☐☐
24.12	M	☒☐
25.12	C.ME.BE	☒☐☐☐☐☐☐☐☐☐
26.12	ME	☒☐
27.12	ME	☒☐
31.12	KC.M.ME. BE	☒☐☐☐☐
1.1.74	KC.ME.BE	☒☐☐☐
2.1	C.ME.BE	☒☐☐☐☐☐☐☐☐☐
4.1	US	☒☐
	US.BE	☒☐☐☐☐☐
	US.BE	☒☐☐
	US.BE	☒☐☐☐
5.1	US.BE	☒☐
	US.BE	☒☐☐☐
	US.BE	☒☐☐
	M	☒☐
6.1	C.ME.BE	☒☐☐☐☐☐☐☐☐☐
	M	☒☐
12.1	US	☒☐
	US.M.ME.BE	☒☐☐☐☐☐
	C.ME.BE (29)	☒☐☐☐☐☐☐☐☐☐
13.1	US.ME	☒☐☐
	US	☒☐
15.1	BE.KC	☒☐☐☐☐
	US.M.BE	☒☐☐☐
	M	☒☐☐
	US	☒☐
	C.ME.BE (30)	☒☐☐☐☐☐☐☐☐☐
	US.M	☒☐☐
16.1	US.M	☒☐☐☐
	US.M	☒☐☐
17.1	M	☒☐☐
	US.M	☒☐☐
	US	☒☐
	C.ME.BE (31)	☒☐☐☐☐☐☐☐☐☐
	US	☒☐
18.1	US	☒☐
	ME	☒☐

BIBLIOGRAPHY*

CRISIS BEHAVIOR OF STATES
(Preface, Chapters 1, 4, 7, 10, 11, and 12)

ALLISON, Graham T. *The Essence of Decision: Explaining the Cuban Missile Crisis.* Boston: Little, Brown, 1971.

———. "Conceptual Models and the Cuban Missile Crisis," *The American Political Science Review,* 63 (September 1969), 689–718.

———, and Morton H. HALPERIN. "Bureaucratic Politics: A Paradigm and Some Policy Implications," in R. Tanter and R. H. Ullman, eds., *Theory and Policy in International Relations.* Princeton, N.J.: Princeton University Press, 1973, pp. 40–79.

AZAR, Edward E. "Conflict Escalation and Conflict Reduction in an International Crisis: Suez, 1956," *The Journal of Conflict Resolution,* 16 (June 1972), 183–201.

BOBROW, Davis B., S. CHAN, and J. A. KRINGEN. "Understanding How Others Treat Crisis: A Multimethod Approach," *International Studies Quarterly,* 21 (March 1977), 199–224.

BRADY, L. P. *Threat, Decision Time and Awareness: The Impact of Situational Variables on Foreign Policy Behavior.* Ph.D. Dissertation, Ohio State University, Creon Publication 31, 1974.

BRECHER, Michael. "India's Devaluation of 1966: Linkage Politics and Crisis Decision-Making," *British Journal of International Studies,* 3 (April 1977), 1–25.

———. "Toward a Theory of International Crisis Behavior," *International Studies Quarterly,* 21 (March 1977), 39–74.

———. *Decisions in Israel's Foreign Policy.* London: Oxford University Press, 1974; and New Haven: Yale University Press, 1975.

———. *Israel, The Korean War and China.* Jerusalem: Academic Press, 1974; and New Brunswick, N.J.: Transaction Books, 1977.

*NOTE: Multiple entries under one author are listed in reverse chronological order.

————. "Research Findings and Theory-Building in Foreign Policy Behavior," in P. J. McGowan, ed., *Sage International Yearbook of Foreign Policy Studies*, 2. Beverly Hills, Calif.: Sage, 1974, pp. 49–122.

————. "Israel and the Rogers' Peace Initiatives: Decisions and Consequences," *Orbis*, 18 (Summer 1974), 402–426.

————. "India's Decision on the Voice of America: A Study in Irresolution," *Asian Survey*, 14 (July 1974), 637–650.

————. "Inputs and Decisions for War and Peace: The Israel Experience," *International Studies Quarterly*, 18 (June 1974), 131–177.

————. "India's Decision to Remain in the Commonwealth," *The Journal of Commonwealth and Comparative Politics*, 13 (March and July 1974), 62–90, 228–230.

————. "Images, Process and Feedback in Foreign Policy: Israel's Decisions on German Reparations," *The American Political Science Review*, 67 (March 1973), 73–102.

————. *The Foreign Policy System of Israel.* London: Oxford University Press, 1972; and New Haven: Yale University Press, 1972.

————, ed. *Studies in Crisis Behavior.* New Brunswick, N.J.: Transaction Books, 1979.

————, Blema STEINBERG, and Janice G. STEIN. "A Framework for Research on Foreign Policy Behavior," *The Journal of Conflict Resolution*, 13 (March 1969), 75–101.

BUTTERWORTH, R. L. *Managing Interstate Conflict, 1945–1974: Data with Synopsis.* Pittsburgh: University Center for International Studies, 1976.

FRYE, R. L., and T. M. STRITCH. "Effects of Timed versus Non-Timed Discussion Upon Measures of Influence and Change in Small Groups," *Journal of Social Psychology*, 63 (1964), 141.

GEIST, Benjamin. "The Six Day War: A Study in the Setting and the Process of Foreign Policy Decision-Making Under Crisis Conditions." Unpublished Ph.D. dissertation, The Hebrew University of Jerusalem, Jerusalem, 1974.

GEORGE, A. L., D. K. HALL, and S. A. SIMONS. *The Limits of Coercive Diplomacy: Laos, Cuba, Vietnam.* Boston: Little, Brown, 1971.

GEORGE, A. L. "Case studies and theory development: The method of structured, focused comparison," in P. G. Lauren (ed.), *Diplomacy: New Approaches in History, Theory and Policy* (New York, 1979).

GEORGE, A. L., and R. SMOKE. *Deterrence and Defense in American Foreign Policy: Theory and Practice.* New York: Columbia University Press, 1974.

GUETZKOW, H., and J. GYR. "An Analysis of Conflict in Decision-Making Groups," *Human Relations*, 7 (1954), 367–381.

HAZLEWOOD, Leo, and J. J. HAYS. *Planning for Problems in Crisis Management.* Washington, D.C.: CACI Inc., 1976.

HERMANN, Charles F. "Threat, Time, and Surprise: A Simulation of International Crises," in C. F. Hermann, ed., *International Crises: Insights from Behavioral Research.* New York: The Free Press, 1972, pp. 187–214.

————. *Crises in Foreign Policy: A Simulation Analysis.* Indianapolis: Bobbs-Merrill, 1969.

————. "International Crisis as a Situational Variable," in J. N. Rosenau, ed., *International Politics and Foreign Policy.* New York: The Free Press, 1969, pp. 409–421.

————. "Some Consequences of Crisis Which Limit the Viability of Organizations," *Administrative Science Quarterly,* 8 (1963), 61–82.

————, ed. *International Crises: Insights from Behavioral Research.* New York: The Free Press, 1972.

HILTON, G. "The 1914 Studies: A re-assessment of the Evidence and Some Further Thoughts," *Peace Research Society (International) Papers,* 13 (1970), 117–141.

HOFFMANN, S. "International Relations: The Long Road to Theory," *World Politics,* 11 (April 1959), 346–377.

HOLST, J. J. "Surprise Signals and Reaction," *Cooperation and Conflict,* 1 (1966), 31–45.

HOLSTI, O. R. "Foreign Policy Formation Viewed Cognitively," in R. Axelrod, ed., *Structure of Decision.* Princeton, N.J.: Princeton University Press, 1976.

————. *Crisis, Escalation, War.* Montreal: McGill-Queens University Press, 1972.

————. "Time, Alternatives, and Communications: The 1914 and Cuban Missile Crises," in C. F. Hermann, ed., *International Crises: Insights from Behavioral Research.* New York: The Free Press, 1972, pp. 58–80.

————. "Cognitive Dynamics and Images of the Enemy: Dulles and Russia," in D. J. Finlay, O. R. Holsti, and R. Fagen, eds., *Enemies in Politics.* Chicago: Rand McNally, 1967, chap. 2.

————. "The 1914 Case," *The American Political Science Review,* 59 (June 1965), 365–378.

————, and A. L. GEORGE. "The Effects of Stress on the Performance of Foreign Policy-Makers," *Political Science Annual,* 6 (1975), 255–319.

————, R. A. BRODY, and R. C. NORTH. "Measuring Affect and Action in International Reaction Models: Empirical Materials from the 1962 Cuban Crisis," *Journal of Peace Research,* 3–4 (1964), 170–190.

————, R. C. NORTH, and R. A. BRODY. "Perception and Action in the 1914 Crisis," in J. D. Singer, ed., *Quantitative International Politics.* New York: The Free Press, 1968, pp. 123–158.

HOPPLE, G. W., and P. J. ROSSA. "International Crisis Analysis: An Assessment of Theory and Research." Unpublished paper, 1978, pp. 6–25.

International Encyclopedia of the Social Sciences, David L. Sills, ed., 17 volumes. New York and London: Collier Macmillan, 1968.

JANIS, Irving L. *Victims of Groupthink: A Psychological Study of Foreign Policy Decisions and Fiascos.* Boston: Houghton Mifflin, 1972.

————. "Groupthink," *Psychology Today* (November 1971), 43–76.

————, and Leon MANN. *Decision-Making.* New York: The Free Press, 1977.

JERVIS, Robert. *Perception and Misperception in International Politics.*

Princeton, N.J.: Princeton University Press, 1976.

———. "The Costs of the Quantitative Study of International Relations," in K. Knorr and J. N. Rosenau, eds., *Contending Approaches to International Politics*. Princeton, N.J.: Princeton University Press, 1969, chap. 10.

KAPLAN, Morton. "Some Problems of International Systems Research," in *International Political Communities, An Anthology*. New York: Doubleday, 1966, pp. 469–501.

———. *System and Process in International Politics*. New York: John Wiley, 1957.

KRINGEN, John A., and S. CHAN. "Chinese Crisis Perception and Behavior: A Summary of Findings," paper prepared for Joint Committee on Contemporary China, Workshop on Chinese Foreign Policy, Ann Arbor, Michigan, 1976.

LAZARUS, Richard S. "The Psychology of Stress and Coping: With Particular Reference to Israel." Address given at the international conference on Psychological Stress and Adjustment in Time of War and Peace, Tel Aviv, January 6–10, 1975.

———. "Stress," in D. L. Sills, ed., *International Encyclopedia of the Social Sciences*. London and New York: Collier Macmillan, 1968, vol. 15, pp. 337–348.

———. *Psychological Stress and the Coping Process*. New York: McGraw-Hill, 1966.

LENTNER, Howard H. "The Concept of Crisis as Viewed by the United States Department of State," in C. F. Hermann, ed., *International Crises: Insights from Behavioral Research*. New York: The Free Press, 1972, pp. 112–135.

McCLELLAND, Charles A. "The Anticipation of International Crises: Prospects for Theory and Research," *International Studies Quarterly*, 21 (March 1977), 15–38.

———. "Warning in the International Event Flow: EFI and ROZ as Threat Indicators," *Threat Recognition and Analysis Project Technical Report*. Los Angeles, California: University of Southern California, July 1976.

———. "Crisis and Threat in the International Setting: Some Relational Concepts," *Threat Recognition and Analysis Project Technical Report*. Los Angeles, California: University of Southern California, June 1975.

———. "The Beginning, Duration, and Abatement of International Crises: Comparisons in Two Conflict Arenas," in C. F. Hermann, ed., *International Crises: Insights from Behavioral Research*. New York: The Free Press, 1972, pp. 83–105.

———. "Access to Berlin: The Quantity and Variety of Events, 1948–1963," in J. D. Singer, ed., *Quantitative International Politics: Insights and Evidence*. New York: The Free Press, 1968, pp. 159–186.

———. "Action Structures and Communication in Two International Crises: Quemoy and Berlin," *Background*, 7 (1964), 201–215.

———. "Decisional Opportunity and Political Controversy, the Quemoy Case," *The Journal of Conflict Resolution*, 6 (September 1962), 201–213.

————. "The Acute International Crisis," *World Politics*, 14 (October 1961), 182–204.

McCORMICK, David M. *Decisions, Events and Perceptions in International Crises, Vol I: Measuring Perceptions to Predict International Conflict.* Ann Arbor, Michigan: First Ann Arbor Corp., 1975.

MARCH, James C., and H. A. SIMON. *Organizations.* New York: John Wiley, 1958.

MILBURN, Thomas W. "The Management of Crisis," in C. F. Hermann, ed., *International Crises: Insights from Behavioral Research.* New York: The Free Press, 1972, pp. 259–277.

MOFFITT, J. W., and R. STAGNER. "Perceptual Clarity and Closure as a Function of Anxiety," *Journal of Abnormal and Social Psychology*, 52 (1956), 350–357.

MOORE, J. A., et al. *Crisis Inventory.* Washington, D.C.: CACI, Inc., 1975.

MORSE, Edward L. "Crisis Diplomacy, Interdependence, and the Politics of International Economic Relations," in R. Tanter and R. H. Ullman, eds., *Theory and Policy in International Relations.* Princeton, N.J.: Princeton University Press, 1972, pp. 123–150.

NAVEH, Hanan, and M. BRECHER. "Patterns of International Crises in the Middle East, 1938–1975," *The Jerusalem Journal of International Relations*, 2–3 (Winter–Spring 1978), 277–315.

NOMIKOS, Eugenia V., and R. C. NORTH. *International Crisis: The Outbreak of World War I.* Montreal: McGill-Queens University Press, 1976.

NORTH, Robert C. "Research Pluralism and the International Elephant," in K. Knorr and J. N. Rosenau, eds., *Contending Approaches to International Politics.* Princeton, N.J.: Princeton University Press, 1969, pp. 218–242.

————, R. A. BRODY, and O. R. HOLSTI. "Some Empirical Data on the Conflict Spiral," *Peace Research Society (International) Papers*, 1 (1964), 1–14.

PAIGE, Glenn D. "On Values and Science: *The Korean Decision* Reconsidered," *The American Political Science Review*, 71 (December 1977), 1603–1609.

————. "Comparative Case Analysis of Crisis Decisions: Korea and Cuba," in C. F. Hermann, ed., *International Crises: Insights from Behavioral Research.* New York: The Free Press, 1972, pp. 41–55.

————. *The Korean Decision.* New York: The Free Press, 1968.

PRUITT, Dean G. "Definition of the Situation as a Determinant of International Action," in H. C. Kelman, ed., *International Behavior.* New York: Holt, Rinehart and Winston, 1966, chap. 11.

ROBINSON, James A. "Crisis: An Appraisal of Concepts and Theories," in C. F. Hermann, ed., *International Crises: Insights from Behavioral Research.* New York: The Free Press, 1972, pp. 20–35.

————. "Crisis," in D. L. Sills, ed., *International Encyclopedia of the Social Sciences.* London and New York: Collier Macmillan, 1968, vol. 3, pp. 510–514.

————. *The Concept of Crisis in Decision-Making.* Washington, D.C.:

National Institute of Social and Behavioral Science, Symposia Studies
Series, No. 11, 1962.
SCHELLING, Thomas A. *Arms and Influence*. New Haven: Yale University
Press, 1966.
SHAPIRO, Howard B., and M. A. GILBERT. *Crisis Management: Psycho-
logical and Sociological Factors in Decision-Making*. Arlington, Vir-
ginia: Office of Naval Research, Advanced Research Projects Agency
AD–A010 211, 1975.
SHLAIM, Avi. "Failures in National Intelligence Estimates: The Case of
the Yom Kippur War," *World Politics*, 28 (April 1976), 348–380.
SIMON, Herbert A. "Political Research: The Decision-Making Frame-
work," in D. Easton, ed., *Varieties of Political Theory*. Englewood
Cliffs, N.J.: Prentice-Hall, 1966, pp. 15–24.
SNYDER, Glenn H. "Crisis Bargaining," in C. F. Hermann, ed., *Inter-
national Crises: Insights from Behavioral Research*. New York: The
Free Press, 1972, pp. 217–256.
———, and Paul DIESING. *Conflict Among Nations: Bargaining, Decision
Making, and System Structure in International Crises*. Princeton, N.J.:
Princeton University Press, 1977.
SNYDER, Richard C., H. W. BRUCK, and B. SAPIN, eds. *Foreign Policy
Decision-Making*. New York: The Free Press, 1962.
STEIN, Janice Gross. "Krishna Menon's View of the World—A Content
Analysis," in M. Brecher, *India and World Politics*. London: Oxford
University Press, 1968, pp. 339–371.
———, and M. BRECHER. "Image, Advocacy and the Analysis of Con-
flict: An Israeli Case Study," *The Jerusalem Journal of International
Relations*, 1 (Spring 1976), 33–58.
———, and R. TANTER. *Rational Decision-Making: Israel's Security
Choices, 1967*. Columbus: Ohio State University Press, forthcoming
1980.
TANTER, Raymond. "International Crisis Behavior: An Appraisal of the
Literature," *The Jerusalem Journal of International Relations*, 3 (Win-
ter–Spring 1978), 340–374.
YOUNG, Oran R. *The Politics of Force: Bargaining During International
Crises*. Princeton, N.J.: Princeton University Press, 1968.
———. *The Intermediaries: Third Parties in International Crises*. Prince-
ton, N.J.: Princeton University Press, 1967.
YOUNG, Robert A., ed. "International Crisis: Progress and Prospects for
Applied Forecasting and Management," *International Studies Quarter-
ly*, 21 (March 1977), 5–248.
ZINNES, Dina A. "A Comparison of Hostile Behavior of Decision-Makers
in Simulated and Historical Data," *World Politics*, 18 (April 1966), 474–
502.
———. "'Pair Comparison' Scaling in International Relations," in R. C.
North, O. R. Holsti, D. Zaninovitch, and D. A. Zinnes, *Content
Analysis*. Evanston, Illinois: Northwestern University Press, 1963,
chap. 5.

THE 1967 CRISIS
(Chapters 2, 5, 8, and Appendix B).

ALLON, Yigal. *The Making of Israel's Army.* London: Vallentine, Mitchell, 1970.

————. *Masakh Shel Hol (Curtain of Sand).* 2nd rev. ed. Tel Aviv: Hakibbutz Hame'uhad, 1968 [in Hebrew].

————. Interview with Michael Brecher, 26 July 1968.

————. "The Last Stage of the War of Independence," *OT* (November 1967), 5–13 [in Hebrew].

————. "'Active Defense': A Guarantee for Our Existence," *Molad,* 1 (212) (July–August 1967), 137–143. [A speech delivered on 22 February 1967, in Hebrew.]

————. Interview, *Lamerhav,* 4 June 1967.

————. Speech in Tel Aviv, 2 June 1967, English Summary issued by the State of Israel, *Government Press Office,* Press Bulletin (mimeo), 3 June 1967.

————. Interview, *Lamerhav,* 14 May 1967.

AMIT, Meir. Interview with Benjamin Geist, 13 July 1973.

AVNER, Gershon. Interview with Benjamin Geist, 25 February 1973.

————. Interview with Michael Brecher, 24 July 1968.

BAR-LEV, Haim. Interview, *Yediot Aharonot,* 5 June 1973.

————. Interview, *Ma'ariv,* 16 May 1973.

————. Interview, *Ma'ariv,* 6 May 1973.

————. Interview, *Ma'ariv,* 18 April 1972.

BAR-ON, Hanan. Interview with Michael Brecher, 6 August 1968.

BAR-ZOHAR, Michael. *Embassies in Crisis: Diplomats and Demagogues Behind the Six Day War.* Englewood Cliffs, N.J.: Prentice-Hall, 1970.

————. *The Longest Month.* Tel Aviv: Levin-Epstein, 1968.

BEGIN, Menahem. "The Meeting of 2 June 1967," *Ma'ariv,* 2 June 1972.

————. Eulogy to Y. Herzog, March 1972.

————. "A Chapter from a Book to be Written," *Ma'ariv,* 18 June and 2 July 1971.

————. Interview, *Yediot Aharonot,* 2 June 1967.

BEN-GURION, David. Interview, *Ma'ariv,* 13 November 1970.

BENKLER, R. "General Rikhye's Truth," *Al Hamishmar,* 13 August 1971.

BEN-PORATH, Yehoshua, and U. DAN. *Mirage Contre MiG.* Paris: R. Laffont, 1967.

BENTOV, Mordekhai. "The Truth and Not 'Nightmares' Are of Educational Value," *Al Hamishmar,* 18 May 1972.

BENZIMAN, Uzi. *Yerushalayim, Ir Lelo Khoma (Jerusalem, City Without Walls).* Jerusalem and Tel Aviv: Schocken, 1973 [in Hebrew].

BITAN, Moshe. Interview with Michael Brecher, 8 August 1968.

BLECHMAN, Barry M. "The Impact of Israel's Reprisals on Behavior of the Bordering Arab Nations Directed at Israel," *Journal of Conflict Resolution,* 16 (June 1972), 155–181.

BRECHER, Michael. *Decisions in Israel's Foreign Policy.* London: Oxford University Press, 1974; and New Haven: Yale University Press, 1975.

————. *The Foreign Policy System of Israel: Setting, Images, Process.* London: Oxford University Press, 1972; and New Haven: Yale University Press, 1972.

British Broadcasting Corporation (BBC). *Summary of World Broadcasts, Part 4, The Middle East and Africa, Second Series (BBC).* Monitoring Service of the British Broadcasting Corporation, Caversham Park, Reading, England, April–June 1967.

British Parliamentary Debates. Hansard, House of Commons, 2nd Session, 27th Parliament, I, 8 May–5 June 1967.

BULL, General Odd. *War and Peace in the Middle East.* London: Leo Cooper, 1976.

BUNCHE, Ralph. Letter to the Editor, *New York Times,* 11 June 1967.

BURDETT, Winston. *Encounter with the Middle East: An Intimate Report of What Lies Behind the Arab-Israeli Conflict.* London: Andre Deutsch, 1970.

BURG, Yosef. Interview with Benjamin Geist, 8 August 1973.

Canadian House of Commons. *Debates, House of Commons, 2nd Session, 27th Parliament, 1, 8 May–5 June 1967.*

CARMEL, Moshe. "Fighting for Survival—Struggling for Peace," *Davar,* 2 June 1972.

————. Interview, *Jerusalem Post,* 2 June 1972.

————. "And Yet: We Were Faced with the Danger of Destruction," *Ma'ariv,* 21 April 1971.

CHRISTMAN, Henry M., ed. *The State Papers of Levi Eshkol.* New York: Funk & Wagnalls, 1969.

CHURCHILL, Randolph S., and Winston S. CHURCHILL. *The Six Day War.* London: Heinemann, 1967.

DAGAN, Avigdor. *Moscow and Jerusalem: Twenty Years of Relations Between Israel and the Soviet Union.* London: Abelard-Schuman, 1970.

DAYAN, Moshe. *Story of My Life.* Jerusalem and Tel Aviv: Steimatzky's Agency, 1976.

————. *Mapa Hadasha—Yahasim Aherim* (New Map—Other Relations). Tel Aviv and Haifa: Sifriyat Ma'ariv-Shikmona, 1969 [in Hebrew].

————. Interview, *Yediot Aharonot,* 16 June 1967.

————. Interview, *Ma'ariv,* 13 June 1967.

————. Interview, *Yediot Aharonot,* 13 June 1967.

—————. Press Conference, 13 June 1967, State of Israel, Government Press Office (mimeo).

————. Broadcast to *Tzahal,* 5 June 1967, State of Israel, Government Press Office (mimeo).

DE GAULLE, Charles. Press Conference, 27 November 1967; excerpts in *New York Times,* 28 November 1967.

Divrei Haknesset (Official Records of the Knesset). Jerusalem and Tel Aviv: Government Printer, 1948–1976.

DRAPER, Theodore. *Israel and World Politics: Roots of the Third Arab-Israeli War.* New York: Viking Press, 1968.

EBAN, Abba. *An Autobiography.* Jerusalem and Tel Aviv: Steimatsky's Agency, 1977.

————. *My Country: The Story of Modern Israel.* London and Jerusalem: Weidenfeld and Nicolson, 1973.

————. "Revelations from the Waiting Period," *Ma'ariv*, 6 May 1973.

————. Interview, *Yediot Aharonot*, 22 April 1973.

————. Interview, *Ma'ariv*, 2 June 1972.

————. Interview, *Ha'aretz*, 5 June 1970.

————. *Voice of Israel.* New York: Horizon Press, 1969.

————. *To Live or Perish* (unpublished manuscript), 1968.

————. Interviews with Michael Brecher, 22 July and 8 August 1968.

————. Interview, *Ma'ariv*, 1 December 1967.

————. Address to the UN Security Council, 6 June 1967, *Israel Information Services.* New York, June 1967.

————. Press Conference in Tel Aviv, 5 June 1967. English text issued by State of Israel, *Government Press Office* (mimeo).

————. Press Conference in Jerusalem, 30 May 1967. English text issued by State of Israel, *Government Press Office* (mimeo).

————. Speech in Rehovot, 17 May 1967, reported in *Ma'ariv*, 18 May 1967.

————. Interview, *Jewish Observer and Middle East Review*, 17 February 1967.

————. "Abba Eban Reviews Diplomatic Results," *Jerusalem Post*, 28 October 1966.

ELAZAR, Lieutenant-General David. Interview, *Yediot Aharonot*, 9 June 1972.

Encyclopaedia Hebraica, vol. 23, cols. 722–750, s.v. "The Six Day War" [in Hebrew].

ESHKOL, Levi. Answer to Question in Knesset, 9 December 1968, *Divrei Haknesset*, 53, 602–603.

————. Interview, *Yediot Aharonot*, 18 October 1967.

————. Interview with the editors of *Ma'ariv*, 4 October 1967.

————. Interview, *Yediot Aharonot*, 7 July 1967.

————. Statement in the Knesset, 12 June 1967, *Divrei Haknesset*, 49, 2327–2331. English version in H. M. Christman, ed., *The State Papers of Levi Eshkol.* New York: Funk & Wagnalls, 1969, pp. 113–134.

————. Address to the Chief Rabbis and Spiritual Leaders of all of Israel's Communities, 7 June 1967. English version in H. M. Christman, ed., *The State Papers of Levi Eshkol.* New York: Funk & Wagnalls, 1969, p. 114.

————. Broadcast to the Nation, 5 June 1967. English version in H. M. Christman, ed., *The State Papers of Levi Eshkol.* New York: Funk & Wagnalls, 1969, pp. 107–110.

————. Letter to Harold Wilson, 5 June 1967, in R. St. John, *Eban.* Garden City, N.Y.: Doubleday, 1972, p. 452.

————. Letter to USSR Premier Kosygin on 1 June 1967. English version in *Jerusalem Post*, 4 June 1967.

————. Statement in the Knesset, 29 May 1967, *Divrei Haknesset*, 49, 2283–2285. English version in H. M. Christman, ed., *The State Papers of Levi Eshkol.* New York: Funk & Wagnalls, 1969, pp. 95–104.

————. Broadcast to the Nation, 28 May 1967. English version in *BBC, Summary of World Broadcasts, Part 4, The Middle East and Africa, Second Series (BBC)*. Monitoring Service of the British Broadcasting Corporation, Caversham Park, Reading, England, April–June 1967, 30 May 1967.

————. Statement in the Knesset, 22 May 1967, *Divrei Haknesset*, 49, 2225–2227. English version in H. M. Christman, ed., *The State Papers of Levi Eshkol*. New York: Funk & Wagnalls, 1969, pp. 77–89.

————. *Appointment Book* for 14 May–10 June 1967 (Eshkol's *AB*).

————. Broadcast on Remembrance Day for Those Who Fell in the Defense of Israel, 13 May 1967, State of Israel, Government Press Office (mimeo). English version in H. M. Christman, ed., *The State Papers of Levi Eshkol*. New York: Funk & Wagnalls, 1969, pp. 69–73.

————. Interview, *U.S. News and World Report*, 17 April 1967.

EVRON, Ephraim. Interview with Michael Brecher, 3 March 1972.

GAVISH, Yeshayahu. Interview with Dov Goldstein, *Yediot Aharonot*, 3 April 1970.

GAZIT, Mordekhai. Interview with Michael Brecher, 15 July 1968.

GEIST, Benjamin. "The Six Day War: A Study in the Setting and Process of Foreign Policy Decision-Making Under Crisis Conditions." Ph.D. dissertation, The Hebrew University of Jerusalem, Jerusalem, 1974.

GILBOA, Moshe. "The Crisis that Reached the Top," *OT*, 31 May 1973.

————. *Shesh Shanim—Shisha Yamim (Six Years—Six Days: Origins and History of the Six Day War)*. Tel Aviv: Am Oved, 1969 [in Hebrew].

HARIF, Yosef. "In the Argument Around the 'Separation of Forces' on the Syrian Frontier, Washington Bases Itself on an Israeli Document of 19 June 1967," *Ma'ariv*, 22 March 1974.

HEIKAL, Mohamed. "The 1967 Arab-Israeli War," *Sunday Telegraph* (London), 21 and 28 October 1973, and *Ma'ariv*, 9 November 1973.

————. *Nasser: The Cairo Documents*. London: New English Library, 1972.

HERZOG, Ya'acov. Interview with Michael Brecher, 10 August 1968.

HIGGINS, Rosalyn. *United Nations Peace Keeping 1946–1967: Documents and Commentary, vol. I—The Middle East*. London: Oxford University Press, 1969.

HUSSEIN, Ibn Talal, King of Jordan. *My "War" with Israel*. As told to and with additional material by V. Vance and P. Lauer. New York: William Morrow, 1969.

International Institute for Strategic Studies, London. *The Military Balance 1966–1967*, and *The Military Balance 1967–68*, published in 1966 and 1967 respectively.

Israel, Government Press Office, Press Releases, Tel Aviv.

Israel, IDF Information Office, Tel Aviv. *This Was Goliath*. Tel Aviv, October 1967.

Israel Information Services. *The Record of Aggression 1958–1967*. New York, 1967.

Israel, Ministry of Defense. *The War of Four Days, the Southern Command, 5 June–9 June 1967*. Jerusalem, June 1969.

Israel, Ministry for Foreign Affairs, Cables and Communications, Jerusalem, 1967.

JABBER, Fuad A. *International Documents on Palestine 1967.* Beirut: Institute for Palestine Studies, 1970.

JOHNSON, Lyndon B. *The Vantage Point: Perspectives of the Presidency 1963–1969.* New York: Holt, Rinehart and Winston, 1971.

KHALIDI, Ahmed S. "The Military Balance 1967–73," in Naseer H. Aruri, ed., *Middle East Crucibles: Studies on the Arab-Israeli War of October 1973.* Wilmette, Ill.: The Medina University Press International, 1975, pp. 21–63.

KIMCHE, David, and D. BAWLY. *The Sandstorm, The Arab-Israeli War of 1967: Prelude and Aftermath.* London: Secker & Warburg, 1968.

KOLLEK, Teddy. *For Jerusalem.* Jerusalem and Tel Aviv: Steimatsky's Agency, 1978.

LAFFIN, John. *Fedayeen: The Arab-Israeli Dilemma.* London: Cassell, 1973.

LALL, Arthur. *The United Nations and the Middle East Crisis, 1967,* 2nd ed. New York: Columbia University Press, 1970.

LAQUEUR, Walter Z. *The Road to War, 1967: The Origins of the Arab-Israel Conflict.* London: Weidenfeld and Nicolson, 1968.

LAU-LAVIE, Naftalie. *Moshe Dayan, A Biography.* London: Vallentine, Mitchell, 1968.

LEGLER, A., and W. LIEBISCH. "Militärische Ereijuisse im Nahen Osten, Juni 1967, Eine Documentation," *Bibliothek für Zeitgeschichte, Jahres-Bibliographie.* Stuttgart, 1967, pp. 321–395 [in German].

MEIR, Golda. Interview, *Jerusalem Post,* 16 June 1972.

Middle East Record 1967, vol. 3 (*MER 1967*). D. Dishon, ed. Tel Aviv: The Shiloah Center for Middle Eastern and African Studies, Tel Aviv University, Jerusalem: Israel Universities Press, 1971.

DE MURVILLE, Maurice Couve. *Une Politique Étrangere 1958–1969.* Paris: Plon, 1971 [in French].

NAKDIMON, Shlomo. "The Moves that Preceded the Occupation of the the Old City," *Yediot Aharonot,* 4 June 1971.

———. *Likrat Sha'at Haefes (Toward the Zero Hour: The Drama that Preceded the Six Day War).* Tel Aviv: Ramdor, 1968 [in Hebrew].

NARKISS, Major-General Uzi. Interview, *Davar Hashavua,* 1 June 1973.

———. Interview, *Ma'ariv,* 8 June 1972.

———. Interview with five generals, including U. Narkiss, *Ma'ariv,* 4 June 1971.

NASSER, Gamal Abdel. Interview, *Newsweek,* 10 February 1969.

O'BALLANCE, Edgar. *The Third Arab-Israeli War.* London: Faber and Faber, 1972.

PELED, Matityahu. "The Beauty Is Untouched," *Ma'ariv,* 15 June 1973.

———. "The Character of Danger," *Ma'ariv,* 24 March 1972.

PERES, Shimon. Interview with Michael Brecher, 15 July 1968.

RA'ANAN, Uri. "Soviet Global Policy and the Middle East," *Midstream,* 15:5 (May 1969), 3–13.

RABIN, Yitzhak. "Six Days and Five More Years," *Ma'ariv,* 2 June 1972.

————. "Analogies with the Present and the Future," *OT,* 3 June 1971.

————. Address on the 15th Anniversary of the passing of Yitzhak Sadeh, 21 September 1967. Excerpts in *Jerusalem Post Weekly,* 9 October 1967.

————. Interview, *Ma'ariv,* 4 October 1967.

RAFAEL, Gideon. "May 1967—A Personal Report," Ma'ariv, 18 and 21 April 1972.

————. Interview, *Yediot Aharonot,* 4 June 1971.

————. Interview with Michael Brecher, 12 August 1968.

————. Interview, *Ma'ariv,* 4 August 1967.

RODINSON, Maxime. *Israel and the Arabs.* London: Penguin Books, 1968.

SAFRAN, Nadav. *From War to War: The Arab-Israeli Confrontation 1948–1967.* New York: Pegasus, 1969.

ST. JOHN, Robert. *Eban.* Garden City, N.Y.: Doubleday, 1972.

SCHIFF, Zeev. "The Three Weeks that Preceded the War," *Ha'aretz,* 4 October 1967.

————. "Three Days of the Campaign," *Ha'aretz,* 9 June 1967.

SERLIN, Joseph. Interview, *Yediot Aharonot,* 5 June 1972.

————. Interview, *Yediot Aharonot,* 26 May 1972.

SHAPIRA, Haim M. Interview with Michael Brecher, 16 July 1968.

SHARON, Ariel. Interview, *Ma'ariv,* 20 July 1973.

————. Interview, *Yediot Aharonot,* 20 July 1973.

SNEH, Moshe. Interview, *Yediot Aharonot,* 16 June 1967.

TEVETH, Shabtai. *Moshe Dayan.* Jerusalem and Tel Aviv: Schocken, 1971 [in Hebrew].

TZIMOUKI, Arie. "Eshkol As I Knew Him," *Yediot Aharonot,* 25 February 1972.

————. "The Longest Month" (A résumé of crisis events), *Yediot Aharonot,* 16, 21, and 25 June 1967.

ULAM, Adam B. *Expansion and Coexistence: The History of Soviet Foreign Policy, 1917–67.* New York: Praeger, 1968.

United Nations. Report on the Withdrawal of the United Nations Emergency Force, by U Thant, Secretary-General of the United Nations, 26 June 1967, *UN Monthly Chronicle,* 4:7 (July 1967), 135–161.

————. UN Document, 8/7953 (8 June 1967).

————. Report of the Secretary-General of the United Nations, U Thant, to the Security Council, S/7906 (26 May 1967).

————. Report by the Secretary-General of the United Nations, U Thant, to the Security Council, S/7896 (19 May 1967).

United States. Senate Documents, Washington, D.C.

VELIE, Lester. *Countdown in the Holy Land.* New York: Funk & Wagnalls, 1969.

WEIZMAN, Major-General Ezer. "A Chapter from My Memoirs," *Ma'ariv,* 26 September 1973.

————. Interview with Dov Goldstein, *Ma'ariv,* 5 June 1973.

————. Text of Speech before *Herut* Center, 14 January 1973, *Yediot Aharonot,* 19 January 1973.

WILSON, Harold. Interview with Benjamin Geist and Michael Brecher, 22 December 1972.

————. *The Labour Government: A Personal Record 1964–1970*. London: Weidenfeld and Nicolson, 1971.

YAFFE, Aviad. "The War of Twenty-Seven Days," *Nitzoz*, September 1967.

YONAH, Major. "The Background of the Six Day War in the Eyes of the Arabs: Egypt and Her Entry Into the War," *Ma'arakhot*, 191–192 (June 1968), 37–40, 73–103.

YOST, Charles W. "The Arab-Israeli War: How It Began," *Foreign Affairs*, 46:2 (January 1968), 304–320.

THE 1973 CRISIS
(Chapters 3, 6, 9, and Appendix B)

AGRANAT COMMISSION REPORTS. Third and Final Report. Press release issued by the Commission of Inquiry—Yom Kippur War (Agranat Commission). Jerusalem: Government Press Office, 30 January 1975 (mimeo).

————. Partial Report issued by the Committee of Inquiry—Yom Kippur War. Jerusalem: as published in the Hebrew press, 3 April 1974.

AL-HAYTHAM al-Ayoubi. "The Strategies of the Fourth Campaign," in N. H. Aruri, ed., *Middle East Crucible: Studies on the Arab-Israeli War of October 1973*. Wilmette, Ill.: The Medina University Press International, 1975, pp. 65–96.

ALLON, Yigal. Interview with (journalist) Uri Millstein, 23 January 1974.

————. Speech to Israeli Labor Party Central Committee, 5 December 1973.

————. Address at the Van Leer Jerusalem Foundation, 26 November 1973.

————. Interview on Israeli Television, 11 November 1973.

————. Address at the Van Leer Jerusalem Foundation, 3 June 1973.

————. Speech to the Israeli Labor Party Central Committee, November 1972.

————. Interview on IDF Radio, 29 January 1972.

ARURI, Naseer H., ed. *Middle East Crucible: Studies on the Arab-Israeli War of October 1973*. Wilmette, Ill.: The Medina University Press International, 1975.

AVNERY, Arieh. *Shamayim Adoumim (Red Sky)*. Tel Aviv: Sifriyat Madim, 1975 [in Hebrew].

BAR-LEV, Haim. Interview, *Ma'ariv*, 21 September 1977.

————. "We Knew Where the Egyptians Would Attack and How—But We Made a Mistake About the Timing," *Ma'ariv*, 1 August 1975.

————. Interview with Michael Brecher, 29 July 1974.

————. Interviews with Uri Millstein, 24 and 31 January, 26 June 1974.

————. Interview, *Ma'ariv*, 9 November 1973.

BAR-TOV, Hanoch. *Dado—48 Years and Another 20 Days*. 2 vols. Tel Aviv: Sifriyat Ma'ariv, 1978 [in Hebrew].

BEGIN, Menahem. Statement in the Knesset, 16 October 1973, *Divrei Haknesset*, 68, 4476–4479.

BEN-PORATH, Yeshayahu, Jonathan GEFEN, Uri DAN, Eitan HABER, Hezi CARMEL, Eli LANDAU, and Eli TABOR. *Hamechdal (The Fiasco)*. Tel Aviv: Hotza'a Meyuhedet, 1973 [in Hebrew].

BRECHER, Michael. *Decisions in Israel's Foreign Policy*. London: Oxford University Press, 1974; and New Haven: Yale University Press, 1975.

DAYAN, Moshe. *Story of My Life*. Jerusalem and Tel Aviv: Steimatzky's Agency, 1976.

————. Interview on U.S. Television, CBS, "Face the Nation," 9 December 1973.

————. Address to Israeli Lawyers' Association, 24 November 1973.

————. Lecture to the Labor Party College, 10 November 1973.

————. Speech to the Knesset, 30 October 1973, *Divrei Haknesset*, 68, 4585–4587.

————. Interview on Israeli Television, 20 October 1973.

————. Interview on Israeli Television, 14 October 1973; text in *Ma'arakhot*, Special Edition (November 1973), 232–233.

————. Confidential Briefing to Israeli Newspaper Editors, 9 October 1973; full text published in *Ha'aretz*, 15 February 1974.

————. Address to the Nation on Israeli Television, 6 October 1973; text in *Ma'arakhot*, Special Edition (November 1973), 232–233.

————. Press Conference, 6 October 1973, Israeli Government Press Office, Press Bulletin (mimeo).

————. Interview, *Time*, 30 July 1973.

————. Address to the Haifa Technion, 27 June 1973.

————. Interview on U.S. Television, CBS, "Face the Nation," 13 February 1972.

DISENTSHIK, Ido. "You Don't Ask for a Cease-fire with Your Back to the Wall," *Ma'ariv*, 21 September 1977.

DRAPER, Theodore. "The Road to Geneva," *Commentary*, 57:2 (February 1974), 23–39.

EBAN, Abba. *An Autobiography*. Jerusalem and Tel Aviv: Steimatsky's Agency, 1977.

————. Interview, *Ha'aretz*, 4 October 1974.

————. Interview with Michael Brecher, 15 July 1974.

————. Interview, *Davar*, 28 December 1973.

————. Interview on U.S. Television, NBC, "Today," 16 November 1973.

————. Reaction to Statement of EEC, 9 November 1973; text in *Israel's Foreign Relations*, 1065–1067.

————. Interview on United Kingdom Television, "Panorama," 30 October 1973.

————. Press Conference in Israel, 24 October 1973, Israeli Government Press Office (mimeo).

————. Press Conference with UN Correspondents Association, 17 October 1973; reported in *New York Times*, 18 October 1973.

————. Interview on U.S. Television, ABC, "Issues and Answers," 7 October 1973.

————. "Kissinger Told Me That He Went to Sleep Quietly After He Received the Israeli Intelligence Appreciation on the Eve of October 5," *Ma'ariv*, 21 September 1977.

ELAZAR, David. "The Yom Kippur War: Military Lessons," in *Military Aspects of the Israeli-Arab Conflict*, Proceedings of an International Symposium, October 12–17, 1975. Tel Aviv: University Publishing Projects, 1975, pp. 245–250.

―――. Memorandum submitted to the Cabinet in May 1975 in response to the Agranat Commission's findings, published in *Ma'ariv*, 20 April 1976.

―――. Interview with Janice Stein, 20 April 1974.

GALILI, Yisrael. Interview with Y. Ben-Porath, *Yediot Aharonot*, 27 October 1978.

GAVISH, General Yeshayahu. Interview, *Yediot Aharonot*, 21 September 1977.

GAZIT, Mordekhai. Interview with Michael Brecher, 27 July 1974.

GAZIT, Shlomo. "Arab Forces Two Years After the Yom Kippur War," in *Military Aspects of the Israeli-Arab Conflict*, Proceedings of an International Symposium, October 12–17, 1975. Tel Aviv: University Publishing Projects, 1975, pp. 188–195.

GOLAN, Aviezer. "Albert," excerpts of biography of *General Abraham Mendler*, published in *Yediot Aharonot*, 7 and 14 January 1977.

GOLAN, Galia. *Yom Kippur and After: The Soviet Union and the Middle East Crisis*. Cambridge, England: Cambridge University Press, 1977.

GOLAN, Matti. *The Secret Conversations of Henry Kissinger: Step-by-Step Diplomacy in the Middle East*. New York: Bantam Books, 1976.

GONEN, General Shmuel. Interview, *Yediot Aharonot*, 21 September 1977.

Government of Jordan Communiqué, 13 October 1973; published in *New York Times*, 14 October 1973.

HAFEZ, General Ismail. Interview with Mohamed Heikal in *Al-Ahram* (Cairo), 18 November 1973.

HALAF, Salah. "Clear Thoughts in a Muddy Situation," *Shaoun Falastin*, January 1974; Hebrew translation in A. Sivan, ed., *Arav Veyisrael*, 5. Tel Aviv and Jerusalem: Am Oved and The Hebrew University of Jerusalem, 1974.

HANDEL, Michael I. "Perception, Deception and Surprise: The Case of the Yom Kippur War," *Jerusalem Papers on Peace Problems*, 19. Jerusalem: Leonard Davis Institute of International Relations, Hebrew University of Jerusalem, 1976.

HAREVEN, Alouf. "A Hierarchy of 'Lies' Against a Hierarchy of Heroes," *Ma'ariv*, 1 October 1976.

HASELKORN, Avigdor. "Israeli Intelligence Performance in the Yom Kippur War," Discussion Paper, Hudson Institute, 17 July 1974.

HAUSNER, Gideon. Statement in the Knesset, 16 October 1973, *Divrei Haknesset*, 68, 4483–4484.

HAZAN, Ya'acov. Statement in the Knesset, 16 October 1973, *Divrei Haknesset*, 68, 4485–4486.

HEIKAL, Mohamed. *The Road to Ramadan*. London: Collins, 1975.

HERZOG, Major-General Chaim. *The War of Atonement*. Jerusalem and Tel Aviv: Steimatsky's Agency, 1975.

HOLST, J. J. "Surprise Signals and Reaction," *Cooperation and Conflict*, 1 (1966), 31–45.

HOROWITZ, Yigal. Statement in the Knesset, 16 October 1973, *Divrei Haknesset*, 68, 4484–4485.

HUSSEIN, Ibn Talal, King of Jordan. Statement in the Jordanian Cabinet, broadcast over Radio Amman, 7 October 1973; text in *Ma'arakhot*, Special Edition (November 1973), 232–233.

Insight Team of *The Sunday Times* (London), *The Yom Kippur War*. London: Andre Deutsch, 1974.

International Institute for Strategic Studies, London. *The Military Balance 1973–74*, published in 1973.

KALB, Bernard, and Marvin KALB. *Kissinger*. Boston and Toronto: Little, Brown, 1974.

KEATING, Ambassador Kenneth, and other U.S. Embassy officials. Interviews with Michael Brecher, 30 July and 12 August 1974.

KISSINGER, Henry. Press Conference, 6 June 1974. Text in *Statements on the Middle East*. Tel Aviv: U.S. Information Service, 1974.

———. News Conference, 21 March 1974. Text in *Statements on the Middle East*. Tel Aviv: U.S. Information Service, 1974.

———. Press Conference, 22 January 1974. Text in *Statements on the Middle East*. Tel Aviv: U.S. Information Service, 1974.

———. Press Conference, 25 October 1973. Reported in *New York Times*, 26 October 1973.

KLINE, Ray. Testimony Before U.S. House of Representatives, Report of Select Committee on Intelligence, September 1975. Published in *Village Voice* (New York, 17 February 1976).

KNORR, Klaus. "Failures in National Intelligence Estimates: The Case of the Cuban Missiles," *World Politics*, 16 (April 1964), 455–467.

KOHLER, Foy D., Leo GOURÉ, and Mose L. HARVEY. *The Soviet Union and the October 1973 Middle East War, The Implications for Detente*. Miami: Monographs in International Affairs, Center for Advanced International Studies, University of Miami, 1974.

KOLLEK, Teddy. *For Jerusalem*. Jerusalem and Tel Aviv: Steimatsky's Agency, 1978.

LUTTWAK, Edward N., and Walter LAQUEUR. "Kissinger and the Yom Kippur War," *Commentary*, 58:3 (September 1974), 33–40.

MEDZINI, Meron, ed. *Israel's Foreign Relations, Selected Documents 1947–1974*. Jerusalem: Ministry of Foreign Affairs, 1976.

MEIR, Golda. *My Life*. Jerusalem and Tel Aviv: Steimatsky's Agency, 1975.

———. Interview, *Ma'ariv*, 16 September 1974.

———. Government Statement to the Knesset on the Disengagement Agreement with Syria, 30 May 1974, *Divrei Haknesset*, 70, 1459–1462.

———. Statement to the Knesset, 22 January 1974, *Divrei Haknesset*, 69,

10–12; English text in *Israel's Foreign Relations,* 1976 (see Medzini), pp. 1111–1116.

―――. Statement to the Knesset, 20 December 1973, *Divrei Haknesset,* 68, 4796–4799 and her summary at the end of the debate, 4829–4833.

―――. Press Conference, 3 November 1973. Reported in *New York Times,* 4 November 1973.

―――. Speech to the Knesset, 23 October 1973, *Divrei Haknesset,* 68, 4507–4510.

―――. Speech to the Knesset, 16 October 1973, *Divrei Haknesset,* 68, 4459–4474.

―――. Press Conference in Israel, 13 October 1973; text in *Ma'arakhot,* Special Edition (November 1973), 232–233.

―――. Address to the Nation on Television, 10 October 1973; English text in *Israel's Foreign Relations,* 1976 (see Medzini), 1035–1037.

―――. Address to the Nation on Television, 6 October 1973; text in *Ma'arakhot,* Special Edition (November 1973), 232–233.

―――. Statement to the Knesset, 25 July 1973, *Divrei Haknesset,* 68, 4274–4284.

―――. Interview on IDF Radio, 29 January 1972.

Military Aspects of the Israeli-Arab Conflict. Proceedings of an International Symposium, October 12–17, 1975. Tel Aviv: University Publishing Projects, 1975.

MONROE, Elizabeth, and A. H. HOCKLEY. *The Arab-Israeli War, October 1973, Background and Events.* London: The International Institute for Strategic Studies, Adelphi Paper No. 111, Winter 1974.

NAKDIMON, Shlomo. "Protocols of Discussions Among the Political and Military Leaders on the 5th and 6th October 1973," *Yediot Aharonot,* 21 September 1977.

―――. "The Days Before and After the War: New Revelations," *Yediot Aharonot* (series of articles), 12, 19, 26 July, 2, 9, 16 August 1974.

―――. "The Full Report of a Group Discussion of the American Secretary of State with Jewish Intellectuals," *Yediot Aharonot,* 15 February 1974.

―――. "The Events that Preceded the War," *Yediot Aharonot* (series of articles), 23, 30 November, 7, 14 December 1973.

NIXON, Richard. *RN: The Memoirs of Richard Nixon.* New York: Grosset and Dunlap, 1978.

―――. Interview with David Frost on U.S. Television, ABC, 12 May 1977; text of verbatim transcript.

PELED, Binyamin. "The Air Force in the Yom Kippur War," *Military Aspects of the Israeli-Arab Conflict.* Proceedings of an International Symposium, October 12–17, 1975. Tel Aviv: University Publishing Projects, 1975, pp. 228–245.

PERES, Shimon. Interview with Michael Brecher, 11 August 1974.

QUANDT, William B. *Decade of Decisions: American Policy Toward the Arab-Israeli Conflict 1967–1976.* Berkeley, Los Angeles, and London: University of California Press, 1977.

RAZ, Mordekhai. "The Decision Making Process of the Pre-Crisis Phase of the 1973 War," M.A. Thesis, The Hebrew University of Jerusalem, December 1975.

RUSH, Kenneth. Statement Before the Senate Committee on Foreign Relations, 13 December 1973; in *Statements on the Middle East*. Tel Aviv: U.S. Information Service, 1974.

SADAT, Anwar. *In Search of Identity: An Autobiography.* New York: Harper & Row, 1978.

————. "The October War: As Seen Through the Eyes of Anwar Sadat," Interviews with Mussa Sabri, *Akhbar el-Yom,* 10 September 1974, published in *Ma'ariv,* 13 September 1974.

SAPIR, Pinhas. Interview with Michael Brecher, 25 June 1974.

SCHIFF, Zeev. "The Full Story of the Encirclement that Ended the Yom Kippur War," *Ha'aretz,* 14 September 1975.

————. *October Earthquake, Yom Kippur 1973.* Tel Aviv: University Publishing Projects, 1974.

————. "The 8th of October: The Most Important Day of the War," *Ha'aretz,* 25 and 30 September 1974.

————, and Eitan HABER, eds. *Israel, Army and Defence, A Dictionary.* Tel Aviv: Zmora, Bitah, Modim, 1976.

SEGUEV, Shmuel. "Kissinger Said: Hit Hard and Fast for the Oil Companies are Putting Pressure on the President," *Ma'ariv,* 26 March 1976.

SHAY, Lt. Colonel Avi. "Egypt Before the Yom Kippur War: War Aims and Plan of Attack," *Ma'arakhot,* 250 (July 1976), 15–38.

SHEEHAN, Edward R. F. "Step by Step in the Middle East," *Foreign Policy,* 22 (Spring 1976), 3–70.

SHLAIM, Avi. "Failures in National Intelligence Estimates: The Case of the Yom Kippur War," *World Politics,* 28 (April 1976), 348–380.

SZYLIOWICZ, Joseph S., and Bard E. O'NEILL, eds. *The Energy Crisis and U.S. Foreign Policy.* New York: Praeger, 1975.

TAL, Major-General Y. Interview, *Yediot Aharonot,* 21 September 1977.

Text of Agreement on Disengagement Between Israel and Syrian Forces, signed on 31 May 1974, published in *New York Times,* 30 May 1974.

United Nations. *UNSC,* S/RES339 (1973), 23 October 1973.

————. *UNSC,* S/7930/ADD. 225–237.

U.S. Government, House of Representatives. Report of Select Committee on Intelligence, September 1975. Published in *Village Voice* (New York, 17 February 1976).

U.S. Information Service, Tel Aviv. *Statements on the Middle East,* 29 November 1973–24 June 1974.

VAN CREVELD, Martin. *Military Lessons of the Yom Kippur War: Historical Perspectives.* Vol. III of the series, *The Washington Papers.* The Center for Strategic and International Studies, Georgetown University, Washington, D.C., London and Beverly Hills: Sage Publications, 1975.

WASSERMAN, B. "The Failure of Intelligence Prediction," *Political Studies,* 8 (June 1960), 156–169.

WHALEY, B. *Codeword Barbarossa.* Cambridge, Mass.: MIT Press, 1973.

WOHLSTETTER, Roberta. "Cuba and Pearl Harbor: Hindsight and Fore-sight," *Foreign Affairs,* 43 (July 1965), 690–705.
————. *Pearl Harbor: Warning and Decision.* Stanford, Calif.: Stanford University Press, 1962.
YARIV, Major-General Aharon. "Israeli Intelligence Believed Already in the Summer of 1972 that Egypt Would Be Ready for War in May 1973," *Ma'ariv,* 18 July 1975.
————. Interview with Michael Brecher, 7 August 1974.
ZUMWALT, Admiral Elmo R. *On Watch, A Memoir.* New York: Quad-rangle/The New York Times Book Co., 1976.

INDEXES

Designer:	Eric Jungerman
Compositor:	Dwan Typography
Printer:	Publishers Press
Binder:	Mountain States Bindery
Text:	Linocomp Caledonia
Display:	Stymie Extrabold
Cloth:	Holliston Roxite B 53544
Paper:	50 lb. Publishers Eggshell 66